COMPUTER LITERACY FOR IC3™

UNIT 2: USING PRODUCTIVITY SOFTWARE

COMPUTER LITERACY FOR IC3™

UNIT 2: USING PRODUCTIVITY SOFTWARE

John Preston

Sally Preston

Robert L. Ferrett

CERTIPORT® APPROVED Instructional Materials

IC3™ INTERNET AND COMPUTING CORE CERTIFICATION GLOBAL STANDARD 3

Prentice Hall

Boston   Columbus   Indianapolis   New York   San Francisco   Upper Saddle River
Amsterdam   Cape Town   Dubai   London   Madrid   Milan   Munich   Paris   Montreal   Toronto
Delhi   Mexico City   Sao Paulo   Sydney   Hong Kong   Seoul   Singapore   Taipei   Tokyo

Library of Congress Cataloging-in-Publication Data

Preston, John M.
    Computer literacy for IC3 / John Preston, Robert L. Ferrett, Sally Preston.
      p. cm.
    Includes index.
    ISBN-13: 978-0-13-506497-9
    ISBN-10: 0-13-506497-X
    1. Electronic data processing personnel—Certification—Study guides. 2. Computer literacy—Examinations—Study guides.
3. Computers—Examinations—Study guides. 4. Internet—Examinations—Study guides. I. Ferrett, Robert. II. Preston, Sally.
III. Title. IV. Title: Computer literacy for IC3.
    QA76.3.P743 2009
    004—dc22

2009004932

VP/Editorial Director: Natalie E. Anderson
Editor in Chief: Michael Payne
Director, Product Development: Pamela Hersperger
Product Development Manager: Eileen Bien Calabro
Editorial Project Managers: Melissa Arlio, Virginia Guariglia
Editorial Assistant: Marilyn Matos
AVP/Director of Online Programs, Media: Richard Keaveny
AVP/Director of Product Development: Lisa Strite
Media Development Manager: Cathi Profitko
Editor, Assessment and Media: Paul Gentile
Editorial Media Project Manager: Alana Coles
Editorial Assistant, Media: Jaimie Howard
Production Media Project Manager: John Cassar
Director of Marketing: Kate Valentine
Marketing Manager: Tori Olsen Alves
Marketing Coordinator: Susan Osterlitz
Marketing Assistant: Angela Frey
Senior Managing Editor: Cynthia Zonneveld
Associate Managing Editor: Camille Trentacoste
Production Project Manager: Ruth Ferrera-Kargov

Manager of Rights & Permissions: Charles Morris
Senior Operations Specialist: Nick Sklitsis
Operations Specialist: Natacha Moore
Senior Art Director: Jonathan Boylan
Interior Design: Frubilicious Design Group
Cover Design: Frubilicious Design Group
Cover Illustration/Photo: © Steve Coleccs/iStockphoto
Illustration (Interior): Black Dot Group
Director, Image Resource Center: Melinda Patelli
Manager, Rights and Permissions: Zina Arabia
Manager, Visual Research: Beth Brenzel
Manager, Cover Visual Research & Permissions: Karen
  Sanatar
Image Permission Coordinator: Jan Marc Quisumbing
Photo Researchers: Sheila Norman and Kathy Ringrose
Composition: Black Dot Group
Full-Service Project Management: Black Dot Group
Printer/Binder: Webcrafters Inc.
Typeface: Adobe Garamond

Microsoft, Windows, Word, PowerPoint, Outlook, FrontPage, Visual Basic, MSN, The Microsoft Network, and/or other Microsoft products referenced herein are either registered trademarks or registered trademarks of the Microsoft Corporation in the U.S.A. and other countries. Screen shots and icons reprinted with permission from the Microsoft Corporation. This book is not sponsored or endorsed by or affiliated with the Microsoft Corporation.

Pearson Education Ltd., London
Pearson Education Singapore, Pte. Ltd
Pearson Education, Canada, Inc.
Pearson Education–Japan
Pearson Education Australia PTY, Limited

Pearson Education North Asia Ltd., Hong Kong
Pearson Educación de Mexico, S.A. de C.V.
Pearson Education Malaysia, Pte. Ltd.
Pearson Education, Upper Saddle River, New Jersey

Prentice Hall
is an imprint of

10 9 8 7 6 5 4 3 2 1
ISBN-13: 978-0-13-506497-9
ISBN-10: 0-13-506497-X

INTERNET AND
COMPUTING CORE
CERTIFICATION

CERTIFICATION ROADMAP

Whether you're seeking further education, entering the job market, or advancing your skills through higher ICT certification, IC³ gives you the foundation you need to succeed.

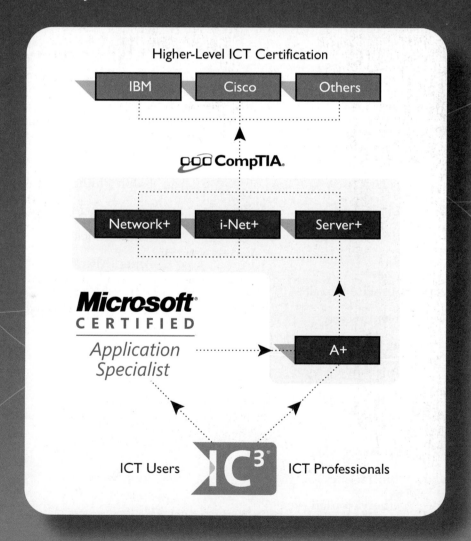

Dedication

We have been working as a collaborative team since 1996. Our many years of friendship have been the glue holding this project together. We would like to dedicate this book to that unique camaraderie.

Acknowledgments

Our thanks go to Michael Payne for asking us to write this book. We appreciate the careful tech edits from Jan Snyder, Elizabeth Lockley, Janet Pickard, and June West, who paid attention to all the little details, and offered helpful suggestions for improvement. We also appreciate the contributions of Melissa Arlio and Eileen Calabro of Pearson Education.

Additionally, we would like to thank the following people for their valuable contributions to this book:

Shelley Allen	Elizabeth Lockley
Michelle August	Thomas McKenzie
Linda Bird	Lawrence Metzelaar
Lynn Bowen	Keith Mulbery
Julie Boyles	Phyllis Pace
Peter Casey	Ralph Phillips
Linda Collins	Janet Pickard
Lew Cousineau	Jennifer Pickle
Doug Cross	Anita P. Ricker
Annette Duvall	Steven Rubin
Denise Farley	Rafaat Saade
Marianne Fox	Cheryl L. Slavik
Anthony Garner	Jan Snyder
Laurie Grosik	Barbara Taylor
Carson Haury	Pam Toliver
Christine Held	Philip Vavalides
Bill Holmes	June West
Cheryl Jordan	

About the Authors

John Preston is an Associate Professor at Eastern Michigan University in the College of Technology in the Technology Management program. He has been teaching, writing, and designing computer courses since the advent of PCs, and has authored and co-authored more than 60 books on computer applications and the relationship between technology and society. He teaches courses in global technologies, managing information systems, project management, and quantitative reasoning. He served as program coordinator of the Energy Management program and has trained commercial energy auditors for all of the major utilities in Michigan. Prior to his tenure at EMU, he was a partner in an energy management consulting firm.

Sally Preston teaches computing in a variety of settings, which provides her with ample opportunity to observe how people learn, what works best, and what challenges are present when learning a new software program. This diverse experience provides a complementary set of skills and knowledge that is blended into her writing. Sally has been writing computer textbooks for nearly 10 years and has authored books for the *GO! Series,* the *Learn Series,* and for the *Essentials Series.* Sally has an MBA from Eastern Michigan University. When she is away from her computer, she is often found planting flowers in her garden.

Robert L. Ferrett recently retired as Director of the Center for Instructional Computing at Eastern Michigan University, where he provided computer training and support to faculty. He has authored or co-authored more than 80 books on Access, PowerPoint, Excel, Publisher, WordPerfect, Windows Vista, and Word. He has been designing, developing, and delivering computer workshops for nearly two decades. Bob has written for the *GO! Series,* and was a series editor for the *Learn 97, Learn 2000,* and *Learn XP* books. He has a BA in Psychology, an MS in Geography, and an MS in Interdisciplinary Technology from Eastern Michigan University. His doctoral studies are in Instructional Technology at Wayne State University. As a sidelight, Bob teaches a four-week Computers and Genealogy class, and has written genealogy and local history books.

IC³ Series Contents

Unit 1: Computing Fundamentals

CHAPTER 1: Identifying Types of Computers

CHAPTER 2: Identifying Computer Components and Their Functions

CHAPTER 3: Evaluating, Purchasing, and Maintaining Computer Equipment

CHAPTER 4: Identifying Software and Hardware Interaction and Types of Software

CHAPTER 5: Identifying Operating System Functions

CHAPTER 6: Using Windows Vista

Unit 2: Using Productivity Software

CHAPTER 1: Starting with Microsoft Office 2007 Applications

CHAPTER 2: Creating a New Word Document and Inserting Graphics and Tables

CHAPTER 3: Formatting and Organizing Paragraphs and Documents

CHAPTER 4: Importing Text and Formatting a Newsletter

CHAPTER 5: Working with Collaborative Tools

CHAPTER 6: Creating and Formatting a Worksheet

CHAPTER 7: Managing Money Formulas and Functions

CHAPTER 8: Giving Meaning to Data Using Charts

CHAPTER 9: Creating a Presentation

CHAPTER 10: Enhancing a Presentation

CHAPTER 11: Creating a Customized Database *(Available online on the Companion Website)*

CHAPTER 12: Retrieving Information from Your Database *(Available online on the Companion Website)*

Unit 2: OpenOffice.org
(Available via our Custom PHIT program www.pearsoncustom.com Keyword search: customphit)

CHAPTER 1: Starting with OpenOffice.org 3.0 Applications

CHAPTER 2: Creating a New Document and Inserting Graphics and Tables

CHAPTER 3: Formatting and Organizing Paragraphs and Documents

CHAPTER 4: Importing Text and Formatting a Newsletter

CHAPTER 5: Working with Collaborative Tools

CHAPTER 6: Creating and Formatting a Worksheet

CHAPTER 7: Managing Money Formulas and Functions

CHAPTER 8: Giving Meaning to Data Using Charts

CHAPTER 9: Creating a Presentation

CHAPTER 10: Enhancing a Presentation

CHAPTER 11: Creating a Customized Database

CHAPTER 12: Retrieving Information from Your Database

Unit 3: Living Online

CHAPTER 1: Understanding the Internet

CHAPTER 2: Searching for Information

CHAPTER 3: Buying, Selling, and Banking Online

CHAPTER 4: Communicating Online

CHAPTER 5: The Future of Living Online

CHAPTER 6: Using Windows Vista

Contents

chapter

one | Starting with Microsoft Office 2007 Applications 2

File Guide 6
Lesson 1:   Starting an Application and Identifying Common On-Screen Elements 6
Lesson 2:   Opening and Saving a File and Closing Applications 11
Lesson 3:   Navigating a Document and Inserting, Selecting, and Editing Text 14
Lesson 4:   Using Buttons and Dialog Boxes 21
Lesson 5:   Checking Spelling and Grammar 24
Lesson 6:   Selecting and Formatting Text 26
Lesson 7:   Copying, Pasting, Cutting, and Moving Text 27
Lesson 8:   Using Galleries, Contextual Tabs, and the Quick Access Toolbar 33
Lesson 9:   Printing Documents 37
Lesson 10: Using Help 40
Advanced Skills or Concepts 42
Check Your Work 46
Key Terms 46
Assessing Learning Outcomes 47
Skill Drill 50
Fix It 54
On the Job 55
Discussion of Advanced Skills or Concepts 59
On Your Own 59
Assess Your Progress 60

chapter

two | Creating a New Word Document and Inserting Graphics and Tables 62

File Guide 66
Lesson 1:   Creating a New Document 66
Lesson 2:   Creating and Modifying a Numbered or Bulleted List 68
Lesson 3:   Formatting, Aligning, and Indenting Text 71
Lesson 4:   Creating a Title with WordArt 75
Lesson 5:   Inserting and Modifying Clip Art 79
Lesson 6:   Inserting and Modifying Pictures 83
Lesson 7:   Inserting Tables 86
Lesson 8:   Formatting Tables 94
Lesson 9:   Inserting a Header or Footer in a Document 99
Lesson 10: Creating a Document from a Template 103
Advanced Skills or Concepts 106
Check Your Work 106
Key Terms 107
Assessing Learning Outcomes 107
Skill Drill 110
Fix It 116

On the Job 117
Discussion of Advanced Skills or Concepts 120
On Your Own 121
Assess Your Progress 122

chapter
three | Formatting and Organizing Paragraphs and Documents   **124**

File Guide 128
Lesson 1:   Customizing Word 128
Lesson 2:   Importing Text from Another Document 131
Lesson 3:   Creating, Applying, and Modifying Styles 134
Lesson 4:   Using Language Tools 138
Lesson 5:   Creating Footnotes 141
Lesson 6:   Managing Citations 143
Lesson 7:   Creating a Bibliography 147
Lesson 8:   Preparing a Document for Printing .150
Advanced Skills or Concepts 151
Check Your Work 153
Key Terms 153
Assessing Learning Outcomes 154
Skill Drill 156
Fix It 165
On the Job 166
Discussion of Advanced Skills or Concepts 167
On Your Own 168
Assess Your Progress 168

chapter
four | Importing Text and Formatting a Newsletter   **170**

File Guide 174
Lesson 1:   Inserting Data from Other Documents 175
Lesson 2:   Creating and Formatting a Multicolumn Document 180
Lesson 3:   Saving a Document as a Template 183
Lesson 4:   Applying Special Formatting 186
Lesson 5:   Adding Symbols 190
Lesson 6:   Setting and Modifying Tab Stops 192
Lesson 7:   Saving a Document Using Different Document Formats 200
Lesson 8:   Adding Hyperlinks and Saving a Document as a Web Page 204
Advanced Skills or Concepts 208
Check Your Work 212
Key Terms 213
Assessing Learning Outcomes 213
Skill Drill 215
Fix It 221
On the Job 222
Discussion of Advanced Skills or Concepts 227

On Your Own 227

Assess Your Progress 228

chapter

five | Working with Collaborative Tools 230

File Guide 236

Lesson 1:   Inserting Comments into a Document 236

Lesson 2:   Tracking Changes in a Document 242

Lesson 3:   Responding to Comments and Document Changes 245

Lesson 4:   Creating a Main Document for Merging 249

Lesson 5:   Opening a Data Source and Inserting Fields into a Document 250

Lesson 6:   Merging a Document with a Data Source 256

Lesson 7:   Using the Mail Merge Wizard to Create Mailing Labels 258

Advanced Skills or Concepts 261

Check Your Work 263

Key Terms 264

Assessing Learning Outcomes 264

Skill Drill 267

Fix It 276

On the Job 277

Discussion of Advanced Skills or Concepts 279

On Your Own 280

Assess Your Progress 281

chapter

six | Creating and Formatting a Worksheet 282

File Guide 286

Lesson 1:   Navigating a Workbook, Selecting Cells, and Entering Text and Data 286

Lesson 2:   Adjust Column Widths 292

Lesson 3:   Inserting or Deleting Rows or Columns 294

Lesson 4:   Summing a Column of Numbers 295

Lesson 5:   Formatting Numbers and Dates 297

Lesson 6:   Aligning Text 304

Lesson 7:   Adding Emphasis, Colors, Shading, and Borders 308

Lesson 8:   Opening, Copying, Inserting, and Deleting Worksheets 312

Lesson 9:   Formatting, Sorting, and Filtering Tables 315

Lesson 10:   Documenting and Printing Worksheets 321

Advanced Skills or Concepts 325

Check Your Work 326

Key Terms 327

Assessing Learning Outcomes 327

Skill Drill 330

Fix It 335

On the Job 336

Discussion of Advanced Skills or Concepts 337

On Your Own 338

Assess Your Progress 339

chapter

seven | Managing Money Using Formulas and Functions   **340**

File Guide		.343
Lesson 1:	Fill Labels and Use Worksheet Functions	.344
Lesson 2:	Using the Payment Function	.351
Lesson 3:	Filling a Sequence of Numbers and Formatting Them as Text	.357
Lesson 4:	Using References to Cells in Other Worksheets and Relative Cell References	.360
Lesson 5:	Calculating a Percentage Increase and Decrease Using Absolute Cell References	.362
Lesson 6:	Using a Cash Flow Analysis	.366
Lesson 7:	Calculating a Simple Payback Using a Hidden Row, the IF function, and Conditional Formatting	.370
Lesson 8:	Using the Internal Rate of Return Function	.377
Lesson 9:	Printing Large Worksheets	.379
Advanced Skills or Concepts		.388
Check Your Work		.390
Key Terms		.391
Assessing Learning Outcomes		.391
Skill Drill		.394
Fix It		.401
On the Job		.402
Discussion of Advanced Skills or Concepts		.407
On Your Own		.408
Assess Your Progress		.408

chapter

eight | Giving Meaning to Data Using Charts   **410**

File Guide		.414
Lesson 1:	Creating a Column Chart	.415
Lesson 2:	Editing Chart Elements	.421
Lesson 3:	Using a Pie Chart	.425
Lesson 4:	Charting a Trend with a Line Chart	.435
Lesson 5:	Formatting Axis Labels and Adding a Trendline	.441
Lesson 6:	Documenting the Chart and Worksheets	.447
Advanced Skills or Concepts		.453
Check Your Work		.454
Key Terms		.455
Assessing Learning Outcomes		.455
Skill Drill		.457
Fix It		.465
On the Job		.466
Discussion of Advanced Skills or Concepts		.469
On Your Own		.469
Assess Your Progress		.471

chapter
nine | Creating a Presentation 472

File Guide 476
Lesson 1:   Creating a Presentation 476
Lesson 2:   Adding Slides to a Presentation and Editing Content 482
Lesson 3:   Adding Graphic Elements 486
Lesson 4:   Applying a Theme to a Presentation 493
Lesson 5:   Adding Information to the Header and Footer 499
Lesson 6:   Adding Slide Transitions and Viewing a Slide Show 504
Lesson 7:   Creating Speaker Notes and Handouts 508
Advanced Skills or Concepts 514
Check Your Work 515
Key Terms 515
Assessing Learning Outcomes 516
Skill Drill 518
Fix It 523
On the Job 524
Discussion of Advanced Skills or Concepts 526
On Your Own 526
Assess Your Progress 527

chapter
ten | Enhancing a Presentation 528

File Guide 532
Lesson 1:   Importing Text from an Outline 532
Lesson 2:   Applying a Theme and Adding Graphics 535
Lesson 3:   Adding Tables to a Presentation 539
Lesson 4:   Adding Charts to a Presentation 548
Lesson 5:   Inserting Diagrams Using SmartArt 553
Lesson 6:   Adding Animations 559
Lesson 7:   Adding Hyperlinks and Saving as a Web Page 567
Advanced Skills or Concepts 575
Check Your Work 576
Key Terms 577
Assessing Learning Outcomes 577
Skill Drill 579
Fix It 585
On the Job 586
Discussion of Advanced Skills or Concepts 588
On Your Own 588
Assess Your Progress 589

Glossary 590

Photo Credits 609

Index 611

Why We Wrote This Book

"I know how to use a computer"

We've probably all heard this statement at some point from our students and employees and wondered exactly what it meant—or, at least, what it meant to them. To those of us in the business of teaching computer skills, it's not just a matter of semantics. There is, in fact, a great deal of confusion out there about what constitutes computer literacy.

We often hear from administrators that the introductory level computer course will soon disappear at the college level. Because students today have greater exposure to computers by the time they leave high school, the argument goes, they feel comfortable enough to skip formal classes altogether. Yet in my experience teaching computer concepts and applications, I have come across such vast differences in the level of computer proficiency that it is nearly impossible to give the same lesson to any one group of students.

Even the best and most prepared students have significant gaps in their knowledge at the basic level. Some know how to surf the Internet, but have only a vague idea of how it works. Others, returning to school as adults, might know a few isolated applications but lack the concepts to learn software more thoroughly. All would benefit from a foundation course that teaches computers in the real world context that students must master in order to succeed—in college and in their careers.

This is where IC^3 comes in. The philosophy behind IC^3 certification helps define the concepts all students must know in order to be considered computer literate. Even if they never take the certification tests, this "common baseline" approach will give your students the confidence to say, "I know how to use a computer" and know exactly what that means.

Why IC^3?

Not just applications
- Unlike other certifications, IC^3 offers a well-rounded approach to computer literacy that covers basic computer concepts, applications, and the Internet.

Software is not vendor specific
- Although we wrote the applications section using Microsoft Office because it is the industry standard, students will learn about other operating systems such as Linux and Mac OS and other applications suites like OpenOffice.org.

Flexibility
- Because of the division of topics into three major areas—Computing Fundamentals, Key Applications, and Living Online—students can choose to focus on areas where they need more work. Faculty have the freedom to be creative while working within IC^3's defined framework. There are also two versions of *Unit 2: Using Productivity Software* allowing for even more flexibility; the traditional version written to Microsoft Office and a new version written to OpenOffice.org that is available through our Custom PHIT Database program.

Why Computer Literacy for IC³?

Comprehensive coverage of objectives
* Each of the IC³ objectives is covered comprehensively so you can be assured that your students are learning everything necessary to meet the standard.

Extensive end-of-project material
* Several levels of reinforcement exercises to choose from at the end of chapter—including **Assess Your Progress, On the Job,** and **On Your Own**—offer a range of choices.

Skills based, hands-on instruction
* Students grasp the material quickly and easily with clearly numbered, bold, step-by-step instructions within these hands-on tutorials.

Typeface Conventions Used in This Book

Computer Literacy for IC³ uses the following typeface conventions to make it easier for you to understand the material.

Monospace type appears frequently and `looks like this`. It is used to indicate text that you are instructed to key in.

Italic text indicates text that appears onscreen as (1) warnings, confirmation, or general information; (2) the name of a file to be used in a lesson or exercise; and (3) text from a menu or dialog box that is referenced within a sentence, when that sentence might appear awkward if it were not set off.

Hotkeys are indicated by underline. Hotkeys are the underlined letters in menus, toolbars, and dialog boxes that activate commands and options, and are a quick way to choose frequently used commands and options. Hotkeys look like this: <u>F</u>ile, <u>S</u>ave.

Student Resources

Companion Website (www.pearsonhighered.com/ic3). This text-specific Website provides students with additional information and exercises to reinforce their learning. Features include: additional end-of-project reinforcement material; online Study Guide; easy access to *all* chapter data files; and much, much more!

Accessing Student Data Files. The data files that students need to work through the chapters can be downloaded from the Companion Website (www.pearsonhighered.com/ic3). Data files are provided for each chapter. The filenames correspond to the filenames called for in this book. The filename indicates the unit, chapter, and topic. For example, where U2 is the unit number, Ch01 indicates the chapter number within that unit, which is followed by a descriptive name. After you open the file, you will save it with the same name followed by your name to identify the file as yours.

Instructor's Resources

The Instructor's Resource Center on CD-ROM is an interactive library of assets and links. The Instructor's Resource Center on CD-ROM writes custom "index" pages that can be used as the foundation of a class presentation or online lecture. By navigating through the CD-ROM, you can collect the materials that are most relevant to your interests, edit them to create powerful class lectures, copy them to your own computer's hard drive, and/or upload them to an online course management system. The new and improved Prentice Hall Instructor's Resource Center on CD-ROM includes tools you expect from a Prentice Hall text:

- The Instructor's Manual in Word and PDF formats—includes solutions to all questions and exercises from the book and Companion Website
- Multiple, customizable PowerPoint slide presentations for each chapter
- Data and Solution Files
- Complete Test Bank
- TestGen Software
- TestGen is a test generator that lets you view and easily edit test bank questions, transfer them to tests, and print in a variety of formats suitable to your teaching situation. The program also offers many options for organizing and displaying test banks and tests. A built-in random number and text generator makes it ideal for creating multiple versions of tests that involve calculations and provides more possible test items than test bank questions. Powerful search and sort functions let you easily locate questions and arrange them in the order you prefer.

CourseSmart

CourseSmart is an exciting new choice for students looking to save money. As an alternative to purchasing the print textbook, students can purchase an electronic version of the same content and save up to 50% off the suggested list price of the print text. With a CourseSmart etextbook, students can search the text, make notes online, print out reading assignments that incorporate lecture notes, and bookmark important passages for later review. For more information, or to purchase access to the CourseSmart eTextbook, visit www.coursesmart.com.

Companion Website @ www.pearsonhighered.com/ic3

This text is accompanied by a Companion Website at www.pearsonhighered.com/ic3. Features of this new site include an interactive study guide, downloadable supplements, additional practice projects, Web resources links. All links to Internet exercises will be constantly updated to ensure accuracy for students.

COMPUTER LITERACY FOR IC3™

Visual Walk-Through

From cover to cover, *Computer Literacy for IC3* makes it easier for you to teach the course you want. In addition to breaking each IC3 unit out into its own separate text, *Computer Literacy for IC3* contains many features that help students learn the material, effectively preparing them for each new lesson.

Know where IC3 standards are targeted within each lesson and direct student focus throughout, with the **Learning Outcomes** feature that closely matches the titles of the step-by-step tutorials.

Lesson	Learning Outcomes	Code	Related IC3 Objectives
1	Create a new document	2.01	1.2.1
1	Display the ruler	2.02	2.1.3
2	Create and modify a bulleted list	2.03	2.1.7, 2.1.16
3	Format text	2.04	1.3.6
3	Change text alignment	2.05	1.3.6
3	Indent text	2.06	2.12
4	Create a title with WordArt	2.07	1.3.7
4	Modify WordArt	2.08	1.3.7
5	Insert, resize and move clip art	2.09	1.3.7
6	Insert, move, and crop pictures	2.10	1.3.7
7	Create a table	2.11	2.1.13, 2.1.16
7	Insert and edit data in a table	2.12	2.1.13, 2.1.16
7	Modify table structure	2.13	2.1.14
7	Insert and delete cells, rows, and columns	2.14	2.1.14
7	Change column width and row height	2.15	2.1.14, 2.1.16
7	Convert text to a table or table to text	2.16	2.1.13
8	Format tables with table styles	2.17	2.1.15
8	Modify table formats using command buttons	2.18	2.1.15
8	Align table cell contents	2.19	2.1.15
8	Merge cells	2.20	2.1.15
8	Add, modify, and remove table and shading	2.21	2.1.15
8	Split cells in a table	2.22	2.1.14
8	Split tables	2.23	2.1.14
8	Sort data in a table	2.26	2.1.15
9	Insert and modify a footer	2.24	2.1.10
10	Use a document template	2.25	1.2.1
Advanced Skills	Use overtype	2.27	1.3.3
Advanced Skills	Transmit documents in electronic format	2.28	1.4.6, 1.4.7

Instructions throughout the lessons are based on the Vista operating system, running Microsoft Office 2007.

? *Why* Would I Do This?

Documents can be based on already existing files or written from scratch to create a new file. In addition, several preformatted and designed documents can be used for specific purposes such as memos or fax cover letters.

Formatting text helps the reader see the organization of the document and identify important information or ideas. Font selection conveys the tone of a document from serious to fun. Simple formatting tools enable you to change font, font size, or text alignment. You can emphasize text to make it stand out from the surrounding text by using bold, italic, underline, color, or special character effects.

Graphics add visual components to your documents that help draw the reader's attention or highlight an important idea or fact. Images should be related to the topic and provide visual interest or information. This can be done with pictures that are stored in a digital format, shapes used to create a drawing, borders and shading to draw attention to information, or electronic images provided with your software. Graphic elements can be resized and repositioned. Adding graphics creates excitement and visual appeal.

Tables are lists that display data in a column-and-row format. They organize and present parallel lists of information and can be used in a variety of circumstances.

Why Would I Do This? effectively explains why each task and procedure is important so that students will be able to apply them in real life scenarios.

Make sure your students see the big picture with the **Visual Summary**, a graphical presentation of the concepts and features in each chapter that also includes the final results of the completed project.

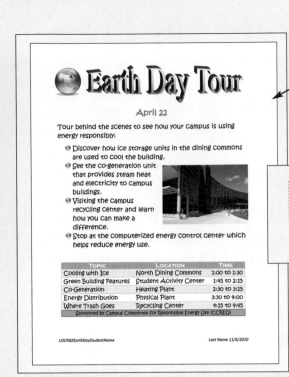

visual
summary | In this chapter, you will create a new document that is a flyer announcing an upcoming Earth Day tour at a local university, and then you will use a preformatted fax cover sheet to distribute the file electronically to the campus community. The documents created are shown in Figure 2.1.

4 Click the Page Layout tab. In the Paragraph group, under Spacing, in the After box, be sure that 10 pt displays. If 10 pt does not display, click in the After box, type 10 and then press ↵Enter. *Spacing after* adds space between paragraphs, which occurs when you press ↵Enter to begin a new paragraph. Recall that a paragraph can be a single line of text. The default spacing following a paragraph in Word 2007 is 10 pt, which creates white space between paragraphs.

5 Click the Home tab, and in the Paragraph group, click the Line Spacing button, and then click 1.0 to set the line spacing to single-space. The default *line spacing*—the spacing between lines of text in a paragraph—is 1.15 in Word 2007. When text is *single-spaced*—1.0—there is no additional space between lines of text in a paragraph.

Provide students with the "learn by doing" **Step-by-Step Tutorials**, a feature that uses one-at-a-time instructions in a clear numbered and bolded format.

6 Type Earth Day Tour press ↵Enter, and then type April 22 Notice that there is space between these two lines of text because of the spacing after feature that is set to 10 pt.

7 Press ↵Enter. Type Tour behind the scenes to see how your campus is using energy responsibly: and then press ↵Enter.

8 On the Quick Access Toolbar, click the Save button 🖫 to display the Save As dialog box. If you have not previously saved your file, the Save As dialog box will display when you click the Save button.

to extend **your knowledge...**

CHANGING FONT SIZE
Another way to change font size is to use the Grow Font or Shrink Font buttons that are in the Font group, just to the right of the Font Size box. Each time you click one of these buttons, the font size is increased with the Grow Font button Aˆ or decreased with the Shrink Font button Aˇ.

Show your students alternative ways to complete a process, give them special hints about using the software, and provide them with extra tips and shortcuts with the **To Extend Your Knowledge** feature.

Capture teachable moments with **Good Design**, a Unit 2 feature that introduces design tips in the most applicable section of the material. This feature is assessed in the **Fix It**, **On the Job**, and **On Your Own** end-of-chapter exercises.

good **design...**

USING LISTS TO ORGANIZE DATA
Lists of data can be presented using several different techniques. It is important to select the best option for the data to be listed. Use bullet lists when there is no particular order to the items listed, and use numbered lists when there is an order, such as steps in a process, order of importance, or chronological order.

Help students anticipate or solve common problems quickly and effectively with **If You Have Problems**, a feature that provides short troubleshooting notes.

if you have **problems...**

If you press ⏎Enter after typing the last item, another number will display on the screen. Press ⌫Backspace as needed to remove the number and return the insertion point to the end of the previous numbered item in the list.

fix *it*

One way to appreciate the value of good design is to fix a file that is not designed well. In this exercise, you open a file that has several errors and design flaws and fix it according to good design elements, using the skills that you practiced in the lessons.

Navigate to the folder with the student files, open **U2Ch02FixIt** and save it as U2Ch02FixItStudentName

Examine this document and format it using the skills you have practiced so that it is a professional, readable flyer that will attract attention and create interest. Make changes to comply with the good design principles that were introduced in this chapter. Here is a list of corrections needed and the design principles introduced in this chapter, along with some tips on how to fix the flyer.

- Create a title for the flyer to attract attention to the topic of energy efficiency.
- Use a clip art that is appropriate to the topic, and position it to break up the opening paragraphs.
- Use a font that is appropriate to the topic, audience, and type of document.
- Use a font size that is easy to read quickly.
- Adjust the alignment and/or indents to create a balanced document.
- Where it is appropriate, convert text to a table, and insert a row with column headings.
- Format the table so that it is clear and easy to read. Center the table on the page.
- Insert the **U2Ch02WDBuilding2** image, which is the building that will be LEED-certified.

Encourage hands-on design practice with **Fix It**. This feature gets students to improve a file containing several errors and design flaws by having them use the skills and good design elements that they practiced in their lessons.

Prepare students to use each lesson outside the classroom with the extensive **end-of-chapter exercises**. These exercises include: **Check Your Work**, **Assessing Learning Outcomes**, **Skill Drill**, **On the Job**, **On Your Own**, and **Assess Your Progress**.

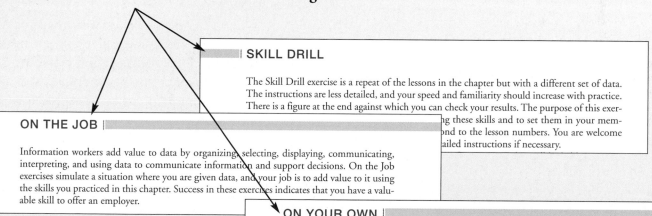

SKILL DRILL

The Skill Drill exercise is a repeat of the lessons in the chapter but with a different set of data. The instructions are less detailed, and your speed and familiarity should increase with practice. There is a figure at the end against which you can check your results. The purpose of this exer-
...ng these skills and to set them in your mem-
...ond to the lesson numbers. You are welcome
...ailed instructions if necessary.

ON THE JOB

Information workers add value to data by organizing, selecting, displaying, communicating, interpreting, and using data to communicate information and support decisions. On the Job exercises simulate a situation where you are given data, and your job is to add value to it using the skills you practiced in this chapter. Success in these exercises indicates that you have a valuable skill to offer an employer.

ON YOUR OWN

Once you are comfortable with the skills in this chapter, you can apply them to new situations of your own choosing. In this section, you choose data that you have in your possession or that you can find elsewhere. To successfully complete this assignment, you must apply good design practices and demonstrate mastery of the skills that were practiced. Refer to the list of skills and design practices in the Fix It exercise.

COMPUTER LITERACY FOR IC3™

UNIT 2: USING PRODUCTIVITY SOFTWARE

chapter **one**

Starting with Microsoft Office 2007 Applications

Lesson	Learning Outcomes	Code	Related IC3 Objectives
1	Start a Windows application	1.01	1.1.1
1	Identify common on-screen elements	1.02	1.1.2
1	Switch between open applications	1.03	1.2.3
2	Open and save files	1.04	1.2.2, 1.2.4
2	Exit an application	1.05	1.1.1
3	Navigate a document	1.06	1.1.3
3	Change views and magnification	1.07	1.1.5, 1.1.6
3	Select a word, line, paragraph, or document	1.08	1.3.2
3	Insert and replace text	1.09	1.3.1, 1.3.2
3	Use the Backspace and Delete keys to edit text	1.10	1.3.2
4	Use command buttons and dialog boxes	1.11	1.1.4
4	Insert a symbol	1.12	2.1.8
4	Use Find and Replace to edit text	1.13	1.3.4
5	Check spelling	1.14	1.3.5
6	Select and format text	1.15	1.3.6
7	Copy and paste text within a document	1.16	1.3.2
7	Copy and paste text between documents	1.17	1.3.2
7	Cut text and move text using drag-and-drop	1.18	1.3.2
8	Use galleries, contextual tabs, and the Quick Access Toolbar	1.19	1.1.4
8	Format text	1.20	1.3.6
8	Use Undo and Redo commands	1.21	1.3.3
9	Print a document	1.22	1.4.2, 1.4.3
9	Close files and exit an application	1.23	1.1.1, 1.2.5
10	Use Help	1.24	1.1.9
Advanced Skills	Identify and prioritize Help resources	1.25	1.1.8
Advanced Skills	Manage print job and resolve printing problems	1.26	1.4.4, 1.4.5

Instructions throughout the lessons are based on the Vista operating system running Microsoft Office 2007. Due to variability in screen size and display settings, as well as personal settings, your screen may not always match the figures included in this chapter.

Why Would I Do This?

Many computer programs use the same methods for accomplishing common tasks. In this chapter, you practice the procedures that are common to several programs. *Application software* is the term used for computer programs that accomplish a specific set of tasks. They are also referred to as applications or *programs*. *Windows-based applications* are computer programs that are written to work on a computer using a Microsoft Windows operating system. *Microsoft Office* is a suite of applications that performs tasks commonly used in an office environment, such as writing documents, managing finances, and presenting information.

Whether you are using a Microsoft Office application or another Windows-based program, you will use the same basic procedures to start and exit each application and to interact with the various programs. Before you can use a software application effectively, you need to know how to work with the program's on-screen elements. Microsoft Office applications use a *graphical user interface*, commonly referred to as *GUI* (pronounced "gooey"), which includes windows, dialog boxes, command buttons, and menus. A mouse and keyboard are the most common input devices used to interact with the on-screen elements. In this chapter, you practice using the Microsoft Office 2007 user interface.

visual summary

In this chapter, you will open several applications and identify elements that are common to all applications. You will then open a file and use common features in Microsoft Office Word 2007 to edit a letter to a customer about green energy technology, as shown in Figure 1.1.

GREEN ENERGY EXPRESS™
One Plaza Drive, Detroit, MI 48231-1001
www.greenenergyexpress.net

August 23, 2010

Rob and Maria Franklin
6236 Daleview Drive
Ypsilanti, MI 48197

Dear Mr. and Mrs. Franklin:

Congratulations! You are the recipients of a donation on your behalf to the *Green Energy Express*™ program. Your benefactors, Jake and Sara Prescott, have purchased a month's supply of green energy for your home.

The *Green Energy Express*™ program helps fund research and develops new sources of electrical energy. The following two projects will produce the electrical energy for your home in the coming month:

- **Wind** – Our newest wind generator is named Express One. It generates one megawatt of electrical power from the wind while producing no exhaust gasses.
- **Biomass** – We are partnering with the largest dairy herd owners in the state to capture the methane gas that is produced by natural processes in the animal waste and burning it to generate electricity.

Because new technologies cost more to get up and running, the electricity costs a bit more but the benefits to our state and country are worth it. Your bill for the following month will not change but an additional $.02 will be added to Jake and Sara Prescott's bill for each kilowatt-hour of electricity you use. The amount you are already paying, plus the small increase funded by your benefactors, will pay for a month's green energy that does not add to air pollution or send your dollars overseas.

At the end of the month, you will have the opportunity to continue to participate in the *Green Energy Express*™ program. You have three options; you can do nothing and your bill will not be affected, you can sign up for the *Green Energy Express*™ program and assume the additional cost yourself, or you can be the benefactor of someone else.

We hope that this experience of using electricity for a month in the most environmentally friendly way possible will be a satisfying experience. We want to invite you to get on the Green Express by continuing the program yourself or by being a benefactor to a friend.

Sincerely,

Student Name
Director, *Green Energy Express*™

FIGURE 1.1

List of Student and Solution Files

In most cases, you will start from a new, empty file and enter text and data or paste content from other files. You will add your name to the file names and save them on your computer's hard drive or portable memory device. Table 1.1 lists the files you will start with and the names you will give them when you save the files.

ASSIGNMENT	STUDENT SOURCE FILE:	SAVE AS:
Lessons 1–10	U2Ch01Energy U2Ch01ExpressLogo	U2Ch01EnergyStudentName Not saved
Skill Drill	U2Ch01Parking U2Ch01ParkingMemo	U2Ch01ParkingStudentName Not saved
Fix It	U2Ch01FixIt	U2Ch01FixItStudentName
On the Job	U2Ch01Coop U2Ch01CoopProject U2Ch01Pricing	U2Ch01CoopStudentName Not Saved U2Ch01PricingStudentName
On Your Own	New file New file	U2Ch01AppreciationStudentName U2Ch01CareerStudentName
Assess Your Progress	U2Ch01Assess	U2Ch01AssessStudentName

TABLE 1.1

▶▶▶ *lesson*

one | Starting an Application and Identifying Common On-Screen Elements

To start a Microsoft Office application, you typically use the Start button found on the *taskbar* at the bottom of your screen. All programs can be started in this same way. In this lesson, you start several Office applications and explore common on-screen elements.

to start an application and identify common on-screen elements

1 **On the taskbar at the bottom of your screen, in the left corner, click the Start button ⊕ to display the Start menu.** The Start menu lists frequently used programs on the left and commonly used folders on the right.

2 **On the Start menu, click All Programs to display the list of programs that are installed on your computer.** If necessary, a vertical scroll bar displays so that you can scroll down the list to see additional programs, as shown in Figure 1.2.

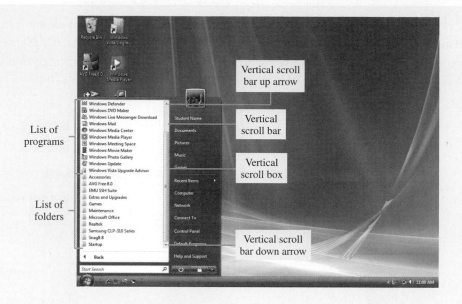

FIGURE 1.2

3 If necessary, scroll down to display Microsoft Office, and then click Microsoft Office to expand the list of available Office programs, as shown in Figure 1.3. The programs listed depend on the version of Microsoft Office that is installed on your computer.

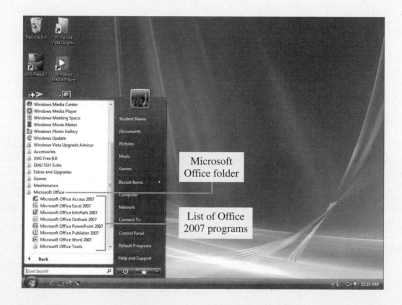

FIGURE 1.3

4 From the displayed list, click Microsoft Office Word 2007 and locate the areas on your screen that are identified in Figure 1.4. Refer to Table 1.2 for a description of each element. The Microsoft Word window opens to a new *document*, which is the main *work area* in Word. Word gives the document a default name, such as *Document1*. This name displays in both the title bar and the taskbar. The work area in each application is different, but the other on-screen elements are very similar. You may see a paragraph mark displayed in the document at the insertion point location. The settings used when Word was last open determine whether this formatting mark displays.

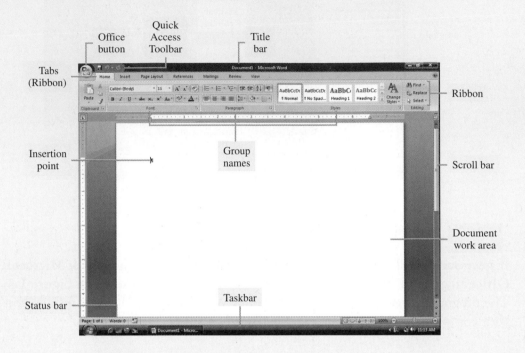

FIGURE 1.4

SCREEN ELEMENT	DESCRIPTION
Title bar	Displays the program icon, the name of the file, and the name of the program. The Minimize, Maximize/Restore Down, and Close buttons are grouped on the right side of the title bar.
Office button	A button that displays commands related to files.
Ribbon	A strip at the top of the screen that contains groups of buttons for the most common commands used in applications.
Tabs (Ribbon)	Used to access lists of commands related to a category of actions for each application. The content of the tabs varies for each application.
Group	A collection of related commands on a tab that enable you to interact with the software.
Work area	The area on the screen where you enter text, numbers, or graphics to create a document, a worksheet, or presentation slides.
Quick Access Toolbar	A customizable toolbar to the right of the Office button that contains the Save, Undo, and Repeat/Redo buttons.
Insertion point	Indicates with a blinking vertical line where text or graphics will be inserted.

Taskbar	Displays the Start button and the names of any open files and applications. The taskbar may also display shortcut buttons for other programs.
Scroll bars	Horizontal and vertical bars that enable you to navigate in a window, menu, or gallery.
Status bar	Displays information about the document or other file on which you are working.
Maximize/Restore Down button	Expands a window to fill the screen or restores it to its previous size.
Minimize button	Reduces a window to a button on the taskbar.
Close button	Closes a file or the application if only one file is open.

TABLE 1.2

5 **On the taskbar, click the Start button** ⊕. **On the displayed Start menu, click All Programs, click Microsoft Office, and then click Microsoft Office Excel 2007 to display the Excel window.** The default file name displayed in the title bar is *Book1*.

6 **If necessary, on the right end of the title bar, click the Maximize button** 🔲 **to expand the Excel window so that it fills your screen.** Notice that two buttons display on the taskbar—one for each open application window.

7 **Examine your screen and locate each of the screen elements in the Excel window that are identified in Figure 1.5.** The same basic screen elements are displayed in both the Excel and Word applications; however, the tabs and commands used in

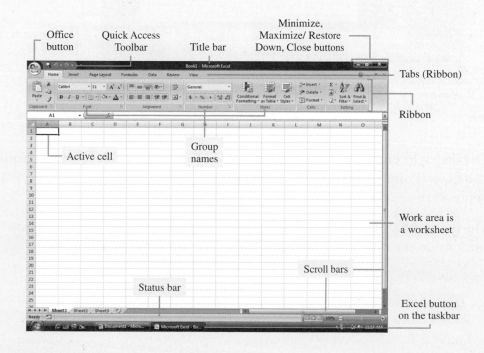

FIGURE 1.5

Starting an Application and Identifying Common On-Screen Elements

Excel are slightly different and include commands that are specific to the Excel program. The Excel window displays a *worksheet* as the main work area, which is a grid of rows and columns. Rows are identified by numbers, and columns are identified by letters. The intersection of each row and column is referred to as a *cell*. Each cell is referred to by its *cell address*, which is the column letter and row number. The first cell's address is A1. Cell A1 has a dark border, which indicates that it is the *active cell*—the cell where data will display when you type.

8 **From the Start menu** 🔵**, display the list of Microsoft Office applications, and then click Microsoft Office PowerPoint 2007. Examine your screen and identify the elements in the PowerPoint window shown in Figure 1.6.** Again, as in Word and Excel, the same basic screen elements display, but the tabs on the Ribbon and the groups of commands are specific to the PowerPoint program. The default file name is *Presentation1*.

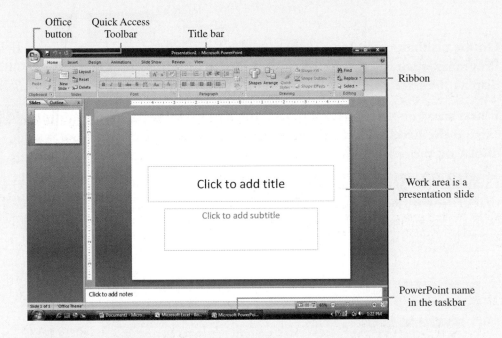

FIGURE 1.6

9 **On the right end of the title bar, click the Minimize button** 🔲 **to minimize the PowerPoint window to the taskbar.** The Excel window—previously the active application—redisplays on the screen.

10 **On the taskbar, click the Word button to display the open Word window.** The buttons on the taskbar can be used to switch between open applications.

11   **Leave all of the applications open to continue to the next lesson.**

to extend **your knowledge**

STARTING APPLICATIONS

There are several ways to start an application. The most common is to use the Start menu, and then point to All Programs to locate the application you need. Application shortcuts can be pinned to the top of the Start menu or added to the desktop. Application shortcuts can also be added to the Quick Launch bar on the left side of the taskbar. Use Windows Help if you would like to use one of these shortcut methods. In this book, you will simply be instructed to start the application—you decide which method to use.

▶▶▶ *lesson*

two | Opening and Saving a File and Closing Applications

When you open an application, you can create a file using the blank document, worksheet, or presentation file that displays. You can also open an existing file, make changes to the file and save it with its current name, or save it with a new name. When you save a file, give the file a name that is related to the contents of the file and specify the location on your computer where you want to save the file. In this lesson, you open a file and save it with a new name. Then you will close applications that are no longer being used.

to open and save a file

1 **With the Microsoft Office Word window displayed, in the upper left corner of the screen click the Office button.** **From the displayed menu, click Open to display the Open dialog box.** In a *dialog box*, you select settings and choose what actions you want the computer to take. The Open dialog box enables you to locate files on your computer. The default folder that displays is usually the Documents folder on your computer's hard drive. The Documents folder may be personalized to display the name of the registered owner of the computer.

2 **Navigate to the location for the student files for this book.** The files may be on a CD-ROM, a network drive, or on your computer's hard drive or USB drive.

3 **Double-click the StudentFiles folder, and then double-click the Chapter01 folder to display the files for this chapter.** Double-clicking a folder opens the folder and displays its contents. Placing files in folders helps to organize your work.

4 **On the Menu bar, click the Views button arrow, and then click List. Click the file U2Ch01Energy one time to select it, as shown in Figure 1.7.**

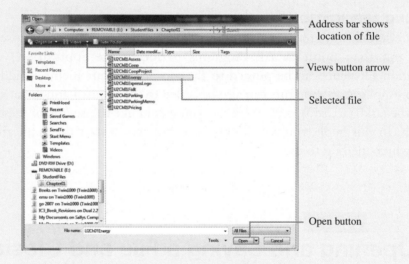

FIGURE 1.7

5 **In the lower right corner of the Open dialog box, click the Open button to open the selected file.** You can also double-click a file name to open it.

6 **In the upper left corner of the Word window, click the Office button, and then from the displayed menu click Save As.** In the displayed Save As dialog box, you can give the file a new name and save it to a location on your computer, USB drive, or network drive.

7 In the Save As dialog box, in the File name box, type U2Ch01EnergyStudentName **replacing the words** *StudentName* **with your own name.** Each time you save a file used in this textbook, you will add your name to the end of the file name so that your work can be easily identified.

8 In the left panel of the Save As dialog box, click Computer, and then double-click the drive location where you want to save your files—such as a USB drive or removable disk.

9 Click the New Folder button, type Chapter01 and then press ⏎Enter. Compare your screen with Figure 1.8. The folder name and path display in the Address bar, with the new file name in the File name box. The new folder is empty. It is helpful to organize your files into folders so that you can locate all of the completed files when it is time to submit your work.

Address bar
displays
location of file

Chapter01 folder
displays in
Address bar

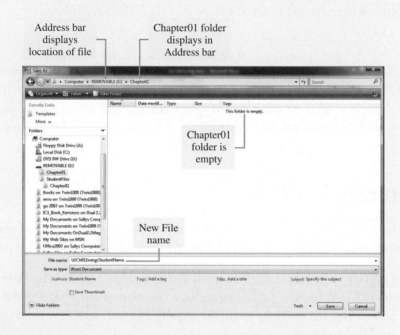

Chapter01
folder is
empty

New File
name

FIGURE 1.8

10 In the lower right corner of the Save As dialog box, click Save. The new file name displays in the title bar of the open Word document. Using the Save As dialog box and renaming the file creates a new document. The original file is preserved and can be opened again.

SAVING AND OPENING FILES

When you save a file, it is important to first select the folder where you want it to be saved. If you open a file and click the save button, it will be saved to the folder and drive in which it was previously stored.

A saved file can be opened from within the computer's file management program or from the desktop. If you save a file to the desktop, you can double-click the file name icon on the desktop to open the file. When you double-click on a file name it launches the program that it was created with, and then displays the file. If you save your files to the Documents folder, you can open the files by selecting Documents from the Start menu, which will display a dialog box with the Documents folder selected. Locate the file you want to open and double-click the file name. Similarly, you can use the Recent Items list from the Start menu and click the file you want to open. The key to good file management is to use folders and to be sure you identify the location where the file is saved before you click the Save button.

When you finish using an application, you should close it to conserve the resources of your computer. This helps to ensure that you have sufficient memory to work with in other active programs. There are several possible techniques for closing an application. If you made changes to a file, the program will prompt you to save your changes before you exit.

to exit an application

1 **On the taskbar, click the PowerPoint button. On the right end of the title bar of the PowerPoint window, click the Close button** [X] **to close the program.**

2 **On the taskbar, click the Excel button. On the right end of the Title bar, click the Restore Down button** [⊡] **to reduce the size of the Excel window.** The Restore Down button changes to the Maximize button, which is used to expand a window to fill the screen.

3 **In the Excel window, click the Office button** 🔘**, and then at the bottom of the menu, click Exit Excel to close Excel.** Notice that only the Word application remains open and it displays the name of the open file.

▶▶▶ *lesson*
three | Navigating a Document and Inserting, Selecting, and Editing Text

One of the main advantages of using a computer is the ability to alter documents by changing the content. The techniques used to navigate and edit are common across most applications. In this lesson, you will practice the fundamental methods used for navigating, inserting, selecting, and editing text.

to navigate a document

1 **With the *U2Ch01EnergyStudentName* file open, on the Ribbon, in the Paragraph group, click the Show/Hide button** ¶ **until it is gold, to indicate that it is active.** Paragraph marks display at the end of each paragraph and between paragraphs, and dots display between words to indicate spaces, as shown in Figure 1.9. In Microsoft Word, when you press ↵Enter, Spacebar, or Tab⇆, characters display to represent these keystrokes. These ***formatting marks*** or ***nonprinting characters*** do not print. When editing a document, it is helpful to display these marks.

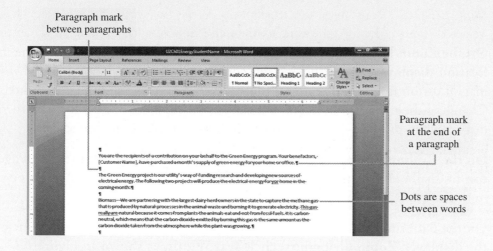

FIGURE 1.9

2 **On the status bar, on the right side, click the Print Layout button** 🗏 **, if necessary.** Each application can be displayed in several different ***views***—different ways to display data on the screen. In Word, these include Print Layout, Full Screen Reading, Web Layout, Outline, and Draft. Views can be changed by clicking the View buttons on the status bar or by clicking the View tab on the Ribbon and then selecting a view from the application's Views group.

3 **On the status bar, to the right of the view buttons, point to the Zoom bar until the Zoom ScreenTip displays, as shown in Figure 1.10. A *ScreenTip* is** a description that displays the name of a screen element, button, or area on a window, and often information on how to use the element. Use these to help you locate buttons and tools in your application window. The ***Zoom bar*** enables you to change the magnification of the document or worksheet. Clicking the Zoom In or Zoom Out buttons on the Zoom bar increases or decreases the magnification of the document workspace on the screen. Dragging the Zoom slider toward the left or right will also change the magnification. The current magnification displays to the left of the Zoom bar; typically the default magnification is 100%.

Current Zoom setting

Zoom bar

Zoom In button

Zoom Out button

Zoom Slider

FIGURE 1.10

4 **On the Zoom bar, click the Zoom In button ⊕ three times or until the magnification displays 130%.** Clicking the Zoom In or Zoom Out buttons changes the magnification first to the nearest 10% and then by 10% each time it is clicked. Changing the magnification does not change the font size or how the document will display when printed—it only changes the way it displays on your screen.

5 **On the Ribbon, click the View tab. In the Zoom group, click the One Page button to display the entire document on the screen.** Notice that the zoom percentage in the Zoom bar decreased.

6 **On the Ribbon on the View tab, in the Zoom group, click the Zoom button. In the displayed Zoom dialog box, click Text Width, as shown in Figure 1.11, and then click OK.** The document is magnified until the text displays from the left edge to the right edge of the screen. The full margin area no longer displays, but text appears larger and is easier to read. On the Zoom bar, the magnification percent is increased.

Zoom options

Text width option selected

Entire document displayed on the screen

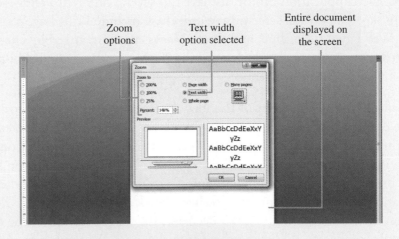

FIGURE 1.11

7 On the right edge of the screen, at the end of the vertical scroll bar, click the Down arrow ⬇ several times to scroll down the screen. If you hold down the left mouse button continuously while pointing to the Down arrow, the page will continue to scroll so that you can see more of the text on the lower half of the document, while the top of the document scrolls up and out of view.

8 On the vertical scroll bar, point to the vertical scroll box and *drag*—hold down the left mouse button and move the mouse. Drag the mouse down until the scroll box reaches the end of the scroll bar and you see the bottom of the page. When you scroll a page, the insertion point does not move; only the text displayed on the screen changes. To move the insertion point, you need to click in a new location.

9 At the bottom of the window, on the horizontal scroll bar, drag the scroll box to the left to display the lower left corner of the page. The horizontal scroll bar enables you to move the document to the left or right on your screen.

10 On your keyboard, click (PgUp) one time to move the document up on the screen. Navigation keys are another method used to move around the screen.

11 Hold down (Ctrl), and then press the (Home) key one time to display the top of the document. Release the (Ctrl) key. When you press two keys at a time, it is a *keyboard shortcut* used to perform an action—in this case to move to the top of the document. Keyboard shortcuts work across all Office applications and in many other applications as well.

to extend your knowledge

MORE INFORMATION ABOUT THE SCROLL BOX

Each scroll bar includes a scroll box, which lets you know your location in a document—it is at the top of the scroll bar when you are at the beginning of the document and at the bottom of the scroll bar when you are at the end of the document. When a document is in Print Layout view, the size of the scroll box, relative to the length of the scroll bar, indicates how the currently visible portion of the document compares in size to the document as a whole; for example, a small box represents a large document. One of the quickest ways to move through a large document is to drag the scroll box up or down. As you scroll through a multipage document, a ScreenTip next to the scroll box displays the current page number.

OTHER WAYS TO NAVIGATE IN A FILE

In this lesson, you practiced just a few of the navigation techniques used to move around in a file. Table 1.3 lists common keyboard shortcuts. Most of these work in a similar fashion in most Microsoft Office applications.

TO MOVE	PRESS THE FOLLOWING KEYS
To the beginning of a file	Ctrl + Home
To the end of a file	Ctrl + End
To the beginning of a line	Home
To the end of a line	End
To the beginning of the previous word	Ctrl + ←
To the beginning of the next word	Ctrl + →
To the beginning of the current word (if the insertion point is in the middle of a word)	Ctrl + ←
To the beginning of the next word (if the insertion point is in the middle of a word)	Ctrl + →
To the beginning of the current paragraph	Ctrl + ↑
To the beginning of the next paragraph	Ctrl + ↓
Up one screen	PgUp
Down one screen	PgDn

TABLE 1.3

to insert text

1 **With the insertion point in the blank line at the top of the document, type** Rob and Maria Franklin **and then press** ↵Enter. As you type, the insertion point and the paragraph mark move to the right. Pressing the ↵Enter key moves the insertion point to a new line.

2 **Type the address for this letter on two lines as follows:**

6236 Daleview Drive

Ypsilanti, MI 48197

Notice that a red wavy line displays under *Daleview* and under other words in the document. These lines indicate words that are unrecognized by the spelling program included with Microsoft Office. Later in this chapter, you will check spelling to resolve these discrepancies.

3 **At the end of the zip code, press** ↵Enter **two times, type** Dear Mr. and Mrs. Franklin: **and then press** ↵Enter. Letters include an *inside address* (the name and address of the recipient of the letter) and a *salutation* (a greeting to the recipient). One line is placed between the inside address and the salutation, and then one line is placed between the salutation and the body of the letter. You can use the ↵Enter key to create a blank line between parts of a letter.

BLOCK-STYLE LETTER

There are a few generally accepted styles for a professional letter or memo. The most common is the block style, which aligns all of the text at the left margin. In a letter, the spacing between the inside address and the salutation is one blank line, created by pressing ⏎Enter two times at the end of a line of text. The inside address is single-spaced and includes the name and address of the person to whom you are writing, as demonstrated in the previous steps and shown in Figure 1.12. The salutation should be personalized using the name or names of the person to whom the letter is being sent.

4 **In the first paragraph in the body of the letter, click to the left of the word** *You*, **type** Congratulations! **and then press** Spacebar. As you type, the text on the line moves to the right, and words move down to the next line as necessary to fit within the established margins. This feature is known as **wordwrap**—words within a paragraph wrap to the next line when text is inserted or typed. It is only necessary to press the ⏎Enter key when you want to end a paragraph or create a new line, as you did with the address lines.

5 **On the Quick Access Toolbar, click the Save button** 💾 **, and then compare your screen with Figure 1.12.** Using the Save button saves the file with the same name, which updates the file to include the changes you have made.

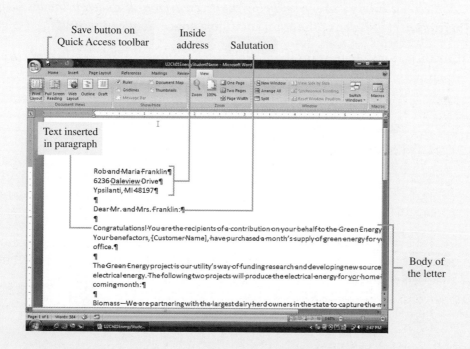

FIGURE 1.12

to select and edit text using the Delete and Backspace keys

1 On the Zoom bar, click the Zoom Out button ⊖ until the magnification displays 110%.

2 In the first paragraph that begins *Congratulations!*, click at the end of the paragraph and press ◄Backspace eleven times to remove the phrase *or office*. Then, type a period at the end of the sentence. The Backspace key removes characters and spaces to the left of the insertion point.

3 In the first line of the paragraph that begins *Congratulations!*, click to the left of the word *contribution*, press the Delete key eight times, and then type dona to change the word to *donation*. The Delete key removes characters and spaces to the right of the insertion point.

4 In the paragraph that begins *The Green Energy project*, in the first line, double-click the word *project*, and then type program Double-clicking a word selects the word. Typing replaces the selected text.

5 On the same line, click to the left of the word *is*, drag to the right to select the phrase *is our utility's way of*; then, with the phrase selected, type helps to replace the phrase with a single word.

6 Using the techniques you have practiced, continue editing this line so it reads: *The Green Energy program helps fund research and develops new sources of electrical energy.* Be sure that you include a space between words.

7 On the Quick Access Toolbar, click the Save button 🖫, and then compare your document with Figure 1.13.

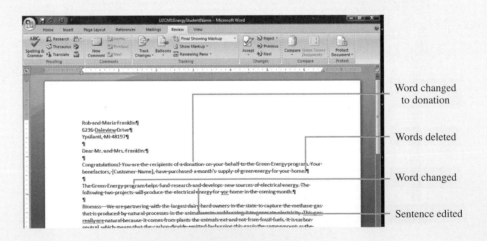

FIGURE 1.13

▶▶▶ *lesson*

four | Using Buttons and Dialog Boxes

The Ribbon is the main tool used to interact with a document. The Ribbon in each application contains several tabs. Each tab includes commands that perform similar tasks. Tabs are further organized into groups of related commands that are activated by clicking on a button. For example, on the Home tab is a Font group which contains buttons used to alter the font displayed. *Font* is a set of numbers and letters that have the same design and shape. In this lesson, you will use the Ribbon as you continue to edit the letter.

to use buttons and dialog boxes to add a symbol

1 **In the paragraph that begins** *Congratulations!,* **click to the right of the word** *Energy* **and press** Spacebar. **Type** `Express` **so that the program name is** *Green Energy Express program.*

2 **In the same paragraph, at the end of the first line, click to the immediate right of the word** *Express.* **Be sure that the insertion point is between the s in** *Express* **and the space, which is indicated by a dot to the right of the word.** Before you insert a symbol, place the insertion point at the location where you want the symbol to display.

3 **On the Ribbon, click the Insert tab. In the Symbols group, click the Symbol button.** A *gallery*—a list of potential results—displays recently used symbols, as shown in Figure 1.14. The symbols in the gallery displayed on your screen will vary from the ones shown in the figure.

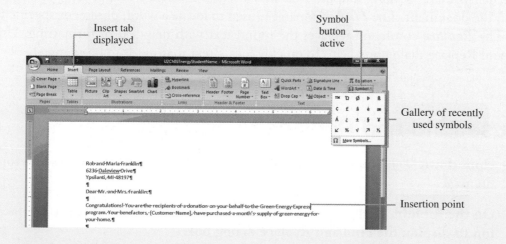

FIGURE 1.14

4 **At the bottom of the Symbols gallery, click More Symbols to open the Symbol dialog box.** If the symbol you want is not displayed in the Symbols gallery, opening the dialog box gives you access to a larger selection of symbols.

5 In the Symbol dialog box, click the Font arrow, and locate and select the Symbol font. Scroll to locate the trademark symbol (™) and click it to make it active, as shown in Figure 1.15. When a symbol is selected, the background of the symbol displays in blue. The bottom row displays recently used symbols (the ones shown in your dialog box may vary).

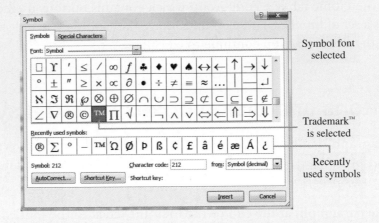

Symbol font selected

Trademark™ is selected

Recently used symbols

FIGURE 1.15

6 In the lower right corner of the Symbol dialog box, click Insert to insert the ™ symbol to the right of the program name, *Green Energy Express*. Click Close to close the Symbol dialog box.

When you are working in a file, you may need to locate a word, phrase, value, or record within the document. The ***Find*** command is used to locate a word, phrase, or specific formatting. The ***Replace*** command replaces the found text with new text or formatting. Using the Find and Replace dialog box helps to quickly locate text that needs to be changed.

to use Find and Replace to edit text

1 Hold down Ctrl, and then press Home to move the insertion point to the top of the page.

2 On the Ribbon, click the Home tab. In the Editing group, click the Replace button to display the Find and Replace dialog box.

3 In the Find what box, type `[Customer Name]` Press Tab, and then in the Replace with box, type `Jake and Sara Prescott` Compare your screen with Figure 1.16. The Find and Replace dialog box is used to locate text in a file. After it is found, you can choose to replace it with other text—as you will here—or you can make other changes to the text, such as deleting it.

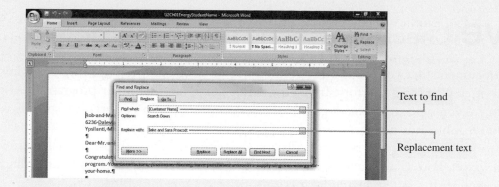

FIGURE 1.16

4 **In the Find and Replace dialog box, click Find Next.** If necessary, point to the title bar of the Find and Replace dialog box, hold down the left mouse button, and drag the dialog box out of the way so that you can see the first instance of the found text that is selected, as shown in Figure 1.17.

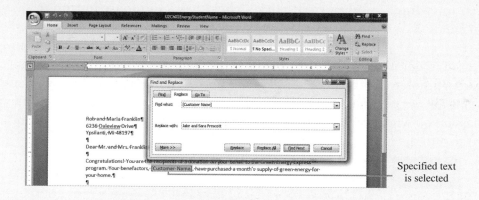

FIGURE 1.17

5 **Click Replace.** The selected text is replaced with *Jake and Sara Prescott*, and the next instance of *[Customer Name]* is highlighted.

6 **Click Replace All.** A message box displays to inform you that one instance of the specified text was replaced.

7 **Click OK to acknowledge the message, and then in the Find and Replace dialog box, click Close.** Using the Replace All command may have some unintended consequences, such as replacing part of a word. Using the Replace command enables you to review the words to be replaced.

8 **In the second occurrence of *Jake and Sara Prescott*, click to the right of *Prescott* and type ' s to make this possessive.**

9 **On the Quick Access Toolbar, click the Save button** 🖫 . Alternatively, press Ctrl + S to save your work.

▶▶▶ *lesson*
five | Checking Spelling and Grammar

Any document that you work on should be free of errors, and the Spelling & Grammar tool makes it easy to remove errors. In Word, the Spelling and Grammar program is set to check spelling as you type and to mark grammar errors as you type. In PowerPoint, spelling is marked as you type, but it is not marked in either Excel or Access. Many commonly misspelled words are corrected as you type, such as replacing *hte* with *the*. This AutoCorrect feature works in Word, Excel, PowerPoint, and Access. When a word is not recognized, it is underlined with a red wavy line. If a potential grammar error is detected, it is underlined with a green wavy line. In this lesson, you will use the Spelling & Grammar tool to remove errors from the letter.

to check spelling and grammar

1   **Press Ctrl + Home to move the insertion point to the top of the document.**

2   **In the inside address, point to the word *Daleview*, which is underlined with a red wavy line, and then right-click—click the right mouse button.** A shortcut menu displays *Dale view* as a suggested replacement for this word, as shown in Figure 1.18. Proper nouns, such as names of people or streets, are often not recognized, but this does not mean the words are misspelled. ***Shortcut menus*** display when you click the right mouse button; they display a list of the most likely actions that you might want to take. Shortcut menus are ***context sensitive***—the choices listed in the menu depend on where you click in your document—and in this case, the options listed are related to the unrecognized word.

Options for Ignoring word or adding it to the Dictionary   Dale view suggested as a replacement   Other related tools   Shortcut menu

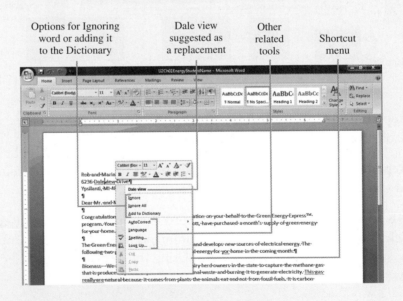

FIGURE 1.18

3   **On the shortcut menu, click Ignore to ignore this instance of the word.** The shortcut menu closes and the red wavy line is removed.

4   **On the Ribbon, click the Review tab, and then in the Proofing group, click the Spelling & Grammar button.** The Spelling and Grammar dialog box displays, and it locates the first word that is not recognized—*yor*—as shown in Figure 1.19.

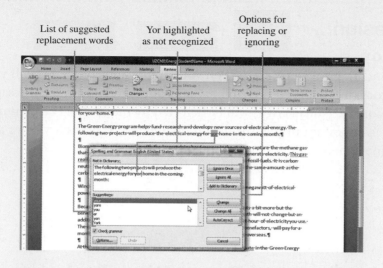

List of suggested replacement words   Yor highlighted as not recognized   Options for replacing or ignoring

FIGURE 1.19

5   **With *your* selected in the Suggestion box, click the Change button.** The change is made, and the next error—marked as a grammar error—displays. If you are uncertain why something is marked as an error, you can click the Explain button.

· ·

if you have **problems...**

ARE OTHER ERRORS FLAGGED?

The errors that are flagged by Word depend on the Proofing settings. Not all of the potential errors noted here may display during your spelling and grammar check. Your document may also stop at potential errors that are not noted here, such as the use of the passive voice in the document. If you encounter words or phrases that are not included here, click the Ignore Once button to move to the next potential error. If the grammar error described in the following steps is not flagged, read the steps and continue with the next misspelled word.

· ·

6   **In the Spelling and Grammar dialog box, click Explain. Read the description that displays in the Word Help box.** The subject and verb do not agree in this sentence, which also affects the word *this*.

7   **Click the Close button** ![X] **to close the Word Help window. With the first option selected—*This gas really is*—click Change.** The next misspelled word—*technlogies*—is located.

8   **Click Change to accepted the suggested word: *technologies*. Continue in this manner to correct the remaining spelling errors in this document.**

9 In the Message box informing you that the spelling and grammar check is complete, click OK. If the Statistics dialog box displays, click OK to close it. Save 💾 your changes.

••

good design...

ACCURACY

Spelling and grammar errors reflect on your ability and competence. If you leave errors in your work, it reduces your credibility and can detract from the message that you are trying to convey. Not all errors will be detected by the Spelling & Grammar tool, however, so it is important to proofread your documents. If necessary, have a trusted friend or colleague review your documents before distribution.

••

▶▶▶ *lesson*
SIX | Selecting and Formatting Text

Formatting changes the appearance of text or numbers and can add clarity to documents and improve the readability of the information. Formatting can include a change in font, font size, or font color. Formatting can also be the emphasis that is added by applying bold, italics, or an underline. You can format a word or multiple words or entire paragraphs. In this lesson, you apply bold emphasis to words and format paragraphs with bullets to help them stand out in the body of the letter.

to select and format text

1 Press Ctrl + Home to return to the top of the document. Position the mouse pointer about 1 inch to the left of the word *Biomass*. When the 𝄃 pointer displays, click once to select the first line of this paragraph.

2 With the line selected, hold down the left mouse button and drag down the white margin area until you have selected the *Biomass* paragraph and the following paragraph, which begins with the word *Wind*. Compare your screen with Figure 1.20. To format text, you must first select it.

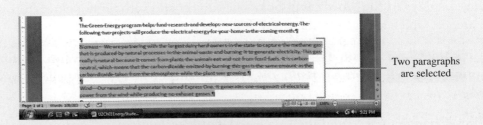

Two paragraphs are selected

FIGURE 1.20

3 On the Ribbon, click the Home tab, and then in the Paragraph group, click the Bullets button [icon]. A bullet is added to each selected paragraph and the paragraphs are indented. This highlights the information about the green energy alternatives.

4 In the first bulleted paragraph, double-click the word *Biomass*, and on the Home tab, in the Font group, click the Bold button [B].

5 In the second bulleted paragraph, select the word *Wind*, and in the Font group, click the Bold button [B].

6 Save [icon] your file.

to extend your knowledge

USING BUTTONS

Buttons on the Ribbon sometimes include an arrow on the right side of the button. When you click the button, the default settings for that command are applied. If you click the button arrow, a gallery or menu of options displays, which can sometimes be further expanded by clicking the More option found at the bottom of the gallery or menu.

▶▶▶ *lesson*
seven | Copying, Pasting, Cutting, and Moving Text

When a section of text needs to be repeated from one location to another in a document—or from one file to another—use the *Copy* command rather than retyping the text. Copying text places it in the *Office Clipboard*, which is a temporary storage location in Microsoft Office applications. Then use the *Paste* command to add the text to the new location. The text you copied remains in its original location and is added to the new location in the document. If you *cut* text, it is removed from its original location but is available in the Office Clipboard for use in another location.

In this lesson, you copy text and paste it into another location in the same document, and then from another file into the letter you are editing.

to copy and paste text

1 In the first line of the paragraph that begins *Congratulations!*, click to the left of the word *Green*, and then hold down the left mouse button and drag to the right to select the phrase *Green Energy Express* (do not select the trademark symbol). When you release the mouse button, move the mouse slightly up; a Mini toolbar displays above the selected phrase, as shown in Figure 1.21. The Mini toolbar is a shortcut toolbar that is used to format selected text. It displays when text is selected.

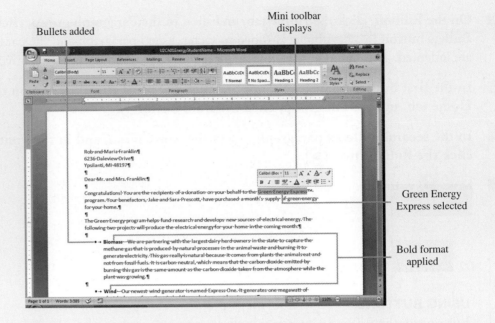

Green Energy
Express selected

Bold format
applied

FIGURE 1.21

2 On the Mini toolbar, click the Italic button $\boxed{I}$ to apply italics to the trademark name.

3 With *Green Energy Express* still selected, press ⬆Shift + → to also select the ™ symbol.

4 On the Home tab, in the Clipboard group, click the Copy button 📋. The selected text is copied and placed in the Office Clipboard. When you copy text, it remains in its original location and is available to be added to other locations.

5 In the Clipboard group, click the Dialog Box Launcher 🔲, as shown in Figure 1.22. Several groups on the Ribbon include a Dialog Box Launcher, which is used to

Dialog Box
Launcher

Clipboard
task pane

Text copied to
Office Clipboard

Selected text

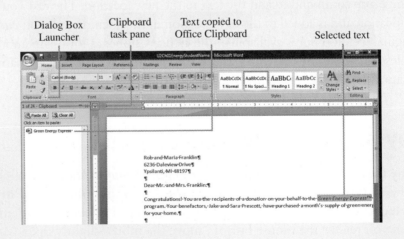

FIGURE 1.22

open a related dialog box or task pane that gives you more options and more control over the choices you make. In this instance, the Clipboard task pane shows the copied phrase. When the Clipboard task pane is displayed, you can collect up to 24 words, phrases, or images in the Office Clipboard, which can then be pasted to another area in your document, to other documents, or to files in other applications.

6 **In the paragraph that begins with *The Green Energy program*, in the first line, select the phrase *Green Energy*. In the Clipboard group, click the top part of the Paste button.** The phrase is replaced with the copied text that is stored in the Office Clipboard. The most recently copied text is what is pasted when you click the Paste button. The Paste Options button displays, as shown in Figure 1.23. The *Paste Options* button provides formatting options for the text that was just inserted. You can ignore the Paste Options button, or you can click it to choose an action to take.

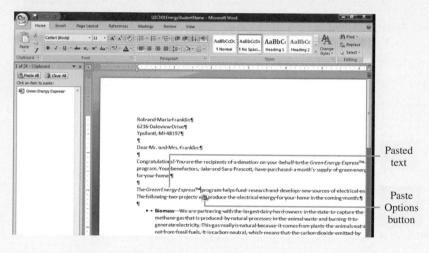

Pasted text

Paste Options button

FIGURE 1.23

7 **Click the Paste Options button** 📋. The default option is listed first—*Keep Source Formatting*—which applies the italics formatting from the copied text. In this case, you want to keep the italics formatting.

8 **Press `Esc` to close the Paste Options menu. Scroll down to the paragraph that begins with *At the end*, and then at the end of the first line, select *Green Energy*. On the Clipboard task pane, click *Green Energy Express*.** When you have multiple items copied to the Clipboard task pane, you can click the phrase in the Clipboard task pane to paste it to a new location.

9 **In the same paragraph, in the second to last line, select *Green Energy*, and then press `Ctrl` + `V` to paste the program name.** Keyboard shortcuts are a quick way to cut (`Ctrl` + `X`), copy (`Ctrl` + `C`), or paste (`Ctrl`+`V`) text. These three letters (X, C, and V) are next to each other on keyboards that use Roman letters and are used throughout a wide variety of programs to cut, copy, and paste text or images.

10 **Save** 💾 **your changes.**

In addition to copying text within a document, you can copy or move text and images between documents and between applications.

to copy text between documents

1 **From the Office menu 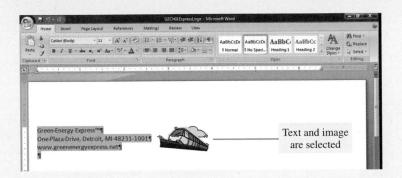, click Open. In the Open dialog box, navigate to your student files for this chapter. Select the file** *U2Ch01ExpressLogo,* **and then click Open.** A document opens that displays the program name and address and a logo that has been selected for the Green Energy Express™ program.

2 **Press** Ctrl **+** A **to select all of the contents of this document.** This keyboard shortcut selects the entire content of a document, as shown in Figure 1.24.

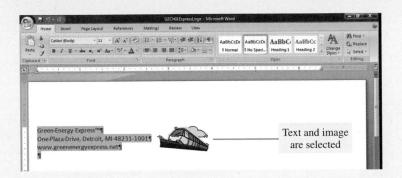

FIGURE 1.24

3 **Press** Ctrl **+** C **to copy the selected text and image.**

4 **In the upper right corner of the title bar, click** ☒ **to close the** *U2Ch01ExpressLogo* **document.** The *Ch01GreenEnergyStudentName* file displays on your screen, and the copied text and image display in the Clipboard task pane.

5 **Press** Ctrl **+** Home **to move to the top of the document, press** ↵Enter **two times, and then press** ↑ **two times to position the insertion point at the top of the letter.**

6 **Press** Ctrl **+** V **to paste the copied text into the letter.** This serves as the letterhead for the letter.

good **design...**

LETTERHEAD

The letterhead in a letter is the name, address, and logo (optional) of the sender of the letter. This should follow the rules for the letter style that is being used. In a block style letter, the letterhead address is aligned at the left margin, along with the rest of the text. Companies may use preprinted letterhead paper, requiring sufficient room at the top to accommodate the letterhead—usually an additional inch from the top margin, or six blank lines.

7 There should be three paragraph marks between the end of the inserted letterhead and the inside address. Click to move the insertion point to the middle paragraph mark, and then type August 23, 2010. Compare your screen with Figure 1.25.

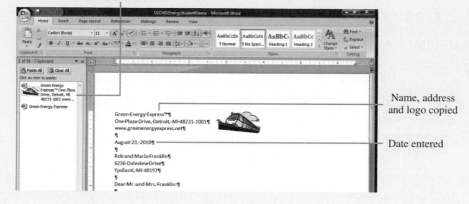

Copied text and logo display at the top of the Clipboard task pane

Name, address and logo copied

Date entered

FIGURE 1.25

8 Save 💾 your changes.

good **design...**

DATES AND SPACING

The date in a letter appears on the first available line at the top of the letter, underneath the letterhead. Usually there are three lines between the date line and the first line of the inside address; however, if it is necessary to ensure that a letter displays on one page, this spacing can be reduced. The date should include the name of the month (spelled out), the day, and then the four-digit year. Do not use numbers or abbreviations for the months.

to cut and move text

1 Press Ctrl + End to move the insertion point to the end of the document at the end of the closing—*Sincerely.*

2 Press ↵Enter four times and type your name. Press ↵Enter again and type Director, Green Energy Express The closing on the letter moves to a second page.

3 Select *Green Energy Express*, and on the Mini toolbar click the Italic button ☐.

4 Use the skills you have practiced to copy the ™ symbol from another location in the document and to paste it to the right of *Green Energy Express* in the closing. If necessary, select the ™ and press Ctrl + I to remove the italic format from the symbol. Alternatively, on the Insert tab, in the Symbols group, click the Symbol button, and then click the trademark symbol.

good **design...**

COMPLIMENTARY CLOSE

The closing in a letter includes a complimentary closing phrase such as *Sincerely,* or *Best regards,* followed by three blank lines and then the writer's name and title on the next two lines. The blank lines between the complimentary close and the writer's name are reserved for the writer's signature.

5 Use the vertical scroll bar to scroll up the document until the two bulleted paragraphs are displayed. In the *Biomass* paragraph, in the second sentence—third line—click to the left of *This.* Drag down to select the last two sentences in this paragraph, but do not select the paragraph mark ¶ at the end of paragraph.

6 On the Home tab, in the Clipboard group, click the Cut button ☒. The text is removed from the document and is added to the Clipboard task pane, as shown in Figure 1.26. The Cut command removes text from its original location but makes it available to paste into another location. In this case, the text was removed to shorten the letter to one page and will not be added elsewhere.

Cut text
displays in the
Clipboard task pane

Text removed
from the
document

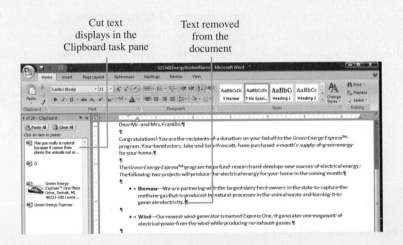

FIGURE 1.26

7 In the Biomass paragraph, triple-click—click the left mouse button rapidly three times—to select the entire paragraph. When text is selected, you can move it by using the mouse to drag it to a new location—known as *drag-and-drop*.

8 Point to the selected text. When the ⟨pointer⟩ pointer displays, hold down the left mouse button and drag down and point at the paragraph mark below the *Wind* paragraph, as shown in Figure 1.27. When you drag, the mouse pointer displays as ⟨pointer⟩, which indicates that text or an object is being moved.

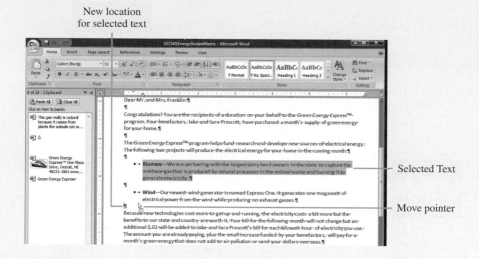

FIGURE 1.27

9 Release the mouse button to complete the move. Click next to the paragraph mark in the blank line above the *Wind* paragraph and press Delete to remove the extra blank line. The Biomass paragraph now follows the Wind paragraph.

10 On the Clipboard task pane, click ✕ to close the task pane, and then Save 💾 your changes.

▶▶▶*lesson*
eight|Using Galleries, Contextual Tabs, and the Quick Access Toolbar

Some command buttons will display a gallery of options from which to choose. Some objects have their own tabs that display on the Ribbon when that type of object is selected. Frequently used buttons are located on the *Quick Access Toolbar*, which can be customized. In this lesson, you change font, font size, and font color, format an image, and then use tools on the Quick Access Toolbar.

to format text using galleries and contextual tabs

1 Scroll up to display the top of the document. In the letterhead address, select *Green Energy Express* ™. Click the Home tab, and in the Font group click the Font button arrow `Cambria ▾`. Some buttons display a menu or gallery of choices. If necessary, a scroll bar may be included so that you can scroll through the list to display all options.

2 Point to Arial Rounded MT Bold, as shown in Figure 1.28.

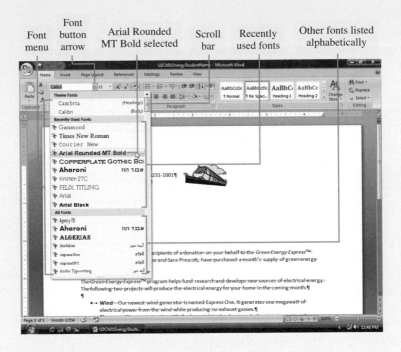

FIGURE 1.28

3 Drag the scroll box down the Font list. Locate and click Felix Titling to change the font for the selected text.

4 With the text still selected, in the Font group, click the Font Size button arrow `12 ▾` and point at 14 and notice that the size of the selected text changes. This *live preview* technology shows the result of formatting changes on selected text, which gives you the opportunity to view multiple options before applying any change. Font size is measured in *points*—abbreviated *pt*—with 11-point being the default font size in Microsoft Office Word 2007. There are 72 points to an inch.

5 Click to select 14-point font. Then, in the Font group, click the Font Color button arrow `A ▾` to display the Font Color gallery. Point to different colors and observe the live preview of the color on the selected text.

6 Under Theme Colors, in the seventh column, point to the last color—Olive Green, Accent 3, Darker 50%—as shown in Figure 1.29; and then click to apply this color to the text. When a gallery displays, ScreenTips often display to describe the options available.

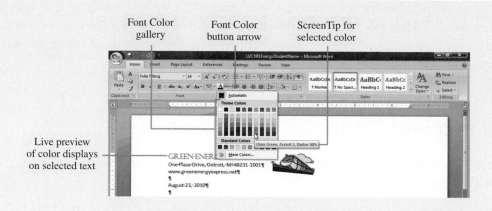

Font Color gallery

Font Color button arrow

ScreenTip for selected color

Live preview of color displays on selected text

FIGURE 1.29

7 To the right of the letterhead name and address, click the image of the train. When an object is selected, *sizing handles* display—small circles, squares, or dots around the perimeter of an object to indicate that the object is selected and can be resized or otherwise modified. The Picture Tools Format tab becomes available on the Ribbon. This is a *contextual tab*—a tab that contains tools that are related to the selected object and only displays when a related object is selected.

8 Click the Picture Tools Format tab. In the Adjust group, click the Recolor button. In the displayed Recolor gallery, under Dark Variations, point to the fourth color—*Accent color 3 Dark*—as shown in Figure 1.30. Notice that live preview displays the color on the selected image.

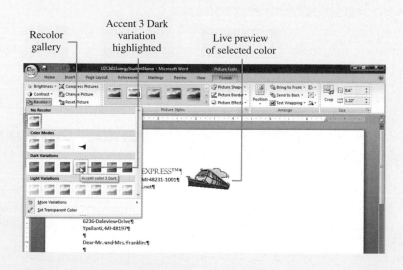

Recolor gallery

Accent 3 Dark variation highlighted

Live preview of selected color

FIGURE 1.30

9 Click the highlighted color to recolor the image. Save your changes.

Sometimes you will apply a format, change a word, move text, or make some other change that was not intended. When you make a mistake, use the ***Undo*** command to reverse one or more of the previous actions. If you reverse more actions than intended, the ***Redo*** command reverses the action of the Undo command.

to use Undo and Redo

1 **On the Quick Access Toolbar, click the Undo button 🔄 to remove the color from the image.**

2 **On the Quick Access Toolbar, click the Undo button arrow 🔄▾ to display the list of actions that you have performed on this letter.** You can use the mouse pointer to select a sequential list of actions that you want to reverse.

3 **Click the Undo button arrow 🔄▾ again to close the list. On the Quick Access Toolbar, click the Redo button 🔄 to reapply the color to the image.** The Redo button reverses the action of the Undo button and is active when you have used the Undo button.

4 **Press** Ctrl **+** Home**, and then save 💾 your changes.**

to *extend* your knowledge

QUICK ACCESS TOOLBAR BUTTONS

By default, the Quick Access Toolbar includes the buttons described in Table 1.4. You can customize this toolbar by adding buttons to it that you use frequently. To add buttons, click the Customize Quick Access Toolbar arrow ▾ that displays on the right side of the toolbar, and then click the commands that you want to add to this toolbar. To display additional command button options, click More Commands.

QUICK ACCESS TOOLBAR: DEFAULT BUTTONS

BUTTON NAME	BUTTON	DESCRIPTION
Save	💾	Saves the current document. If the document has not been saved previously, the Save As dialog box will display.
Undo	🔄	Reverses the previous action or series of actions.
Repeat	🔄	Repeats the previous action; shares the same button with the Redo button.
Redo	🔄	Reverses the action of the Undo button and displays when the Undo button has been used.

TABLE 1.4

nine | Printing Documents

Information can be distributed in printed form or electronically by e-mail or through a website. When documents are printed, use the same basic procedures to ensure that your document will print correctly. Printing techniques that are specific to each application will be covered later. In this lesson, you practice the basic process for printing.

to print a document

1 **Check to be sure that your printer is turned on and connected to your computer. Check the paper tray to ensure that there is enough paper for the document you want to print and that it is the correct type of paper.**

2 **From the Office menu** **, point to Print to display the Print menu shown in Figure 1.31.**

Print submenu   Print command highlighted   ScreenTip displays print keyboard shortcut

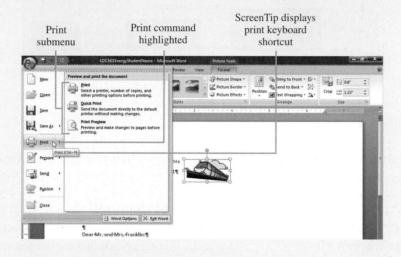

FIGURE 1.31

if you have problems...

DID THE PRINT DIALOG BOX DISPLAY?
If you click Print in the Office menu, the Print dialog box opens. In the Print dialog box, click the Close button and then repeat step 2. Be sure that you point to Print and do not click it.

3 **In the displayed Print menu, click Print Preview.** Compare your screen with Figure 1.32. The full document displays on the screen as it will look when it is printed. If your printer is not a color printer, the green color will display as shades of black and gray. Notice that the formatting marks—paragraph marks and spaces—do not show. You should review a document in Print Preview to ensure that it looks as you intended so that you do not waste paper. In this case, it is important that the letter is on one page and evenly balanced between the top and bottom margins.

Print
Preview
tab

Full
document
displays

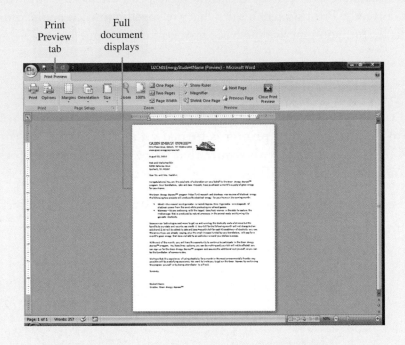

FIGURE 1.32

4 **On the Print Preview tab, in the Zoom group, click the 100% button to increase the magnification of the document.**

5 **In the Preview Group, click the Magnifier button until the check mark is removed. Click anywhere on the document and notice that the insertion point displays.** You can make editing changes in Print Preview if you see something that needs to be corrected.

6 **On the Print Preview tab, in the Print group, click the Print button.** The Print dialog box displays, with the default printer indicated in the Name box. You can change the printer by using the list arrow on the right of the Name box to display other printers that may be installed for your computer.

7 **Verify that the Print range is set to All and the Number of copies is set to 1, as shown in Figure 1.33.**

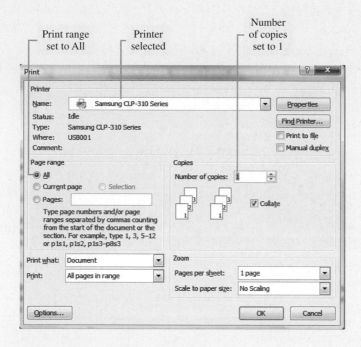

Print range
set to All

Printer
selected

Number
of copies
set to 1

FIGURE 1.33

8 **In the Print dialog box, click OK to print the document and close the Print dialog box.** If required by your instructor, submit the printed document for evaluation.

9 **On the Print Preview tab, in the Preview group, click the Close Print Preview button to return to Print Layout view.**

10 **From the Office menu ⊞, click Close to close the document, but leave Word open. Click Yes when prompted to save your changes.** When you close a file, if you have not saved your most recent changes, the program will prompt you to do so.

good **design...**

BALANCED ON THE PAGE

A letter needs to appear balanced on the page, from top to bottom and from left to right. Using Print Preview helps you determine if the end of the letter has moved to a second page—as it originally did in this letter—or if everything is bunched at the top of the letter, in the case of a short letter. To help ensure that your letter is balanced on the page, adjust the spacing between the date line and top of the letter or the letterhead, or between the date line and the first line of the inside address. The standard is to space down six times before typing the date; typically, this leaves enough space for the letterhead at the top of the letter. At a minimum, the date should be 0.5 inches below the letterhead.

▶▶▶ *lesson*
ten | Using Help

Software applications come with installed Help programs designed to assist you in using the applications. These Help programs can be searched by keywords or by broader topics. You can often receive additional help online if you are connected to the Internet. In this lesson, you will practice using the Help program that is part of Microsoft Office Word 2007. The Help tools for other Microsoft Office 2007 applications work the same way.

to use Help

1 **In the upper right corner of the Word window, click the Help button** ❓. The Word Help dialog box displays a list of topics, as shown in Figure 1.34. At the top of the dialog box is a search box in which you can type a word or phrase.

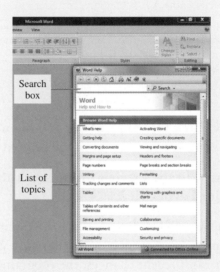

FIGURE 1.34

2 **On the Word Help toolbar, click the Change Font Size button** 🅰, **and then, from the displayed menu, click Larger.**

3 **In the Word Help dialog box under Browse Word Help, click** *What's new.* When you point to topics, the 👆 pointer displays, which indicates that you are clicking a *hyperlink*—text or an object that connects to another document or location where the information is located.

4 **Under the list of topics, click Reference:** *Locations of Word 2003 commands in Word 2007.* This topic displays and includes a brief introduction and a list of the topics that will be covered in the article.

5 **Use the scroll bar on the right of the dialog box to scroll down and review the content of the topic.** The topic summarizes the major components of Microsoft Office 2007 that have been introduced in this chapter.

6 **On the Help toolbar, click the Back button  to return to the previous list of topics.** The Back button works the same as it does when your are browsing on the Internet or searching through files on your computer—it returns you to the previous screen or location.

7 **Click in the Search box and type** `help` **and then press ⏎Enter to display a list of related topics, as shown in Figure 1.35.**

Help entered in Search box

List of topics

FIGURE 1.35

8 **Click the topic** *Work with the Help window.* **Scroll down and read the topic** *Resize or reposition the Help window.*

9 **Follow the instructions provided in this Help topic to resize the Word Help dialog box so it is in the upper right corner of the window, below the Ribbon, and fills approximately half of the screen, as shown in Figure 1.36.**

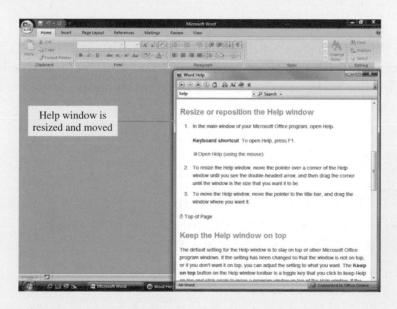

Help window is resized and moved

FIGURE 1.36

10 Scroll down and read the *Keep the Help window on top* topic. Click the term *ScreenTip* to display the definition. When a definition is available, the term displays in blue.

11 Beginning with the topic title—*Keep the Help window on top*—select the text in the topic down through the end of Step 2.

12 On the Word Help toolbar, click the Print button 🖨, and then, in the displayed Print dialog box under Page Range, click Selection. Compare your screen with **Figure 1.37.** If there is a topic you want to print for later use, you can print the entire topic or a portion of it.

Print range set to Selection   Print button   Selected text

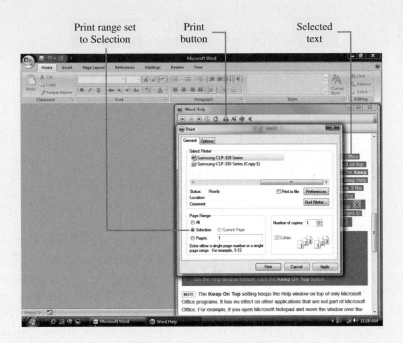

FIGURE 1.37

13 In the Print dialog box, click Print. In the Word Help dialog box title bar, click the Close button ❌, and then in the Word window title bar, click the Close button ❌ to exit the Word program. If no files are open, the Close button will close the application.

Advanced Skills or Concepts

In this section, you are introduced to skills that are not taught with step-by-step instructions.

Prioritizing Help Resources

In addition to the installed Help program, there are other resources available when you need assistance. The following is a list of available Help resources and the order in which they should be used:

- Online help within software (such as operating systems and applications)
- Online help available via the Internet (including a software manufacturer's online Help websites and product user-group websites)
- Coworkers, classmates, or teachers
- Printed documentation
- Help desk for your organization
- Help desk of the product manufacturer

To become a self-sufficient user of software, first search the Help program installed with the software. Many companies, such as Microsoft, offer online help with their Help program; therefore, it is important that you are connected to the Internet when using Help so that you have access to all available Help topics. Often there is a user group that posts questions and responses from other users or from software specialists. These discussions provide a wealth of information about little-known software problems or peculiarities. Sometimes software user groups are part of the software vendor's website; other times they exist independently of the vendor. By searching the Internet, you can usually locate a user group related to the software you are using.

Look for printed documentation from the software manufacturer or find a good reference book on the software. Sometimes a coworker, classmate, friend, or teacher can provide you with assistance. If you are not able to find the help you need on your own, then you can seek help from a professional. Many companies provide computer support to staff members through a company help desk. Help desk personnel are trained to respond to questions about the software they support and to assist you in using the software. Oftentimes, problems you encounter are unique to the particular installation protocol that is used at your company or may be related to network, hardware, or other nonsoftware-related issues. It is always good to check with your help desk to see if the problem you are experiencing has been reported as a problem by others. Most companies have a policy that requires you to use their help desk before turning to the software vendor's help desk. As a last resort, most software vendors provide a help desk to support their software. Before you call the software vendor's help desk, you want to make sure you have tried to find the answer yourself. Some software vendors charge for this service, or you must pay a membership fee to get help.

Managing Printers

When you purchase a printer, it needs to be connected to the appropriate port on your computer, and the appropriate ***print driver***—software that communicates between the computer and the printer—must be installed on your computer. Use the installation disk that comes with your printer to install the driver. If you upgrade your computer system (e.g., change the operating system), you may need to install a new driver. Print drivers can usually be located on the printer manufacturer's website and downloaded and installed.

After a printer is installed, it can be designated as the ***default printer***. If you have access to more than one printer, the default printer is the one that is used when you click the Print button. You can also share the printer with other computers. Use the Control Panel dialog box to set the default printers and to share printers on a network.

When you click the Print button, the active document is sent to the default printer. The printer may be on your desk or down the hall in another room. If your computer is connected to a printer over a network, along with several other computers, your file is sent to a ***print queue*** to wait its turn to be printed. If you want to see where your document is in the queue, locate the printer icon in the tray on the right side of the taskbar and double-click it. This will open the print queue dialog box and display the progress of your document. You can also use this window to stop, pause, or cancel a print job.

Resolving Printing Problems

When you print a document, a complex process takes place to transfer the document from your computer's memory to the printed page. Success depends on the proper functioning of each component in the process. If the document does not print, here is a list of possible reasons to check, from simple and most likely to more difficult and less likely.

Document Settings The document does not match the paper size or the printer's ability to print close to the edge.

- *Confirm that the document can be printed by the default printer.* If an error message says that the document will not fit within the margins of the paper, you need to change the layout of the document. Click the Office button, point to Print, and click Print Preview to see if the document will fit. Click the Page Layout tab and use the Page Setup group to change the orientation or margins.

- *Confirm that the header and footer print correctly.* Some printers can get closer to the edge of the paper than others. The footer may not print completely on some printers. If this problem occurs, click the Page Layout tab, choose Margins from the Page Setup group, and click Custom Margins. Check the size of the top and bottom margins. Click the Layout tab and check the distance of the header and footer from the edges of the paper. Increase these values until the header and footer print correctly.

Printer Hardware Look for connection problems and consumable supply issues.

- *Confirm that the printer is receiving power.* Look for a power indicator light, and check to see that the power cord is plugged into the wall and the back of the printer.

- *Confirm that the computer is connected to the printer.* Check both ends of the cable that connects the computer and printer to be sure they are both seated properly.

- *Confirm that the printer is online.* The term "online" means that the printer's own diagnostic program has determined that it is ready to print. The online status is usually indicated by an indicator lamp. If the printer is offline, the lamp may flash or a red light may display. If the printer is offline, check its display panel or indicator lights for confirmation of the problem. The most common problems are paper jams and low ink or toner. Follow the directions in the printer's manual to clear paper jams or replace ink or toner cartridges.

Printer Software Settings Look for incorrect settings or problems with the print queue. Display the Control Panel, and click Printer under Hardware and Sound.

- *Confirm that the document was sent to the correct printer.* When you clicked the Print button, your document was sent to the default printer. If your document cannot be found at the printer where you expected it to be, it is probably in the out-tray of the default printer. To make a different printer the default printer for your computer, right-click on the desired printer, click Printing Preferences, and then click Default.

- *Confirm that the printer is ready.* Check the status of the default printer. Right-click the default printer. If it says Resume Printing, then the printing has been paused; click Resume Printing.

Security You may not have permission to use this printer or—in a work or lab setting—to use it during the evening or weekends. Display the Control Panel, and click Printer under Hardware and Sound. Right-click the printer icon and choose Properties to open the Properties dialog box for the printer.

- *Confirm that you have permission to use this printer.* If you share a printer over a network, the administrator may not have included your computer on the list of those that may use the printer. Click the Security tab to confirm that you are a member of one of the groups that is allowed to use the printer.

- *Confirm that the printer is available at the current time of day.* If you use a printer on a network, the network administrator may have blocked access to the printer at night to prevent unauthorized use. Click the Advanced tab and check to see that the printer is available.

Printer Installation If you recently upgraded the operating system or added the printer to your computer, look for installation problems with the drivers and assigned printer ports. Display the Control Panel and click Printer under Hardware and Sound. Right-click the printer icon and choose Properties to open the Properties dialog box for the printer. If you find a problem in this list, it is usually better to install the printer again. This process is the last item on the list.

- *Confirm that the printer is assigned to a port.* The computer should be programmed to send the document to a specific port for this computer. Click the Ports tab. Confirm that one of the Port boxes is checked for the printer. If the printer is plugged into the parallel port in the back of the system unit, the port may be an LPT1. Printers may also use USB ports. If the printer is not listed, install the printer again.

- *Confirm that the correct driver is installed.* Click the Advanced tab. The printer name and model number listed in the Driver box should match your printer; if not, install the printer again.

- *Reinstall the printer.* In many cases, you must run the installation program provided with the printer before you connect the printer to the system unit. If you upgrade to a new operating system, you may need to download an upgraded version of the print driver to work with the new operating system. Download a new print driver or confirm that you have the installation discs that come with the printer and that they work with the operating system on your computer. Right-click the printer icon and choose Delete. Place the disc that comes with the printer into your computer, and run the Setup program if it does not start automatically. Follow the directions. Connect the printer and turn it on after the software is installed. The installation program should assign the port correctly and install the correct driver.

If the document does not print after you have performed these steps, make a note of what you have tried and seek help from a qualified technician. Tell the technician what you have tried and the results. This is valuable information, and the technician will be able to solve your problem more quickly if he or she does not have to check these items.

CHECK YOUR WORK

Here is a list of items your instructor will probably look for when grading your work. To improve your evaluation, take time to check the items yourself before you turn in your work.

Green Energy Letter
- Letterhead name, address, and logo pasted at the top of the page
- Font, font size, and font color in the letterhead name changed
- Color of image changed to green
- Date inserted one line below the letterhead address
- Inside address entered one line below the date, and a salutation one line below the address
- *Congratulations!* inserted at the beginning of the first paragraph
- *Contribution* replaced with *donation* in the first line
- *Project* replaced with *program* in the second paragraph, and the paragraph edited
- The program name changed and formatted to *Green Energy Express* in five locations
- The trademark symbol (™) inserted after the program name in five locations
- Bullet points added to the *Wind* and *Biomass* paragraphs
- Text cut from the *Biomass* paragraph
- *Biomass* paragraph moved to below the *Wind* paragraph
- The words *Biomass* and *Wind* formatted in bold
- *[Customer Name]* found and replaced with *Jake and Sara Prescott* in two places
- Spelling and grammar errors located and corrected, or ignored, as appropriate
- Your name on the fourth line under *Sincerely,* with *Director, Green Energy Express*™ on the following line
- Document printed

KEY TERMS

active cell	drag-and-drop	Microsoft Office
application software	Find	Minimize button
cell	font	nonprinting characters
cell address	formatting marks	Office button
Close button	gallery	Office Clipboard
context sensitive	graphical user interface (GUI)	Paste
contextual tabs		Paste Options
Copy	group	point (pt)
Cut	hyperlink	print driver
default printer	insertion point	print queue
dialog box	keyboard shortcut	programs
document	live preview	Quick Access Toolbar
drag	Maximize/Restore Down button	Redo

Repeat

Replace

Ribbon

ScreenTip

scroll bars

shortcut menu

sizing handles

status bar

tabs (Ribbon)

taskbar

title bar

Undo

Views

Windows-based applications

wordwrap

work area

worksheet

Zoom bar

ASSESSING LEARNING OUTCOMES

SCREEN ID

Identify each element of the screen by matching call-out numbers shown in Figure 1.38 to a corresponding description.

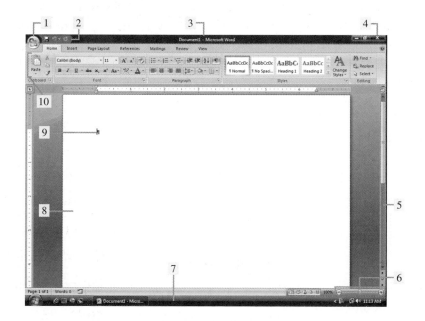

FIGURE 1.38

____ **A.** Close button

____ **B.** Insertion point

____ **C.** Office button

____ **D.** Quick Access Toolbar

____ **E.** Ribbon

____ **F.** Taskbar

____ **G.** Title bar

____ **H.** Vertical scroll bar

____ **I.** Work area

____ **J.** Zoom bar

MULTIPLE CHOICE

Circle the letter of the correct answer for each of the following. The lesson in which the term or concept was introduced is indicated at the end of the sentence.

1. In Microsoft Office 2007 applications, groups of buttons that display commands used in applications are found on the _____. [L1]
   a. menu
   b. Ribbon
   c. toolbar
   d. command bar

2. To switch between open applications, click the related button on the _____. [L1]
   a. menu bar
   b. program bar
   c. sidebar
   d. taskbar

3. To open a file from within an application, click the _____ button. [L2]
   a. File
   b. Office
   c. Open
   d. Start

4. To display the top of a document, you can do all of the following **except** _____. [L3]
   a. press Ctrl + Home
   b. drag the scroll box up to the top of the vertical scroll bar
   c. click the Home tab on the Ribbon
   d. click the up scroll arrow continuously until the top of the document is displayed

5. To change the magnification of a document from 80% to 100%, _____. [L3]
   a. all of the following would work
   b. drag the Zoom slider to the middle of the Zoom bar until 100% displays
   c. click the 100% button on the Views tab
   d. on the Zoom bar, click the Zoom In button twice

6. To correct spelling errors in your document, _____. [L5]
   a. proofread the document and correct any word that displays a red wavy underline
   b. right-click on each word with a red wavy underline, and replace it with a correctly spelled word, or choose to ignore it
   c. use the Spelling & Grammar dialog box to review and correct both grammar and spelling errors
   d. any of the above would work

7. When you cut or copy text or images, they are stored in a temporary storage location know as the _____. [L7]
   a. Office Clipboard
   b. Holding Tank
   c. Recycle Bin
   d. Storage Locker

8. Some buttons include a list or gallery of possible results that displays the change to selected text or an image using live _____ technology. [L8]

a. evaluation

b. preview

c. review

d. sample

9. To immediately reverse an action, click the _____ button. [L8]

a. Redo

b. Repeat

c. Reverse

d. Undo

10. In the Print dialog box, you can do all of the following except _____. [L9]

a. change the selected printer

b. change the number of copies to print

c. change the default printer

d. change the range of pages in a document that will print

MATCHING

Match the term or concept to its description.

_____ 1. Pressing two or more keys at a time to perform some action

_____ 2. A collection of related commands on a tab that enable you to interact with the software

_____ 3. The area on the screen where you enter text, numbers, or graphics to create a document, a worksheet, or presentation slides

_____ 4. In Word, indicates with a blinking vertical line where text or graphics will be inserted

_____ 5. A button that displays options for a recently completed action

_____ 6. A description that displays the name of a screen element, button, or area on a window

_____ 7. A set of tools—including dialog boxes, command buttons, and menus—that is manipulated with a mouse and keyboard to interact with software

_____ 8. A list of potential results

_____ 9. When you click the right mouse button, a list of actions that displays, which are related to the area on which you clicked

_____ 10. A customizable area containing a Save button and an Undo button

A. Gallery

B. Graphical user interface

C. Group

D. Insertion point

E. Keyboard shortcut

F. Paste Options button

G. Quick Access Toolbar

H. ScreenTip

I. Shortcut menu

J. Work area

The Skill Drill exercise repeats the lessons in the chapter but with different data. The instructions are less detailed, and your speed and familiarity should increase with practice. There is a figure at the end against which you can check your results. The purpose of this exercise is to build your confidence and speed in using the skills introduced in this chapter and to set them in your memory for later recall. The section numbers correspond to the lesson numbers. You are welcome to refer back to the lessons referenced and the detailed instructions, if necessary.

In this exercise, you edit a memo to employees about a change in parking alternatives. Print copies of the letter if your instructor requires it.

1. Starting an Application and Identifying Common On-Screen Elements

1. On the taskbar, click the **Start** button. Click **All Programs,** and scroll as necessary to display the Microsoft Office folder.

2. From the list of programs, click the **Microsoft Office** folder, and then click **Microsoft Office Word 2007.**

2. Opening and Saving a File

1. Click the **Office** button, and from the displayed menu click **Open.**

2. In the Open dialog box, navigate to the drive and folder that contain the student files for this chapter. Locate and select the file **U2Ch01Parking**, and then click **Open.**

3. From the **Office** menu, click **Save As**.

4. In the Save As dialog box, in the File name box, type Ch01ParkingStudentName using your own name for *StudentName*. Navigate to and open the **Chapter01** folder that you created previously.

5. In the Save As dialog box, click **Save**.

3. Navigating a Document and Inserting, Selecting, and Editing Text

1. On the **Home** tab, in the **Paragraph** group, click the **Show/Hide** button until it turns gold to indicate that it is active. If necessary, on the right end of the status bar, click the **Print Layout** button.

2. On the Ribbon, click the **View** tab, and then in the **Zoom** group, click the **Zoom** button. In the displayed Zoom dialog box, click **Page Width,** and then click **OK.**

3. On the second line of the memo, click to the right of *To:*, press Tab two times, and then type All Employees

4. Click to the right of *From:*, press Tab two times, and then type your name, CEO and President

5. Click to the right of *Subject:*, press Tab two times, and then type Parking

6. In the paragraph that begins *We found*, in the first line, select *found out* and type were informed

7. In the paragraph that begins *We have considered*, at the end of the first line, click to the left of *almost*. Press Delete six times to remove this word, and then type `more than`

8. Scroll down to display the paragraph that begins *Some spaces*, click at the end of the first line, and then press ←Backspace until the phrase *during the day* is removed. Be sure only one space remains between *travel* and *as*.

9. Press Ctrl + Home to move to the top of the document. On the Quick Access Toolbar, click the **Save** button.

4. Using Buttons and Dialog Boxes

1. At the top of the memo, click to the right of *Date:*, press Tab⇆ two times, and type the current date.

2. Click the **Home** tab. In the **Editing** group, click the **Replace** button.

3. In the displayed Find and Replace dialog box, in the **Find what** box, type `5th street` and be sure that you type all lowercase letters in *street*. Press Tab⇆, and in the **Replace with** box, type `Fifth Street`

4. Click **Find Next**, and when the phrase is located, click **Replace**. When the second instance of *5th street* is located, click **Replace,** and then click **OK** to close the message box. Click the **Close** button to close the Find and Replace dialog box.

5. On the Quick Access Toolbar, click the **Save** button.

5. Checking Spelling and Grammar

1. Press Ctrl + Home to move to the top of the document.

2. Click the **Review** tab, and then in the **Proofing** group, click the **Spelling & Grammar** button.

3. The first unrecognized word—*comittment*—displays in the Not in Dictionary box, and *commitment* displays as the correct spelling in the Suggestions box. With *commitment* selected, click **Change.** *Note:* If the first unrecognized word that is shown is your name, click **Ignore** to accept it and move to the next word in the document.

4. Continue in this manner to change the next two unrecognized words to *environment* and *descriptions*, respectively.

5. When the sentence with *street* highlighted is selected , click the **Explain** button and read the explanation about capitalization. Click the **Close** button to close the Word Help dialog box, and then click **Change.** *Note:* If the Spelling and Grammar program stops on other exceptions, click **Ignore.**

6. Click **OK** to acknowledge the message box, and then **Save** your changes.

6. Selecting and Formatting Text

1. Press Ctrl + Home to move to the top of the document.

2. Select the word *Memo*. Point to the Mini toolbar, and then click the **Bold** button.

3. Click the **Home** tab, and then in the **Font** group, click the **Font Size** button arrow. Move the mouse pointer over the size and notice that the font size shows as a live preview on the selected text.

4. Click **18** to apply this font size to the selected text.

7. Copying, Pasting, Cutting, and Moving Text

1. Click the **Office** button, and then click **Open.** In the Open dialog box, navigate to the student files for this chapter. Locate and click the **U2Ch01ParkingMemo** file, and then click **Open.** This memo contains a list of parking alternatives for employees.

2. Scroll down the memo to display the indented paragraphs. In the white margin area, point to the line that begins *Pay for commuter bus passes.* Drag down the margin to select the six indented lines.

3. With the six lines selected, on the **Home** tab, in the **Clipboard** group, click the **Copy** button. Click the **Office** button, and then click **Close** to close this document.

4. In the **U2Ch01ParkingStudentName** file, scroll down and click on the empty line between the fourth and fifth paragraphs, after the phrase *we propose the following options.*

5. Press ⏎Enter, and then on the **Home** tab, in the **Clipboard** group, click the **Paste** button to insert the copied text from the other memo.

6. Select the second option: *Provide lockable, weatherproof storage for bicycles.* Press Ctrl + X to cut the text from this location.

7. Click to the left of the word *Pay* in the first option listed, and then press Ctrl + V to paste the cut text. This moves the option related to bicycles to be first in the list. **Save** your changes.

8. Using Galleries, Contextual Tabs, and the Quick Access Toolbar

1. Select the six indented lines of parking alternatives that you inserted in the previous section.

2. With the text selected, on the **Home** tab, in the **Paragraph** group, click the **Bullets** button arrow to display the gallery of bullet options. Move your mouse pointer over the options and observe the live preview displayed on the selected text. Click the right-pointing arrowhead shape.

3. Scroll to the top of the document and click the image of a bicyclist. Notice that the Picture Tools Format contextual tab is available when you click the image.

4. Click the **Picture Tools Format** tab. In the **Adjust** group, click the **Recolor** button. In the displayed gallery, under **Color Modes,** click the second color option—**Sepia.**

5. With the image still selected, on the **Picture Tools Format** tab, in the **Adjust** group, click the **Recolor** button; and under **Light Variation,** click the fifth color—**Accent color 4 Light.**

6. On the Quick Access Toolbar, click the **Undo** button to reverse the last action. Click **Undo** again to remove the sepia color, and then click the **Redo** button once to reapply the Sepia color mode. **Save** your changes.

9. Printing Documents

1. From the **Office** menu, point to **Print**, and then click **Print Preview.** Observe that there is a little space left at the bottom of the memo and that the spacing between the subject line and the body of the memo could be larger.

2. On the **Print Preview** tab, in the **Zoom** group, click the **100%** button. In the Preview group, click the Magnifier button to remove the check mark.

3. On the Subject line, click to the right of *Parking*, and then press ⏎Enter to add another blank line between the Subject line and the body of the memo. Spacing between the Subject line and the body of a memo should be one or two lines.

4. In the **Zoom** group, click the **One Page** button to see the entire memo.

5. In the **Print** group, click the **Print** button. In the Print dialog box, be sure that the printer you want to use is selected in the Name box. Also verify that the Print range is set to *All* and the Number of copies is set to *1*, and then click **OK.**

6. On the **Print Preview** tab, in the **Preview** group, click the **Close Print Preview** button.

7. **Save** your changes. Click the **Office** button, and then click **Close.** Submit the file as directed by your instructor.

10. Using Help

1. Open Microsoft Office Word 2007 if necessary. On the Ribbon, at the right end of the tabs, click the **Help** button.

2. In the Search box, type `Quick Access Toolbar` and then press ⏎Enter.

3. If you are connected to the Internet, in the displayed results, click *Demo: Place your favorite commands on the Quick Access Toolbar.*

4. When the topic displays, click **Play Demo.** To listen to the demo, you need to be connected to the Internet and have speakers connected to your computer and turned on. If you are not connected to the Internet, go to the next step.

5. Scroll down and click the *Customize the Quick Access Toolbar* link and read both topics: *Move the Quick Access Toolbar* and *Add a command to the Quick Access Toolbar.*

6. At the end of the Quick Access Toolbar, click the **Customize Quick Access Toolbar** button. From the displayed list click **Print Preview** to add this button to the Quick Access Toolbar. **Close** the Word Help window.

7. If the computer you are using is your own, you may want to add other command buttons to the Quick Access Toolbar or change its location.

8. If the computer you are using is not your own, on the Quick Access Toolbar, right-click the **Print Preview** button, and then click **Remove from Quick Access Toolbar.**

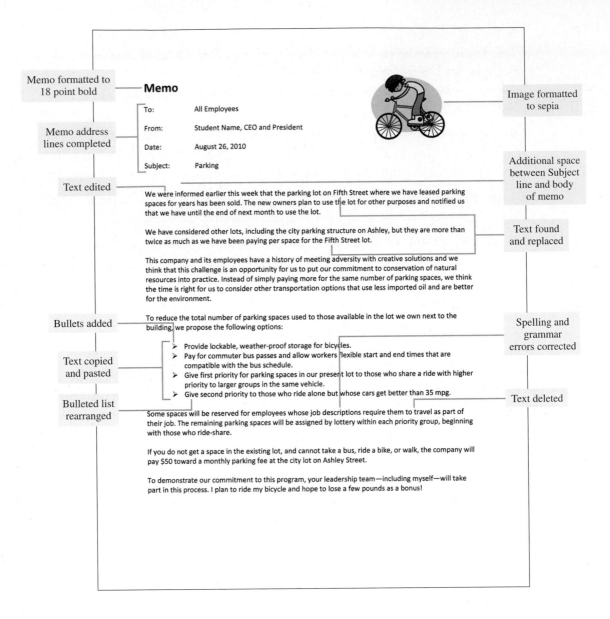

Memo formatted to 18 point bold — **Memo**

Image formatted to sepia

To: All Employees

Memo address lines completed

From: Student Name, CEO and President

Date: August 26, 2010

Subject: Parking

Additional space between Subject line and body of memo

Text edited — We were informed earlier this week that the parking lot on Fifth Street where we have leased parking spaces for years has been sold. The new owners plan to use the lot for other purposes and notified us that we have until the end of next month to use the lot.

We have considered other lots, including the city parking structure on Ashley, but they are more than twice as much as we have been paying per space for the Fifth Street lot.

Text found and replaced

This company and its employees have a history of meeting adversity with creative solutions and we think that this challenge is an opportunity for us to put our commitment to conservation of natural resources into practice. Instead of simply paying more for the same number of parking spaces, we think the time is right for us to consider other transportation options that use less imported oil and are better for the environment.

Bullets added — To reduce the total number of parking spaces used to those available in the lot we own next to the building, we propose the following options:

Spelling and grammar errors corrected

Text copied and pasted
- Provide lockable, weather-proof storage for bicycles.
- Pay for commuter bus passes and allow workers flexible start and end times that are compatible with the bus schedule.
- Give first priority for parking spaces in our present lot to those who share a ride with higher priority to larger groups in the same vehicle.
- Give second priority to those who ride alone but whose cars get better than 35 mpg.

Bulleted list rearranged

Text deleted

Some spaces will be reserved for employees whose job descriptions require them to travel as part of their job. The remaining parking spaces will be assigned by lottery within each priority group, beginning with those who ride-share.

If you do not get a space in the existing lot, and cannot take a bus, ride a bike, or walk, the company will pay $50 toward a monthly parking fee at the city lot on Ashley Street.

To demonstrate our commitment to this program, your leadership team—including myself—will take part in this process. I plan to ride my bicycle and hope to lose a few pounds as a bonus!

FIGURE 1.39

fix *it*

One way to appreciate the value of good design is to fix a file that is not designed well. In this exercise, you open a file that has several errors and design flaws and fix it according to good design elements, using the skills that you practiced in the lessons.

Navigate to the folder with the student files, open **U2Ch01FixIt**, and save it as U2Ch01FixItStudentName

Examine the letter and make the changes that are necessary to correct errors and comply with the good design principles that were introduced in this chapter.

Here is a list of corrections needed and the design principles introduced in this chapter, along with some tips on how to fix the letter.

- Recolor the recycle symbol in the letterhead to dark green (*Accent color 3 Dark*).

- The Recycle Center name was recently changed to *Green City Recycling*™. Replace all references to Recycle Center to the new name, including the trademark symbol.

- Replace *Date* with the current date and space per the stated design principles for a letter.

- This letter is being sent to Joseph Paellas, at 367 Huntington Drive, Toledo, OH 43604. Enter the inside address in the proper location.

- Enter the proper spacing between the date line, inside address, salutation, and the body of the letter.

- Correct all spelling and grammar errors.

- Move the last sentence in the letter so that it is the third sentence in the first paragraph.

- Move the sentence that begins *Be sure food containers are rinsed* so that it is the fourth sentence in the first paragraph.

- Format into a bulleted list the list of items that can be recycled.

- Following the phrase *Toxic Waste Center*, type `located at 3500 E. Hogback Road`

- Place a single space (line) between paragraphs.

- In the last paragraph, in the second sentence, delete the word *the* that precedes the name of the program.

- Add an appropriate closing phrase.

- In the closing area, use your name and the title *Assistant Director*. On the third line of the closing, enter the name of the recycling program.

- Preview the letter and adjust the spacing in the appropriate areas, per the design principles, to balance the letter top to bottom.

Submit the file as required by your instructor. Save and close the file.

ON THE JOB

Information workers add value to data by organizing, selecting, displaying, communicating, interpreting, and using data to communicate information and support decisions. On the Job exercises simulate a situation where you are given data, and your job is to add value to it using the skills you practiced in this chapter. Success in these exercises indicates that you have a valuable skill to offer an employer.

1. Customer Response Letter

In this On the Job exercise, the director of the Green Coop Community Development Project has asked you to prepare a letter in response to an inquiry. Refer to the request from the director, and then, using the skills you have practiced in this chapter, organize the information into a letter.

Joe,

I've received a request for information from Henrico Gallo, 2819 Glacier Way, Boulder, CO 80303, and I'd like you to handle the response. Mr. Gallo would like information about the mission of our organization and recent projects. He is particularly interested in farm-related energy alternatives. I've attached some information that you can use.

Susan

1. Open the file **U2Ch01Coop** and save it as U2Ch01CoopStudentName

2. Enter the date, inside address, and salutation below the letterhead.

3. Write an introductory sentence or two, thanking Mr. Gallo for his inquiry.

4. Review the information that was provided by the director, which is found in file U2Ch01CoopProject. Include the appropriate information from this file in the letter.

5. Add a closing paragraph that offers Mr. Gallo a method of obtaining more information.

6. Adjust the font, if necessary, to be sure that the font used in the letter is all the same.

7. Add a closing, and use your name and the title Administrative Assistant in the closing.

8. Format the letter according to good design principles discussed in the chapter.

9. Preview the letter to ensure that it is balanced on the page and will print on one page.

10. Print or submit the file as directed by your instructor. Save the file and close it.

GREEN COOP COMMUNITY DEVELOPMENT PROJECT
11000 Calloway Park, Suite 58A
Eugene, OR 97406
greencoopcommunitydevelopment.net

August 30, 2010

Henrico Gallo
2819 Glacier Way
Boulder, CO 80303

Dear Mr. Gallo,

Thank you for your inquiry about Green Coop Community Development Project. We are very excited about the projects that we have sponsored and the enthusiastic response of the participants in our community programs.

The Green Coop Community Development Project is a cooperative based program committed to meeting energy needs using alternative, renewable energy sources. We look for opportunities to turn the natural by-product of a business into a renewable energy source. We have been involved in projects across the country, which have included photovoltaic installations, hydroponic systems, biomass, and biogas projects. Our goal is to help businesses and communities improve their energy efficiency while reducing their energy costs.

We have been involved in several projects related to farm energy production. In Michigan, we installed underground bunkers at dairy farm to turn the methane gas from rotting manure into renewable energy to provide electricity to run the milking machines and other farm operations. We have also installed hydroponic systems that use rotting plants in tomato farms or other types of farms, to create a richer environment in which the plants can grow, while generating biomass fuel to help run the electricity needed to operate the business.

If you need more information contact me at 734.555.1002, or go to our Web site at greencoopcommunitydevelopment.net.

Sincerely,

Student Name
Administrative Assistant

FIGURE 1.40

2. Energy Pricing Options Letter

The annual letter to customers about energy pricing for the upcoming heating season needs to be updated and revised. Refer to the request from the boss, and then, using the skills you have practiced in this chapter, revise the information in the letter to reflect the changes indicated.

Marlene,

Here is the customer pricing letter that we used last year. Please update it to reflect the changes we made to our pricing plans. The monthly budget plan has been changed to eleven months from ten. The prepay price plan needs to be locked in by August 1. The prepay price and price ceiling numbers will be available by July 1 rather than June 20. Change the price guarantee fee to $79. I also think that it would read better if the second sentence were changed to a fourth option with the heading None of the Above.

Sam

1. From the student files, open **U2Ch01Pricing**. Save it as U2Ch01PricingStudentName

2. Review the letter and make the changes that are specified in the memo.

3. Move the second sentence to be the last pricing option, with the heading suggested in the memo. Change *If* to lowercase to match the format used in the other four options.

4. Use the techniques you have practiced to include the long dash between the heading and the specifics in the fourth option, so that it matches the first three options.

5. Format the pricing options with a bulleted list.

6. Format the logo in the letterhead to dark blue.

7. Change the font on the company name in the letterhead to Arial Rounded MT Bold, and the font size to 12 point.

8. Add the date to the letter: May 1 of the current year.

Your Energy Company
P.O. Box 820
Bridgeport, CT 06604-0820

May 1, 2010

Dear Customer,

At Your Energy Company we offer several choices to help you control the cost of heating for the coming season. Choose from the following options:

- 11-Month Budget Plan—we will estimate your consumption based on past usage and divide your energy bill into eleven equal payments. Payments begin in September. A final credit or amount due bill will be issued in July.

- Pre-Pay Plan—prepay for your estimated usage for the year by August 1, to lock in your price. The prepay price will be available by July 1.

- Price Guarantee—for a low fee of $79, you can receive the benefits of competitive market prices while guarantee the highest price that you will pay. The price ceiling will be available after July 1.

- None of the Above—if you prefer to pay for the energy at market prices each month, do nothing and you will continue to enjoy the excellent service provided by Your Energy Company.

Since 1976 we have been delivering excellent service and value. Thank you for your continued business. If you have questions about the payment options listed contact our office at (734) 555-0232, or send us an e-mail at yourenergyco.net.

Sincerely,

Student Name
Office Manager

FIGURE 1.41

9. Review the design principles listed in the Fix It exercise and apply those that are relevant. (This letter will not be personalized with an inside address, so the salutation will be *Dear Customer*.)

10. Add a closing to the letter, and use your name with Office Manager as the title.

11. Adjust the spacing in the letter so that it is balanced on the page.

12. Print or submit the file as directed by your instructor. Save the file and close it.

DISCUSSION OF ADVANCED SKILLS OR CONCEPTS

The questions in this section are based on the topics in the Advanced Skills or Concepts section of the chapter.

1. Examine a letter that you have received recently from a company. Identify the parts of the letter and the formatting that has been used to help convey the information. Demonstrate your knowledge of the topics in this chapter in your answer. Describe any errors that you find in the letter.

2. Describe an example from your experience where you have had difficulty printing a document. What steps did you take to resolve the problem?

3. Describe an experience you have had using a computer where you needed to get assistance to use a software program. What methods did you use first to try to resolve the problem on your own? Describe any online sources or searches that you employed. Did you get the help you needed, and from what source? Do you now remember how to perform that particular task?

4. If this is the first time you have used the Office 2007 interface, describe your impressions. Did you find the organization of the buttons to be logical? Were you able to quickly find the buttons you wanted?

5. When you type numbers, do you use the numbers above the letters or the keypad on the side? Why is that your choice?

6. Do you prefer to use the mouse or keyboard shortcuts to select commands? What is your reason for this preference?

ON YOUR OWN

Once you are comfortable with the skills in this chapter, you can apply them to new situations of your own choosing. In this section, you choose data that you have in your possession or that you can find elsewhere. To successfully complete this assignment, you must apply good design practices and demonstrate mastery of the skills that were practiced. Refer to the list of skills and design practices in the Fix It exercise.

1. Write a letter of appreciation.

When companies spend more to conserve energy or pay extra for alternative energy, they do so at the risk of displeasing their investors. If you know of a company or organization that has made an effort to conserve energy or use energy sources that reduce imports of foreign oil, you can help the administrators of those organizations by writing a letter of appreciation. Use the skills you have practiced to write a letter of appreciation to a company for its efforts.

1. Open a new document and save it as U2Ch01AppreciationStudentName

2. Enter the date and address.

3. Enter a salutation.

4. Write two or three paragraphs in which you describe what you observed and what you feel about their efforts.

5. Write a closing.

6. Check what you have written for spelling errors.

7. Save your work and submit the file as directed by your instructor.

2. Ask about job training for careers in alternative energy.

Alternative energy generation will involve inventing, designing, manufacturing, marketing, selling, installing, and maintaining equipment and devices. Write a letter asking for advice on how to prepare for a job that is related to alternative energy generation.

1. Choose a training organization, a college, or a company that deals with alternative energy devices and identify their mailing address.

2. Open a blank document. Enter the date and address.

3. Enter a salutation.

4. Write two or three paragraphs in which you ask for advice on how to prepare for a career related to generating energy using alternative means. Describe your strengths and interests that might be relevant and what motivates you to work in this area.

5. Check what you have written for spelling errors.

6. Save your work as U2Ch01CareerStudentName and submit the file as directed by your instructor.

ASSESS YOUR PROGRESS

At this point, you should have a set of skills and design concepts that are valuable to an employer and to you. You may not realize how much you have learned unless you take a few minutes to assess your progress.

1. From the student files, open **U2Ch01Assess**. Save it as U2Ch01AssessStudentName

2. Read each question in column A.

3. In column B, answer Yes or No.

4. If you identify a skill or design concept that you don't know, refer to the learning objective code next to the question and the table at the beginning of the chapter to find the skill and review it.

5. Print the worksheet if your instructor requires it. The file name is already in the header, so it will display your name as part of the file name.

6. All of these skills and concepts have been identified as important by surveying hundreds of individuals working at over 200 companies worldwide. If you cannot answer all of the questions affirmatively even after reviewing the relevant lesson, seek additional help from your instructor.

chapter two

Creating a New Word Document and Inserting Graphics and Tables

Lesson	Learning Outcomes	Code	Related IC3 Objectives
1	Create a new document	2.01	1.2.1
1	Display the ruler	2.02	2.1.3
2	Create and modify a bulleted list	2.03	2.1.7, 2.1.16
3	Format text	2.04	1.3.6
3	Change text alignment	2.05	1.3.6
3	Indent text	2.06	2.12
4	Create a title with WordArt	2.07	1.3.7
4	Modify WordArt	2.08	1.3.7
5	Insert, resize and move clip art	2.09	1.3.7
6	Insert, move, and crop pictures	2.10	1.3.7
7	Create a table	2.11	2.1.13, 2.1.16
7	Insert and edit data in a table	2.12	2.1.13, 2.1.16
7	Modify table structure	2.13	2.1.14
7	Insert and delete cells, rows, and columns	2.14	2.1.14
7	Change column width and row height	2.15	2.1.14, 2.1.16
7	Convert text to a table or table to text	2.16	2.1.13
8	Format tables with table styles	2.17	2.1.15
8	Modify table formats using command buttons	2.18	2.1.15
8	Align table cell contents	2.19	2.1.15
8	Merge cells	2.20	2.1.15
8	Add, modify, and remove table and shading	2.21	2.1.15
8	Split cells in a table	2.22	2.1.14
8	Split tables	2.23	2.1.14
8	Sort data in a table	2.26	2.1.15
9	Insert and modify a footer	2.24	2.1.10
10	Use a document template	2.25	1.2.1
Advanced Skills	Use overtype	2.27	1.3.3
Advanced Skills	Transmit documents in electronic format	2.28	1.4.6, 1.4.7

Instructions throughout the lessons are based on the Vista operating system, running Microsoft Office 2007.

? *Why* **Would I Do This?**

Documents can be based on already existing files or written from scratch to create a new file. In addition, several preformatted and designed documents can be used for specific purposes such as memos or fax cover letters.

Formatting text helps the reader see the organization of the document and identify important information or ideas. Font selection conveys the tone of a document from serious to fun. Simple formatting tools enable you to change font, font size, or text alignment. You can emphasize text to make it stand out from the surrounding text by using bold, italic, underline, color, or special character effects.

Graphics add visual components to your documents that help draw the reader's attention or highlight an important idea or fact. Images should be related to the topic and provide visual interest or information. This can be done with pictures that are stored in a digital format, shapes used to create a drawing, borders and shading to draw attention to information, or electronic images provided with your software. Graphic elements can be resized and repositioned. Adding graphics creates excitement and visual appeal.

Tables are lists that display data in a column-and-row format. They organize and present parallel lists of information and can be used in a variety of circumstances.

visual **summary** |

In this chapter, you will create a new document that is a flyer announcing an upcoming Earth Day tour at a local university, and then you will use a preformatted fax cover sheet to distribute the file electronically to the campus community. The documents created are shown in Figure 2.1.

FIGURE 2.1A

FIGURE 2.1B

List of Student and Solution Files

In most cases, you will start from with a blank document and enter text and data or paste content from other files. You will add your name to the file names and save them on your computer or portable memory device. Table 2.1 lists the files you start with and the names you give them when you save the files.

ASSIGNMENT	STUDENT SOURCE FILE:	SAVE AS:
Lessons 1–10	New document Fax template U2Ch02Building	U2Ch02EarthDayStudentName U2Ch02FaxCoverStudentName
Skill Drill	New file Fax template U2Ch02Transformer	U2Ch02LectureSeriesStudentName U2Ch02LectureFaxStudentName
Fix It	U2Ch02FixIt U2Ch02Building2	U2Ch02FixItStudentName
On the Job	New file U2Ch02Ship Memo template U2Ch02Bus	U2Ch02NaturalGasStudentName U2Ch02BusStudentName
On Your Own	New file Resume template	U2Ch02FlyerStudentName U2Ch02ResumeStudentName
Assess Your Progress	U2Ch02Assess	U2Ch02AssessStudentName

TABLE 2.1

▶▶▶ *lesson*
one | Creating a New Document

Many times when you write a letter, memo, or other document, you create it from the beginning. When you open Word, a blank document displays on the screen, and you enter text and save the file, which creates a new document file.

to create a new document

1 **Start Word.** A new document named *Document1* displays on the screen.

2 **On the Home tab, in the Paragraph group, click the Show/Hide button ¶ until it is active and the paragraph marks display on the page.**

3 **Click the View tab, and in the Zoom group, click the Zoom button. In the Zoom dialog box, click Page Width, and then click OK. On the View tab, in the Show/Hide group, click the Ruler check box if necessary to display the horizontal and vertical rulers.** Alternatively, at the top of the vertical scroll bar, click the View Ruler button to display the ruler. The View Ruler button at the top of the scroll bar is an example of a *toggle* button—a button that activates or deactivates a feature or command. Click one time to display to the ruler, and click it again to hide the ruler—similar to using a light switch. Rulers display along the top of the page and along the left side, as shown in Figure 2.2. The rulers are displayed to help you align text and graphic images.

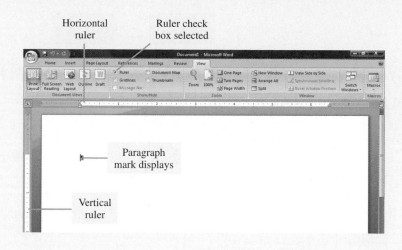

FIGURE 2.2

4 **Click the Page Layout tab. In the Paragraph group, under Spacing, in the After box, be sure that 10 pt displays. If 10 pt does not display, click in the After box, type 10 and then press ⏎Enter.** *Spacing after* adds space between paragraphs, which occurs when you press ⏎Enter to begin a new paragraph. Recall that a paragraph can be a single line of text. The default spacing following a paragraph in Word 2007 is 10 pt, which creates white space between paragraphs.

5 **Click the Home tab, and in the Paragraph group, click the Line Spacing button** ⏸, **and then click 1.0 to set the line spacing to single-space.** The default *line spacing*—the spacing between lines of text in a paragraph—is 1.15 in Word 2007. When text is *single-spaced*—1.0—there is no additional space between lines of text in a paragraph.

6 **Type** Earth Day Tour **press** ⏎Enter, **and then type** April 22 Notice that there is space between these two lines of text because of the spacing after feature that is set to 10 pt.

7 **Press** ⏎Enter. Type Tour behind the scenes to see how your campus is using energy responsibly: and then press ⏎Enter.

8 **On the Quick Access Toolbar, click the Save button** 💾 **to display the Save As dialog box.** If you have not previously saved your file, the Save As dialog box will display when you click the Save button.

9 Navigate to the drive where you are saving your files. Click the New Folder button, type Chapter02 and then press ⏎Enter.

10 Click in the File name box, which will select the text. Using your own name in place of *Student Name*, type U2Ch02EarthDayStudentName and then click Save. The new file name displays in the title bar and your document is saved.

▶▶▶ *lesson*
twO | Creating and Modifying a Numbered or Bulleted List

Lists present data in an easy-to-read format and draw the reader's attention to key points. Word enables you to create two professional-looking list types quickly. The first is a ***bulleted list***, which is a list with each piece of information preceded by a small symbol—often a round black dot—called a ***bullet***. Bulleted lists generally are used when there is no particular order to the items in the list. ***Numbered list*** items are preceded by numbers and are usually used to display data that has some type of order: chronological, importance, or sequence.

In this lesson, you create a bulleted list and then you modify the bullet.

to create numbered or bulleted lists

1 With the insertion point next to the last paragraph mark, on the Home tab, in the Paragraph group, click the Numbering button [⬛▾]. Number *1.* displays on the page, followed by a tab indicator. On the ruler, notice that the left indent indicator is indented to the .5-inch mark and the first line indent indicator is at the .25-inch mark. These indicators show where the number and the text will be aligned, which is slightly inside the left margin.

2 Type Discover how ice storage units in the dining commons are used to cool the building. Press ⏎Enter to move to the next line. Number 2. displays on the next line. Notice that there is no 10-point after spacing between the first and second lines in this numbered list. Numbered and bulleted lists are single-spaced by default.

3 Continue in this manner to enter the next three numbered list items as follows, and then compare your screen with Figure 2.3.

See the co-generation unit that provides steam heat and electricity to campus buildings.

Visit the campus recycling center and learn how you can make a difference.

Stop at the computerized energy control center which helps reduce energy use.

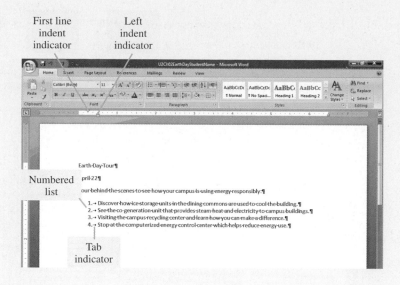

First line indent indicator

Left indent indicator

Numbered list

Tab indicator

FIGURE 2.3

• •

if you have **problems...**

If you press ⏎Enter after typing the last item, another number will display on the screen. Press ⬅Backspace as needed to remove the number and return the insertion point to the end of the previous numbered item in the list.

• •

4 **In the left margin, point to the first numbered item. When the** 🔎 **pointer displays, drag down to select the four items in the numbered list. On the Home tab, in the Paragraph group, click the Bullets button** ▤▾ **to change this to a bulleted list.** This is a random list and should use bullets rather than numbers, which imply a specific order.

5 **With the list still selected, in the Paragraph group, click the Bullets button arrow** ▤▾ **to display the Bullets gallery.** Here you can select another bullet style or define a custom bullet.

6 **At the bottom of the Bullets gallery, click Define New Bullet. In the Define New Bullet dialog box, click Picture.** You can customize a bullet for a particular purpose by clicking the Symbol or Picture buttons, or you can change the color and size of the bullet by clicking the Font button.

7 **In the Picture Bullet dialog box, be sure the *Include content from Office Online* check box is selected. In the *Search text* box, type** Earth **and then press** ⏎Enter **to activate the search. Scroll the list and select the image displayed in Figure 2.4, or one that is similar.**

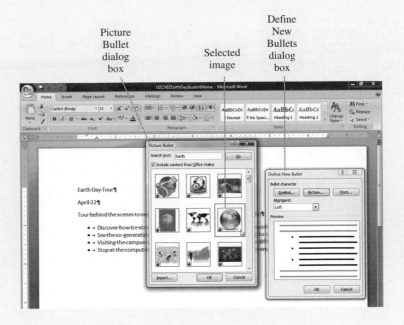

Picture Bullet dialog box

Selected image

Define New Bullets dialog box

FIGURE 2.4

8 **With the image of the earth selected, in the Picture Bullet dialog box, click OK, and then click OK to close the Define New Bullet dialog box.** The bullet is changed to the selected earth image, as shown in Figure 2.5.

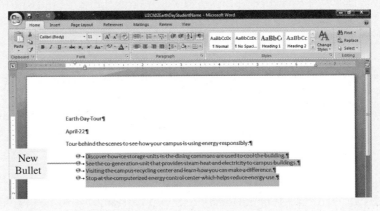

New Bullet

FIGURE 2.5

9 Save 🖫 your work.

· ·

good design...

USING LISTS TO ORGANIZE DATA

Lists of data can be presented using several different techniques. It is important to select the best option for the data to be listed. Use bullet lists when there is no particular order to the items listed, and use numbered lists when there is an order, such as steps in a process, order of importance, or chronological order.

· ·

three|Formatting, Aligning, and Indenting Text

Text can be formatted by changing the font, font size, font color, or by applying bold, italic, or underline styles to add emphasis. There are two types of fonts: serif and sans serif. ***Serif fonts*** have lines or extensions on the ends of the letters and are typically used with large amounts of text, such as in a report or research paper. ***Sans serif fonts*** do not have lines or extensions and are used for shorter documents or for headings. Cambria, Courier, and Times New Roman are examples of serif fonts, and Arial, Calibri, and Verdana are examples of sans serif fonts. The font used should match the length and purpose of the document.

to format text

1   **Press** Ctrl **+** A **to select all of the text in the document. On the Home tab, in the Font group, click the Font button arrow** Cambria **to display the list of available fonts. Scroll the list and point to Kristen ITC.** Notice the live preview of the font applied to the selected text. This feature works when you select fonts using the Font button on the Ribbon. If you use the Mini toolbar, the same selections are available, but the live preview technology is not active.

2   **Click Kristen ITC to apply this font. With the text still selected, click the Font Size button arrow** 12 **and scroll the list to see the live preview of the font sizes applied to the selected text. Click 16 to change the font size. Compare your screen with Figure 2.6.**

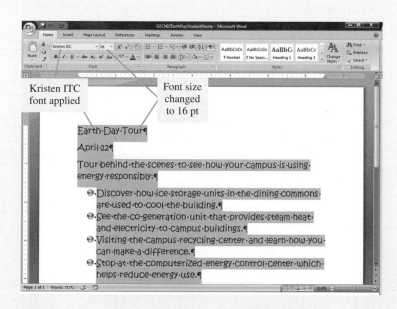

FIGURE 2.6

good **design...**

3 Select *April 22*. **Move your pointer onto the displayed Mini toolbar, click the Font Size button arrow, and then click 20.** Notice that live preview does not display when you use the Mini toolbar.

4 **With April 22 still selected, on the Mini toolbar, click the Bold button** **B**. **Bold changes the style of the font to add emphasis.** You can also use keyboard shortcuts to apply styles: Ctrl + B for Bold, Ctrl + I for Italic, and Ctrl + U for Underline.

5 **With April 22 still selected, on the Home Tab, in the Font group, click the Font Color button arrow** **A** ⌄ **to display the color gallery. Move your pointer over the colors and notice the live preview of colors applied to the selected text.** Colors are displayed in groups by the ***theme*** that is applied to the document. A theme is a collection of design elements that are applied to documents to create a uniform look, such as font, font size, and the color palette. The default theme used in Word 2007 is named Office. Each color in the Font Color gallery displays a ScreenTip when you point to it that describes the color and its intensity.

6 **Under Theme Colors, in the seventh column—Olive Green—point to the fifth color, *Olive Green, Accent 3, Darker 25%*, and compare your screen with Figure 2.7. Then click to apply this color to the selected text.**

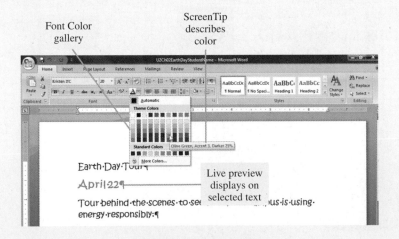

FIGURE 2.7

7 **Save** 💾 **your work.**

Alignment is the horizontal placement of text, whether it is between the left and right margins in a Word document, in a cell on an Excel worksheet, on a PowerPoint slide, or in a graphic object. In documents, most text is arranged on the page so that there is a uniform white space between the left edge of the paper and the beginning of each line. Because the words in each line are of different lengths, the right edge of the paragraph is usually uneven. This type of alignment is called *left-aligned* because the words are evenly aligned on the left. The opposite alignment—with the right edge aligned and the left edge uneven—is called *right-aligned*. *Center* alignment places text in the center of an area. If text is aligned evenly on both sides—known as *justified*—the computer adjusts the size of the spaces between the words in each line to ensure that the text aligns evenly.

Text can also be *indented*—moved in—from the left or right margins. Indenting is used for the first line of a paragraph, for bulleted or numbered lists, or to move a long quote in from both margins so that it stands out. In a flyer, indenting is used to place text in a particular location in the document.

to align and indent text

1 **Select the title *Earth Day Tour*, and on the Home tab, in the Paragraph group, click the Align Text Right button .**

2 **Select *April 22*, and then on the Mini toolbar, click the Center button .** The Center button is the only alignment button that displays on the Mini toolbar.

3 **Select the four bulleted points. On the Home tab, in the Paragraph group, click the Justify button to stretch this text so that it is aligned evenly on both the left and right margins.**

4 **With the bulleted list still selected, on the ruler, point to each of the indent markers to display the ScreenTip that identifies each one. Examine Table 2.2 and identify each marker and read its purpose.**

to extend **your knowledge**

INDENTING TEXT

The indent markers identified in the table display on the ruler and can be used to indent text, or you can use the Paragraph dialog box to change indents or text alignment.

MARKER	SCREENTIP	PURPOSE
▽	First Line Indent	Indicates indent for the first line in a paragraph
△	Hanging Indent	Indicates indent for all but the first line in a paragraph
⊡	Left Indent	Indent from the left margin
⊓	Right Indent	Indent from the right margin

TABLE 2.2

5 **With the bulleted list still selected, on the ruler, point to the Left indent marker ⊡ and drag it to the right to the 1-inch mark.** Notice that the first line indent marker also moves—to the .75-inch mark.

· ·

if you have problems...

If you drag the hanging indent marker △, the first line indent marker will not move on the ruler and the bullet point will remain at the .5-inch mark. If this happens, on the Quick Access toolbar, click Undo and try again. Be sure to point to the lower part of the left indent marker to display the Left Indent ScreenTip, and then drag this portion of the marker to the 1-inch mark on the ruler.

· ·

6 **On the Home tab, in the Paragraph group, click the Dialog Box Launcher ⊡ to display the Paragraph dialog box. Compare your screen with Figure 2.8.** Notice

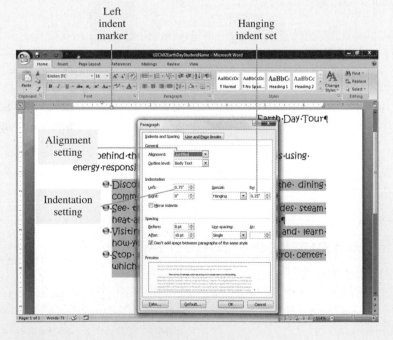

FIGURE 2.8

that the Alignment box is set to Justified under Indentation, Left is set to .75 inch—the location of the first line indent—and the Special box displays a Hanging indent of .25 inches, which is a quarter inch to the right of the first line indent. This indent setting ensures that text wraps to the line of text at the 1-inch mark, rather than to the bullet point, which is at the .75-inch mark.

7 **Click OK to close the dialog box. Compare your screen with Figure 2.9, and then Save** 💾 **your work.**

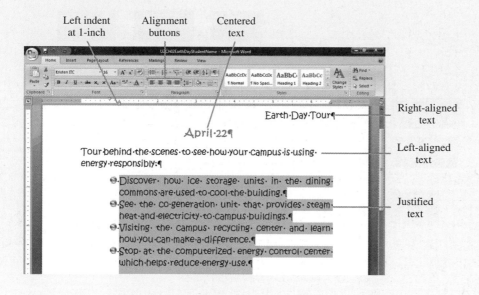

FIGURE 2.9

good design...

ALIGN AND INDENT TEXT TO CREATE BALANCE

Most documents are aligned on the left side of the page. On short documents, such as flyers or announcements, use alignment and indentation to arrange the data so that it is balanced on the page. For example, a short bulleted list might be indented to make it stand out more from the rest of the text, particularly in a document such as a flyer where key points need to be brief and effective.

▶▶▶ *lesson*

four | Creating a Title with WordArt

To make a title stand out from the rest of the text, you can use emphasis (bold, italic, underline), a larger font size, or an unusual font, but you are limited to straight lines of text. *WordArt* is a tool that turns text into graphics to create a more decorative title. It gives you great flexibility for creating very artistic titles.

In this lesson, you change the title on the Earth Day flyer using WordArt.

to create a title with WordArt

1 **Select the text** *Earth Day Tour*—**do not select the paragraph mark at the end of this line. Click the Insert tab, and then in the Text group, click the WordArt button.** A gallery of WordArt styles display, as shown in Figure 2.10. When you point to a style, a ScreenTip displays *WordArt style* followed by a number.

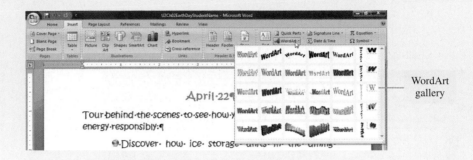

WordArt gallery

FIGURE 2.10

2 **In the fourth row, second column, click WordArt style 20.** The Edit WordArt Text dialog box displays. Here you can type text and change the font, font size, or font style.

3 **Click OK to accept the default settings, and then compare your screen with Figure 2.11.** The text displays as an image and *sizing handles*—small dots or squares displayed around the perimeter of the image—indicate that the image is selected. When sizing handles display, an image can be moved, deleted, formatted, or resized.

WordArt Tools
Format contextual
tab displays

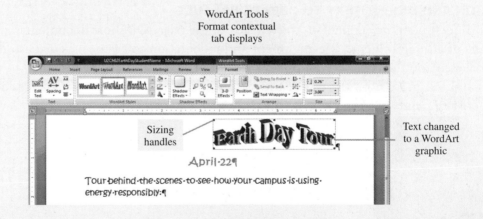

Sizing handles

Text changed to a WordArt graphic

FIGURE 2.11

4 **Click the WordArt image to select it. Point to the lower left sizing handle, and when the ⤢ pointer displays, drag to the left to the 1-inch mark on the**

horizontal ruler and down to approximately the 1.25-inch mark on the vertical ruler, as shown in Figure 2.12; then release the mouse button. An outline of the shape displays on the screen as you drag, to show the approximate size of the image as it is expanded. When you release the mouse, the image is expanded. If you do not like the results, click Undo and try again, or drag the sizing handle again to adjust the size of the image.

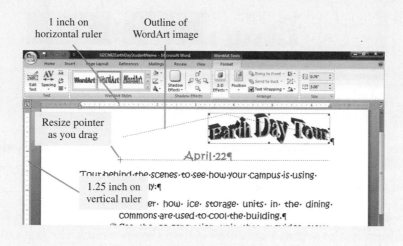

FIGURE 2.12

5 Save 💾 your work.

WordArt images can be modified using a variety of tools found on the WordArt Tools Format tab. This tab is available when a WordArt image is selected. You can select a different style, edit the text, change the text effects, alter the color scheme, add or change shadow effects, or apply 3-D—three dimensional—effects.

to modify WordArt

1 **Click the WordArt Tools Format tab. In the WordArt Styles group, click the Change WordArt Shape button** 🅰️⌄ **to display a gallery of shapes.** As you point at different shapes, notice that the live preview displays the change on the WordArt graphic. This enables you to preview a change before it is applied.

2 **Under Warp, in the second row, third column, click the** *Inflate* **shape.**

3 **In the WordArt Styles group, click the Shape Fill button arrow** 🅰️⌄ **to display the gallery of fill colors. In the seventh column—Olive Green—point to the fifth color,** *Olive Green, Accent 3, Darker 25%,* **as shown in Figure 2.13; then click this color to apply it.**

Fill Color
gallery

Selected color
description

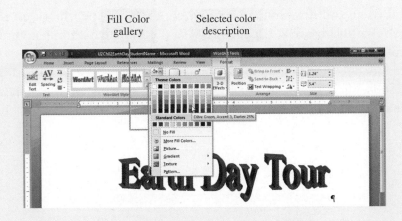

FIGURE 2.13

4 **Click the 3-D Effects button, and then click 3-D Effects to display the gallery.** As you move your pointer over the gallery of 3-D options, live preview displays the effects on the WordArt.

5 **At the bottom of the 3-D Effects list, point to 3-D Color, and then from the color gallery, in the seventh column—Olive Green—click the last color:** *Olive Green Accent 3, Darker 50%.*

6 **In the WordArt Styles group, click the Shape Fill button arrow** 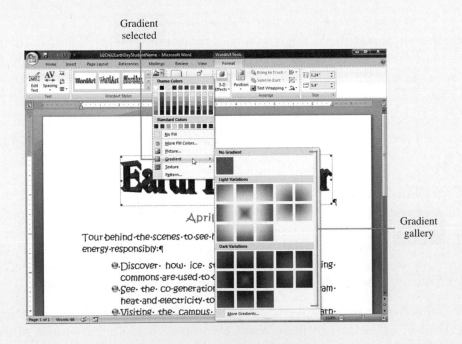**, and then near the bottom of the list, point to Gradient to display the Gradient gallery, as shown in Figure 2.14.** Gradients are applied to shade the colors that are used so that there is a variety in the tone of the color. In this case, the green needs to be lightened.

Gradient
selected

Gradient
gallery

FIGURE 2.14

7 In the Gradient gallery, under Light Variations, in the third row, second column, click the Linear Up gradient.

8 Save 🖫 your changes.

··

good **design...**

CREATING A TITLE

Titles should be at the top of a document. In a flyer, a title should be large enough to be read from a distance and designed to attract attention. WordArt creates a decorative graphic title that can be used to meet these goals.

··

▶▶▶ *lesson*
five |Inserting and Modifying Clip Art

Microsoft Office includes several *clip art* images—electronic images used to illustrate a document. Clip art images cover a wide range of topics and styles, from black-and-white stick art to detailed color drawings. When you need an illustration for a flyer, poster, or brochure, you can usually find one that is appropriate. If your computer is connected to the Internet, you can access a larger selection of clip art images through Microsoft Office Online. Several software vendors also offer clips that you can include in your documents. These are generally available as a purchased software program or through a website.

In this lesson you will insert, resize, and move clip art.

to insert, resize, and move clip art

1 Click at the beginning of the paragraph that begins *Tour behind the scenes.* Click the Insert tab, and then in the Illustrations group, click the Clip Art button. The Clip Art task pane displays on the right. Here you enter keywords to search for images that are related to your topic.

2 In the Clip Art task pane, in the *Search for* box, select any text that might display in the box, and then type earth In the *Search in* box, be sure that *All collections* displays. Click the *Results should be* arrow, and then clear all check boxes except the one next to Clip Art. Click the list arrow again to close it. Compare your screen with Figure 2.15.

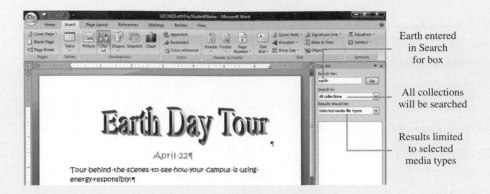

Earth entered
in Search
for box

All collections
will be searched

Results limited
to selected
media types

FIGURE 2.15

3 **To the right of the _Search for_ box, click Go to activate the search.** Images related to the keyword display in the Clip Art task pane. If you are connected to the Internet, images that are available from Office Online are also included.

4 **Scroll the list and point to the image shown in Figure 2.16. If this image is not available, point to a similar image in your results.** When you point to an image, a ScreenTip displays the related topics, dimensions of the image, file size, and image type.

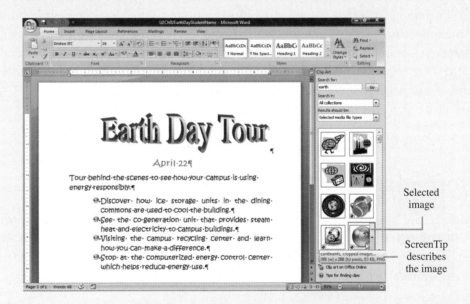

Selected
image

ScreenTip
describes
the image

FIGURE 2.16

5 **Click the image to insert it.** The image is inserted and sizing handles display around the border of the image to indicate that the image is selected. A **_rotation handle_**—used to rotate an image in a circle—displays at the top of the image. A selected image can be moved, deleted, formatted, or resized. When an image is first inserted, it behaves like a character that is on the same line as other text at the point of insertion.

6 With the image selected, point to the lower right sizing handle, and when the ⬉ pointer displays, drag up and to the left to the middle of the image to reduce the size of the image until it is approximately one-quarter of its original size.

7 In the Arrange group, click the Text Wrapping button. Notice that the *In Line with Text* option is selected by default, and then click Square. Before you can move an image, the text-wrapping setting must be changed to something other than *In Line with Text*.

8 Point in the middle of the image, and when the ⊕ pointer displays, drag the image up to the left of the Earth Day Tour title, as shown in Figure 2.17. Notice the *anchor* that displays on the screen, which indicates the paragraph to which a selected image is attached.

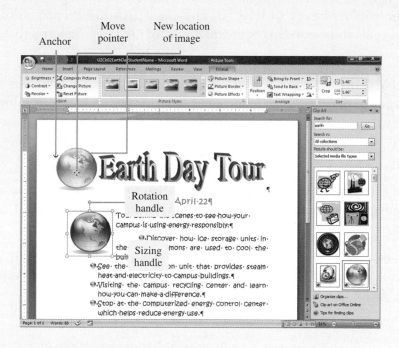

FIGURE 2.17

9 If necessary, scroll to the top of the page. Point to the top edge of the page, and then when the ⬍ pointer displays, double-click to hide the white space at the top of the page. This places the image closer to the horizontal ruler and helps you judge the size of the image. Compare your screen with Figure 2.18.

Image displays   Show/Hide white
next to ruler   space pointer

FIGURE 2.18

10 **Click the clip art image to select it, and then click the Picture Tools Format tab.** The tools shown on this contextual tab are used to format pictures and clip art.

11 **On the Format tab, in the Size group, click in the Shape Height box** ⬚ 3.5" ⬚**, type** 1 **and then press** ⏎Enter**.** Both the Shape Height and Shape Width boxes change to 1". You can also use the up spin arrow and down spin arrow in each box to adjust the size of an image. The image jumps to the upper margin area of the document and may be out of sight.

12 **Point to the upper edge of the page, and when the** ⊞ **pointer displays, double-click to display the image, which jumped to the margin area when you adjusted the size.**

13 **In the Clip Art task pane, click the Close button** ☒**. Drag the clip art image down to the left of the WordArt image, as shown in Figure 2.19. Save your changes** 💾**.**

Image resized
and moved

FIGURE 2.19

SIX| Inserting and Modifying Pictures

Clip art is designed to convey an idea using a variety of drawn images, photos, cartoon-like images, sound, or movie clips. Sometimes you will want to use photographs available in the clip art collection, or digital photographs that you have taken with a camera (either film or digital). Digital images are more appropriate when you need a visual of a specific location, process, person, or subject matter. When they are available, photographs create a more powerful impression.

In this lesson, you add a digital photograph to your document.

to insert and modify pictures

1 Press Ctrl + End to move the insertion point to the end of the document. Press ↵Enter to move to a new line, **and then on the Home tab, in the Paragraph group, click the Bullet button** to remove the bullet point.

2 **On the Home tab, in the Paragraph group, click the Decrease Indent button** to move the insertion point to the left margin—set at 1 inch.

3 **Click the Insert tab, and then in the Illustrations group, click the Picture button to display the Insert Picture dialog box.** Here you navigate to the location that contains the image you want to insert.

4 **Navigate to the location that contains your student files for this chapter. Click to select the U2Ch02Building image, and then click Insert.** The inserted image is larger than the space available and may display on a second page. The Picture Tools Format tab displays.

5 **On the Picture Tools Format tab, in the Size group, click in the Shape Height box** and type 2.2 **Press** ↵Enter**, and then scroll as necessary so that you can see the resized image. Compare your screen with Figure 2.20**. The image displays under the last line of text. In the Size group, the Shape Width box automatically adjusts to maintain the height and width proportion of the original image.

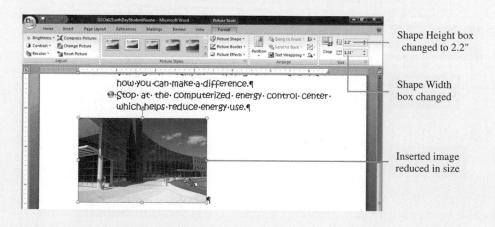

FIGURE 2.20

6 **With the image selected, on the Format tab, in the Size group, click the Crop button, and then move the mouse pointer onto the document.** Crop marks display around the edge of the picture and the mouse pointer displays a crop tool, as shown in Figure 2.21. You can further reduce the size of a picture by removing unwanted parts from the sides. Cropping is like cutting off the edges of a printed picture.

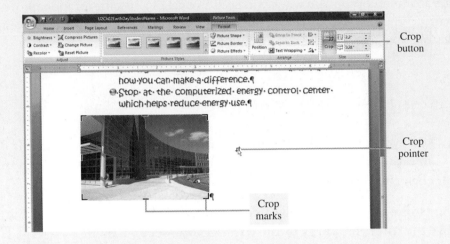

FIGURE 2.21

7 **Move the pointer to the lower middle crop mark and drag up to the top of the corner crop marks, approximately one third of an inch.**

8 **Point to the crop mark in the middle of the right side of the image and drag toward the center of the image until the brick portion of the building is hidden, as shown in Figure 2.22.** When you crop a picture, the cropped portion of the image is hidden and can be redisplayed by reversing the cropping.

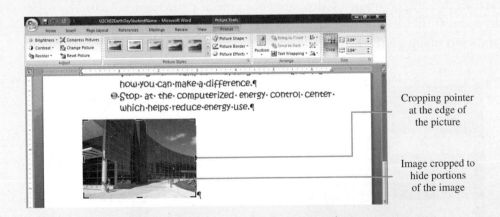

FIGURE 2.22

9 **In the Size group, click the Crop button to deselect the cropping tool.** Alternatively, press (Esc) to deselect the cropping tool.

10 **With the image selected, in the Arrange group, click the Text Wrapping button, and then click Tight.** This text wrapping option enables the text to wrap tightly around the image.

11 **Scroll up as necessary to display the bullet list and the picture. Click the picture and drag it up to the right side of the bullet list to the location shown in Figure 2.23.**

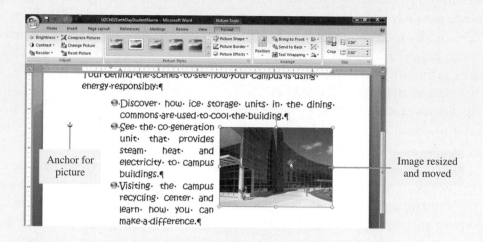

FIGURE 2.23

12 **Select all of the bulleted text. Click the Home tab, and in the Paragraph group, click the Dialog Box Launcher.** In the Paragraph dialog box, click the **Alignment arrow, and then click Left. Under Indentation, in the Left box, type .25 and then click OK.** The bullet list is left-aligned and indented to the .25-inch mark on the ruler.

13 **Save your work.**

good **design...**

USE GRAPHIC IMAGES THAT ARE APPROPRIATE TO THE DOCUMENT AND TOPIC

Graphic images need to be appropriate to the topic, type of document, and audience. For example, other than the company logo, images are not appropriate in business letters but might be used in personal letters. Clip art can be used in newsletters, flyers, announcements, and other more informal documents where attracting attention is important. Digital images may be used in a wider range of documents where the image is used to illustrate a topic. Position images to break up the text or to fill in white space.

seven|Inserting Tables

Tables are lists of information set up in a column-and-row format. The intersection of an individual row and column creates cells that can contain text, numbers, or graphics. Tables are especially useful when you need to create lists of parallel information, especially when the quantity of information varies from one column to the next—tables organize the information so that you can follow the related information as you read across a row. They are excellent for two-column tasks such as résumés, where the topic is on the left and the details are on the right. Tables are also used to organize information on forms that need to be completed electronically or in paper format.

The same formatting tools that are used throughout a document can be applied to a table. You can change font and font size, add bold, italic, or underline emphasis to text, and add borders and shading to rows, columns, or individual cells. Data can be aligned both horizontally and vertically in a cell. Formatting can be applied to an individual cell, multiple cells, or an entire table at once.

Lists of information that is displayed as text can be converted to a table, and a table can also be converted to text. You can also draw a table with variable dimensions in different rows and columns. Cells can be merged or split and column width and row height can be adjusted to your specifications. In all, tables provide a very flexible method for displaying information in columns.

In this lesson, you will create, modify, and format a table for the Earth Day flyer.

to insert a table

1 **Press** Ctrl **+** End **to move to the last line under the last bullet point.** Be sure that you are on a blank line under the last bullet point.

2 **Select the paragraph mark that displays on the line under the bullet list. On the Home tab, in the Font group, click the Font Size button arrow, and then click 14 to change the font size. In the Paragraph group, click the Align Text Left button** ▤ **.**

3 **With the paragraph mark still selected, in the Paragraph group, click the Line Spacing button** ⬍▾ **, and then click Remove Space After Paragraph.**
The paragraph mark controls the format that will be applied to the next line of text—in this case, the new table you will insert. Reducing the font size, changing the alignment to left-aligned, and removing the default spacing that is added after a paragraph will provide more space for the table.

4 **Click next to the paragraph mark to deselect the paragraph mark. Click the Insert tab, and in the Tables group, click the Table button to display the Table menu. Move the pointer across three columns and down four rows as shown in Figure 2.24.** You can drag a range of rows and columns to create the size table you need. The table dimensions display at the top of the table grid—*3x4 Table*—and an outline of the table displays on the document.

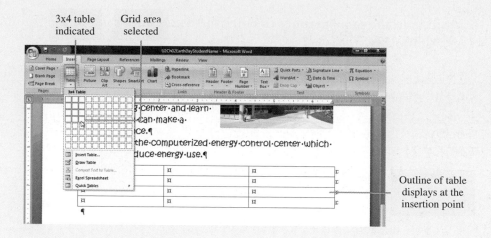

3x4 table indicated **Grid area selected**

Outline of table displays at the insertion point

FIGURE 2.24

5 **Click the 3x4 cell to insert the table. Click in the first cell in the table, type** `Topic` **and then press** (Tab↹). The heading for the first column displays in the first cell, and the insertion point moves to the right to the next cell in the top row. The Table Tools Design and Layout contextual tabs are available on the Ribbon when a table is active.

6 **Type** `Location` **and press** (Tab↹). **Type** `Time` **and then press** (Tab↹). The next two column headings are entered and the insertion point moves to the first cell in the second row, as shown in Figure 2.25. Use the (Tab↹) key to move across rows and from the end of one row to the beginning of the next row. Pressing (⬆Shift) + (Tab↹) moves the insertion point to the left. You can also use the arrow keys to navigate within a table. If you press (↵Enter), it creates a second line within the same cell, thereby increasing the height of the entire row. If you do this, press (←Backspace) to remove the extra line in the row.

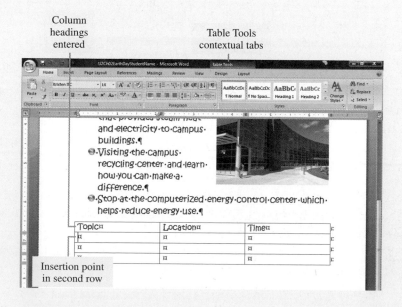

Column headings entered **Table Tools contextual tabs**

Insertion point in second row

FIGURE 2.25

7 Continue in the same manner to enter the data under each of the column headings as follows:

Cooling with Ice	North Dining Commons	1:00 to 1:30
Green Building Features	Student Activity Center	1:45 to 2:15
Where Trash Goes	Recycling Center	4:15 to 4:45

8 Save 💾 your file.

You can add and delete rows or columns in a table. In the next part of this lesson, you add a row at the end of the table, one in the middle of the table, and then delete a column.

to add and delete rows and columns

1 With the insertion point in the last cell in the table, press (Tab⇆) to create a new row at the end of the table. Enter the following information:

| Controlling Energy Distribution | Physical Plant | 3:30 to 4:00 |

2 Move the pointer to the margin area left of the fourth row—*Where Trash Goes*. When the ⌐ pointer displays, click to select the fourth row in the table, as shown in Figure 2.26. Click the **Table Tools Layout tab.** Tools to change the

Selected row

Table Tools Layout tab displayed

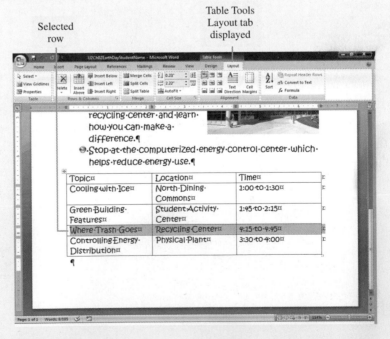

FIGURE 2.26

layout of the table are located on this contextual tab. Here you can insert rows or columns, change the alignment and text direction in cells, merge or split cells, change other table properties, or delete rows, columns, or the entire table.

3 On the Table Tools Layout tab, in the Rows & Columns group, click the Insert Above button to add a row above the selected row.

4 In the new row, enter the following information:

| Co-Generation | Heating Plant | 2:30 to 3:15 |

5 Point to the top border of the first column of the table—just above *Topic*. When the ↓ pointer displays, click to select the first column in the table, as shown in Figure 2.27.

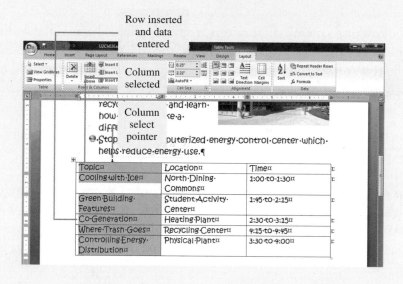

FIGURE 2.27

6 Right-click the selected column, and then from the shortcut menu, click Delete Columns to remove the selected column from the table. Alternatively, on the Layout tab, in the Rows & Columns group, click the Delete button, and then click Delete Columns.

7 On the Quick Access Toolbar, click the Undo button ↻ to return the column to the table. When you make a mistake, you can usually recover what you have lost using the Undo button.

8 Save 💾 your changes.

CREATING A TABLE USING THE INSERT TABLE BUTTON

When you click the Table button, you can click *Insert table* to display the Insert Table dialog box. Here you can enter the number of rows and columns that you want in your table, rather than dragging the table grid to select the dimensions.

CREATING A TABLE BY USING THE DRAW TABLE COMMAND

If you need a table of irregular dimensions with cells of different sizes in each row, you can use the Draw Table command in the Table menu. When you choose this command, the pointer changes to a pencil icon. Drag the pencil tool to draw horizontal or vertical lines on your document. When you finish drawing the table, press Esc to return the pointer to its default shape and function. In this manner, you can draw a table to your match your needs.

In a table, the row and column dimensions are evenly divided across the width of the page, within the left and right margins. As text is entered, the row height is adjusted as needed. The dimensions of the rows and columns can be changed to specific measurements, or they can be made to fit the content of the cells or the width of the page.

to AutoFit table content

1 **Click in any cell in the table. On the Table Tools Layout tab, in the Cell Size group, click the AutoFit button, and then click AutoFit Contents. Compare your screen with Figure 2.28.** The width of each column adjusts to fit the content. In some rows, this enables the text to display on one line, but in the *Time* column, the

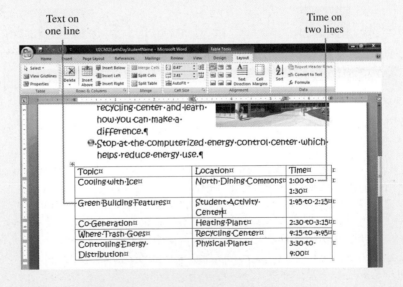

FIGURE 2.28

data displays on two lines in some of the cells. You may need to make further adjustments when you use the AutoFit command.

2 Move the pointer to the border between the first and second columns. When the ◄‖► displays, drag to the left to the 2.5-inch mark on the horizontal ruler. Compare your screen with Figure 2.29.

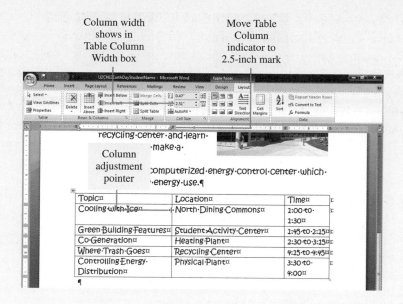

Column width shows in Table Column Width box

Move Table Column indicator to 2.5-inch mark

Column adjustment pointer

FIGURE 2.29

3 Click in a cell in the third column. On the Table Tools Layout tab, in the Cell Size group, click in the Table Column Width box ⊞6" ⬍ , edit the size to `1.25` and then press ⏎Enter . You can change the width of a column or the height of a row by entering a specific dimension in the height or width box in the Cell Size group. You can also drag the Move Table Column indicator on the ruler to increase or decrease the size of a column. When you are adjusting the size of a column or row, it is important that you do not select a single cell in the column; if you do, only that cell will be adjusted, not the entire column.

4 Save 🖫 your changes.

···

good **design...**

WHEN TO USE A TABLE VERSUS A LIST
Use tables when you need to present data in a column-and-row arrangement. They are particularly useful when the data in one or more columns is significantly longer than the related data in another column. In a table, the text wraps within a cell to create a parallel arrangement of the data across the page. Formatting a table—such as using different formats for column or row headings or for column or row totals—helps the reader understand the relationship of information in the table.

···

Data in a table can be converted to text and vice versa. When you create a table in Word, the nonprinting tab character is used to move from one column to the next and from the end of a row to the next. To successfully convert text to a table format, there needs to be a similar consistent symbol or keystroke between each of the intended columns in the text and at the end of each row of data. In the next part of this lesson, you practice converting the table you have created to text and then back to a table format.

to convert a table to text

1 **Click in a cell in the table. On the Layout tab, in the Table group, click the Select button, and then from the list, click Select Table.** The entire table is highlighted to indicate that it is selected. When you move the pointer near a table, the Select All button ⊞ displays in the upper left corner of that table, as shown in Figure 2.30. Clicking this button is an alternative way to select the entire table.

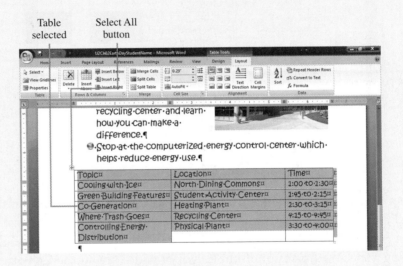

FIGURE 2.30

2 **On the Layout tab, in the Data group, click the Convert to Text button.**

3 **In the displayed Convert Table to Text dialog box, be sure that the Tabs option is selected, and then click OK. Compare your screen with Figure 2.31.** If necessary, on the Home tab, in the Paragraph group, click the Show/Hide button to display the nonprinting formatting marks. The data now displays as a tabbed list with tab marks between the columns. The last row of the table moves to a second page.

Data from the last cell is on another line   Tab marks between columns   Paragraph marks at the end of each row

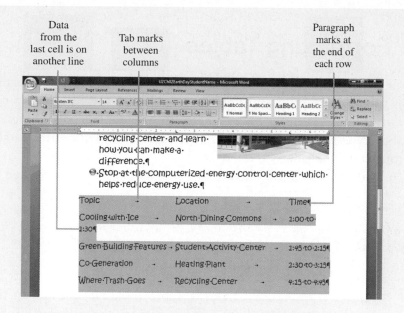

FIGURE 2.31

4 With the data still selected, click the Insert tab. In the Tables group, click the Table button, and then click **Convert Text to Table**. Compare your screen with Figure 2.32.

Tab used to separate the text into columns   Number of columns detected   Number of rows

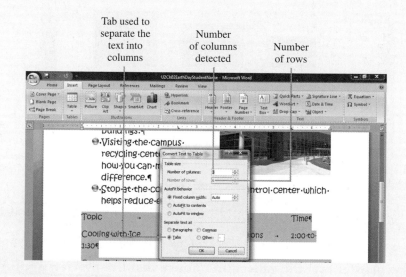

FIGURE 2.32

5 In the Convert Text to Table dialog box, confirm that the number of columns displayed is **3**, and that under *Separate text at* Tab is selected. Click **OK.** The data is returned to a table format, but the column-width adjustments you made earlier are no longer in effect.

6 Save your work.

►►► *lesson*
eight|Formatting Tables

When you create a table, all of the text in the table looks the same. You can use standard formatting tools to emphasize important points, headings in rows and columns, or totals in the last row or column. It is easier, however, to use the Table Tools Design tab to apply preformatted table styles and then modify the styles as needed. Formatting a table gives it an easy-to-read, professional look.

In this lesson, you apply a table style and then modify the format as needed.

to format tables

1   **If necessary, in the upper left corner, just outside of the table, click the Select All button ⊞ to select the table. Click the Table Tools Design tab. In the Table Styles group, click the More button ▼ to display the gallery of Table Styles shown in Figure 2.33.**

Table Styles
gallery

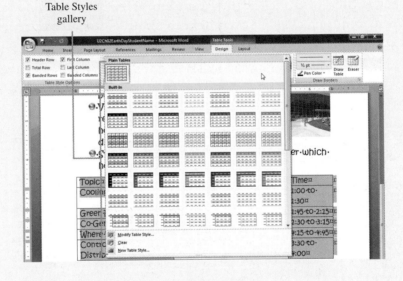

FIGURE 2.33

2   **Move the pointer over the gallery and notice that live preview applies the styles to the table so that you can preview the results.**

3   **In the fourth column and fourth row, click *Medium Shading 1, Accent 3* to apply this style to the table.** This applies a darker tone to the column headings and banded shading to the rest of the table, while bold is applied to the first column.

4   **Click a cell in the first column. On the Design tab, in the Table Styles Options group, click the First Column button to clear the check mark, which removes the bold format from this column.**

5 Move the pointer to the left margin next to the top row. When the [⇗] pointer displays, click to select the first row. Right-click the selected top row. On the Mini toolbar, click the Font button arrow, and then scroll down and click Copperplate Gothic Bold.

6 With the top row still selected, click the Table Tools Layout tab, and then in the Alignment group, click the Align Center button [▦]. This button aligns the text in the middle of the cell both horizontally and vertically. You can also align text vertically at the top or bottom of a cell.

7 Point to *1:00 to 1:30* in the second row. When the [↗] pointer displays, drag down to select the time in all five rows.

8 On the Layout tab, in the Alignment group, click the Align Top Right button [▤] to align the time on the right side of the cells.

9 Point just above the Time column heading, and when the [↓] pointer displays, click to select the column. On the Layout tab, in the Cell Size group, in the Table Column Width box [▤ 6″ ▤], click the up spin arrow until 1.3 displays.

10 Click in the center column, and using the technique you just practiced, change the Table Column Width to 2.5″.

11 In the first cell in the last row, double-click the word *Controlling*, and then press [Delete] to reduce the amount of text so that it will display on one line. Change the width of the first column to 2.5″. Compare your screen with Figure 2.34.

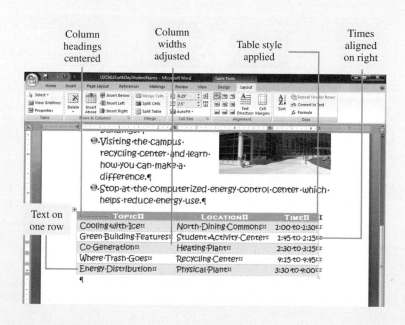

Column headings centered · Column widths adjusted · Table style applied · Times aligned on right

Text on one row

FIGURE 2.34

12 Save [▤] your changes.

Data in tables can be sorted. This is useful if the data needs to be sorted in chronological, numerical, or alphabetical order. In this part of the lesson, you will sort the table so that the times are displayed in chronological order.

to sort a table

1 Click a cell in the table to make the table active.

2 On the Table Tools Layout tab, in the Data group, click the Sort button.

3 In the Sort dialog box, under My list has, be sure the Header Row option is selected so that the column headings in the first row are not sorted with the data.

4 In the Sort by box, click the arrow, and then click Time. If you want to sort on more than one column, you can do so by using the *Then by* boxes.

5 In the Type box, confirm that Date displays, and confirm that the Ascending option button is selected. Compare your screen with Figure 2.35. The Type box will display Number, Text, or Date to match the type of data that is used for the sort column. You can sort in ascending or descending order. To sort dates or time in chronological order, select *ascending* as the sort order.

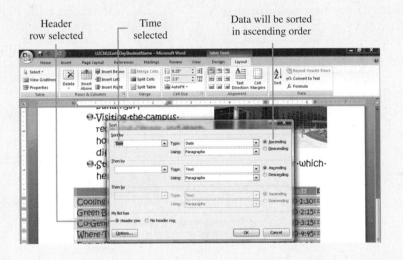

FIGURE 2.35

6 Click OK. Notice that Energy Distribution at 3:30 is now in the fifth row of the table.

7 Save your changes.

Table cells can be merged together to create a larger cell. This is useful if you need to create a heading for more than one column or row of information. You can also split cells if you decide that information needs to be divided into more than one cell. In this task, you will add a row, enter data, and then merge the cells in the row into one cell.

to merge cells

1 In the last cell in the table, click to the right of the time and press `Tab↹` to add a new row.

2 Type `Sponsored by Campus Committee for Responsible Energy Use (CCREU)` As you type, the new row expands so that all of the text is in the first cell in the row, which may expand to a second page.

3 Point to the last row in the table, and when the `⬚` pointer displays, click to select the row. Click the Table Tools Layout tab, and then in the Merge group, click the Merge Cells button. The cells are merged together, and the text is aligned on the right and is wider than the table, so it still displays on two lines.

4 With the text still selected, right-click the selected row, and on the Mini toolbar, click the Font Size button arrow, and then click 11 pt.

5 On the Layout tab, in the Alignment group, click the Align Top Center button `▤`.

6 With the last row still selected, click the Design tab. In the Table Styles group, click the Shading button arrow to display the color gallery. In the first row, click *Olive Green, Accent 3* to apply a color to this row so that it appears to be part of the table.

7 With the last row still selected, in the Table Styles group, click the Borders button arrow, and then click Outside Borders to add a border around this merged cell.

8 In the upper left corner of the table, click the Select All button `⊞` to select the entire table. Click the Home tab, and then in the Paragraph group, click the Center button `≣` to center the table between the left and right margins.

9 Click outside the table and compare your screen with Figure 2.36; then Save `💾` your changes.

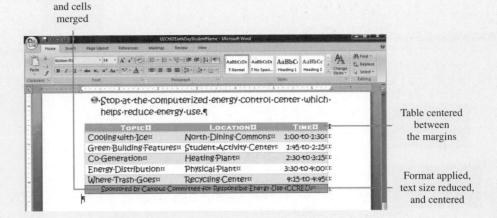

Row added
and cells
merged

Table centered
between
the margins

Format applied,
text size reduced,
and centered

FIGURE 2.36

to extend your knowledge

SPLITTING CELLS IN A TABLE

The process of splitting cells in a table is similar to merging cells. Select the cell you want to split, and then on the Table Tools Layout tab, in the Merge group, click the Split Cells button. You can also right-click the selected cell and choose Split Cells from the shortcut menu. In the Split Cells dialog box, enter the number of columns or rows into which the data should be split. Remember, if the results are not what you expected, you can always click Undo.

SPLITTING A TABLE

Tables can be split into more than one table. To split a table, click in the row where you want to split the table, and then on the Table Tools Layout tab, in the Merge group, click the Split Table button. The table will split in two at the row that contains the insertion point. If a Table Style has been applied, the top row in the new table—the one that contains the insertion point—will be formatted as the heading row for the table.

CHANGING THE VERTICAL ALIGNMENT

In addition to changing the horizontal alignment of text in a cell, you can also change the vertical alignment to control whether the text is placed at the top, middle, or bottom of a cell. This is useful when you have cell headings that take more than one line and you want to align all of the text in the row to be on the bottom or in the middle of the row. To do this, right-click the cell you want to change, and then point to Cell Alignment from the shortcut menu. Select the alignment option that you want from the displayed palette of options. This shortcut menu option can be used for both vertical and horizontal alignment of text in table cells.

CHANGING TEXT ORIENTATION

If necessary, text can be oriented vertically in a cell. This is useful when you want to minimize the space that is used by row headings. To do this, right-click the cell you want to change and, from the shortcut menu, click Text Direction. In the Text Direction dialog box, select the orientation you want to use, and then click OK.

▶▶▶ *lesson*

nine | Inserting a Header or Footer in a Document

Headers and *footers* are reserved areas at the top (header) or bottom (footer) of each page in a document. Here you can insert text, graphics, or data such as the current date, page number, file name and location, or the author of the document. Information entered in these areas appears on each page in the document unless it is specifically excluded from the first page. In the rest of this book, you will use the footer area to display the file name of each document.

to insert a footer

1 **Press** Ctrl **+** Home **to move to the top of the document. Click the Insert tab, and then in the Header & Footer group, click the Footer button.** A gallery of built-in footer styles displays, as shown in Figure 2.37. If you want to enter your own text, use the Edit Footer command.

Footer
gallery

FIGURE 2.37

2 **Use the Footer scroll bar to scroll the list and see the styles that are available. At the bottom of the list, click Edit Footer.** The end of the page displays and the insertion point is blinking in the Footer area, as shown in Figure 2.38. Notice that the text area appears dimmer because the footer area is now active. The Header & Footer Tools Design tab displays, which enables you to format and edit this area of your document.

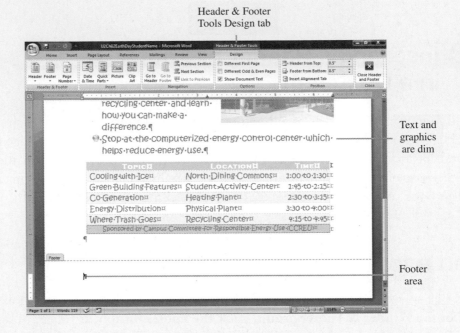

FIGURE 2.38

3 **On the Design tab, in the Insert group, click the Quick Parts button, and then click Field to display the Field dialog box.** A *field* is a category of data—such as file name, date, time, or page number—which can be inserted into a document.

4 **Under Field names, use the vertical scroll bar to scroll the list of fields until you locate FileName. Click FileName, and then compare your screen with Figure 2.39.**

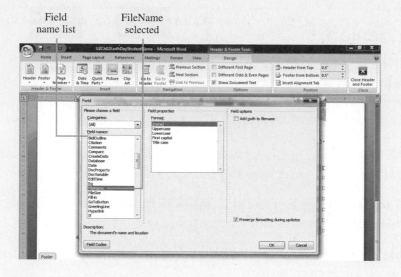

FIGURE 2.39

5 With FileName selected, click OK to place the name of your file in the lower left corner of the Footer.

6 Press Tab⇆ two times to move to the right side of the footer area. Type your last name and press Spacebar. In addition to the file name, document the authorship of a document in the footer area.

7 On the Design tab, in the Insert group, click the Date & Time button to display the Date and Time dialog box. Here you can select a date and time format. Including the date in the footer of the flyer provides a reference date so that university departments can tell how long a flyer has been posted.

8 With the first format selected—mm/dd/yy—click OK to insert the current date. Compare your screen with Figure 2.40.

File name
displays in
footer area

Your last
name and the
current date
display on
the right

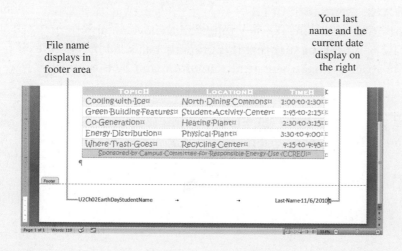

FIGURE 2.40

good **design...**

USE THE FOOTER AREA FOR DOCUMENTATION

The footer area is a good place to document the file name and author. If the material is time sensitive, include a date in this area as well.

9 On the Design tab, in the Close group, click the Close Header and Footer button. The footer area closes and the top of the document displays.

10 Scroll to the end of the page and notice that the footer text displays, but it is in gray because this area is not currently active.

11 Double-click the footer to make that area on your document active. Notice that the Design tab is again active.

12 Select all of the text displayed in the footer. On the Mini toolbar, click the Italic button *I*. Double-click in the document to close the Footer area.

13 From the Office button, point to Print, and then click Print Preview. Review the flyer to see if all of the information is balanced on the page so that all of the elements are not bunched together and there is enough white space between each area. On the flyer, there is more white space between the table and the end of the page that is not used.

14 In the Preview group, click the Close Print Preview button to return to the flyer. Click at the end of the last bullet point, press ⏎Enter and then press ⌫Backspace to remove the bullet point. This increases the white space between the bullet list and the table and improves the balance of the table and the end of the document.

good **design...**

REVIEW THE FINAL RESULTS

Before printing, use Print Preview to review the overall appearance of your document. In the case of a flyer, be sure that it is properly balanced between text, visual elements, and white space so that it will attract attention and be easy to read.

15 Save 💾 your work. Print the file or submit it as directed by your instructor. Click the Office button, and then click Close to close the flyer.

›››› *lesson*
ten| Creating a Document from a Template

There are several *templates*—preformatted documents—that come with each Microsoft Office application. Templates can help save time because they provide the basis for standard forms such as memos, fax cover letters, resumes, or standard letters, which can be used repeatedly. They can include text formatting, graphics, and layout of the document. Templates can be customized to create a uniform look and style with personalized information such as a company name, address, and logo.

In this lesson, you will use a template to create a fax cover letter that can be sent with the flyer you just created.

to create a document from a template

1 **Click the Office button 🔘, and then from the displayed menu, click New. In the displayed New Document dialog box, in the left panel under Templates, click Installed Templates, and then compare your screen with Figure 2.41.** The center panel displays a preview of the installed templates.

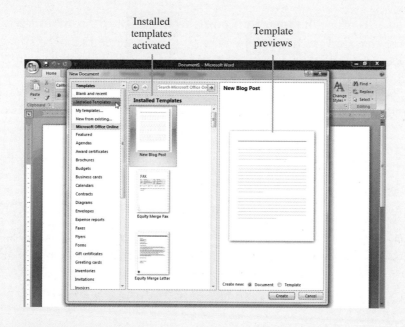

Installed templates activated

Template previews

FIGURE 2.41

2 **In the center panel, use the vertical scroll bar to scroll the list of templates.** These templates are named for a theme. Each theme may include several types of documents such as a memo, a fax cover, a letter, a report, and a resume.

3 **Scroll the template list and locate and click the Origin Fax to select it; then click Create.** The fax cover letter displays, as shown in Figure 2.42. Areas within brackets can be selected and replaced by typing.

Origin Fax template

FIGURE 2.42

4 On the right side of the Fax cover letter, click *Pick a date*, and then click the *Pick a date* arrow to display the calendar for the current month. At the bottom of the calendar, click Today.

5 Press Tab⇄ to move the insertion point to the right of From and type your name. The name that displays here is the name of the registered owner of the software. When you tab to this area, a box displays as a ***field area***—an area that is coded to insert a specific value—in this case, the owner of the software.

6 To the right of Phone, click to select the text inside of the brackets and type 248.555.0023. Continue in this manner to enter the remaining information for the top part of the fax cover letter.

Fax: 248.555.0032

Company Name: Campus Committee for Responsible Energy Use (CCREU)

To: All Departments

Fax: Distribution List

Company Name: University Community

7 In the *To* area, to the right of *Phone*, click the field placeholder, and then press Delete to remove this from the address area.

8 Under Comments, select the placeholder text *[Type Comments]* and then type

Please post the attached flyer in a prominent area in your office and on the public bulletin boards in your area.

9 Press ↵Enter and type Thank you. Press ↵Enter again and type CCREU. Compare your screen with Figure 2.43.

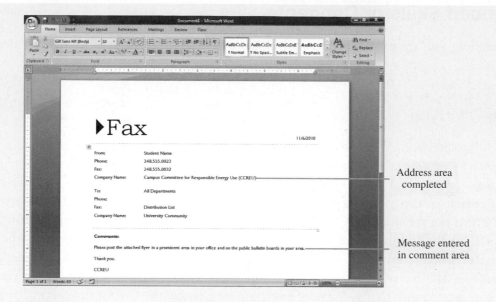

FIGURE 2.43

10 On the Quick Access Toolbar, click the Save button 🔲. In the displayed Save As dialog box, navigate to the Chapter02 folder that you created for this chapter. In the File name box, type U2Ch02FaxCoverStudentName and then click Save.

11 Click the Insert tab, and in the Header & Footer group, click the Footer button. At the end of the menu, click Edit Footer.

12 On the Design tab, in the Insert group, click the Quick Parts button, and then click Field. In the Field dialog box, scroll the Field names list, and then click FileName. Click OK to insert the file name in the left footer area. Double-click in the document to close the Footer area.

13 Follow the instructions provided by your instructor to submit your work. Close the file and save it when prompted to do so, and then exit Word.

to extend your knowledge

TEMPLATES ONLINE

If you select one of the template categories listed under Microsoft Office Online, examples for that particular category display. A License Agreement for the Community Templates page may display, which details the terms of use for the templates. It requires that you have a validly licensed copy of Microsoft Office and that you agree to the terms for using the template.

Advanced Skills or Concepts

In this section, you are introduced to skills that are not taught with step-by-step instructions.

Using Overtype

By default, when you type text into a document, the existing text moves to the right and the new text is inserted at the insertion point. It is also possible to replace existing text by using overtype.

To switch to overtype, right-click the status bar to display the Customize Status Bar menu. From the menu, click Overtype to display an Insert button on the Status bar. When you click the Insert button on the Status bar, it changes to Overtype, and then when you type, existing text is replaced. To deactivate the Overtype mode, click the Overtype button on the status bar to change it back to Insert. To remove the Insert/Overtype button from the status bar, first be sure that you are in Insert mode. Display the Customize Status Bar menu, and then verify and remove the check mark next to Overtype.

Unless you have a specific reason to use this feature, it is generally better to select and delete text that you want to replace or select text and type new text to replace the selected text.

Transmitting Files Electronically

Documents are often sent from one location to another by e-mail or by fax.

Using e-mail, you can distribute documents to a distribution list or to several individuals at once. To send a document by e-mail, it must first be saved. If it is open, from the Office menu, point to Send, and then click E-mail. A Send Message window will display with the document shown as an attachment. Enter the e-mail addresses and message to the recipients, and then send the message. Alternatively, open your e-mail program, click the attachment button, and then locate and attach the file that you want to transmit.

A fax copy of a document that has been signed creates a facsimile signature, which may be acceptable for business transactions or contracts that require a legal signature. To send a document using a traditional fax machine, print the document and then use a fax machine to send it. To send a document using an Internet fax service, from the Office menu, click Send, and then click Internet Fax. Follow the instructions to sign up for an Internet fax service supplied by a third party vendor that can transmit Microsoft Office files.

CHECK YOUR WORK

Here is a list of items your instructor will probably look for when grading your work. To improve your evaluation, take time to check the items yourself before you turn in your work.

Earth Day Flyer
- Earth Day Tour title changed to a WordArt graphic.
- The WordArt shape changed to *Inflate*.
- Colors on the WordArt graphic changed to shades of olive green.

- Clip art image inserted, resized, and moved to the left of the WordArt title.
- Date centered under the title and formatted in Kristen ITC 20 pt bold font.
- The font in the rest of the document formatted in Kristen ITC 16 pt font.
- A list of four bullet points is in the center of the document.
- The bullets are changed to an image of the world.
- Picture of a building inserted, cropped, and moved to the right side of the bulleted list.
- The bulleted list is aligned on the left after the picture is inserted.
- A table is created under the bulleted list with six rows of data in three columns.
- The table is formatted using the Medium Shading 1, Accent 3 style.
- The text on the title row is centered and changed to Copperplate Gothic Bold.
- The data in the *Time* column is aligned on the right.
- A row is added to the end of the table, data is entered, the three cells are merged.
- The last row of the table is formatted with Olive Green, Accent 3, and the font size is reduced to 11 pt.
- The file name is added to the left side of the footer area, and your last name and the date are on the right side of the footer.

Fax Cover Memo
- A fax cover template is used to create a fax cover letter.
- The address information is entered on the upper portion of the fax cover letter.
- A single line of instructions is typed in the comments area.
- The file name is added to the left side of the footer area.
- Placeholders at the top of the memo are replaced with appropriate information.

KEY TERMS

alignment	header	serif fonts
anchor	indent	single-spaced
bullet	justified	sizing handle
bulleted list	left-aligned	spacing after
center	line spacing	table
clip art	numbered list	templates
field	right-aligned	theme
field area	rotation handle	toggle
footer	sans serif fonts	WordArt

ASSESSING LEARNING OUTCOMES

SCREEN ID

Identify each element of the screen by matching callout numbers shown in Figure 2.44 to a corresponding description.

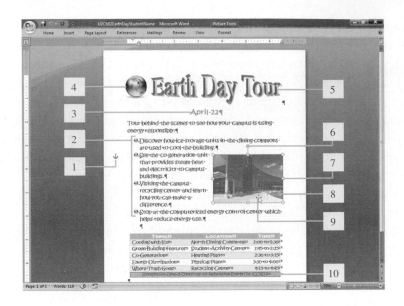

FIGURE 2.44

_____ **A.** Bullet list   _____ **E.** Merged cells   _____ **I.** Sizing handle

_____ **B.** Centered text   _____ **F.** Move pointer   _____ **J.** WordArt

_____ **C.** Clip art   _____ **G.** Picture anchor

_____ **D.** Digital image   _____ **H.** Rotation handle

MULTIPLE CHOICE

Circle the letter of the correct answer for each of the following. The lesson in which the term or concept was introduced is indicated at the end of the sentence.

1. To move an image around on a document, you need to change the _____. [L5]

   a. image magnification

   b. text wrapping

   c. size of the image

   d. format settings

2. Use a numbered list for all of the following **except** items that are listed _____. [L2]

   a. randomly

   b. sequentially

   c. chronologically

   d. by importance

3. Examples of a serif font include _____. [L3]

   a. Times New Roman, Courier, Arial

   b. Comic Sans, Cambria, Verdana

   c. Courier, Times New Roman, Cambria

   d. Verdana, Calibri, Arial

4. The difference between indent and alignment is: [L3]

   a. There is no difference—they both are used to line up text on the left.

   b. Indent is used to line up text at the margins, and alignment moves text in from the left or right margin.

c. Alignment is set using the ruler or a dialog box, and indents are set using buttons on the Ribbon.

d. Indent is used to move text in from the left or right margin, and alignment lines up text at the margins.

5. You may add graphics in all of the following circumstances except to _____. [L4–6]

a. illustrate a point

b. embellish every type of document

c. attract the reader's attention

d. provide information

6. Digital images should be resized and cropped to _____. [L6]

a. make the image fit in the available space

b. focus attention on the significant portion of the image

c. remove clutter from an image

d. do any of the above

7. When you need to create lists of parallel information, use a _____. [L7]

a. table

b. numbered list

c. bulleted list

d. outline

8. To create a table, you can _____. [L8]

a. drag the dimensions in the Insert Table grid

b. use the Draw Table command

c. convert text to a table

d. do any of the above

9. To display the file name and author on every page of a document, use the _____. [L9]

a. top and bottom area

b. margin area

c. header and footer area

d. keyboard to type the information on each page of a document

10. All of the following are true about using a template **except:** [L10]

a. Templates can only be used once.

b. Templates can be used repeatedly.

c. Templates are available to create a resume.

d. Templates can be customized.

MATCHING

Match the term or concept to its description.

_____ 1. Fonts that do not have lines or extensions on the ends of letters

_____ 2. A collection of design elements that are applied to documents to create a uniform look

_____ 3. An area reserved at the top of a document for information that should appear on every page in a document

_____ 4. A category of data such as file name, date, or page number that is inserted into a document

_____ 5. Preformatted and designed document that can be used repeatedly

_____ 6. A font that has lines or extensions on the ends of the letters

A. Alignment

B. Field

C. Footer

D. Header

E. Justified

F. Sans serif

G. Serif

H. Template

I. Theme

J. WordArt

_____ 7. The horizontal placement of text

_____ 8. Text that is aligned evenly between both the left and right margins

_____ 9. A tool used to turn words into a graphic to create a decorative title

_____ 10. An area reserved at the bottom of a document for information that should appear on every page in a document

SKILL DRILL

The Skill Drill exercise is a repeat of the lessons in the chapter but with a different set of data. The instructions are less detailed, and your speed and familiarity should increase with practice. There is a figure at the end against which you can check your results. The purpose of this exercise is to build your confidence and speed in using these skills and to set them in your memory for later recall. The section numbers correspond to the lesson numbers. You are welcome to refer back to the lessons illustrated and the detailed instructions if necessary.

In this exercise, you create a flyer to announce a lecture series that will be held on energy independence.

1. Creating a New Document

1. **Start** Word. On the **Quick Access Toolbar,** click the **Save** button. Navigate to the **Chapter02** folder you created earlier. In the **File name** box, type `U2Ch02LectureSeriesStudentName` and then click **Save.**

2. If necessary, on the **Home** tab, in the **Paragraph** group, click the **Show/Hide** button to make it active. If the ruler does not display, click the **View** tab. In the **Show/Hide** group, click the **Ruler** check box.

3. On the **Home** tab, in the **Paragraph** group, click the **Line Spacing** button and then click **1.0.** Click the **Line Spacing** button again, and click **Remove Space After Paragraph.**

4. Type `Energy Independence Lecture Series` and then press Enter two times.

5. Type `The campus committee on global awareness is sponsoring a lecture series to bring experts to campus to discuss the future of energy in the world. This year's topic is:` Press Enter three times.

6. Type `The Road to Energy Independence` Press Enter two times. **Save** your work.

2. Creating and Modifying a Bulleted List

1. Type `Sponsored by:` and then press ⏎Enter two times.

2. On the **Home** tab, in the **Paragraph** group, click the **Bullets** button, and then type the following on four lines:
   `Central Utilities Coop`
   `Chemicals for Modern Living`
   `Farmer's Group Products`
   `Campus Committee for Responsible Energy Use`

3. Select the four bulleted lines you just typed. On the **Home** tab, in the **Paragraph** group, click the **Bullets** button arrow. From the **Bullets** gallery, click the **black square bullet** symbol.

4. **Save** your work.

3. Formatting, Aligning, and Indenting Text

1. Press Ctrl + A to select all of the text. On the **Home** tab, in the **Font** group, click the **Font** button arrow. Scroll the font list and then click **Verdana.**

2. With the text still selected, in the **Font** group, click the **Font Size** button arrow, and then click **14** pt.

3. Select the line *The Road to Energy Independence*. On the Mini toolbar, click the **Bold** button, the **Italic** button, and the **Center** button. On the **Home** tab, in the **Font** group, click the **Grow Font** button twice to increase the font size to **18** pt.

4. Select the next line *Sponsored by:* and click the **Center** button.

5. Select the four lines of bulleted text. On the **Home** tab, in the **Paragraph** group, click the **Dialog Box Launcher.** In the Paragraph dialog box, under **Indentation,** in the **Left** box, type `1.5` and then click **OK.**

6. **Save** your work.

4. Creating a Title with WordArt

1. Select the first line: *Energy Independence Lecture Series*. Click the **Insert** tab, and in the **Text** group, click the **WordArt** button. From the displayed gallery, in the second row, second column, click **WordArt style 8.**

2. In the **Edit WordArt Text** dialog box, click the **Bold** button, and then click **OK.**

3. On the **Format** tab, in the **Size** group, click **Size.** In the **Height** box, type 1 and then press ⏎Enter. Alternatively, click the up spin arrow to increase the size until 1" displays.

4. On the **Format** tab, in the **WordArt Styles** group, click the **Change WordArt Shape** button. In the displayed gallery, under **Wrap,** in the first row, click the fourth shape—**Can Down.**

5. In the **WordArt Styles** group, click the **Shape Fill** button arrow. In the displayed gallery, in the sixth column—*Red*—click the fifth color: **Red Accent 2, Darker 25%.**

6. In the **WordArt Styles** group, click the **Shape Outline Fill** button arrow to display the outline color gallery. In the fourth column, click the fifth color: **Dark Blue, Text 2, Darker 25%.**

7. In the **Shadow Effects** group, click the **Shadow Effects** button, and then click **No Shadow Effect** to remove the shadow from this graphic.

8. **Save** your work.

5. Inserting and Modifying Clip Art

1. Click to the left of the line of text under the WordArt graphic: *The campus committee.* Press ⏎Enter two times to move this down on the page.

2. Click the **Insert** tab, and then in the **Illustrations** group, click the **ClipArt** button.

3. In the Clip Art task pane, in the **Search For** box, type oil and then press ⏎Enter.

4. Click the clip art of the oil derrick shown in Figure 2.45 (the image is green and will be recolored) to insert it in the document.

5. With the inserted clip art selected, on the **Format** tab, in the **Arrange** group, click the **Text Wrapping** button, and then click **Tight.**

6. Drag the clip art so that it is positioned to the left of the entire first paragraph, as shown in Figure 2.45.

7. On the **Format** tab, in the **Size** group, click in the **Shape Height** box, and then click the down spin arrow until **1.5"** is displayed.

8. Move the image to the left of the first paragraph, and position it under the middle of the word *Energy* in the WordArt title. Refer to Figure 2.45 to confirm the placement of the clip art.

9. On the **Format** tab, in the **Adjust** group, click the **Recolor** button, and then under **Dark Variations,** click the third color: **Accent color 2, Dark.**

10. Close the Clip Art task pane. **Save** your changes.

6. Inserting and Modifying Pictures

1. Click to the right of the last word in the first bulleted line: *Coop.*

2. Click the **Insert** tab, and then in the **Illustrations** group, click the **Picture** button. Navigate to the folder that contains the student files for this chapter. Click the figure named **U2Ch02Transformer,** and then click **Insert.**

3. With the inserted picture selected, on the **Picture Tools Format** tab, in the **Size** group, click the **Crop** button.

4. On the left side of the picture, position the crop pointer on the left middle crop mark and drag into the middle of the image to the vertical pole that is just right of the center of the image. The two high towers on the right should remain in the picture as shown in Figure 2.45.

5. On the **Format** tab, in the **Arrange** group, click the **Text Wrapping** button, and then click **Square.**

6. In the **Size** group, in the **Shape Height** box, type 1.5 Position the image so that it is on the right of all four bullet points, at approximately the 4.75-inch mark on the horizontal ruler.

7. Compare your results with Figure 2.45, and then **save** your changes.

7. Inserting Tables

1. Click on the blank line under *The Road to Energy Independence*. Press ⏎Enter, then click the **Home** tab, and in the **Paragraph** group, click the **Center** button. Type Topics and Speakers include: and then press ⏎Enter two times.

2. Click the **Insert** tab, and in the **Tables** group, click the **Table** button. Drag the grid to insert a **3 × 3** table—three columns and three rows.

3. Click in the first cell of the table and enter the following information, using the Tab⇆ key to move from cell to cell.

Our Partnership with Canada to End Mideast Oil Imports	Dr. Mohammed Kalid	October 30
The Potential of Tar Sands	Dr. Josephine McIntyre	November 20
Diesel Fuel from City Sewage: The Future of Biodiesel	Dr. Samuel Abrams	December 15

4. Click in a cell in the first row of the table, and then right-click. On the shortcut menu, point to **Insert,** and then click **Insert Rows Above.** Type the following column headings in this row: Topic, Speaker, Date

5. Point to the left of the second row and drag down to select the last three rows of the table. Click the **Home** tab, and in the **Paragraph** group, click the **Left Align** button. Recall that when you insert a table, it assumes the format of the previous paragraph, which was center-aligned.

6. Click the **Table Tools Layout** tab, and in the **Cell Size** group, click the **AutoFit** button, and then click **AutoFit Contents.**

7. **Save** your changes.

8. Formatting Tables

1. With the table still selected, click the **Table Tools Design** tab, and in the **Table Styles** group, click the **More** button. In the displayed gallery, in the second row, second column, click the **Light List Accent 1** style.

2. In the **Table Styles Options** group, click **First Column** to remove the check mark, which removes the bold format from the text in the first column.

3. Select the three rows under the column headings. Click the **Layout** tab, and in the **Cell Size** group, in the **Table Row Height** box, click the up spin arrow until **.7"** displays.

4. On the **Layout** tab, in the **Alignment** group, click the **Align Center Left** button to move the text vertically to the middle of each cell.

5. Point to the top of the first column and click to select the first column. On the **Layout** tab, in the **Cell Size** group, click in the **Table Column Width** box, and then click the down spin arrow until **3.3"** displays.

6. Using the technique you just practiced, reduce the *Speaker* column width to **1.7"**. This adjusts the columns so that the dates display on one row instead of two.

7. Select the three dates in the Date column, and on the **Layout** tab, in the **Alignment** group, click the **Align Center** button.

8. Click to the right of the last word in the last cell of the table, and then press `Tab` to insert a new row. Type `Times and locations to be announced`

9. Select the last row in the table. On the **Layout** tab, in the **Merge** group, click the **Merge Cells** button. In the **Cell Size** group, in the **Table Row Height** box, click the down spin arrow until the height displays as **0.3"**.

10. Click the **Design** tab, and in the **Table Styles** group, click the **Shading** button arrow. In the displayed gallery, in the fourth column, third row, click **Dark Blue, Text 2, Lighter 60%**.

11. **Save** your changes.

9. Inserting a Header or Footer in a Document

1. Click the **Insert** tab, and in the **Header & Footer** group, click the **Footer** button. At the end of the list, click **Edit Footer.**

2. On the **Header & Footer Tools Design** tab, in the **Insert** group, click the **Quick Parts** button, and then click **Field.**

3. In the **Field** dialog box, under Field names, scroll the list to locate FileName. Click **FileName,** and then click **OK.**

4. Press `Tab` two times. Type your last name and press `Spacebar`. In the **Insert** group, click the **Date & Time** button and then click **OK** to insert the default date using the default date format.

5. In the **Footer** area, select all of the text, and then on the Mini toolbar, click the **Bold** button and the **Italic** button.

6. On the **Design** tab, in the **Close** group, click the **Close Header and Footer** button.

7. **Save** your changes. Submit the file as directed by your instructor. Click the **Office** button, and then click **Close.**

10. Creating a Document from a Template

1. **Start** Microsoft Office Word 2007 if necessary. From the **Office** menu, click **New.**

2. In the New Document dialog box, under **Templates,** click **Installed Templates.** Scroll the templates displayed in the middle of the dialog box. Locate and click the **Equity Fax** template, and then click **Create.**

3. On the **Home** tab, in the **Paragraph** group, click the **Show/Hide** button if necessary to hide the formatting marks. On the right of *To:*, click the placeholder text and type `Academic Departments`. If your name does not display next to *From:*, click the text displayed and type your name.

4. On the next line, next to *Fax*, replace the placeholder text by typing 555.0611 and next to *Pages:*, type 2

5. Next to *Phone*, delete the placeholder text, and then next to *Date:*, enter the current date. Next to *Re:*, type Lecture Series and then next to *CC:*, delete the placeholder text.

6. Under *Comments*, select the placeholder text and type: Please ask your faculty to announce our lecture series in their classes. Attendance at all three lectures will fulfill one credit toward the Learning Beyond the Classroom requirement.

7. In the sentence you just typed, select *Learning Beyond the Classroom*, and then on the Mini toolbar, click the **Italic** button.

8. **Save** the document in your **Chapter02** folder with the name U2Ch02LectureFaxStudentName

9. Click the **Insert** tab, and in the **Header & Footer** group, click the **Footer** button. Use the procedure you followed in part 9 to insert the FileName field in the left footer area. Compare your results with Figure 2.45.

10. **Save** the file and submit it as directed by your instructor. **Close** the file, and then **exit** Word.

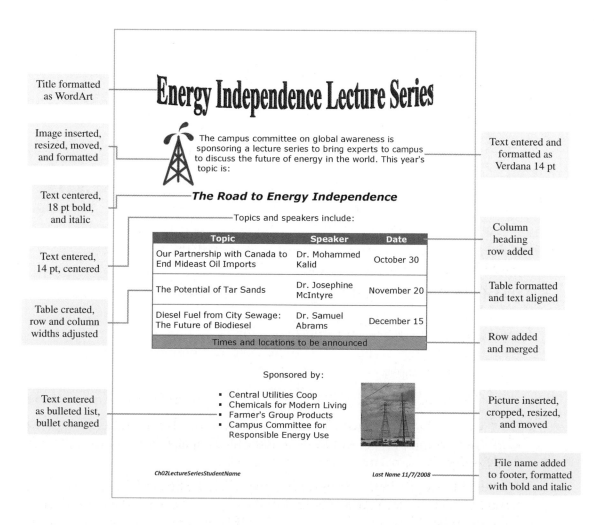

FIGURE 2.45A

FIGURE 2.45B

fix *it*

One way to appreciate the value of good design is to fix a file that is not designed well. In this exercise, you open a file that has several errors and design flaws and fix it according to good design elements, using the skills that you practiced in the lessons.

Navigate to the folder with the student files, open **U2Ch02FixIt** and save it as U2Ch02FixItStudentName

Examine this document and format it using the skills you have practiced so that it is a professional, readable flyer that will attract attention and create interest. Make changes to comply with the good design principles that were introduced in this chapter. Here is a list of corrections needed and the design principles introduced in this chapter, along with some tips on how to fix the flyer.

- Create a title for the flyer to attract attention to the topic of energy efficiency.
- Use a clip art that is appropriate to the topic, and position it to break up the opening paragraphs.
- Use a font that is appropriate to the topic, audience, and type of document.
- Use a font size that is easy to read quickly.
- Adjust the alignment and/or indents to create a balanced document.
- Where it is appropriate, convert text to a table, and insert a row with column headings.
- Format the table so that it is clear and easy to read. Center the table on the page.
- Insert the **U2Ch02WDBuilding2** image, which is the building that will be LEED-certified.

- Crop and resize the image, and position it to balance the meeting information items on the page.
- Use a numbered or bulleted list whichever is appropriate to the list.
- Place the file name in the footer and your last name and the date on the right side of the footer.
- Preview the flyer and adjust the spacing between information to create a balanced, attractive flyer.
- Submit the file as required by your instructor. Save and close the file.

ON THE JOB

Information workers add value to data by organizing, selecting, displaying, communicating, interpreting, and using data to communicate information and support decisions. On the Job exercises simulate a situation where you are given data, and your job is to add value to it using the skills you practiced in this chapter. Success in these exercises indicates that you have a valuable skill to offer an employer.

1. Natural Gas Lecture Flyer

In this On the Job exercise, you create a flyer to announce the upcoming guest lecturer for the Energy Independence Lecture Series. Refer to the memo from the program coordinator, and then, using the skills you have practiced in this chapter, organize the information into a flyer.

Susan,

Please create a flyer announcing a lecture by Dr. R. F. Lewis, a leading expert on natural gas exploration and transportation. The lecture will be held on September 12 from 3:00 to 5:00 in the Boone Lecture Hall in the Patterson Science Building. The lecture is free to students and $5.00 for the general public. The title of the lecture is: Transporting Natural Gas Overseas— LNG Safety Issues. The lecture will include the following topics:
Our domestic natural gas resources
Why natural gas burns cleaner than coal
Pipeline bottlenecks
How much of it is imported and from whom
Role of Algeria and Venezuela in heating the northeast
Liquefied Natural Gas (LNG) for transport by ship
Handling LNG safely
Protecting LNG ships and facilities from accidents
Be sure to include in the flyer the picture of the ship that Dr. Lewis supplied. This should go out under the title of Energy Independence Lecture Series so that everyone knows this is part of that series. Also, include the fact that this lecture is sponsored by the Campus Committee for Responsible Energy Use (CCREU).

David

1. Create a new document and save it in your Chapter02 folder as
   U2Ch02NaturalGasStudentName

2. Create a graphic image for the name of the lecture series.

3. Write an introduction to announce Dr. Lewis and his credentials. Include the name of the sponsoring committee in your introductory announcement.

4. Next introduce the title of the lecture.

5. Add the list of lecture topics in a bulleted list.

6. Add the ship image, which is in the student files: **U2Ch02Ship.** Crop the image to show just the ship, and place it under the list of topics. Refer to Figure 2.46.

7. Select a font and font size to create a bold statement that is appropriate and easy to read.

8. Create a table to list the details about the time, location, and cost of the lecture. Format appropriately and center between the margins under the ship.

9. Insert the file name on the left side of the footer and your last name and the date on the right side of the footer.

10. Print or submit the file as directed by your instructor. Save the file and then close it.

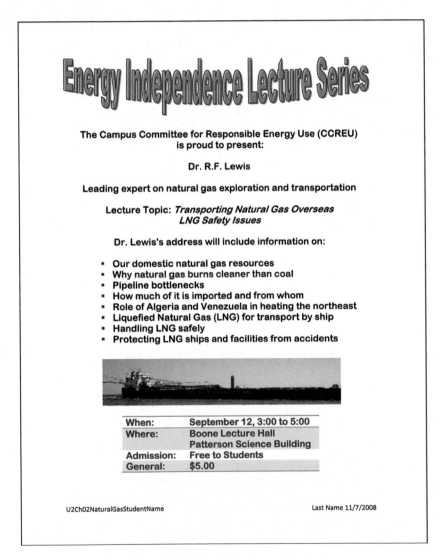

FIGURE 2.46

2. Bus Schedule and Flextime Procedures

Human Resources has just been given approval to offer flextime to employees who elect to take a bus to work. In addition, the company will cover the cost of the bus pass. Refer to the memo from the boss, and then using the skills you have practiced in this chapter, create a flyer that can be e-mailed to all employees as an e-mail attachment.

Carol,

Draft a memo to employees to announce the implementation of our Bus to Work program. Attached is a schedule of the bus arrival times in the morning and departure times in the afternoon and evening. Provide a list of benefits to encourage people to sign up for this program. We need to create interest and generate enthusiasm. Also include the steps to apply for the program, which include determining which bus they will take, getting approval from their supervisor, and completing a form to request a bus pass.

Joshua

1. Create a new memo by using a memo template. Under Microsoft Office Online, scroll the list and click Memo, and then download the Memo Professional Design template.

2. Delete the company name block on the right side of the memo. This is a table format, so you can use the Table Tools Layout tab to delete this table from the memo.

3. Address the memo to All Employees from Human Resources and you (your name). Use the current date for the date and *Bus to Work Program* as the subject. Delete any unused lines that are included in the memo header area.

4. Announce the program and create a list of the benefits.

5. Open the file **U2Ch02Bus,** copy the bus schedule into the memo, and then convert the schedule to a table. Route 8 lists two different schedules, depending on the time of day. Merge the cells in each column for route 8 so that this row displays as one row with two listings for the route.

6. Format the table so that it is attractive and easy to read.

7. Sort the table in ascending order by the route number.

8. Put the steps in a list that describe how to apply for the program.

9. Adjust the font, font size, alignment, and indents to make it easy to read, balanced on the page, and attractive.

10. Add a clip art that is appropriate to the topic at the top right of the memo address area.

11. Adjust the spacing as needed to balance the information on the page.

12. Save the file as U2Ch02BusStudentName Add the file name to the left side of the footer.

13. Print or submit the file as directed by your instructor.

Memo

To: All Employees

From: Human Resources, Student Name

Date: 9/21/2010

Re: Bus to Work Program

Sign up now for the Bus to Work program and receive a paid bus pass to ride to work. The benefits are many:

- Your transportation to work is paid for by the company
- You save gas
- You save wear and tear on your vehicle
- You help save the environment
- You can work a flex time schedule to meet the bus route for your neighborhood
- You can read the paper and relax while riding to work

The schedule of bus routes that arrive at our location are listed in the following table:

Route	Days of Operation	Hours of Service	Arrival Frequency
2	Mon – Fri	6:30 am -7:00 pm	Every 15 minutes
7	Mon-Sat	6:15 am - 8:00 pm	Every 20 minutes
8	Mon – Fri	6:40 am – 7:00 pm	Every 10 minutes
		7:00 pm – 1 am	Every 15 minutes

To sign up for the Bus to Work program, follow these steps:

1. Determine the bus schedule you will use
2. Obtain approval from your supervisor
3. Complete the bus pass request form

U2Cn02BusStudentName

FIGURE 2.47

DISCUSSION OF ADVANCED SKILLS OR CONCEPTS

The questions in this section are based on the topics in the Advanced Skills or Concepts section of the chapter.

1. When would you sort data in a table? Give an example of when you might sort a table on more than one column.

2. When you sort a table, why is it important to indicate that there is a header row? If you do not indicate that you have a header row, and sorting moves the header, how would you recover from that error?

3. Give an example of when it would save time to use overtype.

4. What are the advantages or disadvantages of using fax rather than e-mail to transmit information electronically? When would you use one versus the other?

5. Describe the equipment and software requirements necessary to send a document using an electronic fax service.

6. What is required to send a document as an e-mail attachment from within the Word application?

ON YOUR OWN

Once you are comfortable with the skills in this chapter, you can apply them to new situations of your own choosing. In this section, you choose data that you have in your possession or that you can find elsewhere. To successfully complete this assignment, you must apply good design practices and demonstrate mastery of the skills that were practiced. Refer to the list of skills and design practices in the Fix It exercise.

1. Create a Flyer for an Activity

Flyers are used by many organizations to announce activities or events. Create a flyer for an organization with which you are familiar.

1. Open a new document and save it as `U2Ch02FlyerStudentName`

2. Create a title for the flyer using WordArt.

3. Type the information that is necessary to announce the activity or event. Change the font, font size, alignment, and indent.

4. Create two of the following to convey information: numbered list, bulleted list, or table.

5. Format the lists and tables.

6. Add clip art or picture images that support the topic of the flyer.

7. Document the file name, your name, and the date in the footer.

8. Save your work and submit the file as directed by your instructor.

2. Use a Résumé Template

Résumés present information about your education, work experience, volunteer work, and accomplishments. They should be succinct and create a positive impression. Microsoft Word includes several résumé templates that offer a format for writing your resume. Many of them use a basic table format to help you align data into columns.

1. Choose one of the résumé templates listed in the Installed Templates list.

2. Locate an ad or a job description for a job you would like to have.

3. Enter the personal data in the résumé. Include an objective statement that matches the qualities needed for the job to which you aspire.

4. List your education, with the most recent listed first. Use the format provided to include the completion date and the type of degree. List any noteworthy accomplishments related to your education.

5. List your work experience, with the most recent experience listed first.

6. List skills or accomplishments that are relevant for the job to which you aspire.

7. Save the file as `U2Ch02ResumeStudentName` and submit the file as directed by your instructor.

ASSESS YOUR PROGRESS

At this point, you should have a set of skills and design concepts that are valuable to an employer and to you. You may not realize how much you have learned unless you take a few minutes to assess your progress.

1. From the student files, open **U2Ch02Assess.** Save it as U2Ch02AssessStudentName

2. Read each question in column A.

3. In column B, answer Yes or No.

4. If you identify a skill or design concept that you don't know, refer to the learning objective code next to the question and the table at the beginning of the chapter to find the skill and review it.

5. Print the worksheet if your instructor requires it. The file name is already in the header, so it will display your name as part of the file name.

6. All of these skills and concepts have been identified as important by surveying hundreds of individuals working at over 200 companies worldwide. If you cannot answer all of the questions affirmatively even after reviewing the relevant lesson, seek additional help from your instructor.

chapter **three**

Formatting and Organizing Paragraphs and Documents

Lesson	Learning Outcomes	Code	Related IC3 Objectives
1	Customize Word options	3.01	1.1.7
1	Create AutoCorrect entries	3.02	1.1.7
2	Import and modify text	3.03	1.3.1, 1.3.2
2	Format header text	3.04	2.1.10, 2.1.16
2	Insert page numbers	3.05	2.1.9, 2.1.16
2	Insert current date and time	3.06	2.2.2, 2.1.16
3	Change line spacing	3.07	2.1.1
3	Change paragraph spacing	3.08	2.1.1
3	Create a style	3.09	2.1.11
3	Apply a style	3.10	2.1.11
3	Indent text	3.11	2.1.2
3	Modify a style	3.12	2.1.11
4	Change spelling and grammar errors using the Shortcut Menu	3.13	1.3.5, 2.2.1
4	Change spelling and grammar errors using spelling and grammar checker	3.14	1.3.5, 2.2.1
4	Use a thesaurus to find synonyms	3.15	2.2.1
4	Display document statistics	3.16	2.2.1
5	Create footnotes	3.17	2.2.2
5	Use the Go To command	3.18	1.1.3
6	Create print citations	3.19	
6	Create Web citations	3.20	
7	Create a bibliography	3.21	
7	Insert page breaks	3.22	2.1.6, 2.1.5
8	Prepare a document for printing	3.23	1.3.8
8	Preview multiple pages per screen	3.24	1.4.2
Advanced Skills	Use information found on the Web	3.25	2.2.1
Advanced Skills	Use an outline to organize documents	3.26	2.1.16
Advanced Skills	Create a table of contents	3.27	
Advanced Skills	Change paper size	3.28	1.4.1

Instructions throughout the lessons are based on the Vista operating system, running Microsoft Office 2007.

?Why Would I Do This?

The four major Office applications—Word, Excel, PowerPoint, and Access—provide easy ways to customize the programs to fit your needs and preferences. When you begin working on a different project, it is easy to change the settings to fit your new needs.

When you attend classes or take a job in the business world, you will likely be asked to write research papers or business reports. Word has a number of features that enable you to write these reports effectively and add the required components, such as footnotes, citations, and reference pages. Each type of report has its corresponding style manual, which needs to be followed to format a report properly.

To help you locate and correct errors, Word also provides language tools that check your spelling, grammar, and word usage.

visual summary | In this chapter, you will create a research paper about offshore wind energy. The document created is shown in Figure 3.1.

Student Name

Warren Liedermeyer

Introduction to Technology

April 17, 2010

Offshore Wind Farms

The need for clean, renewable sources of energy is growing. Wind, hydro, geothermal, and solar power are all set to become power players in the changing world of energy production.

The U.S. Department of Energy (DOE) estimates that more than 900,000 MW (close to the total current installed U.S. electrical capacity) of potential wind energy exists off the coasts of the United States, often near major population centers, where energy costs are high and land-based wind development opportunities are limited. Slightly more than half of the country's identified offshore wind potential is located off the New England and Mid-Atlantic Coasts, where water depths generally deepen gradually with distance from the shore. Resources on the Gulf Coast and Great Lakes Regions have not been fully characterized (Offshore Wind Collaborative Organizing Group 11).

Wind Farm Design

Wind turbines exist in two basic designs: a vertical axis turbine, which resembles an old-fashioned eggbeater, and the more common horizontal axis design.[1] Wind power plants, or wind farms, use the horizontal axis design.

The construction of a wind turbine begins when a suitably shallow offshore location is found. Piles are driven into the seabed, and a tower is built to support the turbine assembly. The turbine itself is a three-bladed rotor connected through a drive train to the generator. Wind direction sensors turn the nacelle, a shell that combines the gearbox, generator, and blade hub, to face the wind. Wind moving

_____

[1] These look like large airplane propellers.

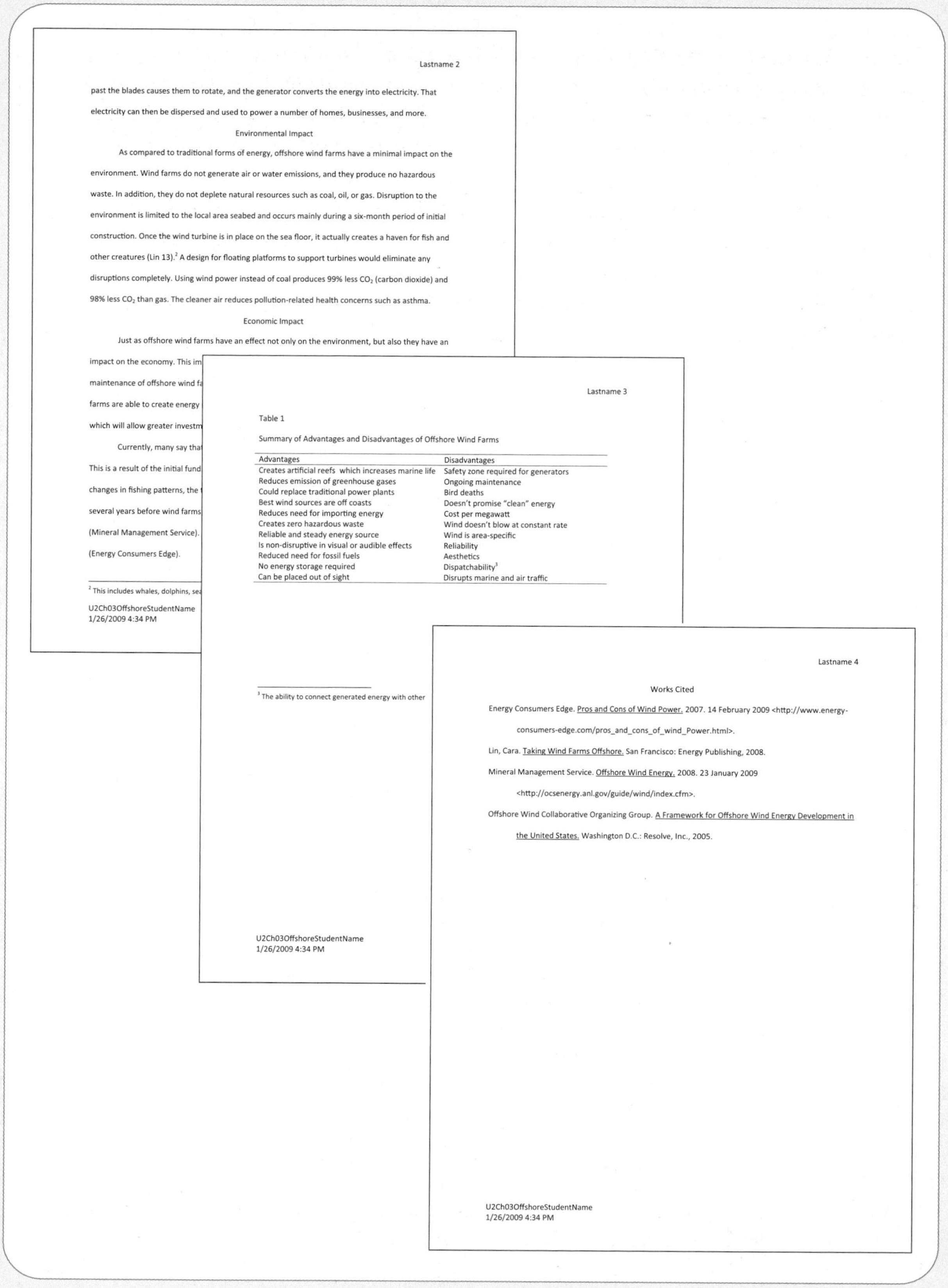

past the blades causes them to rotate, and the generator converts the energy into electricity. That

electricity can then be dispersed and used to power a number of homes, businesses, and more.

Environmental Impact

As compared to traditional forms of energy, offshore wind farms have a minimal impact on the

environment. Wind farms do not generate air or water emissions, and they produce no hazardous

waste. In addition, they do not deplete natural resources such as coal, oil, or gas. Disruption to the

environment is limited to the local area seabed and occurs mainly during a six-month period of initial

construction. Once the wind turbine is in place on the sea floor, it actually creates a haven for fish and

other creatures (Lin 13).[2] A design for floating platforms to support turbines would eliminate any

disruptions completely. Using wind power instead of coal produces 99% less CO_2 (carbon dioxide) and

98% less CO_2 than gas. The cleaner air reduces pollution-related health concerns such as asthma.

Economic Impact

Just as offshore wind farms have an effect not only on the environment, but also they have an

impact on the economy. This im

maintenance of offshore wind fa

farms are able to create energy

which will allow greater investm

Currently, many say that

This is a result of the initial fund

changes in fishing patterns, the

several years before wind farms

(Mineral Management Service).

(Energy Consumers Edge).

[2] This includes whales, dolphins, sea

U2Ch03OffshoreStudentName
1/26/2009 4:34 PM

Table 1

Summary of Advantages and Disadvantages of Offshore Wind Farms

Advantages	Disadvantages
Creates artificial reefs which increases marine life	Safety zone required for generators
Reduces emission of greenhouse gases	Ongoing maintenance
Could replace traditional power plants	Bird deaths
Best wind sources are off coasts	Doesn't promise "clean" energy
Reduces need for importing energy	Cost per megawatt
Creates zero hazardous waste	Wind doesn't blow at constant rate
Reliable and steady energy source	Wind is area-specific
Is non-disruptive in visual or audible effects	Reliability
Reduced need for fossil fuels	Aesthetics
No energy storage required	Dispatchability[3]
Can be placed out of sight	Disrupts marine and air traffic

[3] The ability to connect generated energy with other

U2Ch03OffshoreStudentName
1/26/2009 4:34 PM

Works Cited

Energy Consumers Edge. Pros and Cons of Wind Power. 2007. 14 February 2009 <http://www.energy-

consumers-edge.com/pros_and_cons_of_wind_Power.html>.

Lin, Cara. Taking Wind Farms Offshore. San Francisco: Energy Publishing, 2008.

Mineral Management Service. Offshore Wind Energy. 2008. 23 January 2009

<http://ocsenergy.anl.gov/guide/wind/index.cfm>.

Offshore Wind Collaborative Organizing Group. A Framework for Offshore Wind Energy Development in

the United States. Washington D.C.: Resolve, Inc., 2005.

U2Ch03OffshoreStudentName
1/26/2009 4:34 PM

FIGURE 3.1

List of Student and Solution Files

In most cases, you will start with a new, empty file and enter text and data or import content from other files. You will add your name to the file names and save them on your computer or portable memory device. Table 3.1 lists the files you start with and the names you give them when you save the files.

ASSIGNMENT	STUDENT SOURCE FILE:	SAVE AS:
Lessons 1–8	New document U2Ch03Offshore	U2Ch03OffshoreStudentName
Skill Drill	New document U2Ch03BatteryCars	U2Ch03BatteryCarsStudentName
Fix It	U2Ch03FixIt	U2Ch03FixItStudentName
On the Job	U2Ch03SolarFarms U2Ch03HydrogenFuel	U2Ch03SolarFarmsStudentName U2Ch03HydrogenFuelStudentName
On Your Own	New file	U2Ch03StylesStudentName U2Ch03ConservationStudentName
Assess Your Progress	U2Ch03Assess	U2Ch03AssessStudentName

TABLE 3.1

▶▶▶ *lesson*
one | Customizing Word

Word enables you to determine what types of mistakes the proofing tools will examine, how your editing commands work, and even where your files will be saved by default. You can also have the program correct frequent typing mistakes that you make.

to customize system settings

1 **Start Word.** A new document named *Document1* displays in the Word window.

2 **On the Home tab, in the Paragraph group, click the Show/Hide button ¶ as necessary to display formatting marks.** In this chapter, it will be helpful to see the formatting marks.

3 **Click the Office button 🅑, and then at the bottom of the Office menu, click Word Options. In the left pane of the Word Options dialog box, click Proofing.** Settings for the spelling and grammar checkers display.

4 **Under *When correcting spelling in Microsoft Office programs*, be sure only the first four check boxes are selected.** Notice that the changes you make will be reflected in *all* of the Microsoft Office programs.

5 Under *When correcting spelling and grammar in Word*, **click the *Writing Style* box arrow, and then click Grammar Only.** This will restrict the program to grammar errors, not style issues (such as passive voice). Notice that the changes you make will be reflected in *only* the Word program. Compare your screen with Figure 3.2.

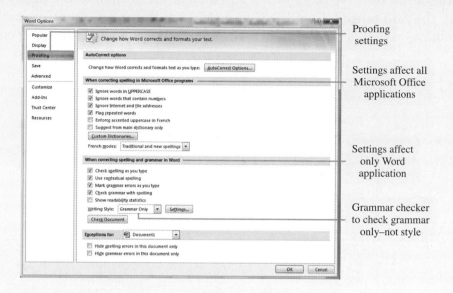

Proofing settings

Settings affect all Microsoft Office applications

Settings affect only Word application

Grammar checker to check grammar only–not style

FIGURE 3.2

6 **In the left pane of the Word Options dialog box, click Advanced. Under Editing Options, clear the second check box: *When selecting, automatically select entire word.*** This enables you to select part of a word or phrase without unwanted text being selected.

7 **Leave the Word Options dialog box open for the next exercise.**

Everyone has words that they type incorrectly on occasion, such as *teh* for *the* or *gril* for *girl*. Many of these common errors are anticipated by the program and corrected when made. However, you may have a word that is not included in the list of common mistakes. You can add your own words to the list.

to customize AutoCorrect settings

1 **With the Word Options dialog box still open, in the left pane, click Proofing. Under AutoCorrect options, click the AutoCorrect Options button.** The AutoCorrect dialog box displays.

2 **Click the AutoFormat tab and examine the options that are available.**

3 In the AutoCorrect dialog box, click the AutoCorrect tab.

4 Under *Replace text as you type*, in the Replace: box, type Ofshore and then press Tab⇥.

5 In the With: box, type Offshore and then at the bottom of the dialog box, click the Add button. Compare your screen with Figure 3.3. AutoCorrect will match the capitalization shown here when it replaces this word in your document.

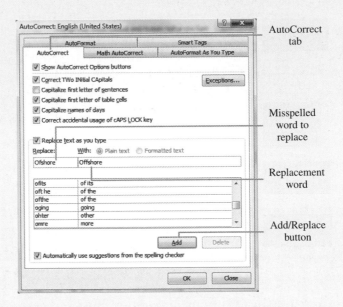

FIGURE 3.3

···

if you have **problems...**

If someone has done this exercise before you on the same computer, the information will already be there, and the Add button will change to a Replace button instead. If this happens, click the Replace button.

···

6 In the AutoCorrect dialog box, click the OK button, and then Close ☒ the Word Options dialog box. The changes are saved.

to extend **your knowledge**

CONTROLLING AUTOMATIC FORMATTING

If your Word program is making automatic formatting changes that you do not want it to, such as beginning lists automatically or changing Web addresses to live links, you can change the settings to disable automatic formatting in the AutoCorrect dialog box. To turn off AutoCorrect options, you need to change them on both the AutoFormat tab and the AutoFormat As You Type tab.

▶▶▶ *lesson*
two | Importing Text from Another Document

If two or more people are working on the same document, or if you have two parts of a document saved in different files, you can import the text from one file into the other.

to import text from another document

1 **In the first line of the new document, type your first and last names, and then press ⏎Enter. Type** Warren Liedermeyer **and then press** ⏎Enter. **This research paper will be written using the Modern Language Association (MLA) style. In that style, the first line of the document is the name of the person writing the report, and the second line is name of the person for whom the report is being written—typically an instructor or a supervisor.**

....

good design...

USING STYLE MANUALS TO FORMAT REPORTS

When you write a research paper or a report for college or business, you will need to follow a format prescribed by one of the standard style guides. The two most commonly used academic styles are those created by the ***Modern Language Association (MLA)*** and the ***American Psychological Association (APA)***; there are several others. Business reports typically use formats defined in business communication references, the most popular being *The Gregg Reference Manual* by William A. Sabin (New York: McGraw-Hill). Some of the differences between style manuals include margins, line spacing, notes, the way citations are presented, and whether to include a cover page or a bibliography. The research paper in this chapter uses the MLA style.

....

2 **In the next three lines, type the following, and press** ⏎Enter **after each line. Be sure to misspell** *Ofshore* **as shown. Notice that when you press** Spacebar, **the word autocorrects to** *Offshore.*

Introduction to Technology

April 17, 2010

Ofshore Wind Farms

3 **Press** ⏎Enter **to move the insertion point to a new line. Click the Insert tab, and then in the Text group, click the Object button arrow. From the menu, click Text from File. Navigate to the location where you are storing your student files, click the** *U2Ch03Offshore* **file, and then click Insert.** The contents of the file are pasted at the insertion point.

4 Press **⟨←Backspace⟩** to remove the extra paragraph mark at the end of the page, and then press **⟨Ctrl⟩** + **⟨Home⟩** to move to the beginning of the document. Compare your screen with Figure 3.4. Notice that several words and phrases have wavy underlines of different colors. These indicate potential spelling and grammar errors.

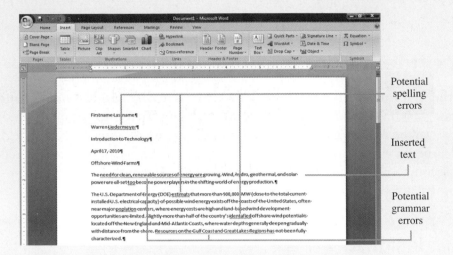

FIGURE 3.4

5 On the Quick Access Toolbar, click the Save button 🖫 to display the Save As dialog box.

6 Navigate to the drive where you are saving your files. Click the New Folder button, type `Chapter03` and then press **⟨←Enter⟩**.

7 In the File name box, using your own name, type `U2Ch03OffshoreStudentName` and then click Save.

....

good **design...**

USING SPACES BETWEEN SENTENCES

When typewriters were used for reports, two spaces were always added between sentences. Because of the way word processors handle spacing, most style guides now call for only one space between sentences; in fact, only one space after any punctuation mark.

....

The MLA style requires that the author's name and the page number appear at the top right of every page except the first page. This should be added in the header area so that the page number is automatically changed on each page. When you are working on a report that you will probably revise several times, it is also good practice to add the current date and time to the footer area. You can remove it when the paper is complete and ready to be printed.

to add a header and footer

1 In an open area in the top margin of the document, right-click, and then from the shortcut menu, click Edit Header.

2 Type your last name, and then press (Spacebar). On the Design tab, in the Header & Footer group, click the Page Number button. In the menu, point to Current Position, and then click Plain Number. The page number is positioned at the insertion point location.

3 Click the Home tab. In the Paragraph group, click the Align Text Right button ▤. Scroll to view the top of Page 2. The name and page number display in the header, as shown in Figure 3.5.

Name and page number in the header

FIGURE 3.5

4 On the Design tab, in the Navigation group, click the Go to Footer button. In the Insert group, click the Quick Parts button. From the menu, click Field, scroll down in the Field names box, click FileName, and then click OK. The file name is added to the footer area.

5 Press (↵Enter). In the Insert group, click the Date & Time button. In the Date and Time dialog box, under Available formats, click the MM/DD/YYYY – HH/MM AM/PM format, for example, 4/17/2010 1:15 PM. At the bottom of the dialog box, select the *Update automatically* check box, and then click OK. The current date and time display in the footer below the file name, as shown in Figure 3.6. The date will automatically update every time you open the document. Your date will be different because the options show the current date.

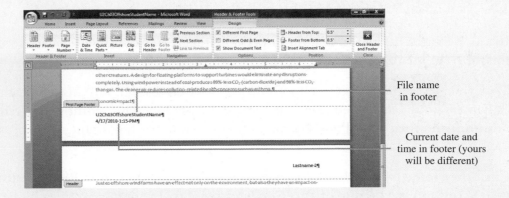

File name in footer

Current date and time in footer (yours will be different)

FIGURE 3.6

6 **On the Design tab, in the Options group, select the Different First Page check box.** The name and page number will display on every page in the document *except* the first page, which is the format the MLA style requires.

7 **Double-click anywhere in the document to close the footer area, and then press** Ctrl + Home **to move to the beginning of the document. Save** 🖫 **your changes.**

▶▶▶ *lesson*
three | Creating, Applying, and Modifying Styles

Microsoft Word contains built-in formats called *styles*. A ***style*** contains formatting, such as font, font size, font emphasis, paragraph indents, line spacing, and so on. A style can be created for paragraphs, text, lists, or tables and are applied from the ***Quick Style gallery*** with a single click. The Quick Style gallery is located on the Home tab. Styles can be created (new) or modified. When you modify a style, all instances of that style are modified at the same time. Businesses may require standardized styles for correspondence, which can be created and added to the style gallery.

In this lesson, you create and apply two different paragraph styles.

to create and apply a style

1 **Near the top of the document, locate the paragraph that begins *Offshore Wind Farms* and click anywhere in the paragraph.** This is one of the titles in the document.

2 **On the Home tab, click the Center button** ≣ **. In the Styles group, click the More button** ⤓ **, and then from the menu, click *Save Selection as a New Quick Style*. In the Name box, type** `MLA Title` **and then compare your screen with Figure 3.7.**

FIGURE 3.7

3 **In the Create New Style from Formatting dialog box, click OK.** In the Styles group, notice that the new style has been added to the Quick Style gallery, as shown in Figure 3.8.

FIGURE 3.8

4 **Locate the *Wind Farm Design* title, click anywhere in the paragraph, and then in the Quick Style gallery, click MLA Title.** Notice that the formatting of the paragraph now matches the formatting of the first title.

5 **Scroll down and repeat the procedure you used in Step 4 to change the style of the last two titles—*Environmental Impact* and *Economic Impact*. Press Ctrl + Home to move to the top of the document.**

6 **In the paragraph that begins *The need for clean*, click anywhere. Click the Page Layout tab, and then in the Paragraph group, click the Dialog Box Launcher. In the Paragraph dialog box, under Indentation, click the Special arrow, and then click First line. Verify that the By box displays 0.5". Under Spacing, click the Line spacing arrow, and then click Double.** MLA style requires that all elements in a document be double-spaced and that the first line of all paragraphs be indented 0.5 inches to the right compared to the rest of the paragraph, know as a *first line indent*. Compare your dialog box with Figure 3.9.

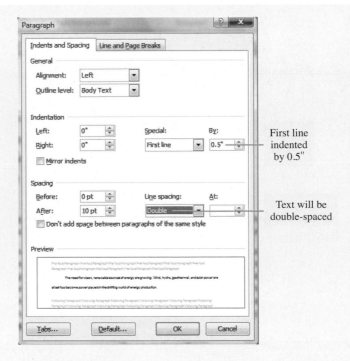

First line
indented
by 0.5"

Text will be
double-spaced

FIGURE 3.9

7 In the Paragraph dialog box, click OK.

8 On the Home tab, in the Styles group, click the More button ⎤, and then from the menu, click *Save Selection as a New Quick Style*. In the Name box, type MLA Paragraph and then click OK.

9 Apply the new MLA Paragraph style to the other six text paragraphs in the document. Do not apply the style to the titles or the table.

10 Press Ctrl + Home to move to the beginning of the document, and then Save 🖫 your work.

When you create a style or use a default style that comes with the Word program, the style might be close to what you want but may need to be modified slightly to meet your exact needs. The new MLA Paragraph style that you just created did not remove the spacing after the paragraphs.

to modify a style

1 On the Home tab, in the Styles group, click the Dialog Box Launcher ▣. The Styles pane displays, typically on the right side of the Word window. Notice that your two new styles are included in the Styles list.

2 In the Styles pane, move the pointer to the arrow to the right of the MLA Paragraph style. The details of the style display in a ScreenTip, as shown in Figure 3.10.

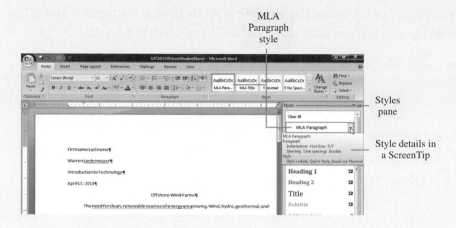

MLA
Paragraph
style

Styles
pane

Style details in
a ScreenTip

FIGURE 3.10

3 Click the arrow, and then from the menu, click Modify.

4 Near the bottom of the Modify Style dialog box, click the Format button, and then from the menu, click Paragraph.

5 In the Paragraph dialog box, under Spacing, click the After down spin arrow two times to change the space after the paragraph to 0 pt. Compare your screen with Figure 3.11.

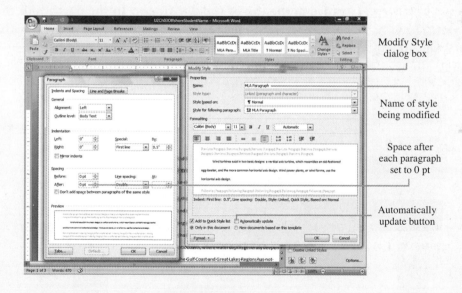

Modify Style
dialog box

Name of style
being modified

Space after
each paragraph
set to 0 pt

Automatically
update button

FIGURE 3.11

6 In the Paragraph dialog box, click OK. Near the bottom of the Modify Style dialog box, select the *Automatically update* check box, and then click OK. Scroll through the document and notice that the change has been made to all of the paragraphs that used the MLA Paragraph style.

7 In the Styles pane, move the pointer over the MLA Paragraph style. Use the ScreenTip to confirm that the style has been changed to After: 0 pt.

8 Close ☒ the Styles pane, and then Save 🖫 your document.

▶▶▶ *lesson*

four | Using Language Tools

Word compares the text you type to words in the Office dictionary and compares your phrases and punctuation to a list of grammar rules. Words that are not in the Office dictionary are marked with a wavy red underline. Phrases and punctuation that differ from the built-in grammar rules are marked with a wavy green underline. A list of grammar rules applied by a computer program can never be exact, and a computer dictionary cannot contain all known words and proper names; thus, you will need to check any words flagged by Word with wavy underlines. Word also places a wavy blue underline under a word that is spelled correctly but used incorrectly, such as the misuse of *their*, *there*, and *they're*.

to use the language tools

1 Press Ctrl + Home to move to the top of the document. In the paragraph that begins *The U.S. Department*, right-click *estimats*—a misspelled word with a wavy red underline. Notice that the shortcut menu suggests three possible replacements. Notice also that you can choose to ignore the word one time, ignore the word throughout the document, or add the word to the Office dictionary, as shown in Figure 3.12.

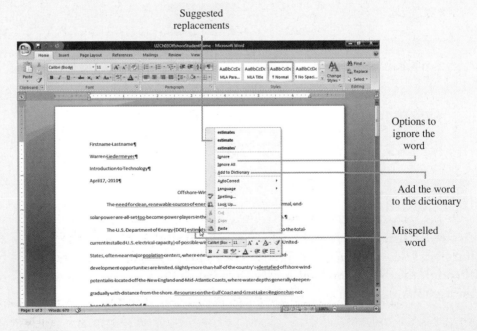

FIGURE 3.12

An unrecognized word, such as a person's name, is an example of a word that you might want to add to the dictionary so that it is not flagged repeatedly.

2 **From the shortcut menu, click *estimates*.** Notice that the word has been corrected in the document and the wavy red underline is gone.

3 **In the paragraph that begins *The need for clean*, right-click any of the words with wavy green underlines.** Two suggested replacements for the grammar error are suggested, either of which is correct.

4 **From the shortcut menu, click the first choice—the phrase that ends with the word *is*.**

5 **Press** Ctrl **+** Home **to move to the beginning of the document.** When you run the Spelling & Grammar checker, it begins checking from the location of the insertion point.

6 **Click the Review tab. In the Proofing group, click the Spelling & Grammar button.** The Spelling and Grammar dialog box opens and the first flagged word is displayed—*Liedermeyer*—in this case, a correctly spelled proper name.

7 **In the Spelling and Grammar dialog box, click the Ignore Once button.** The wavy red underline is removed and the next flagged word displays—a possible word-choice error, as shown in Figure 3.13.

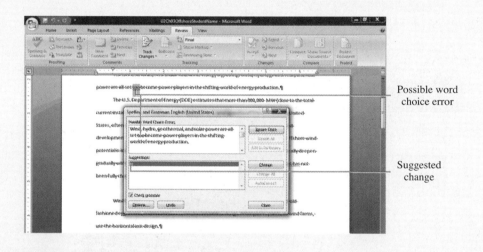

Possible word choice error

Suggested change

FIGURE 3.13

8 **In the Spelling and Grammar dialog box, click the Change button.** The wavy blue underline is removed, *too* is changed to *to*, and the next flagged word displays— a misspelled word.

9 **In the Spelling and Grammar dialog box, continue with the changes, accepting the changes of *poplation* to *population*, *identafied* to *identified*, and the *Resources* grammar error. Ignore Once the *dispatchability* potential misspelling, and then click OK when the check is finished.**

10 **Move to the top of the document. In the paragraph that begins *The need for clean*, right-click the word *shifting*. From the shortcut menu, point to Synonyms, and**

then from the list, click *changing*. The word is replaced. A **synonym** is a word that has the same meaning, or close to the same meaning, as another word.

11 **In the second line of the next paragraph, select the word *possible*. On the Review tab, in the Proofing group, click the Thesaurus button.** The Research task pane displays. A **thesaurus** is a dictionary of similar words and will suggest replacement words for the one selected, as shown in Figure 3.14.

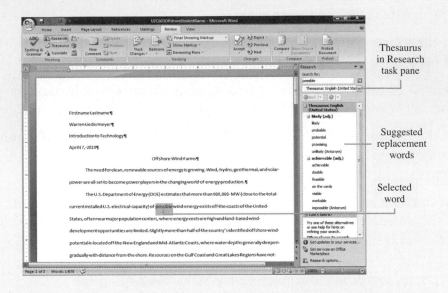

FIGURE 3.14

12 **From the list of replacement words, point to *potential*, click the arrow to the right of the word, and then click Insert.** The word *potential* replaces the word *possible*.

13 **Close [X] the Research task pane. In the Proofing group, click the Word Count button [ABC/123].** The Word Count dialog box displays the number of pages, words, characters, paragraphs, and lines, as shown in Figure 3.15. These numbers are particularly important when you have a limit on the size of a document.

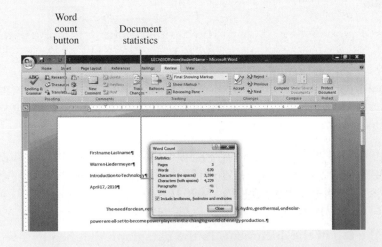

FIGURE 3.15

14 Close ❎ the Word Count dialog box, and then Save 💾 your work.

▶▶▶ *lesson*
five|Creating Footnotes

When there is information that needs to be explained but does not belong in the body of the paper, footnotes or endnotes are used. A ***footnote*** is a reference placed at the bottom of the page and containing a number reference, while an ***endnote*** is a reference placed at the end of a document or chapter. Footnotes and endnotes are not citations; they are used for additional explanatory text that might otherwise be shown in parentheses, or to refer the reader to more information about a particular topic. This information is placed in a footnote or endnote to avoid interrupting the flow of the main topic of the text.

In this lesson, you add three footnotes to the document.

to create footnotes

1 Press Ctrl + End **to move to the end of the document. In the second column of the table, click to the right of the word** *Dispatchability.*

2 **Click the References tab. In the Footnotes group, click the Insert Footnote button.** Word creates a footnote in the footnote area at the bottom of the page and adds a footnote number to the text at the insertion point location. Footnote 1 displays at the top of the footnote area, and the insertion point moves to the right of the number. A short horizontal line is added just above the footnote area. You do not need to type the footnote number.

3 **Type** The ability to connect generated energy with other sources. The footnote text is entered as footnote number 1.

4 **Scroll to the top of Page 2. In the paragraph under** *Environmental Impact,* **in the sixth line, position the insertion point to the right of the period after the word** *creatures.* **Use the procedure you used in Steps 2 and 3 to add the following footnote:** This includes whales, dolphins, sea turtles, and coral reefs. Notice that this footnote is now number 1; the other footnote has been changed to number 2.

5 **Scroll to the middle of Page 1. In the paragraph under** *Wind Farm Design,* **in the second line, position the insertion point to the right of the period following the words** *axis design.* **Use the procedure you used in Steps 2 and 3 to add the following footnote:** These look like large airplane propellers. Compare your screen with Figure 3.16.

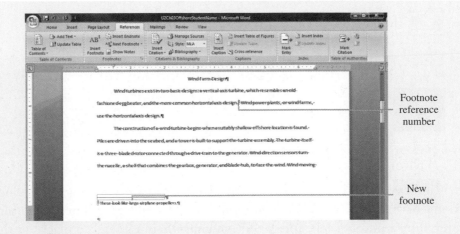

FIGURE 3.16

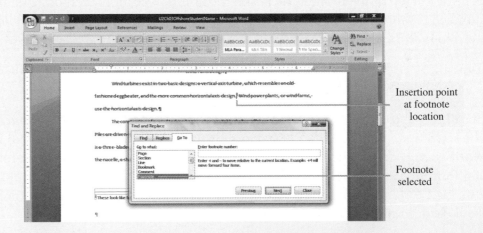 *(label at top right)* Footnote reference number

(label at right) New footnote

6 Scroll down to view the other two footnotes, and notice that the numbers have been changed to display in the proper order. Save 🖫 your work.

7 Press Ctrl + Home to move to the beginning of the document. On the Home tab, in the Editing group, click the Replace button. In the Find and Replace dialog box, click the Go To tab. The Go To tab enables you to search through your document by page numbers, tables, graphics, or a number of other objects, including footnotes.

8 In the Find and Replace dialog box, under *Go to what*, click Footnote, and then click Next. The program finds the next footnote reference in the document and moves the insertion point to that location, as shown in Figure 3.17.

(label at right) Insertion point at footnote location

(label at right) Footnote selected

FIGURE 3.17

9 In the Find and Replace dialog box, click Close.

SIX | Managing Citations

When writing a research paper, you will likely cite several books, articles, and websites. Some of your research sources may be cited more than once, others only one time. A ***citation*** is a reference in a text to the source of the information. The source usually includes the name of the author, the full title of the work, the year of publication, and other publication information. In MLA style, citations to sources within the text of your research paper are indicated in an *abbreviated* manner surrounded by parentheses, called a ***parenthetical citation***. However, as you enter a citation for the first time, you can also enter the *complete* information about the source. Then, when you have finished your paper, you will be able to automatically generate the list of sources that must be included at the end of your research paper.

In this lesson, you insert two print citations and then insert two Web citations.

to insert print citations

1 **Near the top of Page 2, in the paragraph below the *Environmental Impact* title, locate the footnote reference and click to the left of the period after *other creatures*. Click the References tab, and in the Citations & Bibliography group, click the Style box arrow, and then click MLA.** This tells the program how to format citations.

2 **In the Citations & Bibliography group, click the Insert Citation button, and then click Add New Source.** The first time you cite a source, you need to add the source details, which will be used on a page of sources.

3 **In the Create Source dialog box, click the *Type of source* box arrow, and then click Book.** Different types of sources require different information.

4 **In the Create Source dialog box, fill in the information as shown below, and then compare your screen with Figure 3.18.**

Author:	Lin, Cara
Title:	Taking Wind Farms Offshore
Year:	2008
City:	San Francisco
Publisher:	Energy Publishing

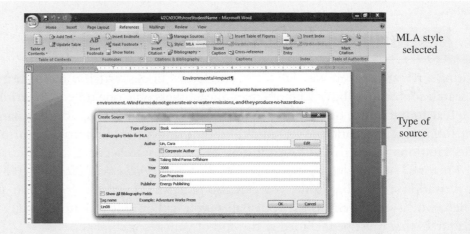

MLA style selected

Type of source

FIGURE 3.18

5 **In the Create Source dialog box, click OK.** The author's last name is enclosed in parentheses and displays at the insertion point.

6 **Click the parenthetical citation and notice that a box with an arrow surrounds the citation. Click the arrow, and then from the menu, click Edit Citation. In the Edit Citation dialog box, in the Pages box, type** 13 **and then compare your screen with Figure 3.19.**

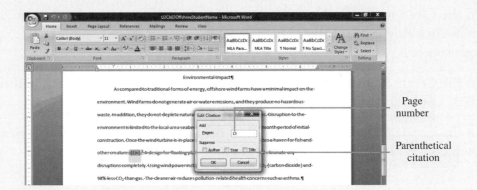

Page number

Parenthetical citation

FIGURE 3.19

7 **In the Edit Citation dialog box, click OK.** Notice that the page number follows the author's last name, and there is no comma between the name and the page number, which is MLA style.

8 **Move to the middle of Page 1. In the paragraph that begins** *The U. S. Department,* **click to the left of the period at the end of the paragraph.**

9 **On the References tab, in the Citations & Bibliography group, click the Insert Citation button, and then click Add New Source. In the Create Source dialog box, select the Corporate Author check box.** A corporate author is used when any organization is listed as the author of a document.

10 Use the procedure you practiced in Steps 3 through 5 to add the following Book citation, and then compare your screen with Figure 3.20.

Corporate Author:	Offshore Wind Collaborative Organizing Group
Title:	A Framework for Offshore Wind Energy Development in the United States
Year:	2005
City:	Washington, D.C.
Publisher:	Resolve, Inc.

FIGURE 3.20

11 In the Create Source dialog box, click OK to save the citation. Click the new parenthetical citation, click the arrow, and then click Edit Citation.

12 In the Edit Citation dialog box, in the Pages box, type 11 and then click OK.

13 Save 🖫 your document.

When you cite Web pages, the citation information is a little different from that of books and magazines. In this task, you will insert two Web citations.

to insert Web citations

1 Move to the bottom of Page 2. In the fourth line of the paragraph that begins *Currently*, position the insertion point between *efficient* and the period.

2 On the References tab, in the Citations & Bibliography group, click the Insert Citation button, and then click Add New Source.

3 In the Create Source dialog box, click the Type of Source arrow, and then scroll down and click Web site. Select the Corporate Author check box.

4 Fill in the boxes using the following information, and then compare your screen with Figure 3.21. Not all of the fields have entries.

Corporate Author:	Mineral Management Service
Name of Web Page:	Offshore Wind Energy
Year:	2008
Month:	
Day:	
Year Accessed:	2009
Month Accessed:	January
Day Accessed:	23
URL:	http://ocsenergy.anl.gov/guide/wind/index.cfm

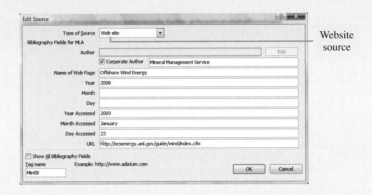

FIGURE 3.21

5 **In the Create Source dialog box, click OK.** The parenthetical citation is inserted. Web pages have no page numbers, so it is not necessary to add one here.

6 **In the next sentence, position the insertion point between** *farms* **and the period, and then add the following web Web site source, using a Corporate Author:**

Corporate Author:	Energy Consumers Edge
Name of Web Page:	Pros and Cons of Wind Power
Year:	2007
Month:	
Day:	
Year Accessed:	2009
Month Accessed:	February
Day Accessed:	14
URL:	http://www.energy-consumers-edge.com/pros_and_cons_of_wind_power.html

7   **In the Create Source dialog box, click OK.** The parenthetical citation is inserted, as shown in Figure 3.22.

Web sources do not have page numbers

FIGURE 3.22

8   **Save** 💾 **your document.**

▶▶▶ *lesson*

seven | Creating a Bibliography

A **bibliography** is a list of sources used in the paper, which are listed at the end of a document. Bibliographical sources are sorted alphabetically by author. In MLA style, the bibliography is called **works cited**, the text is double-spaced, and all but the first line of each source is indented.

In this lesson, you create the bibliography for your research paper.

to create a bibliography

1   **Press** Ctrl + End **to move the insertion point to the end of the document. Press** Ctrl + ↵Enter. A **manual page break** is inserted, and the insertion point moves to the top of the new page. A manual page break is a break between pages that is inserted to control the flow of text, also referred to as a hard page break.

2   **Scroll back up to the top of page 3.** Notice that a Page Break marker displays below the table, as shown in Figure 3.23. If the nonprinting characters are turned off, there is no marker to indicate a manual page break.

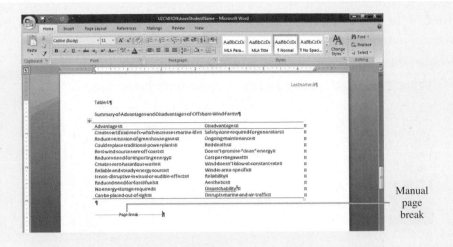

Manual page break

FIGURE 3.23

3 Press Ctrl + End to move to the top of Page 4. Type Works Cited and then press ⏎Enter.

4 On the References tab, in the Citations & Bibliography group, click the Bibliography button. At the bottom of the menu, click Insert Bibliography. The sources used in the document are placed on the page. Notice that they are displayed in alphabetical order, but they are not double-spaced.

5 Move the pointer to the left of the first item in the list of sources to display the ⤢ pointer. Drag down to select all of the items in the list.

6 Click the Home tab. In the Paragraph group, click the Dialog Box Launcher ⯐. Under Spacing, click the After box down spin arrow to change the spacing after to 0. Click the Line Spacing box arrow, and then click Double.

7 Under Indentation, click the Special box arrow, and then click Hanging. A *hanging indent* is a paragraph style that leaves the first line at the left margin and the rest of the lines of the paragraph indented to the right of the first line. By default, the indent is 0.5", which is the MLA style. See Figure 3.24.

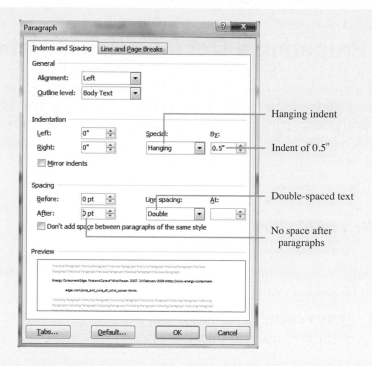

FIGURE 3.24

8 In the Paragraph dialog box, click OK. Click in the Works Cited title. In the Styles group, click the MLA Title button to apply this style to the title. Compare your screen with Figure 3.25.

Hanging indents   Centered title

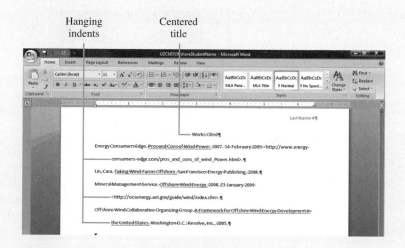

FIGURE 3.25

9 Save 💾 your document.

▶▶▶ *lesson*
eight | Preparing a Document for Printing

Before you print a document, besides checking the document for errors, it is a good idea to look at the pages in Print Preview, which displays the document as it will appear on the printed page. It is also important to check to be sure that the pages break in the places you desire and that any headers or footers display on the pages and locations you want.

In this lesson, you will preview your document.

to prepare your document for printing

1 **Read through your document to be sure you have not left out words and that everything is worded properly.**

2 **Press** Ctrl + Home **to move to the beginning of the document. Click the Office button** 🔲, **point to Print, and then click Print Preview.**

3 **On the Print Preview tab, in the Zoom group, click the Two Pages button.** The first two pages of the document display, as shown in Figure 3.26. Notice that the header and footer display on the second page but not on the first, which is the result of selecting the Different First Page button on the Header & Footer Tools Design tab.

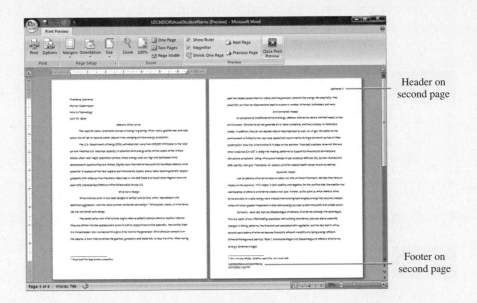

Header on second page

Footer on second page

FIGURE 3.26

4 **Use the vertical scroll bar to display pages 3 and 4.** Notice that the headers and footers display on both pages.

5 **On the Print Preview tab, in the Preview group, click the Close Print Preview button.**

6 Print the document or submit it as directed by your instructor. Close [X] the document, then exit Word.

good design...

MANAGING PAGE BREAKS

When you preview your document, look for awkward page breaks. Titles should be on the same page as at least the first two lines of the paragraph that they introduce. Whenever possible, tables should be on one page and not be split between pages. If moving a table to a single page creates a large white space in the document, you may want to control where the table splits and repeat the table column headings on the second page where the table appears.

Advanced Skills or Concepts

In this section, you are introduced to skills that are not taught with step-by-step instructions.

Using Information Found on the Web

When you used the Research task pane in Lesson 4, you used the thesaurus built into Word. You can also use the Research task pane to go to the Web and find information using such resources as the Encarta Encyclopedia and other electronic books, along with financial and company information.

Nearly everything you find on the Internet—including sources you find through the Microsoft website—is protected by *copyright* law, which protects authors of original works, including text, art, clip art, photographs, and music. Copyright gives the author of intellectual property ownership of the property and the right to choose who uses it. If you want to use text or graphics that you find online, you will need to get permission. One of the exceptions to this law is the use of small amounts of information for educational purposes, which falls under fair use guidelines. If you find information that you use in a paper, you must give credit to the source, even if you change the wording of the information.

Copyright laws in the United States are open to different interpretations, and copyright laws can be very different in other countries. As a general rule, if you want to use substantial portions (or all of) someone else's material, always get permission first.

Creating a Word Outline to Organize Documents

When writing a research paper, after deciding on a topic, you typically gather information for the paper by researching the topic. In a class, you might be required to write an outline for your paper. Outlines help you organize research and formulate the main themes and topics of a paper.

Word includes an Outline view that is used to create an outline. By default, the Outline view uses heading levels, which are styles, to differentiate between one level and another in your outline. The highest topic level uses Heading 1, the next level uses Heading 2, and so forth. You can apply the traditional outline numbering and lettering format—I., A., 1., a.—by selecting this option from Multilevel List button on the Home tab. The Outlining view has its own tab with buttons that are used to promote or demote a topic from one level of importance to another; and other buttons that move topics up or down in the organization of your outline.

Outlines are a good tool to use whenever you need to organize your thoughts, whether it is for a research paper in school, procedures that need to be followed at work, or for a presentation that you need to make.

Creating a Table of Contents

When you create a long document, it is often a good idea to create a table of contents (TOC) to let the reader know where to find various sections of the document. To create a table of contents:

- For the headings that you want as the main items in the TOC, use the Heading 1 style from the Quick Style gallery. You can change the format of the style to match the style guide you are using for the document.

- For subheadings, use the Heading 2 style.

- When you have your heading styles set, from the References tab, in the Table of Contents group, click the Table of Contents button, and then click Insert Table of Contents.

- If you want to include text that does not use one of the heading styles, select the text. In the Table of Contents group, click the Add Text button, and then select the level at which you want the new item to display. The level that you set will appear at the equivalent level in the heading levels list.

Unlike page numbers and footnote numbers, which update automatically when changes are made, a TOC must be updated manually. When you make a change to the document, on the References tab, in the Table of Contents group, click the Update Table button.

Changing Paper Size

The three standard paper sizes in the United States are Letter (8.5" × 11"), Legal (8.5" × 14"), and Tabloid or Ledger (11" × 17"). These sizes are standards in the U.S. and Canada, but the rest of the world uses a different standard, based on ISO 216. The equivalent letter size in this system is A4, which is about 8.3" × 11.7". The advantage of the international system is that when you fold a sheet of paper in half, the same length-to-width proportions are maintained. Microsoft Office supports a number of different paper sizes. To change the paper size:

1. On the Page Layout tab, click the Dialog Box Launcher.

2. In the Page Setup dialog box, click the Paper tab.

3. Click the Paper size box arrow, and then click the paper size you want to use.

On the same tab, you can select the location of the paper for the first page of the document and the location of the paper for the rest of the pages of the document. This is helpful when the first page is going to be printed on letterhead paper.

CHECK YOUR WORK

Here is a list of items your instructor will probably look for when grading your work. To improve your evaluation, take time to check the items yourself before you turn in your work.

Offshore Wind Farms Research Paper
- Text imported from another document.
- Last name and page number right-aligned in header.
- File name added to the footer.
- Current date and time added to the footer.
- MLA Title style created.
- MLA Title style applied to four titles.
- MLA Paragraph style created.
- MLA Paragraph style applied to seven paragraphs.
- MLA Paragraph style updated to remove space after paragraphs, and this style applied to all paragraphs.
- The word *estimats* changed to *estimates*.
- The sentence beginning *The need for clean* corrected for grammar.
- The word *too* changed to *to*.
- The word *poplation* changed to *population*.
- The word *identafied* changed to *identified*.
- The word *shifting* changed to *changing* using thesaurus.
- The word *possible* changed to *potential* using thesaurus.
- Footnote added to Page 1.
- Footnote added to Page 2.
- Footnote added to Page 3.
- Two print citations added, with page numbers.
- Two Web citations added, without page numbers.
- Manual page break added at the bottom of the table on Page 3.
- *Works Cited* title added to the top of Page 4, and the MLA Title style applied.
- Four bibliography entries added to Page 4.
- Bibliography entries double-spaced.
- Hanging indents added to bibliography entries.
- Spaces after paragraphs removed from bibliography entries.

KEY TERMS

American Psychological Association (APA)

bibliography

citation

copyright

endnote

first line indent

footnote

hanging indent

manual page break

Modern Language Association (MLA)

parenthetical citation

Quick Style gallery

style

synonym

thesaurus

works cited

SCREEN ID

Identify each element of the screen by matching callout numbers shown in Figure 3.27 to a corresponding description.

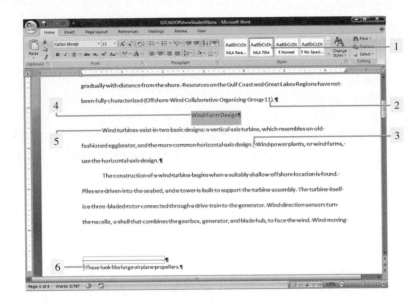

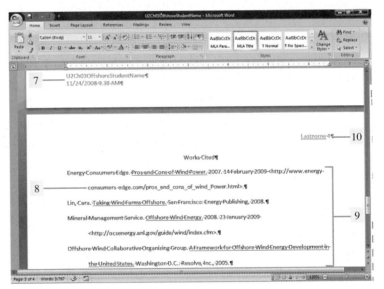

FIGURE 3.27A, B

___ **A.** Bibliography

___ **B.** Citation

___ **C.** First line indent

___ **D.** Footer

___ **E.** Footnote

___ **F.** Footnote reference

___ **G.** Hanging indent

___ **H.** Header

___ **I.** Quick Style button

___ **J.** Title style applied

MULTIPLE CHOICE

Circle the letter of the correct answer for each of the following. The lesson in which the term or concept was introduced is indicated at the end of the sentence.

1. To check for style such as passive voice, change the _____ options in the _____ dialog box. [L1]

   a. Grammar Checking, Spelling and Grammar

   b. Grammar Checking, Word Options

   c. Writing Style, Word Options

   d. Quick Style, Spelling and Grammar

2. To automatically correct a frequently mistyped word, use the _____ dialog box, which is accessed from the _____ pane in the Word Options dialog box. [L1]

   a. AutoFormat, Popular

   b. AutoCorrect, Proofing

   c. AutoFormat, Customize

   d. AutoCorrect, Advanced

3. To import text from another document, use the _____ button found on the _____ tab. [L2]

   a. Object, Insert

   b. Insert, Page Layout

   c. Text, Home

   d. Import, File

4. Which of the following is a paragraph style in which the first line of a paragraph extends to the right of the rest of the paragraph? [L3]

   a. first line indent

   b. hanging indent

   c. paragraph indent

   d. right indent

5. In addition to paragraph styles, what other styles are available in Word? [L3]

   a. text styles

   b. list styles

   c. table styles

   d. all of the above

6. Words that are underlined in _____ indicate possible incorrect word usage. [L4]

   a. red

   b. green

   c. purple

   d. blue

7. A reference in a document to the source of information is a(n) _____. [L6]

   a. endnote

   b. footnote

   c. citation

   d. bibliography

8. The keyboard shortcut to insert a page break is _____. [L7]

   a. Alt + ↵Enter

   b. Ctrl + ↵Enter

   c. Insert + ↵Enter

   d. ↑Shift + ↵Enter

9. Which of the following is a paragraph style in which the first line of a paragraph extends to the left of the rest of the paragraph? [L7]

   a. first line indent

   b. hanging indent

   c. paragraph indent

   d. right indent

10. The paper size used by the ISO 216 standard that is comparable to the 8.5" × 11" standard letter size used in the United States and Canada is _____. [ADV]

    a. A1

    b. A2

    c. A3

    d. A4

MATCHING

Match the term or concept to its description.

_____ 1. A reference that is placed at the end of a document or section of a document

_____ 2. Ownership of intellectual property and the right to choose who uses it

_____ 3. A reference that is placed at the bottom of a page

_____ 4. One of two commonly used styles for formatting research papers and reports

_____ 5. A list of available styles in a document; found on the Home tab

_____ 6. A reference in a text to the source of the information

_____ 7. A citation in the MLA style that uses the author's last name and the page number, surrounded by parentheses

_____ 8. A research tool that provides a list of synonyms

_____ 9. The name of a bibliography in a document that uses the MLA style

_____ 10. A list of sources used in a paper, which are listed at the end of a document

A. APA

B. Bibliography

C. Citation

D. Copyright

E. Endnote

F. Footnote

G. Parenthetical citation

H. Quick Style gallery

I. Thesaurus

J. Works cited

SKILL DRILL

The Skill Drill exercise is a repeat of the lessons in the chapter but with a different set of data. The instructions are less detailed, and your speed and familiarity should increase with practice. There is a figure at the end against which you can check your results. The purpose of this exercise is to build your confidence and speed in using these skills and to set them in your memory for later recall. The section numbers correspond to the lesson numbers. You are welcome to refer back to the lessons illustrated and the detailed instructions if necessary.

In this exercise, you create a research paper about battery-operated cars for an Introduction to Technology class.

1. Customizing Word

1. **Start** Word. Click the **Show/Hide** button to display the formatting marks, if necessary. From the **Office** menu, click the **Word Options** button. In the left pane of the Word Options dialog box, click **Proofing**.

2. Under *When correcting spelling in Microsoft Office programs*, verify that only the first four boxes are checked. Under *When correcting spelling and grammar in Word*, in the *Writing Style* box, verify that **Grammar Only** displays.

3. Under AutoCorrect options, click the **AutoCorrect Options** button and be sure that the AutoCorrect tab displays. Then in the **Replace** box, type BO press Tab↹, type Battery-Operated and then click **Add.**

4. In the AutoCorrect dialog box, click the **OK** button, and then **Close** the Word Options dialog box.

2. Importing Text from Another Document

1. In the first line of the document, type your first and last names, and then press ↵Enter. Type Cecilia Murano and then press ↵Enter.

2. In the next three lines, type the following, pressing ↵Enter after each line. Be sure to type BO as shown, and notice that when you press Spacebar, the word autocorrects to *Battery-Operated.*

   Intro to Technology

   November 13, 2010

   BO Cars: Will They Make the Grade?

3. Press ↵Enter. On the **Insert** tab, in the **Text** group, click the **Object** button arrow, and then click **Text from File.** Navigate to the location where you are storing your student files, click the **U2Ch03BatteryCars** file, and then click **Insert.**

4. Delete the last paragraph mark at the end of the document. Display the Save As dialog box. Navigate to the **Chapter03** folder that you created earlier. Save the file with the name U2Ch03BatteryCarsStudentName

5. Move to the top of the document. In the top margin area, right-click, and then click **Edit Header.**

6. Type your last name, and then press Spacebar. On the **Design** tab, in the **Header & Footer** group, click the **Page Number** button. In the menu, point to **Current Position,** and then click **Plain Number.** On the **Home** tab, in the **Paragraph** group, click the **Align Text Right** button.

7. On the **Design** tab, in the **Navigation** group, click the **Go to Footer** button. In the **Insert** group, click the **Quick Parts** button. From the menu, click **Field,** scroll down in the **Field Names** box and click **FileName,** and then click **OK.**

8. Press ↵Enter. In the **Insert** group, click the **Date & Time** button. In the Date and Time dialog box, click the **MM/DD/YYYY H:MM AM/PM** format. Click **OK.**

9. On the **Design** tab, in the **Options** group, select the **Different First Page** check box. Double-click anywhere in the document to close the footer area, and then **Save** your changes.

3. Creating, Applying, and Modifying Styles

1. Near the top of the document, in the fifth line that begins *Battery-Operated Cars,* right-click to display the Mini toolbar, and then click the **Center** button to center this title on the page.

2. In the **Styles** group, click the **More** button to display the menu. Click **Save Selection as a New Quick Style.** In the **Name** box, type Title MLA and then press ↵Enter to set this style.

3. Click the **Limitations** title, and in the **Styles** group, click the **Title MLA** button to apply this style. Repeat this procedure to apply the Title MLA style to the remaining three titles: **Charging Stations, Tax Incentives,** and **Long-Term Survival.**

4. Near the top of the document, in the paragraph that begins *On the market today,* click anywhere. On the **Home** tab, in the **Paragraph** group, click the **Dialog Box Launcher.** In the Paragraph dialog box, under **Indentation,** click the **Special** arrow, and then click **First line.** Under **Spacing,** click the **Line spacing** arrow, click **Double,** and then click **OK.**

5. On the **Home** tab, in the **Styles** group, click the **More** button, and then from the menu, click **Save Selection as a New Quick Style.** In the **Name** box, type `Para-MLA` and then click **OK.**

6. Click in each of the five multi-line paragraphs in the paper, and from the **Quick Styles,** click the **Para-MLA** button to apply this style. Do not apply this style to titles, tables, or labels for tables.

7. In the **Styles** group, click the **Dialog Box Launcher.** In the Styles task pane, point to **Para-MLA,** click the arrow that displays, and then click **Modify.**

8. In the Modify Style dialog box, click the **Format** button, and then click **Paragraph.** In the Paragraph dialog box, change the space after the paragraph to **0 pt** Click **OK.**

9. In the Modify Style dialog box, click the **Automatically update** check box, and then click **OK.**

10. Close the Styles task pane, and then **Save** your document.

4. Use Language Tools

1. Move the insertion point to the top of the document. Click the **Review** tab, and in the **Proofing** group, click the **Spelling & Grammar** button.

2. The first unrecognized word is a proper name: *Murano.* In the Spelling and Grammar dialog box, click the **Ignore Once** button to remove the red wavy line. (If the Spelling and Grammar dialog box stops on your name first, click Ignore All to remove the red wavy lines.)

3. The next word encountered is *hybids.* From the suggested list, be sure that *hybrids* is selected, and then click the **Change** button. Replace the next word—*vibility*— with *viability.*

4. The next word that is highlighted is *their,* which is underlined in blue, indicating a possible incorrect word usage. Change *their* to *there.*

5. Next, a sentence is highlighted due to a grammar error that is shown in the Spelling and Grammar dialog box: *this cars.* Be sure *these cars* is selected, and then click **Change.**

6. In one of the tables, *NiMH* is highlighted as not in the dictionary. Click the **Ignore Once** button. Continue in this manner to correct the remaining errors by changing *infastucture* to *infrastructure, enviromentalists* to *environmentalists,* and *enviroment* to *environment.*

7. Choose to ignore *Prius* and your last name if necessary.

8. On the first page, in the paragraph that begins *On the market today*, at the end of the third line, select the word **rise.** On the **Review** tab, in the **Proofing** group, click the **Thesaurus** button. In the **Research** task pane, point to **increase,** click the displayed arrow, and then click **Insert** to replace *rise* with *increase*.

9. In the paragraph under the *Limitations* title, in the third line, locate the word *total*, and then right-click **total** to display the shortcut menu. Point to **Synonyms,** and then from the list, click **overall** to replace the selected word.

10. Close the Research task pane and **Save** your work.

5. Creating Footnotes

1. In the paragraph under the *Charging Stations* title, position the insertion point at the end of the paragraph, to the right of the period after the word *table*. Click the **References** tab. In the **Footnotes** group, click the **Insert Footnote** button. In the footnote area, type `Lithium-ion batteries show the most promise.`

2. On Page 2, in Table 2, position the insertion point to the right of *Full Credit*. Use the procedure you used in step 1 to add the following footnote: `January 1, 2006-December 31, 2007`

3. Use the same procedure to add the following two footnotes for the remaining column headings in Table 2:

   50% Credit `January 1, 2008-June 30, 2008`

   25% Credit `July 1, 2008-December 31, 2008`

4. Press Ctrl + Home. On the **Home** tab, in the **Editing** group, click the **Replace** button. In the Find and Replace dialog box, click the **Go To** tab. Under *Go to what*, click **Footnote,** and then click **Next.** Review the first footnote and click **Next** to review the next three footnotes. Close the Find and Replace dialog box.

5. **Save** your changes.

6. Managing Citations

1. On Page 1, in the paragraph that begins *On the market today*, in the third line, click to the left of the period after *hybrids*. Click the **References** tab, and then in the **Citations & Bibliography** group, click the **Style** box arrow, and then click **MLA.**

2. In the **Citations & Bibliography** group, click the **Insert Citation** button, and then click **Add New Source.** In the Create Source dialog box, click the **Type of Source** box arrow, and then click **Book.**

3. In the Create Source dialog box, fill in the information as shown below, and then click **OK.**

Author:	Sunez, D.B.
Title:	On the Road with EVs
Year:	2007
City:	Bloomington
Publisher:	Laslo Publishing, Inc.

4. Click the parenthetical citation, and then click the arrow. From the menu, click **Edit Citation.** In the Edit Citation dialog box, in the **Pages** box, type 37 and then click **OK.**

5. In the paragraph under the *Limitations* title, in the third line, place the insertion point to the left of the period following the word *vehicle.*

6. Click the **Insert Citation** button, and then click **Add New Source.** In the Create Source dialog box, in the **Type of Source** box, select **Article in a Periodical.**

7. Fill in the information shown below, and then click **OK.**

Author:	Gorski, Lance
Title:	"Death of the EV?"
Periodical Title:	Automotive Times
Year:	2007
Month:	January
Day:	31
Pages:	55–58

8. Click the parenthetical citation. Display the menu, click **Edit Citation,** in the **Pages** box type 56 and then click **OK.**

9. At the end of the paragraph under the *Charging Stations* title, click to the left of the period that follows the word *table.* Display the Create Source dialog box and use the procedure you have practiced to enter the website citation information listed below:

Author:	Lampton, Christopher
Name of Web Page:	How Electric Car Batteries Work
Year:	2008
Month:	September
Day:	28
Year Accessed:	2009
Month Accessed:	July
Day Accessed:	14
URL:	http://auto.howstuffworks.com/electric-car-battery2.htm

10. At the end of the paragraph, under the *Tax Incentives* title, click to the left of the period that follows the word *Government*. Display the Create Source dialog box and use the procedure you have practiced to enter the website citation information listed below:

Name of Web Page:	New Energy Tax Credits for Hybrids
Year:	
Month:	
Day:	
Year Accessed:	2009
Month Accessed:	July
Day Accessed:	12
URL:	http://www.fueleconomy.gov/feg/ tax_hybrid.shtml

11. **Save** your changes.

7. Creating a Bibliography

1. Press Ctrl + End to move the insertion point to the end of the document. Press Ctrl + ↵Enter to insert a manual page break.

2. At the top of Page 4, type Works Cited and then press ↵Enter. Select the *Works Cited* title, and on the **Home** tab, in the **Styles** group, click the **Title MLA** button.

3. Click next to the paragraph mark under the title. On the **References** tab, in the **Citations & Bibliography** group, click the **Bibliography** button, and then click **Insert Bibliography.**

4. Select all of the items in the bibliography list. On the **Home** tab, in the **Paragraph** group, click the **Dialog Box Launcher.** Under **Spacing,** change the **After** spacing to **0.** Under **Line Spacing,** change the spacing to **Double.** Under **Indentation,** click the **Special** box arrow, and then click **Hanging.** Click **OK.**

5. **Save** your changes.

8. Preparing a Document for Printing

1. Proofread the document to be sure that no words have been omitted and that everything is worded properly.

2. Press Ctrl + Home to move to the beginning of the document. From the Office menu, point to **Print,** and then click **Print Preview.**

3. If necessary, in the **Zoom** group, click the **Two Pages** button. Notice that the table at the bottom of Page 1 breaks at the end of the page, and part of the table displays at the top of Page 2. The table label, title, and table should display on one page so that it is easier to understand.

4. On the **Print Preview** tab, in the **Preview** group, click the **Magnifier** check box to clear the check mark. The magnifier pointer changes to a select arrow point, which enables you to edit the document in the Print Preview window.

5. Near the end of Page 1, click to the left of the *Table 1* label and then press Ctrl + ↵Enter to move the Table 1 label, table title, and the first row of the table to the top of Page 2. Notice that the *Long-Term Survival* title is now displayed alone at the bottom of Page 2. This title should be on the same page as the beginning of the paragraph that follows it.

6. Click to the left of the *Long-Term Survival* title and press Ctrl + ↵Enter to move this title to the top of Page 3 so that it is on the same page as the paragraph it introduces.

7. Click the **Close Print Preview** button. **Save** your work and print the document or submit it as directed by your instructor. **Close** the document, and then exit Word.

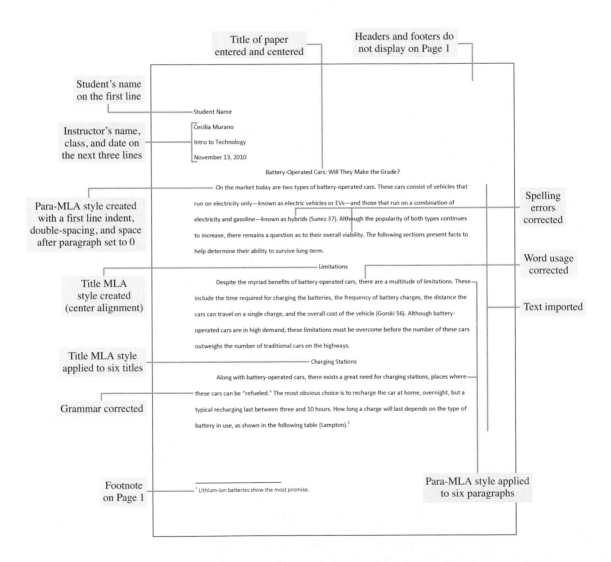

FIGURE 3.28A

Table label, title, and table together

Header on Pages 2-4 display student's last name and an automatic page number

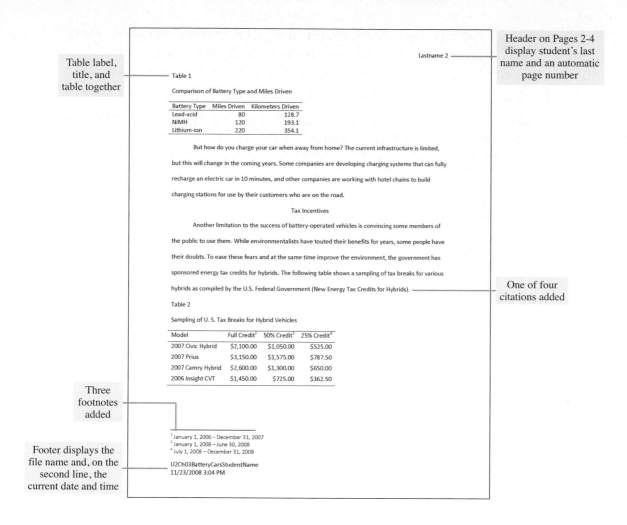

Table 1

Comparison of Battery Type and Miles Driven

Battery Type	Miles Driven	Kilometers Driven
Lead-acid	80	128.7
NiMH	120	193.1
Lithium-ion	220	354.1

But how do you charge your car when away from home? The current infrastructure is limited, but this will change in the coming years. Some companies are developing charging systems that can fully recharge an electric car in 10 minutes, and other companies are working with hotel chains to build charging stations for use by their customers who are on the road.

Tax Incentives

Another limitation to the success of battery-operated vehicles is convincing some members of the public to use them. While environmentalists have touted their benefits for years, some people have their doubts. To ease these fears and at the same time improve the environment, the government has sponsored energy tax credits for hybrids. The following table shows a sampling of tax breaks for various hybrids as compiled by the U.S. Federal Government (New Energy Tax Credits for Hybrids).

One of four citations added

Table 2

Sampling of U. S. Tax Breaks for Hybrid Vehicles

Model	Full Credit[2]	50% Credit[3]	25% Credit[4]
2007 Civic Hybrid	$2,100.00	$1,050.00	$525.00
2007 Prius	$3,150.00	$1,575.00	$787.50
2007 Camry Hybrid	$2,600.00	$1,300.00	$650.00
2006 Insight CVT	$1,450.00	$725.00	$362.50

Three footnotes added

[2] January 1, 2006 – December 31, 2007
[3] January 1, 2008 – June 30, 2008
[4] July 1, 2008 – December 31, 2008

U2Ch03BatteryCarsStudentName
11/23/2008 3:04 PM

Footer displays the file name and, on the second line, the current date and time

FIGURE 3.28B

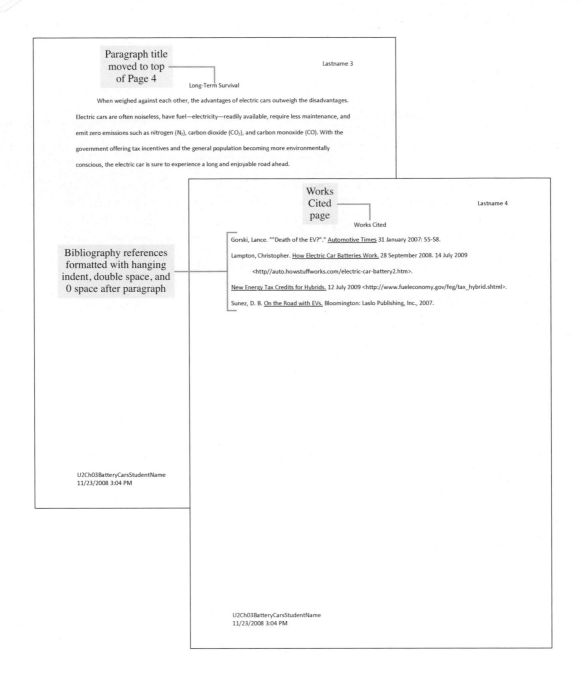

Paragraph title moved to top of Page 4

Long-Term Survival

When weighed against each other, the advantages of electric cars outweigh the disadvantages. Electric cars are often noiseless, have fuel—electricity—readily available, require less maintenance, and emit zero emissions such as nitrogen (N_2), carbon dioxide (CO_2), and carbon monoxide (CO). With the government offering tax incentives and the general population becoming more environmentally conscious, the electric car is sure to experience a long and enjoyable road ahead.

Lastname 3

U2Ch03BatteryCarsStudentName
11/23/2008 3:04 PM

Works Cited page

Works Cited

Lastname 4

Bibliography references formatted with hanging indent, double space, and 0 space after paragraph

Gorski, Lance. ""Death of the EV?"." Automotive Times 31 January 2007: 55-58.

Lampton, Christopher. How Electric Car Batteries Work. 28 September 2008. 14 July 2009
        <http//auto.howstuffworks.com/electric-car-battery2.htm>.

New Energy Tax Credits for Hybrids. 12 July 2009 <http://www.fueleconomy.gov/feg/tax_hybrid.shtml>.

Sunez, D. B. On the Road with EVs. Bloomington: Laslo Publishing, Inc., 2007.

U2Ch03BatteryCarsStudentName
11/23/2008 3:04 PM

FIGURE 3.28C

fix *it*

One way to appreciate the value of good design is to fix a file that is not designed well. In this exercise, you open a file that has several errors and design flaws and fix it according to the good design elements in the lessons.

Navigate to the folder with the student files, open **U2Ch03FixIt,** and save it as U2Ch03FixItStudentName

Examine this document and format it using the skills you have practiced. Format this research paper about home energy conservation using the MLA style. Make changes to comply with the good design principles that were introduced in this chapter. Here is a list of corrections needed and the design principles introduced in this chapter, along with some details about the footnotes and citations to insert.

- Add your name at the top of the document.
- Using MLA style, add the instructor's name, Margot Espinoza, course name, Intro to Environmental Sciences and the current date.
- Enter the title as Home Energy Conservation and format according to the MLA style.
- Create a paragraph style that uses the format specified for MLA and apply it to the full paragraphs in the paper. Name the style MLA-Para.
- Correct any spelling, grammar, or word usage errors.
- In the paragraph that begins *The most important,* replace *effectiveness* with an appropriate synonym.
- In the paragraph that begins *If you choose,* in the third line, add a footnote following *12 months.* The footnote is: If you no longer have copies of your bills, your utility company can provide the information to you.
- Locate the sentence about the ENERGY STAR program and add a footnote to their website.
- Citations have been added, but page 34 needs to be added to the Kincaid citation.
- Based on the citations that have been entered, create a Works Cited page and format it according to the MLA style used in this chapter.
- Create a proper MLA header and do not display it on Page 1.
- Place the file name and current date in the left side of the footer.
- Review the document and be sure the font is the same throughout—Calibri—including in the headers and footers, footnotes, bibliography, and body of the document.
- Submit the file as required by your instructor. Save and close the file.

ON THE JOB

Information workers add value to data by organizing, selecting, displaying, communicating, interpreting, and using data to support decisions. On the Job exercises simulate a situation where you are given data, and your job is to add value to it using the skills you practiced in this chapter. Success in these exercises indicates that you have a valuable skill to offer an employer.

1. Solar Farms Journal Paper

In this On the Job exercise, you will format a paper about solar farms that your boss has drafted for publication in an industry journal. Refer to the note from your boss and then, using the skills you have practiced in this chapter, format the paper and add citations and references, using the MLA format. Use the file named **U2Ch03SolarFarms** and save it as `U2Ch03SolarFarmsStudentName`

> *Jake,*
>
> *Attached is a draft of a paper on solar farms. Format the paper according to the journal specifications listed below and return it to me by the end of the day. I noted my sources in square brackets at the relevant points, but these need to be turned into proper citations. Convert parenthetical comments into footnotes. Needless to say, if you find any errors, please fix them!*
>
> *Gabriella*

Requirements for Journal Submissions

All papers submitted for publication must be in the following form:

1. Follow MLA format specifications for paragraphs and titles.

2. Include your last name and the page number on the right side of the header on all but the first page.

3. Tables or figures should be labeled sequentially according to their appearance in the text; for example, Table 1, Table 2, or Figure 1, Figure 2. Also include an appropriate title.

4. All citations should be in MLA format, with appropriate page references.

5. The Works Cited page must be on a separate page, in MLA format.

6. Footnotes should be numbered sequentially using Arabic numerals.

Open the file named **U2Ch03SolarFarms** and save it as `U2Ch03SolarFarms StudentName` In addition to the requirements listed above, demonstrate your ability to apply the skills practiced in this chapter by creating a paragraph style and applying it to all paragraphs in the paper. Be sure to remove any extra paragraph marks between paragraphs. Be sure the font is consistent throughout the paper. Include the file name and date in the footer. Preview the paper in Print Preview and make any necessary adjustments to page breaks. Submit the file as directed by your instructor.

2. Hydrogen Fueled-Cars Research Paper

Your boss has written a paper on the use of hydrogen-fueled cars that is the basis for a presentation he will make at the Alternative Energy Conference. He has drafted the paper and has asked you to format it according to the requirements listed below from the conference committee that approves presentation topics.

Open the file named **U2Ch03HydrogenFuel** and save it as `U2Ch03Hydrogen FuelStudentName` Using the skills you have practiced in this chapter, format the paper according to the specifications listed. Include the file name and date in the footer. Four bibliographical references are scattered throughout the paper and noted as sources within square brackets. Change these to MLA format citations, including page numbers when appropriate. Enter the information necessary for a Works Cited page. Change four parenthetical notations—including the ones in the tables—into footnotes. Add labels to the tables.

Requirements for Papers Submitted for Consideration

All papers submitted for consideration for the Alternative Energy Conference must be in the following form:

1. Follow MLA format specifications for paragraphs and titles.

2. Include your last name and the page number on the right side of the header on all but the first page.

3. Tables or figures should be labeled sequentially according to their appearance in the text; for example, Table 1, Table 2, or Figure 1, Figure 2. Also include an appropriate title.

4. All citations should be in MLA format, with appropriate page references.

5. The Works Cited page must be on a separate page, in MLA format.

6. Footnotes should be numbered sequentially using Arabic numerals.

Preview the paper in Print Preview and make any necessary adjustments to page breaks. Submit the file as directed by your instructor.

DISCUSSION OF ADVANCED SKILLS OR CONCEPTS

The questions in this section are based on the topics in the Advanced Skills or Concepts section of the chapter.

1. What are the policies at your school regarding using copyright materials in papers that you may write for your classes? What are the consequences, if any, for violating your school's copyright policies?

2. What role does a table of contents play in a book or magazine? Describe a situation when you used a TOC to locate an article you wanted to read in a magazine. Was it helpful or not helpful?

3. Give examples of when you might use different paper sizes. Have you received something from another country that used a different paper size? How did it compare to the sizes used in the United States and Canada?

4. Describe a situation where you used an outline for a paper you had to write, or a report that you had to give. Was the outline helpful? What experience, if any, have you had with the outlining tools in Word?

ON YOUR OWN

Once you are comfortable with the skills in this chapter, you can apply them to new situations of your own choosing. In this section, you choose data that you have in your possession or that you can find elsewhere. To successfully complete this assignment, you must apply good design practices and demonstrate mastery of the skills that were practiced. Refer to the list of skills and design practices in the Fix It exercise.

1. Format a Paper Using Another Style

The Modern Language Association is only one of several styles that might be specified for writing educational or research papers. Use the Internet to learn more about other styles that are commonly used, and write a brief paper with citations and bibliographical references that compares and contrasts the MLA style to one other style. In the paper, demonstrate your understanding of the alternative style by writing your paper using that style. Employ the Quick Style, Spelling & Grammar, footnotes, citation, bibliographical, thesaurus, and paragraph format tools that you have worked with in this chapter. Ensure that you follow your school's policy regarding the use of copyright material. Save the paper as U2Ch03StylesStudentName and add the file name to the footer.

2. Gather Information for a Research Paper

When you write a research paper, it is important to include all of the necessary data related to your sources. Use the Internet to research information related to an energy conservation topic of your choice. Assemble the references that you would use in a paper, including potential quotes. Create a list of topics and the sources that you would use for each. Add the sources, using the citation and bibliography tools that you have just practiced. Save the paper as U2Ch03ConservationStudentName and add the file name to the footer.

ASSESS YOUR PROGRESS

At this point, you should have a set of skills and design concepts that are valuable to an employer and to you. You may not realize how much you have learned unless you take a few minutes to assess your progress.

1. From the student files, open **U2Ch03Assess.** Save it as U2Ch03AssessStudentName

2. Read each question in column A.

3. In column B, answer Yes or No.

4. If you identify a skill or design concept that you don't know, refer to the learning objective code next to the question and the table at the beginning of the chapter to find the skill and review it.

5. Print the worksheet if your instructor requires it. The file name is already in the header, so it will display your name as part of the file name.

6. All of these skills and concepts have been identified as important by surveying hundreds of individuals working at over 200 companies worldwide. If you cannot answer all of the questions affirmatively even after reviewing the relevant lesson, seek additional help from your instructor.

chapter four

Importing Text and Formatting a Newsletter

Lesson	Learning Outcomes	Code	Related IC3 Objectives
1	Set document margins	4.01	1.4.1
1	Create a WordArt image	4.02	1.3.7
1	Format a WordArt image	4.03	1.3.7
1	Insert text from another document	4.04	1.3.7
1	Use Paste Special to insert data from another application	4.05	1.3.2
1	Change spacing after a paragraph	4.06	2.1.16
2	Create multiple columns	4.07	2.1.12
2	Modify column width and alignment	4.08	2.1.12
3	Save a document as a template	4.09	1.2.4
4	Apply special text formatting	4.10	1.3.6
4	Use the Format Painter to apply formatting	4.11	1.3.6
4	Apply paragraph borders	4.12	2.1.16
4	Apply shading to paragraphs	4.13	2.1.16
4	Apply page borders	4.14	
4	Insert a manual line break	4.15	2.1.6
5	Add symbols to a document	4.16	2.1.8
5	Apply a superscript	4.17	1.3.6
6	Insert tab stops	4.18	2.1.4
6	Modify tab settings	4.19	2.1.4
6	Add dot leaders to tabs	4.20	2.1.4
6	Insert a manual column break	4.21	2.1.5, 2.1.12
6	Insert a clip art image	4.22	1.3.7
7	Customize the Quick Access Toolbar	4.23	1.1.7
7	Save a document in PDF format	4.24	1.2.4, 1.4.6
8	Add a Web hyperlink to a document	4.25	2.2.2
8	Add an e-mail hyperlink to a document	4.26	2.2.2
8	Save a document as a Web page	4.27	1.4.6
Advanced Skills	Identify and solve problems related to working with files	4.28	1.2.6

Instructions throughout the lessons are based on the Vista operating system, running Microsoft Office 2007.

?Why **Would I Do This?**

Documents are often assembled from files that have been prepared by others, or saved in different files and then combined together in one document. Files can be imported in their entirety, or parts of files can be copied from one document and pasted into another.

When you create a newsletter, the text is easier to read in multiple columns, similar to that found in newspapers and magazines. You can change column widths and lengths to make the columns fit the newsletter space and artificially end columns when necessary.

A document that has been formatted to meet your needs can also be saved as a template so that the same document can be reused in the future with new content. When the document is complete, you can save it as a document to be printed, save it in a special format that can be read on nearly all computers, or save it as a Web page.

visual summary |

In this chapter, you will create a two-page conservation newsletter. The bottom half of the second page will be left blank so that the document can be folded in half so that mailing labels can be added at a later time. The document created is shown in Figure 4.1.

NANOTECHNOLOGY: THE SMALLEST THING IN ALTERNATIVE ENERGY

Nanotechnology is a big word with great promise. In essence, nanotechnology is science and engineering on a molecular scale—working at the level of atoms, molecules, and supramolecular structures. Ultimately, nanotechnology increases the potential for sustainable material design and resource use.

In the area of transportation, nanotechnologies will improve energy transduction and storage in batteries, and in agriculture, nanotechnologies will remove pesticides and clean water. Further, it is expected that nanotechnologies will bring about improvements in storing and transporting energy, something that will become increasingly important as we reduce our reliance on fossil fuels.

Several commercial, private, educational, and governmental institutions are making nanotechnology a top priority. For more information, you can review a copy of Nanotechnology and the Environment, which can be found at www.nano.gov.

U2Ch04RecycleStudentName

News from Green Alternative Energy

This newsletter is a monthly publication from Green Alternative Energy™ and is distributed electronically. If you prefer to be removed from our distribution list, please send your request to newsletter@greenae.com.

CONSERVATION BEGINS WITH RECYCLING

Recycling is a key player in the conservation of natural resources. Reusing or recycling paper, glass, metals, and plastics that are used everyday reduces the energy and fossil fuels needed to produce new and replacement versions of these items.

For example, it takes 20 times more energy to make a new aluminum can than to recycle one. Paper recycling uses 60% less energy and conserves 7,000 gallons of water. Recycling also keeps these products out of landfills, as shown in the following chart.

Product	Time to Degrade
Glass	1 million years
Aluminum cans	80-100 years
Plastic	700 years
Paper cups	20 years

To conserve energy and the environment, everyone needs to participate. Over the next six months, Green Alternative Energy will ask for your help as it begins its sponsorship of National Disposal's recycling program.

GAE HELPS JAMESON CHARTER SCHOOL GO GREEN

You've heard of green homes and businesses, but what about green schools? Green schools are a growing trend, and as part of its commitment to give back to the community, GAE recently donated $75,000 in labor and supplies toward the upcoming renovation of Jameson Charter School.

As part of the renovation, GAE will install a rooftop photovoltaic system. GAE will also purchase several highly energy-efficient systems for heating and cooling.

Studies show that students in green schools have fewer absences and have higher test scores. GAE is excited to be a part of improving not only the performance of the school but also the performance of its students.

The U.S. Department of Energy estimates that U.S. schools spend approximately $125 per student in annual utility costs. Green schools save up to $50 annually per student, cutting costs while improving the environment.

YOU CAN MAKE A DIFFERENCE

Did you know that with little steps you can make great strides in improving the energy efficiency in your home this winter? No, this doesn't mean you have to replace your current heating system or install solar panels. Below are simple, everyday things you can do to reduce your utility bills.

Turn down your thermostat. By turning down your thermostat by 10 to 15 F at night, you reduce utility costs by 10%.

Close your curtains. In the winter, close the curtains on any windows that don't receive sunlight. By doing so, you reduce heat loss by 10%.

Lower your hot water temperature. For each 10 degrees you lower the temperature, you save 3-5% in energy costs.

Insulate your water heater tank. Using a minimum R-24 insulation saves you 4-9% in heating costs and reduces heat loss by 25-45%.

The following chart shows potential cost savings over a three-month period for a 3,000 sq. ft. home.

Month	Thermostat	Water
December	$17.62	$7.48
January	$21.32	$10.21
February	$18.91	$9.18

U2Ch04RecycleStudentName

FIGURE 4.1

List of Student and Solution Files

In most cases, you will start with a new, blank file and enter text and data or import content from other files. You will add your name to the file names and save them on your computer or portable memory device. Table 4.1 lists the files you start with and the names you give them when you save the files.

ASSIGNMENT	STUDENT SOURCE FILE:	SAVE AS:
Lessons 1–8	New document U2Ch04Community U2Ch04Conservation U2Ch04Efficiency U2Ch04Nanotechnology U2Ch04Savings	U2Ch04RecycleStudentName.docx U2Ch04RecycleStudentName.mht U2Ch04RecycleStudentName.pdf U2Ch04NewsletterTemplateStudentName.dotx
Skill Drill	New document U2Ch04HeatPumps U2Ch04Read U2ch04Sales U2Ch04Prices	U2Ch04EmployeeNewsStudentName.docx U2Ch04EmployeeNewsStudentName.mht U2Ch04EmployeeNewsStudentName.pdf U2Ch04EmpNewsTemplateStudentName.dotx
Fix It	U2Ch04FixIt U2Ch04LunaViews1 U2Ch04LunaViews2 U2Ch04LunaViews3	U2Ch04FixItStudentName.docx U2Ch04FixItStudentName.mht U2Ch04FixItStudentName.pdf
On the Job	U2Ch04CMG U2Ch04CMG1 U2Ch04CMG2 U2Ch04CMG3 U2Ch04CMG4	U2Ch04CMGStudentName.docx U2Ch04CMGTemplateStudentName.dotx U2Ch04CMGStudentName.mht
	New document U2Ch04Liestal1 U2Ch04Liestal2 U2Ch04Liestal3 U2Ch04Liestal4 U2Ch04Liestal5	U2Ch04LiestalStudentName.docx U2Ch04LiestalTempStudentName.dotx U2Ch04LiestalStudentName.pdf U2Ch04LiestalStudentName.mht
On Your Own	New document New document	U2Ch04HealthNewsStudentName U2Ch04CampusStudentName
Assess Your Progress	U2Ch04Assess	U2Ch04AssessStudentName

TABLE 4.1

▶▶▶ *lesson*
one | Inserting Data from Other Documents

When you create a new document, you can set the *margins*—the space between text and the left, right, top, and bottom of the paper. By default, in Word 2007, the margins are set to one inch on all sides: top, bottom, left and right. If you decide to change the margin settings, it is a good idea to do it first, before you start typing, to ensure that the document margins are consistent throughout. Then you can insert text from other documents at anytime and it will conform to the established margins.

To begin, you will set the margins and create and format a title for the newsletter using WordArt.

to set margins and use WordArt

1 **Start Word, and then if necessary, display the formatting marks.** A new document displays in the Word window.

2 **Type** `News from Green Alternative Energy` **and then press** ⏎Enter. **Type the following, and then press** ⏎Enter.

`This newsletter is a monthly publication from Green Alternative Energy and is distributed electronically. If you prefer to be removed from our distribution list, please send your request to newsletter@greenae.com.`

⋯⋯

if you have **problems...**

If the e-mail address that you typed—newsletter@greenae.com—turns blue and displays an underline, right-click the text, and then from the shortcut menu, click Remove Hyperlink.

⋯⋯

3 **Click the Page Layout tab. In the Page Setup group, click the Margins button, and then from the menu, click Custom Margins. In the Top box, type** `.5` **and then press** Tab⇄. **Change the margins to** `.75` **for the Bottom, Left, and Right margins.** Compare your screen with Figure 4.2.

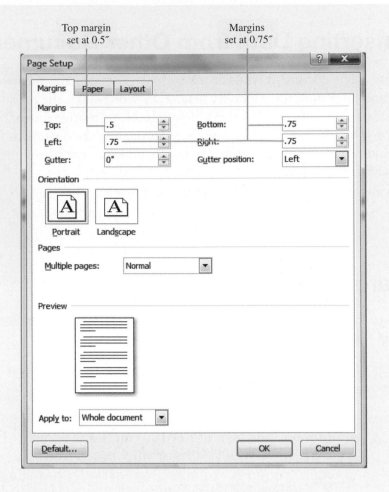

Top margin
set at 0.5″

Margins
set at 0.75″

FIGURE 4.2

4 **Click OK.** Notice that the margins are changed.

5 **Move the pointer to the left of the first line of the document to display the** ⟨pointer icon⟩ **pointer, and then click one time to select the text.**

6 **Click the Insert tab. In the Text group, click the WordArt button, and then in the second row, click the fifth style—WordArt style 11. In the Edit WordArt Text dialog box, click OK.** The WordArt image stretches from the left margin to the right margin.

7 **On the Format tab, in the Size group, click the Shape Height up spin arrow** ⟨icon 3.5″⟩ **until the height of the image is 1.0″. In the WordArt Styles group, click the Shape Fill button arrow** ⟨icon⟩ **, and then under Standard Colors, click the sixth color—Green.** Compare your screen with Figure 4.3.

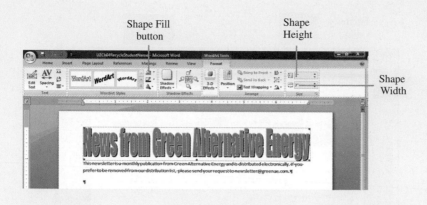

Shape Fill button

Shape Height

Shape Width

FIGURE 4.3

8 In the Quick Access Toolbar, click the Save button 💾. Navigate to the location where you are saving your files, and then click the New Folder button. Name the folder `Chapter04` and then in the File name box, type `U2Ch04RecycleStudentName` **Click Save.**

Articles included in a newsletter often come from a variety of sources and authors. You can insert Word files using the Insert Object button if you want to use all of the text in a document. It is a good idea to review and edit the Word document in its original file before importing it into your newsletter layout. The files that you will import have already been edited and are ready to be added to the newsletter.

to insert text from Word documents

1 Press Ctrl + End. The insertion point moves to the blank line at the end of the document.

2 Click the Insert tab. In the Text group, click the Object button arrow, and then click Text from File. Navigate to the location of your student files for this chapter, click U2Ch04Conservation, and then click Insert. All of the contents of the file are inserted at the insertion point location, as shown in Figure 4.4.

Inserted
file

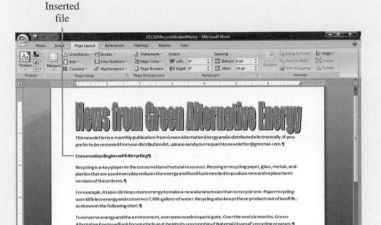

FIGURE 4.4

3 Use the technique you practiced in Step 2 to insert the following three files in the order shown: *U2Ch04Community*, *U2Ch04Efficiency*, and *U2Ch04Nanotechnology*. Do not remove the blank line at the end of the document.

4 Move to the top of the document. Select the text from the paragraph that begins *This newsletter* through the end of the document, including the paragraph mark in the last (blank) paragraph.

5 Click the Page Layout tab. In the Paragraph group, under Spacing, click the Spacing After down spin arrow one time to display 6 pt. In Word 2007, the default spacing after paragraphs is 10-point. The Spacing After spin arrows are used to increase or decrease this spacing; when the spacing is 10-point, clicking the down spin arrow once changes it to 6-point.

· ·

good **design...**

USE ONE FONT FOR THE BODY OF YOUR NEWSLETTER

When you gather documents that have been written by several other people, the font, font size, and other formatting may be inconsistent. Be sure to apply one font and font size for all of the paragraphs in the body of the text. Titles or headings may use a different font, font size, or style to add emphasis and set these apart from the rest of the text.

· ·

In addition to inserting entire documents, you can copy a portion of a file and paste it into another. You can also copy data from other programs, such as Excel or Access, and paste that data into a Word document.

to copy and paste data from an Excel file

1 Click the Start button 🌐, and then click Computer to display the drives and folders on your computer. Navigate to the location of your student files for this chapter, right-click U2Ch04Savings, and then click Open. The U2Ch04Savings Excel file opens.

2 In the Excel file, click in the upper left cell—cell A1—and drag down and to the right until all of the cells with data are selected, as shown in Figure 4.5.

Twelve cells selected

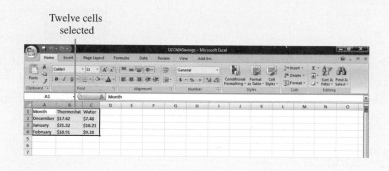

FIGURE 4.5

3 On the Home tab, in the Clipboard group, click the Copy button 📋. Close ❎ the Excel file.

4 If necessary, on the taskbar, click the button for your Word document. On the bottom of the first page of the document, in the sentence above the Nanotechnology article title, click at the end of the sentence and press ↵Enter.

5 On the Home tab, in the Clipboard group, click the Paste button arrow—the bottom half of the Paste button. From the menu, click Paste Special. In the Paste Special dialog box, click Unformatted text. Compare your screen with Figure 4.6. The options listed in your dialog box may vary.

Unformatted
Text

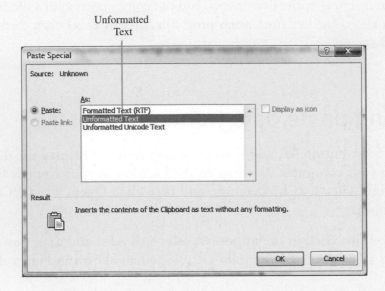

FIGURE 4.6

6 **At the bottom of the Paste Special dialog box, click OK.** The text is pasted at the insertion point location. Because you used the Paste Special option, the data from the Excel worksheet is separated by tabs, as indicated by the arrows. If you had used the simple Paste command, the text would have been inserted as a table.

7 **Save** 🖫 **your document.**

▶▶▶ *lesson*
tWO | Creating and Formatting a Multicolumn Document

Newspapers and most magazines and newsletters use multiple columns for articles, because text in narrower columns is easier to read than text that stretches across a page. Word has a tool that enables you to change a single column of text into two or more columns and then format the columns. If a column does not end where you want, you can end the column at a location of your choice.

In this lesson, you change text to a two-column format and then format the columns.

to create multiple columns

1 **Press** Ctrl + Home **to move to the top of the document. In the article title that begins** *Conservation Begins*, **position the insertion point at the beginning of the title.** The WordArt graphic and the first paragraph will be left in single-column format.

2 **Scroll to the end of the document, hold down** ⟨⬆Shift⟩**, and then click to the right of the paragraph mark in the last (blank) paragraph.** All of the text below the title and the opening paragraph of the newsletter is selected.

3 **Click the Page Layout tab. In the Page Setup group, click the Columns button, and then click Two. Move to the top of the document.** Notice that all of the selected text is changed to a two-column format, as shown in Figure 4.7. A section-break formatting mark displays after the paragraph below the WordArt graphic; because it is so short, the section-break text does not display. A *section* is a portion of the document that is formatted differently from surrounding text.

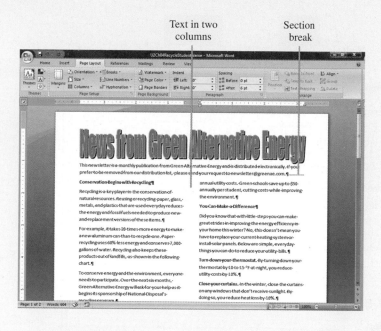

FIGURE 4.7

4 **Save** 🖫 **your document.**

In most cases, multiple-column text should be justified. Recall that justified text is aligned on both the right and left sides. Also, the default space between columns may be wider than necessary, which can be adjusted.

to format columns

1 **Select all of the text in columns.**

2 **On the Page Layout tab, in the Page Setup group, click the Columns button, and then click More Columns.** The Columns dialog box displays, enabling you to change the column widths, set different column widths for different columns, or add a line between the columns.

3 **In the Columns dialog box, under *Width and spacing*, click the Spacing down spin arrow three times. In the Apply to box, be sure *Selected text* displays.** The *Spacing* should be 0.2" and the *Width* should be 3.4" as shown in Figure 4.8.

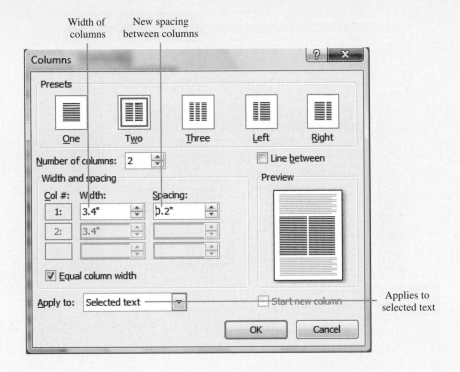

FIGURE 4.8

4 **Click OK to accept the changes.** Notice that the distance between columns is narrower.

5 **With the column text still selected, click the Home tab. In the Paragraph group, click the Justify button** ▤. The left and right edges of each column are aligned.

6 **Press** Ctrl **+** Home **to move to the top of the document, and then compare your document with Figure 4.9.**

Space between
columns is reduced

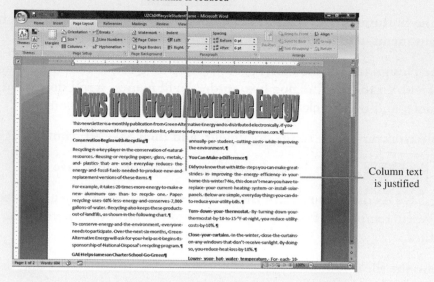

Column text
is justified

FIGURE 4.9

7 Save 💾 your document.

good **design...**

DETERMINING THE RIGHT NUMBER OF COLUMNS

When you are using columns on letter-sized paper (8.5" × 11" or A4), two columns are usually best, because the short line length in a three-column format can cause awkward-looking gaps between words, especially if the text is justified. If the left and right margins are set to 0.5", however, three-column formatting will sometimes work. Test your document using both column formats to see which one looks best.

▶▶▶ *lesson*

three | Saving a Document as a Template

When you create a document that needs to be reused on a regular basis—such as a monthly newsletter, a letterhead, or a memo—it is a good idea to create a template to save time. With a template, you can reuse the headings, titles, font, and other formatting rather than having to redo these elements each time. When you open a template, it opens as an unnamed document, and you then replace the appropriate text and pictures and give the document a new name. The original template is not changed and can be used again in exactly the same manner.

In this lesson, you save your newsletter as a template. First, you will add the file name to the footer so that it is included in this document before it is submitted for evaluation.

to save a document as a template

1 Near the bottom edge of Page 1, in an open area, right-click, and then from the shortcut menu, click Edit Footer.

2 On the Design tab, in the Insert group, click the Quick Parts button, and then click Field. In the Field dialog box, under Field names, scroll down and click FileName, and then click OK. This file name is placed in the footer.

3 Double-click anywhere in the document, and then Save 💾 your changes.

4 Click the Office button 🔘, and then from the menu, click Save As.

5 In the Save As dialog box, click the *Save as type* arrow, and then from the list, click Word Template. If necessary, navigate to the location where you are saving your files.

6 Rename the file `U2Ch04NewsletterTemplateStudentName`, and then click Save. The file is saved as a template.

to extend your knowledge

FILE EXTENSIONS

Files created using application software typically have a three- or four-character *file extension*. These file extensions are what the operating system uses to determine which program to use to open a file. For example, the full file name of the document on which you are working is *U2Ch04RecycleStudentName.docx*. Microsoft Word files from older versions of Office used a *.doc* extension. Some of the more common file extensions are shown in Table 4.2. The first four are Microsoft Office formats, with the Office 2007 extensions shown first and the older extensions shown second. In Microsoft Office 2007, you can save files with the older file format so that they can be opened with earlier versions of the software; this is known as *compatibility mode*.

FILE EXTENSION	ASSOCIATED PROGRAM
.docx, .doc	Word document
.dotx, .dot	Word template
.xlsx, .xls	Excel workbook
.pptx, .ppt	PowerPoint presentation
.pdf	Adobe Portable Document Format
.jpg, .tif, .gif	Popular image formats

TABLE 4.2

7 Close [X] your newly created template. Click the Start button, and then click Computer to display your computer's drives and folders. Navigate to the location where you save your files, locate the new template, and then double-click the file name. A copy of the file opens unnamed, as shown in Figure 4.10. The original template file is preserved for later use. This enables you to make changes for another newsletter without making changes to the original template. In this case, the original articles serve as sample text so that the styles and formatting are shown. In many cases, the text would be removed or translated to another language to make it apparent that the text is sample text only.

Template file
opens unnamed

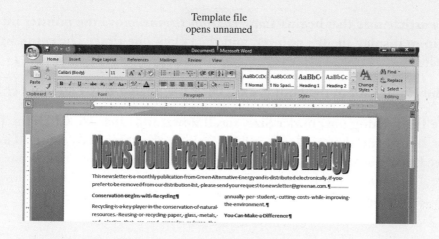

FIGURE 4.10

8 Close [X] the file without saving it. Reopen your U2Ch04RecycleStudentName document.

to extend **your knowledge**

EDITING A TEMPLATE

When you double-click a template file from the Computer window, an unnamed copy of the file opens with all the properties and formatting of the template. Use this to create a new version of the file, which preserves the original template. If you want to edit the template directly, open Word, and from the Office menu, click Open. Locate and open the template. It will open under the template name and enable you to make changes to the template itself.

▶▶▶ *lesson*

four | Applying Special Formatting

Formatting text from the Ribbon gives you many options; formatting text from the Font dialog box gives you several more options and enables you to make several changes at one time. If you make a number of formatting changes to text in one location, you can use the Format Painter to quickly transfer those changes to other text.

to apply special text formatting

1 **In the article title that begins *Conservation Begins*, move the pointer into the margin to display the 🔏 pointer, and then click one time.** The entire article title is selected.

2 **On the Home tab, in the Font group, click the Dialog Box Launcher 🔲 .**

3 **In the Font dialog box, under Size, scroll down and click 16. Click the Font Color arrow, and then under Standard Colors, click the sixth color—Green. Under Effects, select the Small caps check box.** Compare your dialog box with Figure 4.11. *Small caps* is a font effect typically used in titles, where the lowercase letters are capital letters but are the same height as lowercase letters.

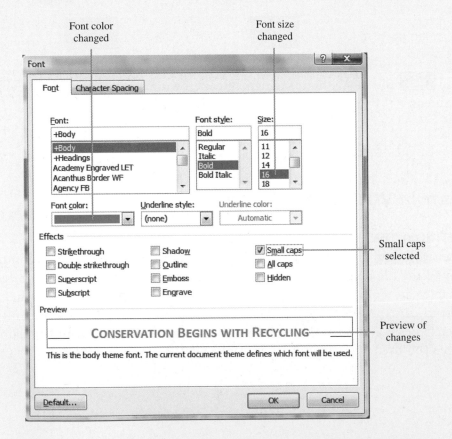

FIGURE 4.11

4 In the Font dialog box, click OK. In the Paragraph group, click the Center button ![icon]. The text formatting is applied, and the title is centered.

5 In the Clipboard group, click the Format Painter button ![icon]. Move the ![icon] pointer to the left column to the title that begins *You Can Make* and drag to select the entire title, including the paragraph mark. The formatting from the first title is applied to the new title, as shown in Figure 4.12. The pointer returns to its original shape—the Format Painter is turned off after it is used.

New formatting applied to two titles

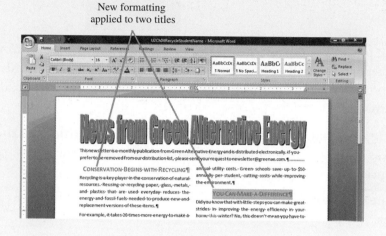

FIGURE 4.12

6 With the title still selected, in the Clipboard group, double-click the Format Painter button ![icon]. When you double-click the Format Painter button, it remains on until you turn it off.

7 Scroll down and use the Format Painter to change the formatting of the title that begins *GAE Helps* and the title that begins *Nanotechnology*. Notice that the Format Painter remains active.

8 Press (Esc) to turn off the Format Painter. You can also click the Format Painter button a second time to turn it off.

9 Scroll as necessary to position the title that begins *GAE Helps*, near the top of the screen. Notice that the text is unbalanced on the two lines.

10 Select the space to the right of *Jameson*. Hold down (⇧Shift) and press (↵Enter). A *manual line break* is entered. This technique enables you to split a line but keep the text in the same paragraph. A special formatting character, shown in Figure 4.13, indicates where a manual line break has been entered.

Manual line
break indicator

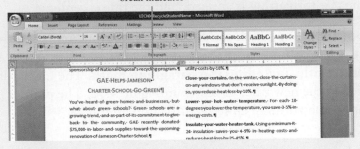

FIGURE 4.13

11 Move to the top of the document. In the title that begins *Conservation Begins*, click anywhere in the title, and then click the Page Layout tab. In the Paragraph group, click the Spacing After down spin arrow to change the space after the paragraph to 0 pt.

12 In the article title that begins *You Can Make*, click in the title, and then in the Quick Access Toolbar, click the Repeat button ↻. The most recent paragraph format is repeated.

13 Use the Repeat button ↻ to remove the spacing after the other two green article titles.

14 Save 💾 your document.

***

good design...

USING CONSISTENT SPECIAL FORMATS

When you use color, small caps, or other special formatting for a document element such as a subtitle, you should use the same formatting for similar elements throughout the document.

***

In addition to text formatting, you can add borders around pages and borders and shading to paragraphs.

to add borders to paragraphs and pages

1 In the second column on the first page, select the four paragraphs that begin with bold text—beginning with *Turn down your thermostat.*

2 On the Home tab, in the Paragraph group, click the Borders button arrow ⊞ ▾, and then click Outside Borders. A border is placed around the four paragraphs.

3 In the Paragraph group, click the Shading button arrow 🪣 ▾, and then under Theme Colors, in the second row of colors, click the seventh color—Olive

Green, Accent 3, Lighter 80%. Click anywhere in the document to deselect the text. Notice that the border displays around the paragraphs and that all four paragraphs have light green shading, which draws the eye to the information in the box, as shown in Figure 4.14.

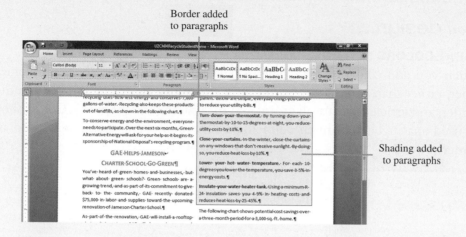

Border added
to paragraphs

Shading added
to paragraphs

FIGURE 4.14

4 **Click the Page Layout tab. In the Page Background group, click the Page Borders button.**

5 **In the Borders and Shading dialog box, under Setting, click Box. Click the Color arrow, and then under Standard colors, click the sixth color—Green. Click the Width arrow, and then click 1 1/2 pt.** A preview of the page border displays on the right side of the dialog box, as shown in Figure 4.15.

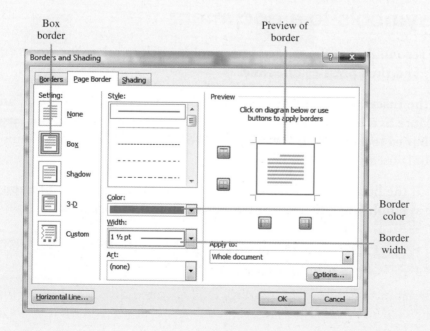

Box
border

Preview of
border

Border
color

Border
width

FIGURE 4.15

6 **In the Borders and Shading dialog box, click OK.** The border is added to both pages.

7 **Save** 🖫 **your document.**

good **design...**

USING COLORS IN A DOCUMENT

When you add colors to a document, it is best to use colors that complement each other, rather than using a number of different colors. In this newsletter, the title, page border, and article titles are all green, and the shading is light green. Colors should also be used sparingly; too much color makes the document look "busy" and makes it harder to read.

▶▶▶ *lesson*
five | Adding Symbols

Symbols are characters that are not displayed on the keyboard but are available from the Insert tab. Some of the more commonly used symbols are copyright (©), trademark (™), and paragraph (¶). You can also create your own symbols using subscripts and superscripts.

to add symbols to a document

1 **In the second line of the shaded box, double-click to select the word *degrees*. Type F and then press ⏎ one time.**

2 **Click the Insert tab. In the Symbols group, click the Symbol button, and then click More Symbols. If necessary, click the Font box arrow, and then use the scroll bar to locate and click the Symbol font.** The Symbol font contains most commonly used symbols.

3 **Scroll to the bottom of the list of symbols, and then scroll up until you see the degree symbol. Click the degree symbol, as shown in Figure 4.16.**

Degree   Symbol
symbol   font

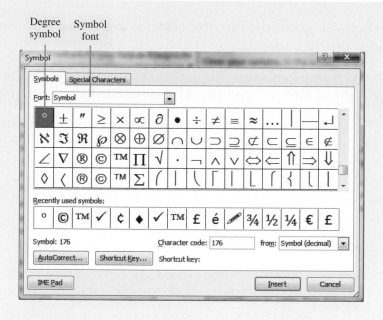

FIGURE 4.16

4 **With the degree symbol selected, click Insert, and then click Close.** The degree symbol, along with the capital *F*, indicates *degrees Fahrenheit*.

5 **Scroll to display the article about nanotechnology. In the paragraph that begins** *Nanotechnology is a big word*, **locate and select the two dashes between** *scale* **and** *working*.

6 **In the Symbols group, click the Symbol button, and then click More Symbols. In the Symbol dialog box, click the Special Characters tab, and be sure Em Dash is selected, as shown in Figure 4.17.** An *em dash* is a long dash that marks a break in thought—similar to a comma but stronger.

Special
Characters
tab   Em dash

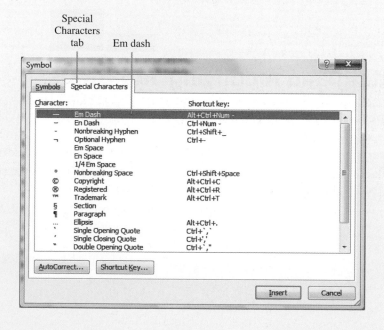

FIGURE 4.17

7 **In the Symbol dialog box, click Insert, and then click Close.** An em dash replaces the two dashes that were selected.

8 **Move to the top of the document. In the paragraph below the WordArt image, click to the right of *Energy*. Type** TM **and then select the text you just typed.**

9 **Click the Home tab. In the Font group, click the Superscript button** ![x² button] **. Click anywhere in the document to deselect the text.** A *superscript* is text that is raised above the regular text; a *subscript* is text that is moved below the level of the regular text. Notice that the text size is also reduced, as shown in Figure 4.18. The trademark symbol is also available from the Symbol dialog box, but this technique assures that the symbol uses the same font as the surrounding text.

Superscript
added

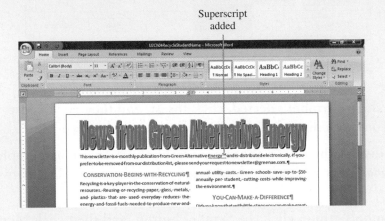

FIGURE 4.18

▶▶▶ *lesson*

SIX | Setting and Modifying Tab Stops

Tab stops mark specific locations on a line of text; use tab stops to indent and align text. Press ⏹Tab to move the insertion point to the next tab stop that has been set for a line of text. There are default tabs every half inch. Pressing ⏹Tab will stop at each half-inch mark until other tabs are set, which replaces the existing tabs for that line of text. Once tab stops are set, they can be moved, modified, or deleted.

In this lesson, you set and modify tab stops. You will also move text by moving the related tab stops.

to set tab stops

1 In the article title that begins *Conservation Begins,* in the second paragraph of the article, position the insertion point at the end of the paragraph—to the right of the period following the word *chart*—and then press ⏎Enter.

2 On the left end of the ruler, locate the Tab button ⌊L⌋. This button will display one of seven different tab types shown in Table 4.3.

TAB TYPE	TAB BUTTON	DESCRIPTION
Left	⌊L⌋	Text is left aligned at the tab stop and extends to the right.
Center	⊥	Text is centered around the tab stop.
Right	⌋	Text is right aligned at the tab stop and extends to the left.
Decimal	⊥	The decimal point aligns at the tab stop.
Bar			A vertical bar is inserted in the document at the tab stop.
First Line Indent	▽	Indents the first line of a paragraph.
Hanging Indent	⊔	Indents all lines but the first in a paragraph.

TABLE 4.3

if you have problems...

If the ruler does not display, click the View button. In the Show/Hide group, select the Ruler check box.

3 **Click the Tab button ⌊L⌋ several times to see the different tab markers.** When you point to the Tab button, a ScreenTip displays the name of the currently displayed tab marker. Whichever tab marker displays in the Tab button is the type of tab that will be inserted into the ruler.

4 **Click the Tab button ⌊L⌋ until the Left Tab stop displays. In the ruler, click one time at 0.25 inches.** A left tab is inserted at that location.

5 **Click the Tab button ⌊L⌋ until the Right Tab stop displays. In the ruler, click one time at 3.25 inches.** A right tab is inserted at that location. Compare your screen with Figure 4.19. If the tab does not display at the desired location, point to the tab mark and drag it off of the ruler, and then try again.

Tab
button

Left tab
stop at 0.25"

Right tab
stop at 3.25"

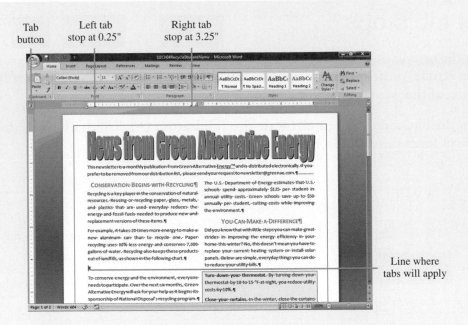

Line where
tabs will apply

FIGURE 4.19

6 Press `Tab`, type `Product` and then press `Tab`. Type `Time to Degrade` and then press `Enter`. Notice that when you type text at the second tab, the text moves from the tab location to the left.

7 Use the procedure you used in Step 6 to finish entering the data. Do not press `Enter` after the last item.

Glass	1 million years
Aluminum cans	80–100 years
Plastic	700 years
Paper cups	20 years

8 Select the first four rows in the tabbed list. Click the Page Layout tab. In the Paragraph group, under Spacing, click the Spacing After down spin arrow to remove the extra spacing between paragraphs.

9 Select the first row of the tabbed list, and then from the Mini toolbar, click the Bold button **B**.

10 Select the last four rows of the tabbed list. Double-click the right tab stop at the 3.25" mark.

11 **In the Tabs dialog box, under** *Tab stop position,* **click 3.25" to select the right tab. Under Leader, click the 2 option button, and then click Set.** Compare your dialog box with Figure 4.20. A *leader* is a series of characters that fill in the gap between two tabbed items. A dot leader is the most commonly used type of leader, with a dot as the *leader character*.

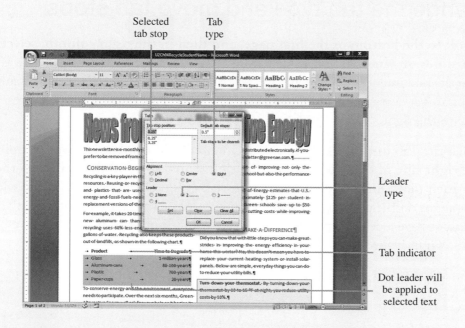

FIGURE 4.20

12 **In the Tabs dialog box, click OK.** Notice that the dots lead the eye from the item on the left of the list to the item on the right. Dot leaders are often used in a table of contents to help guide the eye from the topic on the left side of the page to the page number on right side of the page.

13 **Save** your document.

to extend your knowledge

USING THE TAB DIALOG BOX TO CORRECT TAB SETTINGS

The Tabs dialog box can be used to clear tabs that are set and then set new tabs at the desired location. In the Tabs dialog box, select a tab you want to change and click the Clear button. Then set a new tab at the desired location and click the Set button. To display the Tabs dialog box, click the Paragraph Dialog Box Launcher. In the bottom of the Paragraph dialog box, click Tabs to open the Tabs dialog box.

After you have set tab stops, or if you import data from another document, you may need to modify the type and location of the tab stops.

to change the tab type and move tab stops

1 **Scroll to the bottom of the first page, and then in the right column, select the four lines of data that you pasted from Excel.** Recall that when the data was pasted into the document, tabs were placed between each item in each row. By default, tab stops are set every half inch on the ruler, and tabbed data moves to the nearest tab stop to the right.

2 **Click the Tab button** ⬜ **until the decimal tab** ⬛ **displays. Move the pointer to the right side of the ruler—above the right column—and then click on the 1.5-inch mark on the ruler.** Notice that the second column of data in the selected text aligns on the decimal point. The top item—Thermostat—is not a number and does not have a decimal point, so the entire word displays to the left of the tab stop, as shown in Figure 4.21.

Numbers aligned on the decimal tab stop

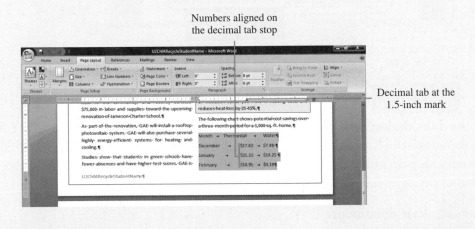

Decimal tab at the 1.5-inch mark

FIGURE 4.21

3 **Move the pointer to the 3-inch mark on the ruler and click to add an additional decimal tab stop.** The third column aligns at the new tab stop.

4 Click anywhere in the first line you just changed, which begins with *Month*. Double-click the tab stop at the 1.5-inch mark.

5 In the Tabs dialog box, under *Tab stop position*, select 3". Under Alignment, click the Center option button, and then click Set. In the same box, select the 1.5" tab stop, click the Center option button, and then click Set. Compare your screen with Figure 4.22.

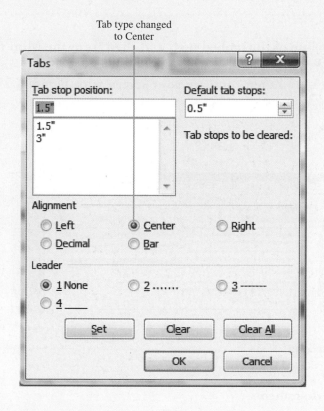

Tab type changed
to Center

FIGURE 4.22

6 In the Tabs dialog box, click OK. On the Page Layout tab, in the Paragraph group, click the Spacing After down spin arrow to change the space after the paragraph to 0 pt.

7 Click in the second and third lines of the new tabbed list, and change the space after each paragraph to 0 pt.

8 Select the last three lines of the tabbed list. In the ruler, point to the decimal tab stop at 1.5". When a ScreenTip displays, drag the tab stop to 1.75" on the ruler. Notice that by selecting several lines of tabbed data, you can move an entire column by moving the associated tab stop.

ALIGN TITLES AND DATA IN TABBED LISTS

In a tabbed list, be sure that the titles align properly over the list of data. All of the data in the table should have a consistent tab format for each line. As necessary, adjust the placement and type of tab stop used for the titles that display at the top of each column of data.

9 Select the first line of the tabbed text, and then from the Mini toolbar, click the Bold button **B** . On the ruler, drag the center tab at the 1.5-inch mark to the 1.75-inch mark, and then compare your screen with Figure 4.23.

Tab stop moved

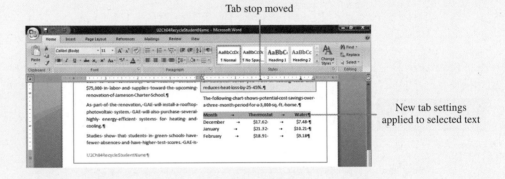

New tab settings applied to selected text

FIGURE 4.23

10 Save 💾 your document.

WHEN TO USE LEADERS

When there is a long gap between items in a tabbed list, it is hard for the eye to follow across the page. When you have a large gap, use a dot or other type of leader to draw the eye across the page.

When you format text in two columns, the ends of the columns of text on the last page seldom align. You can add a ***manual column break*** to end a column so that the columns line up, or you can end one column to leave enough space in the next column to insert a graphic. It is a good idea to finish your document before adding the column break, as each edit changes the lengths of the columns.

to add a manual column break

1 Press Ctrl + End to move to the blank line at the end of the document.

2 In the third paragraph below the *Nanotechnology* title, position the insertion point to the left of the first line—the line that begins *Several commercial*.

3 **Click the Page Layout tab. In the Page Setup group, click the Breaks button, and then from the menu, click Column.** There is space at the bottom of the second column for a clip art image, as shown in Figure 4.24.

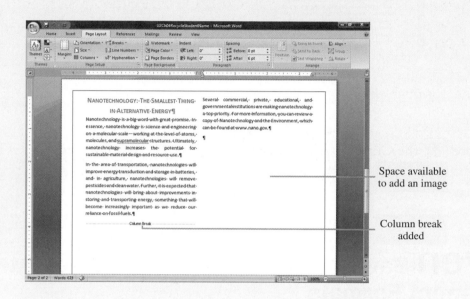

FIGURE 4.24

4 **Position the insertion point in the blank line at the end of the document, and then press ↵Enter.**

5 **On the Insert tab, in the Illustrations group, click the Clip Art button.**

6 **In the Clip Art task pane, in the *Search for* box, type** `conservation` **and then click Go.**

7 **Scroll down and insert the clip art image shown in Figure 4.25. If that image is not available, use a different image and resize it to match the size shown in the figure.**

8 **With the clip art image selected, click the Home tab. In the Paragraph group, click the Center button ▣ to center the image in the column.** Compare your screen with Figure 4.25. Recall that the bottom portion of the second page has purposely been left blank so that it can be used for a mailing address after the newsletter is folded. In Chapter 5, you will learn how to create mailing labels.

Clip art
image centered

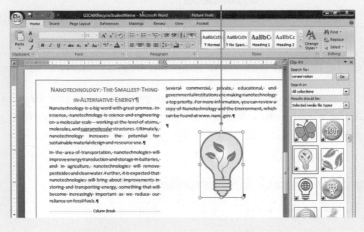

FIGURE 4.25

9 Close ☒ the Clip Art task pane, and then Save 💾 your document.

►►► *lesson*
seven | Saving a Document Using Different Document Formats

You can save Word documents in different formats for different purposes. By default, Word 2007 documents are saved with a *.docx* file extension. If you are sending the document to someone using an earlier version of Word, you can save the document so that it can be opened and edited in earlier versions of Word.

If you need to create a file that can be opened by other word processing programs, even on computers that are using a different operating system, you can save the document in a universal file format called ***rich text format (RTF)***, which uses an *.rtf* extension. An RTF file saves most of the Word formatting, including font styles—such as bold or italic—and paragraph formatting. If formatting is not important, you can save the document in ***plain text format***, which uses a *.txt* extension. This format removes most text formatting, although paragraph marks are included. If the file needs to be read on a different platform—a different operating system—but not edited, you can save the file in the Adobe ***Portable Document Format (PDF)***, which uses a *.pdf* extension.

In addition to saving files with different file formats, you will also customize the Quick Access Toolbar to display buttons that you use frequently or that are not available on the Ribbon.

In this lesson, you will add buttons to the Quick Access Toolbar, and then you will save the open document as a PDF file.

to customize the Quick Access Toolbar

1 **On the Quick Access Toolbar, click the Customize Quick Access Toolbar button ⊽**. The buttons that display on the toolbar have check marks. Three buttons—Save, Undo, and Redo—are displayed on the toolbar by default. Your toolbar may vary. Notice in Figure 4.26 that you can move the toolbar below the Ribbon to make it closer to the document.

Buttons currently on the Quick Access Toolbar

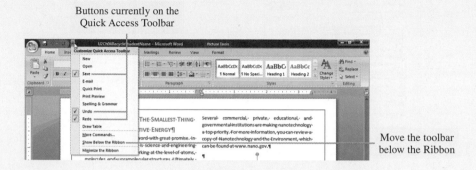

Move the toolbar below the Ribbon

FIGURE 4.26

2 **From the menu, click the Open button.** The Open button is added to the Quick Access Toolbar. This means that you no longer need to open the Office menu to open a document.

3 **On the Quick Access Toolbar, click the Customize Quick Access Toolbar button ⊽. From the menu, click More Commands to display the Word Options dialog box. In the *Choose commands from* box, click the arrow, and then click All Commands.** A list of all possible Word commands is displayed.

4 **Scroll down and click Save As. Click the Add button.** The Save As button is added to the list of buttons on the Quick Access Toolbar, as shown in Figure 4.27.

List of all
Word buttons

Add
button

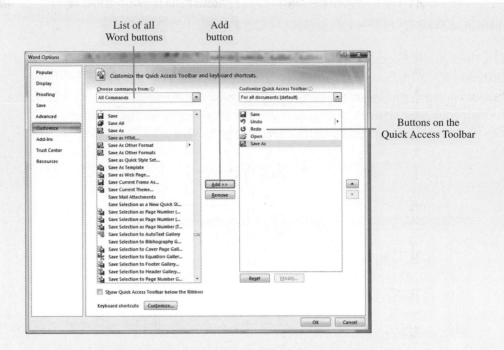

Buttons on the
Quick Access Toolbar

FIGURE 4.27

5 **In the Word Options dialog box, click OK.** Notice that two new buttons have been added to the toolbar, as shown in Figure 4.28.

Open
button

Save As
button

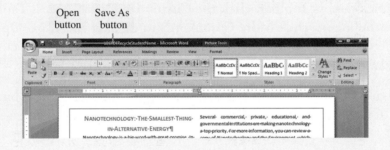

FIGURE 4.28

to extend your knowledge

REMOVING BUTTONS FROM THE QUICK ACCESS TOOLBAR
To remove buttons from the Quick Access Toolbar, right-click the button, and then from the menu, click Remove from Quick Access Toolbar.

You will use the buttons you added to the Quick Access Toolbar in the following task to save a document with different file formats.

to save a document in a different format

1 On the Quick Access Toolbar, click the Save As button.

2 In the Save As dialog box, click the *Save as type* arrow. Compare your screen with Figure 4.29.

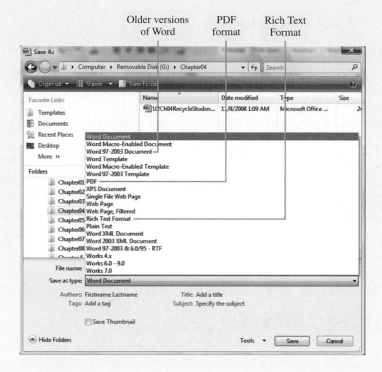

FIGURE 4.29

3 In the list of file types, click PDF. If necessary, navigate to the Chapter04 folder, and then click Save. The file is saved in PDF format, but the Word document remains open. Depending on your computer's settings, Adobe Acrobat Reader may or may not open to display the document.

if you have problems...

If the PDF option does not display on your computer, you may not be able to complete this lesson. If you have access to the Internet and are working on your own computer, you can download an update that will add the PDF file type to your Office program. Go to www.microsoft.com/downloads, click Office, and look for an add-in for saving PDF and XPS files. Follow the instructions to install the add-in.

4 If the file opens in Adobe Acrobat Reader, scan through the document, and then close the file.

5 Click the Start button 🌐, and then click Computer. Navigate to the Chapter04 folder. Notice that there are two versions of your file—a Microsoft Word 2007 file and an Adobe Acrobat document (PDF) file—in addition to the template you created.

6 In the Computer window, click the Minimize button ⬜.

··

to extend your knowledge

DISPLAYING FILE EXTENSIONS

In the Computer window, the file extensions may be turned off. To change this setting, on the menu bar, click Tools, and then click Folder Options. In the Folder Options dialog box, click the View tab. Locate *Hide extensions for known file types* and clear the check mark to display the file extensions, and then click OK. If these are not displayed, on the toolbar, click the Views button, and then click Details. The Type column lists the file type for each file listed.

··

▶▶▶*lesson*
eight | Adding Hyperlinks and Saving a Document as a Web Page

Microsoft Word has tools that enable you to create Web pages directly from word processing documents. *Hyperlinks* can be added to move to related sites quickly. Hyperlinks are text or graphics that you click to move to a file, another page in a website, or a page in a different website.

to add hyperlinks to a document

1 If necessary, scroll to the end of the document. In the last paragraph, select the Web address *www.nano.gov*, but do not select the period at the end of the sentence.

2 Click the Insert tab. In the Links group, click the Hyperlink button.

3 Under Link to, be sure Existing File or Web Page is selected. In the Address box, be sure *www.nano.gov* displays. Compare your screen with Figure 4.30.

Existing File or Web Page | Web address

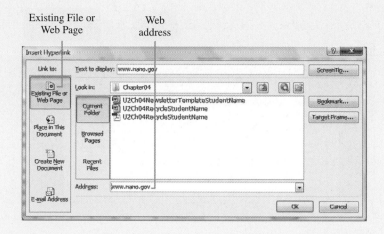

FIGURE 4.30

4 In the Insert Hyperlink dialog box, click the ScreenTip button. In the Set Hyperlink ScreenTip dialog box, under ScreenTip text, type `National Nanotechnology Initiative` and then compare your screen with Figure 4.31. The ScreenTip will display when you move the pointer over this hyperlink.

New ScreenTip

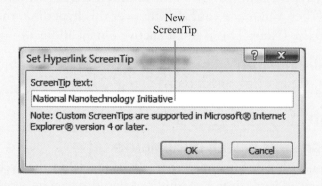

FIGURE 4.31

5 Click OK two times to close the open dialog boxes. Notice that the text is blue and is underlined, indicating a hyperlink. During the editing process, if you press the ⏎Enter key following this Web address, it will already be displayed with the hyperlink formatting.

6 Move the pointer over the new hyperlink. The ScreenTip you typed displays, along with instructions on how to activate the hyperlink. See Figure 4.32.

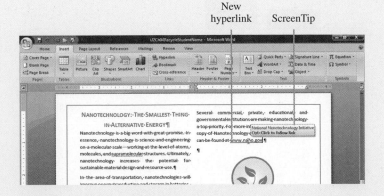

New hyperlink   ScreenTip

FIGURE 4.32

7 Press Ctrl + Home. **In the paragraph that begins** *This newsletter*, **select the text** *newsletter@greenae.com*, **but do not include the period at the end of the sentence.**

8 **In the Links group, click the Hyperlink button. Under Link to, click E-mail Address. In the** *E-mail address* **box, type** newsletter@greenae.com **and then in the Text to display box, delete** *mailto:.*

9 **Click the ScreenTip button. In the Set Hyperlink ScreenTip dialog box, under ScreenTip text, type** Unsubscribe **and then click OK two times to close the dialog boxes.** When you move your pointer over this hyperlink, the ScreenTip will display *Unsubscribe*. (Note: This is not an active e-mail address.)

10 Save 💾 **your document.**

·····································

good design...

INCLUDE HYPERLINKS IN WEB DOCUMENTS
If you plan to publish a document so that it is available on the Web, change any Web addresses or e-mail addresses into hyperlinks so that they can be accessed from the Web.

·····································

In the following task, you use the Save As button that you added to the Quick Access Toolbar to save the newsletter as a Web page.

to save a document as a Web page

1 **On the Quick Access Toolbar, click the Save As button.**

2 **In the Save As dialog box, click the** *Save as type* **arrow. From the list, click Single File Web Page.**

3 Near the bottom of the Save As dialog box, click the Change Title button. In the Set Page Title dialog box, under Page title, type `Green Alternative Energy Newsletter` and then click OK. The page title will display in the browser title bar.

4 In the Save As dialog box, click Save. Notice that some features supported by Word are not supported by Web pages, as shown in Figure 4.33.

Small caps are
not supported

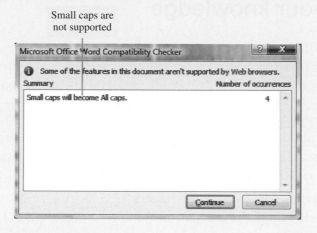

FIGURE 4.33

5 In the Microsoft Office Word Compatibility Checker dialog box, click Continue. The text displays as it will display in a browser. Notice that during the conversion, the two-column format was also lost.

6 Close the document. In the taskbar, click the Computer window button. If necessary, navigate to your Chapter04 folder.

7 Double-click the U2Ch04RecycleStudentName.mht file, which is the MHTML document. The Web page opens in the browser, as shown in Figure 4.34. Notice the page title in the title bar. If you want to fix the minor problems with this Web page, you will

Page title
in title bar

Two-column
format is lost

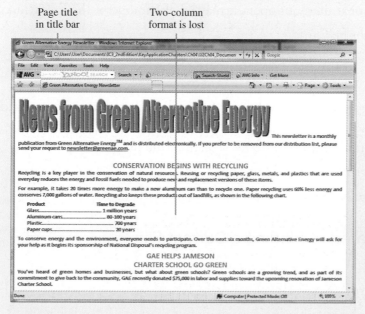

FIGURE 4.34

need to use a program that enables you to change the HTML code. Alternatively, you can make changes to the Word document and resave it as a Web page.

8 Close **X** the browser. Submit your files as directed.

to extend **your knowledge**

SAVING DOCUMENTS IN WEB FORMAT

If you have a website that is shared with your intended audience, saving documents in a Web format is a good way to distribute documents when you want everyone on that site to view the information. To distribute content as a Web page, the file must be saved using ***HTML format (Hypertext Markup Language)***—a set of symbols or codes that are inserted in a file to indicate how it should be displayed on the Web. Alternatively, the file can be saved as a single-file Web page, which uses ***MHTML format (MIME HTML)***—an HTML format that binds the components of a file together in one file. The HTML format saves supporting files, such as images, in a separate folder that must also be uploaded to the website. With MHTML format, all of the supporting files are stored together with the document, using one file name.

Advanced Skills or Concepts

In this section, you are introduced to skills that are not taught with step-by-step instructions.

Resolving Common Problems Related to Working With Files

A variety of problems may cause you to be unable to open a file or lose some of your work. If a file is missing or it does not open, it may be due to one of the following problems.

- The file cannot be found.
- The most recent version of the file cannot be found.
- The location where the file is stored is not available.
- The operating system does not know what application program is associated with the file.
- The application program you have will not open a file created in a similar application program or by a newer version of the program.
- The file is corrupted and will not open.
- Recent changes to a file were lost due to a power failure.

Problems Related to Finding a Current File

There are several reasons that a file might be hard to find.

File Does not Exist   Do not jump to this conclusion. MS Office and Windows have several features that help you avoid losing your work but there are still a few ways that it can happen.

If you close a new document without saving it, it will not be available to use later. It is a good idea to get into the habit of saving a new file to a known location with an easily identifiable name as soon as you open it.

If you save a different file or an empty file using the same name, and then confirm that you want to overwrite the existing file, the existing file is lost. If you are keeping more than one version of the same document, use different names that include the version number. If you save an old version using the same name as the newer one, your recent work will be lost.

If you use a public computer in a lab that is shared by many people and save a file to the Desktop, it could be erased by the security software before you use the computer again. If you are using a public computer, be sure to save your work to your own portable drive, a network or Internet storage area, or send it to yourself as an e-mail attachment.

If you open a file directly from a different computer on a network, the file might open in *Read Only* mode if you do not have permission to save files to that location. You must save the edited file to a location where you have permission to save files. If you close the edited file without saving it to a different location, the work will be lost.

File Exists But You Cannot Find It   When a computer has hundreds or thousands of files, you must separate them into smaller groups. Organize your files into folders with names that will help you locate your files. Use names for your folders and files that are descriptive of their content so the name has meaning to you later. When you close a file, be sure to respond appropriately to the *Do you want to save the changes to your file?* message box, and then pay attention to the folder in which the file will be saved.

A list of file names can be sorted alphabetically in most dialog boxes by clicking on the column heading. Consider this fact when you choose the name of the file. If you want several files to appear next to each other in a sorted list, begin the files with the same letters. If you plan to number the files, be aware that numbers in the file name are treated like letters for sorting purposes. If the largest numbers use two digits, be sure to use two digits for all of the numbers less than ten, such as 01, 02, and 03, so they sort properly.

If you are unable to locate a file, open the Computer window and use the search tools to search for the file by topic, key word, or date modified.

If you open a file directly from a website, the file might be saved in a temporary folder within an obscure folder in the operating system. This folder might not be included in a normal search so it will appear that the file is lost. To avoid this problem, download the file to a known folder before you open it or save it to a known folder before you start work on it. If you have already edited a file after opening it from a website and cannot find it, use the advanced search options to search hidden folders or open the file again from the website and start the Save As procedure to show where your computer stores these files. Do not complete the Save As procedure because you might overwrite the previous version of the file that contains your work.

If you are searching for a file using the Open dialog box within an application, the list of files is usually restricted to the files that match that application. For example, if you are looking for a Word file from the Open dialog box in Excel, the Word documents do not display by default unless you choose the All Files option.

Make backup copies of your files. If you save files to an external storage device, such as a flash drive (memory stick), network drive, or an Internet location, these storage devices may not be available when you need them later. In particular, it is easy to lose a flash drive. Be sure that you have your name on the device if you use it in a public location such as a computer lab at school. Apply a self-adhesive return address label to your memory stick to identify your ownership and contact information.

Problems Related to Availablility

There are several reasons that a file might not be available.

The storage device is not available   If you store a file on a network device, it might be out of service temporarily for maintenance or backup. This work is typically done during off-hours when it affects the fewest people. If this is the problem, wait a while and try again.

The portable media was removed   If the file was saved to a flash drive, the drive must be inserted into the computer. The computer will assign a temporary letter to the drive that is not always the same. If you do not see the usual drive letter when you list the available resources, try the other drive letters.

The connection to the network or Internet is not active   If the file is stored on a remote device that is accessible through a network or Internet connection, the connection must be active. Check the physical and logical connections between your computer and the network to see if your cables are plugged in and your login is accepted. Contact the network administrator for assistance.

Problems Related to File Associations

The Windows operating system associates files with the applications that create and read them by using a period followed by a three- or four-character code called a *file extension* at the end of each file name to identify which application is associated with the file. When you install a new application program, it registers the codes for its files with Windows. If you double-click a file name, Windows looks for the file extension. If the file has an extension, Windows looks into its list of extensions to see what application is associated with that extension, starts the application, and then instructs the application to open the file. For example, Word 97–2003 uses *.doc* to identify its files, and Word 2007 uses .docx. This system works pretty well, but it can break down if one of the following situations occurs.

The file is renamed without the file extension   Windows can be set to hide the file extensions for known file types, or it can be set to display them all. If a file name is displayed with its file extension, the extension must be included when you rename the file. For example, if the file MySummerVacation.docx were renamed WhatIdidThisSummer without the file extension, it would not be associated with Word. However, if the files are displayed with the extensions hidden, you could rename MySummerVacation as WhatIdidThisSummer, and Windows would automatically add the extension for you without showing it. To avoid this type of problem, always include the file extension when you rename a file if the original file has its extension displayed.

A new application has reassigned the file extension   Some files may be used by several different application programs. Two examples are Web page files that end with .htm and graphics files that end with .jpg. If you install a new application that uses either of these types of files, it may ask if you want it to be the default program for these types of files or it may simply go ahead and change the Windows file that associates extensions with applications. From that moment onward, when you double-click one of these files, the new application program will start instead of the previous program. To avoid this problem, do not agree to allow a program to be your default application for a certain type of file when you install it.

The file extension is missing or misspelled   If you are in an application program and choose to open a file, the list of files displayed in the dialog box is usually restricted to the list of files that have the associated file extension. If the file you are looking for does not have the correct extension, it will not be listed unless you change the Files of type option to All Files. If that is the only problem, you can still open the file.

Problems Related to Versions of Your Application Program

Application programs include special features that distinguish them from their competitors. To keep ahead of the competition and to continue to improve the performance of their products, companies add new features and release new versions of their application programs every few years. Unfortunately, these features use codes that are not recognized by the competition or by earlier versions of the same program. Most companies make sure that new versions of their application programs can open files that were created by older versions—even though the new version may not use the obsolete codes. These applications are ***backwardly compatible***. If you have a file that contains proprietary codes that your application program cannot read, you may be able to open the file using one of the following techniques.

The file was created by a competitor's program   Run your application's installation program again and look for optional conversion programs that translate the proprietary codes of other brands of application programs into ones your program can read. This method will not work for applications that came out after your installation disc was created.

If your program does not have a conversion program for the file type, ask the person who created the file to save it in a format that is compatible with your application program. Provide them with the file extension used by your program. Alternatively, you can ask them to save the file in a generic format such as RTF for word documents or CSV format for spreadsheets.

The file was created by a more recent version of the same application program Download and install a conversion program from the company's website. Many companies make conversion programs available that will translate the newer codes into codes that may be read by older versions of the software. These programs may be downloaded from the company's website and installed on your computer. Microsoft offers a compatibility pack to use with older versions of Word that works with Word 2007 files.

Problems Related to Corrupted Files

There are special programs that can read damaged files and recover some of the data if you get a corrupted file error message. Prevention is much easier than curing the problem. If your file is stored on magnetic media—an internal or external hard drive—some of its data may be lost if the media is exposed to magnetic fields. Keep your magnetic disks away from magnets, including the strong magnets in music speakers. The data on optical discs may be lost if the plastic disc is scratched, or it may be hard to read if the surface is dirty. When using flash drives, be sure to close all files and the programs that they used before removing the drive. Click the storage device icon in the tray area of the taskbar to ensure that it is safe to remove the drive before doing so.

Protect the discs during storage and clean them carefully if they are dirty. In some cases, your application program can repair some of the damage and open the corrupted file, but if you get a corrupted file error message, it is usually too late to recover the data easily. Make backup copies of important files to reduce the risk of loss.

Problems Related to Power Failures or System Crashes

When you open a file, a copy is placed in the computer's temporary memory and edits are made to that copy. When you save the file, the copy is written to long-term storage media such as a hard disk or your flash drive. The temporary memory needs continuous power. If the power goes off or the computer stops functioning, the work that has been done to the version in temporary memory since the last time it was saved is lost. To limit this loss, MS Office saves a backup of open files using the **AutoRecover** feature. The default setting for saving a backup is every ten minutes. When you restart your computer after an unexpected shut down, you have the option of opening the backup file. Open the file and save it using a new name. This feature can be turned on or off and the time between backups can be set by clicking the Office button, the Word Options button, and then, in the dialog box, click the Save option.

CHECK YOUR WORK

Here is a list of items your instructor will probably look for when grading your work. To improve your evaluation, take time to check the items yourself before you turn in your work.

Green Alternative Energy Newsletter
- Top margin set to 0.5".
- Left, bottom, and right margins set to 0.75".
- WordArt title created.
- Height of the WordArt title changed to 1".
- Color of the WordArt title changed to Green.
- Four Word documents inserted.
- All but the WordArt title and the following paragraph changed to two-column format.
- Spacing between columns changed to 0.2".
- Template file created.
- Article titles changed to small caps, 16-point, Green.
- Border and light green shading added to four paragraphs.
- Page border added.
- Page border formatted using 1.5" line width and green color.
- Superscripted trademark symbol added to paragraph below the WordArt title.
- Em dash added to paragraph on the second page.
- Five lines added to first column using a left and right tab stop.
- Dot leader added to four lines in the tabbed list.
- Tabs added at 1.75" and 3" in the tabbed list in the second column.
- Tabs in first row of list are center tab stops.
- Tabs in second through fourth rows of list are decimal tab stops.
- Column break added before last paragraph.
- Clip art image inserted and centered at bottom of last column.
- Document saved in PDF format.
- Web hyperlink added to second page of newsletter.
- E-mail hyperlink added to first page of newsletter.
- Document saved as single-file Web page.

KEY TERMS

AutoRecover

backwardly compatible

compatibility mode

em dash

file extension

hyperlink

Hypertext Markup
Language (HTML)

leader

leader character

manual column break

manual line break

margin

MHTML format
(MIME HTML)

plain text format

Portable Document Format
(PDF)

rich text format (RTF)

section

small caps

subscript

superscript

tab stop

ASSESSING LEARNING OUTCOMES

SCREEN ID

Identify each element of the screen by matching callout numbers shown in Figure 4.35
to a corresponding description.

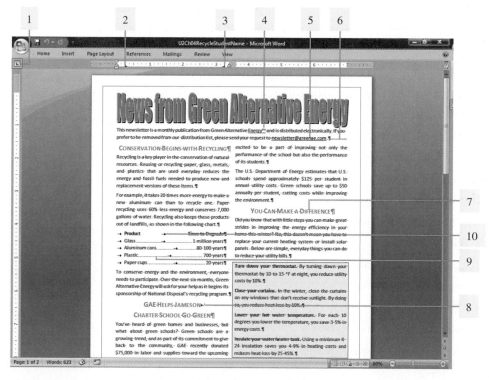

FIGURE 4.35

____ **A.** Hyperlink	____ **E.** Right tab stop	____ **I.** Tab button
____ **B.** Leader	____ **F.** Section break	____ **J.** Tab indicator
____ **C.** Left tab stop	____ **G.** Small cap effect	
____ **D.** Manual line break	____ **H.** Superscript format	

MULTIPLE CHOICE

Circle the letter of the correct answer for each of the following. The lesson in which the term or concept was introduced is indicated at the end of the sentence.

1. In a Word 2007 document, the default margin settings are _____. [L1]

   a. 1 inch on all sides

   b. 1.25 inches for the left and right margins, and 1 inch for the top and bottom margins

   c. 1 inch for the left and right margins, and 1.25 inches for the top and bottom margins

   d. 0.75 inch on all sides

2. To include data from Excel in a Word document so that it does not display as a table, use the Paste Special command and choose _____. [L1]

   a. Paste as text

   b. Plain text

   c. Rich Text Format

   d. Unformatted text

3. When you format a document with multiple columns, you can do all of the following **except** _____. [L2]

   a. control the space between the columns

   b. display a line between the columns

   c. you must format the entire document in the same number of columns

   d. set different column widths for different columns

4. The best way to edit a template is to _____. [L3]

   a. open Word, and then open the .dotx file from the Open dialog box

   b. click New From Existing in the New dialog box

   c. open the Computer window and double-click the template file name

   d. open the file as a document and resave it as a template

5. To repeat a format that was just applied to another area, use the _____. [L4]

   a. Copy and Paste buttons

   b. Format Painter or the Repeat button

   c. Repeat the Format button

   d. Copy and Format buttons

6. To insert a manual line break, press _____. [L4]

   a. Alt + ↵Enter

   b. Ctrl + ↵Enter

   c. ⬆Shift + ↵Enter

   d. Alt + Ctrl

7. The Tab button displays all of the following stops **except** the _____. [L5]

   a. bar tab

   b. decimal tab

   c. hanging indent

   d. right indent

8. To display the Tab dialog box, _____. [L6]

   a. click the Tab Dialog Box Launcher

   b. double-click a tab stop on the ruler

   c. double-click the Tab button

   d. double-click a tab marker in a line of text

9. You can save a Word document in any of the following file formats **except** _____. [L7]

   a. .dotx, .doc, .txt

   b. .ptf, .pdf, .docx

   c. .rtf, .doc, .pdf

   d. .mht, .docx, .pdf

10. To save a Word document as a Web page from the Save as type box, choose _____. [L8]

    a. Single File Web Page

    b. MHTML

    c. Web Document

    d. Rich Text Format

MATCHING

Match the term or concept to its description.

_____ 1. A universal document format that can be read by nearly all word processing programs

_____ 2. Text or graphics that provide a shortcut to a file or website

_____ 3. Characters that are placed below the rest of the text in a line

_____ 4. The space between the edge of the paper and the text

_____ 5. Three or four letters at the end of a file name that identify the type of file

_____ 6. A language that defines the way everything looks on a Web page

_____ 7. Characters that are placed above the rest of the text in a line

_____ 8. The ability of a newer version of a program to open and display files that were created using an earlier version of the program

_____ 9. A series of dots that provide a visual connection between widely separated text

_____ 10. An artificial end to a line without creating a new paragraph

A. Backwardly compatible

B. Dot leader

C. File extension

D. Hyperlink

E. HTML

F. Manual line break

G. Margin

H. RTF

I. Superscript

J. Subscript

SKILL DRILL

The Skill Drill exercise is a repeat of the lessons in the chapter but with a different set of data. The instructions are less detailed, and your speed and familiarity should increase with practice. There is a figure at the end against which you can check your results. The purpose of this exercise is to build your confidence and speed in using these skills and to set them in your memory for later recall. The section numbers correspond to the lesson numbers. You are welcome to refer back to the lesson's illustrated and detailed instructions if necessary.

In this exercise, you assemble and format an employee newsletter for Green Alternative Energy employees.

1. Inserting Data from Other Documents

1. **Start** Word, and then if necessary, display the formatting marks. Type `Green Alternative Energy Employee News` and then press `⏎Enter`. Type `Living and Selling Green` and then press `⏎Enter`.

2. On the **Page Layout** tab, in the **Page Setup** group, click the **Margins** button, and then click **Custom Margins**. Change the Top margin to .5 and the Bottom, Left, and Right margins to .75 and then click **OK.**

3. Select the first line—the newsletter title. On the **Insert** tab, in the **Text** group, click the **WordArt** button. In the first column, second row, click **WordArt style 7**, and then in the Edit WordArt Text dialog box, click **OK.**

4. On the **Format** tab, in the **Size** group, click the **Shape Height** up spin arrow until the height of the image is **0.8"**. In the **WordArt Styles** group, click the **Shape Fill** button arrow, and then under **Theme Colors**, in the seventh column, click the fifth color—**Olive Green, Accent 3, Darker 25%.**

5. Press Ctrl + End to move to the blank line at the end of the document. On the **Insert** tab, in the **Text** group, click the **Object** button arrow, and then click **Text from File.** Navigate to the location of your student files for this chapter, click **U2Ch04HeatPumps**, and then click **Insert.**

6. Repeat this process to insert the **U2Ch04Read** and **U2Ch04Sales** files. Do not remove the blank line at the end of the document.

7. On the Quick Access toolbar, click the **Save** button. Navigate to the Chapter04 folder that you created earlier, and save this file as U2Ch04EmployeeNewsStudentName

8. Click the **Start** button, and then click **Computer.** Navigate to the location of your student files for this chapter, right-click **U2Ch04Prices,** and then click **Open.** In the Excel file, click in cell **A1** and drag down and to the right until all of the cells with data are selected. Press Ctrl + C to copy this data. Close Excel.

9. If necessary, on the taskbar, click the button for your Word document. Just before the *Eco-Reading* article title, click at the end of the preceding paragraph, and then press ⏎Enter. On the **Home** tab, in the **Clipboard** group, click the **Paste** button arrow, and then click **Paste Special.** In the Paste Special dialog box, click **Unformatted text**, and then click **OK** to insert this data just above the *Eco-Reading* article title.

10. **Save** your work.

2. Creating and Formatting a Multicolumn Document

1. Move the insertion point to the top of the document. In the first article, position the insertion point at the beginning of the title *GAE Partners*. Scroll to the end of the document, hold down ⇧Shift, and then click to the right of the paragraph mark in the last (blank) paragraph.

2. On the **Page Layout** tab, in the **Page Setup** group, click the **Columns** button, and then click **Two.**

3. With the column text still selected, click the **Home** tab. In the **Paragraph** group, click the **Justify** button. In the **Font** group, click the **Grow Font** button one time to increase the font to **12 pt.**

4. At the top of the document, under the WordArt newsletter title, select the *Living and Selling Green* text.

5. On the **Home** tab, in the **Font** group, click the **Dialog Box Launcher**. In the Font dialog box, under **Font style,** click **Bold;** under **Size,** click **16.** Click the **Font color** arrow and click **Olive Green, Accent 3, Darker 50%.** Under **Effects,** click the **Small caps** check box. Click the **Underline style** arrow, and then scroll down and click the underline style that is third from the bottom of the list. Click **OK.**

6. **Save** your work.

3. Saving a Document as a Template

1. Near the bottom edge of Page 1, in an open area below the paragraph mark, right-click, and then from the shortcut menu, click **Edit Footer.**

2. On the **Design** tab, in the **Insert** group, click the **Quick Parts** button, and then click **Field.** In the Field dialog box, locate and click **FileName,** and then click **OK.**

3. Double-click anywhere in the document, and then **Save** your changes.

4. From the **Office** menu, click **Save As.** In the Save As dialog box, click the *Save as type* arrow, and then click **Word Template.** If necessary, navigate to the location where you are saving your files.

5. Rename the file U2Ch04EmpNewsTemplateStudentName and then click **Save.**

6. Close the template document.

4. Applying Special Formatting

1. Reopen the **U2Ch04EmployeeNewsStudentName** document. Select the first article title—*GAE Partners with HeatCo*—being sure to include the paragraph mark at the end of the line.

2. On the **Home** tab, in the **Font** group, click the **Dialog Box Launcher.** In the Font dialog box, under **Size,** click **16.** Click the **Font color** arrow, and under Theme Colors, click **Olive Green, Accent 3, Darker 25%.** Under Effects, select the **Small caps** check box and the **Engrave** check box. Click **OK.**

3. In the **Paragraph** group, click the **Center** button. On the **Page Layout** tab, in the **Paragraph** group, click the **Spacing After** down spin arrow one time to change the space after the paragraph to **6 pt.**

4. On the **Home** tab, in the **Clipboard** group, double-click the **Format Painter** button. Recall that when you double-click this button, you can use it multiple times. Move the 🔏 pointer to the left to the article title that begins *Eco-Reading,* and drag to select the entire title, including the paragraph mark.

5. Repeat this process to paint the format to the *GAE Sales Sweep* title. Press Esc to turn off the Format Painter.

6. Move to the top of the document. In the paragraph that begins *HeatCo,* click anywhere in the paragraph, and then click the **Page Layout** tab. In the **Paragraph** group, click the **Spacing After** down spin arrow to change the space after the paragraph to **6 pt.**

7. Click in the next paragraph that begins *Sales staff*, and on the Quick Access Toolbar, click the **Repeat** button. Using either the Format Painter or the Repeat button, change the spacing after paragraphs to **6 pt** for each paragraph, including the tabbed list.

8. Click the **Page Layout** tab. In the **Page Background** group, click the **Page Borders** button. In the **Borders and Shading** dialog box, under **Setting**, click **Box**. Click the **Color** arrow, and then click **Olive Green, Accent 3, Darker 50%**. Click the **Width** arrow, and then click **1 1/2 pt.** Click **OK.**

9. **Save** your work.

5. Adding Symbols

1. In the *Eco-Reading* article title, select the two dashes between *Reading* and *Join*.

2. On the **Insert** tab, in the **Symbols** group, click the **Symbol** button and then click **More Symbols**. In the Symbol dialog box, click the **Special Characters** tab. Be sure **Em Dash** is selected, and then click **Insert**. **Close** the dialog box.

3. At the top of the document, in the first article title, click to the right of *HeatCo* and type TM Select the *TM* you just typed, and then on the **Home** tab, in the **Font** group, click the **Superscript** button.

4. Repeat step 3 to add the trademark symbol next to the other two occurrences of *HeatCo* in this article.

5. **Save** your changes.

6. Setting and Modifying Tab Stops

1. Select the five lines of text that you imported from Excel, which appear in a tabbed list. On the **Home** tab, in the **Paragraph** group, click the **Line Spacing** button, and then click **1.0"** to change the line spacing. Select the first four lines of the tabbed list, click the **Line Spacing** button again, and then click **Remove Space After Paragraph.**

2. Select the five lines of the tabbed list. At the left end of the ruler, click the **Tab** button until the **Decimal** marker displays. On the ruler, click at **1.5** inches and at **3** inches.

3. On the ruler, point to the decimal tab at the 1.5-inch mark and drag it to **1.75** inches.

4. Click in the first line of the tabbed list, and then on the ruler, double-click the decimal tab at the 1.75-inch mark. In the Tab dialog box, click **1.75**, and then click the **Clear** button. Click **3,** and then click the **Clear** button.

5. In the **Tab stop position** box, type 2 and under **Alignment**, click **Right,** and then click the **Set** button. Repeat this process to set a right tab at **3.25** inches. Click **OK.**

6. Select the five lines of the tabbed list. On the **Home** tab, in the **Paragraph** group, click the **Borders** button arrow, and then click **Outside Borders.**

7. Click the **Borders** button arrow again, and then click **Borders and Shading**. In the dialog box, click the **Color** arrow, and then click **Olive Green, Accent 3, Darker 50%**. Click the **Shading** tab. Click the **Fill** arrow, and then click **Olive Green, Accent 3, Lighter 80%**. Click **OK**.

8. Select the first row in the tabbed list. Click the **Borders** button arrow, and then click **Bottom Border**.

9. In the second column, under the last paragraph, select the (blank) paragraph mark at the end of the newsletter. Use the **Line Spacing** button to change the line spacing for this paragraph to **1.0"**, and then remove the space after the paragraph.

10. On the ruler, click the **Tab** button until the **Center** marker displays, and then on the right side of the ruler, click on **2** inches and on **3** inches to insert a center tab stop at these two locations.

11. Type the data shown below, using ⌞Tab⌝ to move between each column of data.

NAME	PRICE	INCENTIVE
Clemens Cordless EX	$519.99	$520.00
Green Products Vac	$499.99	$500.00
ESKO Mover 365	$750.00	$750.00

12. Select the last three rows of the tabbed list. On the ruler, double-click on one of the tab stop markers to display the Tabs dialog box. Using the procedure you have practiced, change both tab stops to decimal tabs at **2** inches and **3** inches.

13. Select the four rows of the tabbed list. Repeat steps 6 through 8 to apply the same border and shading format as is applied to the tabbed list in the first column.

14. Compare your results with Figure 4.36 and **Save** your changes.

7. Saving a Document Using Different Document Formats

1. On the Quick Access Toolbar, click the **Customize Quick Access Toolbar** button. From the list of buttons, click **Print Preview**. Display the list of buttons again and click Spelling and Grammar.

2. From the Quick Access Toolbar, click the **Spelling & Grammar** button to check the spelling and grammar in this newsletter. Ignore *Vac, HeatCo,* and *SEER,* and correct any other spelling errors that you may encounter.

3. If the Save As button is on the Quick Access Toolbar, click it to display the Save As dialog box. Otherwise, from the **Office** menu, click **Save As**.

4. In the Save As dialog box, click the **Save as type** arrow. In the list of file types, click **PDF**. If necessary, navigate to the Chapter04 folder, and then click **Save**. If the PDF option does not display on your computer, you may not be able to complete this step. If the file opens in Adobe Acrobat Reader, scan through the document, and then close the file.

8. Adding Hyperlinks and Saving a Document as a Web Page

1. In the last paragraph of the first column, select *http://www.energystar.gov*. Click the **Insert** tab, and in the **Links** group, click the **Hyperlink** button.

2. Under Link to, be sure **Existing File or Web Page** is selected. In the Address box, be sure *http://www.energystar.gov* displays.

3. Click the **ScreenTip** button. In the Set Hyperlink ScreenTip dialog box, under ScreenTip text, type `Home Energy Tips` Click **OK** two times to close the dialog boxes.

4. Point to the new hyperlink to display the ScreenTip you typed and the directions to activate the hyperlink.

5. In the preceding paragraph, in the third line, click to the right of *Burton* and type `(jburton@greenae.com)` Select the text inside the parentheses—do not select the parentheses. Right-click the selected text, and then click **Hyperlink.**

6. Under Link to, click **E-mail Address.** In the *E-mail address* box, type `jburton@greenae.com` In the *Text to display* box, delete *mailto:*

7. Click the **ScreenTip** button. In the Set Hyperlink ScreenTip dialog box, under ScreenTip text, type `Contact Jan Burton` and then click **OK** two times to close the dialog boxes. **Save** your changes.

8. Display the Save As dialog box. Click the **Save as type** arrow, and from the list, click **Single File Web Page.**

9. Click the **Change Title** button. In the Set Page Title dialog box, under Page title, type `GAE Employee News` and then click **OK.** In the Save As dialog box, click **Save.**

10. In the Microsoft Office Word Compatibility Checker dialog box, notice that the underline, small caps, and engraved formatting will be lost. The color will be changed to gray for the engraved title fonts. Click **Continue.**

11. Close the document. In the taskbar, click the **Computer** window button. If necessary, navigate to your Chapter04 folder. Double-click the **U2Ch04EmployeeNewsStudentName** MHTML Document.

12. Close the browser and submit your files as directed.

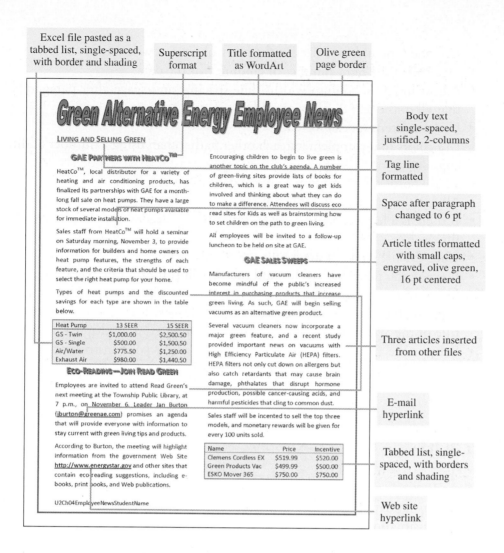

Excel file pasted as a tabbed list, single-spaced, with border and shading

Superscript format

Title formatted as WordArt

Olive green page border

Body text single-spaced, justified, 2-columns

Tag line formatted

Space after paragraph changed to 6 pt

Article titles formatted with small caps, engraved, olive green, 16 pt centered

Three articles inserted from other files

E-mail hyperlink

Tabbed list, single-spaced, with borders and shading

Web site hyperlink

FIGURE 4.36

fix *it*

One way to appreciate the value of good design is to fix a file that is not designed well. In this exercise, you open a file that has several errors and design flaws and fix it according to good design elements, using the skills that you practiced in the lessons.

Navigate to the folder with the student files, open **U2Ch04FixIt,** and save it as U2Ch04FixItStudentName

Examine this document and format it using the skills you have practiced so that it is a professional, readable newsletter that will attract attention and create interest. Insert the three files that are listed in the document, in the order indicated, and delete the instruction text. Make changes to comply with the appropriate good design principles that were introduced in this chapter. Here is a list of corrections needed and the design principles introduced in this chapter, along with some tips on how to fix the newsletter. Not all of the good design principles are necessarily appropriate to the content.

- Use one font and font size for the body of your newsletter.
- Determine the right number of columns for the data.
- Adjust margins, column widths, line spacing, and space after paragraphs so that all of the text displays on one page.
- Use consistent special formats.
- Use colors that complement each other, rather than using a number of different colors.
- Apply borders and shading to make data stand out.
- Align titles and data in tabbed lists.
- If there is a large gap, use a dot or other type of leader to draw the eye across the page.
- Place the file name in the footer.
- Preview the newsletter to be sure that it will print on one page. Save it as a .docx file.
- Save the file as a PDF file and as a Web file—with *Luna Vista Views* as the title of the Web page—so that it can be distributed in multiple formats.
- Submit the three files you create as required by your instructor. Save and close the file.

ON THE JOB

Information workers add value to data by organizing, selecting, displaying, communicating, interpreting, and using data to communicate information and support decisions. On the Job exercises simulate a situation where you are given data, and your job is to add value to it using the skills you practiced in this chapter. Success in these exercises indicates that you have a valuable skill to offer an employer.

1. Community Medical Group Newsletter

In this On the Job exercise, the marketing director of Community Medical Group needs your help assembling the weekly newsletter. Refer to the note from the marketing director, and then, using the skills you have practiced in this chapter, organize the information into a one-page newsletter.

Leticia,

This week's newsletter focuses on our efforts to "go green." We have received articles about biking to work (U2Ch04CMG1), paper recycling (U2Ch04CMG2), and E85 gasoline stations (U2Ch04CMG3). We have also received a list of E85 stations in the area from Jerry in an Excel spreadsheet (U2Ch04CMG4). Be sure to include that data with the related article. Contact HR and find out who bikes to work regularly, and include some specific recognition for those individuals. While you are at it, create a template so we don't have to keep creating a new newsletter from scratch each week. Use our corporate colors.

Alex

1. Open the file **U2Ch04CMG** and save it in your Chapter04 folder as U2Ch04CMGStudentName

2. Under the newsletter title, type: This month's *Headliner* has gone green. In this issue, you'll find features on employees who bike to work, E85 gas stations, and the new paper recycling program.

3. Select the words *gone green*. Change the font to Standard Green, Bold, and apply the All caps font effect.

4. Insert the three Word documents listed in the note from Alex.

5. Open the Excel file and copy the data. Just above the last paragraph, in the article about E85 gasoline, use Paste Special to paste this data as unformatted text.

6. Format all of the inserted text as two columns, and select the Line Between check box. Justify the text.

7. Select one of the article titles and open the Font dialog box. Select Copperplate Gothic Bold, 16-point font. Change the font color to Purple, Accent 4, Darker 25%, and add the underline that is second from the bottom of the list. Center the title. Apply this font to the other two article titles.

8. In the *E85* article title, insert a manual line break after the word *Only*.

9. Between the last two paragraphs in the article about biking to work, enter a tabbed list of the following information that was obtained from HR about the people who bike to work the most:

Troy Alcantar   401.3
Kunika Onodera   378.2
Anabel Serrano   285.1

10. For this list of data, set a decimal tab at the 3-inch mark and use a dot leader between the name and the miles.

11. Format this tabbed list with a border that uses the Shadow setting, a 3/4-inch line, and Purple, Accent 4, Darker 25% as the line color. Add shading that is Purple, Accent 4, Lighter 60%.

12. Format the inserted Excel data as a tabbed list. For the title row, set a center tab at 1.5 inches and a right tab at 3.25 inches. For the four rows of data, set a center tab at 1.5 inches and a decimal tab at 3 inches, and use a dash as the leader style. Apply the same shading and borders as you applied to the tabbed list in column one.

13. Under the tabbed list in column one, locate the e-mail address for HR and change this to an e-mail hyperlink.

14. Add a page border that is Shadow style, 4 1/2 pt wide, and Purple, Accent 4, Darker 25% as color.

15. Add the file name in the footer. Save the file. Compare your results with Figure 4.37. Save the file as a template file named U2Ch04CMGTemplateStudentName and as a Web page file with *CMG Headliner* as the Web title.

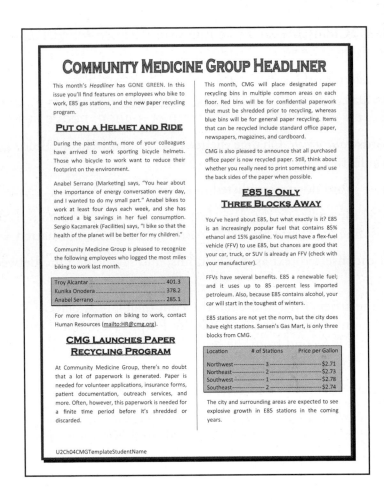

COMMUNITY MEDICINE GROUP HEADLINER

This month's *Headliner* has GONE GREEN. In this issue you'll find features on employees who bike to work, E85 gas stations, and the new paper recycling program.

PUT ON A HELMET AND RIDE

During the past months, more of your colleagues have arrived to work sporting bicycle helmets. Those who bicycle to work want to reduce their footprint on the environment.

Anabel Serrano (Marketing) says, "You hear about the importance of energy conversation every day, and I wanted to do my small part." Anabel bikes to work at least four days each week, and she has noticed a big savings in her fuel consumption. Sergio Kaczmarek (Facilities) says, "I bike so that the health of the planet will be better for my children."

Community Medicine Group is pleased to recognize the following employees who logged the most miles biking to work last month.

Troy Alcantar	401.3
Kunika Onodera	378.2
Anabel Serrano	285.1

For more information on biking to work, contact Human Resources (mailto:HR@cmg.org).

CMG LAUNCHES PAPER RECYCLING PROGRAM

At Community Medicine Group, there's no doubt that a lot of paperwork is generated. Paper is needed for volunteer applications, insurance forms, patient documentation, outreach services, and more. Often, however, this paperwork is needed for a finite time period before it's shredded or discarded.

This month, CMG will place designated paper recycling bins in multiple common areas on each floor. Red bins will be for confidential paperwork that must be shredded prior to recycling, whereas blue bins will be for general paper recycling. Items that can be recycled include standard office paper, newspapers, magazines, and cardboard.

CMG is also pleased to announce that all purchased office paper is now recycled paper. Still, think about whether you really need to print something and use the back sides of the paper when possible.

E85 IS ONLY THREE BLOCKS AWAY

You've heard about E85, but what exactly is it? E85 is an increasingly popular fuel that contains 85% ethanol and 15% gasoline. You must have a flex-fuel vehicle (FFV) to use E85, but chances are good that your car, truck, or SUV is already an FFV (check with your manufacturer).

FFVs have several benefits. E85 a renewable fuel; and it uses up to 85 percent less imported petroleum. Also, because E85 contains alcohol, your car will start in the toughest of winters.

E85 stations are not yet the norm, but the city does have eight stations. Sansen's Gas Mart, is only three blocks from CMG.

Location	# of Stations	Price per Gallon
Northwest	3	$2.71
Northeast	2	$2.73
Southwest	1	$2.78
Southeast	2	$2.74

The city and surrounding areas are expected to see explosive growth in E85 stations in the coming years.

U2Ch04CMGTemplateStudentName

FIGURE 4.37

2. Liestal Marquis Hotel Group Newsletter

Your boss has just been made editor of the company newsletter and has asked you to assemble and format the information. She has edited four articles and given you a list of instructions for the overall format. Save your file as U2Ch04LiestalStudentName

Marlene,

I need you to create the Liestal Marquis Hotel Group Happenings newsletter. Attached are four articles and some spreadsheet data to include in this month's newsletter. The files are in the usual location and labeled U2Ch04Liestal1, U2Ch04Liestal2, U2Ch04Liestal3, and U2Ch04Liestal4. This should fit on a page-and-a-half so that there is room for a mailing label on the second page. I have listed formatting particulars below. Let me know if you have any questions.

Jeanne

1. In a new document, create a WordArt title with WordArt style 7 and using the title noted above. Use a fill color of Dark Blue, Text 2, Darker 25% and a shadow color of White, Background 1, Darker 25%. (Use the Shadow Effects button and click Shadow Color.)

2. Under the newsletter title, type: `Welcome Aboard, Jeanne!` and on the next line type: `This month's` *Happenings* `is pleased to introduce its new editor-in-chief—Jeanne Laforest.` Be sure to insert an em dash as shown.

3. Insert the three articles in the order listed above, and then save the file as `U2Ch04LiestalStudentName`

4. Format all of the text—except the newsletter title—as two columns, with a line between the columns and the text justified.

5. Format the five titles using small caps, 16-point bold font, with the same blue color that was applied to the newsletter title. Center the titles, and in the article title for the last article, insert a manual break to balance the title on two lines.

6. Copy the data from the U2Ch04Liestal5 workbook and paste it in the Water Conservation article, just before the last paragraph. Set the tabs so that the data is evenly spaced and balanced under the titles.

7. Format this data with the White, Background 1, Darker 15% shading and a 1-point Dark Blue, Text 2, Darker 25% border. Bold the column titles, and add a bottom border under the titles.

8. At the end of the Going Green article, add the following award table. Set tabs so that the data is balanced under the headings, and use dot leaders so it is easier to read.

```
Votes    Dollar Award    LMHG Nights
1-3      $500            2
4-5      $750            3
7-8      $1000           4
9-10     $2000           6
```

9. Format this data the same as the other tabbed list.

10. Under the tabbed list at the end of the newsletter, type `Thank you for all that you do!` This should be left aligned so that it doesn't look odd.

11. On the second page, insert a column break just before the paragraph that begins *Effective immediately* to balance the column on this page.

12. Find the EnergyStar reference and change it to a hyperlink to the www.energystar.gov website. Use `Light Bulb Ratings` as the ScreenTip.

13. In the article about *Sensors*, locate the word *degrees*, replace it with the degree symbol, and add `F` for Fahrenheit—10°F.

14. Add a page border using a 2.25-point Dark Blue, Text 2, Darker 25% border.

15. Add the file name to the footer. Save the file.

16. Save the file as a PDF file, as a Word template named `U2Ch04LiestalTempStudentName` and as a Web page with `LMHG Happenings` as the title that will display on the browser title bar.

17. Submit your files as directed by your instructor.

Page 1 (upper document)

sensor activates the temperature set-back function on the in-room air conditioning unit. The temperature set-back will be 10 F, but will vary depending on the time of year, time of day, and the overall occupancy of the hotel.

The sensors will provide substantial energy savings both for LMHG and the environment.

GOING GREEN ISN'T WITHOUT GROWING PAINS

In this issue, we've covered several initiatives undertaken by LMHG to improve the environment. But the effect isn't limited just to the environment; it affects you, too!

LMHG recognizes that recent changes affect the way you do your jobs and your work environment. You're working harder and smarter, and we want to reward you.

Effective immediately, nomination boxes will be provided in all departments for both managers and staff to nominate those who have gone above and beyond. One winner will be drawn monthly from each department, and then management will vote on a grand-prize winner. Prizes will be chosen based on the number of votes received, and recipients can choose from a cash reward or free nights in any LMHG suite, as shown in the following chart.

Votes	Dollar Award	LMHG Nights
1-3	$500	2
4-5	$750	3
7-8	$1000	4
9-10	$2000	6

Thank you for all that you do!

Page 2 (lower document)

Liestal Marquis Hotel Group Happenings

WELCOME ABOARD, JEANNE!

This month's *Happenings* is pleased to introduce its new editor-in-chief—Jeanne Laforest.

WATER CONSERVATION PROGRAMS

This quarter LMHG launches a new water conservation effort for all of its U.S.-based laundry services departments. July sees changes on the west coast, August brings changes out east, and September tackles the Midwest.

To begin, state-of-the-art energy efficient laundry system that filter and reuse water using ozone water technology will be installed as older units require repair and replacement. Further, all washing machines will be set a minimum of two degrees lower, and only full loads will be washed.

During the first quarter, LMHG initiated its water conservation program in grounds maintenance, and the second quarter saw a 27% decrease in overall water use. The following chart shows the actual savings in each region.

Region	Q1 Decrease	Q2 Decrease
West coast	8.3%	11.2%
Midwest	6.7%	7.1%
East coast	7.0%	8.7%

Given the success of the grounds program, the laundry program is expected to flourish also.

LAMPS ARE NOW ENERGY EFFICIENT

LMHG recently began replacing broken and worn-out incandescent light bulbs with energy-efficient CFLs (compact fluorescent light bulbs), as recommended by the U.S. Environmental Protection Agency. Bulbs with the agency's ENERGY STAR rating use up to 75 percent less energy and last up to 10 times longer.

The new CFLs can be found in guest rooms and in all general hotel lighting, including hallways, service areas such as the kitchen and laundry areas, and grounds lighting. Neither guests nor staff should notice a discernable difference in lighting quality.

Because CFLs contain mercury, LMHG will also implement safety guidelines for handling bulbs and changing broken bulbs. Always screw and unscrew bulbs from the base, not the glass, to prevent breakage. If a bulb breaks, follow posted guidelines for cleanup, which differ for hard surfaces, such as tile, and soft surfaces, such as carpet.

SENSORS TURN DOWN THE TEMP

On any given day, room vacancies at LMHG hotels and resorts are inevitable despite the best efforts of all staff. While this means reduced water usage both in individual rooms and laundry services, it doesn't necessarily equate to reduced energy consumption—until now that is.

Starting in March of next year, all rooms will be equipped with ceiling-mounted occupancy sensors. These sensors are a combination of a door-switch and room motion sensor that will detect the presence of guests and LMHG staff. When the sensor detects that the room has been unoccupied for at least four hours, the

FIGURE 4.38

DISCUSSION OF ADVANCED SKILLS OR CONCEPTS

The questions in this section are based on the topics in the Advanced Skills or Concepts section of the chapter.

1. Describe a circumstance when you were unable to open a file. What steps did you take to resolve the problem?

2. If you have a file that cannot open on your computer, based on the Advanced Skills and Concepts section, what steps should you take to try and resolve the problem?

3. Have you opened files created with a newer version of the software using compatibility mode? Describe your experience.

4. Do you have Office 2007 or 2003? Have you worked with files that were created in one version of the software and tried to open them with a different version? What happened? Have you downloaded the compatibility package for Office 2007?

5. What is the purpose of a file extension? What happens when the file extensions are displayed and you rename a file in the Computer window without including the file extension?

6. What does *backwardly compatible* mean?

7. What are some examples of encoding standards that are used with computer programs? What are the differences, and why would one standard be used over another?

8. How can a file become corrupted? What steps should you take to be sure that you do not lose your files?

ON YOUR OWN

Once you are comfortable with the skills in this chapter, you can apply them to new situations of your own choosing. In this section, you choose data that you have in your possession or that you can find elsewhere. To successfully complete this assignment, you must apply good design practices and demonstrate mastery of the skills that were practiced. Refer to the list of skills and design practices in the Fix It exercise.

1. Create an Improved Health Practices Newsletter

Newsletters are used by many organizations to keep members informed of upcoming events, encourage desirable behavior, reinforce company values, and create a sense of community.

1. Do some research on the Internet related to healthy practices in the workplace. Write three brief articles (100 to 150 words) that would be suitable for a newsletter related to healthy workplace practices. Include references to your Web sources.

2. Open a new document and save it as U2Ch04HealthNewsStudentName

3. Create a title for the newsletter using WordArt.

4. Insert the articles you have written in a two-column format. Include an appropriate title for each article.

5. Include at least one tabbed list.

6. Format the titles, text, list, and newsletter using the skills and design practices that you have practiced in this chapter.

7. Format your Web references as hyperlinks.

8. Apply borders and shading to an area of your newsletter to make it stand out.

9. Add the file name in the footer. Save your file as U2Ch04HealthNewsStudentName in the form indicated by your instructor, and submit the file as directed.

2. Conservation on Campus

The formatting techniques used in this chapter are used in other types of documents, such as articles published in a magazine or newspaper. Demonstrate your mastery of the skills by writing an article for the student newspaper about campus conservation.

1. Write a one-page article for submission to the student newspaper about campus conservation. The article could be about conservation that is practiced on campus or have suggestions for ways to improve campus conservation.

2. Format the article in two columns.

3. Include two to three subtitles, and apply a consistent format for the titles that demonstrates your ability to apply special font effects.

4. Include a tabbed list of data, and apply borders and shading to the list.

5. Include a hyperlink to related information on your school's website or to sites with related topics.

6. Add the file name in the footer. Save your file as U2Ch04CampusStudentName and submit the file as directed by your instructor.

ASSESS YOUR PROGRESS

At this point, you should have a set of skills and design concepts that are valuable to an employer and to you. You may not realize how much you have learned unless you take a few minutes to assess your progress.

1. From the student files, open **U2Ch04Assess.** Save it as U2Ch04AssessStudentName

2. Read each question in column A.

3. In column B, answer Yes or No.

4. If you identify a skill or design concept that you don't know, refer to the learning objective code next to the question and the table at the beginning of the chapter to find the skill and review it.

5. Print the worksheet if your instructor requires it. The file name is already in the header, so it will display your name as part of the file name.

6. All of these skills and concepts have been identified as important by surveying hundreds of individuals working at over 200 companies worldwide. If you cannot answer all of the questions affirmatively even after reviewing the relevant lesson, seek additional help from your instructor.

chapter five

Working with Collaborative Tools

Lesson	Learning Outcomes	Code	Related IC3 Objectives
1	Read comments	5.01	2.2.3
1	Use Word options to personalize Word	5.02	1.1.7
1	Display comments and changes in balloons	5.03	2.2.3
1	Insert a comment into a document	5.04	2.2.3
1	Edit a comment	5.05	2.2.3
2	Track changes in a document	5.06	2.2.3
3	Accept or reject tracked changes	5.07	2.2.3
3	Delete comments	5.08	2.2.3
4	Create a mail merge main document	5.09	
5	Open a data source for mail merge	5.10	
5	Sort the data in a data source	5.11	
5	Insert a mail merge address block	5.12	
5	Insert a mail merge field	5.13	
5	Insert a date field	5.14	
6	Merge a data source and a main document	5.15	
6	Preview a merged document	5.16	
6	Create a single document with merged documents	5.17	
7	Use the Mail Merge Wizard to create mailing labels	5.18	
Advanced	Use AutoRecover to recover files	5.19	1.2.6
Advanced	Change the frequency of the AutoRecover feature	5.20	1.1.7
Advanced	Describe the methods used to protect a document from unauthorized use	5.21	2.2.4
Advanced	Describe how to print envelopes using mail merge	5.22	
Advanced	Print an envelope	5.23	

Instructions throughout the lessons are based on the Vista operating system, running Microsoft Office 2007.

Why **Would I Do This?**

As you write, you may need to consult with other people in your department or organization. Collaboration tools enable you to easily gather input from various sources. The Track Changes feature in Word provides a visual indication of deletions, insertions, and formatting changes in a document. If the document is edited by more than one person, the changes are displayed in a different color for each reviewer. After the document has been reviewed by the appropriate individuals, the author can locate the changes and accept or reject the edits. Each person reviewing the document can also add comments that will not print when the document is printed. These comments can be used to identify potential problems in the document, to question a fact, or to suggest changes.

When a document is completed, you will often want to send it to several people. You can create a personalized cover letter that is merged with a data source of names and addresses. You can also use the data source to create mailing labels.

In this chapter, you work with the Track Changes feature to record and review changes and comments. You also create a mail merge main document and merge the main document with a data source. Your documents will look similar to those in Figure 5.1.

visual summary

In this chapter, you will work with comments and track the changes made in a request for proposal (RFP) document related to an electric vehicle initiative. You will also use a data source to merge data with a main document and use a wizard to create mailing labels to send the letter to potential bidders for this RFP. The documents created are shown in Figure 5.1 A, B, C, D.

Comments and Tracked Changes

Bidding Procedure

All contractors will need to submit an official proposal to the Chamber. The following information is required as part of this proposal:

- Complete contact information and brief company history
- Explanation of why contractor wants to participate in the "Electric Vehicle Corridor" program
- Advantages contractor brings to the project
- Detailed description of the work to be performed
- Detailed analysis of costs, including a breakdown of labor and supplies
- Minimum and maximum costs for the project
- Timeline for completion[MH4]

Contractor E

All contractors should have <u>a minimum </u>of five years experience in electric vehicle charging station install current references[SNS]. Finally, all contractors must be

Submission Proced

Written proposals should be submitted to Meghan Le Patriot Dr., Merrill, OR, 97633 or mlesbaum@merrillc the Web at www.merrillchamber.gov/EVparking.

All bids submitted via postal mail must be postmarked submitted via the Web must be submitted by midnight

---

Request for Proposal

Project Overview

The Merrill ~~Chamber of Commerce~~<u>COC</u> is committed to finding innovative ways to support the city's ~~"Electric Vehicle Corridor"~~ initiative, which was ~~actually~~ launched earlier this year. As part of this initiative, the Chamber is currently in search of a contractor to wire its parking lot for 5 to 20[MH1] electric vehicles. Details of the project and directions for proposal submissions are listed below. The Chamber is an equal opportunity employer and welcomes all submissions that meet the ~~guidelines~~ <u>objectives </u>described in this document.

Project Details

As described, the Chamber is looking to equip its parking lot with wiring to support 5 to 20[MH2] electric vehicles. As part of this project, the contractor ~~would~~ <u>will </u>need to resize the existing parking spaces to accommodate cars, trucks, sport utility vehicles, and at least three handicap-accessible electric vehicles. The contractor ~~would~~ <u>will </u>also need to rework existing parking lot lighting to accommodate the electric vehicle spaces, including additional lighting for the recharging units. The current timeline for project completion is July 11, 2011[DDD3].

Site Tour

The Chamber will host a site tour at 8:00 a.m. on Tuesday, March 8, 2011. At this time the Chamber will provide a more detailed overview of project needs, provide an onsite tour, and <u>clarify </u>any questions. For contractors who are interested in bidding on the project but are unable to attend the official site tour, a separate tour can be arranged by calling Meghan Lesbaum at (541) 555-3500 prior to March 8.

FIGURE 5.1A

Comments and Tracked Changes Resolved

Bidding Procedure

All contractors will need to submit an official proposal to the Chamber. The following information is required as part of this proposal:

- Complete contact information and brief company history
- Explanation of why contractor wants to participate in the "Electric Vehicle Corridor" program
- Advantages contractor brings to the project
- Detailed description of the work to be performed
- Detailed analysis of costs, including a bre
- Minimum and maximum costs for the pro
- Timeline for completion

Any proposals that do not include all of the prece

Contract

All contractors should have a minimum of five ye
experience in electric vehicle charging station ins
current references. Finally, all contractors must b

Submission Pro

Written proposals should be submitted to Megha
Patriot Dr., Merrill, OR, 97633 or mlesbaum@me
the Web at www.merillchamber.gov/EVparking.

All bids submitted via postal mail must be postma
submitted via the Web must be submitted by mid

U2Ch05EVRevisedStudentName

Request for Proposal

Project Overview

The Merrill Chamber of Commerce is committed to finding innovative ways to support the city's *Electric Vehicle Corridor* initiative, which was launched earlier this year. As part of this initiative, the Chamber is currently in search of a contractor to wire its parking lot for ten electric vehicles. Details of the project and directions for proposal submissions are listed below. The Chamber is an equal opportunity employer and welcomes all submissions that meet the objectives described in this document.

Project Details

As described, the Chamber is looking to equip its parking lot with wiring to support ten electric vehicles. As part of this project, the contractor will need to resize the existing parking spaces to accommodate cars, trucks, sport utility vehicles, and at least three handicap-accessible electric vehicles. The contractor will also need to rework existing parking lot lighting to accommodate the electric vehicle spaces, including additional lighting for the recharging units. The current timeline for project completion is July 11, 2011.

Site Tour

The Chamber will host a site tour at 8:00 a.m. on Tuesday, March 8, 2011. At this time the Chamber will provide a more detailed overview of project needs, provide an onsite tour, and clarify any questions. For contractors who are interested in bidding on the project but are unable to attend the official site tour, a separate tour can be arranged by calling Meghan Lesbaum at (541) 555-3500 prior to March 8.

U2Ch05EVRevisedStudentName

FIGURE 5.1B

Merged Letter

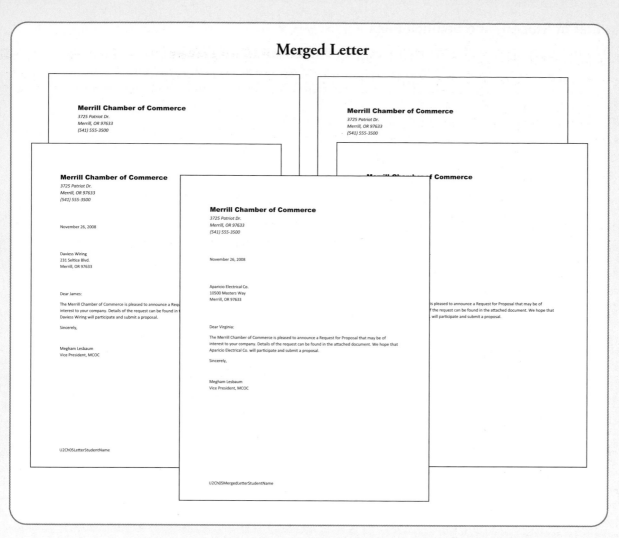

FIGURE 5.1C

Merged Labels

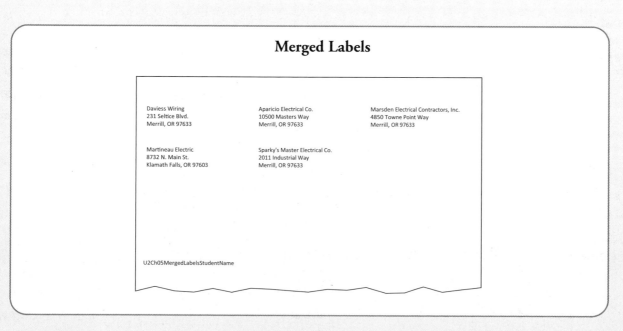

FIGURE 5.1D

List of Student and Solution Files

In most cases, you will start with a new file and enter text and data or import content from other files. You will add your name to the file names and save them on your computer or portable memory device. Table 5.1 lists the files you start with and the names you give them when you save the files.

ASSIGNMENT	STUDENT SOURCE FILE:	SAVE AS:
Lessons 1–7	New document U2Ch05EV U2Ch05Contractors	U2Ch05EVStudentName U2Ch05EVRevisedStudentName U2Ch05LetterStudentName U2Ch05MergedLetterStudentName U2Ch05MergedLabelsStudentName
Skill Drill	New document U2Ch05LEED U2Ch05Library	U2Ch05LEEDStudentName U2Ch05LEEDRevisedStudentName U2Ch05LibraryStudentName U2Ch05LibraryMergedStudentName U2Ch05LibraryLabelsStudentName
Fix It	U2Ch05FixIt	U2Ch05FixItStudentName
On the Job	New document U2Ch05Green U2Ch05Directors U2Ch05LadogaHills	U2Ch05GreenStudentName U2Ch05GreenRevisedStudentName U2Ch05DirectorLetterStudentName U2Ch05DirectorMergedStudentName U2Ch05DirectorLabelsStudentName
	New document U2Ch05Memo U2Ch05Departments	U2Ch05MemoStudentName U2Ch05MemoRevisedStudentName U2Ch05DeptLabelsStudentName
On Your Own	New documents	U2Ch05ReunionStudentName U2Ch05ReunionRevisedStudentName U2Ch05ReunionReviewedStudentName U2Ch05AddressesStudentName U2Ch05AddressLabelsStudentName U2Ch05CollaborationStudentName
Assess Your Progress	U2Ch05Assess	U2Ch05AssessStudentName

TABLE 5.1

▶▶▶ *lesson*
one | Inserting Comments into a Document

A ***comment*** is a note that an author or reviewer adds to a document. Word displays the comment either in a balloon-shaped graphic in the margin of the document or in a reviewing pane at the bottom or side of the document. Comments are a good way to communicate when more than one person is involved in the editing process or when you want to leave yourself notes for future actions.

to read comments from reviewers

1 **Start Word, and then if necessary display the formatting marks.** A new document named Document1 displays in the Word window.

2 **Click the Office button 🔵, and then click Open. Navigate to the location where you store your student files, click U2Ch05EV, and then click Open.** The document will open with several tracked changes marked and several comments displayed, as shown in Figure 5.2. The configuration and layout of these changes and comments on your screen may be different from what you see in the figure. The settings will be changed in this lesson.

Changes to Comments (yours may Initials of person
the document display in balloons) making the comment

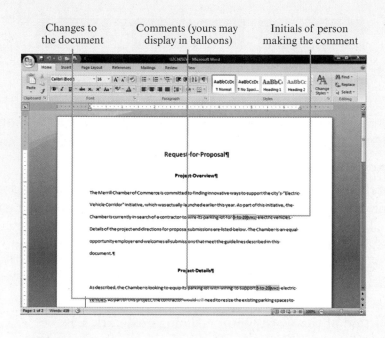

FIGURE 5.2

3 **Click the Office button 🔵, and then click Save As. In the Save As dialog box, navigate to the location where you are saving your files, and then click the New Folder button. Name the folder** Chapter05 **and then in the File name box, type** U2Ch05EVStudentName **and click Save.**

4 **Click the Office button 🔵, and then click Word Options. In the left pane, be sure Popular is selected.** This page of the Word Options dialog box provides options such as displaying the Mini toolbar, Live Preview, and ScreenTips.

5 **Under *Personalize your copy of Microsoft Office*, in the User name box, type your name, and then in the Initials box, type your initials.** Compare your screen with Figure 5.3. It is important to add your name and initials because any comments that you add or changes that you make will be identified with you. If your name and initials already display, you do not need to retype them.

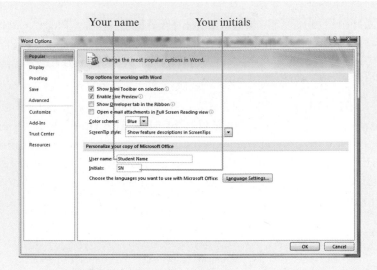

Your name   Your initials

FIGURE 5.3

---

good **design...**

IDENTIFY YOURSELF

It is important that you are associated with any comments or changes you make to a document. If you are using someone else's computer, change the user name and initials before making changes or adding comments to a document. If the author has questions or wants to respond to suggestions, he or she needs to be able to identify the name of each reviewer.

---

6   **At the bottom of the Word Options dialog box, click OK.**

7   **Click the Review tab. In the Tracking group, click the Balloons button, and then click Show Revisions in Balloons.** This option will display all comments and most changes in balloons in the margin, with the exception of insertions, which will be marked with a different color and underlined. A vertical line in the margin to the left of the change also shows where a change has been made.

to extend **your knowledge**

LOCATION OF BALLOONS ON THE SCREEN

The balloons may display on the left or right on your screen, depending on the last setting used for this feature. To change the location of the balloons, on the Review tab, in the Tracking group, click the Track Changes button, and then click Change Tracking Options. In the Track Changes Options dialog box, under Use Balloons, change the setting in the Margin box.

8 **On the Review tab, in the Comments group, click the Next button. Move the pointer over the highlighted area in the document.** The first comment in the document is highlighted, and a ScreenTip displays the name of the person who made the comment, the date and time the comment was made, and the comment text, as shown in Figure 5.4.

Name of person making the comment

Date and time of the comment

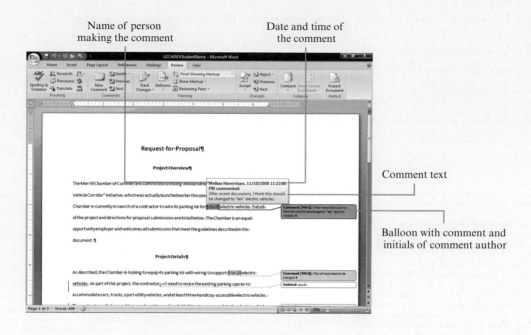

Comment text

Balloon with comment and initials of comment author

FIGURE 5.4

9 **In the Comments group, click the Next button to view the final three comments.** Notice that comments by different people are displayed using different colors.

to extend **your knowledge**

OTHER OPTIONS

There is another way to display the Word Options dialog box so that you can change the user name and initials. On the Review tab, in the Tracking group, click the Track Changes button arrow, and then click Change User Name. This will display the Word Options dialog box.

You can add comments to a document at any time. When you add a comment, it displays in the balloons or in a ***Reviewing pane*** at the bottom or side of your screen, depending on how you have set up your tracking options.

to add comments to a document

1 **Press** Ctrl **+** End **to move to the end of the document.**

2 **In the paragraph that begins *All Contractors*, select the last word in the paragraph:** *licensed.* You can insert a comment with selected text or at the insertion point location.

3 **In the Comments group, click the New Comment button.** A balloon displays in a different color in the balloon area, and your initials and the comment number display. The comments are numbered sequentially regardless of the person making the comment.

4 **Type** Should the contractor also be bonded? Compare your screen with Figure 5.5.

Your initials and
comment number

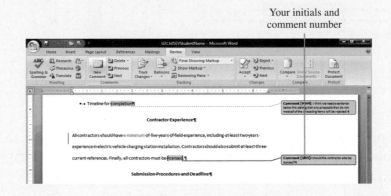

FIGURE 5.5

5 **In the same paragraph, select *three current references*. In the Comments group, click the New Comment button. Add the comment** Should we specify the type of references? Notice that this comment number is 5 and that the previous one you wrote changes to comment number 6 because it comes after the comment you just typed.

6 **Scroll to the middle of Page 2. Locate the comment labeled *MH4* and click in the balloon at the end of the comment.**

7 **Press** ⏎Enter **two times, and then type** `I agree.` **and type your name.** You can respond to other comments, but your name will not display. You need to add your name if you append a comment to another comment instead of adding a new comment. Compare your screen with Figure 5.6.

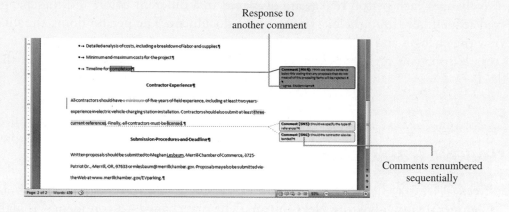

Response to another comment

Comments renumbered sequentially

FIGURE 5.6

8 **Save** 💾 **your document.**

to extend **your knowledge**

ANOTHER WAY TO RESPOND TO COMMENTS

Rather than clicking in a comment to make a response, you can click the comment and then click the New Comment button. A new comment balloon displays below the comment you selected and shows a reply number that matches the original comment; for example, SN5R4, indicating that it is a reply to the fourth comment. If you use this method, then your initials will display in the second comment that has been added and you will not need to type your name.

good **design...**

WRITE CLEAR AND CONCISE COMMENTS

Comments should be short and to the point. Be sure that your comments are helpful, kind, and unambiguous. The reviewer should know what action is needed without feeling insulted. Any criticism needs to be constructive, with a suggestion for how to improve the document. Look for opportunities to compliment the author.

▶▶▶ *lesson*

tWO | Tracking Changes in a Document

Track Changes is a feature that records changes and comments made to a document by others. Once this feature is activated, each change is identified by the name of the person making the change and the date and time the change was made. If more than one person edits a document, the changes each person makes are displayed in a different color, and the changes are numbered sequentially from the beginning of the document. The person doing the final edit can review the changes and accept or reject the changes that have been suggested.

In this lesson, you review the tracked changes and then make some changes that are tracked.

to review tracked changes

1 **Press** Ctrl **+** Home **to move to the top of the document. On the Review tab, in the Changes group, click the Next button.** The first change—a comment—is highlighted. The Next button in the Changes group moves to the next change—either an editing change or a comment. The Next button in the Comments group only stops on comments and does not move to the next editing change.

2 **In the Changes group, click the Next button two more times.** The deleted word *would* is selected and displays in the balloon on the right.

3 **In the Changes group, click the Next button again.** The word *will* is highlighted. In this change, the word *would* was selected and *will* was typed over it. When you replace a selected word or phrase with another word or phrase, two changes are made: a deletion and an insertion. See Figure 5.7. Notice that the inserted word displays in the text, the deleted word displays in a balloon, and a vertical line displays to the left of the the change to indicate that a change was made.

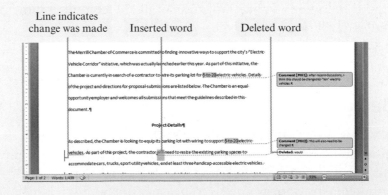

FIGURE 5.7

4 **Click the Next button several more times.** Notice that comments, insertions, deletions, and even manual page breaks are highlighted. When you reach the end, a message box displays, asking if you want to continue searching from the beginning.

5 **In the message box, click Cancel. Press** Ctrl + Home **to move back to the top of the document.**

To track the changes that you make to the document, you need to activate the Track Changes feature.

to create tracked changes

1 **On the Review tab, in the Tracking group, click the top half of the Track Changes button.** When the button turns orange, it means that the Track Changes feature is turned on.

· ·

good **design...**

TRACK CHANGES YOU MAKE

When you are asked to review a document, be sure that you turn on the Track Changes feature before you begin. If you make changes without doing this, the originator of the document will not be able to tell what changes have been made, unless he or she runs the document comparison feature. Tracked changes inform the author of the changes you have made, which avoids surprises.

· ·

2 **In the paragraph that begins** *The Merrill Chamber,* **select the text** *Chamber of Commerce.* **Type COC and move the pointer over your change.** Notice that the text you typed is inserted, the text you deleted displays in a balloon, and the ScreenTip displays your name, the current date, and the inserted text. Compare your screen with Figure 5.8.

Inserted text   Your name   Deleted text

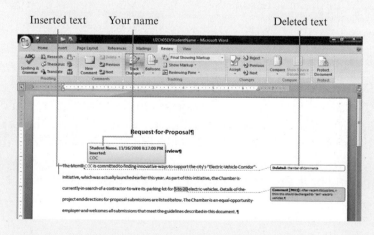

FIGURE 5.8

3 In the following line, select and delete the word *actually*. In the last line of the same paragraph, select the word *guidelines* and type `objectives`

4 In the first line of the same paragraph, delete the two quotation marks, and then select *Electric Vehicle Corridor*. From the Mini toolbar, click the Italic button *I*. Notice that the formatting change also displays in a balloon. Also notice that all of the lines of text changed with Track Changes turned on display a vertical line to the left of the change, as shown in Figure 5.9.

Vertical lines indicate tracked changes   Formatting change

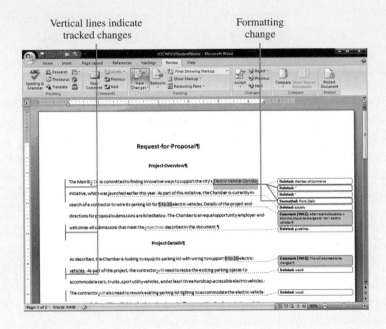

FIGURE 5.9

5 Press Ctrl + Home to deselect the text. Save your document. Submit the document as directed. You will submit this document in two ways: with the changes still marked, as you saved it here, and after the changes have been accepted or rejected, which is done in the next lesson.

good design...

BE CAREFUL NOT TO INTRODUCE ERRORS

When you make editing changes in a document, be careful that you do not introduce errors. Pay particular attention to spacing between words so that words do not run together. If necessary, change the Display for Review box from the default *Final Showing Markup* to *Final* so that you can detect errors such as words that run together or other spelling or grammar errors that you may have made.

▶▶▶ *lesson*
three | Responding to Comments and Document Changes

Once all of the changes are made to a document and all of the comments have been added, the document's final author responds to all of them. This involves accepting or rejecting changes and responding to and deleting comments. It is often a good idea to keep the marked-up document for future reference and work on a new version of the document.

In this lesson, you save the document using a different name, and then you respond to changes and comments in the document.

to respond to changes

1 Click the Office button ⊞, and then click **Save As**. Change the name of the file to `U2Ch05EVRevisedStudentName` **then navigate to your Chapter05 folder and click Save.**

2 On the Review tab, in the Tracking group, click the Balloons button, and then click **Show All Revisions Inline.**

3 In the Tracking group, click the Reviewing Pane button arrow, and then click **Reviewing Pane Vertical. If necessary, at the top of the Reviewing pane, click the Show Detailed Summary button** ⊻ . The balloons are removed and the changes are displayed in the document text. A Reviewing pane displays on the left side of the screen. The Reviewing pane gives more details about the changes, including a summary at the top of the pane, as shown in Figure 5.10.

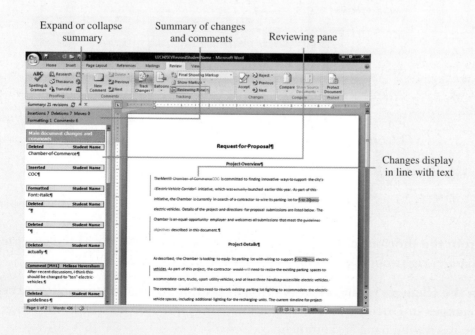

FIGURE 5.10

4 In the Tracking group, click the top half of the Track Changes button to turn off the Track Changes feature.

5 Press Ctrl + Home to move to the beginning of the document. In the Changes group, click the Next button. The first change—the deletion of the phrase *Chamber of Commerce*—is highlighted.

6 In the Changes group, click the Reject button. The change is rejected and the next change is highlighted. Recall that you highlighted *Chamber of Commerce* and replaced it with *COC*. This involved two steps: a deletion and an insertion.

7 In the Changes group, click the Reject button. The insertion is rejected and the next change is highlighted.

8 Triple-click to select the paragraph with the selected change. In the Changes group, click the Accept button. All of the changes in the selected paragraph are accepted. The comment in the paragraph is selected but not changed or removed.

9 In the paragraph that begins *As described*, in the second line, right-click the deleted word *would*. A shortcut menu displays, as shown in Figure 5.11.

Shortcut menu

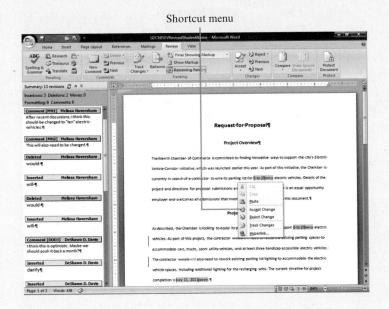

FIGURE 5.11

10 From the shortcut menu, click Accept Change. To the right of the accepted change, right-click *will*, and then click Accept Change.

11 In the Changes group, click the Accept button arrow, and then click Accept All Changes in Document. The rest of the changes are accepted. The only items left in the Reviewing pane are comments.

to extend your knowledge

HIDING TRACKED CHANGES IN A DOCUMENT

If you have a number of tracked changes and comments in a document, the document is often hard to read. You can view the document with the changes and comments hidden. To hide the changes and comments, on the Review tab, in the Tracking group, click the Display for Review button arrow—which will display *Final Showing Markup*—and then click Final. The changes will be shown as if they had been accepted.

You need to respond to each comment individually; there is no way to remove all of the comments at one time.

to respond to comments

1 **In the first paragraph that contains a comment, right-click the comment, and then click Delete Comment.** The comment is deleted. You can right-click either the comment noted in the text or the comment in the Reviewing pane.

2 **In the same paragraph, select the text that was highlighted for the comment: *5 to 20*. Type** ten **to replace the selected text, and then compare your screen with Figure 5.12.** The comment is deleted and the new text replaces the selected text.

New text

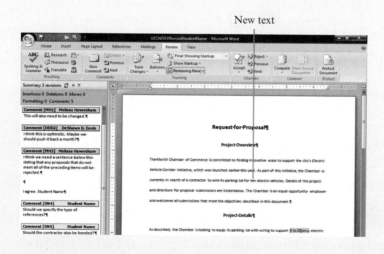

FIGURE 5.12

3 **In the paragraph that begins *As described*, repeat the procedure you practiced in Steps 1 and 2 to change the comment text *5 to 20* to** ten **and then delete the comment.**

4 In the Comments group, click the Next button to highlight the comment attached to *July 11, 2011*. In the Reviewing pane, right-click the top comment, which is now numbered 1 and is from DeShawn D. Davis. From the displayed list, click Delete Comment.

5 In the Comments group, click the Next button, which selects the comment from Melissa Haversham, attached to the word *completion*. Click to the right of the comment, and then press ⏎Enter. A new line with a bullet displays.

6 At the top of Page 2, click anywhere in the paragraph that begins *All contractors*. Click the Home tab. In the Clipboard group, click the Format Painter button 🖌.

7 Move the 🔲 pointer to the new blank bulleted paragraph and click one time. The bullet is removed, and the paragraph indent is removed so that this paragraph is formatted the same as the one preceding the bulleted list.

8 Type Any proposals that do not include all of the preceding items will be rejected. Compare your screen with Figure 5.13.

New paragraph   Comment not deleted

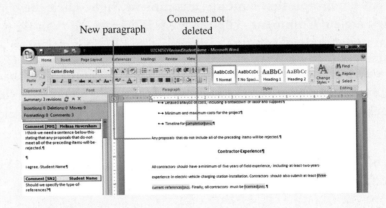

FIGURE 5.13

9 In the Reviewing pane, right-click each of the remaining three comments, and then click Delete Comment. All of the changes and comments are removed from the Reviewing pane.

10 Close ✕ the Reviewing pane.

11 Double-click in the footer area. On the Design tab, in the Insert group, click the Quick Parts button, and then click Field. Under *Field names*, scroll down and click FileName, and then click OK.

12 Save 💾 your changes and submit the document as directed. Click the Office button 🔘, click Close to close the file, but leave Word open.

▶▶▶ *lesson*

four | Creating a Main Document for Merging

If you have ever received a form letter with your name and some personal information in the text of the letter, you have received a letter that was created by merging a document with a data source. Customized letters are created using a merge feature that can also be used to create mailing labels, print envelopes, and customize e-mail messages.

Word's **mail merge** feature joins a main document and a data source to create customized letters, labels, or envelopes. The **main document** contains the text or formatting that remains constant. In the case of labels, the main document contains the formatting for a specific label size. The **data source** is a file that contains organized data that includes the names and addresses of the individuals for whom the labels are being created, along with any other necessary information.

to create a main document for mail merge

1 **Open a new document and display formatting marks.** Type `Merrill Chamber of Commerce` **and press** ⏎Enter. **Type the following, pressing** ⏎Enter **after each line:**

```
3725 Patriot Dr.
Merrill, OR 97633
(541) 555-3500
```

2 **Select the four paragraphs of text that you just typed, but do not include the blank paragraph mark on the line after the text. Click the Page Layout tab. In the Paragraph group, under Spacing, click the After down spin arrow two times or until the Spacing After displays 0.**

3 **Select the first line of text. On the Mini toolbar, click the Bold button** B. **Click the Font button arrow, and then click Arial Black. Click the Font Size button arrow, and then click 16.**

4 **Select the second through the fourth lines—the address and phone number—and from the Mini toolbar, click the Italic button** I. **Click the Font Size button arrow, and then click 12. Click anywhere in the document to deselect the text.** The new letterhead is formatted, as shown in Figure 5.14.

Letterhead
formatted

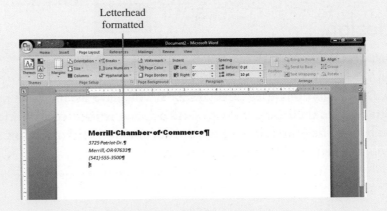

FIGURE 5.14

5 Press `Ctrl` + `End` and then press `⏎Enter` two times. Click the Insert tab. In the Text group, click the Date & Time button, and then click the December 15, 2010 format. Select the *Update automatically* check box and click OK. The Date field is added and will be updated to the current date whenever the document is opened. The date displayed on the letter will be the current date.

6 On the Quick Access toolbar, click the Save button 💾. In the Save As dialog box, navigate to your Chapter05 folder. In the File name box, type `U2Ch05LetterStudentName` and then click Save.

7 Add the FileName field to the footer, and then double-click in the body of the letter. Save 💾 your changes.

▶▶▶ *lesson*
five|Opening a Data Source and Inserting Fields into a Document

When you merge a letter with a mailing list, the names, addresses, and other information are stored in a separate data source file. The data source can be any organized group of data in a Word table, an Excel worksheet, an Access database table, or an Outlook contact list. In this lesson, you will use an Access database table. It does not matter if you have Access as one of the programs available on your computer; the mail merge feature will still be able to insert the necessary information from an Access file.

As you continue to create the main document, you insert the *field placeholders* for the data that will later be merged with the letter. The placeholders reserve spaces in the letter for the actual data that will be inserted when the letter is merged with the data source. To begin, you first attach the data source to the letter.

to open and sort a data source

1 **Click the Mailings tab. In the Start Mail Merge group, click the Start Mail Merge button.** Notice the different types of merge documents that you can create.

2 **Click the Start Mail Merge button again to close the menu. In the Start Mail Merge group, click the Select Recipients button, and then click Use Existing List. Navigate to the student folder for this chapter, click U2Ch05Contractors, and then click Open.** The list is attached to the document, although nothing displays on the screen. Before you can insert fields into a main document, you have to attach the letter to a source document.

3 **In the Start Mail Merge group, click the Edit Recipient List button.** The list of contractors displays in the Mail Merge Recipients dialog box, as shown in Figure 5.15. The data displays in columns, with the name of each *field* displayed at the top of the column. A field is a category of data that is organized and named, such as Address, City, or State. The field names indicate the type of data contained in the fields. You select the field names that you want to include in the mail merge process.

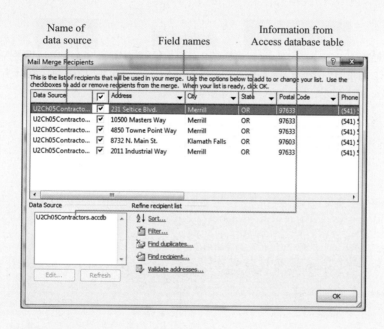

FIGURE 5.15

4 **In the Mail Merge Recipients dialog box, scroll to the right to display the Contractor Name field. In the Contractor Name column header, click the arrow, and then click Sort Ascending.** The column is sorted in ascending alphabetical order.

5 **At the bottom of the Mail Merge Recipients dialog box, click OK.**

6 **Save** 💾 **your document.**

to extend your knowledge

ADDING RECORDS OR EDITING THE DATA SOURCE

All of the information about an individual or company that is displayed in a single row of a data source is a *record.* There are two ways to edit data source information or add records to the data source. First, you can open the data source in its own application—Word, Excel, Access, or Outlook. You can also make these changes in the Mail Merge Recipients dialog box. In the Data Source box, click the data source file name. Near the bottom of the dialog box, click Edit. In the Edit Data Source dialog box, edit the data or click New Entry to add a record.

Once you have identified the data source and made any necessary changes, you can insert the fields from the data source into the main document. As you do so, you will enter the rest of the text for the letter.

to insert fields into the main document

1. **Click at the end of the date and then press** ⏎Enter **three times. In the Write & Insert Fields group, click the Address Block button.** The Insert Address Block dialog box displays. Notice that neither a company name nor a person's name appears in the Preview box, as shown in Figure 5.16. When the program cannot determine which field to use, you have to do it manually.

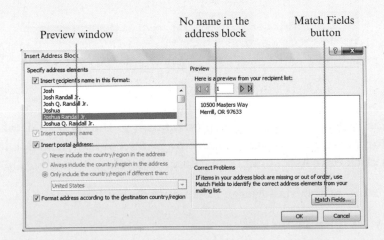

FIGURE 5.16

2 In the Insert Address Block dialog box, click the Match Fields button. Click the Company arrow, and then click Contractor Name. The Contractor Name field is now associated with the Company field for the Address Block, as shown in Figure 5.17. Notice that the Address, City, State, and Postal Code fields are already matched.

Company associated with
Contractor Name field

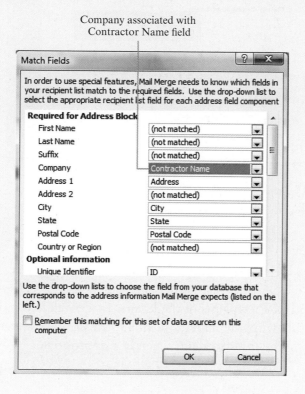

FIGURE 5.17

3 In the Match Fields dialog box, click OK. When prompted to confirm the match, click Yes. In the Preview box, notice that the company name is now part of the Address Block.

4 In the Insert Address Block dialog box, click OK. The address block field is added at the insertion point location, surrounded by chevrons: «AddressBlock».

5 Press ↵Enter two times, type Dear and then press Spacebar. In the Write & Insert Fields group, click the Insert Merge Field button arrow, and then compare your screen with Figure 5.18. Notice that all of the fields in the Access database table display. The field names in the database have spaces between the words, but the underscores are added by Word because field names in mail merge cannot contain spaces.

Address block   Underscores replace spaces in field names   Fields in Access database table

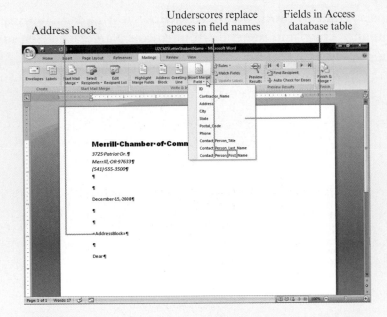

FIGURE 5.18

6   **In the Insert Merge Field menu, click the Contact_Person_First_Name field, and then type a colon** : A personal first name salutation is used because the sender is on a first-name basis with the recipients of the letters. In a block letter, the colon is preferred punctuation following the salutation. In a form letter, be sure to include the punctuation following the inserted fields when it is appropriate.

....

good **design...**

USE APPROPRIATE SALUTATIONS

For the salutation, consider who the recipients are. If you are on a friendly basis with the recipients, using a first name is acceptable. In most circumstances, however, it is preferable to use a formal salutation that includes a title such as Mr., Ms., or Dr. and the last name of the recipient rather than the first name. If a formal title is used, be sure that your data source includes punctuation with the title if it is appropriate. In those circumstances, it is important that the data source include a field for the title and that you include the title, a space, and then the last name field in the salutation.

....

7   **Press** ⏎Enter. **Type** The Merrill Chamber of Commerce is pleased to announce a Request for Proposal that may be of interest to your company. Details of the request can be found in the attached document. We hope that

8 Press ⟨Spacebar⟩ after the word *that*. In the Write & Insert Fields group, click the Insert Merge Field button, and then click Contractor_Name to insert the company name. Press ⟨Spacebar⟩ and type `will participate and submit a proposal.` Merge fields can be inserted in the middle of paragraphs, and word wrap will adjust the paragraph text. Be sure to include the necessary spacing around inserted fields.

9 Press ⟨←Enter⟩ and type `Sincerely,` Press ⟨←Enter⟩ two times and type `Meghan Lesbaum` Press ⟨←Enter⟩ and type `Vice President, MCOC` The body of the letter and the closing is added.

10 Select Megan Lesbaum. On the Page Layout tab, in the Paragraph group, click the Spacing After down spin arrow until 0 pt displays.

11 Move your pointer over the new Date field. Notice that the entire date is highlighted, indicating that the date is a field—a value that is inserted from another source—as shown in Figure 5.19. In this case, the current date is inserted from your computer's internal clock.

Highlight indicates a field   Inserted fields from the Access database table

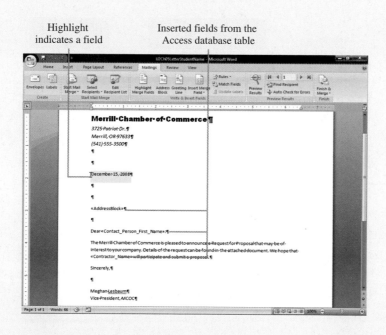

FIGURE 5.19

12 Save 💾 your changes.

· ·

good design...

INCLUDE SPACING AND PUNCTUATION

In a form letter, be sure to include punctuation following inserted fields when it is appropriate. Also be careful to include spacing before and after fields that are inserted into the middle of a sentence.

· ·

SIX | Merging a Document with a Data Source

When you add the merged fields from the data source into the main document, you need to preview the results, make any necessary modifications, and then either print the merged documents directly or perform a final merge to create a single document. Merging into a single document will enable you to go through the letters and add further personal notes, if necessary.

to merge a document with a data source

1 **Press Ctrl + Home to move to the top of the document.**

2 **On the Mailings tab, in the Preview Results group, click the Preview Results button.** The field placeholders are replaced with the data from the first record in the database table. The address block takes on the formatting of the existing paragraph, which includes 10-point spacing after each paragraph, as shown in Figure 5.20.

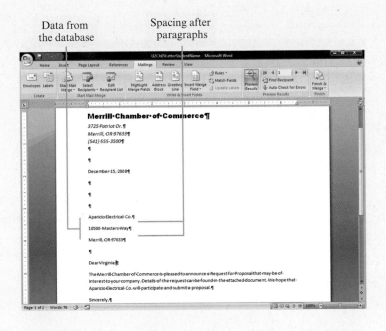

FIGURE 5.20

3 **On the Mailings tab, in the Preview Results group, click the Preview Results button.** The field placeholders display again.

4 **Select the address block, including the paragraph mark. Click the Page Layout tab. In the Paragraph group, click the Spacing After down spin button as necessary to remove the spacing after the selected paragraphs.**

5 **On the Mailings tab, in the Preview Results group, click the Preview Results button.** Notice that the spacing after the paragraph has been removed for all three lines of the address block.

6 In the Preview Results group, click the Next Record button ▶ four times. Letters to each of the five records in the database table are displayed, customized for each company.

7 In the Finish group, click the Finish & Merge button, and then click Edit Individual Documents. The Merge to New Document dialog box displays, as shown in Figure 5.21.

Space after
paragraphs removed

Merge to New
Document dialog box

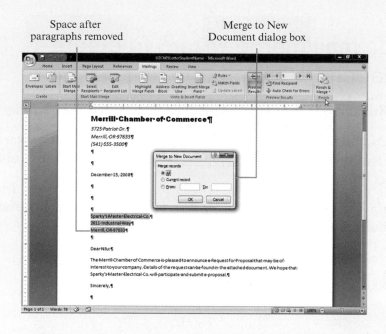

FIGURE 5.21

8 In the Merge to New Document dialog box, be sure the All option button is selected, and then click OK. The new document is five pages long—one page for each record in the database table. Notice that the name of the document is Letters1.

9 Scroll down through the document and notice that each page ends with a section break.

10 Save the file in your Chapter05 folder as U2Ch05MergedLetterStudentName and then double-click anywhere in the footer area. Scroll up to the footer on Page 1 and select the existing footer, including the paragraph mark.

11 On the Design tab, in the Insert group, click the Quick Parts button, and then click Field. Under *Field names*, scroll down and click FileName, and then click OK. The file name is updated to the current file name on Page 1 only because each page is a different section. When you merged the documents, the FileName field in each section footer was changed to regular text and is no longer a field, so it cannot be updated automatically.

12 Close ✕ both Word files, saving your changes if prompted. Submit the documents as directed.

▶▶▶ *lesson*

seven | Using the Mail Merge Wizard to Create Mailing Labels

The Microsoft Word mail merge feature can be used to print mailing labels. Preformatted mailing labels come in different sizes and shapes. All you need to set up the labels for printing is the brand and product number of the labels you are going to use.

to use the mail merge wizard to create mailing labels

1 **Start Word and display a new blank document. Click the Mailings tab.**

2 **On the Mailings tab, in the Start Mail Merge group, click the Start Mail Merge button, and then click Step by Step Mail Merge Wizard.** The Mail Merge task pane displays.

3 **In the Mail Merge task pane, under *Select document type*, click the Labels option button.** Compare your screen with Figure 5.22.

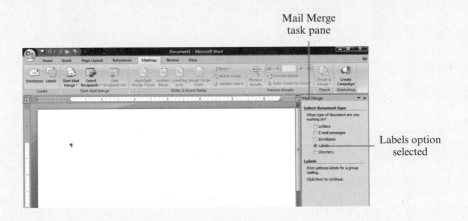

FIGURE 5.22

4 **At the bottom of the Mail Merge task pane, click Next: Starting document. Under *Change document layout*, click *Label options*.**

5 **In the Label Options dialog box, under Printer information, click the Tray box arrow, and then click *Auto Select, Auto Selection,* or something similar that indicates an automatic selection. Under Label information, click the Label vendors arrow, and then click Avery US Letter.** Avery labels are the most commonly used labels in the U.S. and they come in letter-size sheets. The options in the Tray box are controlled by the printer and may vary from one printer to the next.

6 **Under Product number, scroll to the middle of the list and click 5160.** The Avery 5160 labels come in three columns and ten rows per page. Compare your screen with Figure 5.23.

Label
product number

Paper
source

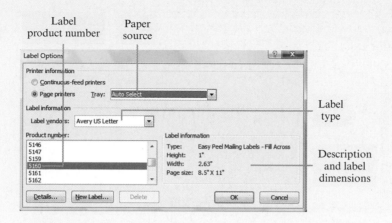

Label
type

Description
and label
dimensions

FIGURE 5.23

7 **In the Label Options dialog box, click OK. At the bottom of the Mail Merge task pane, click Next: Select recipients. Under Select recipients, be sure the** *Use an existing list* **option button is selected. Under** *Use an existing list*, **click Browse.**

8 **Navigate to the location of your student files, click U2Ch05Contractors, and then click Open. At the bottom of the Mail Merge Recipients dialog box, click OK.**

9 **At the bottom of the Mail Merge task pane, click Next: Arrange your labels. Under** *Arrange your labels*, **click Address Block. In the Insert Address Block dialog box, click Match Fields.**

10 **In the Match Fields dialog box, click the Company arrow, click Contractor Name, and then click OK. When prompted, click Yes, and then in the Insert Address Block dialog box, click OK.**

11 **In the upper left corner of the label sheet, select «Address Block». Click the Page Layout tab. In the Paragraph group, click the Spacing Before button down spin arrow one time, and then compare your screen with Figure 5.24.** The formatting change is applied only to the label in the upper left corner.

Address
block

Before spacing
changed to 0

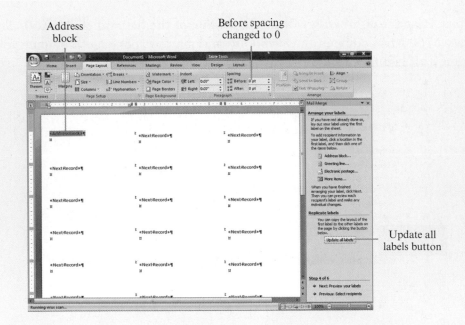

Update all
labels button

FIGURE 5.24

12 In the Mail Merge task pane, click the *Update all labels* button, and then click Next: Preview your labels. The labels are previewed, as shown in Figure 5.25.

Label
preview

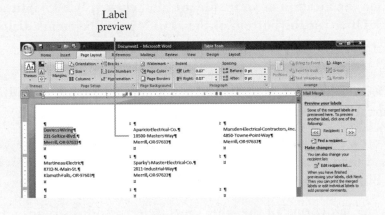

FIGURE 5.25

13 In the Mail Merge task pane, click Next: Complete the merge. Under Merge, click *Edit individual labels*. In the Merge to New Document dialog box, click OK. All of the data from the data source is merged with the main document.

14 Save the document in your **Chapter05 folder as** U2Ch05MergedLabelsStudentName **Add the file name to the footer and Save** 🖫 **the document again.** A second page is added to the document, but the second page is blank.

15 Submit the document as directed. If you are submitting printed copies, just print Page 1. Close the document and close Word. Do not save changes to the unnamed document.

Advanced Skills or Concepts

In this section, you are introduced to skills that are not taught with step-by-step instructions.

Changing Default Settings

In addition to changing the settings for the user name and initials, you can also change other default settings for applications such as the default file location used for saving your files. Control of the default settings is found in the Options dialog box for each application, which is accessed from the Office button. For example, in Word, display the Office menu and click Word Options to display the Word Options dialog box. In the left pane, click Save to display the Save option settings. Here you can use the Browse button to change the default folder that displays when you use the Save, Save As, or Open commands.

If the *AutoRecover* feature is enabled, the computer automatically saves your open documents at specified time intervals, such as every ten minutes. If you lose power or have some other computer malfunction, a version of your file will display in the AutoRecovery task pane, which enables you to recover your work up to the last AutoRecovery Save. On the Save page of the Word Options dialog box, you can also change the frequency with which files are automatically saved and the default folder where those files are stored. If you lose power, Word will display the most recently saved copies of your open files, including the AutoRecover file. You then choose which file to retain and display so that you can continue to work.

If you want to change print settings, in the left pane of the Word Options dialog box, click Advanced. The Advanced page displays several categories of options that you can customize to your particular needs or preferences, including print settings. For example, you can change settings to allow a document to be printed on two sides or printed in reverse order. The Word Options dialog box can be displayed from within the Print dialog box by clicking the Options button.

If you are using someone else's computer, it is impolite to change default settings without their knowledge or permission. Changes to default settings should only be made on your own computer unless you have permission from the owner to change settings on someone else's computer.

Lastly, changes to default settings are specific to each application. If you want to make changes to Excel, PowerPoint, or Access, use the Options dialog box for each of those applications.

Protect a Document from Unauthorized Use

When you send a document, such as a Request for Proposal or a contract using electronic media, it may be important to protect the document from unauthorized changes. One simple method is to save the file as a PDF file, as you did in Chapter 4. There are more sophisticated techniques that can be used, some of which are found on the Office menu under the Prepare option. Here is a brief description of some of the commands from this menu and their purposes:

- *Properties*—displays the document properties pane, which includes the author, document title, subject, keywords for searching, or other information. If you want a document to be anonymous, use this pane to remove or control the information that displays.

- *Encrypt Document*—enables you to set a password for a file. If you encrypt a document with a password, it is critical that you record the password so that you can retrieve it. If you lose or forget the password, you will not be able to display the file again.

- *Restrict Permission*—enables you to specify the users who have permission to read, change, or have full control over a document. This option is available with Office 2007 Ultimate, Professional Plus, and Enterprise editions and may not display on your Prepare list of options.

- *Mark as Final*—changes a document to a Read-only status, which prevents inadvertent changes to the document. However, anyone can remove the Read-only status and make changes, so this should not be considered a security feature.

Printing Envelopes Using Mail Merge

In addition to using mail merge to merge data with a letter or mailing labels, you can also use mail merge to print envelopes. This is a brief description of the steps involved:

- **Enter return address.** On the Mailings tab, in the Create group, click the Envelopes button. If necessary, in the Envelopes and Labels dialog box, type a new address in the Return address box, and then close this dialog box.

- **Select envelope size and font.** In the Start Mail Merge group, click the Start Mail Merge button, and then click Envelopes. In the Envelope Options dialog box, select the envelope size and font, and then click OK to display an envelope form.

- **Select data source.** Click the Select Recipients button, and then click Use Existing List or one of the other options. Navigate to the file that you want to merge with your envelopes.

- **Insert the address block.** Click in the middle of the envelope to display the placeholder reserved for the address. In the Write & Insert Fields group, click Address Block. If necessary, use the Match Fields button to ensure that all parts of the address are included.

- **Preview results and merge data.** Click the Preview Results button and make any necessary adjustments. Click the Finish & Merge button, and then click Edit Individual Documents to display the envelopes in one document.

- **Set up printer for manual feed.** Display the Print dialog box, change the settings to print the envelopes, and set the tray options to manual feed.

To create and print a single envelope, follow these steps:

- Change your printer settings to manual feed and select the paper size to match the envelope size you intend to use. You may need to use the Properties button to change to the envelope size and the Options button to change to manual feed.

- Remove paper from the printer and have the envelope ready to use.

- Click the Mailings tab, and in the Create group, click Envelopes.

- In the Envelopes and Labels dialog box, type the Delivery address and the Return address. Click Options and then select the envelope size and font. Click Print.

CHECK YOUR WORK

Here is a list of items your instructor will probably look for when grading your work. To improve your evaluation, take time to check the items yourself before you turn in your work.

Original Electric Vehicle Proposal—U2Ch05EVStudentName
- Tracked changes show your name and initials.
- *Chamber of Commerce* replaced with *COC*.
- Quotes removed from Electric Vehicle Corridor and italic applied.
- The word *actually* is deleted.
- The word *guidelines* is replaced with *objectives*.
- Two comments are added to the Contractor Experience paragraph.

Revised Electric Vehicle Proposal—U2Ch05EVRevisedStudentName
- All of the tracked changes are accepted or rejected.
- All comments are removed.
- *Chamber of Commerce* displays in the first line rather than *COC*.
- In the paragraphs under Project Overview and Project Details, *5 to 20* is changed to *ten*.
- On the second page, under *Timeline for completion*, a sentence is added at the left margin and without a bullet point.
- The file name is in the footer.

Main Document—U2Ch05LetterStudentName
- *Merrill Chamber of Commerce* is formatted in 16-point Arial Black font.
- The address is 12-point italic and the Space After format is removed.
- Two paragraph marks show before DATE is inserted.
- Two paragraph marks show before COMPANY ADDRESS is inserted.
- One paragraph mark shows before Dear FIRSTNAME: is inserted.
- An introductory paragraph is typed that includes COMPANY in the last line.
- The closing has the Space After format removed between the name and the title.

Merged Letter—U2Ch05MergedLetterStudentName
- DATE, COMPANY ADDRESS, FIRSTNAME, and COMPANY fields are replaced with merged data.
- Document displays five merged letters with a section break at the end of each letter.
- The file name is changed in the footer on the first page.

Merged Labels—U2Ch05MergedLabelsStudentName
- Five merged labels show the company name and address, using the Avery 5160 style—three columns and ten rows.
- The file name is in the footer.

KEY TERMS

AutoRecover	field placeholders	record
comment	mail merge	Restrict Permission
data source	main document	Reviewing pane
Encrypt Document	Mark as Final	Track Changes
field	Properties	

ASSESSING LEARNING OUTCOMES

SCREEN ID

Identify each element of the screen by matching callout numbers shown in Figure 5.26 A, B to a corresponding description.

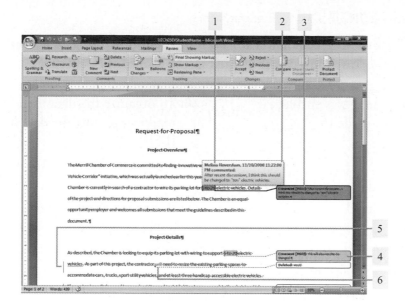

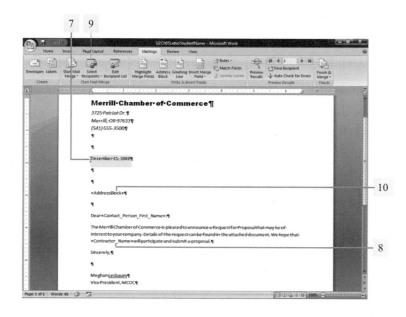

FIGURE 5.26 A, B

_____ **A.** Author of comment

_____ **B.** Change indicator

_____ **C.** Comment text

_____ **D.** Grouped field placeholder

_____ **E.** Inserted field

_____ **F.** Inserted text

_____ **G.** Single field placeholder

_____ **H.** Used to attach a data source

_____ **I.** Reviewer's initials

_____ **J.** Time stamp for comment

MULTIPLE CHOICE

Circle the letter of the correct answer for each of the following. The lesson in which the term or concept was introduced is indicated at the end of the sentence.

1. When Track Changes is enabled, it records changes made to _____. [L1, L3]
   a. formatting
   b. text that is added
   c. text that is deleted
   d. all of the above

2. Tracked changes and comments are numbered _____. [L2]
   a. sequentially from the beginning of the document
   b. chronologically in the order in which the changes or comments were made
   c. sequentially by each reviewer
   d. separately from each other

3. To hide the changes that have been made on the screen, change the Display for Review box to _____. [L3]
   a. Hide changes
   b. Hide comments
   c. Final
   d. Conceal comments and changes

4. Tracked changes are displayed on the screen in _____. [L1, L3]
   a. balloons along the right side of the page
   b. the Reviewing Pane at the bottom of the window
   c. ScreenTips on the page
   d. all of the above

5. To change the user name and initials in the Word Options dialog box, display the _____ page. [L1]
   a. advanced
   b. popular
   c. customize
   d. proofing

6. To organize the data used in a mail merge, sort the data in _____. [L5]
   a. the Edit Recipient List dialog box
   b. the Mail Merge task pane
   c. the mail merge letter
   d. any of the above

7. A data source can be information that is stored in _____. [L5]
   a. Outlook
   b. Access
   c. Excel
   d. all of the above

8. To control who has access to a document and what they can do, display the Prepare menu and select the _____ command. [Adv]
   a. Properties
   b. Encrypt Document
   c. Restrict Permission
   d. Mark as Final

9. When data is merged with a letter using the Edit Individual Documents command, it displays all the letters in one document with _____ between each letter. [L6]
   a. a page break
   b. a section break
   c. a line break
   d. no break

10. To set up labels for printing, you need to know the _____. [L7]
    a. number of labels you need to print
    b. size and shape of the labels
    c. brand and product number of the labels
    d. label manufacturer

MATCHING

Match the term or concept to its description.

_____ 1. A category of data from a data source that is organized and named

_____ 2. All of the information about an individual or company that displays in a single row of a data source

_____ 3. In a mail merge, the document that contains the text and formatting that remains constant

_____ 4. A feature that saves files on your computer at regular intervals to reduce the amount of data lost in the event of a computer malfunction

_____ 5. A pane at the bottom or side of the screen that displays comments and tracked changes

_____ 6. A feature that records changes and comments made to a document by others

_____ 7. A command that enables you to set a password for a file

_____ 8. A note that an author or reviewer adds to a document that displays in either a balloon-shaped graphic or in the Reviewing pane

_____ 9. A Word feature that joins a main document and a data source to create customized letters, labels, or envelopes

_____ 10. A file that contains organized data that includes names, addresses, and other information necessary to merge with a document for mailing purposes

A. AutoRecover

B. Comment

C. Data source

D. Encrypt Document

E. Field

F. Mail merge

G. Main document

H. Record

I. Reviewing pane

J. Track Changes

SKILL DRILL

The Skill Drill exercise is a repeat of the lessons in the chapter but with a different set of data. The instructions are less detailed, and your speed and familiarity should increase with practice. There is a figure at the end against which you can check your results. The purpose of this exercise is to build your confidence and speed in using these skills and to set them in your memory for later recall. The section numbers correspond to the lesson numbers. You are welcome to refer back to the lesson's illustrated and detailed instructions if necessary.

In this exercise, you review a Request for Proposal document about renovations to the Klamath Falls Public Library. You will add tracked changes and comments to the proposal, review the changes, and accept or reject them. Then you will create a main document for mailing the proposal to contractors and merge the letter with the mailing list. Finally, you will create mailing labels for the envelopes.

1. **Inserting Comments into a Document**

    1. **Start** Word and display formatting marks. From the Office menu, display the Open dialog box. Locate and open the **U2Ch05LEED** file. **Save** the file in your Chapter05 folder as U2Ch05LEEDStudentName

    2. Click the **Office** button, and then click **Word Options.** Be sure *Popular* is selected. If necessary, under *Personalize your copy of Microsoft Office*, in the User name box, type your name, and then in the Initials box, type your initials. Click **OK.**

    3. Click the **Review** tab. In the **Tracking** group, click the **Balloons** button, and then click **Show Revisions in Balloons.** On the **Review** tab, in the **Comments** group, click the **Next** button. Move the pointer over the bold insertion mark that shows where the comment was placed to display the comment in a ScreenTip. Because the comment was attached to a word—*profitable*—that the reviewer subsequently deleted, only the comment insertion mark displays.

    4. In the **Comments** group, click the **Next** button to view each of the remaining comments.

    5. On Page 2, at the end of the last item in the bulleted list, select the word *project*. On the **Review** tab, in the **Comments** group, click the **New Comment** button. In the comment box, type Include a timeline for completion in the list of requirements.

    6. In the paragraph under Contractor Experience, in the first line, select the word *seven*. Click the **New Comment** button and type This requirement seems particularly limiting. I would favor five years.

    7. On Page 1, click at the end of the text in the first comment box. Press ⏎Enter two times and type I agree. Then type your name.

    8. **Save** your document.

2. **Tracking Changes in a Document**

    1. Press Ctrl + Home. On the **Review** tab, in the **Changes** group, click the **Next** button. Continue to click the **Next** button to review each of the tracked changes. When you get to the end, click **Cancel** in the message box. Press Ctrl + Home to move back to the top of the document.

    2. On the **Review** tab, in the **Tracking** group, click the top half of the **Track Changes** button to begin to track your changes.

    3. On the first page, in the paragraph under *Overview of Project*, in the fifth line, select the word *that* following *contractors*. Type who In the next line, click to the immediate right of LEED and type (R) which is a shortcut for creating the registered symbol—®. It should display as a superscript: LEED®.

4. Select **LEED**® and press Ctrl + C to copy this to the Office Clipboard. Press Ctrl + F to open the Find dialog box. In the **Find what** box, type LEED Click the **Replace** tab, click in the **Replace with** box, and press Ctrl + V to paste **LEED**®. Click **Find Next** until you find the next instance of LEED, and then click **Replace.** Click **Find Next** again, and then click **Replace All.** There should be a total of six replacements, including the first one you made. When you get to the end of the document, click **No**—do not start at the beginning. Close the Find and Replace dialog box.

5. Review your document and be sure that there are six occurrences of LEED® and that they all display correctly. **Save** your work. Submit the document as directed by your instructor.

3. Responding to Comments and Document Changes

1. Click the **Office** button, and then click **Save As.** Change the name of the file to U2Ch05LEEDRevisedStudentName navigate to your **Chapter05** folder, and then click **Save.**

2. On the **Review** tab, in the **Tracking** group, click the **Balloons** button, and then click **Show All Revisions Inline.** Click the **Reviewing Pane** button arrow, and then click **Reviewing Pane Vertical.**

3. In the **Tracking** group, click the top half of the **Track Changes** button to turn off the Track Changes feature. Press Ctrl + Home to move to the beginning of the document.

4. In the **Changes** group, click the **Next** button. The first comment and change, which deletes *profitable,* is selected. In the **Changes** group, click the **Accept** button. The deletion of the word *profitable* is accepted and the next change is highlighted.

5. The deleted word—*that*—is selected. In the **Changes** group, click the **Reject** button two times to reject the replacement of *that* with *who.*

6. The next change—®—following LEED is highlighted. Click the **Accept** button.

7. In the paragraph under the title *Details of Project,* triple-click the paragraph to select the entire paragraph. In the **Changes** group, click the **Accept** button to accept all of the changes in this paragraph.

8. In the comment that still displays in the paragraph—attached to the word *points*—right-click the comment, and from the shortcut menu, click **Delete Comment.**

9. In the **Changes** group, click the **Accept** button arrow, and then click **Accept All Changes in Document.**

10. Under *Site Tour,* at the comment, select the extension *13* and type 402 Then right-click the comment about the extension and click **Delete Comment.**

11. On Page 2, using the skills you have practiced, delete the comment attached to the word *project.* Click at the end of the last bullet point and press ↵Enter. Type Timeline for completion

12. Delete the last comment attached to the word *seven*, and then change the word *seven* to `five`. Verify that all of the comments and changes have been reviewed, and then close the Reviewing pane.

13. Scroll to the end of Page 1. Double-click in the footer area. On the **Design tab,** in the **Insert** group, click the **Quick Parts** button, and then click **Field.** Scroll the Field names list, click **FileName,** and then click **OK.**

14. Double-click in the document. **Save** your work and close the file. Submit the file as directed.

4. Creating a Main Document for Merging

1. Open a new document and display formatting marks. Type `Klamath Falls Public Library` and press `⏎Enter`. Type the following, pressing `⏎Enter` after each line:

   `Board of Governors`
   `9700 W. Towne Center Pkwy`
   `Klamath Falls, OR 97602`

2. Select the four paragraphs of text that you just typed, but do not include the blank paragraph mark following the selected text. Click the **Page Layout** tab. In the **Paragraph** group, under **Spacing,** click the **After** down spin arrow to display **0.**

3. Select the first line of text. On the Mini toolbar, change the font to **Verdana,** the font size to **16,** and then click the **Italic** button.

4. Select the next three lines, and from the Mini toolbar, change the font to **Verdana** and the font size to **12.**

5. Press `Ctrl` + `End` and then press `⏎Enter` two times. On the **Insert** tab, in the **Text** group, click the **Date & Time** button. Select the December 15, 2010 format and then click **OK.** Press `⏎Enter` three times.

6. Click the **Office** button, and then click **Save As.** In the Save As dialog box, navigate to your **Chapter05** folder. In the File name box, type `U2Ch05LibraryStudentName` and click **Save.**

7. Add the FileName field to the footer. **Save** your changes.

5. Opening a Data Source and Inserting Fields into a Document

1. Click the **Mailings** tab. In the **Start Mail Merge** group, click the **Select Recipients** button, and then click **Use Existing List.** Navigate to your student folder for this chapter, click **U2Ch05Library,** and then click **Open.** Recall that the list is attached to the document even though nothing displays on the screen.

2. In the **Start Mail Merge** group, click the **Edit Recipient List** button. In the Mail Merge Recipients dialog box, scroll to the right to display the Contractor Name field. In the Contractor Name column header, click the arrow, and then click **Sort Ascending.** Click **OK** and **Save** your document.

3. With the insertion point at the last paragraph mark, in the **Write & Insert Fields** group, click the **Address Block** button.

4. In the Insert Address Block dialog box, click the **Match Fields** button. Click the **Company** arrow, and then click **Contractor Name.** Click the **Courtesy Title** arrow, and then click **(not matched).** Click **OK.** When prompted to confirm the match, click **Yes,** and then click **OK.**

5. Press ⏎Enter two times, type `Dear` and press Spacebar. In the **Write & Insert Fields** group, click the **Insert Merge Field** button arrow, and then click **Title.** Press Spacebar. Display the Mail Merge Field list again, click **ContactLastName** and then type a colon :

6. Press ⏎Enter and type `The Klamath Falls Public Library is`
`pleased to announce a Request for Proposal that may be of`
`interest to your company. Details of the request can be`
`found in the attached document. We hope that`

7. Press Spacebar. Display the **Insert Merge Field** list, click **Contractor_Name,** and then press Spacebar. Continue to type the rest of the letter as follows, including the closing for the letter spaced as you have done previously:

   `will participate and submit a proposal.`

   `Sincerely,`

   `Marybeth Sorenson`
   `President, Board of Governors`

8. In the paragraph with the text *Marybeth Sorenson*, click anywhere in the paragraph. On the **Page Layout** tab, in the **Paragraph** group, click the **Spacing After** down spin arrow until **0** displays.

9. **Save** your changes.

6. Merging a Document with a Data Source

   1. Move the insertion point to the beginning of the letter. Select the address block, including the paragraph mark. Click the **Page Layout** tab. In the **Paragraph** group, click the **Spacing After** down spin arrow two times to remove the spacing after in the address block paragraphs.

   2. Click the **Mailings** tab, and in the **Preview Results** group, click the **Preview Results** button. In the **Preview Results** group, click the **Next Record** button four times.

   3. In the **Finish** group, click the **Finish & Merge** button, and then click **Edit Individual Documents.** In the Merge to New Document dialog box, be sure the *All* option button is selected, and then click **OK.**

   4. Scroll through the document and verify that five letters display, each ending with a section break.

   5. **Save** the file in your **Chapter05** folder as `U2Ch05LibraryMergedStudentName` and then double-click anywhere in the footer area. Scroll up to the footer on Page 1, and select the existing footer, including the paragraph mark.

6. On the **Design** tab, in the **Insert** group, click the **Quick Parts** button, and then click **Field.** Under *Field names*, scroll down and click **FileName,** and then click **OK.**

7. **Close** both Word files, saving your changes if prompted. Submit only the **U2Ch05LibraryMergedStudentName** document as directed.

7. **Using the Mail Merge Wizard to Create Mailing Labels**

1. Display a new blank document. Click the **Mailings** tab. In the **Start Mail Merge** group, click the **Start Mail Merge** button, and then click **Step by Step Mail Merge Wizard.**

2. In the Mail Merge task pane, under *Select document type*, click the **Labels** option button. At the bottom of the Mail Merge task pane, click **Next.** Under *Change document layout*, click **Label options.**

3. In the Label Options dialog box, under Printer information, click the **Tray** box arrow, and then click *Auto Select* or the automatic option for your printer. Under Label information, click the **Label vendors** arrow, and then click **Avery US Letter.** Under **Product number,** scroll to the middle of the list, click **5160,** and then click **OK.**

4. At the bottom of the Mail Merge task pane, click **Next.** Under **Select recipients,** be sure the *Use an existing list* option button is selected. Under *Use an existing list*, click **Browse.**

5. Navigate to the location of your student files, click **U2Ch05Library,** and then click **Open.** At the bottom of the Mail Merge Recipients dialog box, click **OK.**

6. At the bottom of the Mail Merge task pane, click **Next.** Under *Arrange your labels*, click **Address Block.** In the Insert Address Block dialog box, click **Match Fields.**

7. In the Match Fields dialog box, click the **Company** arrow, and then click **Contractor Name.** Click the **Courtesy Title** arrow and then click **(not matched).** Click **OK.** When prompted, click **Yes,** and then in the Insert Address Block dialog box, click **OK.**

8. In the upper left corner of the label sheet, select «Address Block». Click the **Page Layout** tab. In the **Paragraph** group, click the **Spacing Before** button down spin arrow one time.

9. In the Mail Merge task pane, click the **Update all labels** button, and then click **Next.** In the Mail Merge task pane, click **Next.** Under Merge, click **Edit individual labels.** In the Merge to New Document dialog box, click **OK.**

10. **Save** the document in your **Chapter05** folder as U2Ch05LibraryLabelsStudentName Add the file name to the footer and **Save** the document again.

11. Submit the documents as directed. If you are submitting printed copies, just print Page 1 of the labels. Close the document and close Word.

Change tracked–*that*
replaced with *who*

Inserted®

LEED changed to
LEED® 6 times

Comments with
your initials

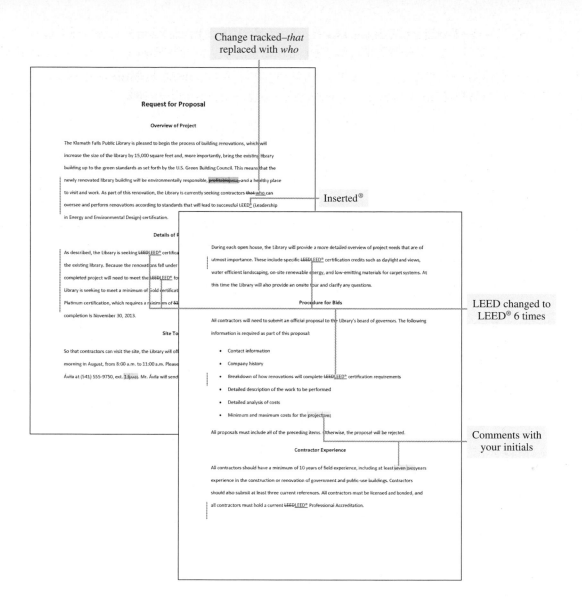

FIGURE 5.27A

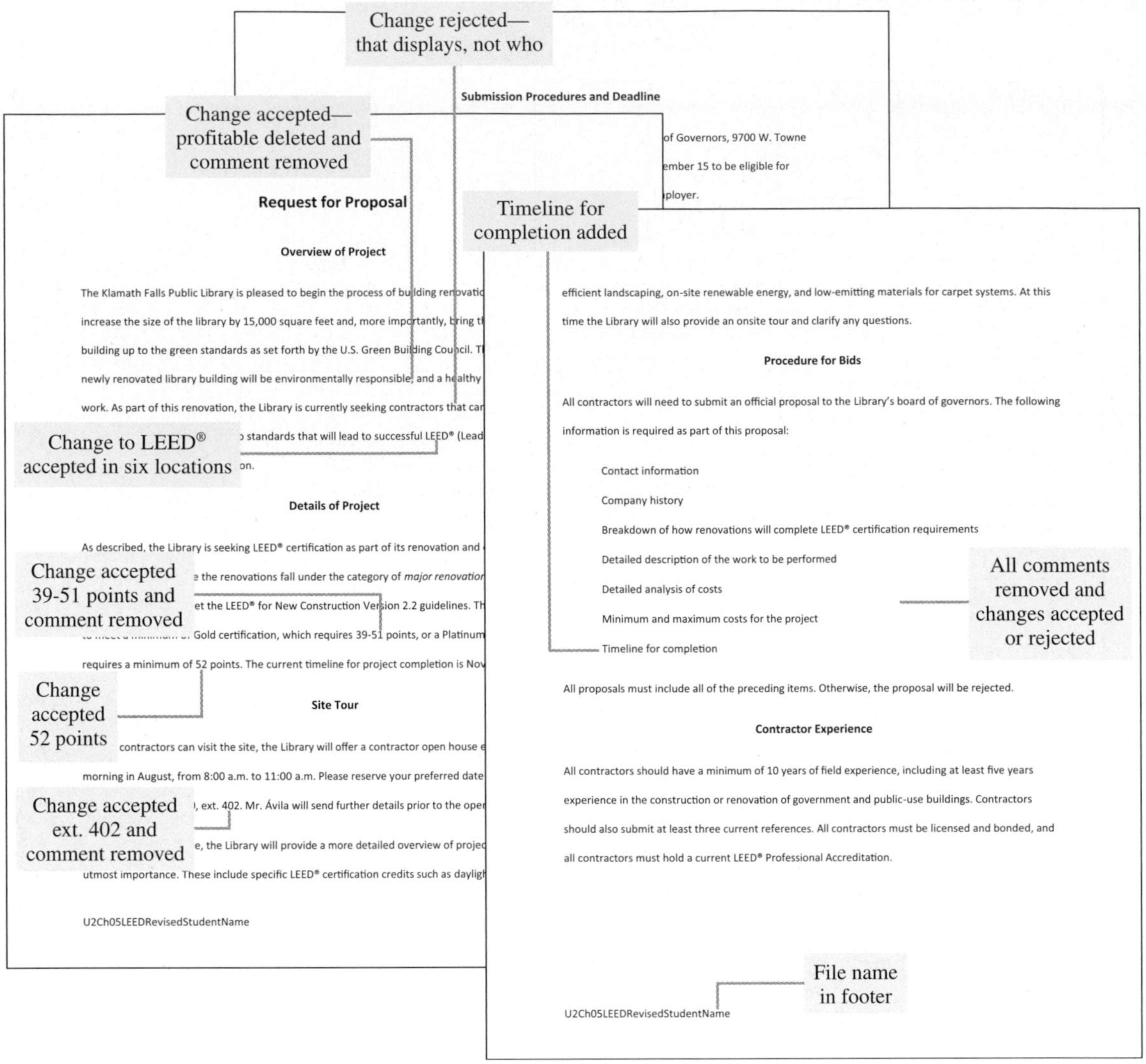

Change rejected— that displays, not who

Change accepted— profitable deleted and comment removed

Timeline for completion added

Request for Proposal

Submission Procedures and Deadline

of Governors, 9700 W. Towne

ember 15 to be eligible for

ployer.

Overview of Project

The Klamath Falls Public Library is pleased to begin the process of building renovatio

increase the size of the library by 15,000 square feet and, more importantly, bring t

building up to the green standards as set forth by the U.S. Green Building Council. T

newly renovated library building will be environmentally responsible, and a healthy

work. As part of this renovation, the Library is currently seeking contractors that can

Change to LEED® accepted in six locations

standards that will lead to successful LEED® (Lead

on.

Details of Project

As described, the Library is seeking LEED® certification as part of its renovation and

Change accepted 39-51 points and comment removed

e the renovations fall under the category of *major renovatio*

et the LEED® for New Construction Version 2.2 guidelines. T

Gold certification, which requires 39-51 points, or a Platinu

requires a minimum of 52 points. The current timeline for project completion is Nov

Change accepted 52 points

Site Tour

contractors can visit the site, the Library will offer a contractor open house

morning in August, from 8:00 a.m. to 11:00 a.m. Please reserve your preferred date

Change accepted ext. 402 and comment removed

, ext. 402. Mr. Ávila will send further details prior to the ope

e, the Library will provide a more detailed overview of proje

utmost importance. These include specific LEED® certification credits such as dayligh

U2Ch05LEEDRevisedStudentName

efficient landscaping, on-site renewable energy, and low-emitting materials for carpet systems. At this

time the Library will also provide an onsite tour and clarify any questions.

Procedure for Bids

All contractors will need to submit an official proposal to the Library's board of governors. The following

information is required as part of this proposal:

Contact information

Company history

Breakdown of how renovations will complete LEED® certification requirements

Detailed description of the work to be performed

Detailed analysis of costs

Minimum and maximum costs for the project

Timeline for completion

All comments removed and changes accepted or rejected

All proposals must include all of the preceding items. Otherwise, the proposal will be rejected.

Contractor Experience

All contractors should have a minimum of 10 years of field experience, including at least five years

experience in the construction or renovation of government and public-use buildings. Contractors

should also submit at least three current references. All contractors must be licensed and bonded, and

all contractors must hold a current LEED® Professional Accreditation.

File name in footer

U2Ch05LEEDRevisedStudentName

FIGURE 5.27B

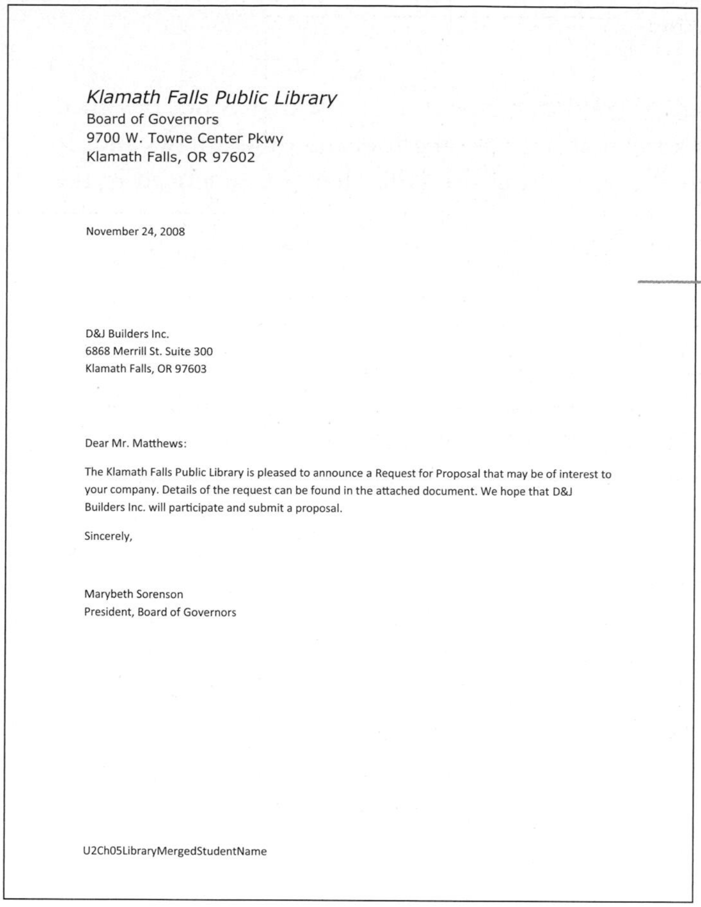

Klamath Falls Public Library
Board of Governors
9700 W. Towne Center Pkwy
Klamath Falls, OR 97602

November 24, 2008

One of the five
merged letters

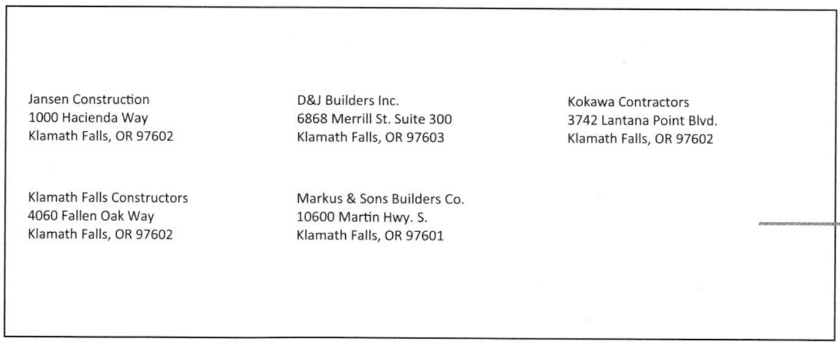

D&J Builders Inc.
6868 Merrill St. Suite 300
Klamath Falls, OR 97603

Dear Mr. Matthews:

The Klamath Falls Public Library is pleased to announce a Request for Proposal that may be of interest to your company. Details of the request can be found in the attached document. We hope that D&J Builders Inc. will participate and submit a proposal.

Sincerely,

Marybeth Sorenson
President, Board of Governors

U2Ch05LibraryMergedStudentName

Jansen Construction 1000 Hacienda Way Klamath Falls, OR 97602	D&J Builders Inc. 6868 Merrill St. Suite 300 Klamath Falls, OR 97603	Kokawa Contractors 3742 Lantana Point Blvd. Klamath Falls, OR 97602
Klamath Falls Constructors 4060 Fallen Oak Way Klamath Falls, OR 97602	Markus & Sons Builders Co. 10600 Martin Hwy. S. Klamath Falls, OR 97601	

Merged mailing
labels

FIGURE 5.27C, D

fix *it*

One way to appreciate the value of good design is to fix a file that is not designed well. In this exercise, you open a file that has several errors and design flaws and fix it according to the good design elements using the skills that you practiced in the lessons.

Navigate to the folder with the student files, open **U2Ch05FixIt,** and save it as U2Ch05FixItStudentName

Read this document. You will make changes as the facilities manager who has been copied on this memo. Craig has asked for your input before he sends the memo to the CEO. Add comments and make changes using the Track Changes feature. Use the good design principles that were introduced in this chapter. Here is a list of corrections needed and the design principles introduced in this chapter.

- Track changes you make.
- In two locations, change Student Name to your name.
- Write clear and concise comments.
- In Craig's comment, respond that the initiatives are under way.
- Identify yourself by entering your name in the edited comment.
- In the first paragraph of the memo, add a comment recommending the use of bullet points to list the initiatives.
- In the first paragraph, remind Craig to include the *Bike to Work* program.
- Be careful not to introduce errors.
- Change all of the font to black.
- Move the last sentence of the first paragraph so that it is the first sentence of the second paragraph.
- In the sentence that is moved, delete *Also,*
- In the second sentence in the second paragraph, delete *We should*, and then capitalize *Also.*
- In the third paragraph, change *me* to your name.
- In the last paragraph replace *you should* with *to.*
- Delete the paragraph about talking with Kim Yates. Add a comment that it is premature and that the CEO does not need to be involved in that meeting.
- Add a comment to the suggested meeting date and recommend two other dates before then that would work better for you.
- Attach a comment to Craig's name and thank and praise him for taking the initiative in getting the managers involved.
- Place the file name in the footer.
- Submit the file as required by your instructor. Save and close the file.

ON THE JOB

Information workers add value to data by organizing, selecting, displaying, communicating, interpreting, and using data to communicate information and support decisions. On the Job exercises simulate a situation where you are given data, and your job is to add value to it using the skills you practiced in this chapter. Success in these exercises indicates that you have a valuable skill to offer an employer.

1. Green Initiatives Report

In this On the Job exercise, you will review the Green Initiatives Report for the Ladoga Hills Retirement Community before it is sent to the Board of Directors in their monthly packet prior to the board meeting. You will respond to comments, add comments, and make changes. Then you will save the document with a new name and accept or reject the changes and remove all comments. Afterward, you will create a cover letter and merge it with the directors' names and addresses for mailing purposes. Finally, you will create mailing labels for use on the envelopes.

1. Open the **U2Ch05Green** document and save it in your Chapter05 folder as U2Ch05GreenStudentName

2. If necessary, in the Word Options dialog box, change the User name and Initials to your name and initials.

3. Activate Track Changes and display the changes in balloons. Review the changes made to this document.

4. In the first paragraph, under the report title, move *six months ago* so that it follows *undertook* on the same line.

5. At the end of that paragraph, insert a comment to recommend the phrase *in the future* rather than *in the years to come*.

6. In the paragraph under *Reduced Energy Expenses*, in the second line, delete *overall*.

7. In the same paragraph, at the end of the fifth line, select *dishwashers*, and add a comment that *most* not *all* dishwashers were replaced.

8. On Page 2, under *Public Transportation*, remove the quotation marks around *Leave the Drive Behind*, and format the program name in italic.

9. On Page 2, in the comment about the amount of credits earned, from the information provided, determine if this figure seems reasonable or not. Then add a response to the comment from Patricia Sawyer to this effect. Verify the number of miles driven to see if it is accurate. If it is not, in your comment, suggest a new figure and how you determined that number. Be sure to identify yourself in your response.

10. In the last paragraph, select the $53,000 and add a comment to ask if this is an additional savings over and above the amount saved this year.

11. Save the file with the changes and comments you have made, and submit the file as directed.

12. Save the file with a new name: U2Ch05GreenRevisedStudentName

13. Turn off Track Changes. Remove the Balloons, and display the changes and comments in the vertical Reviewing pane.

14. Accept the changes in the first paragraph. Replace *years to come* with `future` and then delete the comment with this suggestion.

15. In the paragraph under *Reduced Energy Expenses*, accept the changes, delete the comment, and replace *all* with `most` so that it reads *most dishwashers were replaced*.

16. Accept the remaining changes and delete the remaining comments. Review the document and correct any inadvertent errors that may have been introduced.

17. Add the file name to the footer. Save your file and submit it as directed.

18. Open the **U2Ch05LadogaHills** file and save it in your Chapter05 folder, naming it `U2Ch05DirectorLetterStudentName`

19. On the Mailings tab, click the Select Recipients button and attach the **U2Ch05Directors** data source file to the letter.

20. At the third paragraph mark, under the last line of the letterhead, insert the date field.

21. Press Enter two times and insert the Address Block field placeholder, and then press Enter.

22. Under the Address Block placeholder, click next to the second paragraph mark. In the Write & Insert Fields group, click the Greeting Line button. In the Insert Greeting Line dialog box, select the full first name format—*Joshua*. The Insert Greeting Line dialog box includes Dear as the salutation and a comma following the person's name so that you do not have to type this information.

23. Add the file name to the footer, and then save the file.

24. Click the Preview Results button. Adjust the line spacing in the address to remove the Space After format, and save the file again.

25. On the Mailings tab, click the Finish & Merge button and merge the files so that you can edit individual letters. Save the merged letters as `U2Ch05DirectorMergedStudentName`

26. In the footer on the first letter, delete the file name, and then insert the new file name using the Quick Parts button. Save the merged document and close the file.

27. Open a new document. Start the Mail Merge Wizard and create mailing labels for the directors, using the Avery label 5160. Be sure to remove the Space Before spacing from the address block. Save the file as `U2Ch05DirectorLabelsStudentName`

28. Add the file name to the footer and save the file again. Submit all of your files as directed.

2. Think Green Memo

The director of Human Resources at Pratt Manufacturing has distributed a memo for comments and changes before sending it out to department heads for distribution to employees. You will add your changes and comments to the memo before it is reviewed by the HR director. Then you will accept or reject changes as directed, remove comments, make other necessary changes, and distribute the memo to department heads by merging it with the mailing list data source.

1. Open the **U2Ch05Memo** file and save it in your Chapter05 folder as `U2Ch05MemoStudentName`

2. If necessary, change the User name and Initials in the Word Options dialog box. Turn on Track Changes.

3. In the memo title, remove the quotation marks and apply italic to *Think Green Program*. Add italic to the program name in the first sentence that follows the title.

4. In the second paragraph in the body of the memo, in the fourth line, between the words *With consent*, type `the` At the end of that paragraph, select *garden* and add a comment asking how people sign up for a garden section.

5. In the third paragraph, select the word *mandatory* and add a comment asking if there will be penalties.

6. In the footer, delete the page number. Save the file.

7. Save the file with a new name: `U2Ch05MemoRevisedStudentName`

8. Turn off Track Changes. In the *From* line of the address area, change it to `Lea Chen, Vice President, Human Resources` and delete the comment. Accept the change to the title line.

9. In the body of the memo, accept the changes in the first and second paragraphs.

10. At the end of the second paragraph, delete the comment and add the following sentence: `Go to the company website and click on` *Think Green* `to sign up for a garden plot.`

11. In the third paragraph, accept the change in the first line, and remove the word *mandatory* and the comment attached to it.

12. Accept the changes in the next paragraph, and remove the extra spaces following the word *travel*. In the fifth paragraph, select *Lea Chen, Vice President of* and replace it with `Julie McMurray in`

13. Accept any remaining changes and delete all comments. Add the file name in the footer, and then **Save** and close the file.

14. Open a blank document. Using the Mail Merge Wizard, create mailing labels to attach to interoffice envelopes using the U2Ch05Departments file as the data source. Use the Avery 5159 label. Include the name of the department head, their title, and the department name on the label.

15. In the Edit Recipient List dialog box, remove the check mark from Lea Chen—her office is sending the memo and does not need a mailing label. Merge the data source with the labels; there should be four labels, each on two lines.

16. Be sure to remove the Space Before paragraph spacing and add the file name to the footer. Save the file as `U2Ch05DeptLabelsStudentName` Submit your files as directed.

DISCUSSION OF ADVANCED SKILLS OR CONCEPTS

The questions in this section are based on the topics in the Advanced Skills or Concepts section of the chapter.

1. Have you changed any default settings on your own computer? Which settings did you change and why?

2. Describe an experience you have had when you have lost power or had a program lock up so that you had to close it. Were you able to recover your files? How often does the AutoRecover feature save your files? Has this feature helped you recover files and save your work?

3. Describe a circumstance when you might need to protect a document before it is distributed electronically. Which of the options described would you favor and why? Have you used any of these features? Have you worked with a password-protected file?

4. Have you printed envelopes using the mail merge feature? Have you printed one envelope at a time for mailing correspondence? Describe an experience when you have used the Create Envelope feature. Was it easy to figure out and use?

ON YOUR OWN

Once you are comfortable with the skills in this chapter, you can apply them to new situations of your own choosing. In this section, you choose data that you have in your possession or that you can find elsewhere. To successfully complete this assignment, you must apply good design practices and demonstrate mastery of the skills that were practiced. Refer to the list of skills and design practices in the Fix It exercise and throughout the lessons.

1. Collaborate on a Reunion

Collaborate on a flyer for a reunion—family, class, or group—and distribute the file to a mailing list of five or more people.

1. Open a new document and save it as U2Ch05ReunionStudentName

2. Using the skills you have practiced in the Word chapters, create a flyer for a reunion.

3. Ask a classmate to review it with Track Changes turned on and to make changes and add comments to the flyer.

4. Save the file that is returned to you as U2Ch05ReunionReviewedStudentName

5. Review the changes, accepting or rejecting them as seems appropriate to you. Remove the comments and make changes that are required to improve your flyer. Save the file as U2Ch05ReunionRevisedStudentName

6. In a new file, create a list of names and addresses in a Word table, and save the file as U2Ch05AddressesStudentName

7. Using the Mail Merge Wizard, create mailing labels using the U2Ch05AddressesStudentName file as your data source.

8. Save the merged label file as U2Ch05AddressLabelsStudentName Be sure the file name is in the footer on all of your documents. Save your work and submit the files as directed by your instructor.

2. Collaborate with Friends

Work with one or two classmates to write a group poem, story, or limerick. Your work must be original.

- Choose one or two classmates to work on this project.
- Agree on the topic and the form of the collaborative paper: poem, short story, limerick, or some other writing.
- One person starts the process. Type the title of your work, and then turn on Track Changes and write the opening line, sentence, or paragraph. Save the document as U2Ch05CollaborationStudentName
- Send the document to the next person in the group. The second person should be sure that their name will display when changes are made. Add comments or changes to what has already been written. Add the next line, sentence, or paragraph. Continue this process for each person in the group.
- The originator receives the final document and has the opportunity to edit or review changes and comments made by others.
- Save the final file and leave all changes and comments showing. Submit the file as directed.

ASSESS YOUR PROGRESS

At this point, you should have a set of skills and design concepts that are valuable to an employer and to you. You may not realize how much you have learned unless you take a few minutes to assess your progress.

1. From the student files, open **U2Ch05Assess.** Save it as U2Ch05AssessStudentName

2. Read each question in column A.

3. In column B, answer Yes or No.

4. If you identify a skill or design concept that you don't know, refer to the learning objective code next to the question and the table at the beginning of the chapter to find the skill and review it.

5. Print the worksheet if your instructor requires it. The file name is already in the header, so it will display your name as part of the file name.

6. All of these skills and concepts have been identified as important by surveying hundreds of individuals working at over 200 companies worldwide. If you cannot answer all of the questions affirmatively even after reviewing the relevant lesson, seek additional help from your instructor.

chapter **six**

Creating and Formatting a Worksheet

Lesson	Learning Outcomes	Code	Related IC3 Objectives
1	Navigate a worksheet and a workbook	6.01	1.1.3, 1.1.4, 1.3.1
1	Select cells	6.02	3.1.1, 3.1.3
1	Design a basic worksheet	6.03	3.1.1, 3.1.2
1	Enter text and numbers into cells	6.04	3.1.3
1	Shift values to other cells	6.05	1.3.2, 3.1.4
2	Adjust column width	6.06	3.1.4
3	Insert and delete rows and columns	6.07	3.1.4
4	Sum a column of numbers using sum function	6.08	3.2.5, 3.26
5	Format numbers and dates	6.09	3.15
6	Align text	6.10	3.17
7	Add emphasis, borders, colors, and shading	6.11	3.1.6, 3.1.10
8	Opening, copying, inserting, and deleting worksheets	6.12	1.2.3, 3.1.4
9	Sort, filter, and format tables of data	6.13	3.2.1, 3.2.2
10	Use a custom header to document printouts	6.14	3.1.9
Advanced	Draw simple conclusions	6.15	3.2.10
Advanced	Identify elements of a well-organized worksheet	6.16	3.1.2
Advanced	Recognize the importance of accurate data	6.17	3.1.2

Instructions throughout the lessons are based on the Vista operating system, running Microsoft Office 2007. Due to variability in screen size and display settings, as well as personal settings, your screen may not match the figures included in this chapter.

?Why Would I Do This?

Word processing programs, such as Microsoft Office Word, can display tables of labeled data. When you deal primarily with numbers that might change and there are calculations that need to update automatically, you need to use Microsoft Office Excel. Tables that organize and calculate financial data are called *spreadsheets*, and they are an important tool of any business or organization. They are used to manage expenses, budgets, and sales projections. If you work with money at home or on the job, you will probably use a spreadsheet program like Excel to manage it. Therefore, you need to be familiar with how numbers and text are entered, edited, formatted, and printed.

In this chapter, you create spreadsheets that can be used to calculate the cost of installing photovoltaic solar cells or a wind generator for a single-family home.

visual summary

In these lessons, you will set up a worksheet that shows the costs associated with buying and installing photoelectric solar panels that could provide part of the power for a single-family home (Figure 6.1). You will copy a worksheet from another file that contains a table of data showing the amount of solar energy available by state, then sort it to determine which states are best suited for generating electricity from the sun. See Figure 6.1.

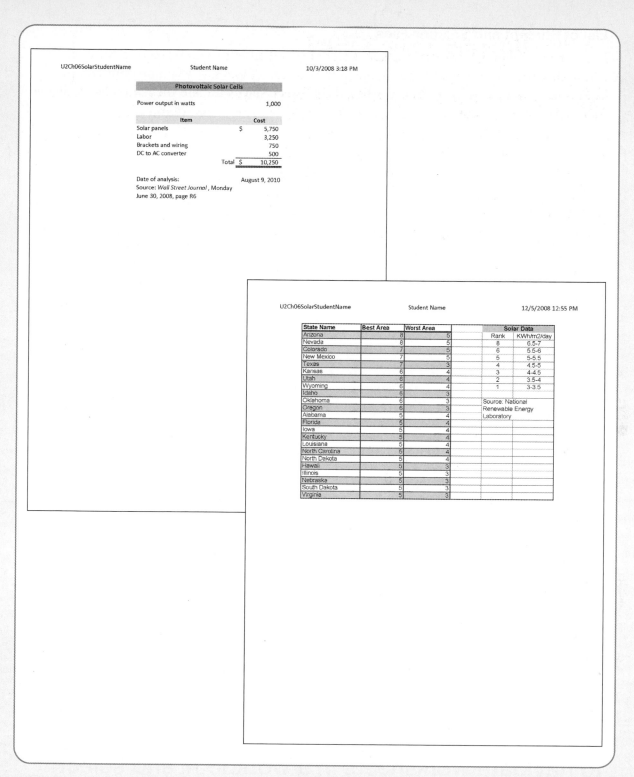

FIGURE 6.1

List of Student and Solution Files

In most cases, you will start with a new, empty file and enter text and data or paste content from other files. You will add your name to the file names and save them on your computer or portable memory device. Table 6.1 lists the files you start with and the names you will give them when you save the files.

ASSIGNMENT	STUDENT SOURCE FILE:	SAVE AS:
Lessons 1–10	New file U2Ch06States	U2Ch06SolarStudentName Not saved
Skill Drill	New file U2Ch06WindEnergy	U2Ch06WindStudentName Not saved
Fix It	U2Ch06FixIt	U2Ch06FixItStudentName
On the Job	New file U2Ch06HydroData	U2Ch06HydroStudentName U2Ch06HydroDataStudentName
On Your Own	New file New file	U2Ch06CostsStudentName U2Ch06DataStudentName
Assess Your Progress	U2Ch06Assess	U2Ch06AssessStudentName

TABLE 6.1

▶▶▶ *lesson*
one | Navigating a Workbook, Selecting Cells, and Entering Text and Data

A Microsoft Office Excel file is a *workbook* that consists of one or more *worksheets*. A *worksheet* is the primary work area in an Excel workbook and consists of a grid of rows and columns. The intersection of a row and a column forms a box known as a *cell*, into which data is entered. Cells can contain text, numbers, or formulas. Worksheets are identified by tabs at the bottom of the workbook window and can be named to identify the content of the worksheet.

to navigate worksheets in a workbook and select cells

1 **Start Microsoft Office Excel 2007.** A blank workbook opens with three blank worksheets, as shown in Figure 6.2.

FIGURE 6.2

2 **Click the Sheet2 tab.** The second empty worksheet displays. Several related worksheets are saved together in a single workbook. Additional worksheets may be added. For example, a workbook might include a worksheet for each month of the year to track annual expenses.

3 **Click the Sheet1 tab to redisplay the first worksheet.**

4 **Double-click the Sheet1 tab, type** `Costs` **and then press** ⏎Enter**.** The name on the tab is changed from *Sheet1* to *Costs*.

5 **Click the first cell in the upper left corner of the worksheet.** When you click a cell, it becomes the ***active cell***—the location where data will display when you type. The active cell is identified by a dark border around the border of the cell. Cells are named using a combination of the column letter and the row number—known as the ***cell address***. The address of the first cell in a worksheet is *A1*, and it displays in the ***Name box***—the area in the Excel window that displays the cell address or the name of the currently selected cell, as shown in Figure 6.3.

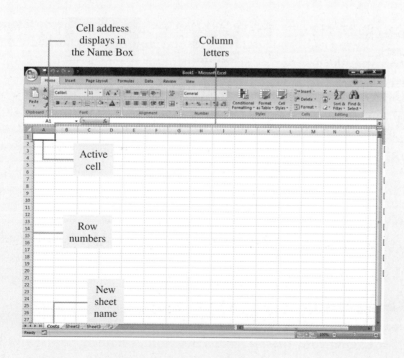

FIGURE 6.3

Navigating a Workbook, Selecting Cells, and Entering Text and Data   287   **Chapter 6**

6 **Move the pointer to the cell at the intersection of column D and row 5—cell D5. Hold down** Shift**, and then click D5.** The range of cells from A1 to D5 is selected, as shown in Figure 6.4. A *range* is a contiguous group of cells that are identified by the cell at the upper left, a colon, and the cell at the lower right. The notation for this range is A1:D5, which means that all the cells in this range are selected. The Name box continues to display the first cell—A1—in the selected range. Notice that the row numbers and column letters of the selected range display in gold, which helps identify the range of selected cells.

Highlighted
area—A1:D5—is
selected

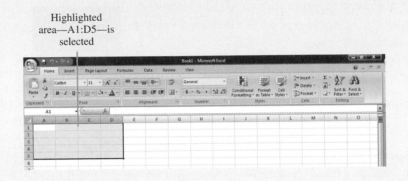

FIGURE 6.4

7 **At the bottom of the vertical scroll bar, click and hold down the arrow** ▼ **until row 50 displays on the screen, and then release the mouse button.** Rows are numbered sequentially. The maximum row number in Microsoft Office Excel 2007 is 1,048,576.

8 **Drag the box in the vertical scroll bar back to the top. Click the horizontal scroll bar arrow** ▶ **on the right repeatedly to display columns Z and AA.** Column labels use two letters after the first twenty-six columns. The second series of column labels begins with A, such as AA and AB. The third group begins with B, such as BA and BB. Microsoft Excel 2007 can have up to 16,384 columns, the last of which is XFD.

· ·

good **design...**

BEGIN IN THE UPPER LEFT CORNER
Use the cells in the upper left corner of the worksheet first. Use the cells that are normally off the screen, to the right or below, only if necessary.

· ·

9 **Drag the box in the horizontal scroll bar to the left to display cell A1.** Notice that the range A1:D5 is still selected.

10 **On the Quick Access Toolbar, click the Save button** 💾 **. Navigate to the location where you are saving your files. Create a new folder named** Chapter06 **In your Chapter06 folder, and using your own name in place of** *StudentName***, name the file** U2Ch06SolarStudentName **and then click Save.**

Text is used to label data, provide titles for worksheets, or give explanations concerning the data. Numbers are entered in cells, upon which mathematical formulas can be performed. In this task, you create labels and enter data that show the costs of buying and installing solar panels that are capable of generating 1,000 watts of electrical power.

to enter labels and data into a worksheet

1 On the Costs sheet on the Zoom bar, click the Zoom In button ⊕ until the Zoom percent displays 130%. Recall that increasing the zoom changes the magnification and makes it easier to display the data entered on the screen but does not affect the printed worksheet.

2 Click cell A1, type `Photovoltaic Solar Cells` and then press ⏎Enter. Click cell A3, type `Power output in watts` and then press ⏎Enter. Do not be concerned if the text overlaps the cell to the right. You will adjust the column widths in the next lesson.

....

if you have **problems...**

DID YOU MAKE A MISTAKE?

If you make a typing mistake, click the cell to select it and type the label again. Press ⏎Enter or click another cell to finish. What you type will replace the incorrect contents.

....

3 Click cell A5. Type `Item` and then press ⏎Enter. Notice that the cell selection moves to the next cell in the column.

4 Use the procedure described in Steps 2 and 3 to enter the following item labels into cells A6, A7, A8, and A9: `Solar panels`, `Labor`, `Brackets and wiring`, **and** `Total` The item label names are entered in the first column of the worksheet, as shown in Figure 6.5.

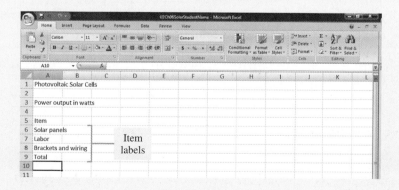

FIGURE 6.5

good **design...**

USE SHORT LABELS

Place labels to the left of data in columns or above data in rows. Use short terms for data labels—they might be used later when space is limited.

5 **Click cell B3, type** `1000` **and then press** ⏎Enter. Notice that when you make an entry in cell B3, the label entered in cell A3 is cut off.

6 **Click cell A3 and examine the formula bar. Notice that the full label remains in cell A3, as shown in Figure 6.6.** The *formula bar* is the area on the Excel window that displays the contents of the currently active cell. The value in cell A3 overlapped cell B3 until a value was entered in cell B3, at which time the entry in cell A3 was truncated. Later, you will widen column A to display the contents of the labels in this column.

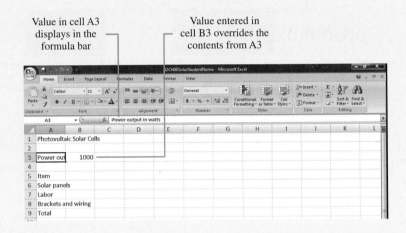

FIGURE 6.6

7 **Click cell B5, type** `Cost` **and then press** ⏎Enter **to move to the next cell in the column. Type** `5750` **and then press** ⏎Enter. The cost of the solar panels is entered in cell B6, and the selection moves to cell B7.

8 **In cell B7, type** `750` **and then press** ⏎Enter. Two of the three costs for the solar panels are entered, as shown in Figure 6.7.

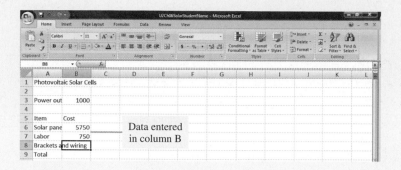

FIGURE 6.7

··

good **design...**

PLACE LABELS ON THE LEFT
When you have a list of numbers that might be summed, they should be in a vertical column with the labels on the left. This is the arrangement that the Excel program assumes if you chart the data at a later time.

··

If you miss a value while entering a column of data, you can insert a value into a cell and shift the remaining cells downward. In the list of data for solar panels, the labor cost was left out and the cost of brackets and wiring is in the wrong cell.

to shift values to other cells

1 **In the Costs worksheet, click cell B7.** This value should be in cell B8.

2 **Right-click cell B7, and from the shortcut menu, click Insert.** The Insert dialog box displays, and the default choice *Shift cells down* is selected.

3 **Click OK.** The value in the cell is moved downward into cell B8, as shown in Figure 6.8. Any other values below cell B8 would also have been moved downward, so this feature must be used with care.

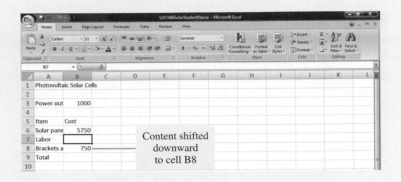

FIGURE 6.8

4 In cell **B7**, type 3250 **and then press** Enter. The value is not recorded until you press Enter.

· ·

to extend **your knowledge**

OTHER TECHNIQUES FOR MOVING CELL CONTENTS

Shifting cells to make room can cause alignment problems with data that is off the screen. The safest way to move data is to use the cut-and-paste method. This works the same way as in a word processor. It is also possible to select cells and drag the content to nearby cells by dragging the edge of the selected cells.

· ·

5 Save the workbook.

▶▶▶ *lesson*

two | Adjust Column Widths

If a column is not wide enough to display a label, the text will overlap the cell or cells to the right if they are empty. If the cells to the right are not empty, only the text that fits in the cell is displayed. The entire text in the cell displays on the formula bar when the cell is selected. If some of the text in a cell is not displayed, it might change the apparent meaning of the text.

If a column is not wide enough to display all of a number, it would certainly change the meaning if only part of the number was displayed. Instead of displaying part of a number, Excel displays pound signs—#####—in a cell when the cell is not wide enough to display the entire number. If you encounter this type of display, widen the column to show the entire number.

to widen a column

1 On the Costs sheet, at the top of the columns, point to the border between A and B, and when the ⊞ pointer displays, hold down the mouse button. Compare your screen with Figure 6.10. The numbers that identify the rows and the letters that identify the columns are called *headings*. A ScreenTip indicates the width of the column to the left in points and pixels, as shown in Figure 6.9. *Pixels* are small picture elements and *points* are 1/72 of an inch.

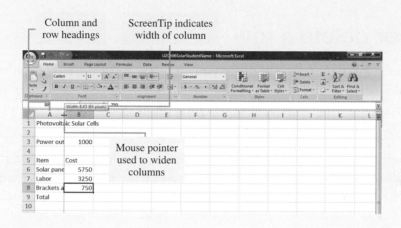

FIGURE 6.9

2 Drag the border line that separates the column headings to the right until the width of the left column—column A—is approximately 20 points, as shown in Figure 6.10.

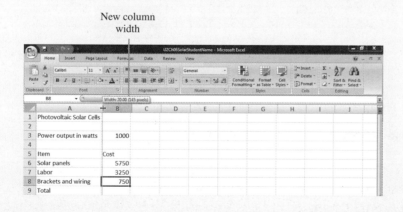

FIGURE 6.10

3 Release the mouse button. Use the procedure described in Steps 1 and 2 to widen column B to 12 points. The columns are now wide enough to display the labels and numbers.

4 Save ⊞ the workbook.

▶▶▶ *lesson*

three | Inserting or Deleting Rows or Columns

When you first design a worksheet, you often do not have all of the information that you will eventually want to include. If you need an additional row or column in a group of data, you can insert either. The displaced data is moved to the adjacent row or column. In this lesson, you add a row to make room for another cost.

to insert or delete a row

1 **With the Costs sheet selected, move your pointer onto the row heading for row 9 to display the ➡ pointer.** Solar cells create direct current, but home electricity uses alternating current. The list of costs for a photovoltaic system should include the cost of a converter, so you need to add a row.

2 **Right-click the row number for row 9.** The Mini toolbar and a shortcut menu displays, as shown in Figure 6.11. On the shortcut menu, you can choose Insert or Delete. The Insert command will insert a new row above the selected row, move the remaining rows downward, and renumber the rows accordingly. The Delete choice will delete the selected rows and move and renumber the remaining rows.

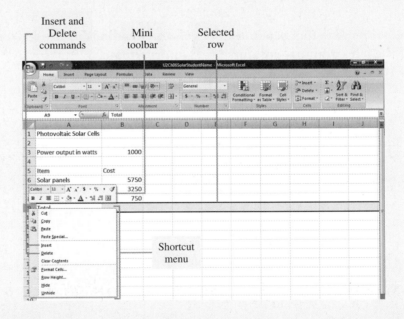

FIGURE 6.11

3 **From the shortcut menu, click Insert to insert a new row 9.** The rows below it are renumbered.

4 Click cell A9 and type DC to AC converter Press ⎢Tab⇆⎥ to move to cell B9, type 500 and then press ⎢↵Enter⎥. The new item and its cost are added to the list, as shown in Figure 6.12. Use the ⎢Tab⇆⎥ key to move to the right across a row of cells, and use ⎢⬆Shift⎥ + ⎢Tab⇆⎥ to move to the left one cell at a time.

New row
is inserted

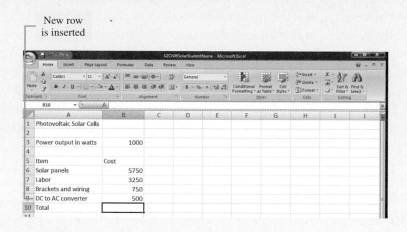

FIGURE 6.12

5 Save 💾 the workbook.

to extend **your knowledge**

INSERTING AND DELETING COLUMNS

You can insert or delete columns using the same method as you just used to insert a row. Right-click on the column letter at the top of the column, and select insert or delete from the shortcut menu that displays.

▶▶▶ *lesson*
four | Summing a Column of Numbers

Excel includes many *functions*—prewritten formulas—that are used to solve mathematical problems or manipulate text fields. One of the most common operations in a spreadsheet is to add up a column of numbers. The **Sum** function chooses adjacent cells that contain numbers, adds the values, and displays the total in the cell that contains the Sum function. The icon on the Sum function button is the Greek letter **Sigma** (Σ), which is regularly used in mathematics to indicate the summation process. In this lesson, you sum the costs.

to sum numbers in a column or row

1 **With the Costs sheet selected, click cell B10.** This cell will contain the sum of the numbers in the Cost column for the photovoltaic cells.

2 **On the Home tab, in the Editing group, click the Sum button** $\boxed{\Sigma \cdot}$. The Sum function is placed in cell B10, and the numbers in the column above are enclosed with a moving border, as shown in Figure 6.13. The program selected the correct set of numbers to sum—B6:B9. The rules that instruct Excel to execute a function are known as *arguments*. All functions begin with an equal sign, followed by the function name, and then the arguments in the order specified by the function are displayed in parentheses. The order of arguments in a function is known as the function *syntax*. In the **SUM** function, the argument is the range of cells that should be summed.

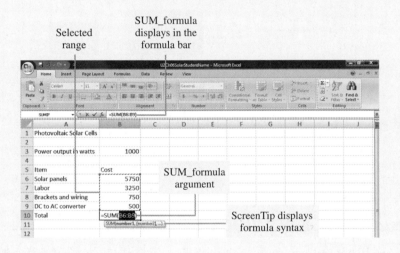

FIGURE 6.13

if you have problems...

ARE THE WRONG CELLS SELECTED?

If the program chooses the wrong cells, you can change the range of selected cells by dragging or typing a new range. This often happens if there is an empty cell in the intended range.

3 **In the Editing group, click the Sum button** $\boxed{\Sigma \cdot}$ **a second time to display the total—10250—in cell B10. Alternatively, press the** $\boxed{\text{←Enter}}$ **key to complete the operation. Notice that the Sum function displays on the formula bar, as shown in Figure 6.14.**

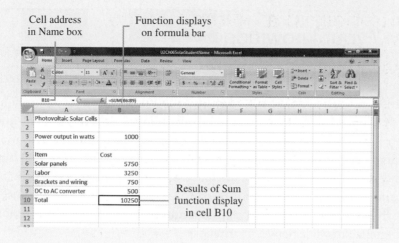

Cell address in Name box

Function displays on formula bar

Results of Sum function display in cell B10

FIGURE 6.14

4 Save 💾 the workbook.

▶▶▶ *lesson*

five | Formatting Numbers and Dates

Data becomes information when you give it meaning. If we place a currency symbol for dollars ($) in front of a number, it tells the reader that the number represents money. Punctuation marks can also be used to make numbers easier to read. Commas separate large numbers into groups of three, and decimal points indicate which part of the number represents a fraction of a unit.

Because Microsoft Office Excel's primary function is to work with numbers, the program includes a variety of formats that can be used to add meaning to numbers and to make them easier to read.

to format currency

1 With the Costs sheet selected, click cell B6.

2 On the Home tab, in the Number group, click the Accounting Number Format button $ ▾.

3 **Notice that a dollar sign is placed to the left, a comma is added between the 5 and 7, a decimal point is added followed by two zeros, and there is a space at the right side of the number.** This formatting style shows two decimal places by default because money is usually rounded to the nearest cent. The style indicates negative numbers by enclosing them in parentheses, so it leaves a space to the right of positive numbers for a closing parenthesis.

to extend your knowledge

USING OTHER CURRENCY SYMBOLS

International trade requires some knowledge of currency symbols and formats used in other countries. In the European Union, it is the Euro (€). In Great Britain and the former British Empire, the pound (£) is still used. In Japan, it is the Yen (¥), and in China it is the Yuan Renminbi (π). In Europe, the decimal point is often replaced by a comma. For example, five Euros would be €5,00. Several countries use the dollar ($), but they do not all have the same value. In that case, the country must be indicated. For example, "$5.00 USD" means U.S. dollars, and "$5.00 CAD" are Canadian dollars. If you change the display of currency values in Excel, it does not automatically convert the amount to adjust for the difference in value between currencies.

---

4 **Notice that the number displayed on the formula bar is still 5750.** The number stored in the cell is what you originally typed. The formatting adds meaning, but it does not change the underlying data.

5 **On the Home tab, in the Number group, click the Decrease Decimal button** ![icon] **two times to remove the decimal point and two zeros, as shown in Figure 6.15.**

Stored value displays in the formula bar   Decrease Decimal button

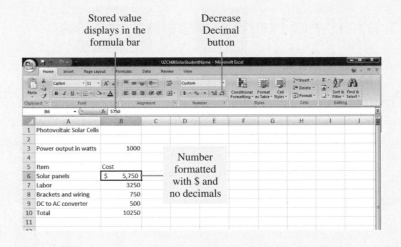

Number formatted with $ and no decimals

FIGURE 6.15

---

good design...

ROUND DISPLAY OF NUMBERS

Many numbers are estimates, and it would be misleading to indicate that you know the values more accurately than you do. In this example, the costs for the solar panels are estimated to the nearest tens of dollars. To indicate this, you do not display any decimal places, and the values are rounded off to the nearest ten.

6 Click cell B7, press ⬆Shift, and then click cell B9. The range from B7 to B9 is selected.

7 On the Home tab, in the Number group, click the Comma Style button 🔲, and then click the Decrease Decimal button 🔲 **two times.** The Comma style places a comma every three digits to make numbers easier to read. It also reserves a space to the right for a parenthesis in case a number is negative.

....

good **design...**

WHEN TO DISPLAY A CURRENCY SYMBOL

In a column of numbers that is all currency and ends with a sum, format the first number in the column and the sum with dollar signs; format the rest of the numbers with just commas. This is done to reduce visual clutter and make the information easier to read.

....

8 Click cell B10. Use the process you used in Steps 1 through 5 to apply the **Accounting Number Format and decrease the decimals so that no decimal places are displayed.** The Accounting Number Format is applied to cells B6 and B10, and the Comma Style is applied to cells B7:B9. No decimal fractions are displayed, as shown in Figure 6.16.

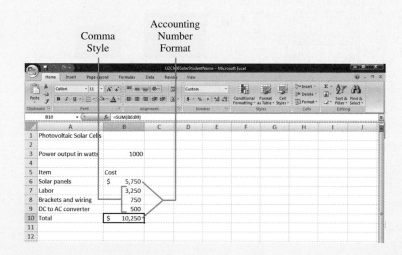

FIGURE 6.16

to extend your knowledge

OTHER NUMBER FORMATS

The Number group contains several shortcuts for formatting numbers. The three that are most commonly used have their own buttons: Accounting, Percent, and Comma. The Percent Style button will display decimal fractions as percentages by moving the decimal point two places to the right and adding the % symbol. Additional options are available by clicking the arrows next to the $ symbol and the Number Format box. A complete set of options is available in the Format Cells dialog box on the Number tab. This dialog box is displayed by clicking the Dialog Box Launcher in the lower right corner of the Number group.

Numbers that represent other types of data can be given meaning using other types of formatting. In this task, you format a number that represents the desired power output.

to format a number

1 **With the Costs sheet selected, click cell B3. On the Home tab, in the Number group, click the Dialog Box Launcher** ⬜ **to display the Format Cells dialog box.** The Number tab is selected. Notice that there are several options for displaying numbers in the Category box. The default option is General, as shown in Figure 6.17. The General format displays numbers without additional formatting.

Number
formatting
categories

General is
default option

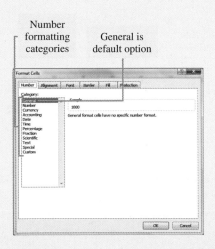

FIGURE 6.17

2 **In the Category box, click Number. In the Decimal Places box, click the down spin arrow two times to change the number of decimal places displayed to *0*. Click the *Use 1000 Separator* check box. Confirm that negative numbers are displayed using a minus sign.** The Sample box displays how the number will be formatted, as shown in Figure 6.18.

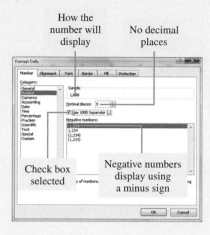

How the number will display

No decimal places

Check box selected

Negative numbers display using a minus sign

FIGURE 6.18

3 **Click OK.** The number is aligned to the right in the cell, with no space for a closing parenthesis, as shown in Figure 6.19.

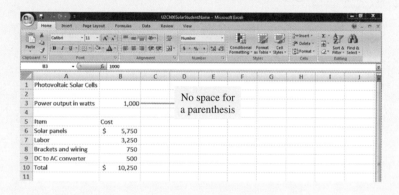

No space for a parenthesis

FIGURE 6.19

good design...

FORMATTING NEGATIVE NUMBERS

One of the Number format options uses parentheses to indicate negative numbers. If you choose to use a minus sign or red color to indicate negative numbers instead of parentheses, the numbers will not align with currency numbers that are formatted with the Accounting or Comma formats. You can use this nonalignment to give meaning to the numbers—specifically that they are not currency. This nonalignment can serve as a warning if you accidentally include a number in a summation range with currency values.

A date is a special type of number. Computers store dates as simple numbers that count from a reference date. For example, January 1, 2010 is stored as 40188 because it is 40,188 days after the beginning of the twentieth century, where January 1, 1900 is Day 1. In this lesson, you enter a date and choose a format that would be understood correctly by people in other countries.

to format a date

1 **With the Costs sheet selected, click A12. Type** `Date of analysis:` **and then press** `Tab↹`.

2 **In cell B12, type** `8/9/10` **and then press** `↵Enter`. Excel is programmed to recognize dates when you type them and to display the year using four digits, as shown in Figure 6.20.

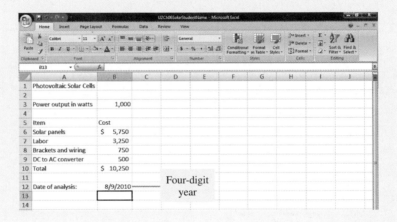

FIGURE 6.20

to extend your knowledge

Excel applies a format that is abbreviated as mm/dd/yyyy, where the letter *d* represents days, *m* represents months, and *y* represents years. Even though you typed *10* for the year, it shows the full year using four digits so that there is no confusion with 1910. If you meant 1910, you would have to type it out fully. When Microsoft Office Excel 2007 is installed, the language and country are specified. Excel refers to this setting. If English (U.S.) is specified, it interprets the first number as the month and the entry 8/9/10 as *August 9, 2010*.

The Excel program stores dates and times as a single number. The time of day is indicated as a decimal fraction of a day. For example, noon on January 1, 2010 is stored as 40188.5, and 6 PM on the same day would be 40188.75. If you chose a date format that included the time, the latter number would display as *1/10/2010 6:00:00 PM* in the U.S.

3 **Click cell B12. On the Home tab, in the Number group, click the Dialog Box Launcher** ⬛. **In the Category box, click General, and then notice the number in the Sample box.** The number 40399 displays. This is the number that was actually stored when you typed the date. It is the number of days after the start of the twentieth century.

4 **In the Category box, click Date. In the Type box, scroll down and click the second instance of 14-Mar-01.** Notice that the Locale is set to *English (United States).* Also notice the display in the Sample box. This format displays the date in dd/mmm/yy format, which forces zeros in single-digit days or months as shown in Figure 6.21.

Locale Sample of
setting selected
   date format

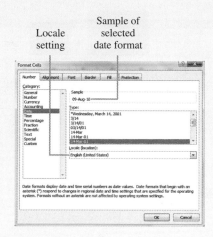

FIGURE 6.21

5 **In the Locale box, click the list arrow. Scroll down the list and click on French (France). In the Type box, scroll up, and then click 14/03/01.** Notice that the date in the Sample box is displayed as 09/08/10 instead of 08/09/10. Many other countries assume that the first number is the day and use the dd/mm/yy format instead of mm/dd/yy that is used on the United States.

good design...

USE INTERNATIONAL DATE FORMATS

Formatting gives meaning to numbers. In the case of dates, the meaning of the position in a date can differ from one country to the next. To avoid confusion, it is a good idea to choose a date format that displays the name of the month and all four digits of the year.

6 **With the Format Cells dialog box still open, click the Locale arrow and choose English (United States). In the Type box, scroll down and select the March 14, 2001 format, and then click OK.** Notice that this format is too wide for the column and a row of #### fills the cell.

7 **Move the pointer to the line between the headings of columns B and C. Double-click the border between the column headings.** Double-clicking the line between the headings is an alternative method of widening the column. The column is *AutoFit*—automatically widened to fit the longest number or text in the column—in this case, the date format in cell B12 shown in Figure 6.22. This date format clearly identifies the month and year. The name of the month might be different in another country, but it would still be clear which parts of the date are the day, month, and year.

Date in formula
bar displays as
it was entered

Format identifies
month and year

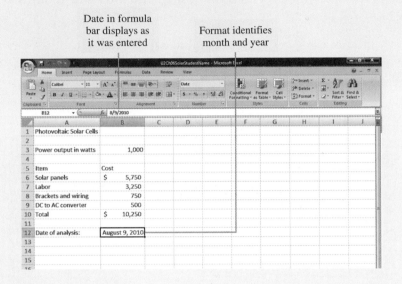

FIGURE 6.22

8 **Save 💾 the workbook.**

▶▶▶*lesson*
SIX | Aligning Text

Text is used as labels, and the alignment of the text within a cell or across columns can identify different types of labels. In this lesson, you change the alignment of text to give it additional meaning.

to align text

1 **With the Costs sheet selected, click cell A1. Notice that this cell contains a long label that is the title for the entire worksheet. Notice also that the data in the worksheet occupies the first two columns.** The title describes the rest of the content in the worksheet. A title is usually placed at the top, and it usually spans all of the columns that contain data.

2 **With the ✥ pointer displayed in the middle of cell A1, drag to the right to cell B1 to select the range A1:B1.** Alternatively, press ⬆Shift and click cell B1 to select both cells.

3 **On the Home tab, in the Alignment group, click the Merge & Center button ⊞ ▾.** The selected cells are treated like one cell and the text is centered across both cells. This places the title of the worksheet across both columns, as shown in Figure 6.23.

Title centered across columns   Merge and Center button

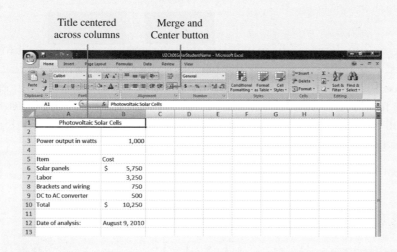

FIGURE 6.23

4 **Click cell A5, and in the Alignment group, click the Center button ≣. Repeat this process to center the title in B5.** The Item and Cost labels are centered on their respective columns.

5 **Click cell A10. In the Alignment group, click the Align Text Right button ≣.** The label is aligned at the right side of the cell, next to the sum to which it refers.

6 **Compare your screen to Figure 6.24, and then save 💾 the workbook.**

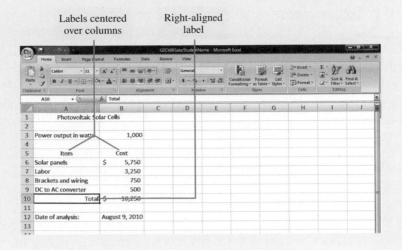

Labels centered over columns

Right-aligned label

FIGURE 6.24

If there is too much text to fit in a cell, it will overlap the cells to the right if they are empty. In many cases, it is better to increase the height of the cell and wrap the text within one cell. Text can be used to document the source of data or to make comments, but either type of text is likely to be too long to fit within a cell of normal width. This type of text is often wrapped within one cell by making the entire row taller. You can use a text-wrap option that works like the automatic text wrapping in a word processing program.

to wrap text

1 **Click cell A13. On the Home tab, in the Alignment group, click the Wrap Text button** 📑. In this cell, you will enter documenting text that is too long to fit in a single column of normal width.

2 **In cell A13, type** `Source: Wall Street Journal, Monday June 30, 2008, page R6` **and then press** ⏎Enter. The text is wrapped within A13 on three lines, as shown in Figure 6.25. The text wraps within the current width of the cell and automatically increases the height of the row as needed.

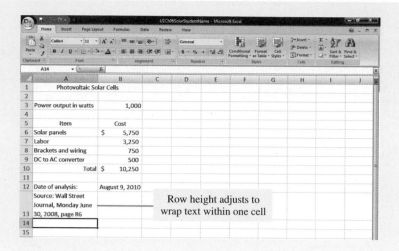

FIGURE 6.25

good design...

DOCUMENT YOUR WORK

Assume that someone else might use your work, and provide them with information such as your data source, who created the workbook, and when it was created. This is called ***documenting*** your work.

3 **With a cell in column A active, on the Home tab, in the Cells group, click the Format button. From the displayed list, click Column Width. In the Column Width dialog box, type** `30` **and then press** `⏎Enter`**.** Notice that the text fits on two lines, but the row height did not decrease accordingly. The row height increases automatically but does not decrease automatically.

4 **Point to the border between the headings for rows 13 and 14. When the** ⬍ **pointer displays, double-click to adjust the row height.** The row height adjusts to the height of the two lines of text in A13, as shown in Figure 6.26.

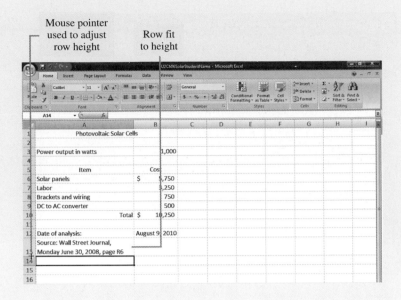

FIGURE 6.26

5 ▸ Save 💾 the workbook.

seven | Adding Emphasis, Colors, Shading, and Borders

The organization of the data and labels is indicated by using different fonts, font sizes, and colors. The cells can be filled with background color, and the edges of the cells can be lines of different styles. In this lesson, you use these tools to indicate the organization of the table and its most important parts.

to add emphasis to fonts

1 ▸ **With the Costs sheet selected, click cell A1.** Because cell A1 is merged with cell B1, they are both selected.

2 ▸ **Press and hold** Ctrl**, and then click cells A5 and B5. Release the** Ctrl **key.** All three cells are selected. Use Ctrl to select cells that are not adjacent to each other, and use ⬆Shift to select a block of adjacent cells.

3 ▸ **On the Home tab, in the Font group, click the Bold button** B **to apply bold to these three titles.**

4   Click cell A13. On the formula bar, drag the name of the paper—*Wall Street Journal*—to select it. In the Font group, click the Italic button ⎡*I*⎤, and then press ⎡↵Enter⎤. The name of the newspaper is italicized to differentiate it from the rest of the source information.

5   Click A1. In the Font group, click the Font Size button arrow ⎡11 ▾⎤, and then click 12. The main title is further emphasized by using a larger font.

6   Save 🖫 your workbook, and then compare your screen with Figure 6.27.

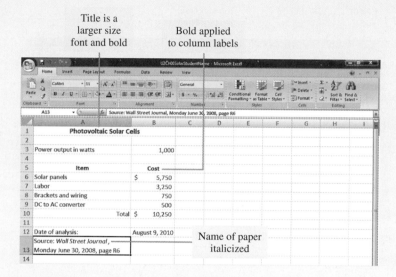

Title is a larger size font and bold

Bold applied to column labels

Name of paper italicized

FIGURE 6.27

good design...

EMPHASIZE THE TITLE

The worksheet title should be in the first row. It is usually centered across the columns and emphasized with a larger font or color. Someone other than the author should be able to tell at a glance what the most important facts are on a worksheet. Use a combination of emphasized fonts, colors, and borders to draw the reader's eye to the titles and totals.

The edges of the cells are defined with **gridlines** that appear on the screen but are not displayed on printouts unless the feature is turned on. When there are many rows or columns, gridlines help your eye stay in the same row or column as you scan a large worksheet. In addition to or in place of gridlines, other lines can be added to the top, bottom, or either side of cells to create groups or to add meaning. These lines are called **borders**. In this task, you add a special border that identifies which number in a column is the total.

to add a border

1 **With the Costs sheet selected, click cell B10.** This is the total of the costs for installing solar panels. Accountants indicate the total at the bottom of a column with a line between the numbers and the total and a double line below the total.

2 **On the Home tab, in the Font group, click the Borders button arrow** 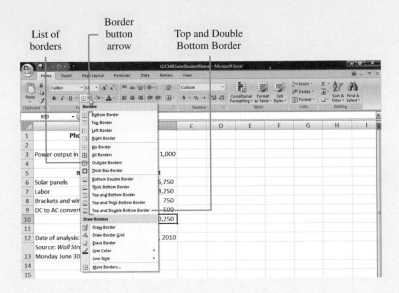 **to display the borders list, shown in Figure 6.28.**

Border
button
List of   arrow   Top and Double
borders   Bottom Border

FIGURE 6.28

3 **On the Borders list, click** *Top and Double Bottom Border.* **Press** Ctrl + Home **to move to cell A1.** You must select a cell that is not adjacent to see the borders. A top line and a double bottom border are added to cell B10, as shown in Figure 6.29.

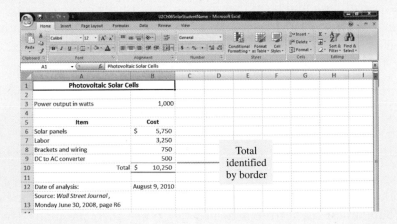

Total
identified
by border

FIGURE 6.29

Color can be used as a background within a cell, or as the color of the font, to add emphasis or to indicate a group.

to add color

1 **With cell A1 selected, on the Home tab, in the Font group, click the Fill Color button arrow** ⬛▾ . The Fill Color gallery displays, shown in Figure 6.30.

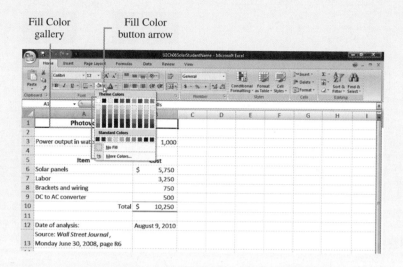

FIGURE 6.30

2 **Under Themes, in the last column, point to the color in the fourth row—** *Orange, Accent 6, Lighter 40%.*

3 **Click** *Orange, Accent 6, Lighter 40%* **to apply this fill background to the selected cell.** Both cells A1 and B1 are filled because they are merged.

4 **Select cells A5 and B5. Use the process described in Steps 1 through 4 to apply the Fill Color** *Orange, Accent 6, Lighter 80%* **to these cells. Compare your screen with Figure 6.31.**

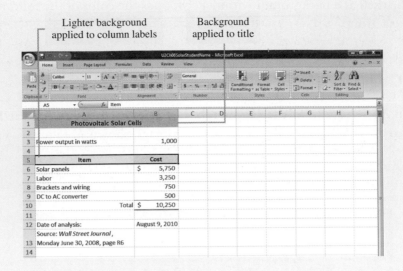

Lighter background applied to column labels

Background applied to title

FIGURE 6.31

5 Save the workbook.

good design...

USE COMPATIBLE AND CONTRASTING COLORS

Background colors should contrast with the font color so that the font is legible. In general, use black for font colors and pastel colors for background colors. Some colors look good together. Excel provides groups of these colors in *themes*, which are collections of colors, fonts, and methods of emphasis that look good together.

▶▶▶ *lesson*

eight | Opening, Copying, Inserting, and Deleting Worksheets

Excel workbooks contain three worksheets by default. You can add or remove worksheets or copy them between workbooks. In this lesson, you open an existing workbook with information about solar resources and copy a worksheet from it into your workbook.

to open an existing workbook and copy a worksheet

1 Click the Office button 🔘, and then click Open.

2 **Navigate to the folder where the student files are located for this chapter and open U2Ch06SolarEnergy.** The SolarEnergy worksheet in this workbook has two groups of data with information about the solar energy that is available each day in each state, as shown in Figure 6.32.

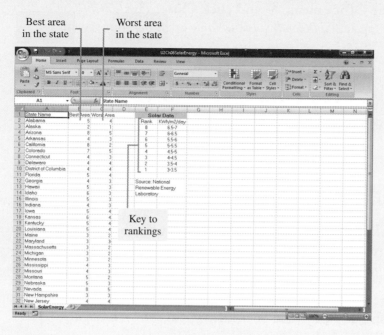

FIGURE 6.32

3 **Point to the SolarEnergy worksheet tab and right-click. On the shortcut menu, click Move or Copy.** The Move or Copy dialog box displays.

4 **Click the To book arrow, and then click U2Ch06SolarStudentName.** A list of worksheets in Ch06SolarStudentName is displayed in the *Before sheet* box.

5 **Click the Create a copy check box. In the Before sheet box, click (move to end). Compare your screen to Figure 6.33, and then click OK.** The display switches to your workbook, where a copy of the SolarEnergy worksheet has been added to your workbook after Sheet 3. The *U2Ch06SolarEnergy* file is still open.

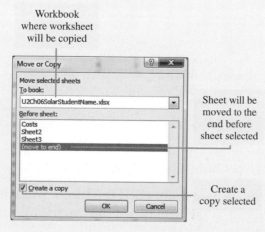

FIGURE 6.33

Opening, Copying, Inserting, and Deleting Worksheets

313 Chapter 6

6 **Click the View tab, and in the Window group, click the Switch Windows button.** A list of the workbooks currently in use displays.

7 **Click U2Ch06SolarEnergy to switch back to this workbook.**

8 **Display the Office menu** 📄 **and click Close.** The *U2Ch06SolarEnergy* workbook closes, leaving *U2Ch06SolarStudentName* open on your screen.

Unused worksheets can be deleted or new worksheets added.

to delete an existing worksheet

1 **Right-click the Sheet2 tab. On the shortcut menu, click Delete.** Sheet2 is removed from the workbook, and the next worksheet in the workbook—Sheet3—displays.

2 **Repeat the process you practiced in step 1 to delete Sheet3.** The workbook has two worksheets—Costs and SolarEnergy—as shown in Figure 6.34.

Solar Energy
worksheet
inserted

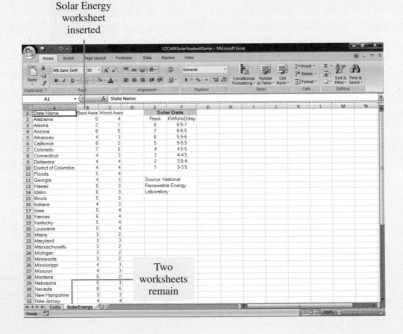

FIGURE 6.34

3 **To the right of the SolarEnergy tab, click the Insert Worksheet tab** 📄 An empty worksheet is added to the workbook. You can use this method to add as many worksheets as needed. Your sheet number might be different, depending on how many times you've practiced this process.

4 **Use the process you just practiced in Steps 1 and 2 to delete the empty worksheet.** The workbook now has two worksheets—Costs and SolarEnergy.

5 **Save** 💾 **the workbook.**

good design...

USE SHORT SHEET NAMES

Each worksheet in a workbook should have a name that indicates the content of the sheet. The names should be short but descriptive. If you use two-word names for sheets, it is best to capitalize the first letter of each word and not use a space. While spaces are accepted in sheet names, if you reference a cell on another sheet, it is easier if the sheet name does not include spaces. Always delete unused worksheets.

▶▶▶ *lesson*
nine|Formatting, Sorting, and Filtering Tables

A *table* is organized in columns, with each type of data in a column and the data for each individual item in a row. One of the advantages of organizing data in labeled columns is that the data can be formatted, sorted, and filtered conveniently using the Excel Table feature.

In this lesson, you apply a table format and then sort and filter the data to determine the states with the most available solar energy, which would be most appropriate for installations of solar power cells.

to define a table and choose a format

1 **With the SolarEnergy worksheet selected, click anywhere in the first three columns of data. Notice that the data in cells E1:F14 are separated from the first three columns by an empty column.** The program will assume that the cells that are adjacent to each other form a group.

good design...

SEPARATE TABLES FROM OTHER DATA

If there will be other data on the worksheet in addition to the values in the table, leave a blank row or column between the table and the other data. This enables the Excel program to identify the range of cells that make up the table.

2 **On the Insert tab, in the Tables group, click the Table button.** The Create Table dialog box displays, shown in Figure 6.35. It selects the cells that are adjacent to the selected cell and assumes that this range of cells comprises the table, and also assumes that the first row of the group contains column labels, called *headers*. This term is different than *headings*, which refers to the row numbers and column letters.

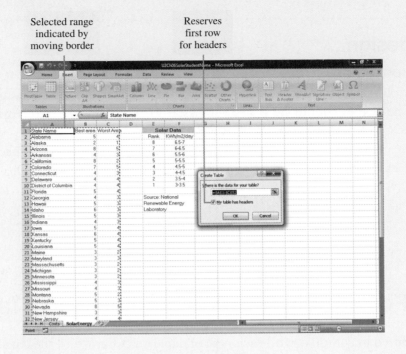

FIGURE 6.35

3 **Click OK.** Fill colors are added to the table, and the header in each column has an arrow button. The Ribbon displays the Table Tools Design tab and highlights the default table style, as shown in Figure 6.36.

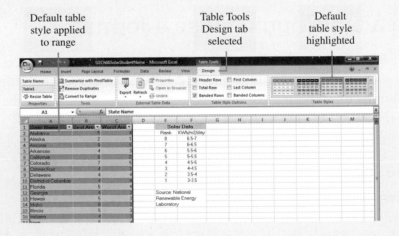

FIGURE 6.36

4 Click the Design tab, and in the Table Styles group, click the More button ▼ to display the gallery of available table styles.

5 Under Light, point to the style in the third row, fourth column—*Table Style Light 17*—as shown in Figure 6.37. Recall that it is good design to choose background colors that contrast with the text to improve legibility. Also notice that the live preview feature applies the style to the table to provide a preview of the style before it is selected.

Live preview
displays the
selected style
on the table

Table Style
Light 17
selected

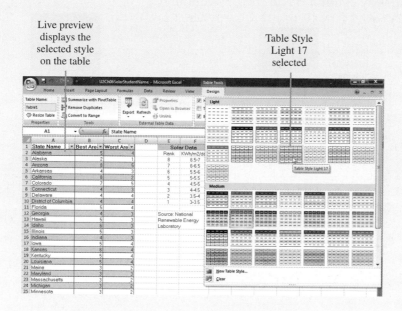

FIGURE 6.37

6 Click *Table Style Light 17* to apply it to the table, and then click a cell outside the table.

7 Point to the border between the headings of columns B and C, and double-click. Repeat this procedure to widen column C. The width of column B and C is increased to display that column header and the arrow button.

Once a table is defined, you can sort it on any of its columns.

to sort a table

1 With the SolarEnergy worksheet selected, click any cell in column B of the table. This indicates which column to sort.

2 Click the Home tab. In the Editing group, click the Sort & Filter button, and then click *Sort Largest to Smallest* ⬇. The header arrow in cell B1 changes to indicate that the column is sorted. The rows of the table are sorted on the values in column B, as shown in Figure 6.38. The states with the best-ranked areas of solar energy—8—are brought to the top of the table. This table has a column for the state's highest-ranked area and the state's lowest-ranked area. Some states have a wide range from high to low. When the values are the same, no further sorting is necessary. To find the states that have the highest values for both their best and worst areas, you can sort first by column B and then by column C.

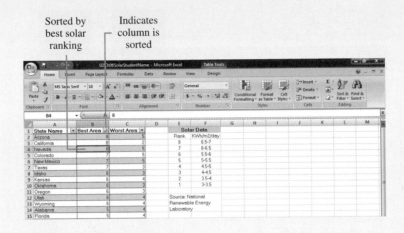

FIGURE 6.38

3 With a cell in column B still selected, in the Editing group, click the Sort & Filter button, and then click Custom Sort. The Sort dialog box displays. You can sort on more than one column by adding levels of sorting. The column heading of column B displays in the *Sort by* box, and the *Order* is Largest to Smallest.

4 In the Sort dialog box, click the Add Level button. Click the Then by arrow and click Worst Area. Click the Order arrow, and then click Largest to Smallest. The options are set up to sort the table first by the Best Area values, from largest to smallest; then, when there are duplicate values, it will subsort those rows based on the values in the Worst Area column. Compare your screen with Figure 6.39.

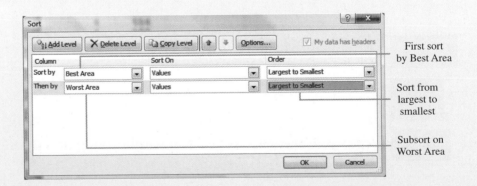

FIGURE 6.39

5 **Click OK. Save** 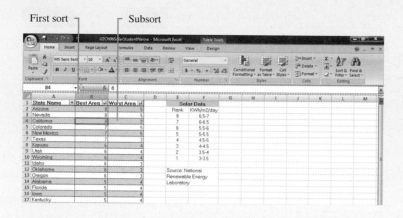 **the workbook.** The table is sorted first by the values in the Best Area column, and then subsorted by the values in the Worst Area column, as shown in Figure 6.40.

First sort   Subsort

FIGURE 6.40

When you define an area as a table, arrows are added to the column headings by default. You can use these arrows to **filter** the table—limit the rows that are displayed in the table to those that match certain conditions—and to sort by individual columns.

to filter a table

1 **With the SolarEnergy worksheet selected, in cell B1, click the arrow.** A menu of sorting and filtering options displays. You can choose to display values that match those on the list by clicking the check boxes.

2 **Click the check boxes next to 2, 3, and 4 to deselect those choices.** Only rows that have values of 5, 6, 7, or 8 will be displayed, as shown in Figure 6.41.

Filtered to
display only
5, 6, 7, or 8

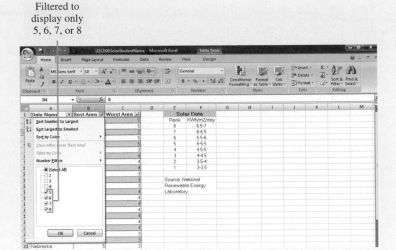

FIGURE 6.41

3 **Click OK.** The arrow icon in B1 changes to indicate that the column is sorted and filtered. You can define the filter using comparison operators. In the Worst Area column, you will limit the values to those greater than 2.

4 **In cell C1, click the header arrow, point to Number Filters, and then click Greater than.** The Custom AutoFilter dialog box displays.

5 **Click the empty box in the first row, and then type** 2 The rows displayed will also have a Worst Area value greater than 2, as shown in Figure 6.42.

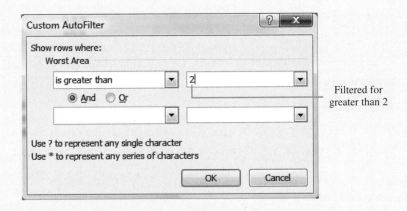

Filtered for greater than 2

FIGURE 6.42

6 **Click OK. Save** 💾 **the workbook.** Only the rows that satisfy both criteria—Best Area values of 5, 6, 7, or 8 and Worst Area greater than 2—are displayed, as shown in Figure 6.43.

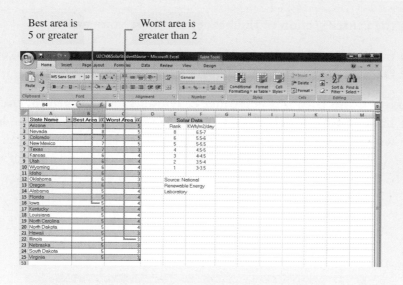

FIGURE 6.43

▶▶▶ *lesson*

ten | Documenting and Printing Worksheets

Documenting refers to the process of providing background and context for the work. One option is to add some of this information to the top or bottom of each printed page. The area reserved at the top of a page for information that will display on each page is called the **header**. The same area at the bottom of the page is known as the **footer**.

In this lesson, you add your name, class, and date to the header, center the worksheets on the page, and then preview the printed version of the Costs and SolarEnergy worksheets.

to document your work in the header

1 **Click the Costs sheet tab. Click cell A1. On the View tab, in the Workbook Views group, click the Page Layout button.** The Page Layout view displays the margins and headers as they would appear on the printed page. Alternatively, on the status bar, click the Page Layout button 🔲.

2 **Click the margin area above the first column.** The Header box changes color, and the insertion point displays in the left section of the header area. The header and footer are divided into three sections. Content in the left section is left aligned, content in the center section is centered, and content in the right section is right aligned.

3 **On the Header & Footer Tools Design tab, in the Header & Footer Elements group, click the File Name button.** A programming code—&*[File]*—is placed in the left section of the header.

4 Click in the center section of the header and type your name.

5 Click in the right section. In the Header & Footer Elements group, click the Current Date button.

6 Press [Spacebar], and then in the Header & Footer Elements group, click the Current Time button. Click cell A1 in the worksheet to deselect the header. The program will reference your computer's internal clock and display the current date and time whenever the worksheet is printed. The date and time on your worksheet will not be the same as the example shown in Figure 6.44.

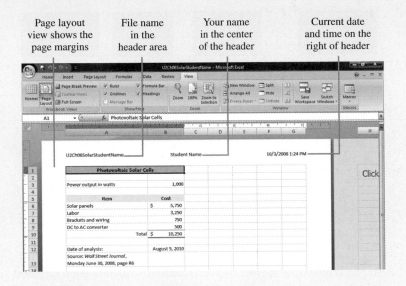

Page layout view shows the page margins   File name in the header area   Your name in the center of the header   Current date and time on the right of header

FIGURE 6.44

Unlike a word processing document, the content of a worksheet might be wider than a single page, or the content might not be centered on the page. You should preview a worksheet to see what it will look like before you send it to the printer.

to prepare a worksheet to print

1 With the Costs sheet selected, on the Page Layout tab, in the Page Setup group, click the Dialog Box Launcher ▣ . The Page Setup dialog box displays. Notice that the default orientation is *portrait*—the page is oriented vertically and is taller than it is wide. If the data on your worksheet is wider than it is tall, select *landscape* orientation so that more data will fit horizontally on each page.

2 In the Page Setup dialog box, click the Margins tab. Under Center on page, click Horizontally to center the content of the worksheet horizontally on the page.

3 **Click the Header/Footer tab.** Notice that your header information displays in the header and the footer is empty. The footer is often used for page numbering.

4 **In the Page Setup dialog box, click the Sheet tab.** The options on this tab are useful when you only want to print part of the data or if the data does not fit on one page.

5 **Under Print, click Gridlines.** The normal view of a worksheet shows the lines that separate the cells, but by default these lines do not print.

6 **In the Page Setup dialog box, click the Print Preview button.** A preview of the printed page displays. The pointer turns into a magnifying glass that indicates that you can change the zoom by clicking on the image of the printout.

7 **Click the Student Name on the printout.** The image is magnified so it is more legible. This version displays the gridlines, as shown in Figure 6.45.

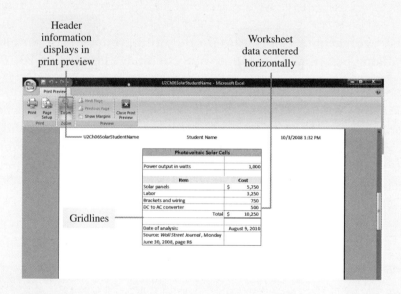

FIGURE 6.45

8 **On the Print Preview tab, in the Print group, click the Page Setup button. On the Sheet tab, click to deselect the Gridlines check box, and then click OK.** This small table does not need gridlines to guide your eye across rows or down columns, so they are omitted, as shown in Figure 6.46.

No gridlines — Documentation in header

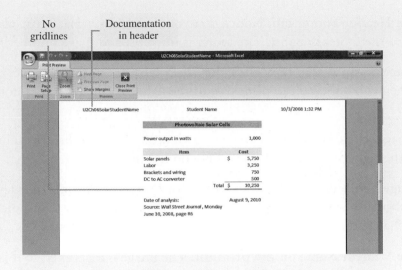

FIGURE 6.46

9 If your instructor requires a printout, in the Print group, click Print, and then in the Print dialog box, click OK. Otherwise, click the Close Print Preview button.

10 Click the SolarEnergy sheet tab. Use the procedures you practiced in Steps 1–9 to prepare the filtered list of states with the solar data. Place the file name in the left section, your name in the center section, and the current date and time in the right section. Display the gridlines and center the content horizontally on this printout. Display the worksheet in the Print Preview window and compare your screen with Figure 6.47.

Documentation in header — Gridlines displayed

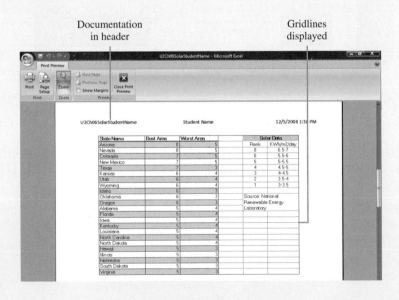

FIGURE 6.47

11 Print the worksheet if your instructor requires it. Otherwise, Close the Print Preview. On the Status bar, click the Normal button ⊞.

12 Click the Costs sheet tab, and then click A1. On the Status bar, click the Normal button ⊞. Save 💾 your changes and then close the workbook.

··

good **design...**

SELECT UPPER CORNER BEFORE SAVING

Before you close your workbook for the last time, select the title of the first worksheet. When the next person opens the workbook, they will be introduced to the workbook at that point.

··

Advanced Skills or Concepts

In this section, you are introduced to skills that are not taught with step-by-step instructions.

Drawing Simple Conclusions

Excel is a decision support tool. This is important to keep in mind when you design a worksheet. In the Costs worksheet, the total cost for a photo cell array was calculated. This value could be used to decide if there is enough money for the project. You sorted and filtered the list of states in the SolarEnergy worksheet to see which states were the best candidates for solar power. This information could be used to decide where to advertise for customers of solar cells.

Identify Elements of a Well-Organized Worksheet

Good design ideas have been identified in the lessons at the points where they are relevant. A well-organized worksheet should have all of those elements. They are summarized as follows:

- The upper left corner of the worksheet is the starting point. Place the title in the first row.

- Merge a title across those columns to which the title applies.

- If the data is in columns, place the labels in the column to the left. If the data is in rows, place the labels above.

- Keep labels short because they might be used later where space is limited.

- If you have a list of numbers to be summed, place them in a column with labels in the column to the left.

- Do not display decimal fractions that imply that you know the values more accurately than you do.
- If you sum a column of currency values, the first number in the list and the total at the bottom display a dollar sign, and the values in between use the Comma Style.
- If you use Accounting Number Format for some currency values in a column, use a format such as Comma Style that reserves a space to the right for a parenthesis so the numbers align properly.
- Use a date format that displays the name of the month to avoid confusion between U.S. and European interpretations.
- If you use background colors, be sure they contrast with the font color so the font is legible.
- Leave an empty row or column between a table and any other data on the same worksheet.
- Each worksheet in the workbook should have a name on the tab, and unused worksheets should be deleted.
- Select the title on the first worksheet before you save and close the workbook so that the next user will open the first worksheet to the title.

Accurate Data Matters

To make valuable conclusions or decisions that are based on the results of a calculation in a worksheet, the data in the worksheet must be accurate. This is one of the reasons that it is important to document the source of the data—so someone else can verify the accuracy of the data.

CHECK YOUR WORK

Here is a list of items your instructor will probably look for when grading your work. To improve your evaluation, take time to check the items yourself before you turn in your work.

Costs sheet
- Header has file name at the left, your name in the center, the current date and time at the right
- Title and column headings in bold
- Title is merged and centered in cells A1 and B1
- Title has a darker background than the two column headings and is in a slightly larger font
- Number in B3 has a comma separator and is right aligned to the edge of the cell
- All costs line up with a space at the right. The value for Solar Panels has a dollar sign, and so does the total. The numbers in between just have commas.
- Total has a border that consists of a single line above and a double line below
- Date in B12 uses a format that displays the name of the month
- Source in A13 is wrapped like word processor text, and A13 is taller than the other cells to accommodate the wrapped text
- Sheet tab is named Costs, and empty worksheets are deleted

- Check the print preview or the printout to be sure the data is centered—you cannot tell this from the Page Layout view.

SolarEnergy Sheet
- Header has file name at the left, your name in the center, and the current date and time at the right
- Table uses the format shown in the Visual Summary at the beginning of the chapter
- Columns of the table are widened so that you can read each column label
- Table of states is filtered to 23 states
- Table is sorted first by the Best Area column
- When states have the same rating for Best Area, the table is subsorted by Worst Area. Check the three states with ratings of 7 for Best Area. Make sure those three are sorted in descending order by the values in the Worst Area column.
- Check the print preview or the printout to be sure the data is centered and the gridlines are displayed—you cannot tell this from the Page Layout view.

KEY TERMS

active cell	function	Sigma Σ
arguments	gridlines	spreadsheet
AutoFit	header	Sum
borders	heading	syntax
cell	landscape	table
cell address	Name box	themes
documenting	pixel	workbook
filter	point	worksheet
footer	portrait	
formula bar	range	

ASSESSING LEARNING OUTCOMES

SCREEN ID

Identify each element of the screen by matching call-out numbers shown in Figure 6.48 to a corresponding description.

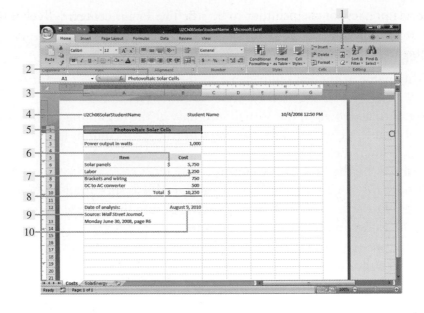

FIGURE 6.48

_____ **A.** Accounting Number Format

_____ **B.** Column headers

_____ **C.** Comma Style

_____ **D.** Date format

_____ **E.** Formula bar

_____ **F.** Header

_____ **G.** Sum button

_____ **H.** Title in merged cells

_____ **I.** Top and double bottom line border

_____ **J.** Wrapped text

MULTIPLE CHOICE

Circle the letter of the correct answer for each of the following. The lesson in which the term or concept was introduced is indicated at the end of the sentence.

1. In Excel, a spreadsheet is called a _____. [L1]
   a. workbook
   b. worksheet
   c. file
   d. spreadsheet

2. If ten rows of data and labels are placed in columns, the labels should be _____ the data. [L1]
   a. to the right of
   b. above
   c. to the left of
   d. below

3. If the number 4311.50 is estimated to the nearest 100 dollars, it would display as _____. [L5]
   a. $4,300.00
   b. $4,310
   c. $4,000
   d. $4,300

4. If Accounting Number Format is used to display currency with dollar signs, the format that right aligns with it by default is _____ format. [L5]
   a. Comma Style
   b. General Style
   c. Number Style
   d. Date

5. To ensure that a date is not misunderstood by someone from another country, the best format to use is _____. [L5]

a. 10-Aug-5

b. 8/5/10

c. August 5, 2010

d. 5/8/10

6. Rules that instruct Excel how to execute a function are called _____. [L10]

a. conclusions

b. arguments

c. reasons

d. logic order

7. The Greek letter that often represents summation is _____. [L5]

a. Delta

b. Omega

c. Pi

d. Sigma

8. The lines between cells that display on screen but not in printouts by default are called _____. [L7]

a. gridlines

b. borders

c. boundaries

d. row and column lines

9. The label at the top of a column of data is called a _____. [L9]

a. heading

b. header

c. title

d. category

10. The row numbers and the column letters are called _____. [L2]

a. headings

b. headers

c. titles

d. categories

MATCHING

Match the term or concept to its description.

_____ 1. Automatic process to adjust the width of a column or height of a row to fit the largest content

_____ 2. Collection of worksheets in a single Excel file

_____ 3. Generic term for financial data arranged in rows and columns with formulas that can recalculate automatically if values in cells change

_____ 4. Limits the rows that display in a table to those that meet certain conditions

_____ 5. Used to identify a total in a column

_____ 6. The column letter and row number used to identify a cell

_____ 7. Providing information about the source, author, and creation date of a workbook

_____ 8. The location where data will display when you type

_____ 9. The area in the Excel window that displays the name of the cell

_____ 10. The location in Excel that displays the formula or contents in the active cell

A. Active cell

B. AutoFit

C. Cell address

D. Documenting

E. Filter

F. Formula bar

G. Name box

H. Spreadsheet

I. Top and double bottom border

J. Workbook

The Skill Drill exercise is a repeat of the lessons in the chapter but with different data. The instructions are less detailed, and your speed and familiarity should increase with practice. There is a figure at the end against which you can check your worksheets. The purpose of this exercise is to build your confidence and speed in using these skills and to set them in your memory for later recall. The section numbers correspond to the lesson numbers. You are welcome to refer back to the lessons illustrated and the detailed instructions, if necessary.

In this exercise, you set up a worksheet that displays the costs of installing a small wind generator and sort a table of data that compares states by their wind resources. Print copies of the worksheets if your instructor requires it.

1. Navigating a Workbook, Selecting Cells, and Entering Text and Data

1. Start Excel and use the blank workbook. Check all three sheets to be sure they are empty. Return to **Sheet1**. Scroll to the right and then toward the bottom to confirm that the sheet is empty beyond the cells that are normally visible on screen.

2. Double-click the **Sheet1** tab, type `Costs` and press `↵Enter`. Click the **Save** button, navigate to the **Chapter06** folder you created previously, and then save the file as `U2Ch06WindStudentName`

3. On the **Costs** sheet in cell **A1**, type the title `Wind Generator` and then press `↵Enter`.

4. In cell **A3**, type `Power Output in watts` In cells **A5** through **A9**, type `Item`, `Turbine`, `Tower`, `Labor`, `Controls and connections`, and `Total` Remember to press `↵Enter` or click another cell after the last entry to complete the process.

5. In cell **B3**, type `1000` In cells **B5** through **B8**, type `Cost`, `2000`, `5000`, and `500` One of the values is left out intentionally.

6. Right-click cell **B8**, and insert an empty cell by shifting the value in the cell downward. Recall that this affects all the cells below it in the same column, but they are still empty at this time.

7. In cell **B8**, type `2000` and then press `↵Enter`.

2. Adjusting Column Widths

1. Notice that column **A** is not wide enough to display all the items. Drag the line between column headings **A** and **B** to widen the column to **24** points, or **173** pixels.

2. Use the same process to widen column **B** to **10** points.

3. Inserting or Deleting Rows or Columns

1. Point to the heading of row **10** and right-click. From the shortcut menu, click **Insert** to insert a new row.

2. Click cell **A10**, and then type `Interface with utility`

3. Click cell **B10**, type `100` and then press `↵Enter`.

4. Summing a Column of Numbers

1. Click cell **B11**. On the **Home** tab, in the **Editing** group, click the **Sum** button.

2. Examine the range of cells and confirm that it includes **B6** through **B10**.

3. Click the **Sum** button again. Alternatively, press ⏎Enter.

5. Formatting Numbers and Dates

1. Click cell **B6.** Hold down Ctrl and click cell **B11**. Recall that holding down the Ctrl key enables you to select cells that are not adjacent.

2. On the **Home** tab, in the **Number** group, click the **Accounting Number Format** button.

3. With both cells still selected, in the **Number** group, click the **Decrease Decimal** button **two** times.

4. Click cell **B7.** Press and hold down ⬆Shift and click cell **B10**. Recall that holding down the ⬆Shift key enables you to select adjacent cells.

5. In the **Number** group, click the **Comma Style** button, and then click the **Decrease Decimal** button **two** times.

6. Click **B3**. In the **Number** group, click the **Dialog Box Launcher.**

7. In the Format Cells dialog box, on the **Number** tab, in the **Category** box, click **Number.**

8. In the **Decimal places** box, click the down spin arrow two times to reduce the decimal places to **0.** Select the **Use 1000 Separator** check box. In the **Negative numbers** box, confirm that a minus sign is used for negative numbers. Click **OK.**

9. Click cell **A13.** Type Date of analysis Click cell **B13,** type 8/9/10 and then press ⏎Enter. Recall that in the United States we use the mm/dd/yy format, and 8/9/10 means August 9, 2010.

10. Click cell **B13** again to select it. Click the **Number** group **Dialog Box Launcher.** In the **Type** box, scroll down and click **March 14, 2001.** Notice that the example in the **Sample** box shows the month name and uses four digits to display the year.

11. Click the **Locale arrow.** Scroll down and click **German (Germany).** In the **Type** box, click **14.03.01.** In the **Sample** box, notice that this date is displayed using dd/mm/yy format, with periods used as separators instead of slashes.

12. Click the **Locale arrow,** and then click **English (United States).** In the **Type** box, click **March 14, 2001,** and then click **OK.**

13. In the column headings, double-click the line between columns **B** and **C** to use the AutoFit feature to adjust the column width.

6. Aligning Text

1. Click cell **A1**, and with the ⬦ pointer displayed, drag to select cell **B1**. On the **Home** tab, in the **Alignment** group, click the **Merge & Center** button.

2. Select cell **A5** through cell **B5**. In the **Alignment** group, click the **Center** button.

3. Click cell **A11**. In the **Alignment** group, click the **Align Text Right** button.

4. Click cell **A14**. In the **Alignment** group, click the **Wrap Text** button. Type `Source: Energy Efficiency and Renewable Energy, U.S. Department of Energy, March 2005` and then press (⏎Enter).

5. On the **Home** tab, in the **Cells** group, click the **Format** button, and then click **Column Width**. In the **Column Width** dialog box, type 32 and then press (⏎Enter) to widen column A.

6. Move the pointer to the line between the headings for rows **14** and **15**. Double-click the line to automatically fit the row height to the wrapped text.

7. Adding Emphasis, Colors, Shading, and Borders

1. Click cell **A1**. Press and hold down (Ctrl) and click cells **A5** and **B5**. On the **Home** tab, in the **Font** group, click the **Bold** button. The title and column headers are bold.

2. Click cell **A14**. On the **formula bar,** select the title of the brochure—*Energy Efficiency and Renewable Energy*. In the **Font** group, click the **Italic** button, and then press (⏎Enter).

3. Click cell **A1**. In the **Font** group, click the **Font Size button arrow,** and then click **12.**

4. Click cell **B11**. In the **Font** group, click the **Borders button arrow,** and then click **Top and Double Bottom Border.** Recall that this type of border indicates the sum of a column of numbers.

5. Click cell **A1**. In the **Font** group, click the **Fill Color button arrow.** On the **Theme Colors** gallery, in the next-to-last column, click **Aqua, Accent 5 Lighter 40%.**

6. Select cells **A5** through **B5**. Repeat the process you practiced in step 5 to add the background color **Aqua, Accent 5 Lighter 80%** to these cells. **Save** your work.

8. Opening, Copying, Inserting, and Deleting Worksheets

1. Click the **Office** button, and then click **Open.** Navigate to the location where the student files are stored for this chapter and open **U2Ch06WindEnergy.**

2. Right-click the **WindEnergy** sheet tab. From the shortcut menu, click **Move or Copy.**

3. Click the **To book** arrow, and then click **U2Ch06WindStudentName.** Click **Create a copy,** and in the **Before sheet** box, click **(move to end).** Click **OK.**

4. On the **View** tab, in the **Window** group, click **Switch Windows.** Click **U2Ch06WindEnergy.** Click the **Office** button, and then click **Close.**

5. With the **U2Ch06WindStudentName** workbook open, right-click the **Sheet2** tab. From the shortcut menu, click **Delete.** Repeat this process to delete **Sheet3.**

9. Formatting, Sorting, and Filtering Tables

1. If necessary, click the **WindEnergy** sheet tab.

2. Click anywhere in the first three columns of data. On the **Insert** tab, in the **Tables** group, click the **Table** button.

3. In the **Create Table** dialog box, confirm that **My table has headers** is selected, and then click **OK.**

4. With the table selected, on the **Design** tab, in the **Table Styles** group, click the **More** button.

5. In the third row, click the style in the seventh column—**Table style light 20.**

6. Drag the line between the headers of columns **B** and **C** to the right to make column **B** 14 points wide. Repeat the procedure to make column **C** 14 points wide.

7. On the **Home** tab, in the **Editing** group, click the **Sort & Filter** button arrow. On the menu, click **Custom Sort.**

8. In the **Sort** dialog box, in the first **Sort by** box, click the arrow, and then click **Wind High.** In the **Order** box, click the arrow, and then click **Largest to Smallest.**

9. In the **Sort** dialog box, click the **Add Level** button. Click the **Then by** arrow and click **Wind Low.** Click the **Order** arrow, and then click **Largest to Smallest.** Click **OK** to sort first by the highest wind ranking and then by the lowest.

10. In cell **B1,** click the arrow. On the menu, click the boxes for **2, 3,** and **4** to **deselect** them, and then click **OK.** Only the states with the highest winds are displayed.

10. Documenting and Printing Worksheets

1. Click the **WindEnergy** sheet tab. On the **View** tab, in the **Workbook Views** group, click **Page Layout.**

2. Click the margin above the first column. On the **Header & Footer Tools Design** tab, in the **Header & Footer Elements** group, click the **File Name** button.

3. Click the center area of the header area and type your name.

4. Click the right area of the header. In the **Header & Footer Elements** group, click the **Current Date** button. Press Spacebar, and then click the **Current Time** button.

5. Click in the worksheet to **deselect** the header. Notice that both tables do not fit on one page. In the column headings, drag the line between columns **D** and **E** to the left to narrow column **D** to **.25** inches. Print the worksheet if your instructor requires it.

6. Click the **Costs** sheet tab. Repeat the process you practiced in steps 1 through 4 to place the file name, your name, and the current date and time in the header.

7. On the **Page Layout** tab, in the **Page Setup** group, click the **Dialog Box Launcher.** Click the **Margins** tab. Under **Center on page,** click **Horizontally.**

8. On the **Margins** tab, click the **Print Preview** button. Confirm that the data is centered horizontally and that the file name, your name, and the current date and time are displayed in the header. If you instructor requires a printout, on the toolbar click the **Print** button. Otherwise, click the **Close Print Preview** button.

9. Compare your worksheets with Figure 6.49. On the **Costs** worksheet, click cell **A1.** On the status bar, click the **Normal** button. **Save** the file, and then **Close** it. Submit your files as directed by your instructor.

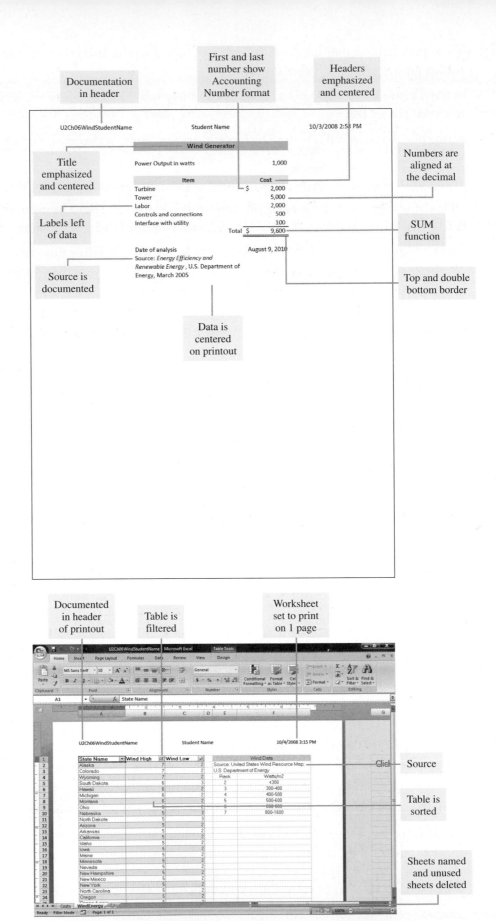

FIGURE 6.49A,B

fix *it*

One way to appreciate the value of good design is to fix a file that is not designed well. In this exercise, you open a file that has several design flaws and fix it according to the good design elements in the lessons.

Navigate to the folder with the student files, open *U2Ch06FixIt*, and then save it as **U2Ch06FixItStudentName.**

Examine the file and make the changes that are necessary to make it comply with the good design principles that were introduced in this chapter. Below is a list of design principles introduced in this chapter, along with some tips on how to fix the worksheet.

- Begin in the upper left corner of the first worksheet. (Tip: Use Cut and Paste to move existing data rather than shifting cell content.)
- Place labels to the left of data in columns or above data in rows.
- Numbers that will be summed are usually arranged in columns rather than rows.
- When using estimated numbers, do not display decimal places if you do not know the numbers that accurately.
- If a column of currency values are summed, the first number and the sum display a currency symbol; the values in between just use comma separators.
- Use formats that align the right side of the numbers, such as Accounting Number Style and Comma Style.
- Use a date format that is not easily misunderstood in other countries, such as 07-Aug-10 or August 7, 2010.
- Place the worksheet title in the first row and center it across the columns that contain data and labels. Use font emphasis, color, or borders to draw attention to it.
- Background colors should contrast with the font color so that the text is legible.
- Name each worksheet tab and delete unused worksheets.
- Tables of data—including headers—should use adjacent cells and be separated from other data or text on the worksheet by empty rows or columns.
- Document the worksheet by providing the source for your data and wrap the text if it is too long to fit in one cell. On the printout, place the file name, your name, and the date and time in a header or footer.
- Center the data horizontally on the page for printing. (Tip: Use Print Preview to confirm that it is centered.)
- Select the title of the first worksheet before you save the workbook for the last time so that the next person to use it is taken to that location first.

Submit the file as required by your instructor. Save and close the file.

Information workers add value to data by organizing, selecting, displaying, communicating, interpreting, and using data to communicate information and support decisions. On the Job exercises simulate a situation where you are given data, and your job is to add value to it using the skills you practiced in this chapter. Success in these exercises indicates that you have a valuable skill to offer an employer.

1. Format Cost Data

Refer to the paragraph below. Extract the data related to the cost of installing a small water turbine, and format it using the skills you practiced in the lessons and in the Skill Drill.

> *Dear Customer,*
>
> *Thank you for your inquiry regarding installation of a water turbine and generator set with a 1000-watt generating capacity. The cost for the turbine is $700. It is connected to a generator that costs $500. The output of the alternator is 12 volts DC, so it needs a converter box to change that to 120 volts AC. The converter costs $500. You mentioned that you already have a naturally occurring waterfall or an existing dam or dyke, so the converter is not included. Piping will cost about $200 for materials and $1,000 for labor.*
>
> *Thank you for your interest,*
> *JP Michaels*
> *Small Hydro Systems*

1. Open a new workbook and save it as `U2Ch06HydroStudentName`

2. Enter appropriate title and column headings.

3. Enter row labels and data.

4. Document the source and the date you created the worksheet.

5. Format the title, column headings, labels, and source according to good design principles.

6. Calculate the total cost.

7. Add appropriate emphasis to the title, headers, and total.

8. Set up the printout to center the data, and put the file name, your name, and the current date and time in the header.

9. Review the design principles listed in the fix *it* exercise and apply those that are relevant.

10. Print or submit the file as directed by your instructor. Save the file and close it.

2. Sort and Filter a Table

The output of a water generator depends on the volume of water flowing through it and the difference in height between the inlet and outlet of the pipes. In this exercise, you sort and filter a table of data to determine the combinations of volume (flow) and height that are necessary to generate 1000 watts of electric power.

1. From the student files, open *U2Ch06HydroData*. Save it as U2Ch06HydroDataStudentName

2. Convert the data to an Excel table. Notice that there is a problem with the column headers. Click Undo and examine the table. Refer to the design principles to determine the problem. Make the necessary change to the worksheet to fix the problem, and then convert the data to an Excel table.

3. Filter the table to show only combinations of volume (flow) and height that can produce 1000 watts or more. Include combinations that produce exactly 1000 watts.

4. Sort the remaining rows on volume flow rate from smallest to largest, and then subsort by height from smallest to largest.

5. Format the table using good design principles, and then add documentation to the worksheet and printout.

6. Add your name, class, and date function to the header. Print the worksheet (optional).

7. Review the design principles listed in the FixIt exercise and apply those that are relevant.

8. Print or submit the file as directed by your instructor. Save the file and close it.

DISCUSSION OF ADVANCED SKILLS OR CONCEPTS

The questions in this section are based on the topics in the Advanced Skills or Concepts section of the chapter.

1. Examine a statement from a bank, utility, or credit card company. How do they use formatting to emphasize the important facts? Demonstrate your knowledge of the topics in this chapter in your answer.

2. What is an example from your experience where the information that went into a spreadsheet was inaccurate, causing the conclusions based on that spreadsheet to be inaccurate?

3. When you look at a bank statement, utility bill, or credit card statement, what simple conclusion do you want to draw from it, and is the document formatted to help you draw that conclusion?

ON YOUR OWN

Once you are comfortable with the skills in this chapter, you can apply them to new situations of your own choosing. In these exercises, you choose data that you have in your possession or that you can find elsewhere. To successfully complete this assignment, you must apply good design practices. Refer to the list of design practices in the Fix It exercise.

1. Format Cost Data

Costs for installing solar panels, wind generators, or small hydro systems depend on many factors and might be significantly higher or lower in your area. You are welcome to contact your local alternative energy system installer and ask for approximate costs for a home system. Alternatively, you may locate data that represents other types of costs that can be summed. Suggestions are monthly utility bills, checkbook registers, or credit card statements.

1. Open a new workbook and save it as U2Ch06CostsStudentName
2. Choose appropriate title and column headers.
3. Enter labels and data.
4. Document the source and the date you created the worksheet
5. Format the title, column headings, labels, and source according to good design principles
6. Calculate the total cost.
7. Add appropriate emphasis to the title, headers, and total.
8. Set up the printout to center the data, and put the file name, your name, and the current date and time in the header.

2. Sort and Filter a Table

Find a table of data that has more information in it than you need to know. Apply what you've practiced to format, filter, and sort the table. Suggestions for tables of data are check registers, credit card statements, or tables of data from the government.

1. Enter data into an empty worksheet. Save the workbook as U2Ch06DataStudentName
2. Sort the table on one or two columns. You do not have to sort on more than one column if it doesn't make sense in your table.
3. Filter the table to limit the number of rows according to a criterion of your choice.
4. Refer to the list of design principles and apply those that are appropriate for a table. Be sure to document the source.
5. Add your name, class, and the current date and time to the header. Submit the file as required by your instructor.
6. Save the file and close it.

ASSESS YOUR PROGRESS

At this point, you should have a set of skills and design concepts that are valuable to an employer and to you. You may not realize how much you've learned unless you take a few minutes to assess your progress.

1. From the student files, open *U2Ch06Assess*. Save it as U2Ch06AssessStudentName

2. Read each question in column A.

3. In column B, answer Yes or No.

4. If you identify a skill or design concept that you don't know, refer to the learning objective code next to the question and the table at the beginning of the chapter to find the skill and review it.

5. Print the worksheet if your instructor requires it. The file name is already in the header, so it will display your name as part of the file name.

6. All of these skills and concepts have been identified as important by surveying hundreds of individuals working at over 200 companies worldwide. If you cannot answer all of the questions affirmatively even after reviewing the relevant lesson, seek additional help from your instructor.

chapter **seven**

Managing Money Using Formulas and Functions

Lesson	Learning Outcomes	Code	Related IC3 Objectives
1	Fills series of labels	7.01	3.1.3
1	Correct circular reference errors	7.02	3.2.8
1	Use statistical functions; MIN, MAX, COUNT, and AVERAGE	7.03	3.2.5
1	Distinguish between zero and null	7.04	—
2	Document changeable values and place them in their own cells	7.05	3.1.2
2	Use arithmetic operators with cell references in a formula	7.06	3.2.4
2	Format percentages	7.07	3.1.5
2	Use the payment (PMT) function	7.08	3.2.7
2	Use arithmetic operators in function arguments	7.09	3.2.7
2	Use positive and negative numbers to indicate direction of cash flow	7.10	—
3	Fill a sequence of numbers and specify the interval	7.11	3.1.3
3	Format numbers as text for use as labels	7.12	3.13
4	Use references to cells in other worksheets	7.13	3.2.4
4	Use and fill formulas with relative cell addresses	7.14	3.1.3, 3.2.3
5	Calculate percentage increase and decrease	7.15	3.2.4
5	Use and fill formulas with absolute cell references	7.16	3.1.3, 3.2.3
6	Calculate annual cash flow	7.17	3.2.7
7	Calculate a cumulative total	7.18	3.2.7
7	Recognize common error codes and their causes	7.19	3.2.8
7	Use an IF function with comparison operators	7.20	3.2.7
7	Use conditional formatting	7.21	3.1.10
7	Determine simple payback	7.22	3.2.7, 3.2.10
7	Hide and unhide rows or columns	7.23	3.1.4
8	Use the internal rate of return (IRR) function	7.24	3.2.7. 3.2.10
9	AutoFit multiple columns	7.25	3.1.4
9	Change page orientation	7.26	1.4.1
9	Repeat columns of labels on each page of a printout	7.27	3.1.9
9	Scale printout to fit a page	7.28	3.1.69
9	Add headers to multiple worksheets	7.29	3.1.9
9	Add page numbers	7.30	2.1.9
9	Set and clear area to print	7.31	3.1.9
Advanced	Drawing conclusions based on calculated values	7.32	3.2.10
Advanced	Designing for What if Analysis	7.33	3.2.10
Advanced	Identify simple trends in tabular data	7.34	3.2.10
Advanced	Identify appropriate use of Excel templates	7.35	1.2.1

Instructions throughout the lessons are based on the Vista operating system running Microsoft Office 2007.

? Why Would I Do This?

The feature that makes a spreadsheet more useful than a table in a word processing document is its ability to make calculations based on the contents of several different cells, and then recalculate quickly if any of those values are changed. Once you know how to write basic formulas and how to use sophisticated financial formulas from a built-in library, you will be able to create worksheets that help you make financial decisions.

visual summary

In this chapter, you will create a worksheet in which you list the heating bills for a year and find the sum, average, minimum, and maximum; then you will count how many months had a heating bill. You will use a financial function to calculate the monthly payment on a loan for a home improvement that adds extra insulation, and then you will use the sum of the heating bills and the loan payment in another worksheet where you evaluate this investment, as shown in Figure 7.1 A, B.

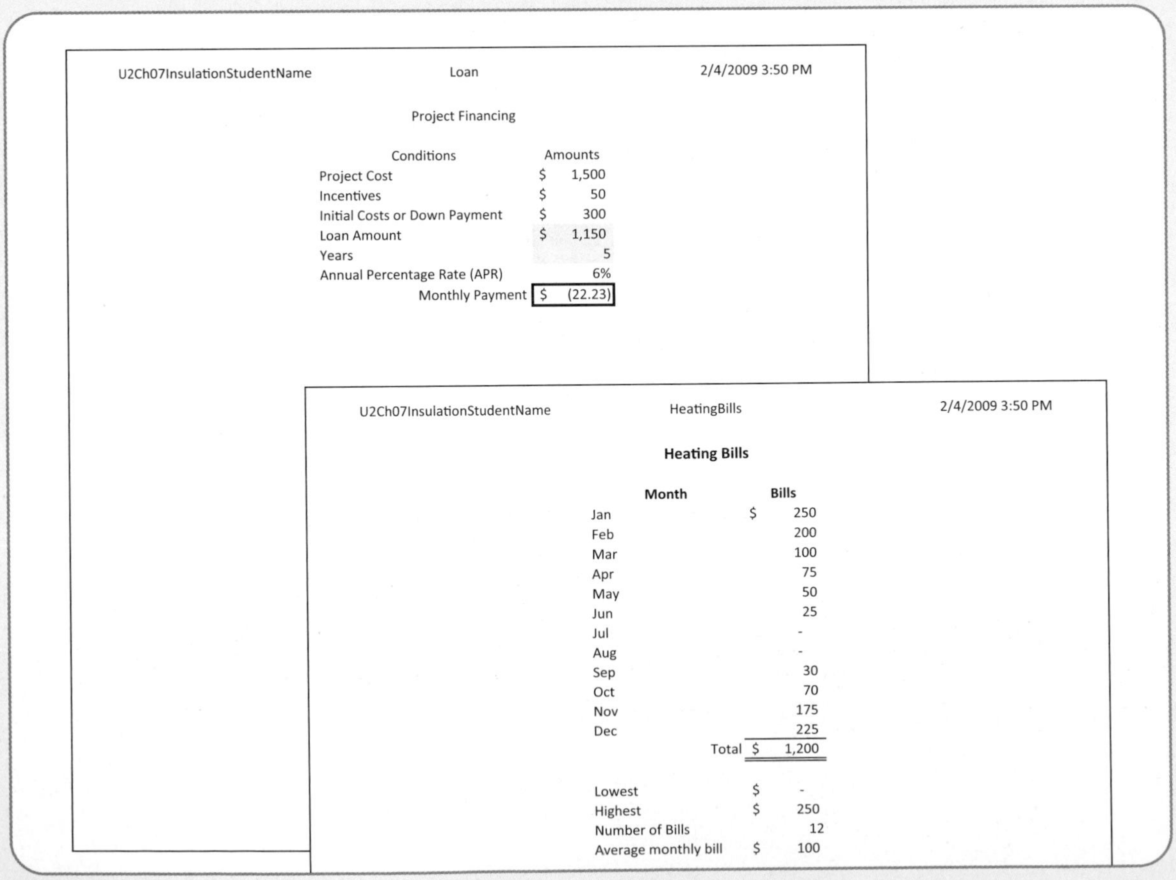

U2Ch07InsulationStudentName	Loan	2/4/2009 3:50 PM

Project Financing

Conditions	Amounts
Project Cost	$ 1,500
Incentives	$ 50
Initial Costs or Down Payment	$ 300
Loan Amount	$ 1,150
Years	5
Annual Percentage Rate (APR)	6%
Monthly Payment	$ (22.23)

U2Ch07InsulationStudentName	HeatingBills	2/4/2009 3:50 PM

Heating Bills

Month	Bills
Jan	$ 250
Feb	200
Mar	100
Apr	75
May	50
Jun	25
Jul	-
Aug	-
Sep	30
Oct	70
Nov	175
Dec	225
Total	$ 1,200

Lowest	$ -
Highest	$ 250
Number of Bills	12
Average monthly bill	$ 100

FIGURE 7.1A

U2Ch07InsulationStudentName   CashFlow   2/4/2009 3:50 PM

Investment Analysis

Annual increase in heating bills	15%
Reduction in heating bills	8%
Years of analysis	20

Year	0	1	2	3	4	5	6	7	8	9
Annual heating bill without added insulation	$ 1,200	$ 1,380	$ 1,587	$ 1,825	$ 2,099	$ 2,414	$ 2,776	$ 3,192	$ 3,671	$ 4,221
Annual heating bill with added insulation		$ 1,270	$ 1,460	$ 1,679	$ 1,931	$ 2,221	$ 2,554	$ 2,937	$ 3,377	$ 3,884
Savings due to added insulation		$ 110	$ 127	$ 146	$ 168	$ 193	$ 222	$ 255	$ 294	$ 338
Project financing *	$ (300)	$ (267)	$ (267)	$ (267)	$ (267)	$ (267)	$ -	$ -	$ -	$ -
Net annual cash flow	$ (300)	$ (156)	$ (140)	$ (121)	$ (99)	$ (74)	$ 222	$ 255	$ 294	$ 338
Cumulative total	$ (300)	$ (456)	$ (596)	$ (717)	$ (816)	$ (890)	$ (668)	$ (412)	$ (119)	$ 219
Negative cumulative totals	1	1	1	1	1	1	1	1	1	0

Payback year	9
Internal Rate of Return (IRR)**	23%

*Assumes a five-year loan
**Assumes 20-year life

3 of 3

FIGURE 7.1B

List of Student and Solution Files

In most cases, you will start with a new, empty file and enter text and data or paste content from other files. You will add your name to the file names and save them on your computer or portable memory device. Table 7.1 lists the files you start with and the names you give them when you save the files.

ASSIGNMENT	STUDENT SOURCE FILE:	SAVE AS:
Lessons 1–9	New file	U2Ch07InsulationStudentName
Skill Drill	New File	U2Ch07WindowsStudentName
Fix It	U2Ch07FixIt	U2Ch07FixItStudentName
On the Job	New file U2Ch07Furnace	U2Ch07HybridStudentName U2Ch07FurnaceStudentName
On Your Own	New file New file	U2Ch07WhatIfStudentName U2Ch07TemplateStudentName
Assess Your Progress	U2Ch07Assess	U2Ch07AssessStudentName

TABLE 7.1

▶▶▶ *lesson*

ONE | Fill Labels and Use Worksheet Functions

Recall that functions are predefined formulas that are used to solve mathematical problems. Previously, you used the Sum function to find the total of a column of numbers. In this lesson, you use other worksheet functions to identify the high, low, and average heating bill and a counting function to find out how many months had no heating bill. You also practice a shortcut for entering a series of common labels.

to enter a series of common labels

1 Start Microsoft Office Excel 2007. Click the Save button 🖫 and navigate to the location where you are saving your files. Create a new folder named Chapter07 and then save the workbook in this folder as U2Ch07InsulationStudentName

2 On the status bar, on the right end of the Zoom bar, click the Zoom In button ⊕ two times until 120% displays.

3 Point to the Sheet1 tab and double-click. Type HeatingBills and then press ↵Enter. In cell A1, type Heating Bills and then press ↵Enter.

4 Select cells A1 and B1. On the Home tab, in the Alignment group, click the Merge and Center button �▾. In the Font group, click the Bold button B. In the Font group, click the Font Size button arrow 11 ▾, and then click 12.

5 Click cell A3. Type Month press Tab⇆, and then type Bills Select cells A3 and B3. In the Font group, click the Bold button B. In the Alignment group, click the Center button ≡.

6 Click cell A4, type Jan and then press ↵Enter. Click cell A4 again to select it. Notice that the dark border that indicates selection has a small square in the lower-right corner. The small square is called the *fill handle*, which can be used to enter a series of related labels or formulas.

7 Point to the fill handle in A4 to display the ⊞ pointer, as shown in Figure 7.2.

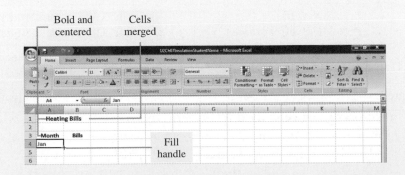

FIGURE 7.2

8 **Drag the fill handle downward to cell A15 and release it.** The program recognizes *Jan* as an abbreviation for January, and when you drag the fill handle, the program assumes you want to fill in a series of month names.

9 **Click cell A16, and then type** `Total` **On the formula bar, click the Enter button** ✓ . The selection stays in A16 when you click the Enter button on the formula bar.

10 **With cell A16 selected, on the Home tab, in the Alignment group, click the Align Text Right button** ▤ .

11 **In cells B4:B9, enter the following numbers:** 250, 200, 100, 75, 50, **and** 25 Recall that a range of cells can be denoted by the first and last cells separated by a colon. Cells B10 and B11 will be left empty.

to extend your knowledge

CONFIRMING CELL ENTRIES

After you enter the contents of the cell, you must complete the process. This can be done on the keyboard by pressing ⏎Enter or by moving the selection to another cell with Tab↹ or one of the four arrow keys. When you use any of these keyboard keys to move the selection to another cell, the program evaluates and formats the content of the cell and displays the results in the original cell.

Do not attempt to complete the entry process by clicking a different cell. The program interprets this as a shortcut method of typing the cell address, and it changes what you have typed in the cell.

To complete the entry process without moving the selection to another cell, you can click the Enter button ✓ . The advantage of using this method is that you can continue to work on the cell without having to move the selection back to it.

In this task, you use the SUM function and edit the function to correct an error.

to correct a circular reference error

1 **In cells B12:B15, enter the following numbers:** 30, 70, 175, **and** 225

2 **Click cell B16. In the Editing group, click the SUM button** Σ ▾ **one time. Notice that the range of cells used in the function is B12:B15.** The program selects adjacent cells that have numbers in them and stops at empty cells. Recall that the ranges and other information needed by the function to perform its operation are called **arguments**. In this example, the SUM function's argument is B12:B15, as shown in Figure 7.3. In the next step, you are instructed to make an error.

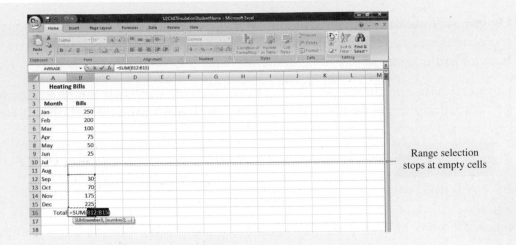

FIGURE 7.3

3 **With the SUM function displayed in B16 and the range B12:B15 chosen as the argument, type** `B4:B16` **and press** `↵Enter`. A warning box displays, informing you that there is a circular reference as shown in Figure 7.4. A *circular reference* error is caused when the cell that contains the formula results is included in the formula argument either directly or indirectly. That cell should not be part of one of the function's arguments.

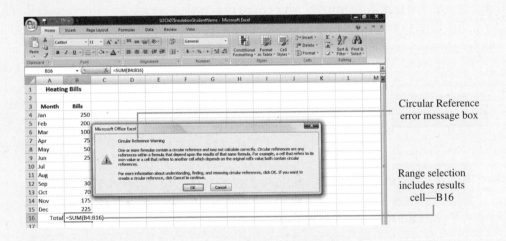

FIGURE 7.4

4 **In the warning box, click Cancel.** If you had clicked OK, an Excel Help dialog box would have opened to explain the problem and offer advice on how to deal with it.

5 **Click cell B16.** Cell B16 is selected and the function is displayed in the formula bar,

6 On the formula bar, in the argument, click to the right of B16. Press ⌫Backspace to delete the 6. Type 5 and then press ⏎Enter. Functions can be edited in the formula bar using arrow keys and the Delete and Backspace keys. The argument is corrected to remove the circular reference error.

7 Click cell B16. In the Font group, click the Borders button arrow ⊞▾, and then click Top and Double Bottom Border.

8 Press Ctrl and click cell B4. On the Home tab, in the Number group, click the Accounting Number Format button $▾. In the Number group, click the Decrease Decimal button ⬚ two times.

9 Click B5, press ⇧Shift and click B15. On the Home tab, in the Number group, click the Comma style button ,. In the Number group, click the Decrease Decimal button ⬚ two times.

10 Save 🖫 your workbook.

The heating bills vary significantly from summer to winter. You can use the MIN function to identify the lowest value and MAX to find the highest.

to use the MIN and MAX functions

1 Click cell A18, type Lowest and then press ⏎Enter.

2 In cell A19, type Highest and then press ⏎Enter.

3 Click cell B18. On the Formulas tab, in the Function Library group, click the **Insert Function button.** The Insert Function dialog box displays. Alternatively, on the formula bar, click the Insert Function button *fx*.

4 Notice that the text in the *Search for a function* box is selected by default. Type lowest value and then click the Go button. In the *Select a function* box, notice the MIN function. You can describe what you want to do in the *Search for a function* box to display a list of functions that might meet your needs, as shown in Figure 7.5.

Likely
functions

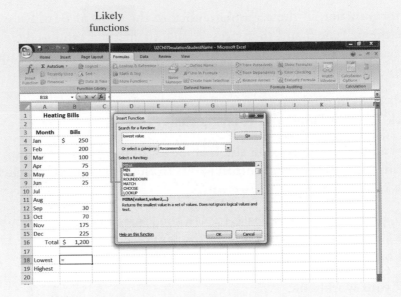

FIGURE 7.5

5   **In the Insert Function dialog box, in the *Select a function* box, click MIN, and then click OK.** The Function Arguments dialog box displays.

6   **In the Function Arguments dialog box, in the Number1 box, notice that the range of cells is B4:B17.** You want to find the minimum heating bill in cells B4:B15.

7   **In the Number1 box, type B4:B15 and then click OK. Notice that the minimum value is $25, not 0.** An empty cell is called a *null* and is not the same as a value of zero. The MIN function ignores the nulls and returns the minimum value in the range, which is 25. Some functions copy the formatting from the first number in the range and automatically apply it to the cell in which the function resides. In this case, the MIN value is formatted in the Accounting Number Format style with the decimal places not showing.

8   **Click cell B19. On the Formulas tab, in the Function Library group, click the Insert Function button.**

9   **In the Insert Function dialog box, click the *Or select a category* arrow. From the list, click Statistical. In the *Select a function* box, scroll down and then click MAX. Click OK.** The Function Arguments dialog box displays.

10   **In the Function Arguments dialog box, in the Number1 box, type B4:B15 The** range of bills is designated, as shown in Figure 7.6. The Function Arguments dialog box provides a definition of the function and each of the arguments when the argument box is active.

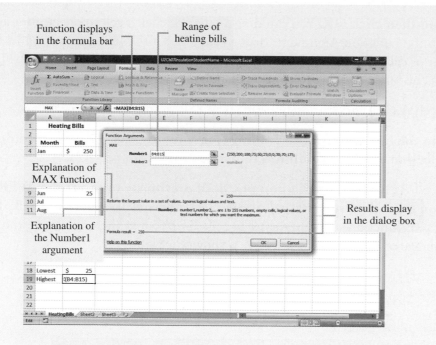

Function displays in the formula bar

Range of heating bills

Explanation of MAX function

Explanation of the Number1 argument

Results display in the dialog box

FIGURE 7.6

11 **Click OK and then Save** 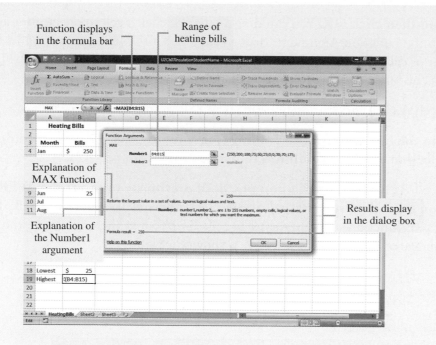 **your workbook.** The highest heating bill—$250— displays in cell B19.

to extend your knowledge

TYPING CELL REFERENCES
When you type a cell reference in a formula, you can use upper or lower case letters. Excel interprets b3 and B3 the same. In this book, upper case letters are used for clarity.

In this task, you use two functions that are affected by the difference between an empty cell and a value of zero.

to use the count and average functions

1 In the *HeatingBills* worksheet, click cell A20. Type Number of bills and then press Tab.

2 In cell B20, display the Insert Function dialog box. From the Statistical category click COUNT, and then click OK. With the Function Arguments dialog box displayed, on the worksheet drag range B4:B15 to place the range in the Value1

box, and then click OK. You can drag a range or click a cell to select it for an argument in the Function Arguments dialog box. The COUNT function counts the number of cells that have numbers in them—10—because cells B10 and B11 are empty. The number displays using a general number format.

3 **Click cell A21. Type** `Average monthly bill` **and then press** (↵Enter).

4 **Point to the line between the headings for columns A and B, and then double-click the line to widen column A to fit the contents of cell A21.**

5 **Click cell B21. Use the skills you practiced previously to insert the AVERAGE function from the list of statistical functions and specify range B4:B15.** The AVERAGE function sums the values in cells B4:B15 and then divides by the count. The average of these ten bills is $120, as shown in Figure 7.7.

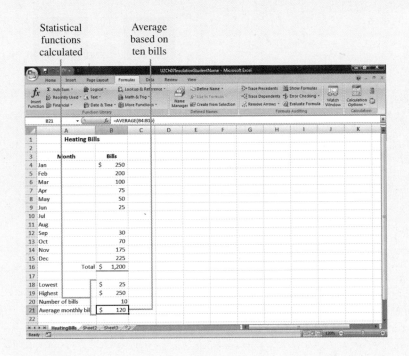

FIGURE 7.7

. . . .

good **design...**

An empty cell in a column of numbers implies that you do not know the value. If you know the value is zero, be sure to enter a zero instead of leaving the cell empty.

. . . .

6 **Click cell B10. Type** *0* **and then press** (↵Enter). **In cell B11, type** *0* **and then press** (↵Enter). **Notice that the lowest value in B18 changed to 0, the count in B20 changed to 12, and the average in B21 changed to $100.** The comma style uses a dash for zero values, and these two values are used in the COUNT and AVERAGE functions, as shown in Figure 7.8.

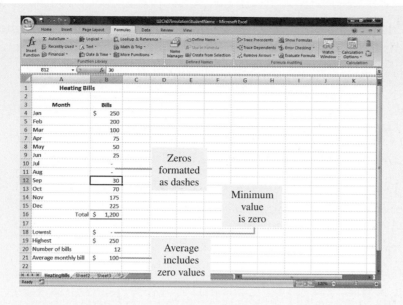

FIGURE 7.8

7 Save ⊟ the workbook.

▶▶▶ *lesson*

two | Using the Payment Function

The library of functions has several functions that are useful for managing money. One of the most commonly used functions calculates the monthly payment necessary to repay a loan. This function can be used for loans with a specified period of time and a fixed interest rate to determine the monthly payment. In this lesson, you consider a loan to pay for adding insulation to the attic to reduce monthly heating bills, and then you calculate the monthly payment to repay the loan. The first step is to document the conditions of the loan.

to document the conditions of the loan

1 Point to the Sheet2 tab, and then double-click. Type Loan and then press ↵Enter. On the Zoom Bar, click the Increase Zoom button ⊕ two times to increase the magnification of the worksheet to 120%.

2 In cell A1, type Project Financing and then press ↵Enter two times.

3 In cell A3, type Conditions and then press ↵Enter. Use this process to enter the following terms in cells A4:A10: Project Cost, Incentives, Initial Costs or Down Payment, Loan Amount, Years, Annual Percentage Rate (APR), and Monthly Payment

4 Point to the line between the headings for columns A and B, and when the ⊕ pointer displays, double-click to widen column A, as shown in Figure 7.9.

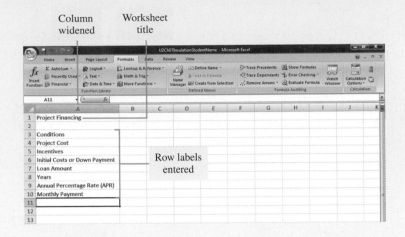

FIGURE 7.9

5 Click cell B3. Type `Amounts` and then press ↵Enter. Continue in cell B4 and enter the following values for each of the conditions. Be sure to leave cell B7—Loan Amount—empty.

Project Cost	1500
Incentives	0
Initial Costs or Down Payment	300
Loan Amount	
Years	5
Annual Percentage Rate (APR)	6%

When you include the percentage sign, the program automatically applies the percentage format to the cell.

· ·

to extend your knowledge

USING PERCENTS IN EXCEL

The term *percent* is a short term that means *per 100*. When you write 6%, it represents the fraction 6/100. In decimal format, it would be .06. If you enter .06 and apply the percentage format, it will display as 6%. However, if you type 6 and then apply the percentage format, you get 600%. In general, it is easier and more reliable to type the percentage sign with the number.

· ·

6 Select cells A1:B1. On the Home tab, in the Alignment group, click the Merge & Center button ⊞ ▾. Select cells A3 and B3 and click the Center ≡ button. Hold down Ctrl and click cells A1, A3, B3, and A10, and then add Bold **B** emphasis.

7 Select cells B4:B7. On the Home tab, in the Number group, click the Accounting Number Format button $ ▾, and then in the Number group, click the Decrease Decimal button .00→.0 two times.

8 Click cell A10. On the Home tab, in the Alignment group, click the Align Text Right button ≡. The terms of the loan are documented, as shown in Figure 7.10.

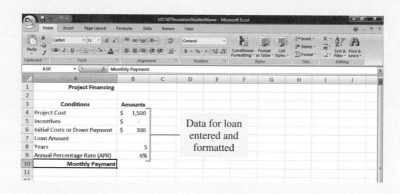

FIGURE 7.10

good **design...**

DESIGNING WORKSHEETS TO RECALCULATE FORMULAS

Each value that will be used as an argument of a function must be in its own cell and should be labeled. This is usually true for values used in formulas that might change. This type of design takes advantage of a spreadsheet's greatest strength: the ability to recalculate formulas and functions quickly if you change one or more of the values used in the function or formula. This enables you to try different combinations of values to see how the changes affect the calculations. This process is called a ***what-if analysis***.

Formulas in Excel are similar to formulas in algebra, with a few differences. Instead of single letters, formulas in Excel use the cell address and then Excel substitutes whatever value is in the cell when the formula is evaluated. The arithmetic operators are the same, and the symbols used for addition, subtraction, multiplication, and division are; +, -, *, and /. The slash used for division is the one that leans forward, not the backward slash (\).

The order in which a formula is evaluated is the same as in algebra. The multiplication and division operations are done first, proceeding from left to right. Then the addition and subtraction operations are done from left to right. If you want to override this method, you enclose part of the formula within parentheses and those operations are done first.

In this task, you write a formula to calculate the amount of the loan, which is the project cost minus any incentive minus the initial payment. Then you use the payment function to determine the monthly payment.

to write a formula with arithmetic operators and use the payment function

1   **With the *Loan* worksheet selected, click B7. Type** =B4-B5-B6 **and then on the formula bar, click the Enter button** ☑. The formula is evaluated based on the contents of cells B4, B5, and B6 and the arithmetic subtraction operator. The result is displayed in cell B7, as shown in Figure 7.11. The cell in which the formula resides is assumed to be the value on the left of the equals sign, which is not written. For example, you can think of the formula you just typed as B7=B4-B5-B6. Because the formula is located in cell B7, it is written as =B4-B5-B6.

Formula displays in the formula bar

Result of formula displays in cell B7

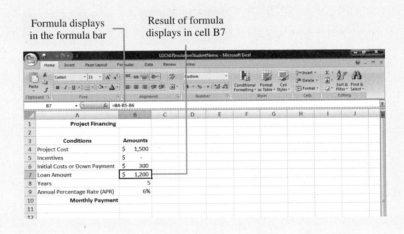

FIGURE 7.11

2   **Click cell B10. On the Formulas tab, in the Function Library group, click the Financial button. Scroll down the menu, and then click PMT.** The Function Arguments dialog box displays, as shown in Figure 7.12. Alternatively, click the Insert Function button and select PMT from the list of functions in the Financial category. The beginning of the formula syntax—=PMT()—displays in the cell and on the formula bar.

Loan   Number of   Rate per
amount   time units   time unit

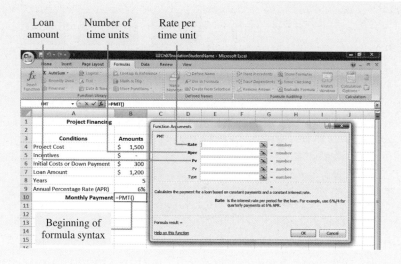

FIGURE 7.12

3 **In the Function Arguments dialog box, click the Rate box, and then type** B9/12
Interest rates—the amount charged to borrow money—are quoted as annual rates (in
this case, 6% per year). Loans can be repaid with payments of different frequency:
annual, quarterly, or monthly. The frequency of payments must be used to determine
the amount of interest per payment. Therefore, to convert the annual rate to a monthly
interest rate to match monthly payments, you divide the interest rate by twelve.

4 **Click the Nper box, and then type** B8*12 By multiplying the number of years in
cell B8 by 12, you calculate the number of time periods—months—of the loan. You
do not use an equals sign in an argument.

5 **Click the PV box, and then type** B7 The value in cell B7 is the ***present value***,
which means the amount of the loan before any of it has been repaid. The three arguments are calculated from cell references, as shown in Figure 7.13. By dividing the

Rate per   Number of   Loan
time unit   time units   amount

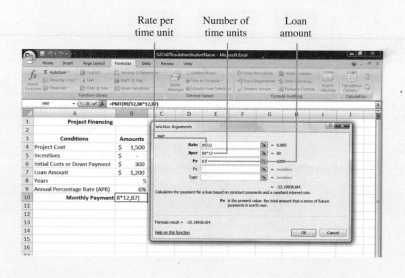

FIGURE 7.13

annual rate by the number of months in the year, you calculate the monthly interest rate. The number 12 is used instead of a cell reference. This assumes that this worksheet will always calculate monthly payments. If that were not a safe assumption, the number of time periods per year would be in its own cell with a label and the 12 in these arguments replaced by the cell reference.

6 **Click OK.** The monthly payment is calculated and displayed as a negative number using the *currency format*. The currency format is similar to the Accounting Number Format, but it places the currency symbol next to the left-most digit.

....

good **design...**

DISPLAYING NEGATIVE NUMBERS

When money is changing hands, positive and negative numbers are used to indicate the direction. If you receive money, the values are represented as positive numbers. If you pay out money, the values are represented as negative numbers. The process of tracking money that is coming in (positive) and going out (negative) is called *cash flow analysis*. It is good design to use a format that makes the difference between positive and negative cash flow very apparent. The Currency Style does this by using a red font and parentheses. Using parentheses to indicate negative numbers is more reliable than using a minus sign, which is small and might be overlooked.

....

7 **With cell B10 selected, on the Home tab, in the Numbers group, click the Accounting Number Format button** $ ▾ **.** The negative number still has parentheses, but it is the normal font color, and the currency symbol is placed at the left to align with the other currency values in this column.

8 **Click cell B5, type** 50 **and then press** ↵Enter **. Notice that the monthly payment in cell B10 is immediately recalculated.** This is an example of using the worksheet to perform a what-if analysis. You can change any of the values in cells B4, B5, B6, B8 or B9 and see the effect on the monthly payment. If you type a value in B7 or B10, it will overwrite the formula or function.

9 **Click cell B7. On the Home tab, in the Font group, click the Fill Color button arrow** ◇ ▾ **. In the Theme Colors gallery, in the first column of the second row, click** *White, Background 1, Darker 5%.* The cell with the formula is shaded to provide a visual cue that this cell is different—a number typed into the cell would overwrite the formula.

10 **Click B10. On the Home tab, in the Font group, click the Borders button arrow** ▦ ▾ **, and then click** *Thick Box Border.* **Click another cell that is not adjacent to B10 so you can see the border.** The most important cell on the worksheet is identified by a thick border, as shown in Figure 7.14. This is not a sum of the values above, so the top and double bottom border is not appropriate.

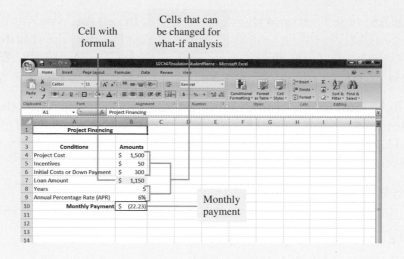

Cell with formula

Cells that can be changed for what-if analysis

Monthly payment

FIGURE 7.14

11 Save ⊟ the workbook.

▶▶▶ *lesson*
three | Filling a Sequence of Numbers and Formatting Them as Text

Column headers may sometimes be numbers, such as years or ages. You can use the fill handle to fill cells with a sequence of these labels if you specify the interval. If these numbers function as text, however, they should be formatted as text to prevent confusion with numbers that could be used in calculations.

to fill a sequence of numbers to be used as labels

1 Point to the Sheet3 tab, and then double-click. Type `CashFlow` and then press ↵Enter.

2 Click cell A1, type `Investment Analysis` and then on the formula bar, click the Enter button ✔. On the Home tab, in the Font group, click the Bold button **B**.

3 Click cell A3, type `Annual increase in heating bills:` and then press →. In cell B3, type `15%` and then press ↵Enter. For this example, you will use an estimate of a 15% increase in heating bills each year. Arrow keys can be used to complete the process of entering numbers.

4 Click cell A5, type `Year` and then press `↵Enter`. In cell A6, type `Annual heating bill without added insulation` Point to the column A heading and right-click. From the shortcut menu, click Column Width. Type `30` and then press `↵Enter` to widen column A to 30 points.

5 Click cell A6, and on the Home tab, in the Alignment group, click the Wrap Text button. Pressing `Tab⇄` has a similar effect to pressing `↵Enter`, except that the selection moves to the right instead of down. This method is useful when entering values in a row.

6 Click cell B5, type `0` and then press `Tab⇄` to move to cell C5. Type `1` and then press `Tab⇄`. The beginning is year zero, and the rest of the numbers in this row refer to how many years have passed since year zero.

7 Select cells B5 and C5. Point to the fill handle in the lower right corner of cell C5. The first two numbers in the sequence of years are selected, as shown in Figure 7.15. The Excel program can fill a series of numbers just as it did the months of the year, but you need to select the first two numbers in the sequence to specify the interval to be used.

First two numbers in the sequence   Fill handle

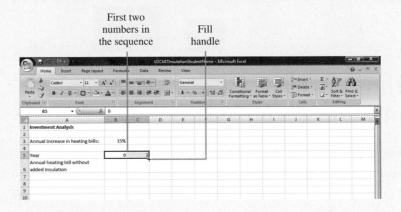

FIGURE 7.15

8 Drag the fill handle to the right to cell V5, and then release the mouse button. A sequence of numbers, with an interval of 1, is filled in row 5 from zero to twenty. The sequence of numbers does not fit on one screen, as shown in Figure 7.16. The AutoFill Options button displays on the screen, which enables you to select other fill options such as *Copy Cells*. In this case, the default option—*Fill Series*—is what you want, so you can ignore the button.

....

if you have **problems...**

DID YOU FILL TOO FAR?
If the screen scrolls past column W, drag to the left to move the fill handle back to column V. Alternatively, on the Quick Access Toolbar, click the Undo button and try again.

....

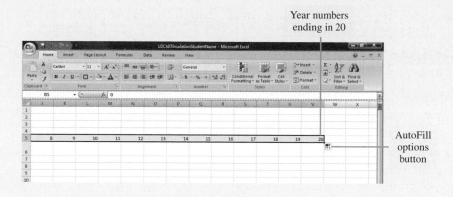

AutoFill
options
button

FIGURE 7.16

If you use a sequence of numbers as if they are labels, they should be formatted as text and center aligned to indicate that they are labels for the columns, not numbers that could be used in a formula.

to format numbers as text

1 With cells B5:V5 selected, on the Home tab, in the Alignment group, click the Center button ≣ to center the year labels.

2 With the range B5:V5 still selected, in the Number group, click the Number Format button arrow `General ▾`. Scroll down the Number Format list and point to Text, as shown in Figure 7.17.

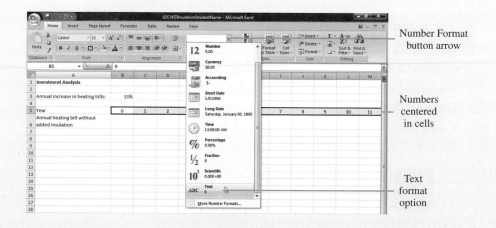

Number Format
button arrow

Numbers
centered
in cells

Text
format
option

FIGURE 7.17

3 Click Text to format the range of numbers as text. Save 💾 the workbook.

four | Using References to Cells in Other Worksheets and Relative Cell References

Some calculations use the same formula repeatedly; each formula uses the results of its predecessor as input. For example, in a savings account, the interest earned is calculated each month by applying an interest rate to last month's balance. Spreadsheets are specifically designed to handle this type of calculation. In this lesson, you refer to the total heating bill from the HeatingBills sheet and then fill formulas into other cells to display the heating bills in other years.

to refer to a cell on a different worksheet

1 In the *CashFlow* worksheet, click cell B6. Formulas can reference cells on other worksheets if the worksheet name is included in the cell reference, followed by an exclamation mark.

2 With B6 selected, type = and then click the *HeatingBills* sheet tab. On the HeatingBills sheet, click cell B16. Notice that the formula on the formula bar includes the worksheet name.

3 Press ⏎Enter. Click cell B6, and notice that the formula in the formula bar refers to cell B16 on the HeatingBills worksheet. The value displayed in cell B6 is the total of the heat bills, as shown in Figure 7.18.

Reference to cell in the HeatingBills worksheet

Value from cell B16 in HeatingBills worksheet

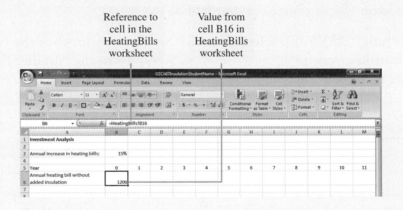

FIGURE 7.18

to extend your knowledge

USING POINT AND CLICK

In formulas, rather than typing a cell address, you can click on the cell you want to use in the formula, as you did in this task. This point and click technique can be used with the Function Argument dialog box or when you are writing a formula in a cell. If you are editing a formula and click on another cell, it alters the formula. Always be sure that you press the Enter key or click on the Enter button to finish a formula. In a dialog box, click OK.

If you need the same formula in several cells, you can use the fill handle to copy the formula across a row or down a column. When you do this, the cells that are referenced in the formula change to adapt to the new position in which the formula is placed. For example, you may have a formula that sums a column of numbers. When you fill this formula across a row, you want it to sum the column of numbers in each subsequent column. By default, formulas use a *relative cell reference*, so when you fill a formula, the cell references used in the formula change so that they are in the same relative position to the results cell. For example, a sum formula in cell A11 to sum cells A3:A10, when filled to cell B11, would sum cells B3:B10; and in cell C11, it would sum cells C3:C10. In this manner, you can write the formula one time and fill it across a worksheet.

to use relative cell references

1 **In the *CashFlow* worksheet, click C6.** To fill in the future estimated heating bills, you will begin by writing a formula that refers to the cell on the left.

2 **In cell C6, type** =B6 **and then on the formula bar, click the Enter button** ✓**.** Notice that the value displayed is the same as the value in the cell to the left.

3 **In cell C6, drag the fill handle to V6. Scroll back to column A, and then click cell C6. Press** Tab **to move to D6. Notice that the formula in the cell that is displayed in the formula bar refers to the cell to the left: C6.**

4 **Press** Tab **several times and notice that each cell has a formula that refers to the cell to the left.**

5 **Save** 💾 **your file.**

· ·

to extend your knowledge

HOW RELATIVE CELL REFERENCES WORK

When you write a cell reference in a formula, the Excel program does not store the actual cell reference. Instead, it stores the position of that cell relative to the cell in which the formula resides. In this example, the formula in C6 was =B6. Excel stores this formula as =RC[-1], which is code for *same row, one column to the left*. When you fill the formulas, this is the code that is actually filled. Each of the resulting formulas displays a reference to the cell on the left.

· ·

▶▶▶ *lesson*
five|Calculating a Percentage Increase and Decrease Using Absolute Cell References

When repeating formulas are used to increase or decrease the balance each month or year by the same percentage, the formula needs to refer to the cell that contains that percentage. This type of cell reference does not change when the formula is filled and is called an ***absolute cell reference.*** In this lesson, you use an absolute reference to the cell that contains the percentage by which you expect heating bills to increase each year, and you fill the formula into a row of cells.

to calculate a percentage increase

1 **With the *CashFlow* sheet selected, click cell C6.** The result of evaluating the formula displays in the cell, and the formula displays in the formula bar.

2 **On the formula bar, point to the right of B6 and click to place the insertion point in the formula bar to the right of =B6.**

3 **Type * (1+B3) and then on the formula bar, click the Enter button ✓.** The formula is now =B6*(1+B3) and the value in cell C6 is 1380, as shown in Figure 7.19. Excel follows the rules of using arithmetical operators. It starts with the portion inside the parentheses. Recall that 15% is the same as the decimal .15; therefore, the evaluation of the part within the parentheses yields 1.15. Next, the program does the multiplication and division from left to right. In this case, it multiplies the value in cell B6—1200—by 1.15, the result of which is 1380.

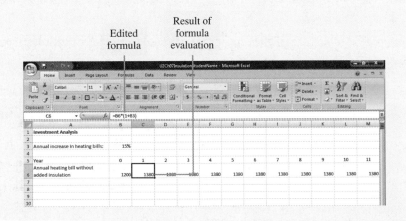

Edited formula   Result of formula evaluation

FIGURE 7.19

4 **With C6 still selected, on the formula bar, in the formula, point to B3. Click to place the insertion point within this cell reference.**

5 **Press F4, and then on the formula bar, click the Enter button ✓.** The reference to B3 has dollar signs to the left of the column letter and the row number, as shown in Figure 7.20. These symbols indicate an absolute cell reference. Cell B3 contains the percent increase and the reference to this cell needs to remain the same when you fill this formula across the row. You can also type the dollar signs before the row number and column letter.

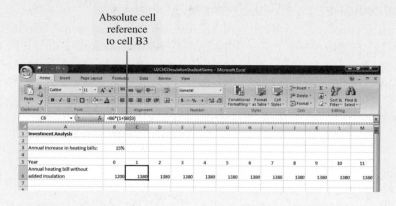

FIGURE 7.20

···

if you have problems...

DID AN ERROR MESSAGE DISPLAY?

If you type the absolute reference incorrectly, an error message appears. The most common error is to enclose the cell reference between dollar signs—$A1$—instead of preceding the column letter and row number with dollar signs—A1. If this happens, click OK in the message box and try again.

···

6 In cell C6, drag the fill handle to cell V6 and release the mouse button. The formula is filled to cells D6:V6.

7 Scroll back to column A, and then click cell D6. Notice that the relative cell reference changed to C6, but the absolute reference still refers to cell B3.

···

to extend your knowledge

HOW ABSOLUTE CELL REFERENCES WORK

Excel stores an absolute cell reference like this one as *=R3C2*, which means *Row 3, Column 2*. When this type of reference is filled or copied into other cells, it does not change. In this example, it would always refer to the cell in row 3, column 2—cell B3.

The use of dollar signs to indicate an absolute reference is an unfortunate choice, because the dollar signs could reasonably be mistaken for having a different meaning that is related to currency formatting, and it is easy to misplace the dollar signs. F4 is programmed to insert the absolute reference symbol—$—into the cell reference in the proper locations.

You can also use a ***mixed cell reference*** in situations where the row or the column needs to remain constant, but not both of them. An example of a mixed cell reference with a constant column is *$C4*, whereas a reference with a constant row is *C$4*. This is useful if you need to fill a table of data where the values are listed in a row and a column at the edge of a table.

···

When you insert a row or column, the data below or to the right is moved. This changes the cell names. The Excel program updates all of the cell references automatically.

to insert a row and calculate a percentage decrease

1 In the *CashFlow* worksheet, point to the row 4 heading and right-click. On the shortcut menu, click Insert to insert a new row.

2 Click cell D7. On the formula bar, notice that the relative cell reference still refers to the cell to the left, but it is now named C7. Notice also that the absolute cell reference to B3 is unchanged, as shown in Figure 7.21. When you insert rows or columns, the program updates the cell references in all the formulas automatically if the name of the cell to which they refer is changed.

Cell
reference
updated

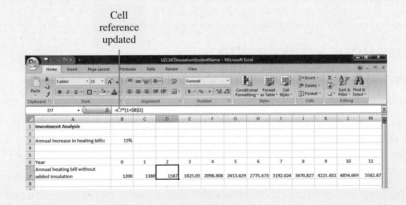

FIGURE 7.21

3 Click cell A4. Type `Reduction in heating bills` and then press `Tab↹`. In cell B4, type 8% and then press `↵Enter`. This is the estimated annual savings in heating bills due to adding insulation.

4 **Click cell A8. Type** Annual heating bill with added insulation **and then on the formula bar, click the Enter button ✔. On the Home tab, in the Alignment group, click the Wrap Text button 📑.** As you begin to type, the value *Annual heating bill without added insulation* displays. This is Excel's ***AutoComplete*** feature: It guesses what you want to enter in a cell based on other entries in the same column. When this displays, if you press ⏎Enter, the suggested value will be entered in the cell. You could then edit the cell to remove *out* from the word *without*. In row 8, you want to calculate the heating bill that is reduced by the percentage in B4.

5 **Click cell C8. Type** =C7*(1–B4) **and then on the formula bar, click the Enter button ✔.** In this case, you want to decrease the heating bill in the cell above by the percentage in cell B4, as shown in Figure 7.22.

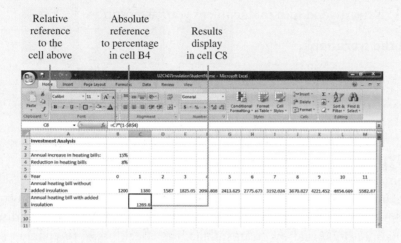

FIGURE 7.22

6 **In cell C8, drag the fill handle to cell V8.** The formulas in row 8 multiply the value in the cell above by 1 plus the percentage in cell B4, as shown in Figure 7.23.

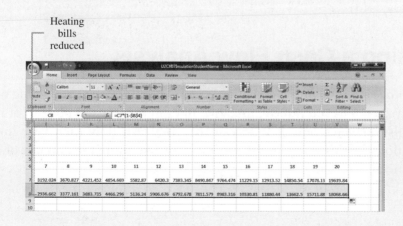

FIGURE 7.23

7 Scroll back to column A. Move the pointer to the heading for row 5 and right-click. On the shortcut menu, click Insert. Click cell A5, type `Years of analysis` and then press (Tab⇆).

8 In cell B5, type `20` and then on the formula bar, click the Enter button ✓. The program assumes you want to format this value as a percentage to match the formats of the cells above it.

9 With cell B5 selected, on the Home tab, in the Number group, click the Number Format box arrow `General ▼`. On the menu, click General. Notice that the program converted 20% to 0.2.

10 With B5 selected, type `20` and then press (↵Enter). The correct value is entered and displayed. A 20-year analysis period was assumed when you extended the row of years. It is always a good idea to document your assumptions.

11 Save 💾 the workbook.

· ·

to *extend* your knowledge

HOW TO TURN OFF AUTOMATIC FEATURES IN EXCEL

The automatic features of Excel can actually cause errors in some cases, as in this example. You can turn these features on or off by clicking the Office button and then clicking the Excel Options button. In the left panel, click Advanced to display a list of options that are organized by groups. Click the check boxes to enable or disable features, and then click OK.

· ·

▶▶▶ *lesson*
SIX | Using a Cash Flow Analysis

Recall that the process of tracking money that is coming in (positive) and going out (negative) is cash flow analysis. It tells you if the cumulative amount of money is positive or negative. You can use the skills you have practiced to calculate the cash flow each year for the cost of installing insulation. The first step in the process is to determine the amount of savings from installing insulation.

to calculate the annual savings due to added insulation

1 With the *CashFlow* sheet selected, click cell A10. Type `Savings due to added insulation` and then press `Tab↹` two times.

2 In cell C10, type `=C8-C9` and on the formula bar, click the Enter button ☑. This formula subtracts the value in the cell above the results cell from the cell that is two rows above it.

3 In cell C10, drag the fill handle to cell V10. Release the mouse button, and then scroll back to column A. The difference between the heating bills with and without added insulation is calculated and displayed in row 10, as shown in Figure 7.24.

Savings shown
as positive
cash flow

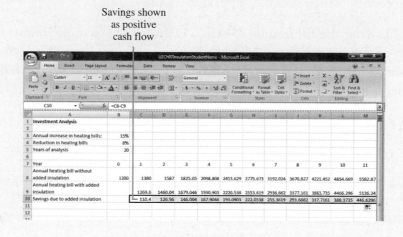

FIGURE 7.24

The next step in the process is to include the cost of financing the insulation to see how it affects the cash flow. The loan payment is money out, so it is recorded as a negative number. The net cash flow is the sum of the positive and negative cash flows.

to use worksheet references to project financing costs

1 Click cell A11. Type `Project financing` and then press `Tab↹`.

2 In cell B11, type `=` and then click the *Loan* sheet tab. On the Loan worksheet, click cell B6. On the formula bar, click the Enter button ☑. The down payment expense—$300—is displayed in year zero.

3 With cell B11 selected, on the formula bar, position the pointer between the = sign and the letter L in *Loan* and click. Type the minus sign (–), and then on the formula bar, click the Enter button ✓. Because this is cash that is paid out, it should be negative.

4 With cell B11 selected, in the Number group, click the Accounting Number Format button $ ▾.

5 Click cell C11, type = and then click the *Loan* sheet tab. On the Loan worksheet, click cell B10, and then on the formula bar, click the Enter button ✓. The monthly loan payment is displayed in cell C11 as a negative number.

6 On the formula bar, double-click cell B10 to select the cell reference in the formula. Type B10*12 and then, on the formula bar, click the Enter button ✓. The cell reference is made absolute. Multiplying by 12 calculates the annual amount paid. If necessary, widen the column to display the results.

7 In cell C11, drag the fill handle to cell G11 to fill the loan payments for the five-year term of the loan. Point to the heading for column C and drag to column G to select columns C:G. Point to a line between any two of the selected column headings, and double-click to widen the columns. The project costs are entered for the five-year term of the loan.

8 Click cell H11. Type 0 and then on the formula bar, click the Enter button ✓. In H11, drag the fill handle to cell V11. Scroll back to column A. The project financing costs are displayed as negative cash flows, as shown in Figure 7.25.

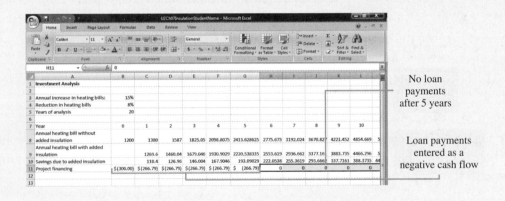

No loan payments after 5 years

Loan payments entered as a negative cash flow

FIGURE 7.25

9 Click cell A11. On the formula bar, click to the right of *financing*. Press Spacebar, and then type *

10 Click cell A19. Type * Assumes a five-year loan and then press ↵Enter.

11 Click the *Loan* sheet tab, and then click cell B8. On the Home tab, in the Font group, click the Fill Color button arrow 🎨 ▾. From the gallery, click the second color in the first column: *White, Background 1, Darker 5%*. This cell is shaded to indicate that it should not be changed.

good design...

DOCUMENT YOUR ASSUMPTIONS

When you build an assumption into a worksheet, be sure to document it to help users avoid errors.

The next step in the cash flow analysis is to determine the annual cash flow by calculating the difference between the positive cash flow—savings due to added insulation—and the negative cash flow—the loan payments for the first five years.

to calculate the annual cash flow

1 Click the *CashFlow* sheet tab. Click cell A12. Type `Net annual cash flow` and then press `Tab⇆`.

2 In cell B12, type `= B10+B11` and then on the formula bar, click the Enter button ✓. You always add cash flows. Because the outgoing amounts are negative numbers, adding them to the total has the same effect as subtracting a positive number.

3 With cell B12 selected, drag the fill handle to cell V12. Widen columns that display ###, and then scroll back to column A. Click cell H12 and notice that the annual cash flow becomes positive in year 6, as shown in Figure 7.26.

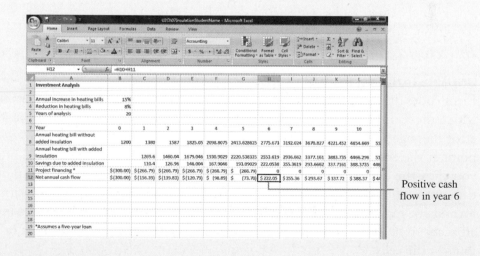

Positive cash flow in year 6

FIGURE 7.26

18 Save 💾 the workbook.

▶▶▶ *lesson*

seven | Calculating a Simple Payback Using a Hidden Row, the IF Function, and Conditional Formatting

The cash flows in the early years of the investment are negative, but they eventually become positive after the loan is paid off and the savings have increased due to higher heating bills. You can add each year's cash flow to the sum of the previous years to calculate a ***cumulative total***. In the early years when the cash flow is negative, the cumulative total becomes more negative each year. Once the cash flows becomes positive, the trend reverses and eventually the cumulative total becomes positive. The number of years that it takes for the cumulative total to become positive is called the ***simple payback period***. This is a measure that is commonly used to compare investments. It tells you how many years it will take to recover your investment before you start to profit from it.

The first step in the process is to calculate a cumulative total for the cash flows.

to calculate a cumulative total

1 **With the *CashFlow* sheet selected, click cell A13. Type** Cumulative total **and press** Tab⇆**.** In the following step, you will be instructed to make an intentional error.

2 **In cell B13, type** =A13+B12 **and then on the formula bar, click the Enter button** ✓**.** The #VALUE! error code displays. A cumulative total adds this year's cash flow to the total in the previous year. The idea behind this formula is correct, but there is no previous year's total in the first year. Therefore, the formula is referring to a cell that contains text—A13—resulting in this error code.

···

to extend your knowledge

UNDERSTANDING ERROR CODES

Error codes display when there is a problem with a formula. In this example, the cell to which the formula refers has text in it instead of a number, which causes the #VALUE! error message to display in the cell. Next to the cell is an *error checking button*. If you point at the error checking button, it displays a message that explains the problem. If you click the button, it provides a menu of options for dealing with the problem. In the corner of the cell that contains the error, a small triangle appears to warn that the formula or function in this cell is different than the formulas or functions in the cells adjacent to it. To fix this type of problem, consider changing the formula or the contents of the cells.

Other common error messages are described in Table 7.2.

···

ERROR CODE	DESCRIPTION
#DIV/0	Division by zero: caused by the denominator of a formula evaluating to zero
#N/A	Required value not available: left out a required argument
#NAME?	Nonexistent function name: usually caused by a misspelling
#NUM!	Invalid number: displays when the number provided as an argument to a function does not meet the function's requirements
#REF!	Cell no longer exists: usually caused by deleting a row or column that contained the cell
#VALUE	Wrong type of data: usually occurs when a formula has arithmetic operators referring to cells that contain text

TABLE 7.2

3 Click cell B13, and then press Delete to remove the formula and error message from this cell. Type =B12 and on the formula bar, click the Enter button ✓. The first item in a cumulative total often has a different formula or value. In year zero, there is no cumulative total from the previous year; therefore, the result is the same as the net cash flow for that year.

4 In cell C13, type =B13+C12 and on the formula bar, click the Enter button ✓. The cumulative total in cell C13 adds this year's cash flow from cell C12 to the cumulative total from the previous year. This is the pattern you want to fill into the remaining cells in this row.

5 In cell C13, drag the fill handle to cell V13, and then scroll back to column A.

6 Click cell B8. Scroll to column V, then press ↑Shift and click cell V13 to select the range of cells. On the Home tab, in the Number group, click the Accounting Number Format button $ ▾. In the Number group, click the Decrease Decimal button ⬓ two times.

7 Click cell K13 and notice that the cumulative total becomes positive in year 9, as shown in Figure 7.27. This means that the simple payback year is year 9.

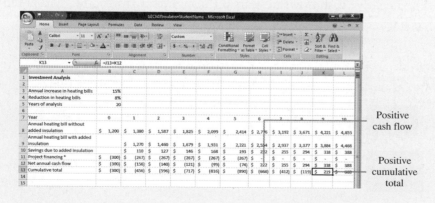

FIGURE 7.27

Calculating a Simple Payback Using a Hidden Row, the IF Function, and Conditional Formatting

Analyzing tables of data involves recognizing when changes occur. You can make this easier to see by using *conditional formatting*, which changes the fill and font colors based on a criterion that you specify.

In this task, you use conditional formats to highlight the negative cash flows.

to use conditional formatting

1 **Click cell B12. Scroll to V12, press ⇧Shift, and click V12.** The Net annual cash flow values are selected.

2 **On the Home tab, in the Styles group, click the Conditional Formatting button. Point to *Highlight Cells Rules*, and then click *Less Than*.** The Less Than dialog box displays.

3 **In the Less Than dialog box, in the *Format cells that are LESS THAN* box, type 0** Notice that the default format is *Light Red Fill with Dark Red Text*, as shown in Figure 7.28.

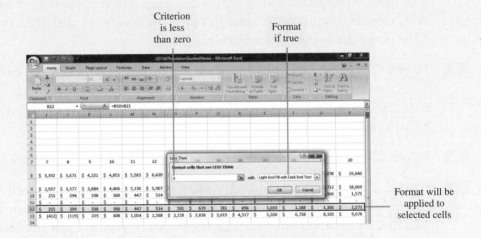

FIGURE 7.28

4 **Click OK. Scroll back to column A. Click a cell outside of row 12 to deselect the range.** The negative cash flows in years 0 through 5 are formatted with a red font on a light red background, as shown in Figure 7.29.

Conditional format
applied to values
less than 0

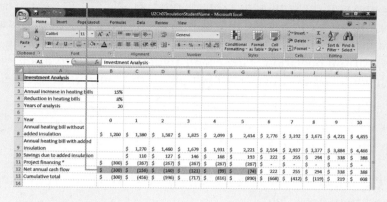

FIGURE 7.29

5 Click in the Name box. Type B13:V13 and then press ⏎Enter to select the **Cumulative total values.** You can use the Name box to select a range of cells.

6 In the Styles group, click the Conditional Formatting button. Point to *Highlight Cells Rules*, and then click *Less Than*.

7 In the Less Than dialog box, in the *Format cells that are LESS THAN* box, type 0

8 In the Less Than dialog box, click the *with* box arrow, and then click *Yellow Fill with Dark Yellow Text*. Click OK and scroll back to column A. Click a cell outside row 13 to deselect the range. The years of negative cumulative total are filled with dark yellow text on a yellow background, as shown in Figure 7.30.

Negative
cumulative
totals

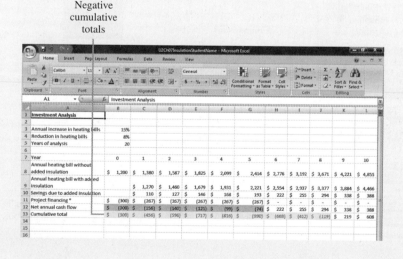

FIGURE 7.30

Calculating a Simple Payback Using a Hidden Row, the IF Function, and Conditional Formatting

There isn't a function in the function library to calculate the payback period, so you will create your own process to calculate the payback year. You will create a row of cells that display a *1* if the cumulative total for that year is positive and a *0* if it is negative. The sum of that row plus 1 will be the first year the cumulative total is positive.

To begin, you will use a conditional function. A conditional function uses arguments, but instead of being a list of inputs for the function to use to calculate a resulting value, the first argument is a comparison operation. The second argument is what to display if the comparison is true, and the third argument is what to display if the comparison is false.

to use an IF function

1 **With the *CashFlow* sheet selected, click cell A14. Type** `Negative cumulative totals` **and then press** Tab.

2 **With cell B14 selected, on the Formulas tab, in the Function Library group, click the Logical button, and then click IF.** The Function Arguments dialog box for the logical IF function displays. Here you enter the arguments to determine if something is true or false.

3 **In the Logical_test box, type** `B13<=0` This is the condition that is being evaluated as true or false

4 **Press** Tab, **and in the Value_if_true box, type** `1` **Press** Tab, **and in the Value_if_false box, type** `0` The function makes a comparison between the value in cell B13 and 0 to see if it is less than or equal to 0. If this is true, 1 will display; if it is not true, 0 will display. In this case, the value in cell B13—negative 300—is less than zero, so the function displays the number 1, as shown in Figure 7.31.

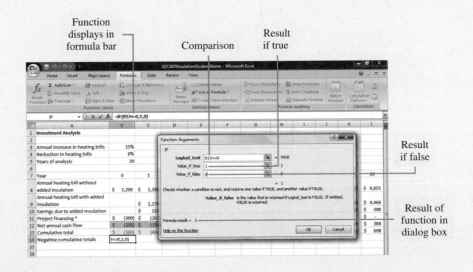

Function displays in formula bar

Comparison

Result if true

Result if false

Result of function in dialog box

FIGURE 7.31

5 **Click OK. In cell B14, drag the fill handle to cell V14. Scroll back to column A.**
Notice that when the cumulative cash flow is negative in the first 8 years, the IF function displays 1 for each year, as shown in Figure 7.32.

1 indicates negative
cumulative cash flow

0 displays
in year 9

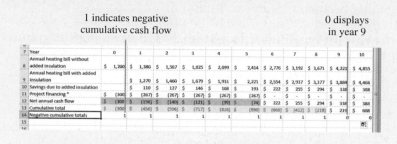

FIGURE 7.32

to extend your knowledge

USING COMPARISON OPERATORS

Comparison operators are symbols used to compare two values—either values in cells to given values or to values in other cells. Commonly used comparison operators are listed in Table 7.3.

OPERATOR	DESCRIPTION
<	Less than: is true if the value to the left is less than the value to the right
<=	Less than or equal to: is true if the value to the left is either less than or equal to the value to the right
>	Greater than: is true if the value to the left is greater than the value to the right
>=	Greater than or equal to: is true if the value to the left is either greater than or equal to the value to the right
<>	Not equal: is true if the two values are not the same

TABLE 7.3

A sum of the values in B14:V14 will be the total number of years the cash flow was negative. The next year is the year in which the cumulative total becomes positive. The values in row 14 are only used to calculate the payback, so the row can be hidden. This is the final step to calculate the simple payback in years.

to calculate the simple payback and hide a row

1 **Click cell A16. Type** `Payback year` **and then press** Tab⇥.

2 **In cell B16, type** `=SUM(B14:V14)` **and then press Enter.** The year in which the cumulative total becomes positive is displayed.

3 **Point to the row 14 heading and right-click. On the shortcut menu, click Hide. Click cell B16.** Row 14 is hidden, but its values are still available for use by the SUM function in cell B16, as shown in Figure 7.33.

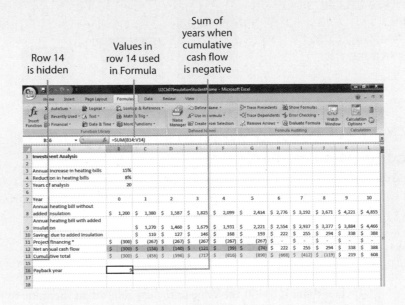

FIGURE 7.33

---

good **design...**

HIDE ROWS OR COLUMNS

Rows or columns that contain supporting calculations that do not add useful meaning to the final printout can be hidden.

---

4 **Point to the heading of row 13, and when the** ➡ **pointer displays, click and drag down to row 15.** Rows 13 through 15 are selected, including the hidden row.

5 **Right-click the selected row headings, and then click Unhide to display the hidden row.** To unhide rows or columns, you must select the rows or columns on either side of the row or column.

6 **On the Quick Access Toolbar, click the Undo button** ↺ **to hide row 14 again.**

7 **Save** 💾 **the workbook.**

▶▶▶ lesson

eight | Using the Internal Rate of Return Function

Determining the simple payback is useful for comparing small projects, but other comparisons are usually necessary if larger amounts are involved. One of these comparison values is called the *internal rate of return (IRR).* It is a financial measurement that is used to evaluate an investment and is comparable to the percent interest you earn on a savings account. Investments with short payback periods and high IRR percentages are usually preferred over investments that take longer to recoup investment money or that have lower IRR values. To make the best use of limited amounts of money, companies, cities, and individuals must make decisions. If alternative energy or conservation projects are to compete for those limited dollars, they need to have short payback periods and fairly high IRR percentages.

to use the IRR function

1 With the *CashFlow* worksheet selected, click cell A17. Type `Internal Rate of Return (IRR)**` and then press Tab⇆.

2 With cell B17 selected, on the Formulas tab, in the Function Library group, click the Financial button. Scroll down and click IRR. The Function Arguments dialog box displays, as shown in Figure 7.34.

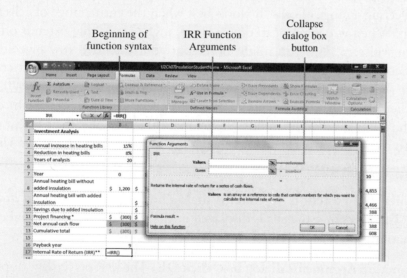

Beginning of function syntax · IRR Function Arguments · Collapse dialog box button

FIGURE 7.34

3 In the Function Arguments dialog box, in the Values box, click the *Collapse dialog box* button [⬛]. You can select a range of cells for the argument, but the dialog box might obscure the worksheet. The Collapse dialog box button shrinks the dialog box to get it out of the way. You can drag the box by dragging its title bar if it is still in the way.

4 **Drag cells B12:V12 and release the mouse button. Scroll back to column A.** The range that includes the annual cash flow values—including year 0—is displayed in the collapsed dialog box, as shown in Figure 7.35.

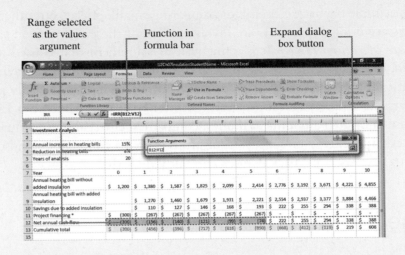

Range selected as the values argument

Function in formula bar

Expand dialog box button

FIGURE 7.35

---

if you have **problems...**

Dragging the pointer across a range of cells with the mouse button held down is a quick way of selecting a range of cells. It works best when the entire range of cells is visible on the screen. When you attempt to drag a large range of cells that extends off the screen, the screen will scroll but you might overshoot your intended row or column. If you have difficulty controlling the scrolling, click the cell in the upper left corner of the range, use the scroll bars to scroll to the cell at the bottom left, hold (⬆Shift), and click.

Another problem with dragging a range to select it is that you might click on the edge of the cell instead of the middle. If you make that mistake, the content of the cell is moved. To recover from accidentally moving the content of a cell, use the Undo button.

---

5 **In the collapsed Function Arguments dialog box, click the *Expand dialog box* button** 📷**.** The range of cells is displayed in the Values box. The initial estimate of the evaluation shows as a decimal in the dialog box.

6 **In the Function Arguments dialog box, click OK.** The IRR percentage displays as 23%.

7 **Using the techniques you have practiced, select the range A16:B17. Right-click the selected range, and on the Mini toolbar, click the Borders button arrow** ⊞▾**, and then click *Thick Box Border.*** Two important statistics that can be used to compare this investment to others are enclosed in a dark border.

8 **Click cell A20. Type** `**Assumes 20-year life` **and then press** ⏎Enter.

9 **Save** 💾 **the file and compare your screen with Figure 7.36.**

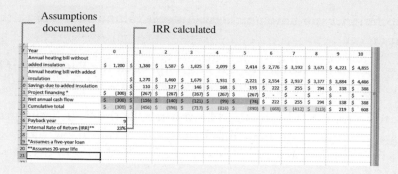

Assumptions documented   IRR calculated

FIGURE 7.36

►►► *lesson*

nine | Printing Large Worksheets

Worksheets are often used to estimate future income and expenses, and they can extend for several columns beyond what would conveniently fit on one page of paper in normal portrait orientation. In this lesson, you choose columns of labels that repeat on each page, and you add page numbers to the footer.

The first thing to do is to make sure you are using the available space efficiently. Then, if the worksheet is still too wide for a single page in portrait orientation, you can change the orientation.

to AutoFit columns and change page orientation

1 **With *CashFlow* worksheet selected, click the heading of column B. Scroll to column V, press ⬆Shift, and then click the heading of column V.** Columns B through V are selected. These columns were widened when the Accounting Number Style was applied, but they remained wide when the decimal places were reduced.

2 **Point to the line between the column U and V headings, and then double-click. The widths of all of the selected columns are adjusted to fit the contents of the columns. Scroll back to column A. Click a cell in column A to deselect columns B:V.** You can double-click any of the lines between any of the selected column headings to adjust all of them.

• •

good **design...**

ADJUST COLUMN WIDTHS

Reduce the total width of a worksheet by adjusting the column widths to the minimum necessary to display the contents of the columns.

• •

3 Using the techniques you have practiced, AutoFit column A to adjust the width to fit its largest cell.

4 On the View tab, in the Workbook Views group, click the Page Layout button. Scroll to the right and notice that the data extends to a third page.

5 Scroll back to column A. On the Page Layout tab, in the Page Setup group, click the Orientation button, and then click Landscape. Scroll to the right. The landscape orientation allows more columns per page, and the data now fits on two pages.

When a worksheet extends to more than one page, it is helpful to include labels on each page so that you can understand the data that is presented. To do this, you can repeat column or row headings on each page of a printout.

to repeat labels on each page of the printout

1 On the *CashFlow* worksheet, on the Page Layout tab, in the Page Setup group, click the **Print Titles button.** The Page Setup dialog box displays with the Sheet tab selected.

2 Click the *Columns to repeat at left* box and type A:B as shown in Figure 7.37.

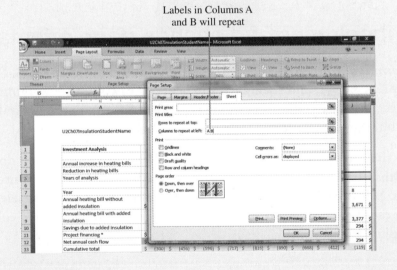

Labels in Columns A and B will repeat

FIGURE 7.37

3 Click OK. Scroll to the right. Notice that the first two columns repeat on each page. Notice also that the third page only displays the last year or two.

good **design...**

TITLES ON LARGE WORKSHEETS

If a worksheet printout will span several pages, place the title in cell A1 but do not merge and center across all of the columns. It will be included on each sheet if the first column of labels is used as a repeating column.

If the data stretches across more pages than is necessary, you can reduce the size of the data so that it will print on fewer pages and then control where the pages break between data so that it makes sense.

to reduce size to fit page and set a page break

1 **On the Page Layout tab, in the Scale to Fit group, click the Width box arrow. On the menu, click 2 pages. Scroll to the right to display page 2.** A scaling factor is calculated that would make the worksheet fit the required width. In this case, it is 79%, as shown in Figure 7.38. Your Scale percent may be different.

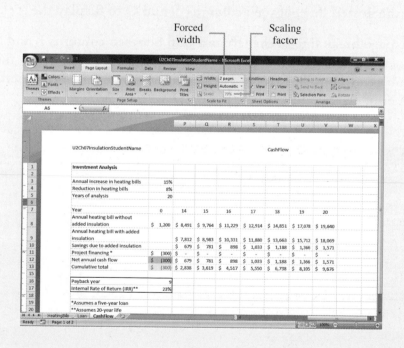

FIGURE 7.38

2 Click the Office button ⊞, point to Print, and then click Print Preview. On the Print Preview tab, in the Preview group, click the Next Page button. Notice that the columns for years 14–20 print on the second page.

3 In the Preview group, click the Close Print Preview button. On the View tab, in the Workbook Views group, click the *Page Break Preview* button. Close the *Welcome to Page Break Preview* dialog box. The pages are labeled and a dotted line indicates where the pages are separated, as shown in Figure 7.39. The dotted line indicates that the position of the page break is calculated by the program.

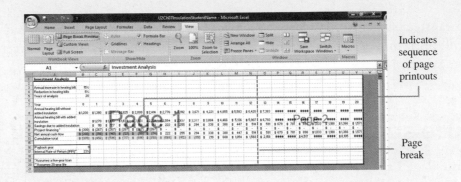

FIGURE 7.39

4 Point to the dotted line between columns N and O to display the ↔ pointer.

5 Drag the page break line to the left and stop between columns L and M. The dotted line becomes a solid line to indicate that it is a page break set by the user, as shown in Figure 7.40. The first ten years will print on Page 1, and the second ten years will print on Page 2.

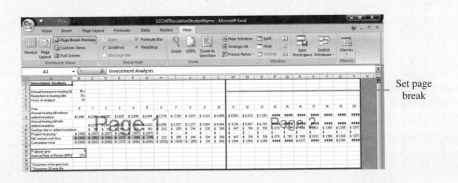

FIGURE 7.40

Document the printout by placing information in the header. When you have multiple-page printouts, add the page number to the footer.

to add page numbers to the footer and scale to fit

1 In the *CashFlow* worksheet, on the View tab, in the Workbook Views group, click the Page Layout button.

2 Click in the left Header area, above *Investment Analysis*. On the Design tab, in the Header & Footer Elements group, click the File Name button. Press Tab⇆ to move to the Center area, and then on the Header & Footer Elements group, click the Sheet Name button. Press Tab⇆, and in the right section, click the Current Date button. Press Spacebar, and then click the Current Time button.

3 Scroll to the bottom of the first page to display the footer area. Scroll to the right side of the first page, below column L, and click in the footer area. In the Header & Footer Elements group, click the Page Number button. Press Spacebar. Type of and then press Spacebar. In the Header & Footer Elements group, click the Number of Pages button. Click a cell in the worksheet. The current page and the total number of pages are placed in the footer, as shown in Figure 7.41.

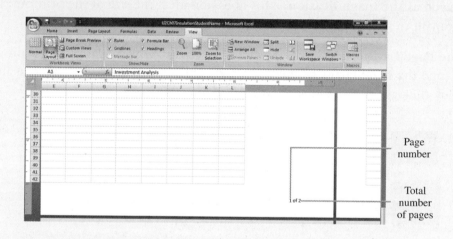

Page number

Total number of pages

FIGURE 7.41

good **design...**

ADD PAGE NUMBERS

If the printout extends to more than one page, add a page number to the header or footer. Display the current page number and the total number of pages. If the pages become separated, you can reassemble them in the correct order and you will know if you have all of them.

4 Click the Office button 🔘, point to Print, and then click Print Preview. The worksheet fits on two pages, but it doesn't use the space available, as shown in Figure 7.42. The scaling factor could be increased.

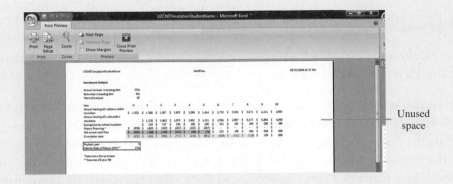

FIGURE 7.42

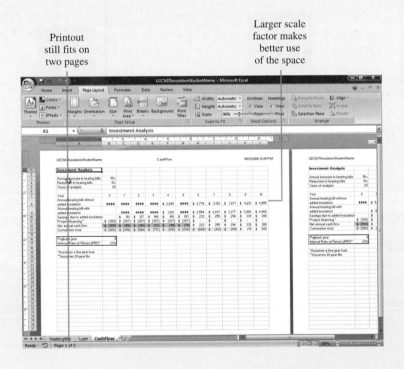

Unused space

5 On the Print Preview tab, in the Preview group, click the **Close Print Preview** button. Press Ctrl + Home to move to cell A1.

6 On the zoom slider, click the Zoom Out button ⊖ several times until 60% is displayed as the magnification. This does not affect the size of the printout; it just enables you to view the whole page on screen.

7 On the Page Layout tab, in the Scale to Fit group, click the **Scale up spin arrow** to change the scale factor to 90%. The worksheet still fits on two pages, as indicated by the page counter in the status bar (shown in Figure 7.43).

Printout still fits on two pages

Larger scale factor makes better use of the space

FIGURE 7.43

In some cases, you might prefer to print a portion of the worksheet. Because the payback occurs in year nine, you set a print area to print just the first 8 years.

to set the print area

1 On the zoom bar, click the Zoom In button ⊕ until the zoom displays 90%. Notice that year 9 is in column K and the last row used is row 20.

2 Select the range A1:K20. On the Page Layout tab, in the Page Setup group, click the **Print Area** button, and then click **Set Print Area.** The selected area is highlighted and a print border displays at the edge of the range.

3 From the Office menu, point to Print, and then click **Print Preview.** The selected print area is set to print as shown in Figure 7.44.

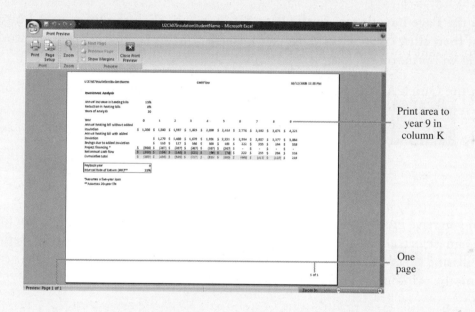

Print area to year 9 in column K

One page

FIGURE 7.44

4 On the Print Preview tab, in the Preview group, click the Close Print Preview button. Zoom to 70%, and notice that the print area is enclosed in a dotted line, as shown in Figure 7.45.

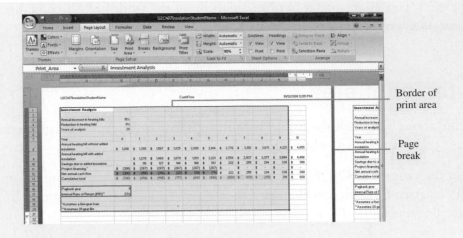

Border of
print area

Page
break

FIGURE 7.45

5 **On the Page Layout tab, in the Page Setup group, click the Print Area button, and then click Clear Print Area.** The default print area is restored and the worksheet will print on two pages.

6 **On the Quick Access Toolbar, click the Undo button** ↺. The print area borders are restored.

7 **Save** 💾 **the workbook.**

When you have more than one worksheet that should have the same page setup for printing, you can select all of the similar worksheets and apply the same page setup. The HeatingBills and Loan worksheets both use portrait orientation, and both of them need to be centered on the printout and have documentation in their headers.

to format the page setup of multiple worksheets

1 **Click the** *HeatingBills* **sheet tab. Press** ⬆Shift **and click the** *Loan* **sheet tab.** Both tabs are highlighted and [Group] is displayed after the file name in the title bar.

2 **On the Page Layout tab, in the Page Setup group, click the Dialog BoxLauncher** ⬚. **Click the Margins tab, and in the** *Center on page* **area, select the Horizontally check box.**

3 **In the Page Setup dialog box, click the Header/Footer tab, and then click the Custom Header button.** The Header dialog box displays.

4 Click in the Left section box, and then click the Insert File Name button .

5 Press Tab⇄, and in the Center section, click the Insert Sheet Name button .

6 Press Tab⇄, and in the Right section, click the Insert Date button . Press Spacebar and click the Insert Time button .

7 In the Header dialog box, click OK. In the Page Setup dialog box, on the Header/Footer tab, click the Print Preview button. Click on Heating Bills to zoom in. The HeatingBills worksheet displays in print preview, as shown in Figure 7.46.

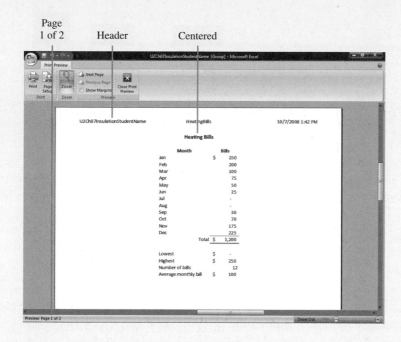

Page 1 of 2   Header   Centered

FIGURE 7.46

8 On the Print Preview tab, in the Preview group, click Next Page. The Loan worksheet preview displays, as shown in Figure 7.47.

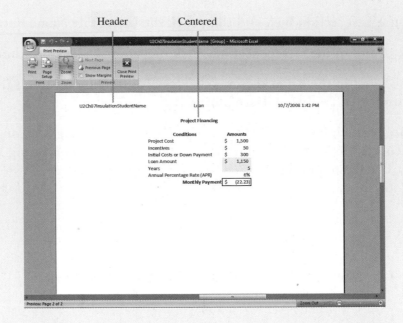

Header   Centered

FIGURE 7.47

9 On the Page Layout tab, in the Page Setup group, click the Close Print Preview button. Press Ctrl + Home to move the active cell to cell A1 for both selected sheets.

10 Click the *CashFlow* sheet tab. On the status bar, click the Normal button, ⊞, and then click cell A1. The first cell in each worksheet is selected before saving.

11 Click the *HeatingBills* sheet tab. Save 💾 the file. The Heating Bills worksheet will be the first to display with the selection in cell A1.

12 Submit the file as directed by your instructor. Close the file.

Advanced Skills or Concepts

In this section, you are introduced to skills that are not taught with step-by-step instructions.

Drawing Conclusions Based on Calculated Values

In this chapter, you used Excel to determine the payback and internal rate of return for an investment in added insulation to reduce heating bills. These two values are very useful for deciding which type of investment to make. For example, in an area that does not receive much sunlight, the payback for a solar photovoltaic cell installation will be longer and the IRR lower than it might be for a wind generator. If you want to convince a company or an organization to support your proposal to invest in alternative energy or conservation projects, it will be much easier to do so if you can show that the payback and IRR values are comparable to other investment options.

Designing for What-If Analysis

If your worksheets are well designed, you can change the values in the cells that document the initial conditions, and all the formulas and functions that depend upon those values will be recalculated. This process is very fast, so you have the opportunity to say *What if we changed the initial conditions?* In this example, on the Loan sheet, you could try different values for the project cost, incentives, initial cost, or annual percentage rate and observe the effect on the monthly payment. Because the initial cost and monthly payment are referred to by formulas in the CashFlow sheet to calculate the payback year and internal rate of return, those comparison values will update immediately and you can see the effect on the project's competitive position. For example, if you install the insulation yourself and lower the project cost from $1,500 to $1,000 on the Loan sheet, it reduces the payback on the CashFlow sheet from eight to six years.

When you design your worksheets, the goal is to place any values that you might want to change in cells with descriptive labels so that it is easy to try out different values to assess their effect on the results. In the design of the Loan worksheet, an assumption was made that the payments would be monthly. This assumption is built in to the functions and formulas. Within the arguments of the PMT function, we multiplied the *Years* value by 12 and divided the *Annual Percentage Rate* by 12; and in the CashFlow worksheet in cell C11, you multiplied the *Monthly Payment* from the Loan sheet by 12 to determine the annual payment. If you wanted to explore the possibility of making payments quarterly or annually, it would be easier if the number of payments was in a cell and that cell reference was used in the formula. Because the number of payments was typed into the formula it would be much harder to explore other payment options because you would have to edit the PMT function arguments and find all the formulas with the number 12 in them. This limitation is reasonably documented by the label *Monthly Payment*.

There are more subtle assumptions built into the CashFlow worksheet that are not apparent to the end user unless you point them out. When you filled the values on the *Project Financing* row, you filled from C11 to G11 to show five years of payments. If you change the number of years in the Loan sheet from 5 to 4, the monthly payment is recalculated, but the formulas remain in C11:G11 instead of automatically changing to C11:F11. The result is an incorrect value for cash flow in the fifth year, which could cause the payback year and IRR calculations to be wrong. This is why you were instructed to document the assumption with an asterisk and a note and shade cell B8 on the Loan sheet. Similarly, the IRR function included all the years from 1 to 20 when you specified its range of B12:V12. Always document your assumptions—especially those that could cause errors if any of the variables are changed.

Identify Simple Trends in Tabular Data

One of the reasons you use gridlines in a spreadsheet is to help your eye follow the numbers across a row or down a column to identify changes, trends, or unusual data. The objective is not to produce the spreadsheet, but to arrange the data so that you can find meaning. To give the data meaning, look for the following:

- Location where values change from positive to negative at one place, like they did in the Cumulative Total row of the CashFlow sheet when payback was achieved
- Cyclical changes where the values go up and down periodically like they did with the heating bills in the Loan worksheet
- Progressively increasing (or decreasing) values like those in the Annual Heating Bill row in the CashFlow worksheet

- Sudden changes like the year when the loan paid off in the Project Financing row in the CashFlow sheet and the values went from $(267) each year to 0 the next year
- Numbers that are significantly different than those before or after them in the data, like the down payment value in year zero of the Project Financing row in the CashFlow sheet. These might be errors; if they are not due to errors, however, they deserve special attention so you know why they are different.

Conditional formatting is a useful tool for helping the user spot sudden changes or values that are outside of expected ranges.

Use Excel Templates

In addition to a library of functions, Excel comes with a library of worksheets that are designed to perform common office functions such as budgets, expense reports, invoices, agendas, and calendars. They are designed to enable you to just fill in the data. They already have the formulas and functions that calculate answers. This is a strength—but it is also a weakness—of templates. Most of them are automated and their formulas and functions are hidden or protected, so they are difficult to modify. To explore Excel templates, click the Office button, and then click New. In the New Workbook dialog box, look at the previews of several different types of templates.

CHECK YOUR WORK

Here is a list of items your instructor will probably look for when grading your work. To improve your evaluation, take time to check the items yourself before you turn in your work.

HeatingBills Sheet
- In Normal view, check formatting: title and column headings in bold, title merged and centered in cells A1 and B1
- Bill for January and total use Accounting Number Style, while the cells between use the comma style.
- Zeros instead of empty cells for the July and August bills
- All of the functions use B4:B15 for the range.
- Functions are used as directed, instead of simple values typed into the cells.
- In Print Preview, check the header for: file name at the left, sheet name in the center, the date and time you printed it at the right

Loan Sheet
- Formula in cell B7 subtracts B5 and B6 from B4
- Function in cell B10 uses calculations in its arguments to convert years to months and annual percentage rate to monthly percentage rate
- Percentage format used in cell B9
- Cell B10 format changed to Accounting Number Style
- In Print Preview, check the header for: file name at the left, sheet name in the center, the date and time you printed it at the right.

CashFlow Sheet
- Changeable values in separate cells B3:B5
- Year numbers formatted as text in row 7
- In cell B8, a reference to cell B16 on the HeatingBills sheet
- In cells C8:V8, a formula that uses a relative reference to the cell on the left and an absolute reference to cell B3
- In cells C9:V9, a formula that uses a relative reference to the cell above and an absolute reference to cell B4
- In cells C10:V10, a formula that subtracts the cell above from the cell two rows above
- In cell B11, a reference to the Loan amount in cell B6 on the Loan worksheet, which has been edited to add a minus sign to make it negative
- In cells C11:V11, formulas that have an absolute reference to cell B10 on the Loan sheet, multiplied by 12
- In cells C12:V12, a formula that adds value from two rows above to the cell one row above
- In cells C13:V13, a formula that adds the value from the cell to the left to the cell above
- Conditional formatting is applied to cells C12:V12 and to C13:V13 to shade negative values.
- Row 14 is hidden. It has the IF function that displays a 1 for negative and 0 for positive values in the cell above. Rehide the row, if necessary.
- In cell B16, the sum of B14:V14
- In cell B17, the IRR function with B12:V12 as the arguments
- Assumptions documented in cells A19 and A20
- In Print Preview, check the header for: file name at the left, sheet name in the center, the date and time you printed it at the right
- In Print Preview, the footer shows the page number and the total number of pages.
- In Print Preview, the print area is set to the first 9 years.

If you make any changes, make sure the final version is in Normal view with cell A1 selected, and then save it.

KEY TERMS

absolute cell reference	conditional formatting	mixed cell reference
argument	cumulative total	null
AutoComplete	currency format	present value
cash flow analysis	fill handle	relative cell reference
circular reference	interest rate	simple payback period
comparison operators	internal rate of return (IRR)	what-if analysis

ASSESSING LEARNING OUTCOMES

SCREEN ID

Identify each element of the screen by matching callout numbers shown in Figure 7.48 to a corresponding description.

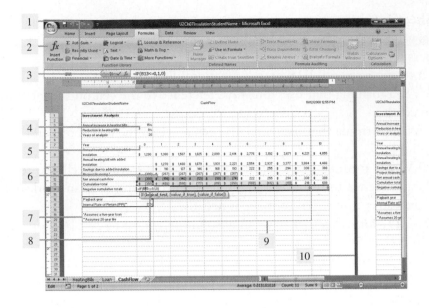

FIGURE 7.48

_____ **A.** Border of print area

_____ **B.** Page break

_____ **C.** Conditional formatting

_____ **D.** Numbers formatted as text

_____ **E.** Changeable values for what-if analysis

_____ **F.** Documentation of assumptions

_____ **G.** Enter button

_____ **H.** Financial functions

_____ **I.** All functions

_____ **J.** Function arguments

MULTIPLE CHOICE

Circle the letter of the correct answer for each of the following. The lesson in which the term or concept was introduced is indicated at the end of the sentence.

1. If the six cells in the range B3:B8 have the content 5, 6, 3, empty, 8, and 10, the COUNT function would display _____. [L1]

a. 5

b. 6

c. zero

d. an error message

2. If the six cells in the range B3:B8 have the content 5, 6, 3, empty, 8, and 10, the MIN function would display _____. [L1]

a. 0

b. 3

c. 5

d. an error message

3. If the six cells in the range B3:B8 have the content 5, 6, 3, empty, 8, and 10, the MAX function would display _____. [L5]

a. 0

b. 10

c. 32

d. an error message

4. Given six cells in the range B3:B8 that have the content 5, 6, 3, empty, 8, and 10, if the function in cell B8 is =SUM(B3:B8), the display would be _____. [L5]

a. 0

b. 32

c. 64

d. an error message

5. A formula with an absolute reference to cell B3 would be _____. [L5]

   a. =B3

   b. =$B3$

   c. =B3

   d. =$B3

6. To represent a payment of $200 to the bank for repayment of a loan, a cash flow statement would display the number as _____. [L10]

   a. $200.00

   b. $200

   c. 200.00

   d. a negative number

7. The second argument of an IF function is _____. [L5]

   a. the criterion

   b. what to display or do if the criterion is true

   c. what to display or do if the criterion is false

   d. the second input number

8. The IRR function returns a value that is similar to _____. [L7]

   a. the monthly payment

   b. the payback period

   c. the interest earned on a savings account

   d. the cumulative total

9. The error code that displays when you misspell a function is _____. [L9]

   a. #DIV/0

   b. #NUM!

   c. #REF!

   d. #NAME?

10. When numbers are used as column or row labels, they should be formatted _____. [L2]

    a. as text

    b. without decimal places

    c. left aligned

    d. with commas

MATCHING

Match the term or concept to its description.

_____ 1. A selected format that is applied if a criterion is met

_____ 2. A cell location that is stored as a given row and column and does not change when a formula is copied

_____ 3. Empty or nonexistent

_____ 4. A process of trying different values to see what happens

_____ 5. A value or expression used by the function

_____ 6. Small box at the lower-right corner of a selected cell

_____ 7. Similar to accounting format, but it places the currency symbol next to the number on the left

_____ 8. A financial measurement that is used to evaluate an investment and is comparable to the percent interest you earn on a savings account

_____ 9. Amount of a loan before it has been repaid

_____ 10. A cell reference that is stored as a certain number of rows and columns from the currently selected cell

A. Absolute reference

B. Argument

C. Conditional

D. Currency

E. Fill handle

F. Internal Rate of Return

G. Null

H. Present Value

I. Relative reference

J. What-if analysis

The Skill Drill exercise is a repeat of the lessons in the chapter but with different data. The instructions are less detailed, and your speed and familiarity should increase with practice. There is a figure at the end against which you can check your worksheets. The purpose of this exercise is to build your confidence and speed in using these skills and to set them in your memory for later recall. The section numbers correspond to the lesson numbers. You are welcome to refer back to the lessons illustrated and the detailed instructions, if necessary.

In this exercise, you set up three worksheets that display monthly heating bills, calculate the loan needed to pay for energy-efficient windows, and calculate a cash flow to determine payback and IRR. Print copies of the worksheets if your instructor requires it.

1. Filling Labels and Using Worksheet Functions

1. Start Excel and use the blank workbook. Double-click the **Sheet1** tab, type `HeatingBills` and press ⏎Enter. Save the workbook in your Chapter07 folder as `U2Ch07WindowsStudentName`

2. In cell **A1,** type `Heating Bills` and then make it bold and center it across cells **A1:B1.**

3. In cell **A3,** type `Month` and then in cell **B3,** type `Bills` Select cells **A3** and **B3.** Make both headers bold and center them within their own cells.

4. In cell **A4,** type `January` and then in cell **A4,** drag the fill handle down to cell **A15** to fill in the sequence of months.

5. In cell **A16,** enter `Total` and then align it on the right side of the cell.

6. In cells **A18** through **A21,** type `Lowest`, `Highest`, `Number of bills`, and `Average bill`

7. In cells **B4** through **B9,** type `300, 250, 150, 125, 100, 50`

8. In cells **B12** through **B15,** type `40, 90, 140, 190`

9. On the line between the column headings of columns **A** and **B,** double-click to adjust the width of column **A.**

10. In cell **B16,** type `=SUM(B4:B15)` and then, on the formula bar, click the **Enter** button.

11. Select cells **B4** and **B16,** and then apply the **Accounting Number Format.** Decrease the decimal places to none. Select **B5:B15,** and then apply the **Comma Style.** Decrease the decimal places to none.

12. Click cell **B16.** Apply the **Top and Double Bottom** border.

13. In cell **B18,** on the **Formulas** tab, in the **Function Library** group, click the **Insert Function** button. Locate and select the **MIN** function and enter `B4:B15` as the argument.

14. Use the procedure you practiced in step 13 to insert the **MAX** function in cell **B19,** the **COUNT** function in cell **B20,** and the **AVERAGE** function in cell **B21.** They should all use B4:B15 as the argument.

15. In cells **B10** and **B11,** type 0 and then notice that the MIN function in cell B18 changes from 40 to a 0 that is displayed as a dash, the COUNT function in cell B20 changes from 10 to 12, and the AVERAGE function in cell B21 changes from 144 to 120.

16. **Save** the workbook.

2. Using the Payment Function

1. Double-click the **Sheet2** tab name, type Loan and then press ↵Enter to rename the sheet tab.

2. In cell **A1,** type Project Financing and then press ↵Enter. Select **A1.** Make it bold and center it across cells **A1:B1.**

3. In cell **A3,** type Conditions and then in cell **B3,** type Amounts Select cells **A3** and **B3.** Make both headers bold and center them within their own cells.

4. In cells **A4** through **A10,** type Project cost, Incentives, Initial cost or down payment, Loan amount, Years, Annual Percentage Rate (APR), and Monthly payment

5. Widen column **A** to fit the labels. Click cell **A10,** apply bold, and align it on the right in the cell.

6. In cells **B4** through **B6,** type 7000, 0, and 1000 Format cells **B4:B7** as **Accounting Number Format** with no decimal places.

7. Click cell **B7.** Type =B4-B5-B6 and then press ↵Enter.

8. In cell **B8,** type 5 and then on the formula bar, click the **Enter** button. In the **Number** group, click the **Number Format box arrow,** and then click **General.**

9. Click cell **B9,** and then type 6%

10. Click cell **B10.** On the **Formulas** tab, in the **Function Library** group, click the **Financial** button. Locate and click the **PMT** function.

11. In the Function Arguments dialog box, in the **Rate** box, type B9/12 In the **Nper** box, type B8*12 and then in the **PV** box, type B7 Click **OK.**

12. In cell **B10,** apply a **Thick Box Border.** Select cells **B7:B8** and apply the **Fill Color** that is *White, Background 1, Darker, 15%.*

13. **Save** the workbook.

3. Filling a Sequence of Numbers and Formatting Them as Text

1. Double-click the **Sheet3** tab, type CashFlow and then press ↵Enter.

2. In cell **A1,** type Investment Analysis and then on the formula bar, click the **Enter** button. With cell **A1** selected, apply **Bold.**

3. In cells **A3** through **A5,** enter Annual increase in heating bills, Reduction in heating bills, and Years of analysis

4. In cells **B3** through **B5,** type 15%, 20%, and 20 If the value in B5 is 20%, change the number format to **General** and type 20 again.

5. In cell **A7,** type `Year` and in cells **B7** and **C7,** type `0` and `1`

6. Select cells **B7:C7.** Drag the fill handle to cell **V7.**

7. With the range still selected, on the **Home** tab, in the **Number** group, click the **Number Format box arrow,** and then click **Text. Center** the labels in their cells.

8. **Save** the workbook.

4. Using References to Cells in Other Worksheets and Relative Cell References

1. Click cell **A8,** type `Annual heating bill with old windows` and then press ⏎Enter. Right-click the column **A** heading, and then click **Column Width.** In the Column Width dialog box, type `29` and then press ⏎Enter.

2. Select cells **A3:A20.** On the **Home** tab, in the **Alignment** group, click the **Text Wrap** button. Labels in this range that are wider than 29 characters will wrap.

3. Click cell **B8.** Type `=` and then click the **HeatingBills** sheet tab. On the HeatingBills worksheet, click cell **B16,** and then press ⏎Enter.

5. Calculating a Percentage Increase and Using Absolute Cell References

1. Click cell **C8.** Type `=B8*(1+B3)` and then on the formula bar, click the **Enter** button.

2. On the formula bar, double-click **B3** to select it. Press F4 to add the symbols that make it an absolute reference. On the formula bar, click the **Enter** button. Alternatively, type `$B$3` when you edit the formula.

3. In cell **C8,** drag the fill handle to cell **V8.** Each formula has a relative reference to the cell to the left and an absolute reference to cell B3.

4. In cell **A9,** type `Annual heating bill with new windows`

5. Click cell **C9.** Type `=C8*(1-$B$4)` and then on the formula bar, click the **Enter** button. In cell **C9,** drag the fill handle to cell **V9.**

6. **Save** the workbook.

6. Using a Cash Flow Analysis

1. Click cell **A10.** Type `Savings due to new windows` and then press Tab⇆ two times.

2. In cell **C10,** type `=C8-C9` and then on the formula bar, click the **Enter** button.

3. In cell **C10,** drag the fill handle to cell **V10.**

4. In cell **A11,** type `Project financing*` and then press Tab⇆.

5. In cell **B11,** type `=` and then click the **Loan** sheet tab. On the Loan worksheet, click cell **B6,** and then press ⏎Enter. Click cell **B11,** and on the formula bar, click between = and **L** and type a minus sign (−) to edit the formula to display =-Loan!B6. This is money that has been paid out, so it needs to display as a negative number.

6. On the **CashFlow** worksheet, click cell **C11.** Type = and then click the **Loan** sheet tab. On the Loan worksheet, click cell **B10.** Press (F4), type *12 and then press (↵Enter). The monthly payment is multiplied by 12 to calculate the annual payment.

7. On the **CashFlow** worksheet, in cell **C11,** drag the fill handle to cell **G11.** The condition of the loan is 5 years. With cells **C11:G11** selected, decrease the decimal places to none.

8. Click cell **H11.** Type 0 and use the fill handle to fill this value to cell **V11.**

9. Click cell **A19.** Type *Assumes a 5-year loan

10. Click cell **A12.** Type Net annual cash flow and then press (Tab⇆).

11. In cell **B12,** type =B10+B11 and then on the formula bar, click the **Enter** button. In cell **B12,** drag the fill handle to cell **V12.**

12. **Save** the workbook.

7. Calculating a Simple Payback Using a Hidden Row, the IF Function, and Conditional Formatting

1. In cell **A13,** type Cumulative total and then press (Tab⇆). In cell **B13,** type =B12 and then press (Tab⇆).

2. In cell **C13,** type =B13+C12 and then on the formula bar, click the **Enter** button. In cell **C13,** drag the fill handle to cell **V13.**

3. Select cells **B8:V13.** Apply the **Accounting Number Format** and decrease the decimals displayed to none.

4. Select cells **B12:V12.** On the **Home** tab, in the **Styles** group, click the **Conditional Formatting** button. Point to **Highlight Cells Rules,** and then click **Less Than.**

5. In the Less Than dialog box, in the box on the left, type 0 and then click **OK.**

6. Select cells **B13:V13.** On the **Home** tab, in the **Styles** group, click the **Conditional Formatting** button. Point to **Highlight Cells Rules,** and then click **Less Than.**

7. In the Less Than dialog box, in the box on the left, type 0 and then click the *with* box arrow. On the menu, click **Yellow Fill with Dark Yellow Text.** Click **OK.**

8. Click cell **A14.** Type Negative cumulative totals and then press (Tab⇆).

9. With cell **B14** selected, on the **Formulas** tab, in the **Function Library** group, click the **Logical** button, and then click **IF.** In the IF Arguments dialog box, in the Logical_test box, type B13<=0 and then press (Tab⇆). In the Value_if_true box, type 1 and in the Value_if_false box, type 0 and then click **OK.** In cell **B14,** drag the fill handle to cell **V14.**

10. Click cell **A16.** Type Payback year and then press (Tab⇆).

11. In cell **B16,** type =SUM(B14:V14) and then press (↵Enter).

12. Point to the heading of row **14,** right-click, and then click **Hide.**

13. **Save** the workbook.

8. Using the Internal Rate of Return Function

1. Click cell **A17.** Type `Internal Rate of Return (IRR)**` and then press Tab.

2. In cell **B17,** on the **Formulas tab,** in the **Function Library** group, click the **Financial** button. Scroll down and click **IRR.**

3. In the Function Arguments dialog box, in the **Values** box, type `B12:V12` and then click **OK.** If necessary, format cell V17 with the Percent Style.

4. Click cell **A20.** Type `**Assumes a 20-year life` and then press Enter.

9. Printing Large Worksheets

1. On the **CashFlow** worksheet, click column heading **C.** Scroll to column **V,** press Shift, and then click the column **V** heading.

2. With columns **C** through **V** selected, double-click one of the lines separating any of the selected column headings. All of the selected columns are resized to fit their widest content.

3. On the **Page Layout** tab, in the **Page Setup** group, click the **Orientation** button, and then click **Landscape.**

4. In the **Page Setup** group, click the **Print Titles** button. The Page Setup dialog box displays with the **Sheet** tab selected. In the **Columns to repeat at left** box, type `A:B` and then click **OK.**

5. In the **Scale to Fit** group, select the **Width** button arrow, and then click **2 pages.**

6. On the **View** tab, in the **Workbook Views** group, click the **Page Break Preview** button. Drag the dotted blue line to a position between columns **L** and **M** to force a page break after the tenth year.

7. Click the **Office** button, point to **Print,** and then click **Print Preview.** On the **Print Preview** tab, click **Next Page.** Notice the repeating columns and the break between years 10 and 11.

8. On the **Print Preview** tab, click the **Close Print Preview** button. On the **View** tab, in the **Workbook Views** group, click the **Normal** button.

9. Select **A1:M20.** On the **Page Layout** tab, in the **Page Setup** group, click the **Print Area** button, and then click **Set Print Area.** This area shows the payback year. In the **Page Break** view adjust the **Scale** percent as necessary to maximize the use of the first page and still show the first 11 years.

10. On the **View** tab, in the **Workbook Views** group, click the **Page Layout** button.

11. Click the left section of the header. Use the buttons in the **Header & Footer Elements** group to insert the **File Name** in the left section, the **Sheet Name** in the center section, and the **Current Date** and **Current Time** in the right section.

12. Scroll to the bottom of the page. Click in the margin area below column L to open the right section of the footer. On the **Header & Footer Tools Design** tab, in the **Header & Footer Elements** group, click the **Page Number** button. Press Spacebar, type `of` and then press Spacebar again. In the **Header & Footer Elements** group, click the **Number of Pages** button. Click a cell in the worksheet to close the footer.

13. Click the **HeatingBills** sheet tab. Press ⬆Shift and click the **Loan** sheet tab. On the **View** tab, in the **Workbook Views** group, click the **Page Layout** button. Use the skills you practiced in the previous step to place the file name in the left section of the header, the sheet name in the center section, and the current date and time in the right section. Click a cell in the worksheet to deselect the header.

14. With the **HeatingBills** and **Loan** sheets still selected, on the **Page Layout** tab, click the Page Setup **Dialog Box Launcher.** In the Page Setup dialog box, click the **Margins** tab and then under *Center on page*, select the **Horizontally** check box. Click **OK.**

15. Click the **CashFlow** sheet tab. Check each worksheet and set it to **Normal** view with cell **A1** selected.

16. Click the **Office** button, point to **Print,** and then click **Print Preview.** Check your work against Figure 7.49. Close **Print Preview** and repeat this process for the other two worksheets. Click the **HeatingBills** sheet tab.

17. **Save** the workbook. Submit the file as directed by your instructor.

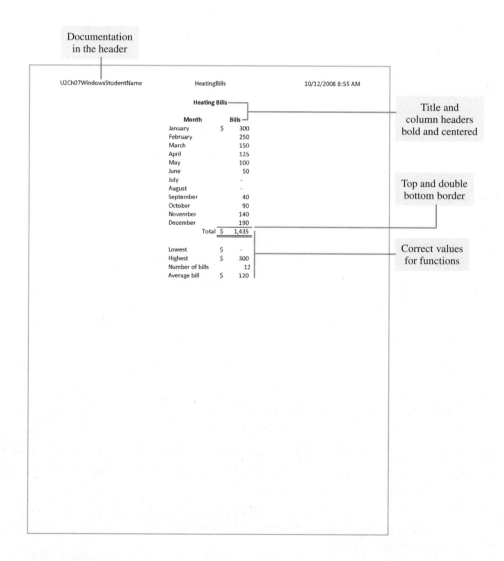

Documentation in the header

Title and column headers bold and centered

Top and double bottom border

Correct values for functions

FIGURE 7.49A

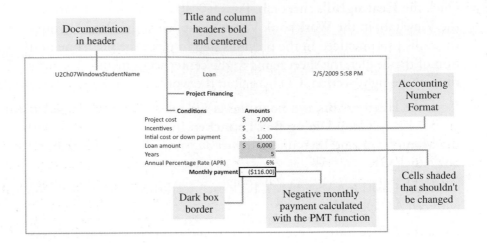

FIGURE 7.49B

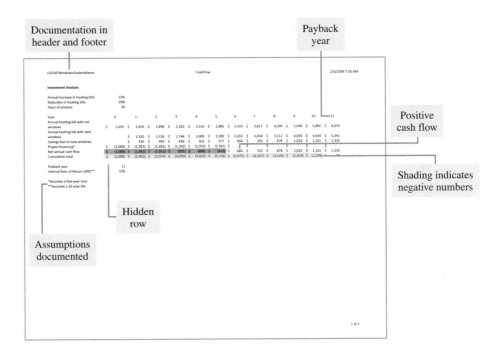

FIGURE 7.49C

fix *it*

One way to appreciate the value of good design is to fix a file that is not designed well. In this exercise, you open a file that has several design flaws and fix it according to the good design elements in the lessons.

Navigate to the folder with the student files, open **U2Ch07FixIt,** and then save it as `U2Ch07FixItStudentName`

Examine the file and make the changes that are necessary to make it comply with the good design principles that were introduced in this chapter. Here is a list of design principles introduced and some common errors to look for to fix the worksheet. There are six intentional errors in this workbook. See if you can find them all. Each time you find an error, fill the cell or cells with yellow and then correct the error.

Good Design
- Cells are not left empty to indicate zero values.
- Values used as arguments in functions are in their own cells and labeled.
- In a cash flow analysis, money coming in is positive and money going out is negative.
- Use parentheses or color to indicate negative numbers. Do not rely upon a minus sign when working with money.
- Use relative and absolute cell references so that formulas can be copied or filled without having to retype them.
- Hide rows containing supporting or interim calculations that might confuse the intended audience.
- Adjust column widths to fit content and reduce width of wide spreadsheets.
- If a worksheet will print across more than one page, place the title in cell A1 and do not merge and center it across all of the columns.
- In multiple-page worksheets, add the page number and total number of pages to the header or footer.

Look for the following types of mistakes:

- Circular logic errors where the cell in which the function is located is included in its own argument
- Incorrect range in a function argument
- Formulas that did not use an absolute reference and the intended reference changed when it was filled or copied
- Formulas that refer to a cell with text in it where the formula or function needs a number
- Incorrect use of positive or negative numbers in a cash flow analysis
- Mixed units of time in financial function arguments
- Cells that display error messages (In some cases, the error is in a cell to which the formula refers and there is nothing wrong with the formula in the cell that displays the error. The message goes away when you fix the other error. This does not count as one of the errors.)

Submit the file as required by your instructor. Save and close the file.

Information workers add value to data by organizing, selecting, displaying, communicating, interpreting, and using data to communicate information and support decisions. On the Job exercises simulate a situation where you are given data, and your job is to add value to it using the skills you practiced in this chapter. Success in these exercises indicates that you have a valuable skill to offer an employer.

1. Hybrid Vehicle

The exercises in this section are related to the following exchange of memos:

> Jane,
>
> *It is time to replace the small SUVs used by our service technicians. I'd like you to find out what it would cost us to use hybrid vehicles. I know it would cost more initially, but I'd like our customers to know we are doing what we can to reduce energy costs. Prepare a cash flow analysis that shows the payback and internal rate of return in the extra amount we would pay to get a hybrid. Ask the service manager for a typical mileage log from one of the techs.*
>
> *John*

In response to a request from Jane, Alphonse—the service manager—responded by e-mail as follows:

> Jane,
>
> *Our service people do most of their calls in the winter and we give them vacation time in the summer, so the miles they drive vary seasonally. I looked over their call logs and here is one that is typical: Jan 1732, Feb 1655, March 1503, April 1323, June 1222, July 835, August 1090, Sept 1250, Oct 1345, Nov 1565, Dec 1634. We keep our cars about six years and they are due for replacement.*
>
> *Alphonse*

Miles Worksheet

1. Open a new workbook and save it as `U2Ch07HybridStudentName` Rename Sheet1 as `Miles`

2. Choose appropriate title and column headings.

3. Enter labels and data.

4. Decide how to deal with the missing data, and document it at the bottom of the sheet. Assume that the service manager is not available when you are preparing the worksheet.

5. Format the title, column headings, labels, and source according to good design principles.

6. Calculate the total, minimum, maximum, count, and average miles.

7. Choose appropriate formats for the numbers.

8. Set up the printout to center the data, and put the file name, sheet name, and the current date and time in the header.

9. Review the design principles listed in the Fix It section and apply those that are relevant. Refer to Figure 7.50.

10. Print or submit the file as directed by your instructor. Save the file and close it.

Loan Worksheet

Jane searched the Internet and found an article at CNNMoney.com with the following information: The highest ranked hybrid SUV was the Ford Escape. It had a cost premium of $5,310 more than a comparable SUV, but it also had a hybrid tax credit of $3,000. It gets 31.4 miles per gallon versus 24 for a similar nonhybrid SUV. The article was posted on July 22, 2008.

1. In the *U2Ch07HybridStudentName* workbook, change the name of Sheet2 to Loan

2. Use the skills you practiced in this chapter to set up a loan calculation table that uses this information to calculate the increase in monthly payments due to buying a hybrid. Assume a three-year loan and a 6% interest rate.

3. Format the table using good design principles, and then add documentation to the worksheet and printout.

4. Add the file name, sheet name, and date information in the header.

5. Review the design principles listed in the Fix It exercise and apply those that are relevant. Refer to Loan sheet in Figure 7.50.

6. Print or submit the file as directed by your instructor. Save the file and close it.

Cash Flow Worksheet

Using the information that Jane previously found on the Internet, complete the cash flow analysis as follows:

1. In the *U2Ch07HybridStudentName* workbook, change the name of Sheet3 to CashFlow

2. Use the skills you practiced in this chapter to set up a cash flow analysis. Begin by documenting the values used in the worksheet in rows 3 through 7. Start with the price of gasoline, the annual increase in gas prices, the annual miles driven from the Miles worksheet, the miles per gallon (MPG) of a comparable nonhybrid, and the MPG of the hybrid. Initially use a price of gas and rate of increase that matches your experience.

3. In row 9, enter labels for years zero through six. Format them as text.

4. In row 10, the label is Annual fuel cost In year zero, write a formula that divides the miles driven by the mileage of the nonhybrid, then multiplies by the price of gasoline.

5. In the Annual fuel cost row 10, in year one, enter a formula that calculates the percent increase of the annual fuel cost using an absolute reference to the annual increase percentage. Fill this formula to year six.

6. In row 11, the label is Annual fuel cost using a hybrid In year zero, enter a formula that starts with the miles driven, divided by the miles per gallon, and then multiplied by the cost of gasoline.

7. In row 11, in year one, enter a formula that calculates the percentage increase using the annual increase in fuel cost. Fill the formula to year six.

8. In row 12, the label is `Annual Savings` In year one, enter a formula that begins with the annual fuel cost and subtract the annual fuel cost using a hybrid. Fill this formula to year six.

9. In row 13, the label is `Project financing*` In row 22, document the assumption of a 3-year loan.

10. In row 13, in year zero, enter a formula that references the initial cost or down payment from the loan sheet.

11. In row 13, in year one, enter a formula that refers to the monthly payment on the Loan sheet and multiplies it by 12 to calculate the annual loan payment. Use an absolute reference to the payment on the Loan sheet and fill the formula to year six.

12. In row 14, enter the label `Net annual cash flow` In row 14, in year zero, enter a formula that adds the annual savings above to the annual loan payment above. Fill the formula to year six.

13. In row 15, enter the label `Cumulative total` In year one, enter a formula that adds the cell to the left to the cell above. Fill this formula to year six.

14. In row 16, the label is `Negative cumulative totals` In year one, enter an IF function that compares the cell above to see if it is less than or equal to zero; if that is true, it displays a 1, if it is not true, it displays a 0. Fill the formula to year six. Hide row 16.

15. Use conditional formatting to show the negative values in row 14 in dark red with a lighter red background, and the negative values in row 15 with dark yellow font and lighter yellow background.

16. In row 18, the label is `Annual fuel savings in gallons` In cell B18, enter a formula that begins with the miles driven divided by the miles per gallon of a nonhybrid, minus the miles driven, divided by the miles per gallon of the hybrid.

17. In cell A19, the label is `Payback year` In cell B19, enter a formula that sums the values in row 16.

18. In cell A20, the label is `Internal Rate of Return (IRR)**` In cell B20, enter the IRR function that uses the values in row 14 as its argument. In cell A23, enter `**Assumes 6-year life`

19. Select A18:B20 and apply a thick box border.

20. Format the table using good design principles, and then add documentation to the worksheet and printout.

21. Add the file name, sheet name, and date function to the header.

22. Review the design principles listed in the Fix It exercise and apply those that are relevant. Refer to Figure 7.50.

23. Enter $2.00 for the price of gasoline, 0% for the annual increase in price, and notice that the payback period exceeds the analysis period and the IRR value is negative. Change the price of gasoline to $4.00 and the annual increase to 10%, and see how much difference this makes to the payback and IRR. If your worksheet is set up correctly to perform this what-if analysis, you should see a payback of 4 years and an IRR of more than 100%.

24. Print or submit the file as directed by your instructor. Save the file and close it.

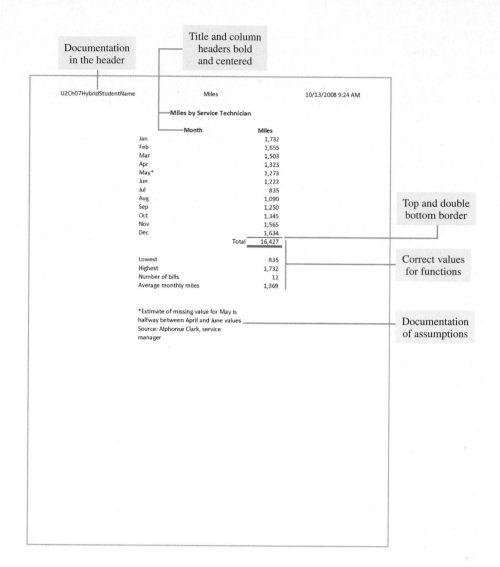

FIGURE 7.50A

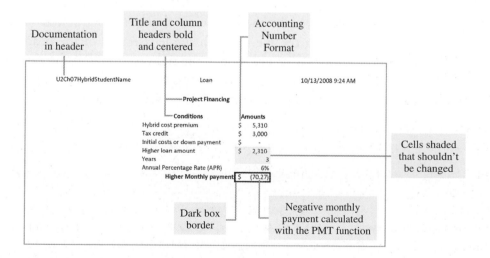

FIGURE 7.50B

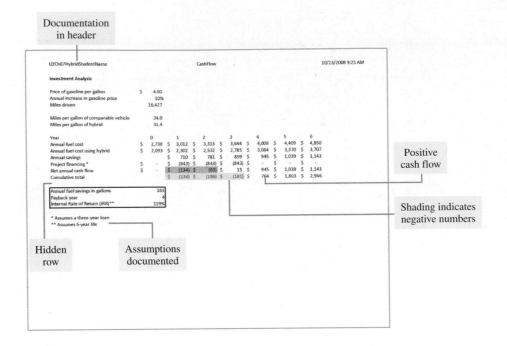

Documentation in header

Positive cash flow

Shading indicates negative numbers

Hidden row

Assumptions documented

FIGURE 7.50C

2. High-Efficiency Furnace

This exercise is based on the following e-mail from a fellow worker:

Jane,

I did a cash flow analysis of a high-efficiency furnace, but the worksheet doesn't fit on one page. Can you help me by formatting it so that it prints sideways on two pages? I'd like to just print the first 15 years and show years 1–10 on the first page and years 11–15 on the second. Can you also get the first two columns of labels to repeat on the second page and add page numbers? Thanks. I owe you one.

Bill

Open the student file named **U2Ch07Furnace** and save it as U2Ch07FurnaceStudentName Make the following changes as requested in the e-mail. Document the printout by putting the file name in the left section of the header, the sheet name in the center, and the current date and time in the right section. Put the page number in the footer so that is shows the current page number and the total number of pages. Refer to Figure 7.51.

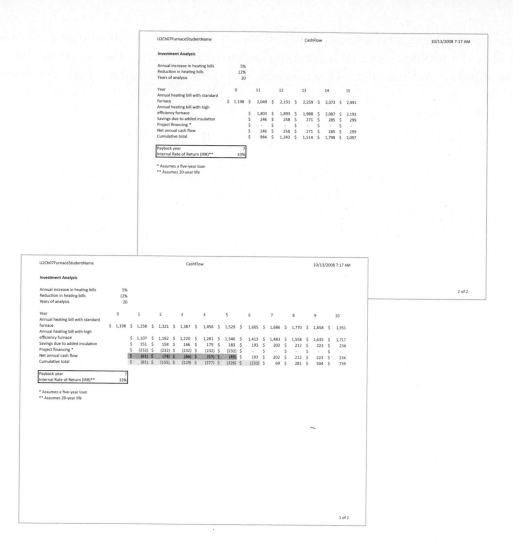

FIGURE 7.51

DISCUSSION OF ADVANCED SKILLS OR CONCEPTS

The questions in this section are based on the topics in the Advanced Skills or Concepts section of the chapter.

1. What are some examples of how you could use the PMT function to try different combinations of loan amount, interest rate, and years to find a monthly payment that is manageable on your current budget?

2. What is the interest rate you are paying on your current loans, such as school, credit cards, home, and car? If you had the chance to spend more money on a high-efficiency device to save money, how would the IRR on that investment have to compare with the other interest rates you are paying before it would be a good investment for you?

3. Have you experienced a situation where an assumption was built into a calculation and it caused a problem because it was not documented? Describe the situation, the assumption, and the effect. Describe how you think it should have been documented.

ON YOUR OWN

Once you are comfortable with the skills in this chapter, you can apply them to new situations of your own choosing. In this section, you choose data that you have in your possession or that you can find elsewhere. To successfully complete this assignment, you must apply good design practices. Refer to the list of design practices in the Fix It exercise.

1. Hybrid Car Choices

Look up costs of automobiles that have higher gas mileage than your current car, but which also cost more. Create or adapt a cash flow analysis worksheet. Find the payback and IRR of three models and print out each one.

- Describe the three models you chose to compare.
- Provide printouts or separate worksheets for each model.
- Provide a summary of models, cost premiums, paybacks, and IRR percentages.
- Perform a what-if analysis on the payback and IRR for one of the models by changing the cost of gasoline and anticipated increases in gasoline price. Determine the price of gasoline, with 0% increase, at which the payback equals the anticipated life of the car. Report your findings.
- Save the file as U2Ch07WhatIfStudentName

2. Explore Excel Templates

Start Excel and choose New. In the New Workbook dialog box, look at several different templates. Choose three of them to open.

1. Enter data into each template. Copy the worksheets into the same workbook. Save the workbook as U2Ch07TemplateStudentName

2. On an empty worksheet, widen the first column to 100 pixels. Format the first four cells in column A to wrap text. In cell A1, type Template descriptions

3. In cells A2:A4, write a short essay describing the characteristics of each of the three templates you used.

4. Add the file name, class, and the current date and time to the header. Delete empty worksheets and save the workbook. Submit the file as required by your instructor.

5. Save the file and close it.

ASSESS YOUR PROGRESS

At this point, you should have a set of skills and design concepts that are valuable to an employer and to you. You may not realize how much you've learned unless you take a few minutes to assess your progress.

1. From the student files, open *U2Ch07Assess*. Save it as U2Ch07AssessStudentName

2. Read each question in column A.

3. In column B, answer Yes or No.

4. If you identify a skill or design concept that you don't know, refer to the learning objective code next to the question and the table at the beginning of the chapter to find the skill and review it.

5. Print the worksheet if your instructor requires it. The file name is already in the header, so it will display your name as part of the file name.

6. All of these skills and concepts have been identified as important by surveying hundreds of individuals working at over 200 companies worldwide. If you cannot answer all of the questions affirmatively even after reviewing the relevant lesson, seek additional help from your instructor.

chapter eight

Giving Meaning to Data Using Charts

Lesson	Learning Outcomes	Code	Related IC3 Objectives
1	Organize data for convenient charting	8.01	3.1.10, 3.2.9
1	Select ranges to chart	8.02	3.2.9
1	Choose column chart to make comparisons	8.03	3.2.9
2	Add a title to the chart	8.04	3.1.10, 3.2.9
2	Add a rotated title to an axis	8.05	3.2.9
2	Change the number format on an axis	8.06	3.2.9
2	Insert a callout to interpret the chart	8.07	1.3.7, 3.1.10
3	Change chart types	8.08	3.2.9
3	Use a pie chart to show contributions to the whole	8.09	3.2.9
3	Format pie chart data labels to show percentages and use leader lines	8.10	3.2.9
3	Modify data and update chart automatically	8.11	3.2.9
3	Preview charts and adapt to printer limitations	8.12	1.4.2
4	Use a line chart to display a trend	8.13	3.2.9, 3.2.10
4	Move a chart to its own sheet	8.16	3.2.9
5	Use an R-squared value to choose the best type of trendline	8.14	3.2.10
5	Use a trendline to estimate future values	8.15	3.2.10
6	Insert a text box to document assumptions in a chart	8.17	1.3.7
Advanced	Choose between chart types	8.18	3.2.9
Advanced	Identifying typical errors in charting	8.19	3.2.10

Instructions throughout the lessons are based on the Vista operating system, running Microsoft Office 2007.

Why Would I Do This?

The purpose of collecting data in a worksheet is to extract meaning from it. In this chapter, you give meaning to data by creating charts that show relationships graphically. You will use charts to make comparisons, to show contributions to the whole, and to show and project trends. Charts create a visual picture of the data that is often easier to see and understand than a table of numbers.

visual summary

In this chapter, you will create charts that are related to the topic of energy independence. By charting data, you can visualize the relative proportions of energy we get from other countries, how energy use in the U.S. compares with that of other countries, and identify historical trends in energy use that enable us to plan for the future, as shown in Figure 8.1.

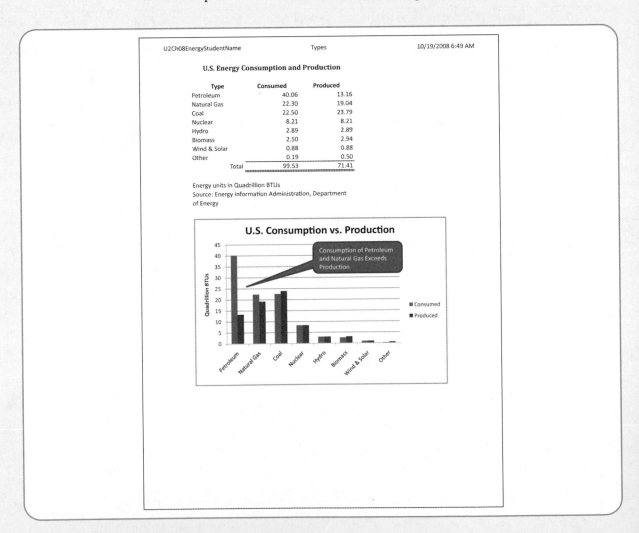

FIGURE 8.1A

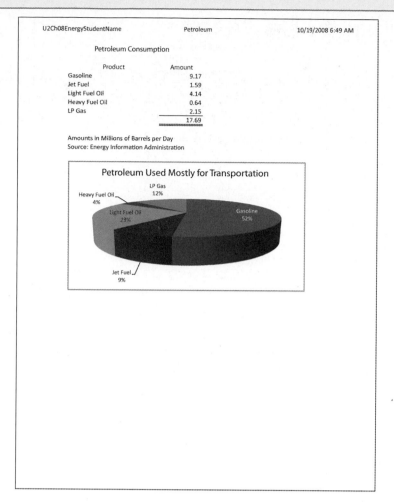

Petroleum Consumption

Product	Amount
Gasoline	9.17
Jet Fuel	1.59
Light Fuel Oil	4.14
Heavy Fuel Oil	0.64
LP Gas	2.15
	17.69

Amounts in Millions of Barrels per Day
Source: Energy Information Administration

Petroleum Used Mostly for Transportation

Heavy Fuel Oil 4%
LP Gas 12%
Light Fuel Oil 23%
Gasoline 52%
Jet Fuel 9%

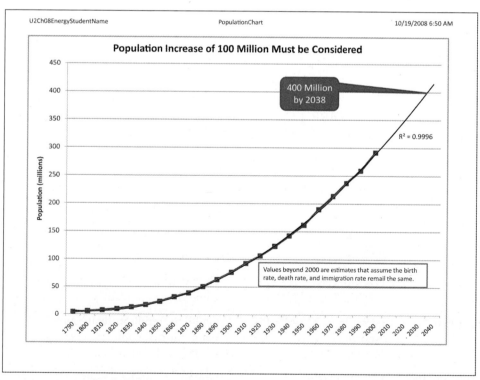

Population Increase of 100 Million Must be Considered

400 Million by 2038

$R^2 = 0.9996$

Values beyond 2000 are estimates that assume the birth rate, death rate, and immigration rate remail the same.

Population (millions)

FIGURE 8.1B, C

Why Would I Do This?   413   **Chapter 8**

U2Ch08EnergyStudentName Population 10/19/2008 6:50 AM

U. S. Population

Census Year	Total Population (millions)
1790	3.9
1800	5.3
1810	7.2
1820	9.6
1830	12.9
1840	17.1
1850	23.2
1860	31.4
1870	38.6
1880	50.2
1890	63.0
1900	76.2
1910	92.2
1920	106.0
1930	123.2
1940	142.2
1950	161.3
1960	189.3
1970	213.3
1980	236.5
1990	258.7
2000	291.4
2010	
2020	
2030	
2040	

Source: U.S. Census Bureau

FIGURE 8.1D

List of Student and Solution Files

In most cases, you will start with a new, empty file and enter text and data or paste content from other files. You will add your name to the file names and save them on your computer or portable memory device. Table 8.1 lists the files you start with and the names you give them when you save the files.

ASSIGNMENT	STUDENT SOURCE FILE:	SAVE AS:
Lessons 1–6	New file	U2Ch08EnergyStudentName
Skill Drill	New file	Ch08ImportsStudentName
Fix It	U2Ch08FixIt	Ch08FixItStudentName
On the Job	U2Ch08Gas U2Ch08Heating	Ch08GasStudentName Ch08HeatingStudentName
On Your Own	New file New file New file	Ch08FutureBillsStudentName Ch08FutureIncomeStudentName Ch08TrendStudentName
Assess Your Progress	U2Ch08Assess	Ch08AssessStudentName

TABLE 8.1

►►► *lesson*
ONE | Creating a Column Chart

In this lesson, you create a chart that shows the types of energy used in the United States, how much of each type is consumed, and how much of each type is produced by the United States. The purpose of the chart is to identify which types of energy are consumed in amounts greater than are produced in order to know where to apply efforts to reduce imports and achieve energy independence.

to enter energy data

1 **Start Microsoft Office Excel 2007 to open a blank workbook. Click the Save button 🖫. In the Save as dialog box, create a new folder named** Chapter08 **and in that folder, save the workbook as** U2Ch08EnergyStudentName

2 **Rename Sheet1 as** Types **and then press** ⏎Enter.

3 **In cell A1, type** U.S. Energy Consumption and Production **and then press** ⏎Enter.

4 **Click cell A1. On the Home tab, in the Font group, click the Font button arrow** [Calibri ▾]**, and then click Cambria. Click the Font Size button arrow** [11 ▾]**, and then click 12. Then click the Bold button** [B] **to finish formatting the title.**

5 **Click cell A3, type** Type **and then press** [Tab⇆]. **Type** Consumed **press** [Tab⇆]**, type** Produced **and then press** ⏎Enter. **Notice that the selection has moved to A4.** When you use the [Tab⇆] key to enter a row of data and then end the sequence with the ⏎Enter key, the selection moves to the cell below the first cell in the sequence to facilitate entry of the next row of data using the keyboard.

6 **Select the range A3:C3 and right-click the selected range. On the Mini toolbar, click the Bold button** [B]**, and then click the Center button** [≡]**. Refer to Table 8.2 and use the method you practiced in step 5 to enter the rest of the labels and data, beginning with cell A4.**

Petroleum	40.06	13.16
Natural Gas	22.30	19.04
Coal	22.50	23.79
Nuclear	8.21	8.21
Hydro	2.89	2.89
Biomass	2.50	2.94
Wind & Solar	.88	.88
Other	.19	.50

TABLE 8.2

Creating a Column Chart   415   **Chapter 8**

7 Notice that the values in cells B9 and C11 do not display two decimal places even though you typed 2.50 and .50. Select the range B4:B11. On the Home tab, in the Number group, click the Number Format arrow, and then click **Number.** All of the numbers display two decimal places and the decimal places of all of the numbers align. When entering numbers, the default format is the General format, which does not display trailing zeros to the right of the decimal place. Changing the format to Number Format displays all of the numbers with two decimal places.

good **design...**

ALIGN DECIMAL POINTS

If you have a column of numbers that have differing numbers of decimal places, format the numbers to align the decimal places, which makes it more convenient to visually add the numbers within the columns.

8 Click cell A12. Type Total and then, on the formula bar, click the Enter button ✓. On the Home tab, in the Alignment group, click the Align Text Right button ☰.

9 Click cell B12. On the Home tab, in the Editing group, click the Sum button Σ ▾. Confirm that the range indicated as the argument for the SUM function is B4:B11, and then click the Sum button Σ ▾ again to confirm the entry. The total energy consumed is displayed in cell B12. The cell references to B4:B11 are relative references, which means that the function in cell B12 can be filled into the adjacent cell and it will sum the column of numbers above.

10 In cell B12, drag the fill handle to cell C12 to display the sum of energy produced in C12.

11 With cells B12:C12 still selected, right-click the selected range, and on the Mini toolbar, click the Borders button arrow ▦ ▾. On the menu, click *Top and Double Bottom Border.* Both columns are totaled and the total is emphasized with a border.

12 Click the column A heading, press (⬆Shift), and then click the column C heading. Right-click the selected columns, and on the shortcut menu, click Column Width.

13 In the Column Width dialog box, type 15 and then press (↵Enter). Select cells A1:C1 and right-click. On the Mini toolbar, click the Merge & Center button ▦ ▾.

14 Click cell A14. Type Energy units are Quadrillion BTUs and then press (↵Enter). In A15, type Source: Energy Information Administration, Department of Energy and then press (↵Enter).

15 Select the range A15: C15. In the Alignment group, click the Merge & Center button arrow ⊞▾, and then click Merge Cells. In the Alignment group, click the Wrap Text button ⊞. The Merge Cells command merges cells and leaves the text aligned on the left of the merged cells. Use this when you want to merge cells but do not want to center the text in the merged cells.

16 Point to the row 15 heading, and when the ⊕ pointer displays, right-click to select the row and display the shortcut menu. Click Row Height, and then in the Row Height dialog box, type 30 and press ↵Enter.

17 Press Ctrl + Home to move cell A1. Save 🖫 the workbook and compare your screen with Figure 8.2. The data and its documentation are complete.

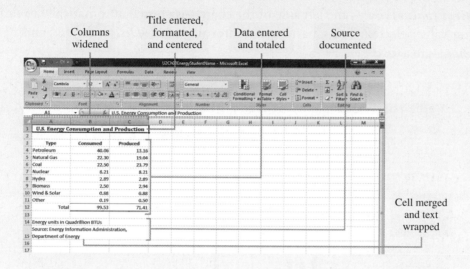

FIGURE 8.2

good **design...**

USE SHORT LABELS

When you enter data that will be used as the basis for a chart, use short words for the labels and headers.

When you chart data, begin by selecting the area you want to chart. Be sure that you include labels in the data that is charted so that the contents of the chart are properly identified. In this task, you select different areas to chart and notice the effect those choices have on the chart.

to select data to chart

1 **Select the range A3:B12.** The first two columns are selected, including the column headers and the total of the Consumed column in B12. Including the total is an error that will be corrected in Step 3.

2 **On the Insert tab, in the Charts group, click the Column button. Under *2-D Column*, click the first choice: *Clustered Column*.** A chart displays. The column header becomes the chart title and the row headers are used as category labels on the *horizontal (category) axis*—bottom of the chart. Notice that the Total column is much larger than all the other columns, as shown in Figure 8.3. The columns are displayed in color and the meaning of the color is explained in the *legend*, which identifies the data series—in this example, the energy consumed. The scale on the *vertical (value) axis*—the left side of the chart—is chosen automatically to fit the largest value selected. The Chart Tools contextual tabs—*Design, Layout,* and *Format*—are active.

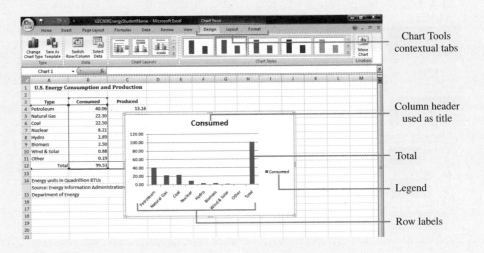

FIGURE 8.3

---

good design...

COMPARE THE SAME TYPES OF DATA

Chart either the totals or the details, but do not chart both on the same chart. When you select data to chart, the data must all be the same type of data to make comparisons meaningful. Do not include the total in the range of selected cells with the individual items. The total is a sum of the individual items, and including it distorts the chart because it causes the scale of the chart to be too large, which makes the other data points in the chart too small.

---

3 **With the chart still selected, press** (Delete). The chart is deleted but the content of the selected cells is not.

4 **Click cell A3, press** (⬆Shift), **and then click cell B11. On the Insert tab, in the Charts group, click the Column button. Under** *2-D Column*, **click the first choice:** *Clustered Column.* The total is not included in this chart. The scale on the vertical axis uses smaller intervals to increase the relative height of the columns, as shown in Figure 8.4.

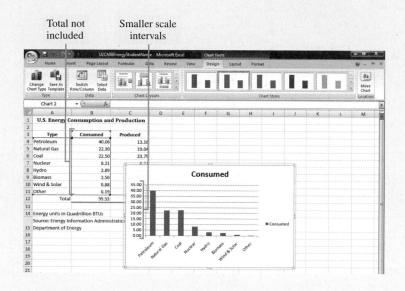

Total not   Smaller scale
included   intervals

FIGURE 8.4

to extend your knowledge

A chart that is similar to a *column chart*—which displays data as vertical columns—is the *bar chart*. In a bar chart, the narrow rectangles that represent data by their length are oriented horizontally instead of vertically.

5 **With the chart still selected, press** (Delete). The chart is deleted.

6 **Select the range A3:A11. Press** (Ctrl), **and then select range C3:C11.** Two nonadjacent ranges of cells are selected, as shown in Figure 8.5: A3:A11 and C3:C11. Notice that both ranges are the same length—the same number of cells. Use the Control key to select ranges of cells that are not adjacent.

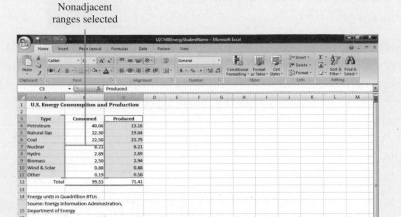

Nonadjacent ranges selected

FIGURE 8.5

7 On the Insert tab, in the Charts group, click the Column button. Under *2-D Column*, click the first choice: *Clustered Column.* The labels from A3:A11 are used on the horizontal axis, the header in C3 is used for the title and legend, and the data from C4:C11 is displayed as columns, as shown in Figure 8.6

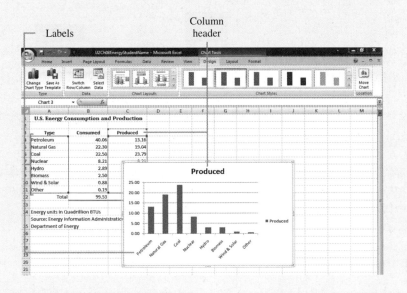

Labels

Column header

FIGURE 8.6

8 With the chart still selected, press ⌫Delete. The chart is deleted.

9 Select the range A3:C11. On the Insert tab, in the Charts group, click the Column button. Under *2-D Column*, click the first choice: *Clustered Column.* The labels in A4:A11 are used along the horizontal axis. The values in B4:B11 and

C4:C11 are shown as pairs—clusters—of columns in different colors, as shown in Figure 8.7. The legend identifies which color is used for each range of data.

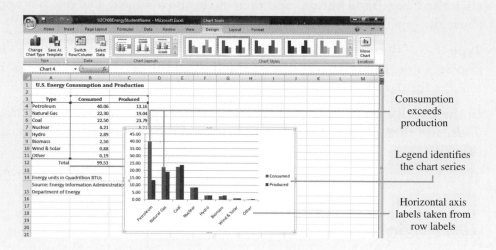

Consumption exceeds production

Legend identifies the chart series

Horizontal axis labels taken from row labels

FIGURE 8.7

10 Save ⊞ the workbook.

good **design...**

COMPARE SIMILAR COLUMNS OR ROWS WITH A COLUMN CHART

To compare columns of data by rows, a ***clustered column chart*** is a good choice. It groups the data by rows so that the columns that represent each value in the row are side by side. This suits the purpose of the chart, which is to compare the consumption and production of each type of energy to see which ones are imported. In this example, it is clear from the chart that more petroleum and natural gas are consumed than produced. The type of chart selected must achieve the purpose of the chart. Have a clear purpose in mind before you choose the range to chart and the type of chart.

If the data is arranged in rows instead of columns, the clustered column chart is useful for comparing similar values in the same column.

▶▶▶ *lesson*
two | **Editing Chart Elements**

Charts should clearly convey information about the data, which may require you to modify the chart in some manner. In this lesson, you edit a chart. The chart needs a title, and the units used on the vertical axis need to be defined. The decimal places displayed on the vertical axis labels should be reduced.

to edit chart elements

1 **With the chart selected, on the Chart Tools Layout tab, in the Labels group, click the Chart Title button, and then click Above Chart.** The title box appears above the top line of the chart with default text.

2 **Type** `U.S. Consumption vs. Production` **and then press** ⏎Enter. The text displays in the formula bar as you type, and when you press ⏎Enter, the new title replaces the default text.

3 **In the Labels group, click the Axis Titles button, point to *Primary Vertical Axis Title*, and then click Rotated Title.** The title of the vertical axis displays parallel to the axis.

4 **Type** `Quadrillion BTUs` **and then press** ⏎Enter. The vertical axis is labeled.

•••

good design...

LABEL THE VERTICAL AXIS UNITS

The vertical axis is typically a series of numbers. Include the units of measure in the label. If this makes the label too long for the space available, rotate the label to display parallel to the vertical axis.

•••

5 **On the Chart Tools Layout tab, in the Axes group, click the Axes button. Point to *Primary Vertical Axis*, and then at the bottom of the list, click *More Primary Vertical Axis Options*.** The Format Axis dialog box displays.

6 **In the left pane, click Number. In the right panel, click the number category, and in the Decimal places box, select the default value; then type** `0` Compare your dialog box to the one shown in Figure 8.8.

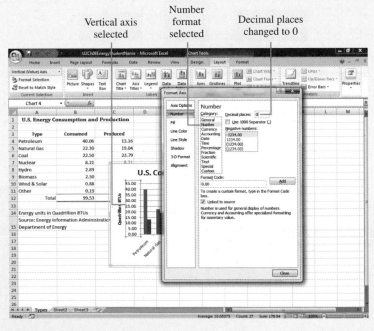

Vertical axis selected   Number format selected   Decimal places changed to 0

FIGURE 8.8

7 In the Format Axis dialog box, click Close to apply the format to the vertical axis.

8 Move the pointer to the edge of the chart to display the ⬚ pointer. Drag the chart below the data. Position its upper left corner in cell A17.

9 Move the pointer to the middle of the lower edge of the chart that is marked by four small dots to display the ⬚ pointer. Drag the bottom edge of the chart downward to row 35. The dots mark the location of the *sizing handles*, which are used to resize graphic objects. The lower edge of the chart is expanded.

10 Point to the sizing handle on the right edge of the chart and drag to the border between columns F and G. Compare your screen with Figure 8.9. You can also adjust the size of a chart by using the sizing handles in the corners of a chart, which are indicated by three dots.

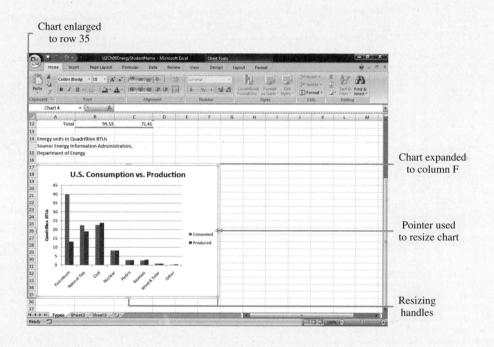

Chart enlarged to row 35

Chart expanded to column F

Pointer used to resize chart

Resizing handles

FIGURE 8.9

Add comments in *callouts* to draw attention to a part of the chart or to state a conclusion. Callouts are shapes that have a pointer and that contain text. In this task, you add a callout to point out the fact that the amount of petroleum and natural gas consumed exceeds the amount produced.

to insert a callout

1 On the Insert tab, in the Illustrations group, click the Shapes button. At the bottom of the displayed gallery, under Callouts, in the first row, click the second choice: *Rounded Rectangular Callout.* The ⊞ pointer displays.

2 Move the ⊞ pointer to the section of the chart below the title and above the short columns. Drag a rectangle in this area, and then release the mouse button. A callout balloon displays. You can adjust the size and position after you enter the text.

3 Type Consumption of Petroleum and Natural Gas Exceeds Production Part of the text appears inside the callout, as shown in Figure 8.10.

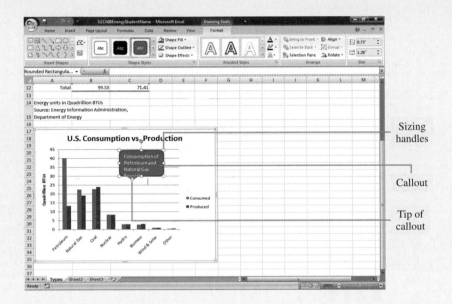

FIGURE 8.10

4 Point to the yellow diamond at the tip of the callout. Drag the yellow diamond to a point between the Petroleum and Natural Gas chart columns. The shape jumps to a new location on the chart; therefore, you need to move the shape to reposition it on the chart.

5 Point to the edge of the callout box border to display the pointer. Drag the box to the position shown in Figure 8.11.

6 Drag the sizing handles on the corners or sides as needed to display all of the text. Compare your screen with Figure 8.11.

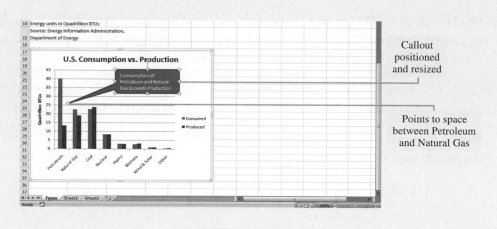

Callout positioned and resized

Points to space between Petroleum and Natural Gas

FIGURE 8.11

7 Save 🖫 the workbook.

good **design...**

USE TITLES OR CALLOUTS TO REINFORCE AN INTERPRETATION
If you think a chart accomplishes the purpose for which it was created and the conclusion is obvious, do not assume that others will see the same thing. Use a title or callout to reinforce your interpretation of the meaning of a chart if you are trying to use it to support a conclusion.

▶▶▶ *lesson*
three|Using a Pie Chart

A *pie chart* uses a circle to represent the whole of a group of data and slices to represent how each piece of data contributes to the whole. The portions are wedge-shaped, which is similar to the way a pie is cut into pieces. It is readily apparent that a larger wedge represents a larger part of the whole pie.

to enter petroleum-use data

1 Click the Sheet2 tab, and rename it `Petroleum`

2 Click cell A1, type `Petroleum Consumption` and then press `↵Enter`.

3 Select cells A1: B1. On the Home tab, in the Alignment group, click the Merge & Center button ⊞▾. In the Font group, change Font Size `11 ▾` to 12 and Font to Cambria, and then click the Bold button **B**.

4 Click A3. Type Product and then press ⇥. Type Amount and then press ↵Enter. Select cells A3 and B3, center the text, and apply bold emphasis.

5 Starting in cell A4, use the method you practiced in step 4 to enter the rest of the labels and data shown below. The value for jet fuel is intentionally incorrect.

Gasoline	9.17
Jet Fuel	15.9
Light Fuel Oil	4.14
Heavy Fuel Oil	.64
Liquid Petroleum (LP) Gas	2.15

6 Click B9. On the Home tab, in the Editing group, click the Sum button Σ ▾ two times. The amount of each type of petroleum product is summed.

7 With B9 selected, in the Font group, click the Borders button arrow ⊞ ▾, and then click *Top and Double Bottom Border*.

8 Click A11. Type Amounts in Millions of Barrels per Day and then press ↵Enter. In A12, type Source: Energy Information Administration and then press ↵Enter.

9 Widen column A to 26 characters and column B to 12 characters. Select cells A11 and B11, and on the Alignment group, click the Merge and Center button arrow ⊞ ▾, and then click Merge Cells. Repeat this to merge cells A12:B12. Compare your screen with Figure 8.12.

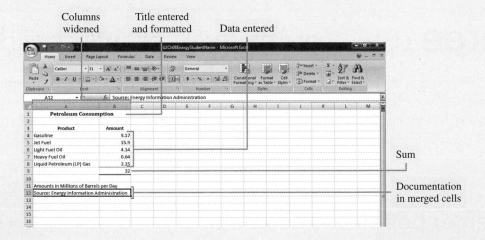

FIGURE 8.12

10 Save 💾 the workbook.

In Excel, it is convenient to change the type of chart to see if another type of chart might be a better choice. In this task, you will create a column chart and then change it to other chart types.

to change chart types

1 **Select the range A3:B8.** The range to chart—without the total—is selected.

2 **On the Insert tab, in the Charts group, click the Column button. Under *3-D Column*, click the first button: *3-D Clustered Column*.** A column chart displays and the columns appear to have depth, as shown in Figure 8.13.

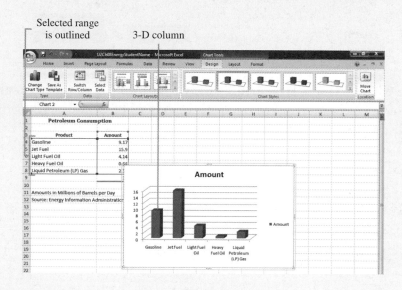

FIGURE 8.13

3 **With the chart selected, on the Chart Tools Design tab, in the Type group, click the Change Chart Type button. In the displayed dialog box, in the pane on the right, scroll down to the Pie area, and then click the second icon: Pie in 3-D.** The *3-D Pie Chart* option is selected, as shown in Figure 8.14. The *3-D pie chart* is a 3-dimensional disk instead of the circle that is used in an ordinary pie chart.

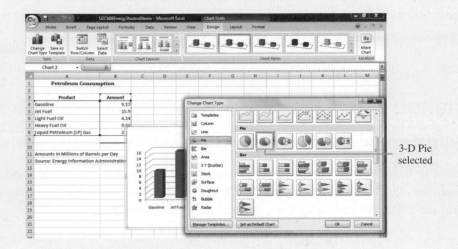

FIGURE 8.14

4 **In the Change Chart Type dialog box, click OK.** The amounts consumed of the five types of petroleum products are shown as pieces of a 3-D disk, as shown in Figure 8.15. The slice for Jet Fuel appears unreasonably large because it is unlikely that the relatively few jet airplanes could use much more petroleum than the millions of cars.

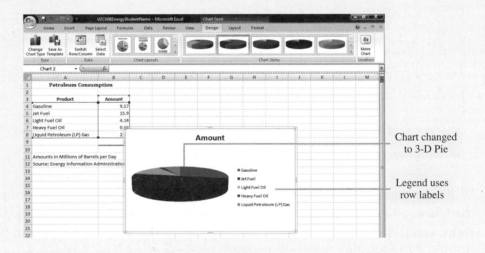

FIGURE 8.15

good **design...**

PIE CHARTS SHOW CONTRIBUTION TO THE WHOLE

If you have data that you can sum, you can use a pie chart to graphically demonstrate how much each piece of data contributes to that sum.

The charts in Excel can be edited to add more information. In this task, you correct an error and edit the title and labels.

to edit data and chart elements

1 **On the Petroleum worksheet, click cell B5. Type** 1.59 **and then press** (↵Enter).
Notice that all of the slices of the pie chart are resized to show how this change affects their relationship to the total amount. The error in the data is corrected, as shown in Figure 8.16.

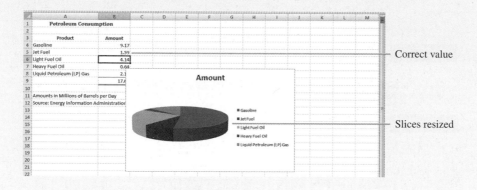

FIGURE 8.16

• •

good design...

USE CHARTS TO CATCH MISPLACED DECIMAL POINTS IN DATA

It is a good idea to chart data to help catch errors. It is hard to see a misplaced decimal point in a group of numbers, but the error is easier to spot when the data is charted and one of the elements appears much too large or too small.

• •

2 **Click the border of the chart to select the entire chart.**

• •

if you have problems...

DID YOU HAVE TROUBLE SELECTING THE CHART?

The chart has many elements. When you click an element of the chart, highlights or borders indicate what you have selected. The Ribbon options often depend on what is selected. If the directions in the book do not seem to match your Ribbon options, check to make sure that the intended portion of the chart is selected. In general, click the edge of the chart to select the entire chart, and click on an element to select it.

If an element is one of a group of similar objects—like all the slices in a pie—the first time you click the element, all of the similar elements are selected. If you click it a second time, the individual element is selected.

• •

3 On the Chart Tools Layout tab, in the Labels group, click the Data Labels button, and then click *More Data Label Options.* The Format Data Labels dialog box displays.

4 In the Format Data Labels dialog box, under Label Options, click the Value check box to clear it. Select the Category Name check box, and then select the Percentage check box. Confirm that *Show Leader Lines* is selected, as shown in **Figure 8.17.** The program will calculate the percentage of each amount of the total. If the slice of the pie is too narrow to display the label, it will be placed on the outside with a *leader line* connecting it to the slice.

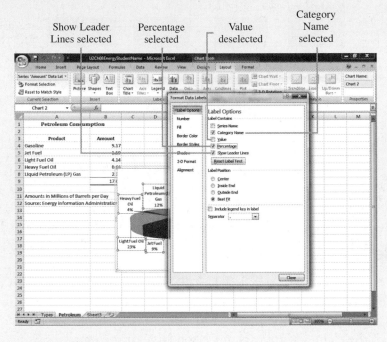

FIGURE 8.17

5 Click Close. The category name and a percentage are added to each slice. A leader line is used where a label is too large for a slice. The category names in the legend are no longer necessary.

6 In the Labels group, click the Legend button, and then click None. The legend is removed and the chart size increases, as shown in Figure 8.18. The black font on the dark blue slice does not contrast well and is difficult to read. All of the labels are still selected.

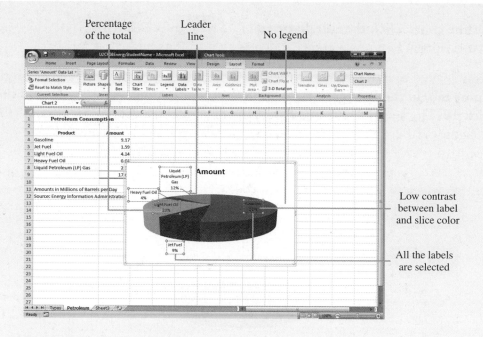

FIGURE 8.18

7 Move the pointer to the Gasoline label on the blue slice and click one time. Click the label one more time to select just that label, and then right-click the label. On the Mini toolbar, click the Font Color button arrow ![A]. In the Theme Color area, in the first column, click the first color: *White, Background 1.* The font color changes to white, which is much easier to read against the dark blue background, as shown in Figure 8.19.

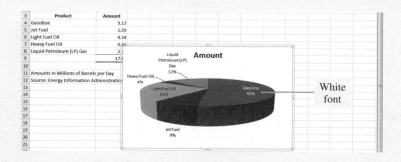

FIGURE 8.19

if you have **problems...**

DID YOU HAVE TROUBLE SELECTING THE INDIVIDUAL LABEL?

The first time you click a slice label, all of the slice labels are selected. The second time you click a label, the individual label is selected. If you click the label a third time, an individual word or number in the label might be selected. It might take you several tries to select and change one slice label. Use the Undo button, if necessary, to reverse an unwanted action.

8 On the chart, click the title. Type `Petroleum Used Mostly for Transportation` As you type, the new title appears in the formula bar.

9 Press `↵Enter` to add the title to the chart. With the chart title still active, on the Home tab, in the Font group, click the Font Size button arrow `11 ▾`, and then click 16. The new title is resized on the chart and the labels are repositioned, as shown in Figure 8.20.

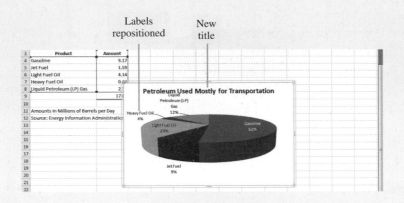

FIGURE 8.20

10 Click cell A8. Type `LP Gas` and then press `↵Enter`. The shorter label fits on the chart below the title.

11 Drag the chart below the data. Position its upper left corner in cell A14, as shown in Figure 8.21. Notice the position of the Jet Fuel label.

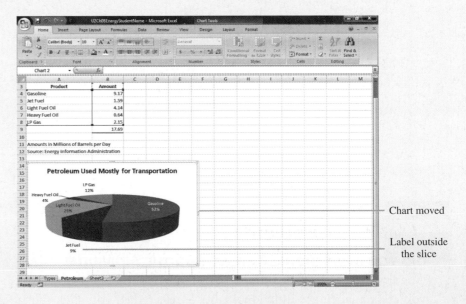

FIGURE 8.21

12 Save 💾 your workbook.

Before you print a worksheet with an *embedded chart*—a chart that is on the sheet with the data—it is important to verify that all of the elements will print as expected. To do this, view the chart using Print Layout and Print Preview.

to preview the chart printout in Page Layout and Print Preview

1 **On the View tab, in the Workbook Views group, click the Page Layout button.** One or more of the labels might be moved onto the slice, depending on the resolution of your screen. The label for Jet Fuel might be displayed on the dark red slice where it would be hard to read. It is not uncommon for the labels to be located differently on a printout or in Page Layout view than they appear in Normal view, depending on the computer's monitor settings.

2 **Point to the label Jet Fuel 9% and click one time.** All of the labels are selected.

3 **Click the same label a second time.** Only the Jet Fuel label is selected.

4 **Point to the edge of the selected label, and when the ![pointer] pointer displays, drag the label off of the pie piece and position it just below the red slice, as shown in Figure 8.22.**

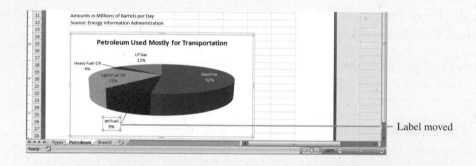

FIGURE 8.22

good **design...**

BE SURE LABELS CAN BE SEEN
The Excel program chooses when to display the slice label on the slice or next to it. If you choose a white font for a label that might be placed in front of a white background, it will seem to disappear. For those labels that might be placed in either position, move the label to a location that you prefer or change the font color to one that will work in both places.

5 **With the chart selected, click the Office button** 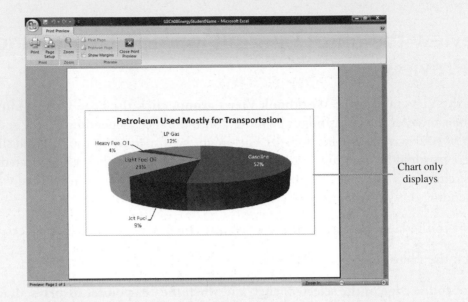 **, point to Print, and then click Print Preview.** A page displays that only has the chart on it, as shown in Figure 8.23. If you are not connected to a color printer, it will not display in color.

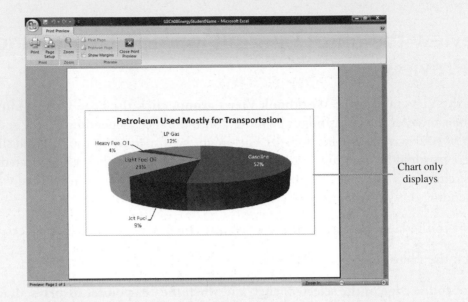

Chart only displays

FIGURE 8.23

6 **On the Print Preview tab, in the Preview group, click the Close Print Preview button. On the worksheet, click a cell outside the chart to deselect it.**

7 **Click the Office button** 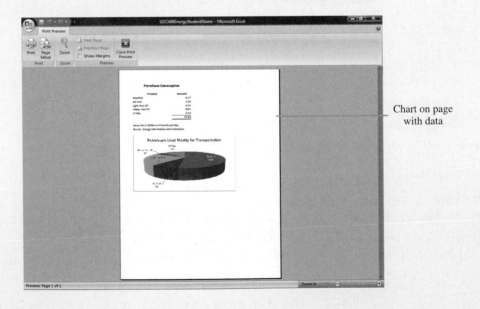 **, point to Print, and then click Print Preview.** The chart and data display on the same page, as shown in Figure 8.24.

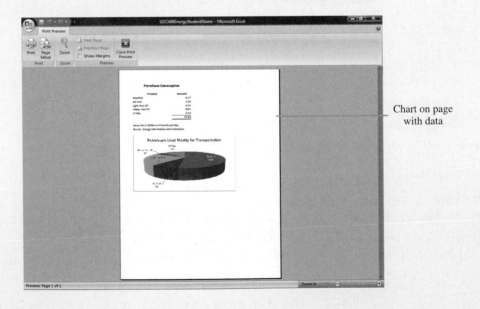

Chart on page with data

FIGURE 8.24

8 On the Print Preview tab, in the Preview group, click the Close Print Preview button.

9 On the View tab, in the Workbook Views group, click the Normal button. Save 💾 the workbook.

to extend **your knowledge...**

ABOUT PRINTING CHARTS

If the chart is selected when you choose Print or Print Preview, only the chart is printed. The chart does not include the worksheet header, so it is not documented properly.

If your printer is not capable of printing in color, the preview will be in black, white, and shades of grey. The default colors for pie charts are not well suited for black-and-white printing. You can change the fill colors on the Chart Tools Format tab, in the Shape Styles group, on the Shape Fill button. The Print Preview illustrations shown in this chapter are in color, assuming that a color printer will be used.

▶▶▶ *lesson*
four | Charting a Trend with a Line Chart

One of the valuable observations you can make about set of data is to recognize a trend that might predict the future. Trends that involve time are best displayed with a *line chart*—a chart that uses lines whose height on the vertical axis represents the value of the data. In this lesson, you chart the population of the U.S. to consider the effect that increasing population will have on efforts to achieve energy independence.

to enter population data

1 Click Sheet3 tab, rename it Population and then press ↵Enter.

2 In cell A1, type U.S. Population and then press ↵Enter.

3 Select cells A1 and B1. On the Home tab, in the Alignment group, click the Merge & Center button 🔲. In the Font group, change Font Size to 12 and Font to Cambria, and then click the Bold button B.

4 Click cell A3. Type Census Year and then press Tab⇄. Type Total Population (millions) and then press ↵Enter. Using the skills you have practiced previously, widen both columns to 18 characters. Center the column title and apply bold emphasis. In cell B3, wrap the text.

5 Click cell A4. Type 1790 and then press ⏎Enter. In cell A5, type 1800 and then press ⏎Enter.

6 Select cells A4 and A5. In cell A5, drag the fill handle down to cell A29. The census is taken every 10 years and the sequence is filled in through 2040. You can create a pattern by entering numbers in two or more cells and then use the fill handle to replicate that pattern in a range of cells.

7 With cells A4:A29 selected, on the Home tab, in the Number group, click the Number format box arrow, and then scroll down and click Text. In the Alignment group, click the Center button ▤. The years are formatted as text and centered.

8 Refer to Table 8.3 and enter the data in cells B4:B25. The population values for 2010 through 2040 are left blank intentionally.

1790	3.9
1800	5.3
1810	7.2
1820	9.6
1830	12.9
1840	17.1
1850	23.2
1860	31.4
1870	38.6
1880	50.2
1890	63.0
1900	76.2
1910	92.2
1920	106.0
1930	123.2
1940	142.2
1950	161.3
1960	189.3
1970	213.3
1980	236.5
1990	258.7
2000	291.4
2010	
2020	
2030	
2040	

TABLE 8.3

9 Select the range B4:B29. On the Home tab, in the Number group, click the Number Format arrow, and then click Number. In the Number group, click the Decrease Decimal button to display one decimal.

10 Click A31. Type `Source: U.S. Census Bureau` and then press Enter. Select cells A31 and B31. In the Alignment group, click the Merge and Center button arrow, and then click Merge cells. The data is entered and documented, as shown in Figure 8.25.

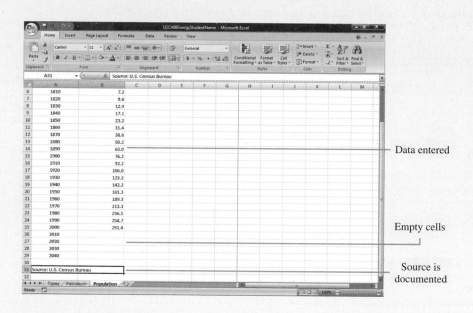

FIGURE 8.25

11 Save your workbook.

good design...

EQUAL TIME INTERVALS

When time is used as a series of labels, it is important that the intervals are the same. If the data you have does not have the same amount of time between each data value, use the *X-Y scatter chart* instead of the line chart. The program that creates the X-Y scatter chart will choose horizontal time intervals that are equal and draw the line so that the shape and angle of the lines have consistent meaning.

When the data is related to units of time, the best choice for displaying trends is usually a line chart—a chart with one or more lines whose height on the vertical axis represents the value of the data.

to create a line chart

1 On the Population sheet, select the range A3:B29, which includes the empty cells.

2 On the Insert tab, in the Charts group, click the Line button. Under 2-D Line, in the second row, click the first choice: *Line with Markers*. A line chart with markers displays small squares—*markers*—along the line at each data point. The program does not recognize the first column as labels. Instead it treats both columns as data that should be charted as lines, as shown in Figure 8.26.

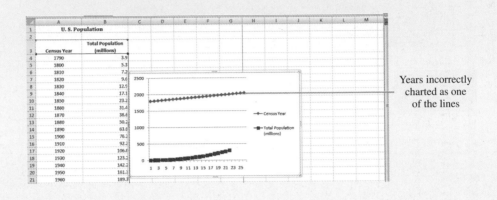

Years incorrectly charted as one of the lines

FIGURE 8.26

if you have problems...

DID EXCEL MISREPRESENT THE LABELS?

If the program makes a mistake in choosing the columns or rows to use as labels, you have to delete the range of data labels from the list of ranges to be charted and then specify it as the range to use as data labels.

3 With the chart selected, on the Chart Tools Design tab, in the Data group, click the Select Data button to display the Select Data Source dialog box.

4 In the Select Data Source dialog box, under *Legend Entries (Series)*, click *Census Year*, and then click the Remove button. Point to the title bar of the dialog box and drag it out of the way so that you can see most of the chart. The line representing census years is removed from the chart, but the horizontal axis does not display the years, as shown in Figure 8.27.

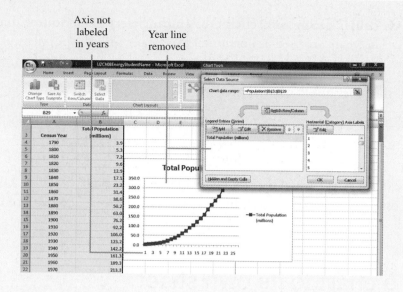

FIGURE 8.27

5 **In the Select Data Source dialog box, in the** *Horizontal (Category) Axis Labels* **area, click the Edit button.** The Axis labels dialog box displays.

6 **On the worksheet, drag to select the range A4:A29.** The range of years—without the column header—is entered as the range of labels for the horizontal axis, as shown in Figure 8.28.

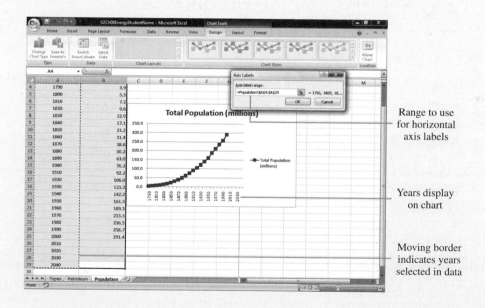

FIGURE 8.28

7 **In the Axis Labels dialog box, click OK. In the Select Data Source dialog box, click OK.** The years are used as horizontal axis labels, and the population data is charted as a line.

8 **Save** 💾 **the workbook.**

If a chart is important enough to print full size on its own page and is self-explanatory without the accompanying data, you can move it to its own sheet in a workbook.

to move a chart to its own sheet

1 **On the Chart Tools Design tab, in the Location group, click the Move Chart button.** The Move Chart dialog box displays.

2 **In the Move Chart dialog box, click the New Sheet option button. In the New Sheet box, notice that the default text is selected. Type** `PopulationChart` **The new sheet will be named, as shown in Figure 8.29.**

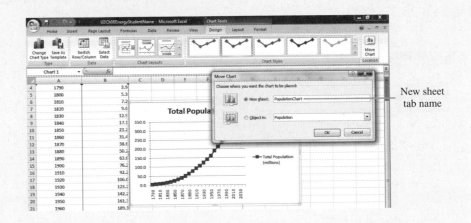

FIGURE 8.29

3 **In the Move Chart dialog box, click OK.** The chart is moved to its own sheet in the workbook. Even though the chart occupies the entire sheet, the font size of the labels did not increase proportionately, as shown in Figure 8.30.

Small fonts
for large chart

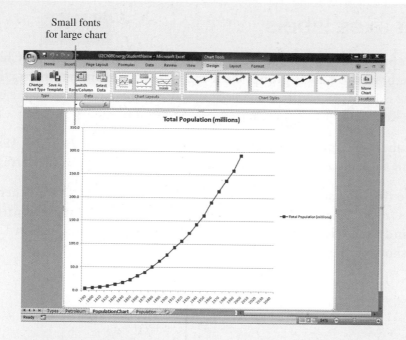

FIGURE 8.30

good **design...**

MOVE CHART TO ITS OWN SHEET

If a chart is important or has a lot of detail that does not fit well on the same sheet as the data on which it is based, move it to its own sheet. You have to choose to add a header to sheets that only have a chart, even if they are sheets selected when you choose header options.

▶▶▶ *lesson*
five | Formatting Axis Labels and Adding a Trendline

Unless the content is obvious, axes should be clearly labeled. This may require adding a label, changing font size, or formatting the data so that it displays an appropriate number of decimal places or other numerical formatting.

to format axes labels

1 **In the PopulationChart worksheet, with the chart selected, on the Chart Tools Layout tab, in the Labels group, click the Legend button, and then click None.** The chart expands to fill the available space. When there is only one line on a chart or one color used in a column chart, the legend is unnecessary.

2 **In the Labels group, click the Axis Titles button. Point to *Primary Vertical Axis Title*, and then click Rotated Title.** A title box displays next to the vertical axis.

3 **With the title box selected, type** `Population (millions)` **and then press ⏎Enter. On the Home tab, in the Font group, click the Font Size button arrow ⎸11 ▾⎸, and then click 12.** The title is placed next to the vertical axis in 12-point font, as shown in Figure 8.31.

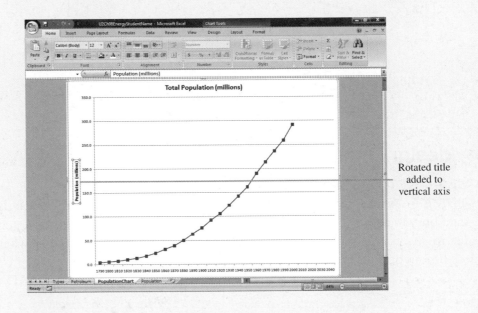

Rotated title added to vertical axis

FIGURE 8.31

4 **On the Chart Tools Layout tab, in the Axes group, click the Axes button. Point to *Primary Vertical Axis*, and then click *More Primary Vertical Axis Options*.** The Format Axis dialog box displays.

5 **In the Format Axis dialog box, in the left pane, click Number. On the right side, move the pointer to the *Decimal Places* box. Select the default number in the box, and then type** `0`

6 **In the Format Axis dialog box, click the Close button. On the Home tab, in the Font group, click the Font Size button arrow ⎸11 ▾⎸, and then click 12.** The vertical axis displays numbers with no decimal places, as shown in Figure 8.32. Notice that the labels on the horizontal axis appear to run together, which makes them hard to read.

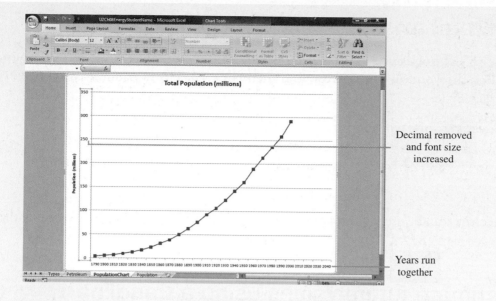

Decimal removed
and font size
increased

Years run
together

FIGURE 8.32

7 On the Chart Tools Layout tab, in the Axes group, click Axes. Point to Primary Horizontal Axis, and then click *More Primary Horizontal Axis Options.*

8 In the Format Axis dialog box, in the left pane, click Alignment. Click the Custom Angle box, and then type -45 Be sure to include the minus sign. The labels on the horizontal axis display at a 45-degree angle so that they do not appear to run together, as shown in Figure 8.33.

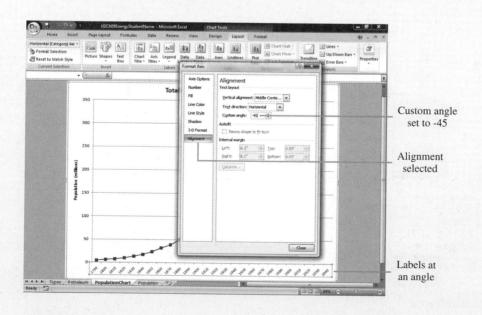

Custom angle
set to -45

Alignment
selected

Labels at
an angle

FIGURE 8.33

Formatting Axis Labels and Adding a Trendline   443   **Chapter 8**

9 On the Format Axis dialog box, click Close.

10 With the horizontal axis labels selected, on the Home tab, in the Font group, click the Font Size box arrow, and then click 12. The horizontal axis displays years at an angle.

11 Save 💾 your workbook.

Line charts can be used to recognize trends and estimate future values by extending the lines.

to estimate future values using a trendline

1 On the PopulationChart worksheet, be sure the chart is selected. On the Chart Tools Layout tab, in the Analysis group, click the Trendline button, and then click More Trendline Options. The Format Trendline dialog box displays with the Linear option selected by default.

2 In the Format Trendline dialog box, point to the title bar. Drag the entire dialog box to the upper left of the screen so you can see the chart. A straight line is drawn through the chart, as shown in Figure 8.34.

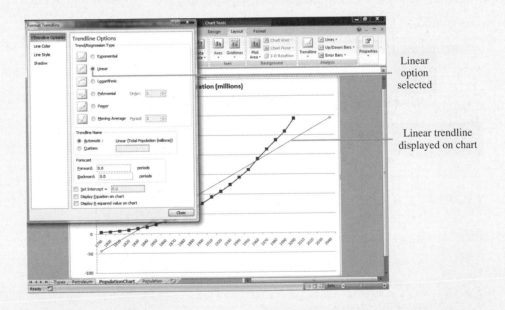

FIGURE 8.34

to extend your knowledge

UNDERSTANDING TRENDLINES

A *trendline* is a line whose points can be determined using a mathematical formula. There are several choices of types of mathematical formulas, the simplest of which is a straight line. The Excel program calculates the *slope*—angle—of the straight line that is the closest fit to the data. It compares each data point to its closest corresponding point on the line and finds the difference. It tries many different slopes until that difference is minimized.

The average difference between the trendline and the data point is summarized in the *R-squared value*. This is a single number that rates how well the trendline fits the actual data.

To calculate the R-squared value, the differences between the actual data and the closest point on the line are squared to make them all positive numbers, and then an average of the squared values is calculated. The next step is to take the square root of the average squared value. This square root of the average of the squared differences is then subtracted from 1. The result is the R-squared value, which is written R^2. If the line is close to the data points, the average difference should be small. When it is subtracted from 1, the result should be slightly less than 1. R^2 values range from 1, a perfect fit, to 0, no fit at all.

Examine the fit of several different trendlines to find the type that has the highest R-squared value—the one that is the closest to 1.

---

3   **In the Format Trendline dialog box, at the bottom right, select the check box next to *Display R-squared value on chart*.** The R-squared value is displayed on the chart. For this line, the value is 0.9166, which is not a very close fit, as shown in Figure 8.35.

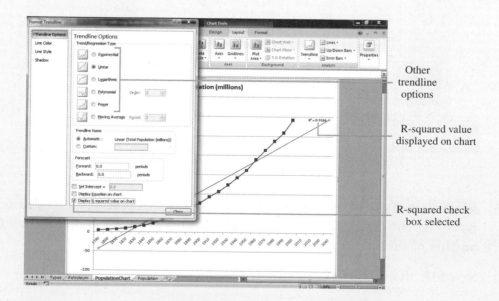

Other trendline options

R-squared value displayed on chart

R-squared check box selected

FIGURE 8.35

4 In the Format Trendline dialog box, under Trend/Regression Type, click the Exponential option button. An exponential trendline has a better R-squared value—.9678—but it is not a very good fit at the end of the line.

5 In the Format Trendline dialog box, under Trend/Regression Type, click the Logarithmic option button. A logarithmic trendline is not a good fit at all with an R-squared value of .6348.

6 In the Format Trendline dialog box, under Trend/Regression Type, click the Polynomial option button. This option has a very good fit with an R-squared value of .9996.

7 In the Format Trendline dialog box, under Trend/Regression Type, click the Power option button. The Power option has an R-squared value of .9426. The best option was Polynomial.

8 In the Format Trendline dialog box, under Trend/Regression Type, click the Polynomial option button. At the bottom right of the Format Trendline dialog box, click Close. The polynomial trendline with its R-squared value is displayed. Because you included the years 2010, 2020, 2030, and 2040, the trendline extends to 2040, as shown in Figure 8.36.

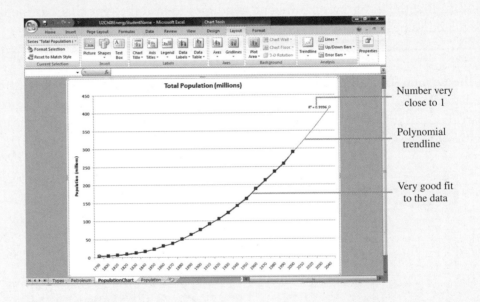

FIGURE 8.36

9 At the top of the chart, click the title, and then select the title text and type `Population Increase of 100 Million Must be Considered` **Click outside of the title text box.**

10 Save the workbook.

to extend your knowledge

FORECASTING USING TRENDLINES

In this exercise, you specified the number of years to extend the trend by including values in the range of axis labels beyond the known data. Alternatively, in the Format Trendline dialog box, in the Forecast area, you can choose the number of additional intervals to extend the line forward or backward, but the program does not calculate or display axis labels for the extended segment of the line.

good design...

EXTEND LINE CHARTS CAREFULLY

When you extend a line to estimate values beyond the end of the known data, the process is called *extrapolation*. To extrapolate, you must assume that the factors that resulted in the known data will not change. It is good design to document those assumptions. In this example, the future increase in population is based on assumptions that the birth, death, and immigration rates remain the same. You can document a chart by using a text box on the chart.

▶▶▶ *lesson*
SIX | Documenting the Chart and Worksheets

In this lesson, you document the worksheets with headers, callouts, and source references.

to document the chart

1. In the PopulationChart sheet, click the R-squared value. Drag the border of this box downward to a position below the extended portion of the line between the horizontal lines that mark populations of 300 and 350.

2. With the R-squared value selected, on the Home tab, in the Font group, click the Font Size button arrow 11 ▾. On the menu, click 12. The R-squared value is repositioned and resized, as shown in Figure 8.37.

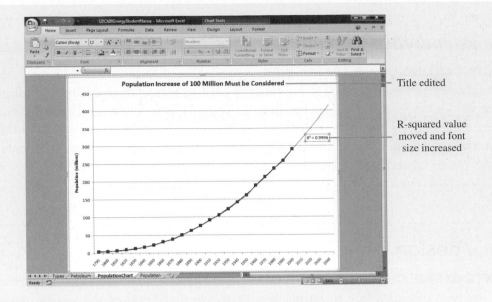

Title edited

R-squared value moved and font size increased

FIGURE 8.37

3 On the Insert tab, in the Illustrations group, click the Shapes button, and then in the Callouts area, click the second choice: **Rounded Rectangle Callout.** The ⊞ pointer displays.

4 Drag a rectangle in the large white area above the line, and then type `400 Million by 2038`

5 On the callout, select the text, point to the displayed Mini toolbar, and click the Center button ▤; then change the Font Size to 16.

6 Drag the sizing handles on the corners of the callout and on the end of the pointer to resize and reposition the callout, as shown in Figure 8.38.

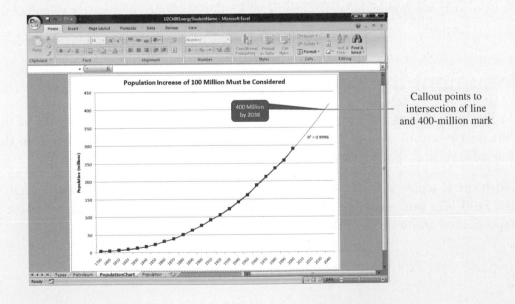

Callout points to intersection of line and 400-million mark

FIGURE 8.38

7 **Point to the last maker on the line.** A ScreenTip displays with the data values. The line with data markers displays the data when you point at one of the markers, as shown in Figure 8.39. If the ScreenTip refers to the trendline, keep trying slightly different positions until the data point value displays.

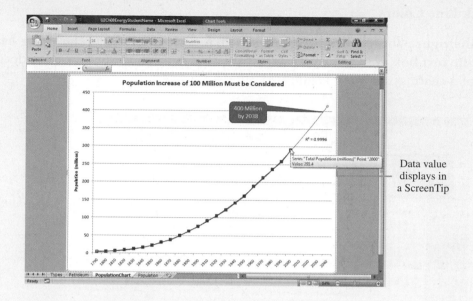

FIGURE 8.39

8 **On the Insert tab, in the Text group, click the Text Box button.** Move the pointer to the area below the data line and drag a short, wide rectangle between the horizontal lines that mark populations of 50 and 100 million; then release the mouse button. A text box displays, as shown in Figure 8.40.

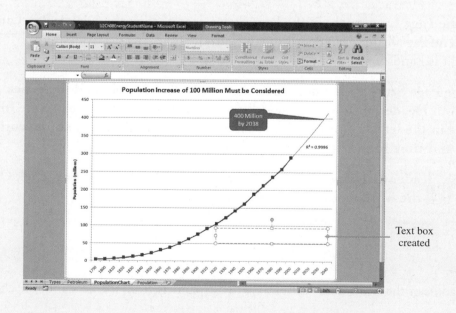

FIGURE 8.40

9 **Type** `Values beyond 2000 are estimates that assume the birth rate, death rate, and immigration rate remain the same.`

10 **With the insertion point in the text box, right-click, and then on the shortcut menu, click Format Shape. In the Format Shape dialog box, in the left pane, click Line Color.**

11 **In the right pane, click Solid Line, and then click Close. Drag the sizing handles on the text box, if necessary, to adjust the size.** A text box can be used to document a chart, as shown in Figure 8.41.

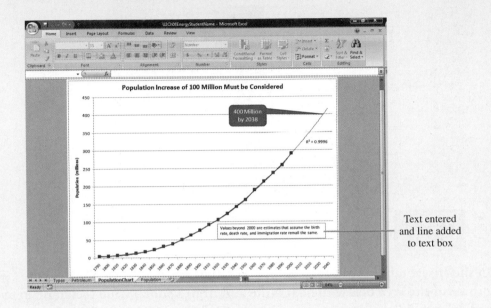

Text entered and line added to text box

FIGURE 8.41

12 **On the Page Layout tab, in the Page Setup group, click the Dialog Box Launcher** ⬚. The Page Setup dialog box displays with the Page tab selected. Notice that the default is Landscape.

13 **In the Page Setup dialog box, click the Header/Footer tab, and then click the Custom Header button. Use the skills you practiced earlier to place the file name in the left section, the sheet name in the center section, and the current date and time in the right section.**

14 **In the Header dialog box, click OK. In the Page Setup dialog box, click OK. Save** 💾 **the workbook.**

The headers of the worksheets must be created separately from the header of the chart sheet.

to use the same header on multiple worksheets

1 **Click the Types sheet tab. Press** Ctrl**, and then click the Petroleum sheet tab and the Population sheet tab.** All three sheet tabs—but not the PopulationChart tab—are selected, as shown in Figure 8.42. The title bar displays [Group] following the file name to indicate that you have grouped sheets.

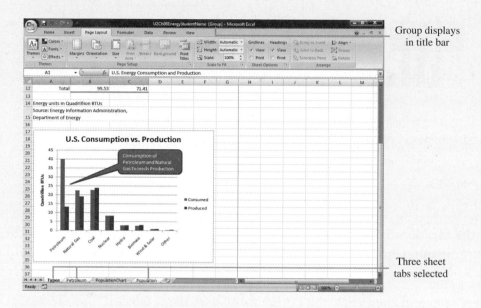

Group displays in title bar

Three sheet tabs selected

FIGURE 8.42

2 **On the Page Layout tab, in the Page Setup group, click the Dialog Box Launcher . Click the Header/Footer tab, and then click the Custom Header button.**

3 **Use the skills you practiced earlier to place the file name in the left section of the header, the sheet name in the center section, and the current date and time in the right section, as shown in Figure 8.43.**

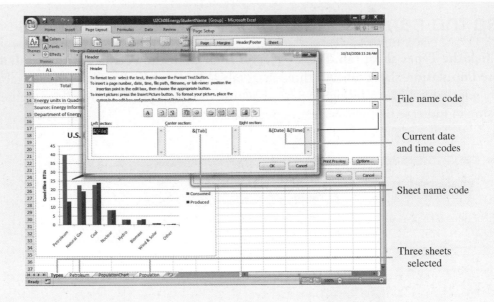

File name code

Current date
and time codes

Sheet name code

Three sheets
selected

FIGURE 8.43

4 In the Header dialog box, click OK. In the Page Setup dialog box, click the Margins tab. Under *Center on Page*, select the Horizontally check box, and then click OK.

5 Press Ctrl, and then click the PopulationChart sheet tab. All four sheets are selected.

6 Click the Office button, point to Print, and then click Print Preview. The Type worksheet displays. The presence of the chart prevents the data from appearing to be centered on the page. If you do not have a color printer, the chart displays in black, white, and shades of gray.

7 On the Print Preview tab, in the Preview group, click Next Page. The Petroleum worksheet printout displays.

8 On the Print Preview tab, in the Preview group, click Next Page. The Petroleum chart printout displays with its header.

9 On the Print Preview tab, in the Preview group, click Next Page. The data on the Population worksheet displays with the same header and is centered.

10 On the Print Preview tab, in the Preview group, click the Close Print Preview button. Click the Population sheet tab. On the Population sheet, confirm that it is in Normal view, and then click A1. Repeat this process for the Petroleum and Types sheets.

11 On the Types sheet, with A1 selected in Normal view, Save your file. Submit the file as directed by your instructor. Close the file, and then close Excel.

Advanced Skills or Concepts

In this section, you are introduced to skills and concepts that are not taught with step-by-step instructions.

Choosing the Correct Chart Type

If you have data that is organized into more than one column—not counting a column of labels—use a clustered column chart to compare the values in the rows to each other. In this chapter, you used a clustered column chart to compare the consumption and production of each type of energy. If a column is summed, you can show how the value in each cell in the column contributes to the sum by using a pie chart. If one of the columns contains time values that increase in equal increments, you can show the trend of the corresponding data using a line chart. Line charts can be extrapolated with a trendline if you are careful to document your assumptions and choose a trendline that fits well.

Identifying If the Chart Accurately Represents the Data

There are several situations where a chart might be misleading. It is important to be aware of them so that you can avoid making this type of mistake or spot them in charts created by others. They are:

- Including different types of data in the same range. The most common example of this error is including the total with the detail data in a column or row.

- Charting the labels as a data series. The Excel program will do this when the labels are numbers.

- Comparing data that have different units of measure using the same vertical axis units.

- Charting intervals between time units on a line chart that are not equal. To correctly interpret the slope of a line, each part of the line must have the same length on the horizontal axis.

- Vertical axis does not start at zero. Small variations in data can be exaggerated visually by limiting the range of the labels on the vertical axis to a small range that begins just below the lowest data point. Do not use this technique yourself unless you document the practice.

It is also important to watch for situations where the chart is accurately displaying incorrect data on the chart. An unexplained dip or rise in a line chart or an unusually large or small slice in a pie chart should alert you to a possible error in the underlying data, such as a typographical error.

CHECK YOUR WORK

Here is a list of items your instructor will probably look for when grading your work. To improve your evaluation, take time to check the items yourself before you turn in your work.

Types Sheet
- The data is formatted using good design principles. Specifically, look for bold and centered titles and headers, with a top and double bottom border on cells with totals.
- Documentation is in merged cells with the text wrapped and row and column sizes that display all of the text of the documentation.
- The chart is placed below the data, with its upper left corner in cell A17.
- The callout in the chart points to an area between the Petroleum and Natural gas columns and all of its text displays.
- In Print Preview, the file name is at the left, the sheet name is in the center, and the date you printed the sheet is at the right.

Petroleum Sheet
- The data is formatted using good design principles. Specifically, look for bold and centered titles and headers, with a top and double bottom border on cells with totals.
- Documentation is in merged cells and row and column sizes that display all of the text of the documentation.
- The chart is placed below the data, with its upper left corner in cell A14.
- The slice labels are on the chart instead of in a legend, and they include percentages.
- The Gasoline label is in white font.
- The Jet Fuel label displays below its related piece.
- In Print Preview, the file name is at the left, the sheet name is in the center, and the date you printed the sheet is at the right.

Population Chart Sheet
- The title is replaced with specified text.
- Vertical axis title is rotated so it is parallel to the axis. The axis labels do not display any decimal places and the font size is 12 points.
- The horizontal axis labels are at a 45-degree angle and range from 1790 to 2040.
- The line has small rectangles at each data point.
- A polynomial trendline with a displayed R-squared value of .9996 extends to 2040.
- A callout points to the intersection of the trendline and the 400-million line. The size of the callout is adjusted to display its text.
- A text box below the line displays the assumptions used to extend the line.
- In Print Preview, the file name is at the left, the sheet name is in the center, and the current date is at the right.

Population Sheet
- The data is formatted using good design principles. Specifically look for bold and centered titles and headers.
- The numbers in column B should all display one decimal place and the decimal points should align.
- The years are formatted as text and are centered in column A.
- In Print Preview, the file name is at the left, the sheet name is in the center, and the date you printed the sheet is at the right. The worksheet is centered horizontally on the page.

If you make any changes, be sure the final version of each sheet is in Normal view with cell A1 selected. Choose the Types sheet and then save the workbook.

KEY TERMS |

3-D pie chart	horizontal axis	sizing handles
bar chart	leader line	slope
callouts	legend	trendline
clustered column chart	line chart	vertical axis
column chart	markers	X-Y scatter chart
embedded chart	pie chart	
extrapolation	R-squared value	

ASSESSING LEARNING OUTCOMES |

SCREEN ID

Identify each element of the screen by matching callout numbers shown in Figure 8.44 to a corresponding description.

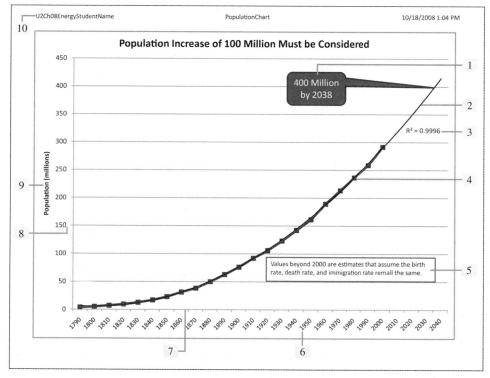

FIGURE 8.44

____ **A.** Angled axis label

____ **B.** Category axis

____ **C.** Callout

____ **D.** Documentation in text box

____ **E.** File name

____ **F.** Line with markers

____ **G.** Polynomial trendline

____ **H.** Rotated axis label

____ **I.** R-squared value

____ **J.** Value axis

MULTIPLE CHOICE

Circle the letter of the correct answer for each of the following. The lesson in which the term or concept was introduced is indicated at the end of the sentence.

1. If a range of cells has numbers that display a mix of decimal places, to display the same number of decimal places, select the range of numbers and change the format to _____ to adjust the decimals. [L1]

   a. General

   b. Currency

   c. Number

   d. Accounting Number

2. Data labels should be _____ if they might be used as chart labels. [L2]

   a. as descriptive as possible

   b. short

   c. all caps

   d. all the same color

3. When you select cells to chart, the values in those cells should be _____. [L1]

   a. the same number of decimal places

   b. formatted as text

   c. the same type

   d. adjacent to each other

4. If you want to create a chart that compares two columns of values and pairs them up by row, use a _____. [L1]

   a. clustered column chart

   b. area chart

   c. pie chart

   d. line chart with markers

5. If you want to demonstrate how the values in a column of numbers contribute to the column's total, use a _____. [L3]

   a. clustered column chart

   b. 3-D column chart

   c. pie chart

   d. line chart with markers

6. If you want to demonstrate how the values change with the passing of time, use a _____. [L4]

   a. clustered column chart

   b. 3-D column chart

   c. pie chart

   d. line chart

7. A common error when choosing a range of cells to chart is to include _____. [Adv]

   a. the total at the bottom of the column

   b. the column header

   c. a column of labels to the left

   d. more than one column of data

8. To correctly interpret the slope of a line chart, _____. [Adv]

   a. intervals on the horizontal axis must be equal

   b. you must use a polynomial trendline

   c. the markers option must be used

   d. a callout must be used

9. A method of exaggerating the difference between values in a line or column chart is to _____. [Adv]

  a. use wider columns or thicker lines

  b. use larger fonts to label one series compared to the other

  c. use a brighter color for one series compared to the other

  d. begin the vertical axis labels at a value other than zero that is just less than the smallest value charted

10. If you do not have a color printer, the Print Preview of a pie chart will display the chart _____. [L6]

  a. in color with a warning box

  b. in black, white, and shades of gray

  c. with all of the labels on the slices in white font

  d. with different patterns of cross-hatching in a pie chart

MATCHING

Match the term or concept to its description.

_____ 1. Identifies each data series on a chart

_____ 2. Extending a line chart beyond known values

_____ 3. The rise or fall of a line

_____ 4. Like a column chart but values are horizontal

_____ 5. Small rectangle on a line chart that displays data values

_____ 6. A calculated line that fits existing data

_____ 7. A shape that has a pointer and contains text, like a cartoon speech or thought balloon

_____ 8. A line that connects a label to a chart element

_____ 9. A calculated value that ranges between 1 and 0 that indicates the quality of the fit of a trendline

_____ 10. Rectangle that displays text

  A. Bar chart

  B. Callout

  C. Extrapolation

  D. Leader

  E. Legend

  F. Marker

  G. R-squared

  H. Slope

  I. Text box

  J. Trendline

SKILL DRILL

The Skill Drill exercise is a repeat of the lessons in the chapter but with a different set of data. The instructions are less detailed, and your speed and familiarity should increase with practice. There is a figure at the end against which you can check your worksheets. The purpose of this exercise is to build your confidence and speed in using these skills and to set them in your memory for later recall. The section numbers correspond to the lesson numbers. You are welcome to refer back to the lessons illustrated and the detailed instructions if necessary.

In this exercise, you set up three worksheets and a chart sheet that compare U.S. imports of oil and gas by world region, compare the different sources of electrical energy in the U.S., and determine the trend in wind energy production in the U.S. Print copies of the worksheets if your instructor requires it.

1. Creating a Column Chart

1. Start **Excel.** Double-click the name of the **Sheet1** tab, type Imports and then press (⏎Enter). **Save** the workbook in your Chapter08 folder as U2Ch08ImportsStudentName

2. In cell **A1,** enter U.S. Imported Gas and Oil and then make it **Bold. Merge and Center** it across cells **A1:C1.** Change **Font Size** to **12** and **Font** to **Cambria.**

3. In cell **A3,** type Region and in cell **B3,** type Natural Gas and then in cell **C3,** type Petroleum Select cells **A3** through **C3.** Make the headers **Bold** and **Center** them within their own cells.

4. Starting in cell **A4,** enter the remaining data.

North America	1,123	2,474
South America	132	906
Mid East	5	1,222
North Africa	55	421
Sub-Saharan Africa	28	1,019
Asia	5	294

5. AutoFit columns **A:C.** Select cells **B4:C9** and format with the **Comma Style** with no decimals.

6. Select cells **A11:C11.** On the **Home** tab, in the **Alignment** group, click the **Merge Center button arrow** and then click **Merge Cells.** In cell **A11,** type Energy in Terawatt Hours Repeat this process to merge cells **A12:C12,** and then in cell **A12,** type Source: Energy Information Administration

7. Select cells **A3:C9.** On the **Insert** tab, insert a **3-D Clustered Column** chart.

2. Editing Chart Elements

1. On the **Chart Tools Layout** tab, in the **Labels** group, create a **Chart Title** above the chart, then type U.S. Imported Gas and Oil and then press (⏎Enter).

2. In the **Labels** group, click the **Axis Titles** button. Point to **Primary Vertical Axis Title,** click **Rotated Axis,** and then type Energy (Terawatt Hours)

3. In the **Axes** group, click the **Axes** button, point to **Primary Horizontal Axis,** and then click **More Primary Horizontal Axis Options.** Click **Alignment,** and in the Custom angle box, type -45 and then press (⏎Enter).

4. Drag the chart below the data and place the upper left corner in cell **A14.** Drag the sizing handles to increase chart height and width so that the lower right corner is in cell **H32.** Be sure that the right edge of the chart does not touch the boundary between columns H and I.

5. On the **Insert** tab, in the **Illustrations** group, click the **Shapes** button, and then click ***Rounded Rectangular Callout.*** On the chart, drag a rectangle between the

1,500 and 2,500 lines and from the Mid East oil to Sub-Saharan oil columns. Type `Need 1,222 TWH of alternatives to replace Mid East oil`

6. Use the sizing handles to adjust the size of the callout so that all of the text displays. **Center** the text in the callout. Point to the yellow diamond and drag the callout pointer to point to the Mid East oil column. Adjust the position of the callout on the chart, as shown in Figure 8.45.

7. **Save** the workbook.

3. Using a Pie Chart

1. Change the name of the **Sheet2** tab to `Electricity`

2. In cell **A1,** type `Sources of U.S. Electricity` and then press [⏎Enter]. Select **A1.** Make it **Bold,** and then **Merge and Center** it across cells **A1:B1.** Change **Font** to **Cambria** and **Font Size** to **12.**

3. In cell **A3,** type `Source` and then in **B3,** type `Energy (TWH)` Select cells **A3** and **B3.** Make both headers **Bold,** and then **Center** them within their own cells. Adjust the width of column **A** to **28** characters and column **B** to **14** characters.

4. Beginning in cell **A4,** enter the data shown below:

Coal	1,990
Petroleum	64
Natural Gas	813
Other Gases*	16
Nuclear	787
Hydroelectric	289
Renewables**	96
Other	14

5. In cell **A12,** type `Total` and then align it to the right side of the cell. In cell **B12,** use the **SUM** function to total the amounts in the cells above. Format cells **B4:B12** with **Comma Style** and no decimals. Format cell **B12** with a **Top and Double Bottom** border.

6. Select cells **A14** and **B14,** merge the cells, apply word wrapping, and then type `*Blast-furnace gas, propane gas, other waste gasses derived from fossil` Adjust the height of **row 14** to **30.**

7. Repeat the process in Step 6 in cells **A15** and **B15** and type `**Wood, municipal solid waste, biomass, solar, and wind` Adjust the row height to **30.**

8. Merge cells **A16** and **B16,** and then type `Energy measured in Terawatt Hours`

9. Merge cells **A18** and **B18,** and then type `Source: Energy Information Administration`

10. Select **A3:B11.** On the **Insert** tab, in the **Charts** group, click the **Pie** button, and then click **3-D pie chart**.

11. Click the chart title to make the title active. Select the displayed title text, and then type `Electricity Energy Sources` Click in an open area on the chart to deselect the title.

12. On the **Chart Tools Layout** tab, in the **Labels** group, remove the legend.

13. In the **Labels** group, click the **Data Labels** button, and then click **More Data Labels Options.** Display the **Category Name** and **Value** showing leader lines.

14. Point to the edge of the chart. Drag the chart below the data so that its upper left corner is in cell **A20.** Drag the sizing handles to increase the size of the chart so that its lower right corner is in the middle of cell **G40.**

15. Click the label on the Coal slice two times to select only the Coal label. Change the font color to **White.**

16. Preview the printout of the Electricity worksheet. Confirm that the pie slice labels have sufficient contrast. **Save** the workbook.

4. Charting a Trend with a Line Chart

1. Rename the **Sheet3** tab to `Wind` and then press ⏎Enter.

2. In cell **A1,** type `Wind Energy` Change **Font** to **Cambria, Font Size** to **12** and apply **Bold. Merge and Center** the title in cells **A1:B1.**

3. In cell **A3,** type `Year` and then in **B3,** type `Energy (TWH)` **Center** each column header in its cell and apply **bold.** Adjust the width of columns **A** and **B** to **14** characters.

4. In cell **A4,** type `2002` and then in **A5,** type `2003` Select cells **A4:A5,** point to the fill handle in cell **A5,** and drag it down to cell **A22**—to the year 2020. With cells **A4:A22** selected, format the numbers as text and center them.

5. In cells **B4:B8,** enter `10.4`, `11.2`, `14.2`, `17.8`, and `26.6`

6. In cell **A24,** type `Measured in Terawatt Hours` and then merge cells **A24** and **B24.**

7. In cell **A25,** type `Source: Energy Information Administration` and then merge cells **A25:C25.**

8. Select cells **A3:B22.** On the **Insert** tab, in the **Charts** group, click the **Line** button, and then click **Line with Markers.**

5. Formatting Axis Labels and Adding a Trendline

1. With the chart selected, on the **Chart Tools Design** tab, in the **Data** group, click the **Select Data** button. In the Select Data Source dialog box, remove the **Year** series. Under **Horizontal (Category) Axis Labels,** click the **Edit** button, and then drag cells **A4:A22.** Click **OK** to close the dialog boxes.

2. On the **Chart Tools Layout** tab, in the **Analysis** group, click the **Trendline** button, and then click **More Trendline Options.**

3. In the Format Trendline dialog box, choose to display the **R-squared** value. Try the first five line types, and then choose the one with the highest R-squared value—the value closest to 1. **Close** the dialog box.

4. Right-click the chart. On the shortcut menu, click **Move Chart.** Choose to place the chart on its own sheet and name it `WindChart` Remove the legend.

5. On the **WindChart** sheet, add a **rotated title** to the primary vertical axis— `Energy (Terawatt Hours)` Format the labels on the primary horizontal axis to `-45` degrees.

6. Select the chart title and edit it to read `Future Wind Energy` Drag the R-squared value below the trendline, just above the horizontal line labeled 250.

7. Insert a callout that points to the end of the trendline that says `About 30% of Mid East oil imports` Adjust the size and position of the callout as shown in Figure 8.45.

8. On the **Insert** tab, in the **Text** group, click the **Text Box** button. Below the trendline, between the horizontal lines for 50 and 100 Terawatt Hours, drag a text box as shown in Figure 8.45.

9. In the text box, type `Estimates beyond 2006 are based on the assumption that the rate of increase is sustained. This extrapolation is based on only five years of data; there-fore estimates should be used cautiously.`

10. Adjust the size and position as necessary to display all of the text. On the **Drawing Tools Format** tab, in the **Shape Styles** group, click the **Shape Outline** button arrow. In the displayed gallery, in the fifth column, click the **Blue, Accent 1** color.

11. **Save** the workbook.

6. Documenting the Chart and Worksheets

1. On the **WindChart** sheet, on the **Page Layout** tab, in the **Page Setup** group, click the **Dialog Box Launcher.** On the **Header/Footer** tab, click the **Custom Header** button. Use the buttons to enter the **file name** in the left section of the header, the **sheet name** in the center, and the **current date** and **time** in the right section. Click **OK** in each dialog box.

2. Click the **Imports** sheet tab. Press Ctrl, click the **Electricity** sheet tab, and then click the **Wind** sheet tab.

3. On the **Page Layout** tab, in the **Page Setup** group, click the **Dialog Box Launcher.** On the **Margins** tab, center the sheets horizontally.

4. On the **Header/Footer** tab, click the **Custom Header** button and enter the **file name** in the left section of the header, the **sheet name** in the center, and the **current date** and **time** in the right section. Click **OK** in both dialog boxes.

5. Press Ctrl and click the **WindChart** sheet tab to include it. Preview all four print-outs to confirm that they all have the file name, the sheet name, and the current date and time in the header.

6. On each worksheet, confirm that it is in **Normal** view with **A1** selected. Do this to the Imports sheet last.

7. **Save** the workbook. Submit the file as directed by your instructor.

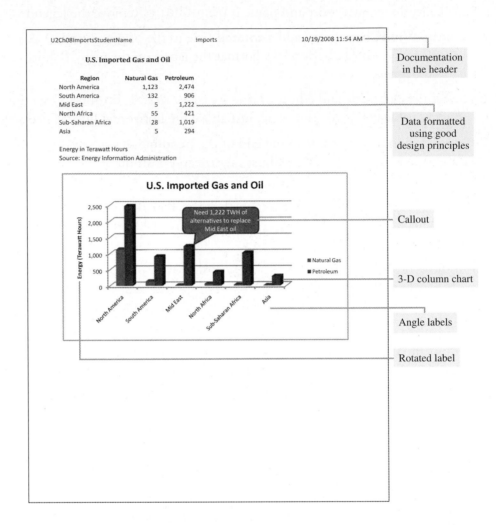

FIGURE 8.45A

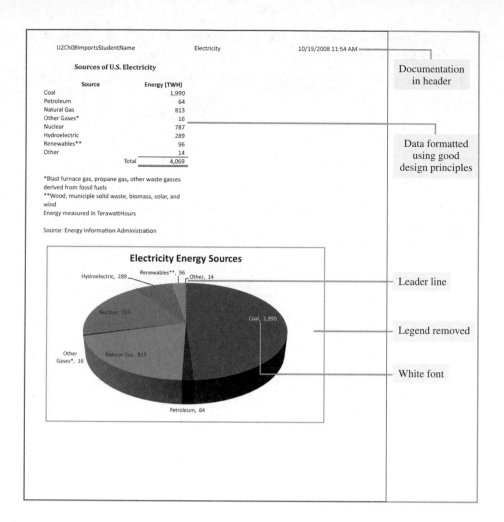

FIGURE 8.45B

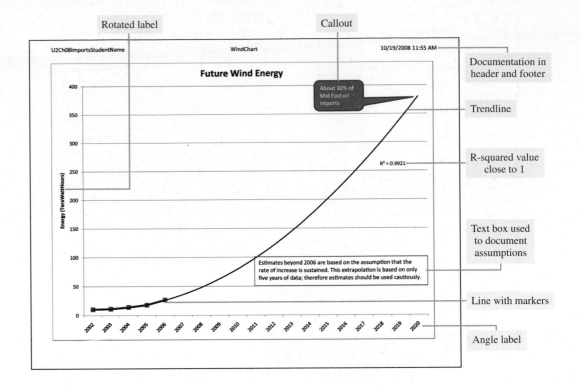

FIGURE 8.45C

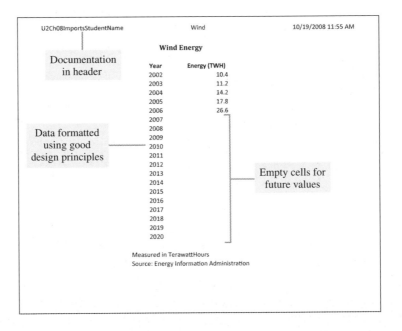

FIGURE 8.45D

fix *it*

One way to appreciate the value of good design is to fix a file that is not designed well. In this exercise, you open a file that has several design flaws and fix it according to the good design elements in the lessons.

Navigate to the folder with the student files, open **U2Ch08FixIt,** and save it in your Chapter08 folder as `U2Ch08FixItStudentName`

Examine the file and make the changes that are necessary to make it comply with the good design principles that were introduced in this chapter. Here is a list of design principles introduced in this chapter and some common errors to look for to fix the worksheet. There are eleven changes that need to be made. See if you can find them all.

Good Design
- Format numbers with commas and no decimals, and non-numerical numbers as text.

- Use short words for column or row headers that might appear on charts.

- Select the same type of data to chart.

- Use a chart that is appropriate to the data and the purpose.

- Use a title or callout to reinforce your interpretation of the data if the purpose is to present an idea or to persuade.

- Examine charts to find data that might be erroneous.

- Be careful when you extrapolate a line chart. Document your assumptions in a text box on the chart.

- Use line charts to show trends over time. Time intervals should increase by the same amount from left to right or from top to bottom.

- If a chart is too large to display well on the same page as the data, move it to its own sheet.

- Label the vertical axis and include the units of measure.

Look for the following types of mistakes:

- The total of a row or column of numbers should not be included in the same range with the data that are part of the sum. (Tip: To correct this type of problem, on the Chart Tools Design tab, in the Data group, click the Select Data button. In the Select Data Source dialog box, use the Edit buttons to display the ranges used for the data and labels; change them.)

- Examine the chart to find typographical errors in the data. In particular, look for misplaced decimal points and revise the data. (Tip: If you did not make the typing mistake, document the change and include the original number in the documentation.)

- Extrapolate a trendline that is not a good fit to the known data. (Tip: Click the line to select it and press Delete), and then try a new line with an R-squared value closer to 1.)

- Vertical axis does not begin at zero and this is not documented.

- The chart and worksheet should have their own headers.

- Apply proper formatting to totals.

- Delete unused worksheets.

Submit the file as required by your instructor. Save and close the file.

Information workers add value to data by organizing, selecting, displaying, communicating, interpreting, and using data to communicate information and support decisions. On the Job exercises simulate a situation where you are given data, and your job is to add value to it using the skills you practiced in this chapter. Success in these exercises indicates that you have a valuable skill to offer an employer.

1. Predict Natural Gas Imports

The exercises in this section are related to the following exchange of memos:

Jane,

We have been approached by a company that manufactures fuel cell systems that convert natural gas to hydrogen and then use it in fuel cells to generate electricity. They would like us to distribute their line of fuel cells in New England for use in commercial buildings as an alternative to using electricity from the grid. I'm not sure that their estimates of the future costs of natural gas are very good. I'd like you to make an estimate of the cost of natural gas for the next five years based on prices in New England. Use data from the Energy Information Administration. Tell me your estimate of the price of natural gas in five years and how confident you are of your number.

John

Navigate to the location where the student files are located. Open **U2Ch08Gas** and save it to your Chapter08 folder as U2Ch08GasStudentName The first worksheet in this workbook has the data you need for this exercise. In this workbook, chart the data and extend it with a trendline for five years beyond the last year in the table. See the following list of elements that will be used to evaluate your final workbook.

GasPrices Worksheet

1. The table should be formatted using good design principles.

2. The row of years should be extended to **2014.**

3. The printout of this sheet should be documented with the sheet name in the center of the header, the file name on the left, and the current date and time on the right of the header.

4. Ensure that the worksheet will print on one page and is centered horizontally.

GasPricesChart

Create a chart that displays the trend in commercial natural gas prices in New England to 2014, based on the data in the GasPrices worksheet.

1. The appropriate chart should be used to estimate future values.

2. The appropriate ranges should be used for the chart and its labels.

3. Include a descriptive chart label and an axis label.

4. The estimate with the highest accuracy should be chosen.

5. Use a text box on the chart to comment on the quality of this estimate based on the fit of the computer's projection to the known data.

6. Draw attention to the part of the chart that shows the estimated price in 2014.

7. The chart sheet should be documented in the header the same as in the GasPrices worksheet.

8. Delete unused worksheets and print or submit the file as directed by your instructor. Save the file and close it.

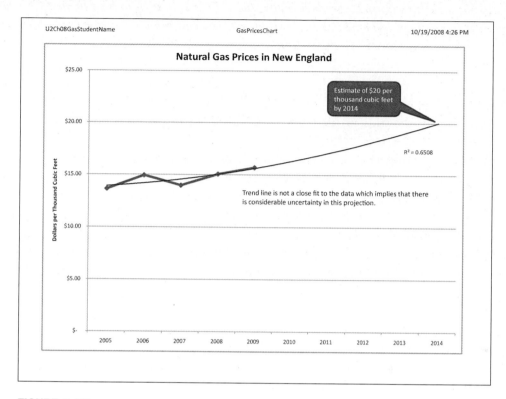

FIGURE 8.46A

Commercial U.S. Natural Gas Prices

	2005	2006	2007	2008	2009	2010	2011	2012	2013	2014
New England	$ 13.63	$ 14.93	$ 13.97	$ 15.06	$ 15.69					
Middle Atlantic	12.01	12.75	12.14	13.93	13.73					
East North Central	10.66	11.41	10.66	11.87	12.19					
West North Central	10.60	10.93	10.46	11.61	12.25					
South Atlantic	12.90	13.63	12.74	14.32	14.19					
East South Central	12.55	13.45	12.34	13.67	13.94					
West South Central	10.62	10.68	10.22	12.03	11.91					
Mountain	9.46	10.63	9.72	10.88	11.66					
Pacific	10.52	10.90	10.86	12.22	12.00					
U.S. Average	11.34	11.99	11.30	12.65	12.87					

Measured in dollars per thousand cubic feet
U.S. Energy Information Administration

FIGURE 8.46B

2. Compare Fuel Costs

This exercise is based on the following e-mail from a fellow worker.

> Jane,
>
> We are planning to sell a new product that reduces the energy used to heat homes. Can you give me a comparison of home heating costs for natural gas, propane, and heating fuel oil by region of the country so that we have an idea where would be the best place to focus our sales efforts?
>
> Bill

Locate and open the student file named **U2Ch08Heating** and save it in your Chapter 08 folder as U2Ch08HeatingStudentName

Create a second table where each value is multiplied by the appropriate conversion factor so that all prices are per million BTUs. Use the skills you practiced to write formulas with absolute references to the conversion factors. Create a chart to compare prices by region using the table you create. Refer to the Fix It exercise to check your work for good design principles and to avoid common errors. Document the printout by putting the file name in the left section of the header, the sheet name in the center, and the current date and time in the right section on the worksheet and the chart sheet. Compare your results with Figure 8.47.

U2Ch08HeatingStudentName   HeatingFuel   10/19/2008 4:37 PM

Heating Fuel Prices by Region

Region	Heating Oil ($ / Gal)	Natural Gas ($/MCF)	Propane ($ / gal)
Northeast	3.87	17.74	2.97
Midwest	3.90	13.11	1.86
South	3.90	18.26	2.78
West	3.99	13.59	2.74

Conversion Factors

Heating Oil: Gallons to millions of BTUs	7.21
Natural gas: MCF to millions of BTUs	0.974
Propane: Gallons to millions of BTUs	10.923

Source: Energy Information Administration

Region	Heating Oil	Natural Gas	Propane
Northeast	$ 27.90	$ 17.28	$ 32.44
Midwest	28.12	12.77	20.32
South	28.12	17.79	30.37
West	28.77	13.24	29.93

Prices in $ per million BTU

FIGURE 8.47A

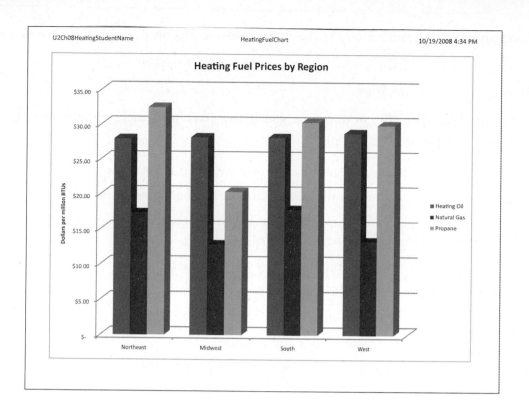

FIGURE 8.47B

DISCUSSION OF ADVANCED SKILLS OR CONCEPTS

The questions in this section are based on the topics in the Advanced Skills or Concepts section of the chapter.

1. What are some examples of tables of data that would be most appropriately represented by a column chart, a pie chart, and a line chart?

2. Consider a situation where a value increases by the same amount each year, but the values are measured at different time intervals. For example, the values are reported every five years, and then the interval between reports is changed to every ten years. What effect would this have on a line chart if the difference in time intervals was not corrected? Explain your answer. You may want to illustrate your answer by creating a table and chart.

3. If the chart reveals an obvious error in someone else's table of data, what should you do? Should you leave the error and add a comment, correct the error, or correct the error and document the change? Provide examples where each solution could be the right choice.

ON YOUR OWN

Once you are comfortable with the skills in this chapter, you can apply them to new situations of your own choosing. In this section, you choose data that you have in your possession or that you can find elsewhere. To successfully complete this assignment, you must apply good design practices and demonstrate mastery of the skills that were practiced. Refer to the list of design practices in the Fix It exercise.

1. Project Your Future Bills

Consider the bills that you, or someone you know, have paid each year for several years. Gather that information into a table.

- Extend the labels of years an additional five years beyond the most recent value.
- Format and document the table according to good design principles.
- Create a line chart on its own sheet that shows the trend, if any, and extend a trendline through the next five years.
- Display and interpret the R-squared value of the trendline.
- Document the chart sheet with its own header.
- Use a callout to point out a trend or a conclusion.
- Document your assumptions and sources.
- Save the file as U2Ch08FutureBillsStudentName
- Submit the file as directed by your instructor.

2. Project Your Future Income

Refer to previous paychecks or income tax forms to identify your net taxable income after deductions for at least five years. You may use data from another person and the person can remain anonymous. Gather that information into a table.

- Extend the labels of years an additional five years beyond the most recent value.
- Format and document the table according to good design principles.
- Create a line chart on its own sheet that shows the trend, if any, and extend a trendline through the next five years.
- Display and interpret the R-squared value of the trendline.
- Document the chart sheet with its own header.
- Save the file as U2Ch08FutureIncomeStudentName
- Submit the file as directed by your instructor.

3. Examine Your Expenses

Create a table of your expenses for one month. Classify expenses according to how you spent your money.

- Format and document the table according to good design principles.
- Include a sum of the expenses for the month.
- Create a pie chart that shows how each category of expense contributed to the whole amount spent for the month.
- Include a chart title.

- Use data labels to show the value and percentage of each piece.
- Be sure that there is good contrast for the data labels.
- Document the chart sheet with its own header.
- Save the file as U2Ch08ExpenseStudentName
- Submit the file as directed by your instructor.

ASSESS YOUR PROGRESS

At this point, you should have a set of skills and design concepts that are valuable to an employer and to you. You may not realize how much you've learned unless you take a few minutes to assess your progress.

1. From the student files, open **U2Ch08Assess.** Save it in your Chapter08 folder as U2Ch08AssessStudentName

2. Read each question in column A.

3. In column B, answer Yes or No.

4. If you identify a skill or design concept that you don't know, refer to the learning objective code next to the question and the table at the beginning of the chapter to find the skill and review it.

5. Print the worksheet if your instructor requires it. The file name is already in the header, so it will display your name as part of the file name.

6. All of these skills and concepts have been identified as important by surveying hundreds of individuals working at over 200 companies worldwide. If you cannot answer all of the questions affirmatively even after reviewing the relevant lesson, seek additional help from your instructor.

chapter *nine*

Creating a Presentation

Lesson	Learning Outcomes	Code	Related IC3 Objectives
1	Create a presentation	9.01	4.1.1
1	Identify the parts of the window in normal view	9.02	4.1.3
1	Enter text using the Slide pane	9.03	4.1.2
1	Enter text using the Outline tab	9.04	4.1.2
1	Increase and decrease bullet-point levels	9.05	4.1.2
1	Move and edit slide content	9.06	4.1.2
2	Add slides to a presentation	9.07	4.1.2
2	Reuse slides from another presentation	9.08	4.1.1
2	Delete a slide from a presentation	9.09	4.1.1
2	Duplicate a slide	9.10	4.1.1
2	Replace text in a slide	9.11	4.1.2
2	Rearrange text in a slide	9.12	4.1.2
2	Use short phases not sentences in bullet points	9.13	4.1.2, 4.1.12
3	Add graphic elements	9.14	4.1.2
3	Navigate between slides	9.15	4.1.1
3	Insert a slide in the middle of a presentation	9.16	4.1.1
3	Change a slide layout	9.17	4.1.4
3	Insert a picture from a file using a content icon	9.18	4.1.2
3	Insert clip art in a slide without using a content icon	9.19	4.1.2
3	Move and modify an inserted graphic	9.20	4.1.2
4	Apply a theme to a presentation	9.21	4.1.5
4	Modify theme color or font	9.22	4.1.5
4	Modify background styles	9.23	4.1.5
4	Hide background graphics	9.24	4.1.5
4	Review and adjust a presentation	9.25	4.1.5
4	Resize placeholders	9.26	4.1.5
5	Add information to a slide header or footer	9.27	4.1.1
5	Do not show header or footer on the first slide	9.28	4.1.1
5	Modify location and format of placeholders using slide masters	9.29	4.1.1, 4.1.3
6	Rearrange slides in slide sorter view	9.30	4.1.3, 4.1.7
6	Add slide transitions	9.31	4.1.6
6	Add different transitions to different slides	9.32	4.1.6
6	Use slide show view	9.33	4.1.3, 4.1.10
6	Use the Mouse, Keyboard, and Onscreen buttons to navigate a slide show	9.34	4.1.11
7	Add speaker notes using the Notes pane	9.35	4.1.9
7	Display the Notes Pages view and add notes	9.36	4.1.3, 4.1.9
7	Change font size of speaker notes	9.37	4.1.9
7	Add header and footer information to note pages and handouts	9.38	4.1.9, 4.1.12
7	Print notes pages	9.39	4.1.9
7	Create handouts with a specified number of slides to a page	9.40	4.1.9
7	Change color mode for printing	9.41	4.1.9
7	Print handouts	9.42	4.1.9

Advanced	Identify common uses for a presentation	9.43	4.1.12
Advanced	Identify methods of distributing a presentation	9.44	4.1.8
Advanced	Identify techniques for using a presentation effectively	9.45	4.1.12
Advanced	Identify techniques for preparing for a presentation	9.46	4.1.12

Instructions throughout the lessons are based on the Vista operating system, running Microsoft Office 2007.

Why Would I Do This?

In your personal or professional life, you may be asked to share information, promote a product, or persuade an audience to a particular point of view. Presentation software can help you get organized, stay on track, cover all the important information, and have fun at the same time. Microsoft Office PowerPoint is a presentation graphics program that helps you convey information to an audience. With this application, you can create visually appealing slides, handouts for the audience, and notes for the presenter. You can even create a slide show to post on the Web for family and friends to view.

In the past, presentations were delivered with transparencies, displayed using a flatbed overhead projector, and in some situations that technology may still be used. More commonly, however, presentations are delivered with an electronic slide show that uses a projector connected to a computer to display each slide. With an electronic slide show, you can animate slides and graphics, which helps control the pace of delivery and creates additional visual interest for the audience.

In this chapter, you create a PowerPoint presentation by adding, deleting, and modifying slides. You add graphics, apply a theme, and insert information in every slide. Finally, you add transitions to slides, preview the slide show, and then create speaker notes and handouts. In addition, you will identify some of the basic principles of effective presentations.

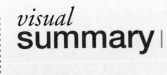

visual **summary** | In this chapter, you will create a presentation to inform an audience about the use of solar energy. When you are done, you will have created a complete presentation with the basic elements that are typically used. Figure 9.1 shows the audience handouts and one of the speaker notes that you will create for the presentation.

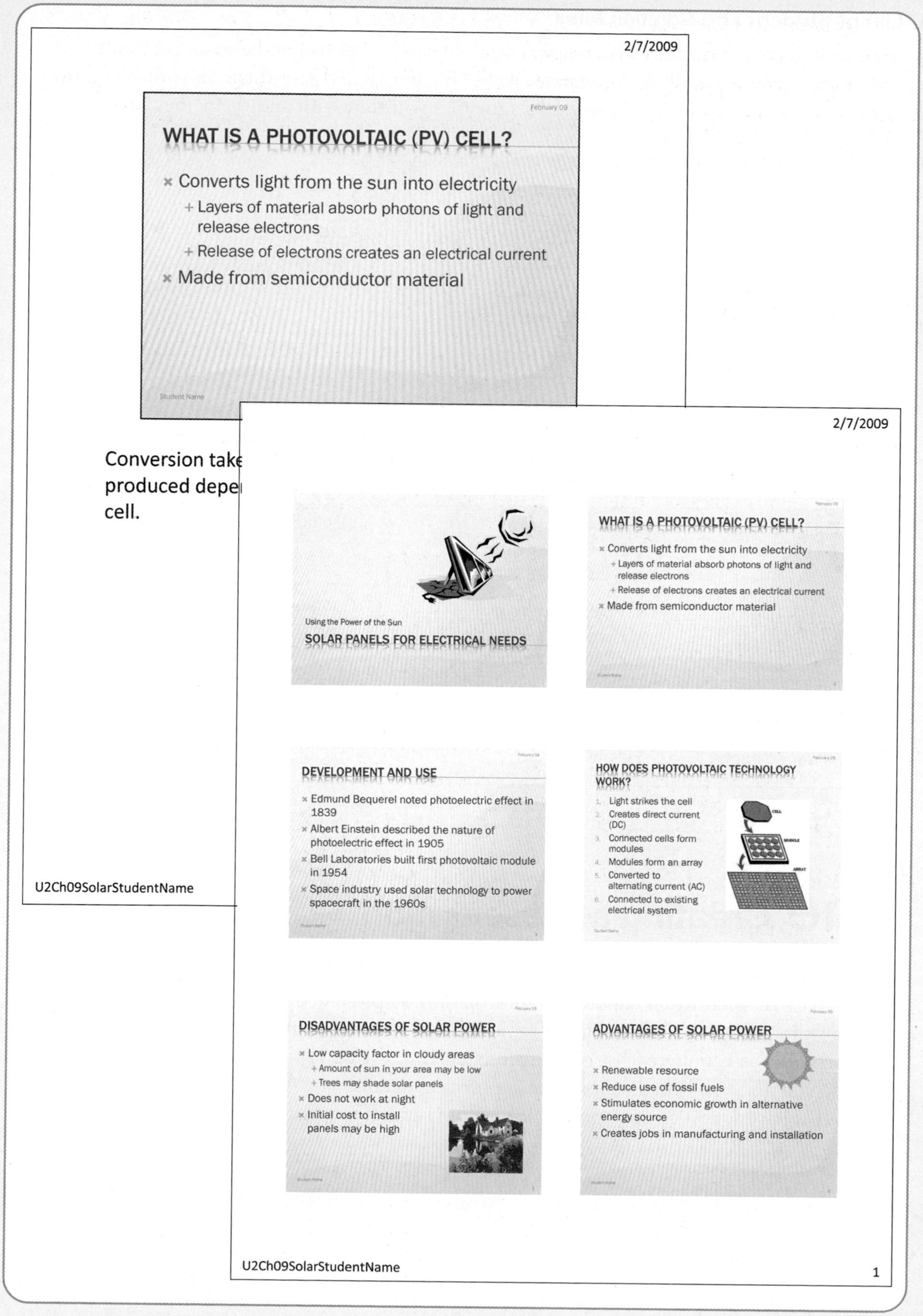

WHAT IS A PHOTOVOLTAIC (PV) CELL?

February 09

× Converts light from the sun into electricity
+ Layers of material absorb photons of light and release electrons
+ Release of electrons creates an electrical current
× Made from semiconductor material

Student Name

Conversion take
produced depe
cell.

Using the Power of the Sun
SOLAR PANELS FOR ELECTRICAL NEEDS

WHAT IS A PHOTOVOLTAIC (PV) CELL?

× Converts light from the sun into electricity
+ Layers of material absorb photons of light and release electrons
+ Release of electrons creates an electrical current
× Made from semiconductor material

DEVELOPMENT AND USE

× Edmund Bequerel noted photoelectric effect in 1839
× Albert Einstein described the nature of photoelectric effect in 1905
× Bell Laboratories built first photovoltaic module in 1954
× Space industry used solar technology to power spacecraft in the 1960s

HOW DOES PHOTOVOLTAIC TECHNOLOGY WORK?

1. Light strikes the cell
2. Creates direct current (DC)
3. Connected cells form modules
4. Modules form an array
5. Converted to alternating current (AC)
6. Connected to existing electrical system

CELL
MODULE
ARRAY

DISADVANTAGES OF SOLAR POWER

× Low capacity factor in cloudy areas
+ Amount of sun in your area may be low
+ Trees may shade solar panels
× Does not work at night
× Initial cost to install panels may be high

ADVANTAGES OF SOLAR POWER

× Renewable resource
× Reduce use of fossil fuels
× Stimulates economic growth in alternative energy source
× Creates jobs in manufacturing and installation

U2Ch09SolarStudentName

U2Ch09SolarStudentName

1

FIGURE 9.1 A, B

List of Student and Solution Files

In most cases, you will start with a new, empty file and enter text and data or paste content from other files. You will add your name to the file names and save them on your computer or portable memory device. Table 9.1 lists the files you start with and the names you give them when you save the files.

ASSIGNMENT	STUDENT SOURCE FILE:	SAVE AS:
Lessons 1–7	New presentation U2Ch09PhotoCell U2Ch09Alternatives	U2Ch09SolarStudentName
Skill Drill	New presentation U2Ch09Reserves U2Ch09Fueling	U2Ch09NaturalGasStudentName
Fix It	U2Ch09FixIt U2Ch09CookingOil U2Ch09BioDiesel	U2Ch09FixItStudentName
On the Job	U2Ch09Wind U2Ch09WindFarm U2Ch09WindSea	U2Ch09WindStudentName
	U2Ch09Geothermal U2Ch09Geysers U2Ch09HotSprings	U2Ch09GeothermalStudentName
On Your Own	U2Ch09GCCD New presentation	U2Ch09GCCDStudentName U2Ch09ConservationStudentName
Assess Your Progress	U2Ch09Assess	U2Ch09AssessStudentName

▶▶▶ *lesson*
ONE | Creating a Presentation

When you create a presentation, start with the content. Answer the questions: What needs to be covered? In what order should the information be presented? A presentation consists of a series of slides. Each slide has a main topic listed as the title of the slide, and the body of the slide typically is a bulleted list of items related to the title topic. It is similar to an outline because you go from broad concepts to supporting details.

In this lesson, you create a presentation from scratch by typing text in slides.

to create a presentation

1 Start PowerPoint 2007. On the Quick Access toolbar, click the Save button . In the Save As dialog box, navigate to the location where you are saving your files. Create a new folder named `Chapter09`. In the new folder, save the file with the name `U2Ch09SolarStudentName`

2 Examine the PowerPoint window, which opens in Normal view, and identify the elements shown in Figure 9.2. *Normal view* is used to create the presentation and includes a *Slides/Outline pane* on the left, a *Notes pane* at the bottom, and a *Slide pane* in center of the screen. The Slides/Outline pane on the left displays the content as thumbnail slides or in an outline. The outline helps you focus on the flow of ideas. The Slide pane in the center helps you focus on one particular topic at a time. As you create your presentation, you may find that you want to add notes to help you remember things you want to say when you cover a particular topic. Notes can be added as you create the slides by inserting comments in the Notes pane of the Normal view. The first slide displays the title slide *layout,* which is an arrangement of *placeholders.* Placeholders are preformatted areas that define the type of information to place in each area on the slide. They typically contain instructions about how to proceed. For example, the first placeholder on the title slide displays *Click to add title,* and the second placeholder displays *Click to add subtitle.*

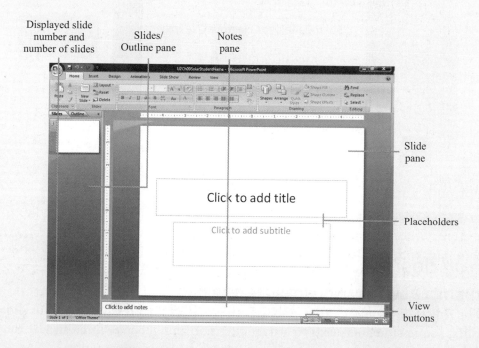

FIGURE 9.2

3 Click in the *Click to add title* placeholder and type: `Solar Panels for Electrical Needs` Notice that on the Home tab, in the Font group, the Font

Size box displays *44,* the Font box displays *Calibri (Headings),* and in the Paragraph group, the *Center* alignment button is selected. Also notice that as you type on the slide, the same text displays in the Slides tab or Outline tab on the left, depending on which tab is currently selected.

4 **Click in the *Click to add subtitle* placeholder and type** `Using the Power of the Sun` **to add the subtitle for your presentation.** Notice that in the Font group, the Font Size box displays *32,* the Font box displays *Calibri (body),* and in the Paragraph group, the *Center* button is again selected. The font, font size, and alignment of the text are preformatted within the placeholder.

5 **On the left side of the screen, click the Slides tab if necessary to display the thumbnail of the slide, and then compare your screen with Figure 9.3.**

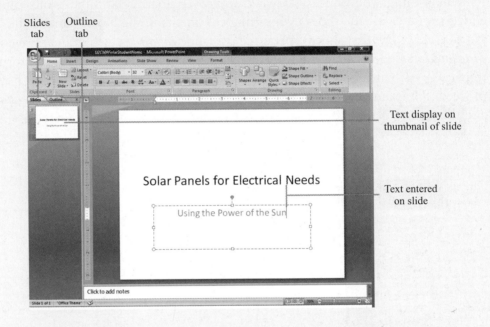

FIGURE 9.3

good **design...**

THE TITLE SLIDE ANNOUNCES THE TOPIC
The title slide should clearly announce the topic of the presentation. This slide creates a first impression and needs to attract attention and generate interest. Use the subtitle area for presenter information or for a subtitle for your presentation.

The main working view in PowerPoint is Normal view. Here you create the presentation. You can add text to slides using the Slide pane or the Outline tab.

to enter text using the slide pane

1   **On the Home tab, in the Slides group, click the top part of the New Slide button.** A new slide displays and by default the Title and Content layout is applied. This is the slide layout that is typically used to add content. You can type text in the slide or use one of the icons displayed on the slide to add a specific type of content such as a graphic image, table, or chart.

2   **Click in the *Click to add title* placeholder and type** What Is a Photovoltaic (PV) Cell?

3   **Press** Ctrl + ⏎Enter **to move the insertion point to the body of the slide. Type** Converts light from the sun into electricity **and then press** ⏎Enter. The first ***bullet point***—a line of text that is preceded by a small dot or other symbol—is added, and the insertion point moves to the second line. Alternatively, you can click in the placeholder to move the insertion point to the placeholder for the body of the slide.

4   **Press** Tab↹ **to indent the bullet point to a second level and type** Layers of material absorb photons of light and release electrons Alternatively, on the Home tab, in the Paragraph group, click the Increase List Level button ⮕. Think of a list as levels where the first level is the highest, most important level and the second level is the next most important. Increasing the list level moves a point from first to second level, from second to third level, and so forth. As you increase indentation, the information becomes more detailed and specific.

5   **Press** ⏎Enter **and type** Release of electrons creates an electrical current This adds another point at the same level.

6   **Press** ⏎Enter, **and then hold down** ⬆Shift **and press** Tab↹ **to move the bullet point up one level.** Alternatively, on the Home tab, in the Paragraph group, click the Decrease List Level ⬅ button to move the bullet point to the first level.

7   **Type** Made from semiconductor material **and then compare your screen to Figure 9.4. Save** 💾 **your presentation.**

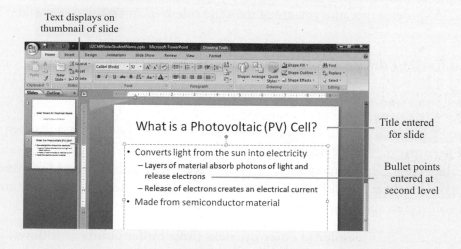

FIGURE 9.4

You can also add text to a slide using the Outline tab.

to enter text using the outline tab

1 On the Slides/Outline pane, click the Outline tab to display the presentation outline. In the displayed outline, click to the right of the last word: *material.*

2 Press ⏎Enter, which adds a bullet point at the same level on this slide. On the Home tab, in the Paragraph group, click the Decrease List Level button 🔲 to create a new slide 3, as shown in Figure 9.5.

New slide displays
in Outline tab

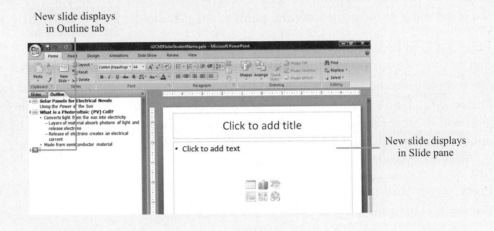

New slide displays
in Slide pane

FIGURE 9.5

3 In the outline, type `Development and Use` and then press ⏎Enter to move to the next line, which creates another new slide. When you are working in the Outline tab, pressing ⏎Enter moves the insertion point to a new line at the same level. In this case, because you are at the slide title level, it creates a new slide, ready for a new slide title.

4 Press Tab⇆ to change the inserted line to the level of a bullet point. Pressing Tab⇆ indents the new line, moving it from the level of a new slide to the level of a bullet point under the Development and Use slide topic.

5 Type `Photoelectric effect noted in 1839 by Edmund Bequerel` and then press ⏎Enter. As you type, the text displays both in the Outline tab and on the Slide pane. The name *Bequerel* is underlined with a red wavy line because it is not recognized by the installed dictionary. In Lesson 7, after the presentation is created, you will review spelling for all of the slides.

6 Continue in this manner to enter the next three bullet points as follows, and then compare your screen with Figure 9.6.

```
Albert Einstein described the nature of photoelectric
effect in 1905
Bell Laboratories built first photovoltaic module in 1954
Space industry used solar technology to power spacecraft in
the 1960s
```

Bullet points added to
slide in the Outline tab

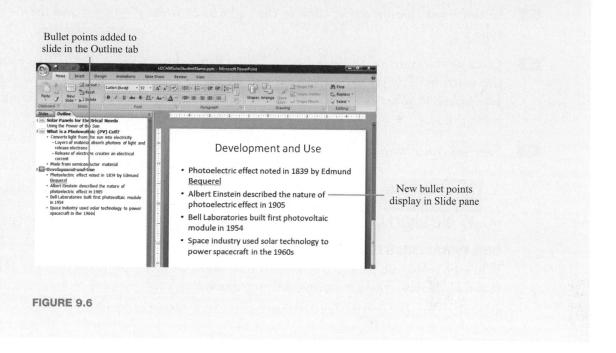

New bullet points
display in Slide pane

FIGURE 9.6

Use the same editing tools you use in Word to edit the content of a slide.

to edit slide content

1 On slide 3, using either the Slide pane or the Outline tab, in the first bullet point, select *Edmund Bequerel*. Point to the selected text, and when the ⬚ displays, drag the selected text to the beginning of the bullet point, as shown in Figure 9.7.

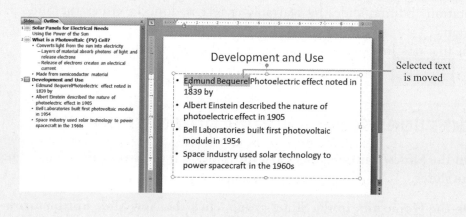

Selected text
is moved

FIGURE 9.7

2 Select the word *noted* and use the drag-and-drop method to move it between *Bequerel* and *Photoelectric*.

3 Click between *Bequerel* and *noted* and press `Spacebar` to add a space between these two words.

4 In the word *Photoelectric*, click to the right of *P*, press `⬅Backspace` and then type p

5 Click at the right of 1839 and press `Delete` three times to remove the space and the word *by*. The edited bullet point should read *Edmund Bequerel noted the photoelectric effect in 1839.* This parallels the phrasing of the other bullet points on the slide.

6 Save 💾 your work.

. . . .

good design...

USE PARALLEL STRUCTURE

When possible, use parallel phrasing in your bullet points. This helps the flow of content and creates a rhythm during the presentation.

. . . .

▶▶▶ *lesson*

two | Adding Slides to a Presentation and Editing Content

Slides can be added to a presentation using several methods. You can add slides one at a time by entering text, as you have been doing. You can also import text from a Word outline into a presentation, insert slides from another presentation, or duplicate an existing slide within a presentation. Editing slides by rearranging text is done in either the Slide pane or the Outline tab.

In the first task in this lesson, you insert a slide from another presentation.

to add slides from another presentation

1 On the Slides/Outline pane click the Slides tab to display thumbnail images of the slides.

2 On the Home tab, in the Slides group, click the New Slide button arrow—the bottom portion of the button—to display the menu options shown in

Figure 9.8. Here you can select a different slide layout for a new slide. You can also duplicate an existing slide, create slides from a Word outline, or reuse slides from another presentation.

New slide layout options

Options for importing or duplicating slides

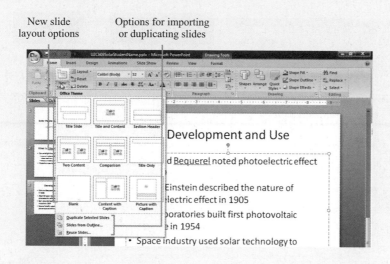

FIGURE 9.8

3 At the end of the displayed list, click **Reuse Slides** to display the Reuse Slides task pane on the right side of the window.

4 Click the Browse button, and then click Browse File. In the Browse dialog box, navigate to the location where your files for this chapter are stored. Locate and click the file *U2Ch09Alternatives*, and then click Open. Thumbnail images of the slides and the first part of each slide title display in the Reuse Slides pane, as shown in Figure 9.9.

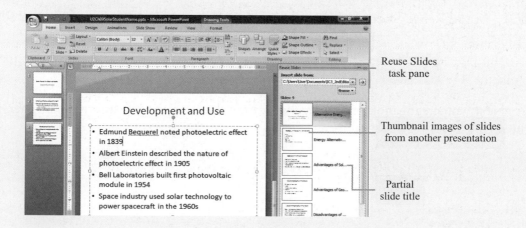

Reuse Slides task pane

Thumbnail images of slides from another presentation

Partial slide title

FIGURE 9.9

5 **Point to the third slide that displays the partial title** *Advantages of Sol.* When you point to the slide, an enlarged image displays to enable you to see the full contents of the slide, as shown in Figure 9.10.

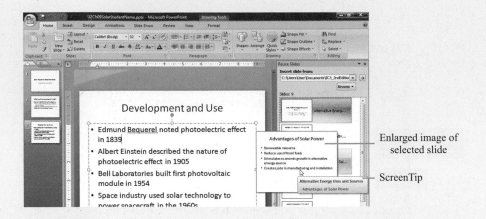

FIGURE 9.10

6 **Click the enlarged image to insert it as the fourth slide in your presentation.** If the slide that you see displayed is not the one you want, merely move the mouse pointer to another location.

If you have problems...

DID YOU INSERT THE WRONG SLIDE?

If you inserted the wrong slide, with the slide selected on the Slides tab, press Delete to remove the slide from the presentation.

7 **In the Reuse Slides task pane, click the Close button** X. **Save** 💾 **your file.**

Next, you create another slide by duplicating the slide you just inserted, and then you edit the text.

to duplicate a slide and edit text

1 With slide 4 as the active slide, on the Home tab, in the Slides group, click the New Slide button arrow. From the displayed list, click Duplicate Selected Slides. A copy of the currently selected slide is added as slide 5, which displays on the Slide pane.

2 With slide 5 displayed on the Slide pane, click in the title and replace *Advantages* with `Disadvantages`

3 Select the list of bullet points and replace them with the following list:

`Amount of sun in your area may be low`
`Trees may shade solar panels`
`Low capacity factor in cloudy areas`
`Initial cost to install panels may be high`

4 On the Slide pane, next to the third bulleted line, click the bullet point to select this line. Point to the selected text and drag it up to the first bullet point position, as shown in Figure 9.11. When you see a faint blue insertion line, release the mouse button to complete the move.

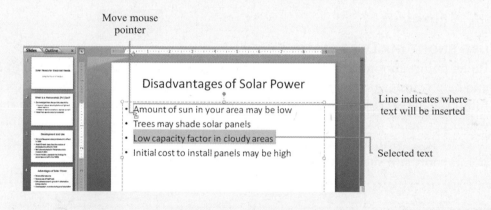

FIGURE 9.11

5 Click in the second bullet point: *Amount of sun in your area may be low.* On the Home tab, in the Paragraph group, click the Increase List Level button to move this to the second level under the first topic listed.

6 Click in the third line—*Trees may shade solar panels*—and repeat the process to move this to a second-level subpoint.

7 Click at the end of this line, after the word *panels*. Press ↵Enter and type `Does not work at night` and then in the Paragraph group, click the Decrease List Level button to move this point to a first-level topic.

8 Save 💾 your presentation and compare your screen with Figure 9.12.

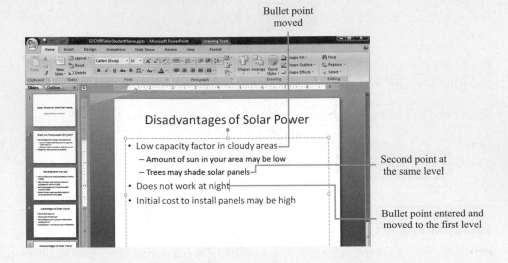

FIGURE 9.12

good **design...**

USE SHORT BULLET POINTS

Bullet points announce topics in a logical order, provide an organizational framework, and help you stay on track when making the presentation. The presenter is expected to fill in the details. Limit the number of bullet points on each slide and the number of words per bullet point. A good rule of thumb is the six-by-six rule: Limit a slide to six lines of text with six words per line. Do not use sentences. In general, keep bullet points short and succinct, and do not use periods.

▶▶▶ *lesson*
three | Adding Graphic Elements

Many of the slide layout options include a content placeholder that offers you a choice of content items to include on a slide. After selecting the slide layout, click the icon for the type of content item that you want to add, such as clip art or pictures. The placeholder determines where the graphic is positioned on the slide and controls the size of the item. You can also add a graphic element to an existing slide without using a content icon. Then you can move and position the item anywhere on the slide. Graphics are added to illustrate a point, add humor, or create interest, but should not be added simply for the sake of adding a graphic. They should be relevant to the topic and enhance the idea that is being presented.

In this lesson, you add a slide that includes text and a picture, and then add clip art to existing slides.

to navigate between slides and Insert a slide with a picture

1 **On the vertical scroll bar, click the Previous Slide button ⬆ two times to move from slide 5 to slide 3.** The arrows at the end of the vertical scroll bar move up and down the presentation one slide at a time.

2 **On the vertical scroll bar, drag the scroll box up the presentation to slide 1 and notice the ScreenTip that displays as you move the scroll box.** A ScreenTip displays the title of each slide and the slide number as you move the scroll box up and down a presentation.

3 **On the Slides tab, click slide 3 to make this the active slide.** Use any of the three techniques used in steps 1, 2, and 3 to navigate between slides in your presentation.

4 **On the Home tab, in the Slides group, click the top part of the New Slide button to insert a new slide after slide 3. In the title placeholder, type** How Does Photovoltaic Technology Work?

5 **Click in the body of the slide. On the Home tab, in the Paragraph group, click the Numbering button ▤▾ to change from a bulleted list to a numbered list.** Use a numbered list for a sequential list, steps in a procedure, or a logical progression in the content. If you have already entered data, select the entire list before clicking the Numbering button.

6 **Type the following list and notice that numbers are used instead of bullets:**

Light strikes the cell
Creates direct current (DC)
Connected cells form modules
Modules form an array
Converted to alternating current (AC)
Connected to existing electrical systems

7 **On the Home tab, in the Slides group, click the Layout button. From the displayed gallery, click the Two Content option.** You can also select the slide layout when you first add a new slide, by clicking the New Slide button arrow and then selecting the slide layout from the gallery that displays. When you change the slide layout, the numbered list displays on the left and a new placeholder box displays on the right. You could type more text here or you could add graphics, chart elements, a table, or other content items by clicking one of the six icons displayed, as shown in Figure 9.13.

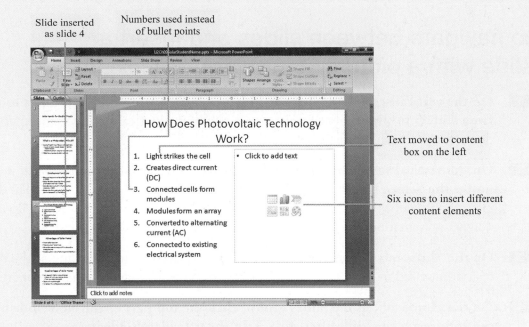

FIGURE 9.13

8 In the right placeholder, point to each of the icons to display the ScreenTip that identifies the type of element that will be inserted when you click that icon.

9 Click the Insert Picture from File icon. In the Insert Picture dialog box, navigate to the folder where the files for this chapter are stored. Locate and click the file *U2Ch09Photocell* to select it.

10 Click Insert to insert the image and close the dialog box. The image is inserted on the right side of the slide and displays sizing handles at the corners and sides of the image. The Picture Tools Format contextual tab displays on the Ribbon.

11 Point to the upper left corner sizing handle, and when the ⬉ pointer displays, drag up to the left to position the top of the image even with the top of the numbered list, as shown in Figure 9.14.

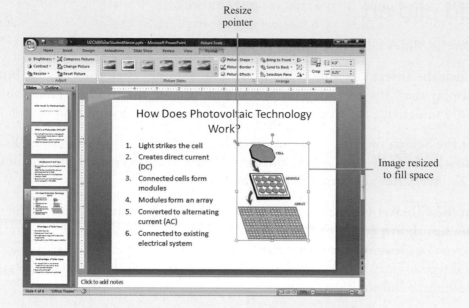

Resize
pointer

Image resized
to fill space

FIGURE 9.14

12 Save 💾 your file.

··

good **design...**

INCLUDE IMAGES TO ILLUSTRATE A CONCEPT

Add images when they add information to a presentation or illustrate a concept. Do not add images just to fill up space. Be sure the image is relevant to the topic.

··

Clip art can also be used to add visual effects that help convey a concept, add humor, or create interest.

to add clip art

1 On the Slides tab, click slide 5 to make it the active slide.

2 Click the Insert tab, and in the Illustrations group, click the Clip Art button to display the Clip Art task pane on the right side of the window. Here you enter a word to describe the type of image that you want to include on your slide.

3 In the Search for box, select any text that may display and type sun Click the *Results should be* box arrow, and clear all check marks except the one next to Clip Art. Click the arrow to close the list.

4 In the Clip Art task pane, next to *sun*, click the Go button. Point to the image of the sun shown in Figure 9.15. The selected image displays a border around it, and a ScreenTip describes the image: size in pixels, *355 (w) x 353 (h)*; storage space, *61 KB*; and type of image, *PNG*. The images displayed in your Clip Art task pane may differ from those shown in the figure.

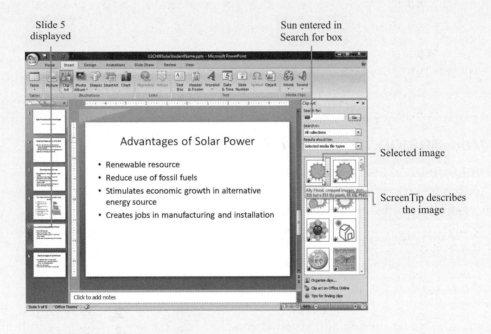

FIGURE 9.15

5 Click the image of the sun to insert it in the slide.

6 Point to the inserted image, and when the ⬚ pointer displays, drag the image to the lower right corner of the slide, as shown in Figure 9.16.

Original
image position

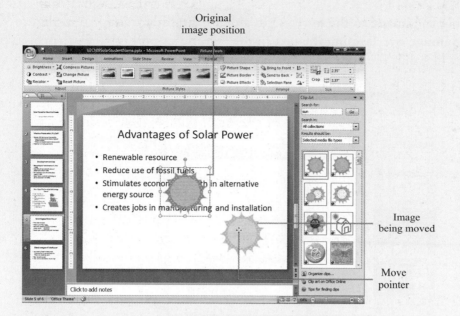

Image
being moved

Move
pointer

FIGURE 9.16

7 **Click slide 6 to make it the active slide. In the Clip Art task pane, in the Search for box, select *sun* and type** homes **Press** ⏎Enter **to activate the clip art search.** If you are connected to the Internet, the list of images will include images from Microsoft Online, which gives you more images to consider.

8 **Click the image shown in Figure 9.17 to insert it into slide 6.**

Image inserted in the
middle of the slide

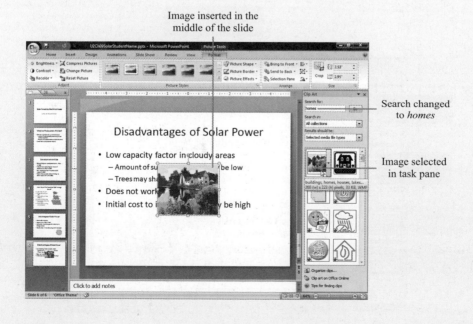

Search changed
to *homes*

Image selected
in task pane

FIGURE 9.17

9 **Drag the image to the lower right side of the slide, as shown in Figure 9.18, with the image overlapping the text in the last bullet point.** When there is a space conflict like this, the text can be forced to a second line or you can resize the image.

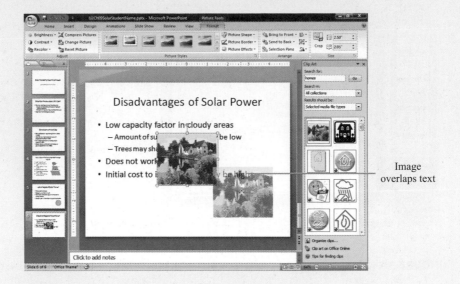

FIGURE 9.18

10 **In the last bullet point, click to the immediate left of the word** *panels.* **Press** (⬆Shift), **and then press** (⏎Enter) **to insert a manual line break in this bullet point.** The text is wrapped to a second line and is no longer hidden by the inserted clip art.

11 **In the Clip Art task pane, click the Close button** ☒. **Compare your screen with Figure 9.19, and then Save** 🖫 **your file.**

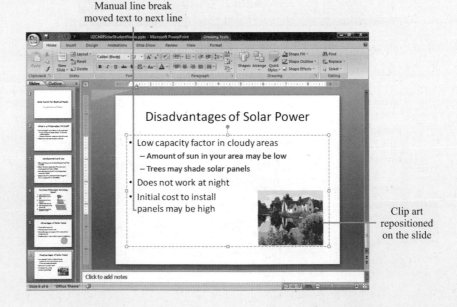

FIGURE 9.19

▶▶▶ *lesson*
four | Applying a Theme to a Presentation

After the content is written and organized, apply a *theme*: a collection of design elements, fonts, colors, and graphics that create a uniform look for a presentation. When you select a theme, keep in mind the environment in which the presentation will be made and the equipment that will be used. With some projection devices, the edges of the screen are black, so a design with a dark or black background works best. If you are using a traditional projection device, a light or white background may be preferable. Room lighting has a great impact on a presentation. Lights directly in front of the screen will create a glare on the screen and make it difficult for the audience to see. All of these issues need to be considered when you apply a theme to your presentation.

In this lesson, you add a theme to the slides and then modify the theme color and the background on one slide.

to apply a theme

1 **Click the Design tab. In the Themes group, click the More button** ⟱ **to display the Themes gallery, as shown in Figure 9.20.** The currently applied design is

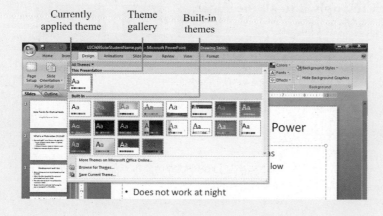

FIGURE 9.20

displayed at the top, followed by Custom themes (if any) and then Built-In themes. The currently applied theme does not include any graphics or background design elements. When you change a theme, it can affect the font and font size, background color, if any, and other graphic design elements.

2 **Slowly move the mouse pointer over the theme templates to display a live preview of each design on the slide.** After a few moments, the slide theme displays on the currently active slide. If you don't like your first selection, simply move to another theme. When you point to a theme, a ScreenTip displays its name. Be cautious in your selection, as some themes may make your content unreadable.

3 **In the last row, point to the *Trek* theme, as shown in Figure 9.21.**

Trek theme
highlighted

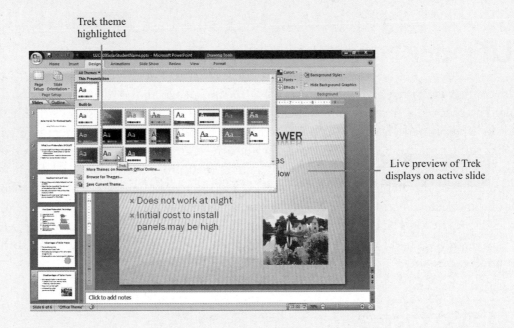

Live preview of Trek
displays on active slide

FIGURE 9.21

4 **Click Trek to apply it to all the slides.**

to extend your knowledge

TEST YOUR PRESENTATION IN THE ACTUAL SETTING
If possible, test your slides in the room in which you will make the presentation. This gives you the opportunity to see how it will look with the available lighting. You may want to dim the lights just in front of the screen to avoid having a glare on the screen. This is not always possible, however, and if you use a dark slide background, the light glaring on the screen can make the slides hard to read. If that is the case, you can easily change the theme background to a color that will be easier for the audience to see. If it is not possible to test the slides in the room prior to your presentation, then print the slides and place them on the floor. If the content is readable from a standing position, then the slides will most likely be readable in a normal room.

After you have applied a theme, you can modify the theme for all slides by changing the colors or fonts. You can also change the background style and hide background graphics on selected slides.

to modify a theme

1 **Click slide 1 to make it active. On the Design tab, in the Themes group, click the Colors button to display the Colors gallery.** Different theme color palettes can be applied.

2 **Move the pointer to different color themes to see the live preview displayed on slide 1. Point at Paper to preview this theme color on the slide, as shown in Figure 9.22.**

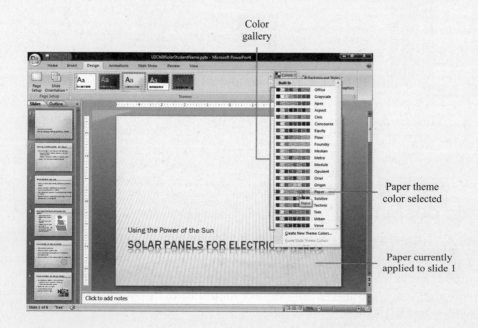

FIGURE 9.22

3 Click the Paper theme color to apply it to all of the slides.

4 In the Themes group, click the Fonts button. Move your pointer over the different font options to see the live preview of the fonts on your slide. Click the Font button again to close the list without changing the font.

5 Click slide 4. On the Design tab, in the Background group, click the Hide Background Graphics check box. Because the title is on two lines, the horizontal line between the title and the content was removed.

6 In the Background group, click the Background Styles button. Point to the different styles to see the live preview applied to the selected slide.

7 In the second column, right-click the first option—Style 2—and then click *Apply to Selected Slides* to apply this background to slide 4 only. This plainer background is a better choice for the slide because of the image that is on the slide; it is less visually confusing.

8 Compare your screen with Figure 9.23, and then Save 🖫 your presentation.

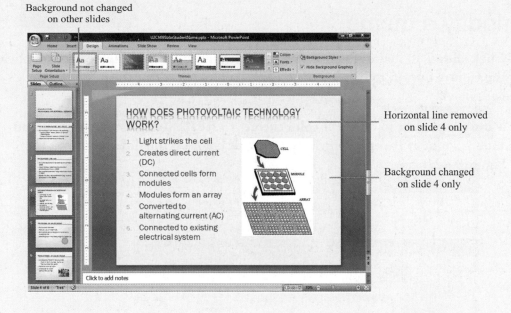

FIGURE 9.23

···

good **design...**

USE A THEME THAT COMPLEMENTS THE TOPIC

The first consideration in selecting a theme is to choose one that will work in the environment in which the presentation will be made. The next consideration is to select a theme that will complement the subject matter of the presentation and be appropriate for the intended audience.

···

After a theme has been added, it is a good idea to review each slide and make adjustments that might be necessary due to a rearrangement of bullet points, font, or graphics that occurred when the theme was applied.

to review and adjust a presentation

1 **Click slide 1.** The top of this slide is a large open area that could benefit from a topical graphic.

2 **Click the Insert tab, and in the Illustrations group, click the Clip Art button.**

3 **In the displayed Clip Art task pane, in the Search for box, select the existing text, type** `solar panels` **and then press** ⏎Enter.

4 **Scroll the list as necessary, and click the image shown in Figure 9.24 to insert it in the title slide.**

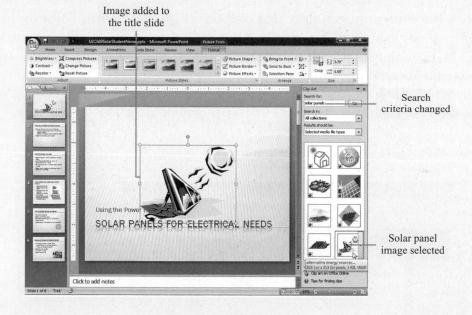

FIGURE 9.24

5 Drag the image to the upper right side of the slide, as shown in Figure 9.25.

Image repositioned
on the slide

FIGURE 9.25

6 Click each slide and review the overall composition of the text and any graphic elements. Stop on slide 5.

7 In slide 5, drag the sun clip art image up until it is just below the horizontal line in the title placeholder.

8 Click the content placeholder that contains the bullet points. Point to the top center sizing handle. When the ⬍ pointer displays, drag down approximately 1/2 inch, as shown in Figure 9.26. Use the vertical ruler on the left side to help judge the distance. Moving the image and adjusting the size and location of the content placeholder helps to balance the content on this slide. Placeholders on slides can be resized and moved just like any other graphic element.

Vertical ruler used   Pointer shape changes as
to guide size   you resize the placeholder

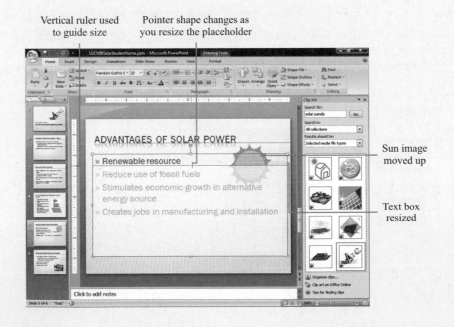

Sun image
moved up

Text box
resized

FIGURE 9.26

9 Close ✕ the Clip Art task pane and Save 💾 the file.

►►► *lesson*
five | Adding Information to the Header and Footer

Information—such as the author's name, file name, presentation topic, date, or slide number—can be added to the header or footer area of each slide. Depending on the theme that has been applied, the information that is added may display in the header area. The placeholders that contain the information can be formatted or moved to another location for all slides, using *slide masters*—slide layout images that contain all of the placeholder formats for each slide layout within a theme.

to add information to the slide header and footer area

1 **Click the Insert tab. In the Text group, click the Header & Footer button.** The displayed Header and Footer dialog box includes a Slide tab, used to add information to the slides, and a Notes and Handouts tab that is used to add information to the handouts or notes that may be created.

2 **On the Slide tab, click the Date and time check box.** In the Preview area, notice that the upper right corner of the preview area is dark. This is the location where the date and time will be inserted.

3 **Under the Update automatically option button, in the box with the date, click the arrow to display the date formatting options.** If the Update automatically option is selected, the date on the presentation will always show the current date. You can include the time if you want and change the format to one of the options displayed. To set a specific date that is not updated, click the Fixed option button and format the date using the text box that displays under the Fixed option button.

4 **From the displayed list, click the option that displays the full name of the current month and the current year, such as *October 10*.**

5 **Click the Slide Number check box, and notice that the lower right corner of the preview area is dark, which indicates the location of the slide number.**

6 **Click the Footer check box, and in the text box, type** `Student Name` **using your own name.** The center area on top of the Preview graphic is dark to indicate the location of this information on the slide. Even though this data is listed as a footer, it will display in the center of the header area on the slide in the Trek theme.

7 Click the *Don't show on title slide* check box to select it, and then compare your screen with Figure 9.27.

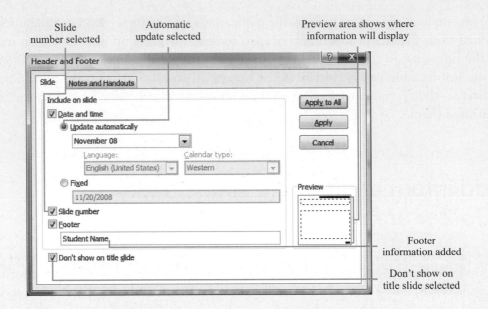

Slide number selected

Automatic update selected

Preview area shows where information will display

Footer information added

Don't show on title slide selected

FIGURE 9.27

8 Click the Apply to All button. Click slide 1 and verify that the header and footer information does not appear on this slide. Click slide 2 and observe the placement of the information on the slide, as shown in Figure 9.28.

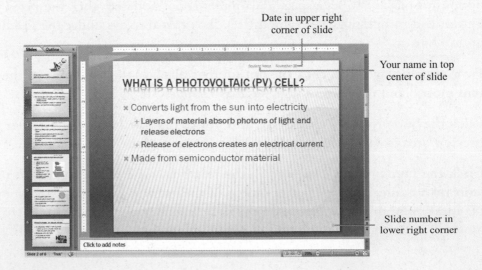

Date in upper right corner of slide

Your name in top center of slide

Slide number in lower right corner

FIGURE 9.28

good design...

USE HEADERS AND FOOTERS TO DOCUMENT OWNERSHIP

The header and footer area is a good place to document the company or author of the presentation. You may also want to display the date of presentation, slide numbers, or file name.

The location and format of the information in the header and footer placeholders can be changed. To do this, you use the **Slide Master view**—a view that contains each slide layout, where you can change placeholder formatting characteristics for the selected theme.

to change the location and format of header and footer information

1 **Click the View tab. In the Presentation Views group, click the Slide Master button.** The pane on the left changes to display slide masters for each layout template that is available for this theme. The Slide pane displays the Title and Content slide master layout—the layout used for the currently active slide. See Figure 9.29.

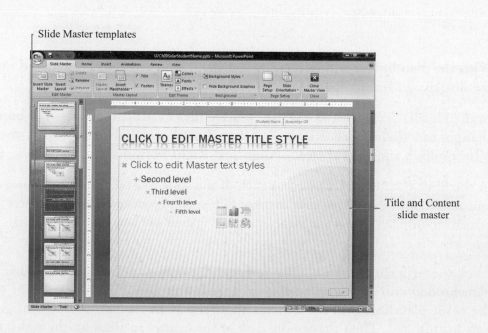

Slide Master templates

Title and Content slide master

FIGURE 9.29

2 In the Master Slide pane on the left, click the first slide master listed to make it the active slide master. In the Slide pane, at the top center of the slide master, click the border of the placeholder that contains your name—**Student Name.** Sizing handles display around the perimeter of the placeholder, and the dotted line changes to a solid line. Now you can format or move this placeholder.

3 Point to the edge of the selected placeholder, and when the 🔲 pointer displays, drag the placeholder to the lower left corner of the slide, below the content placeholder, as shown in Figure 9.30.

Placeholder moved
to the footer area

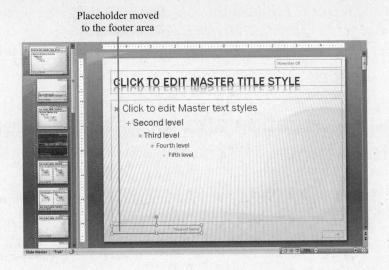

FIGURE 9.30

4 With the placeholder still selected, select the text in the placeholder, and on the displayed Mini toolbar, click the Align Text Left button 📄.

5 In the Header area, click in the date placeholder to make it active—the border changes to a dashed line. Right-click the selected placeholder to display the Mini toolbar, and then click the Align Text Right button 📄.

6 In the Slide Master pane, point to each of the slide master thumbnail images and notice the ScreenTips that display. When you point to each slide master, a ScreenTip displays the layout name and the numbers of the slides that use that layout.

7 Click the fifth slide master—*Two Content Layout*—to select it. Notice that the placeholder with your name displays in the footer area. If necessary, right-click the name placeholder in the footer, and on the Mini toolbar, click the Align Text Left button 📄. Then change the date in the header to align on the right, and then compare your screen with Figure 9.31.

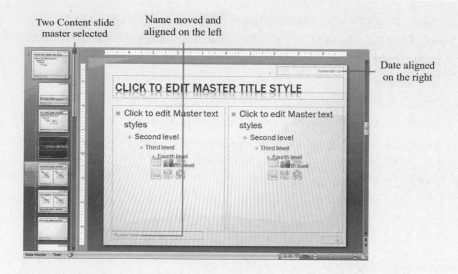

Two Content slide master selected

Name moved and aligned on the left

Date aligned on the right

CLICK TO EDIT MASTER TITLE STYLE

FIGURE 9.31

8 Click the third slide master: *Title and Content Layout.* On this slide master, the alignment has been changed, but the Student Name placeholder is still in the header area on the slide layout.

9 Using the technique you just practiced, drag the placeholder from the header to the lower left corner of the footer area under the main content placeholder. If necessary, right-click the name placeholder in the footer, and on the Mini toolbar, click the Align Text Left button ⊟. If necessary change the date alignment to be right aligned.

10 On the status bar, click the Normal button ⊞ to close the Slide Master view and return to Normal view.

11 Scroll through each slide to verify that your name displays in the lower left corner of the footer, that it is left aligned, and that the date is right aligned in the header. Save ⊟ your file.

good design...

REVIEW HEADERS AND FOOTERS DATA

Review the placement of data in the header and footer areas and adjust it as necessary to be sure that it does not interfere with other text or data on a slide.

▶▶▶ *lesson*

SIX | Adding Slide Transitions and Viewing a Slide Show

In addition to the Normal view and the Slide Master view, PowerPoint also has a ***Slide Sorter view*** that displays thumbnails of slides on a single page. Here you can rearrange slides to adjust the flow of topics and add ***transitions***. Slide transitions control the direction, timing, speed, and manner in which slides enter and exit the screen during a slide show.

In this lesson, you review the slides in Slide Sorter view and add slide transitions, then view the slides in a slide show.

to rearrange slides in slide sorter view

1 **On the status bar, click the Slide Sorter button** 🔳 **to display the Slide Sorter view.** Alternatively, click the View tab, and in the Presentation Views group, click the Slider Sorter button.

2 **On the View tab, in the Zoom group, click the Zoom button. In the displayed Zoom dialog box, click the 100% option button, and then click OK.** The size of the thumbnail images is increased so that it is easier to see the content. When you have a lot of slides in a presentation, Slide Sorter is the best view to use for rearranging slides because you can see more of them on the screen at one time. It is like looking at photographs on a light table.

3 **Click slide 6 to select it.** When it is selected, it is surrounded by a dark border.

4 **Drag slide 6, *Disadvantages*, to the left of slide 5, *Advantages*. When a line displays between slide 4 and 5, as shown in Figure 9.32, release the mouse button.** Placing the Advantages slide at the end creates a more positive conclusion.

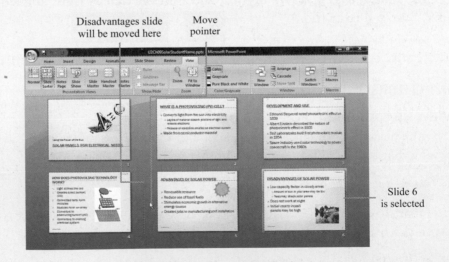

FIGURE 9.32

Transitions add motion to a presentation and make it less static and more interesting. You can select a transition scheme to apply to all of the slides, to each slide individually, or you can apply a random transition scheme that will vary the transition for every slide each time the presentation is shown.

to add transitions

1 **In Slide Sorter view, click slide 1, press ⬆Shift, and then click slide 6 to select all of the slides.** Alternatively, press Ctrl + A to select all of the slides. By selecting the slides first, you designate which slides will be affected by the transition.

2 **Click the Animations tab. In the Transitions to This Slide group, click the More button ⬇ to expand the Transitions gallery, as shown in Figure 9.33.** The transitions are arranged in groups. Each transition button displays an image to indicate the direction in which the slide will move. When you point to a button, a ScreenTip displays the name of that transition.

Transitions gallery

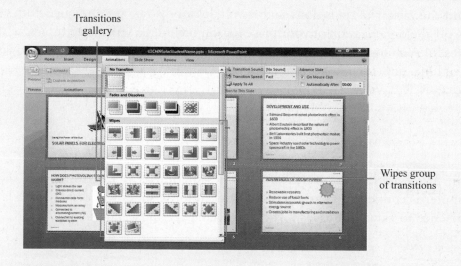

Wipes group of transitions

FIGURE 9.33

3 **Under Wipes, in the first row, locate and click the Wedge transition.** The transition is applied to all the selected slides and the gallery closes. The row in which the selected transition displays in the gallery becomes the active row that displays in the Transitions to This Slide group. A small star on the left under each slide indicates that a transition has been applied to the slide.

4 **In the Transitions to This Slide group, click the More button ⬇ again and try some of the other slide transition options.**

5 **Display the Transitions gallery again. Scroll the list, and under Stripes and Bars, locate and click the Blinds Horizontal button.**

6 In the Transitions to This Slide group, click the Transition Speed arrow, and then click Medium. Each time you make a change, it is quickly demonstrated on the selected slides.

7 In the Preview group, click the Preview button to test the transition on all of the slides. The Preview button demonstrates the transition and more accurately represents the speed.

8 Click slide 1, which deselects the other slides. Display the Transitions gallery, and under the Wipes group, locate and click the *Wheel Clockwise, 4 Spokes* button. This changes the transition on the first slide only.

9 On the status bar, click the Normal 🔲 button. Save 💾 your presentation.

....

good design...

APPLY TRANSITIONS

Add transitions to create motion and generate interest. Do not overdo it, however. Limit the variety of transitions so that you do not distract the audience from your message. If the organization of your presentation includes a few major topics, with several slides for each topic, a change in the slide transition effect can help signal to your audience that a new topic is beginning.

....

Use the *Slide Show view* to deliver your presentation as an electronic slide show. When your computer is connected to an overhead projector, the slides will display on a large screen for the audience to view. In this task, you practice navigating a slide show.

to view a slide show

1 With slide 1 as the active slide, on the status bar, click the Slide Show button. The first slide displays on the screen with the clockwise four-spoke transition that was applied to this slide.

2 Point to the lower left corner of the slide until you locate the four navigation buttons. Beginning with the left-most button, click each button to observe its function. The left-pointing arrow—Previous button—moves to the previous slide; because this is the first slide, your computer may ding because it cannot perform this action. The pen icon displays a list of options for writing instruments that you could use on the slide; the default is to display the normal mouse pointer. The menu icon displays a navigational list for moving between slides. The right arrow—Next button—moves to the next slide; slide 2 displays.

3 **In the middle of slide 2, right-click to display a shortcut menu. Point to Go to Slide to display the submenu shown in Figure 9.34.** Here you can select a specific slide that you want to display.

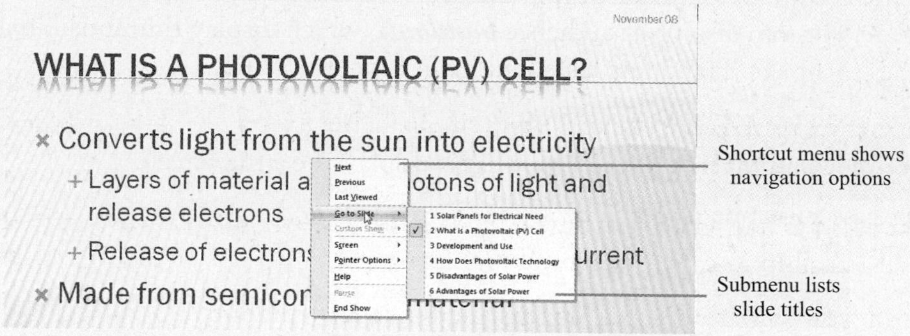

November 08

WHAT IS A PHOTOVOLTAIC (PV) CELL?

× Converts light from the sun into electricity
  + Layers of material a[...]otons of light and release electrons
  + Release of electron[...]urrent
× Made from semicon[...]material

Shortcut menu shows navigation options

Submenu lists slide titles

FIGURE 9.34

4 **From the displayed list, click *4 How Does Photovoltaic Technology* to display the fourth slide.**

5 **On the keyboard, press ⬅ to move back to slide 3.** Use the ⬅ key to move back and the ➡ or ↵Enter key to advance to the next slide.

6 **Right-click to display the shortcut menu. Click Previous to view the slide that comes before the slide that is currently displayed.** If you click Last Viewed, it will move to the last item that has been viewed, regardless of whether it comes before or after the current slide in the presentation.

7 **On the slide, click to move to the next slide.** Simply clicking a slide advances to the next slide. As you view the slides, notice the vertical blinds transition that displays as each slide moves onto the screen.

8 **Right-click, and from the shortcut menu, point to Screen, and then click Black Screen.** If you need to pause your presentation, you can display a black or white screen. You can also use this menu to go to another program where you may have other information that you need to display for your audience.

9 **Click the screen to redisplay the slide.** Alternatively, press Esc to redisplay the slide.

10 **Use one of the methods you have practiced to continue through the presentation. When you get to the end, a black screen displays. Click the screen or press Esc to return to the Normal view.**

▶▶▶ *lesson*

seven | Creating Speaker Notes and Handouts

After the content is created, consider what needs to be printed. It is useful for the presenter to have a set of *speaker notes*. The slide content is printed on the top of each page, and any notes about specific comments to make during the presentation display on the bottom of the page. If appropriate, you can also print audience *handouts*, which display thumbnail images of one to nine slides to a page. Handouts have four main functions. They

- give the audience a place to take notes.
- remove the need for people to write what is displayed on the screen.
- help in case someone is unable to see the screen clearly.
- provide a backup in case of technical problems.

In this lesson, you will create speaker notes and audience handouts.

to create speaker notes

1 **In Normal view, click slide 3. In the Notes pane, at the bottom of the window, click to place the insertion point, and then type:** Bequerel was a French physicist.

2 **Press** ⏎Enter **and type:** Einstein won a Nobel Prize in physics for his work on the photoelectric effect.

3 **Point to the top edge of the Notes pane, and when the** ÷ **pointer displays, drag up slightly to increase the size of the pane so that all of the notes are displayed, as shown in Figure 9.35.** You can resize the panes in Normal view to increase or shrink the Notes pane or the Slides/Outline pane. As you increase the size of one area, the Slide pane is reduced in size.

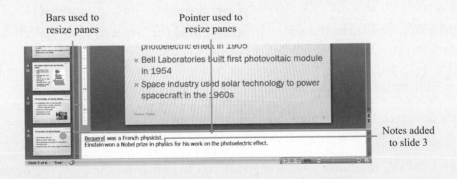

FIGURE 9.35

4 **Click the View tab. In the Presentation Views group, click the Notes Page button to display slide 3 with its notes.**

5 Under the slide, click the text to select the Notes text box. Click the edge of the text box to create a solid border around the Notes text box. Now you can format the text so that it is easier to read.

6 Click the Home tab. In the Font group, click the Increase Font Size button $\boxed{\text{A}}$ 3 times until the font size displays as 18 in the Font Size box. When you create speaker notes, be sure that the font size is large enough to be read at a glance in a dim room. Compare your screen with Figure 9.36.

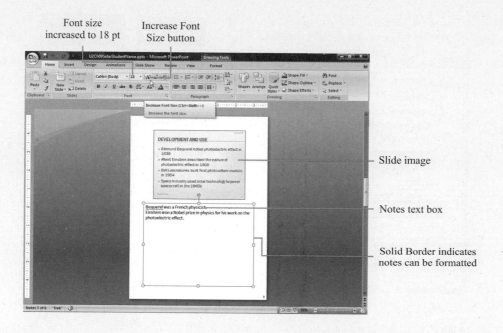

FIGURE 9.36

7 On the vertical scroll bar, click the Previous Slide button $\boxed{\text{≛}}$ to move to the Notes page for slide 2. Click in the Notes text box under the slide. In the Font group, click the Increase Font Size button $\boxed{\text{A}}$ 3 times to increase the font size to 18 pt.

8 In the Notes text box on slide 2, type: Conversion takes place at the atomic level. Current produced depends on amount of sunlight striking the cell.

•••

good **design...**

INCLUDE NOTES FOR THE SPEAKER

Notes help a speaker recall what they intended to say and provide a prompt for the content that is to be discussed for each bullet point. Be sure that the font size is large enough for the speaker to see at a glance in dim lighting.

•••

9 Click the Insert tab, and in the Text group, click the Header & Footer button to display the Header and Footer dialog box, with the Notes and Handouts tab selected.

10 Click the Date and Time check box. Click the Footer check box, and in the footer text box, type U2Ch09SolarStudentName to insert the file name in the footer area of the Notes and Handouts pages. Compare your screen with Figure 9.37.

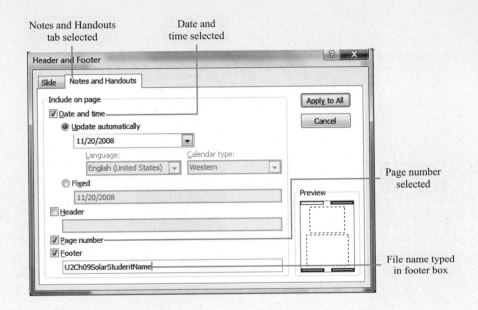

FIGURE 9.37

11 Click Apply to All. Confirm that the date displays in the right side of the header area, the file name in the left side of the footer, and the page number in the right side of the footer.

12 On the status bar, click the Normal view button ⊞. Click slide 1. On the Review tab, in the Proofing group, click the Spelling button. When *Bequerel* is selected, click Ignore All in the Spelling dialog box.

13 Correct any other spelling errors that you may have made, and then when the spelling check is complete, click OK to close the message box. Before you print handouts or make a presentation, be sure the material is free of spelling errors.

Items that are printed, whether they be copies of the slides, speaker notes, or handouts, can be printed in color, black and white, or *grayscale*—shades of gray that represent color. Before selecting your print option, view the selected print options in Print Preview to see how they affect the slide content.

to create handouts

1 **Click slide 1. Click the Office button, point to Print, and then click Print Preview.** The first slide displays in Print Preview. If you are connected to a color printer, it will display in color; otherwise, it will display in black and white.

2 **In the Page Setup group, under Print What, click the arrow to display the options shown in Figure 9.38.**

FIGURE 9.38

3 **Click Handouts, (6 Slides Per Page).** The header and footer information created for the speaker notes displays on the handouts as well. Depending on your audience, you may want to select 3 Slides Per Page, which provides a lined area on the right for the audience to take notes. Here we are using 6 Slides Per Page to save paper in case you are required to print the handout.

4 **In the Print group, click the Options button, point to Color/Grayscale, and then click Grayscale. Compare your screen to Figure 9.39.** Depending on your printer, some of the clip art images may still display with color.

6 Slides Per
Page selected

Handout displays in
grayscale, 6 slides per page

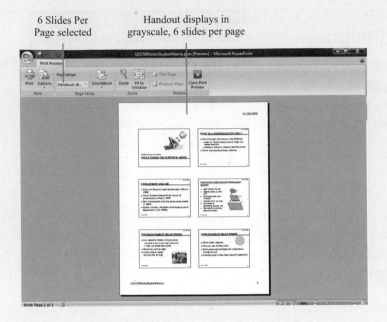

FIGURE 9.39

5 In the Print group, click the Print button. If directed by your instructor, in the displayed Print dialog box, click OK to print a copy of the handouts page; otherwise, click Cancel.

6 Click the Print What arrow, and then click Notes Pages. Click the Next Page button to display slide 2, as shown in Figure 9.40.

Notes
Pages selected

Speaker notes
for slide 2

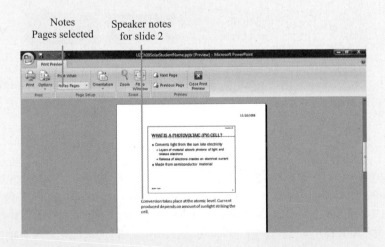

FIGURE 9.40

7 In the Print group, click the Print button. In the Print dialog box, under **Print Range**, click **Slides**, and then type 2 - 3 Confirm that *Notes Pages* displays under Print What and the Color/grayscale box displays Grayscale, as shown in Figure **9.41.** It is only necessary to print those slides that contain notes for the speaker.

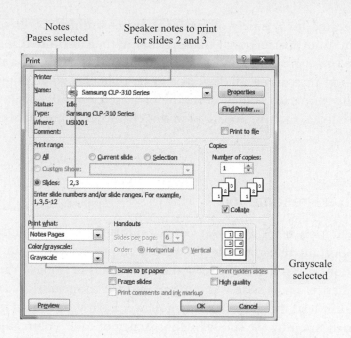

FIGURE 9.41

8 If directed by your instructor, click OK to print these two note pages; otherwise, click Cancel. In the Preview Group, click the Close Print Preview button.

9 Save 💾 your work. On the title bar, click Close ❌ to close the presentation and to close PowerPoint.

•••

good design...

PRINT HANDOUTS FOR THE AUDIENCE

Plan to have handouts available for the audience. Handouts provide a place for people to take notes, write questions, and follow along in case they are not able to see the screen. It also provides insurance in case the electronic equipment does not work as expected.

•••

Advanced Skills or Concepts

In this section, you are introduced to skills that are not taught with step-by-step instructions.

Uses for a Presentation and Distribution Methods

Presentations are created for a variety of purposes and environments. Presentations may be used in a classroom as an instructional training tool, either in printed form or by using a computer connected to a projector. Slides are often created to facilitate a meeting and help distribute information to a group. Slides can also be uploaded to an Internet site to share with a geographically dispersed audience. In any of these circumstances, a presentation can include a variety of media, such as those used in this chapter or more sophisticated media like recordings or videos.

Tips for Making a Presentation

A slide show presentation helps a speaker convey information to an audience. To do this effectively, it is important that the slide show be accurate, relevant, and attractive. When making a presentation, it is important that you do not stand in front of the slides and block the view of the audience. If the slide is important enough to include, make sure your audience can see it. Do not read the slides to your audience. Each slide should focus on one topic that is then expanded upon by the speaker. Consistency of tone, color, and slide transitions creates a unified presentation. Making every slide a different color, using unrelated graphics, or adding frequent sound effects distracts from what the speaker has to say.

Prepare Ahead

A successful presenter is someone who is prepared. After the presentation slides have been created, practice making the presentation. Speak out loud so that you know what you plan to say for each slide and each bullet point. Whenever possible, practice in the room where the presentation will be made. If possible, check out the presentation room ahead of time. If you are relying on someone else's computer and projector, make sure that your presentation will work with their equipment. Room size and lighting controls can affect how well the presentation will be seen by the audience. By viewing the room ahead of time and testing your presentation in that environment, you can make adjustments to the presentation to ensure that it will be clearly visible to the entire room. You also need to be prepared in case any electronic difficulties are encountered. At the very least, have speaker notes prepared and audience handouts available so that if the electronics fail for any reason, you can make the presentation without showing the slides.

CHECK YOUR WORK

Here is a list of items your instructor will probably look for when grading your work. To improve your evaluation, take time to check the items yourself before you turn in your work.

Solar Panels Presentation
- Trek theme applied, color changed to Paper theme colors.
- Clip art of solar panels in middle right of title slide.
- Slide 2 has two main bullet points and two subpoints.
- Slide 3 has four bullet points and uses parallel phrasing.
- Slide 4 uses the two-content layout and includes six items in a numbered list on the left and an inserted picture on the right.
- On slide 4, the background graphics are hidden and the style is changed to Style 2.
- Slide 5 is about disadvantages and contains three main points, two subpoints, and a clip art image.
- Slide 6 is about advantages and contains four bullet points and a clip art image in the upper right side, just below the title.
- On slide 6, the placeholder for the main bullet points has been resized so that it is pushed down the slide by approximately one-half inch.
- Notes display for slides 2 and 3.
- Your name displays in the lower left footer area, and the slide number displays in the lower right corner on all slides except slide 1. The date displays in the upper right corner of the header area.
- The Wheel Clockwise, 4 Spokes transition is applied to slide 1.
- The Blinds Horizontal transition is applied to slides 2 through 6.
- The date displays in the header and the file name and slide number display in the footer for speaker notes and handouts.
- The presentation is set to print as a handout with six slides to a page in grayscale.

KEY TERMS

bullet point	placeholders	Slides/Outline pane
grayscale	slide masters	speaker notes
handouts	Slide Master view	theme
layout	Slide pane	transitions
Normal view	Slide Show view	
Notes pane	Slide Sorter view	

SCREEN ID

Identify each element of the screen by matching callout numbers shown in Figure 9.42 to a corresponding description.

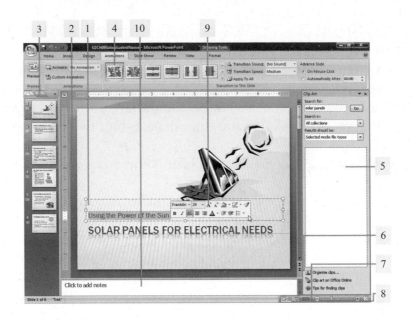

FIGURE 9.42

_____ **A.** Clip Art task pane

_____ **B.** Increase Font Size button

_____ **C.** Next Slide button

_____ **D.** Notes pane

_____ **E.** Outline tab

_____ **F.** Selected transition

_____ **G.** Slide pane

_____ **H.** Slide Show button

_____ **I.** Slide Sorter button

_____ **J.** Placeholder

MULTIPLE CHOICE

Circle the letter of the correct answer for each of the following. The lesson in which the term or concept was introduced is indicated at the end of the sentence.

1. If you need to reorganize several slides in a presentation with 30 or more slides, it is best to use the _____ view. [L6]

   a. Normal

   b. Outline

   c. Slide Master

   d. Slide Sorter

2. Add graphics to your slides for any of the following reasons **except** _____. [L3]

   a. to illustrate a point

   b. to add an image on every slide

   c. to add humor

   d. to create interest

3. To control how slides enter and exit the screen, select _____. [L6]

   a. an animation

   b. an exhibition control

   c. a theme

   d. a transition

4. When using a slide presentation, be sure that you do the following: _____. [LAdv]

   a. stand in front of the display so people won't see any errors you have made

   b. read the slides to your audience in case they can't see them

   c. have only one topic per slide

   d. add a different color on every slide to keep people's interest

5. Presentations can help with all of the following **except** _____. [L1–3]

   a. organizing your content

   b. speaking clearly

   c. staying on track during your presentation

   d. providing the audience a visual focus

6. When applying a theme to a presentation, the most important factor to keep in mind is _____. [L4]

   a. the environment in which the presentation will be given

   b. how many printouts you have to make to be sure you don't run out of ink

   c. the number of people who will be attending the presentation

   d. what you will wear that day so you do not clash with the presentation background

7. Notes for the speaker can be added in the _____. [L7]

   a. Normal view

   b. Slide Sorter view

   c. Notes Pages view

   d. a or c, but not b

8. To display information in the header and footer area of a slide, _____. [L5]

   a. type it on the slide

   b. set the Handout and Speaker Note options in the Header and Footer dialog box

   c. set the Slide options in the Header and Footer dialog box

   d. type it on the master slide

9. Audience handouts are provided for all of the following reasons **except** _____. [L7]

   a. to make people feel like they are part of a group

   b. to remove the need to write what is displayed on the screen

   c. to provide a place to take notes

   d. to ensure that people have printed copies in case they are unable to see the screen

10. In a slide show, to return to the slide that was just viewed prior to the current slide, do any of the following **except** _____. [L6]

    a. press ⬅ on the keyboard

    b. click the Previous button on the slide

    c. press ⬆Shift + Tab⇆ on the keyboard

    d. display the shortcut menu and click Previous

MATCHING

Match the term or concept to its description.

_____ 1. The main view in PowerPoint that is used to create a presentation

_____ 2. In Normal view, the portion of the window at the bottom that is used to create notes for the speaker

_____ 3. The arrangement of placeholders on a slide

_____ 4. Preformatted areas that define the type of information to place in each area on the slide

_____ 5. A collection of design elements, fonts, colors, and graphics that create a uniform look for a presentation

_____ 6. Slide layout images that contain all of the placeholder formats for each slide layout within a theme and are used to change theme formats for all slides

_____ 7. Thumbnail display of slides on a single page that is used to rearrange slides and add transitions

_____ 8. Added to slides to control the direction, timing, speed and manner in which slides enter and exit the screen during a slide show

_____ 9. Displays from one to nine thumbnail images of slides to distribute to an audience

_____ 10. Shades of gray that represent color, which are applied to slide images when they are printed

A. Grayscale

B. Handouts

C. Layout

D. Normal view

E. Notes pane

F. Placeholder

G. Slide masters

H. Slide Sorter view

I. Theme

J. Transitions

SKILL DRILL

The Skill Drill exercise is a repeat of the lessons in the chapter but with a different set of data. The instructions are less detailed, and your speed and familiarity should increase with practice. There is a figure at the end against which you can check your results. The purpose of this exercise is to build your confidence and speed in using these skills and to set them in your memory for later recall. The section numbers correspond to the lesson numbers. You are welcome to refer back to the lessons illustrated and the detailed instructions if necessary.

In this exercise, you create a presentation about using natural gas for transportation.

1. Creating a Presentation

1. **Start** PowerPoint. On the **Quick Access Toolbar,** click the **Save** button. Navigate to the **Chapter09** folder you created earlier. In the **File name** box, type U2Ch09NaturalGasStudentName and then click **Save.**

2. Click in the title placeholder and type Natural Gas in Transportation Click in the subtitle placeholder and type Natural Gas-Powered Vehicles (NGV)

3. On the **Home** tab, in the **Slides** group, click the top part of the **New Slide** button. On the new slide, click in the title placeholder and type Cost of Natural Gas

4. Press Ctrl + ↵Enter to move to the body of the slide. Type Cost of natural gas at the wellhead and press ↵Enter.

5. Press Tab⇆ to indent the next four bullet points as follows:

```
51-57% of cost
Weak production levels
Increase in demand
Environmental issues
```

6. Press Tab⇆ to create subpoints under *Environmental issues* and type:

```
Hurricanes
Cold weather
```

7. Press ↵Enter. On the **Home** tab, in the **Paragraph** group, click the **Decrease List Level** button two times to move the insertion point to the first level. Type Transmission and distribution costs and then press ↵Enter.

8. In the **Paragraph** group, click the **Increase List Level** button and type two subpoints:

```
Moving gas by pipeline
In past has been a higher percent of cost
```

9. On the Slides/Outline pane, click the **Outline** tab. On the **Home** tab, in the **Slides** group, click the **New Slide** button. In the **Outline** tab, click after the new slide icon, type Natural Gas in Automobiles and then press ↵Enter.

10. Press Tab⇆ to move the insertion point to the first bullet point on the third slide. On the **Outline** tab and using the skills that you have practiced, enter the following bullet points:

```
Natural gas is compressed (CNG)
Existing gas-powered vehicles may be converted to CNG
7 million Natural Gas Vehicles (NGVs) worldwide
South America has 48% of global NGVs
In U.S. some buses have been converted to CNG
Auto manufacturers are increasing number of NGVs produced
```

11. **Save** your work.

2. Adding Slides to a Presentation and Editing Content

1. On the vertical scroll bar, click the **Previous Slide** button to make slide 2 active. On the Slide pane, click the bullet mark next to the second bullet point— *Transmission and distribution costs*—which selects the bullet point and the subpoints under this topic.

2. Point to the selected bullet point and drag up to place the entire bullet point first in the body of the slide. When a horizontal line displays before the first bullet point—*Cost of natural gas at the wellhead*—release the mouse button.

3. On the Slides/Outline pane, click the **Slides** tab. On the Slides/Outline pane, right-click **slide 3,** and then click **Duplicate Slide.**

4. Select the title on the new slide 4 and type `How Natural Gas is Used` Select the bullet points in the body of the slide and press ⏣Delete⏣.

5. In the **Paragraph** group, click the **Numbering** button and type the following list:

```
In 62.5% of homes for heat
In electricity generation
In industry
In transportation
```

6. On the **Home** tab, in the **Slides** group, click the **New Slide** button arrow. At the end of the gallery, click **Reuse Slides.**

7. In the Reuse Slides task pane, click the **Browse** button, and then click **Browse File.** Navigate to the folder where the files for this chapter are stored. Locate and select the file **U2Ch09Alternatives** Click **Open.**

8. Point to the slide that displays *Pros and Cons of* and confirm that it is about natural gas for transportation. Click the enlarged image of the slide to insert it. Close the Reuse Slides task pane.

9. **Save** your work.

3. Adding Graphic Elements

1. Click **slide 3.** On the **Home** tab, in the **Slides** group, click the **New Slide** arrow to display the side layout options. Click the **Two-Content** slide layout option.

2. In the title placeholder, type: `Domestic Natural Gas Resources` On the left side of the slide, enter the following three bullet points:

```
Supply estimates vary but exceed 1.3 trillion cubic feet
Difference between proven reserves and potential
Sources concentrated in Alaska, Texas, and Gulf of Mexico
```

3. In the right placeholder, click the **Insert Picture from File** icon. In the Insert Picture dialog box, navigate to the location where the files for this chapter are stored. Locate and click the file **U2Ch09Reserves** to select it, and then click **Insert.**

4. Click **slide 5.** Click the **Insert** tab, and in the **Illustrations** group, click the **Clip Art** button. In the Search for box, type `pipeline` and then press ⏣Enter⏣.

5. Scroll the list and click the image shown in Figure 9.43. If this clip art image is not available, select one that is similar.

6. Drag the image to the lower right corner of the slide. Compare the placement to that shown in Figure 9.43. Close the Clip Art task pane.

7. **Save** your work.

4. Applying a Theme to a Presentation

1. Click **slide 1.** Click the **Design** tab. In the **Themes** group, click the **More** button to display the gallery.

2. Point to different themes to see how they would appear on slide 1, and then click **Civic.**

3. In the **Themes** group, click the **Fonts** button, and then click **Apex** to change the font.

4. With slide 1 displayed, click the **Insert** tab, and in the **Illustrations** group, click the **Picture** button. In the Insert Picture dialog box, navigate to the folder that contains the files for this chapter. Locate and click **U2Ch09Fueling** to select this image, and then click **Insert.**

5. On slide 1, drag the inserted image to the location shown in Figure 9.43.

6. Scroll through the slides to look for adjustments that may be needed. Stop on slide 6. Click in the title placeholder and press Ctrl + A to select all of the text in the placeholder. Right-click the selected text, and on the Mini toolbar, click the **Decrease Font Size** button to reduce the size of the title so that it fits on one line.

7. **Save** your work.

5. Adding Information to the Header and Footer

1. Click the **Insert** tab. In the **Text** group, click the **Header & Footer** button.

2. On the **Slide** tab, click the **Slide number** check box. The slide number in this theme displays in the circle in the center of the slide.

3. Check the **Footer** check box, and then in the text box, type your name.

4. Click the **Don't show on title slide** check box.

5. Click the **Notes and Handouts** tab.

6. Click the **Date and time** check box and be sure that *Update automatically* is selected. Click the date list arrow and click to select the format that displays the day, month, and year as in 31-Oct-10.

7. Click the **Footer** check box, and in the text box, type U2Ch09NaturalGas StudentName and then click **Apply to All.**

8. Scroll through the slides to be sure that your name displays in the left side of the footer, the slide number displays in the circle on each slide except the first slide, and the file name and date display on the note pages. **Save** your changes.

6. Adding Slide Transitions and Viewing a Slide Show

1. On the status bar, click the **Slide Sorter** button. On the Zoom bar, click the **Zoom In** button until 100% displays as the Zoom percent.

2. Click **slide 3**—*Natural Gas in Automobiles*—and drag it to the left of slide 2. When a vertical line displays, release the mouse button to drop this slide between slides 1 and 2 and make it the new slide 2.

3. Press Ctrl + A to select all of the slides. Click the **Animations** tab. In the **Transition to This Slide** group, click the **More** button to display the gallery.

4. Scroll down the list. Under **Wipes,** move your pointer over the transitions to display the transition ScreenTip, and click **Shape Circle** to apply this transition to all of the slides.

5. In the **Transition to This Slide** group, click the **Transition Speed** box arrow, and then click **Medium.**

6. Click **slide 1** to select it and deselect the other slides. Display the Transitions gallery, and under Fades and Dissolves, click **Dissolve** to apply a different transition to the first slide.

7. Click the **Review** tab, and in the **Proofing** group, click the **Spelling** button. Correct any spelling errors that you may encounter, and then click **OK.**

8. If necessary, click **slide 1.** On the status bar, click the **Slide Show** button. Click to progress through the slides. Alternatively, press ➜ or ↵Enter to move through the presentation.

9. **Save** your changes.

7. **Creating Speaker Notes and Handouts**

1. In Normal view, click **slide 2.** Click in the Notes pane, type Natural gas is stored and distributed in cylinders. Press ↵Enter and type Requires more space for fuel storage.

2. Click the **View** tab, and in the **Presentation Views** group, click the **Notes Page** button.

3. Click in the Notes text box under the slide. Select the text and point to the Mini toolbar to make it active. Click the **Increase Font Size** button until the font size increases to **18** pt.

4. Click the **Next Slide** button two times to display slide 4. Click in the Notes text box under the slide. Right-click, and on the Mini toolbar, change the Font Size to **18** pt.

5. Type: Worldwide estimates are not certified by the U.S. Energy Information Administration.

6. Click the **Office** button, point to **Print,** and then click **Print Preview.** In the **Page Setup** group, under **Print What,** click the list arrow, and then click **Handouts, (3 Slides Per Page).** This option places three slides on each page with lines to the right of the slide images for notes.

7. In the **Print** group, click the **Options** button. Point to **Color/Grayscale,** and then click **Grayscale.** If required by your instructor, click the **Print** button, and then click **OK** to print the two handout pages; otherwise, click **Cancel.**

8. In the **Page Setup** group, change the **Print What** box to **Notes Pages.** Click the **Print** button. In the Print dialog box, under Print range, click the **Slides** option button, and then type 2,4 to indicate the two slides that include notes. If required by your instructor, click **OK** to print these two note pages; otherwise, click **Cancel.**

9. Click **Close Print Preview.** Click the **Normal view** button, and then display slide 1. **Save** your changes.

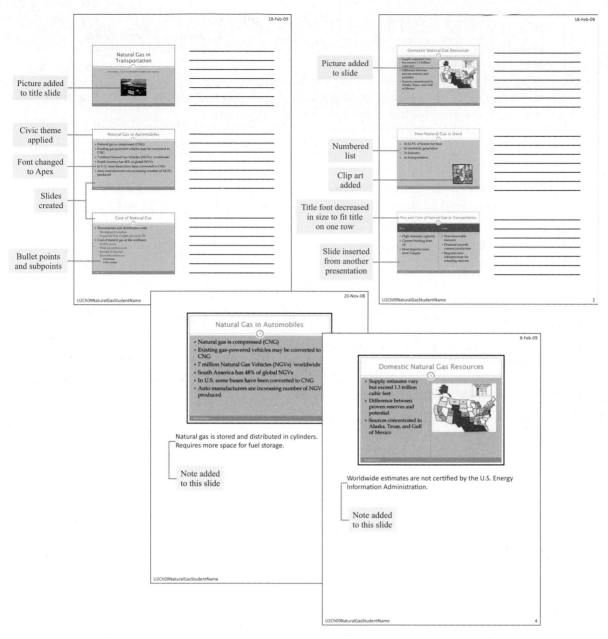

FIGURE 9.43 A, B, C, D

fix *it*

One way to appreciate the value of good design is to fix a file that is not designed well. In this exercise, you open a file that has several errors and design flaws and fix it according to the good design elements in the lessons.

Navigate to the folder with the student files, open **U2Ch09FixIt,** and save it as U2Ch02FixItStudentName

Examine this presentation and modify it using the skills you have practiced so that it is a professional presentation that flows in a logical manner and is appropriately illustrated. Review the content of the file and create a six-slide presentation. Create a handout for the presentation and include the file name and date in the header and footer areas. Make changes to comply with the good design principles that were introduced in this chapter. Here is a list of design principles introduced in this chapter, along with some tips on how to fix the presentation. Use the principles that are appropriate for each slide.

- Create a title slide to announce the topic that will attract attention and create interest. Include a subtitle for the presentation.
- In the bullet points, use parallel phrasing whenever possible.
- Use short bullet points, presented in a logical order. Do not use sentences or periods.
- Include images that illustrate a concept or add information. Two images that are related to this topic are found in your student files: U2Ch09CookingOil and U2Ch09BioDiesel.
- Add clip art images that are related to the topic to add visual interest, create humor, or illustrate a point.
- Use a theme that complements the topic and will work in the environment that will be used for the presentation.
- Add headers or footers to document ownership, date, and slide numbers.
- Adjust placement of header and footer information if necessary so that this does not interfere with the content of the slides.
- Apply transitions to the slides that enhance the presentation and do not distract the speaker or the audience.
- Include notes for the speaker in a font size that is easily readable.
- Review the presentation to remove any spelling errors.
- Create handouts for the audience.

A successful result will include six slides, including a title slide. Each slide will have a title and use bullet points, not sentences. A complementary theme will be applied, transitions will be added, and two pictures and at least one clip art related to the topic will be included. The presentation will be error-free and include documentation in the header/footer area of the handout. Submit the file as required by your instructor. Save and close the file.

ON THE JOB

Information workers add value to data by organizing, selecting, displaying, communicating, interpreting, and using data to support decisions. On the Job exercises simulate a situation where you are given data, and your job is to add value to it using the skills you practiced in this chapter. Success in these exercises indicates that you have a valuable skill to offer an employer.

1. Wind Presentation

In this On the Job exercise, the program coordinator for the Energy Independence Lecture Series has asked you to create slides for a brief wind energy presentation that focuses on offshore wind farms. Refer to the e-mail from the program coordinator, and then, using the skills you have practiced in this chapter, organize the information that is provided in the Word document into a presentation.

Michelle,

I need a short overview presentation about wind farm energy alternatives. Please find my notes in the U2Ch09Wind file. The topics are listed randomly and need to be rearranged in a more logical sequence. Begin with a slide that defines the topic, followed by design and economic impact slides, and end the presentation with a slide about advantages.

I have also included some pictures that I found on the Internet: U2Ch09WindSea and U2Ch09WindFarm. Use whichever image works best. I am counting on your good sense of style and creativeness to create a professional and appealing presentation.

Thanks,
Miguel

1. Create a new presentation and save it in your Chapter09 folder as `U2Ch02WindStudentName`

2. Follow the good design principles listed in the Fix It exercise.

3. Based on the Word file provided, create a six-slide presentation organized as indicated in the note from Miguel.

4. Add one or two pictures and one or two appropriate clip art images.

5. Include a theme and transitions.

6. Add the note indicated in the Word file provided, and be sure the note is large enough to see easily.

7. Remove any errors you encounter.

8. Include the file name in the footer of the handout page and set it to print in grayscale. Include your name in the footer of the slides.

9. Print the handout and notes page or submit the file as directed by your instructor. Save the file and then close it.

2. Geothermal Presentation

In this On the Job exercise, the program coordinator for the Energy Independence Lecture Series has asked you to create slides for a brief geothermal presentation. Refer to the e-mail from the program coordinator, and then, using the skills you have practiced in this chapter, organize the information that is provided in the Word document into a presentation.

Joel,

I made some notes about geothermal energy alternatives for a presentation that I need to make. Locate my notes in the U2Ch09Geothermal file and create a presentation for me. I found a number of locations where geothermal plants are already installed. These all need to be on the same slide, perhaps in side-by-side lists. The Uses of Geothermal topic should follow the first topic slide. Also, place the pros and cons side by side on one slide. End the presentation with a slide about the future of geothermal energy.

I have also included some pictures that you can use. They are named U2Ch09Geysers and U2Ch09HotSprings.

Thanks,
Miguel

1. Create a new presentation and save it in your Chapter09 folder as U2Ch09GeothermalStudentName

2. Follow the good design principles listed in the Fix It exercise.

3. Based on the Word file provided, create a six-slide presentation organized as indicated by Miguel.

4. Add one or two pictures and one or two appropriate clip art images.

5. Include a theme and transitions.

6. Remove any errors you encounter.

7. Include the file name in the footer of the handout page and set it to print in grayscale. Include your name in the footer of the slides.

8. Print the handout and notes page or submit the file as directed by your instructor. Save the file and then close it.

DISCUSSION OF ADVANCED SKILLS OR CONCEPTS

The questions in this section are based on the topics in the Advanced Skills or Concepts section of the chapter.

1. In what circumstances have you used a PowerPoint presentation? Discuss how PowerPoint can help you communicate information to others. Give examples of when you might use it in school, business, or personal situations.

2. Think about presentations, seminars, or lectures you have attended. Describe the circumstances where PowerPoint has been used effectively. What made it effective?

3. Describe a situation where a PowerPoint presentation was ineffective. What made it ineffective and how could it have been improved?

4. When you have to give a presentation to a group, what are the steps you take to prepare for it? What helps you succeed when you make presentations?

ON YOUR OWN

Once you are comfortable with the skills in this chapter, you can apply them to new situations of your own choosing. In this section, you choose data that you have in your possession or that you can find elsewhere. To successfully complete this assignment, you must apply good design practices and demonstrate mastery of the skills that were practiced. Refer to the list of skills and design practices in the Fix It exercise.

1. Create a Presentation for the Green Co-op Community Development Project

The Green Co-op Community Development Project needs a presentation that it can use to inform community members about the organization and the projects it has undertaken in the past year. Create a presentation based on the information in the **U2Ch09GCCD** file.

1. Open a new presentation and save it as U2Ch09GCCDStudentName

2. Create a six-slide presentation that includes a title slide.

3. Organize the information into bullet points that will span the remaining five slides.

4. Include the company name and logo on the opening slide. (Hint: Copy the image from the Word document and paste it into the slide.)

5. Add a theme and transitions.

6. End the presentation with a slide about how to contact the company for more information.

7. Add appropriate clip art or pictures from your file.

8. Include the file name in the footer of the handouts.

9. Save your work and submit the file as directed by your instructor.

2. Create a Presentation on a Related Topic

Create a six-slide presentation on the topic of energy conservation. Research the topic on the Internet. Document your resources by including the Web addresses in the notes area for any pictures or data you include. In addition to the title slide, use two other slide layouts. Include appropriate clip art or pictures. Apply a theme and slide transitions. Include the file name in the footer of the handouts page. Save the file as U2Ch09ConservationStudentName and submit it as directed by your instructor.

ASSESS YOUR PROGRESS

At this point, you should have a set of skills and design concepts that are valuable to an employer and to you. You may not realize how much you have learned unless you take a few minutes to assess your progress.

1. From the student files, open **U2Ch09Assess.** Save it as U2Ch09AssessStudentName

2. Read each question in column A.

3. In column B, answer Yes or No.

4. If you identify a skill or design concept that you don't know, refer to the learning objective code next to the question and the table at the beginning of the chapter to find the skill and review it.

5. Print the worksheet if your instructor requires it. The file name is already in the header, so it will display your name as part of the file name.

6. All of these skills and concepts have been identified as important by surveying hundreds of individuals working at over 200 companies worldwide. If you cannot answer all of the questions affirmatively even after reviewing the relevant lesson, seek additional help from your instructor.

chapter ten

Enhancing a Presentation

Lesson	Learning Outcomes	Code	Related IC3 Objectives
1	Import text from an outline	10.01	4.1.1
1	Modify slide content and layout	10.02	4.1.4
1	Add graphics	10.03	4.1.2
2	Apply a theme	10.04	4.1.2
2	Insert movie clips	10.05	4.1.2
3	Add tables	10.06	4.1.2, 4.1.4
3	Duplicate slides	10.07	4.1.1
3	Modify tables	10.08	4.1.2, 4.1.12
4	Add a chart	10.09	4.1.2, 4.1.12
4	Format a chart	10.10	4.1.2
5	Add SmartArt	10.11	4.1.2
5	Modify SmartArt	10.12	4.1.2, 4.1.12
6	Add transitions and animations	10.13	4.1.6
6	Customize text animations	10.14	4.1.2
6	Animate tables	10.15	4.1.2
6	Customize chart animations	10.16	4.1.2
6	Customize SmartArt animations	10.17	4.1.2
7	Add a hyperlink	10.18	4.1.11
7	Prepare a presentation for Web publication	10.19	4.1.12
7	Add Information to the Slide Footer	10.20	4.1.12
7	Save as a Web page	10.21	4.1.8, 4.1.9
7	View a presentation with a browser	10.22	4.1.10
7	Create handouts	10.23	4.1.8

Instructions throughout the lessons are based on the Vista operating system, running Microsoft Office 2007.

Why Would I Do This?

Now that you have used the basic tools available for creating a presentation, you can expand your skills by using some of the more advanced features. Sometimes you will want to use information that was originally written in a Word document. Rather than retyping the information, it is easier to import an outline from Word as the content for a presentation.

In some circumstances, it is helpful to include a table or a chart. Tables and charts in PowerPoint are similar to the tables you create in Word and the charts you create in Excel. They are better for displaying numerical data than bulleted lists. There is also a wide variety of diagrams that help you show relationships (such as an organizational chart) or processes (such as workflow). In addition to using transitions for a presentation, animations can be applied to customize how the elements on a slide come into view. Finally, presentations are sometimes posted to a Web site as a means of conveying information to a wider audience. When you do this, it is useful to include links to related information that may be of interest to your audience.

In this chapter, you create a PowerPoint presentation by importing an outline, creating slides with tables, creating a chart, using graphic tools, customizing animations, and saving the file in a format that enables you to post it to a Web site. You will also reinforce the skills that were covered in the previous chapter.

visual summary

In this chapter, you will create a presentation to inform an audience about the ways to reduce the cost of heating their homes. when you are done, you will have created a complete presentation with tables, charts, animations, and SmartArt, as shown in the presentation handout in Figure 10.1.

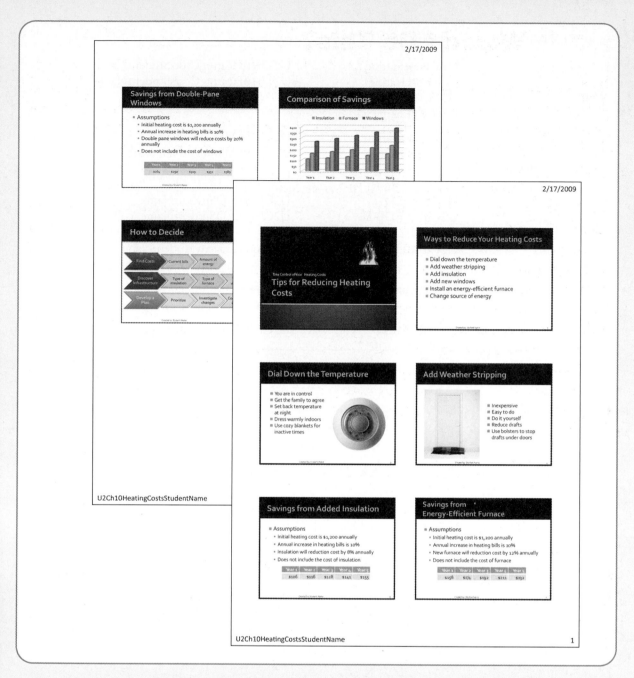

FIGURE 10.1

List of Student and Solution Files

In most cases, you will start with a new, empty file and enter text and data or paste content from other files. You will add your name to the file names and save them on your computer or portable memory device. Table 10.1 lists the files you start with and the names you give them when you save the files.

ASSIGNMENT	STUDENT SOURCE FILE:	SAVE AS:
Lessons 1–7	New Presentation U2Ch10Heating U2Ch10Weather U2Ch10EnergyStarLogo	U2Ch10HeatingCostsStudentName U2Ch10HeatingCostsStudentName.MHT
Skill Drill	New Presentation U2Ch10Oil	U2Ch10OilStudentName U2Ch10OilStudentName.MHT
Fix It	U2Ch10FixIt	U2Ch10FixItStudentName
On the Job	U2Ch10LED U2Ch10LEDBulb U2Ch10Spot U2Ch10Capacity	U2Ch10LEDStudentName U2Ch10LEDStudentName.MHT U2Ch10CapacityStudentName U2Ch10CapacityStudentName.MHT
On Your Own	New Presentation New Presentation	U2Ch10LightsStudentName U2Ch10GasolineStudentName
Assess Your Progress	U2Ch10Assess	U2Ch10AssessStudentName

TABLE 10.1

▶▶▶ *lesson*
one | Importing Text from an Outline

Sometimes the content for a presentation may be taken from another file created by a different program. To import content from Word for slides, the content of the Word document must be in the form of an outline. The outline needs to use heading levels—which are style formats. The top-level heading becomes the title on the slide, and each subsequent level becomes a bullet point under the top heading level or a subpoint under a bullet point.

In this lesson, you open a Word document to view the outline and then import the information into a new presentation. You begin by creating the title slide for the presentation and saving it before you import the content.

to view and import a word outline

1 **Start PowerPoint 2007. On the Quick Access toolbar, click the Save button 🔲. In the Save As dialog box, navigate to the location where you are saving your files. Create a new folder named** Chapter10 **In the new folder, save the file with the name** U2Ch10HeatingCostsStudentName

2 **Click in the title placeholder and type** Tips for Reducing Heating Costs **Click the subtitle placeholder and type** Take Control of Your Heating Costs

3 **Start Word 2007. From your student files, locate and open the** *U2Ch10Heating* **file.** Notice that this outline uses Heading Level 1 as the top-level title and Heading Level 2 for the subpoints. The file displays the Outlining tab. In PowerPoint, Heading 1 topics will become slide titles and Heading 2 topics will become bullet points. Compare your screen with Figure 10.2.

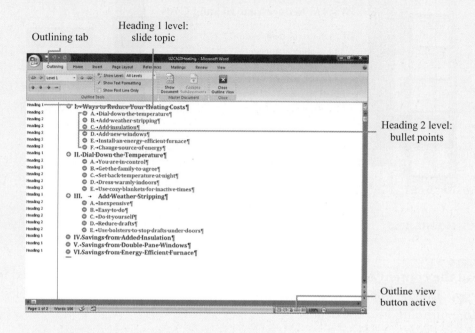

FIGURE 10.2

4 **Close** ▨ **Word. In the PowerPoint window, on the Home tab, in the Slides group, click the New Slide button arrow. From the list, click Slides from Outline.**

5 **In the Insert Outline dialog box, navigate to the student folder for this chapter. Locate and select the** *U2Ch10Heating* **file, and then click Insert.** Compare your screen with Figure 10.3. Six slides are inserted: three with bullet points and three with only a slide title.

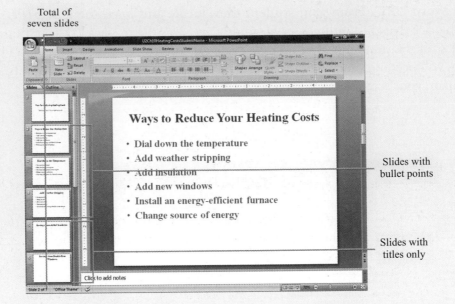

Total of
seven slides

Slides with
bullet points

Slides with
titles only

Ways to Reduce Your Heating Costs

- Dial down the temperature
- Add weather stripping
- Add insulation
- Add new windows
- Install an energy-efficient furnace
- Change source of energy

FIGURE 10.3

6 **Read the content of slide 2.** This is a list of all the topics that will be covered in this presentation. A good practice is to give your audience an overview of the topics before jumping into the details.

7 **Click slide 3. On the Home tab, in the Slides group, click the Layout button. In the Slides layout gallery, click Two Content.** When you review the content of the imported text, consider if the slide layout is appropriate or if it needs to be changed. This slide could be improved by adding a graphic image, which will be done in the next lesson.

8 **Click slide 4. In the Slides group, click the Layout button, and then click Two Content. Select all of the text on the left side of the slide. Press** Ctrl **+** X **to cut this text. Click in the placeholder on the right side of the slide and press** Ctrl **+** V **to paste the text—thereby moving it.** You can also use the Cut and Paste buttons in the Clipboard group or select Cut and Paste from the shortcut menu. Changing the slide layout and moving the text makes room for a graphic illustration on the right. Alternating the placement of your graphics on the left or right creates more visual interest.

9 **Click on each of the next three slides.** Slides 5, 6, and 7 only have titles imported from the outline. Content will be added to these slides in a later lesson.

10 **Save your file** 💾 .

good **design...**

CHOOSE THE APPROPRIATE LAYOUT
Examine each slide and determine which ones need additional illustrations such as graphics, charts, or tables, and change the slide to a layout that matches the content.

▶▶▶ *lesson*

two | Applying a Theme and Adding Graphics

After you import the content from another source, it is a good idea to apply the theme that you want to use. Recall that a theme is a collection of design elements that include graphics, a color palette, and a font selection. It can also affect the placement of items on a slide. Adding a theme later in the process can create the need to rearrange graphics and the placement of other objects on the slides. After you add a theme you can review the slides to see if clip art and other pictures are needed to illustrate the concepts.

In this lesson, you apply a theme and adjust slides to the new theme. Then you add images.

to apply a theme and adjust slides

1 In the Slides/Outline pane, scroll up and click slide 1 to display it on the Slide pane.

2 Click the Design tab. In the Themes group, click the More button [▼] to display the Themes gallery. Under Built-In, locate and click the Module theme to apply it to the slides. Recall that when you point to a theme, a ScreenTip displays the name and the Live Preview feature displays the theme on the currently active slide so that you can preview it.

3 Click slide 2. Click the text in the body of the slide. Click the Home tab and notice that the font is still Times New Roman and the font size is 32. The blue font color, font, and font size from the Word outline were not changed when the theme was applied. The blue font does not display well against the black fill color in the title area.

4 Click slide 5. On the Home tab, in the Slides group, click the Layout button. Notice that the current layout is the Title and Text layout. This is not one of the usual options that is available for a slide layout, but it displays here because of the imported text. Text imported from Word is placed in the Title and Text layout rather than in the more common Title and Content layout. This affects how other objects will display on the slides.

5 Click the Layout button to close the gallery. Click slide 2. On the Home tab, in the Slides group, click the Reset button. The font changes to Corbel and the font color changes to the default colors used with the Module theme.

6 Click slide 3. Using the scroll bar in the Slides/Outline pane, scroll to the end of the slides. Press ⬆Shift and then click slide 7. *Slides 3 through 7 are selected.*

7 On the Home tab, in the Slides group, click the Reset button. *The remaining slides are changed to the Module font and font colors. Compare your screen with Figure 10.4.*

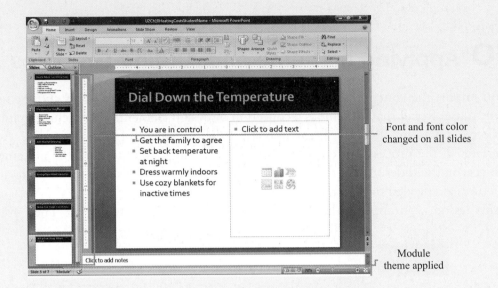

Font and font color changed on all slides

Module theme applied

FIGURE 10.4

8 Save 💾 your changes.

good design...

USE CONSISTENT FONTS AND CAPITALIZATION

The font used in a presentation needs to be consistent throughout. Be sure that the font from the chosen theme is used on all the slides. When you import content, review the font and use the Reset button to change the font to match the rest of the presentation.

In a presentation, each bullet point begins with a capital letter, and each main word in a title is capitalized. If the content you imported does not use capital letters at the beginning of bullet points or title words and the Reset button does not fix this, you need to make the changes manually.

to extend your knowledge

FORMATS FROM IMPORTED TEXT

Slides that are created from an imported outline all use the Title and Text slide layout. The heading-level fonts used in the outline are converted to a font that is the most similar to the font used in the outline. The outline font in Word is Cambria, with various font sizes for different headings. Cambria is not a font that is used in PowerPoint, so this font is converted to Times New Roman, and the font size is increased for each heading level to match the font size typically used in a presentation title or bulleted list.

Illustrations make a presentation more interesting than text alone. Be sure that the images you include are relevant to the topic. In addition to using clip art and digital pictures, you can also use *movie clips*—animated clip art or video clips. This can be as simple as a motion clip selected from the Microsoft Clip Organizer or a video clip that you have saved on your computer.

to add clip art, pictures, and motion clips

1 **Display slide 1 on the Slide pane. Click the Insert tab. In the Media Clips group, click the Movie button arrow, and then click Movie from Clip Organizer.** The Clip Art task pane displays on the screen. All of the clips displayed are motion clips.

2 **Click the *Results should be* arrow and confirm that Movies is the only media type selected. Click in the Search for box and type** `fire` **and then press** ⏎Enter.

3 **Click the fire image shown in Figure 10.5, then move the image and resize it so that it is similar to the image shown in Figure 10.5.** The motion included in a movie clip only displays in Slide Show view.

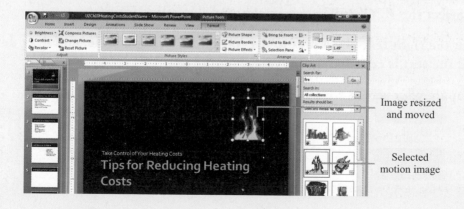

FIGURE 10.5

4 On the status bar, click the Slide Show button 🖳 to view the fire in motion. Then press ⎋Esc to return to Normal view.

5 Click slide 3, and click in the content placeholder on the right to make it active. In the Clip Art task pane, click the *Results should be* arrow, and then click Clip Art and Photographs. Clear the Movies check box. Close the list.

6 In the Search for box, type thermostat and then click Go.

7 Click the thermostat image shown in Figure 10.6 to insert it on the right side of the text box, and then close the Clip Art task pane.

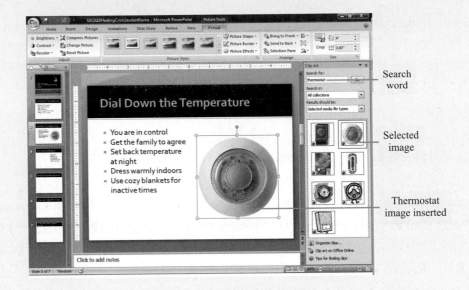

FIGURE 10.6

8 Click slide 4. In the left placeholder, click the Insert Picture from File button 🖼. In the Insert Picture dialog box, navigate to the student files for this chapter. Select the *U2Ch10Weather* image, and then click Insert.

9 Click the right text box. Point to the top center sizing handle, and drag down until the text is centered on the image on the left.

10 Compare your screen with Figure 10.7, and then Save your file 💾.

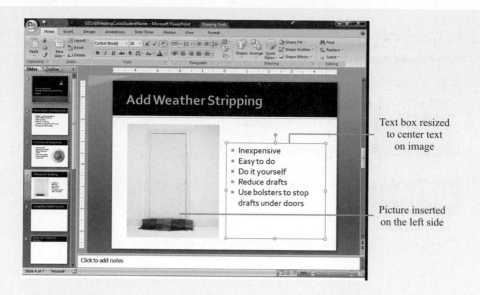

Text box resized to center text on image

Picture inserted on the left side

FIGURE 10.7

good design...

ADD RELEVANT CLIP ART OR PICTURES TO ENHANCE YOUR SLIDES

Sometimes the content on the slide is minimal. When you can find appropriate clip art or pictures to illustrate a slide, it can help to balance the text and give the slide greater visual appeal.

▶▶▶ *lesson*
three | Adding Tables to a Presentation

Some data is best presented in tabular format that uses rows and columns. This may be data that is parallel in nature or a listing of numbers, such as weather data or financial information. Tables in PowerPoint are created in a similar manner to tables created in Word. After the data is entered, the same Design and Layout tabs are available to format the table.

In this lesson, you insert a table in a slide and then add text for additional information.

to add a table to a slide

1 Click slide 5, which is titled *Savings from Added Insulation*.

2 Click the Insert tab. In the Tables group, click the Tables button, and then drag the Insert Table grid to create a 5-column by 2-row table as shown in Figure 10.8. The table displays on the slide at the top of the text box that is reserved for text.

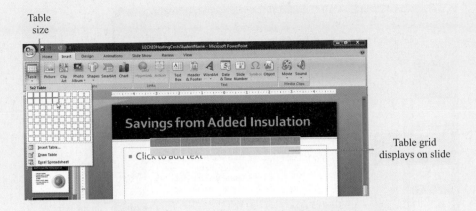

FIGURE 10.8

3 Click to insert the table. Point to the edge of the table, and when the ⬚ pointer displays, drag the table down to near the bottom of the text box and center it horizontally on the slide. You can adjust the placement of the table later.

4 Click in the top left cell of the table. Type `Year 1` and press `Tab⭾` to move to the next cell. Continue in this manner to enter the years in the top row; then press `Tab⭾` and enter the figures shown below in the second row. Compare your screen to Figure 10.9.

Year 1	Year 2	Year 3	Year 4	Year 5
$106	$116	$128	$141	$155

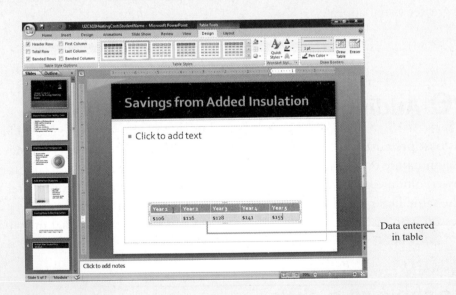

FIGURE 10.9

5 Click next to the bullet point in the text box and type `Assumptions` and then press `⏎Enter`. Press `Tab⭾` to indent the next line and type the following bulleted list:

```
Initial heating cost is $1,200 annually

Annual increase in heating bills is 10%

Insulation will reduce costs by 8% annually

Does not include the cost of insulation
```

6 Compare your screen to Figure 10.10, and adjust the placement of your table as necessary. Save 🖫 your changes.

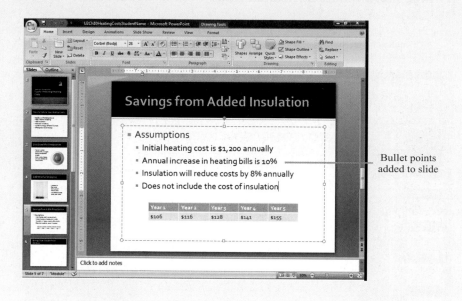

FIGURE 10.10

Tables can also be inserted using the button in the content placeholder rather than the Table button on the Insert tab. In the next task, you change the layout of the slide, use the Insert Table button, and then rearrange the slide placeholders.

to change slide layout and use the insert table button

1 Click slide 6. On the Home tab, in the Slides group, click the Layout button, and then click the Two Content button. This layout includes the content icons on each side of the slide; one will be used for the text and the other for the table. However, the placeholders need to be arranged horizontally in relationship to each other rather than vertically.

2 Click the content placeholder on the left. Point to the bottom center sizing handle, and when the ⬍ pointer displays, drag up to the 1-inch mark that displays below 0 on the vertical ruler. When you click on a sizing handle on a placeholder or object, the numbers on the vertical and horizontal rulers change to show 0 in the center of each ruler, with numbers increasing outward from the center point. This is to help you locate the center of the slide.

3 Point to the right center sizing handle, and when the ⬌ pointer displays, drag to the right to expand the text box to the right edge of the text box on the left—at the 4.5-inch mark on the horizontal ruler. Compare your screen with Figure 10.11.

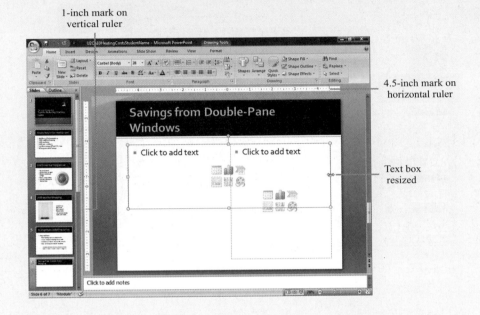

FIGURE 10.11

4 In the content placeholder on the right, click in the lower portion of the box to display the sizing handles and make this placeholder active.

5 Using the technique you just practiced, resize the right placeholder to fill the lower portion of the slide. Place the upper edge at the 1.5-inch mark on the vertical ruler, below the center point, and expand the placeholder horizontally across the slide as shown in Figure 10.12. The two content placeholders are resized into a horizontal rather than vertical arrangement. The bottom placeholder is smaller because the table will not require as much room as the list of assumptions.

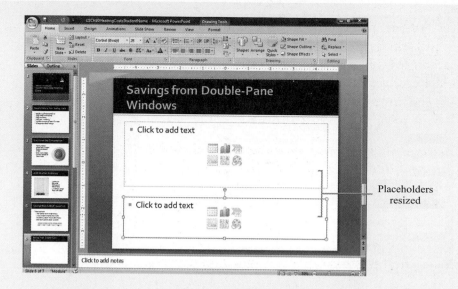

FIGURE 10.12

6 **With the bottom placeholder active, click the Insert Table button** 🔲**.** The Insert Table dialog box displays, and by default the Number of columns box displays *5* and the Number of rows box contains *2*, which is the size of table that is needed.

7 **Click OK. Using the procedure you practiced previously, enter the following data in the table:**

Year 1	Year 2	Year 3	Year 4	Year 5
$264	$290	$319	$351	$389

8 **Click in the top content placeholder and type** Assumptions **and then press** ⏎Enter**. Press** Tab⇄ **and type the following four bullet points:**

Initial heating cost is $1,200 annually

Annual increase in heating bills is 10%

Double-pane windows will reduce costs by 20% annually

Does not include the cost of windows

9 **Save your work** 💾 **and compare your screen with Figure 10.13.**

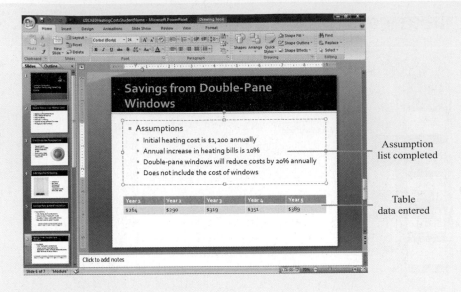

FIGURE 10.13

---

good **design...**

FORMAT TABULAR DATA AS A TABLE

Look for data that would be better displayed using a table so that information is easier to compare and understand.

---

to extend **your knowledge**

CREATING TABLES

The Title and Text layout is used for the slides that were created when the outline was imported. The three slides that contained only a title needed to include both a table and a text box. Two approaches were used for changing these slides to the desired content. This resulted in different font sizes and table sizes between the slides. The two approaches were demonstrated for teaching purposes so that you could see the result of each method. However, when you are creating a presentation, if you plan to use more than one table, it is best to use one method for inserting tables so that the content is consistent across the slides. If necessary, adjust the table size and placement, and expand the cells so that you can maximize the font size.

A third slide needs to display a table and a text box for the topic of installing an energy-efficient furnace. Rather than creating a new slide from scratch, another approach is to duplicate a slide that contains most of the data that you need and make the necessary changes to the content.

to duplicate a slide and edit content

1 Click slide 5 to make it the active slide. Be sure that the Slides tab displays in the left pane.

2 On the Slides tab, right-click slide 5, and then click **Duplicate Slide.** A copy of the currently selected slide is added as slide 6, which displays on the Slide pane.

3 On slide 6, select *Added Insulation* and type `Energy-Efficient Furnace` Click to the left of *Energy* and press (⇧Shift) + (↵Enter) to insert a manual line break, which places the title on two lines.

4 In the second row of the table, replace the figures with the following:

$158	$174	$192	$211	$232

5 In the Assumptions list, edit the third bullet point to read `New furnace will reduce costs by 12% annually` and then in the last bullet point, replace *insulation* with `furnace`

6 Click slide 8—the slide with only the title *Savings from Energy-Efficient Furnace.* This slide is no longer needed and can be deleted.

7 On the Slides tab, right-click slide 8, and then click **Delete Slide to remove it from the presentation.** Alternatively, with the slide selected, press (Delete) on the keyboard; or on the Home tab, in the Slides group, click the Delete button.

8 Save 💾 your presentation. Click slide 6 and compare your screen with Figure 10.14.

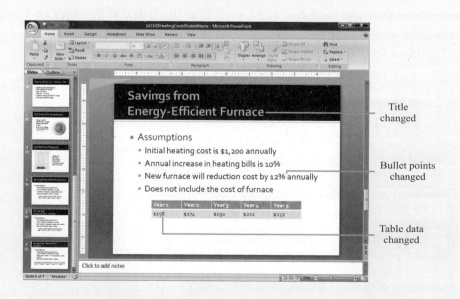

FIGURE 10.14

Table Tools contextual tabs Design and Layout are used to modify tables in PowerPoint. After a theme has been applied to the presentation, you can change the table style, which will change the color and possibly the font used in the table. The layout of the table, including the alignment, font size, and cell size, can be changed at anytime—it is not affected by a change to the theme applied to the presentation.

to format tables and slide content

1 **Click slide 5, and then click the table to make it active.** Contextual Table Tools tabs Design and Layout display on the Ribbon. Recall that contextual tabs display only when that particular type of object is selected.

2 **Click the Layout tab. In the Table group, click the Select button, and then click Select Table.** By selecting the table first, you can alter the dimensions of all of the cells at once and change the text alignment.

3 **In the Alignment group, click the Align Text Right button** ▤ **to align all of the text in the table on the right side of each cell.** Numbers and their headings should be aligned on the right side of cells.

4 **In the Cell Size group, click the Table Row Height box up spin arrow** ▣ 2" ▮ **until 0.5" displays.**

5 **In the Cell Size group, click the Table Column Width box down spin arrow** ▤ 2.67" ▮ **until 1.3" displays.**

6 **With the table still selected, click the Home tab, and in the Font group, click the Increase Font button** A˙ **two times to change the font size to 24.**

7 **In the text box, click the *Assumptions* bullet, and on the Home tab, in the Font group, notice that the font size is 32 pt. Click the listed subpoints and notice that the font size is 28 pt.** You will adjust the font size on slides 6 and 7 as necessary to use the same font size. Compare your screen with Figure 10.15.

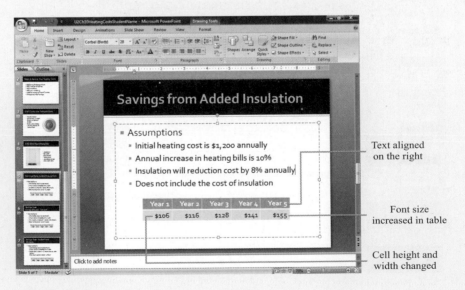

FIGURE 10.15

8 Click slide 6 and repeat steps 2 through 7 to align the table text on the right side, change the size of the cells, and increase the font size in the table to 24. Then verify that the *Assumption* bullet is 32-pt font and the subpoint list is 28 pt.

9 Click slide 7 and repeat steps 2 through 6 to align the table text on the right side, change the size of the cells, and increase the font size in the table to 24.

10 Point to the top border of the table, and when the ⟦⟧ pointer displays, drag the table to the right and center it horizontally under the 0-inch mark on the horizontal ruler.

11 In the text box, click in the *Assumptions* title, and then click the Increase Font Size button ⟦A⟧ one time to display 32 in the Font Size box.

12 Select all four lines of the subpoints list, and click the Increase Font Size button ⟦A⟧ two times to change the font size to 28. The automatic resize feature may resize the title and the text so that it all fits in the text box. The AutoFit options button will display to the left of the text box as shown in Figure 10.16.

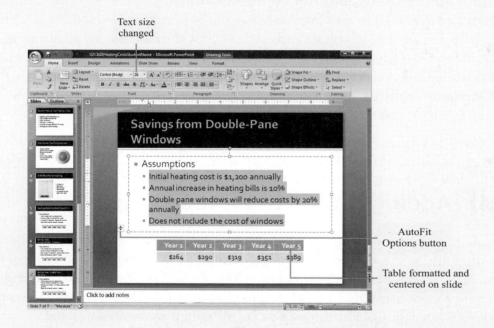

FIGURE 10.16

13 **Click the AutoFit Options button to display the options for fitting the text.** By default, the AutoFit option resizes the font to fit within the text box. If you prefer to resize the text box, you can click *Stop Fitting Text to This Placeholder* and then adjust the font size manually.

14 **Click the AutoFit Options button to close the list. On the lower edge of the text box, point to the sizing handle and drag down to the 1.5-inch mark on the vertical ruler.**

15 **If necessary, move the table down so that the top edge of the table is at the 1.75-inch mark on the vertical ruler. Click the *Assumptions* bullet and verify that the font size is 32. Then verify that the font size for the bulleted list is 28. Save 💾 your work.**

good design...

KEEP FONTS LARGE ENOUGH TO BE READABLE

Font size may need to vary from one slide to the next to accommodate the difference in the amount of text on each slide. Adjust the font size for all elements to ensure that it is large enough to be read from the back of a room. If necessary, insert a new slide and divide the topics between the slides, or reduce the number of words to keep the text large enough to be readable.

▶▶▶ *lesson*
four | Adding Charts to a Presentation

A chart can create a powerful visual in a presentation. Use charts when you need to show comparisons of numbers. The visual representation of numbers in a chart is much easier to understand than a list of numbers in a table. Use line charts to show trends over time, column charts to show comparisons between categories, and pie charts to show the contribution of each part to the whole. The tools used to create a chart are the same as those used in Excel.

In this lesson, you add a slide and then add data to show the comparison of the three heat cost-savings alternatives that were listed in the previous three slides.

to add a chart to a presentation

1 **With slide 7 as the active slide, on the Home tab, in the Slides group, click the New Slide button.** A new slide is inserted that uses the same slide layout as was used in the previous slide—*Two Content*.

2 **In the Slides group, click the Layout button, and then click Title and Content to change the slide layout.** Recall that you can also select the layout you want from the New Slide button if you click the New Slide button arrow to display the slide layout options.

3 **In the title placeholder, type** `Comparison of Savings`

4 **In the content placeholder, click the Insert Chart button** 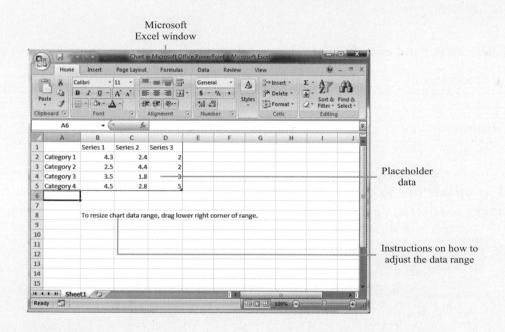 **to display the Insert Chart dialog box.** Here, you select the type of chart you want to create.

5 **On the left side of the Insert Chart dialog box, be sure Column is selected, and then on the right side, in the second row, click Clustered Cylinder and click OK.** After a moment, the *Chart in Microsoft Office PowerPoint – Microsoft Excel* window displays, as shown in Figure 10.17. Placeholder data displays in the cell range A1 to D5. Instructions in row 8 tell you to drag the corner of the data range to resize the range. To create the chart, replace the data shown and drag the corner of the range to increase or decrease the size of the range as necessary to fit your data.

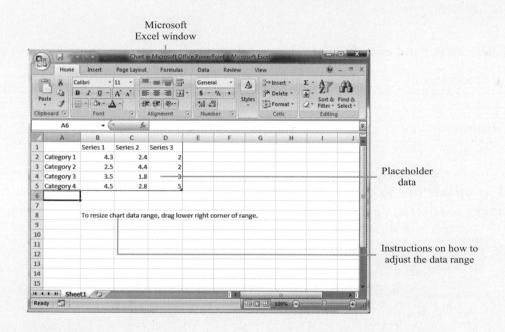

FIGURE 10.17

6 **Click in cell B1—labeled** *Series 1*—**and type** `Year 1` **Press** Tab⇄ **type** `Year 2` **and then press** Tab⇄ **and type** `Year 3` **Press** Tab⇄ **again and notice that the insertion point moves to cell A2 in the next row.** The years need to extend to Year 5, so you need to expand the data range.

7 **Point to the lower right corner of the range in cell D5. When the** ⬉ **pointer displays, drag to the right to the corner of cell F5, as shown in Figure 10.18.** The pattern for the years continues and fills automatically into cells E1 and F1.

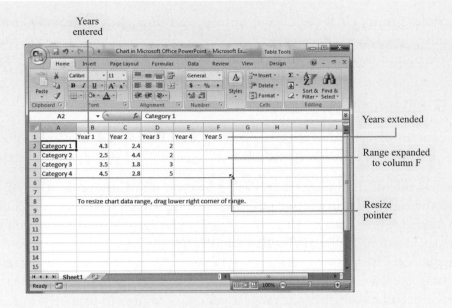

Years entered

Years extended

Years extended

Range expanded to column F

Resize pointer

FIGURE 10.18

8 **Click cell A2 and enter the data shown below, pressing** Tab **to move between cells.**

Insulation	$106	$116	$128	$141	$155
Furnace	$158	$174	$192	$211	$232
Windows	$264	$290	$319	$351	$387

9 **Point to the corner of the range in cell F5, and when the** ⬉ **pointer displays, drag up one row to exclude row 5 from the range.** Alternatively, click the row 5 header to select it, right click the selected row, and then click Delete Row to remove the contents and shrink the range. Compare your screen with Figure 10.19.

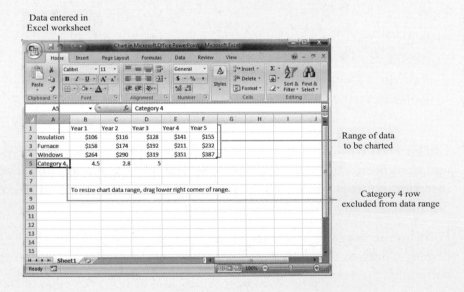

Data entered in Excel worksheet

Range of data to be charted

Category 4 row excluded from data range

FIGURE 10.19

10 In the Microsoft Excel window, click the **Minimize button** [image]. **In the PowerPoint window, Save your changes and compare your screen to Figure 10.20.** The chart displays on the slide, and Chart Tools contextual tabs Design, Layout, and Format are available. If you think you might need to change the data in the worksheet, minimize the Excel window rather than closing it.

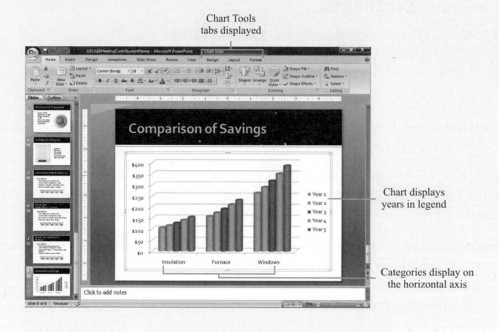

Chart Tools tabs displayed

Chart displays years in legend

Categories display on the horizontal axis

FIGURE 10.20

good design...

INCLUDE CHARTS TO ILLUSTRATE RELATIONSHIPS AND TRENDS IN NUMERICAL DATA

Use an appropriate chart type for the relationship you are trying to demonstrate. Be sure that the range includes all of your data and not any of the sample data.

After a chart is created, you can use the Chart Tools to modify the chart as necessary.

to modify a chart

1 With the chart active—a blue border displays around the edge of the chart—click the Design tab.

2 **In the Data group, click the Switch Row/Column button.** The years display along the horizontal axis, and the legend lists the three categories of energy savings that are being compared. This button is active only if the Microsoft Excel window is still open.

••

if you have **problems...**

IS THE SWITCH ROW/COLUMN BUTTON INACTIVE?

If you closed the Excel window, the Switch Row/Column button will not be active. To display the Excel data again, in the Data group, click the Edit Data button.

••

3 **Click the Chart Tools Layout tab. In the Labels group, click the Legend button, and then click Show Legend at Top.**

4 **Click the legend so that a solid border displays around it. Click the Home tab. In the Font group, click the Increase Font Size button until 24 displays in the Font Size box.**

5 **On the taskbar, click the Excel button, and then close** ☒ **Excel. Compare your screen with Figure 10.21, and then save your changes.**

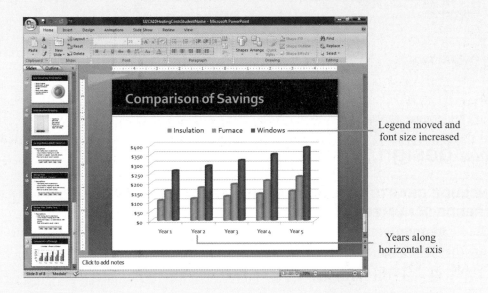

FIGURE 10.21

good design...

**ORGANIZE CHART BY CATEGORY OR SERIES TO
SHOW DESIRED RELATIONSHIP**

Choose to organize the chart by category or series. While the Microsoft Excel worksheet is open, you can use the Switch Row/Column button in the PowerPoint window to choose between using the row headings or column headings as labels on the horizontal axis. Examine both options and choose the one that demonstrates the relationship you are trying to emphasize.

to extend your knowledge

TO CHANGE THE DATA IN A CHART

If you need to change the data or data range of your chart, on the Chart Tools Design tab, in the Data group, click the Edit Data button to display the Microsoft Excel worksheet. Edit the data as necessary, and then drag the range to encompass only the figures you want to chart. View your results on your slide before closing the Excel window.

▶▶▶ *lesson*
five|Inserting Diagrams Using SmartArt

A *SmartArt* diagram creates a visual representation of concepts and information. It can be used to illustrate hierarchies, steps in a process, relationships, cycles, or lists. There is a wide variety of designer-quality SmartArt graphics from which to choose. They can include text, pictures, and several levels of text. You can change the style, effect, and color of a graphic to coordinate with the overall theme of your presentation.

In this lesson, you add a SmartArt diagram, apply a theme, and then modify the graphic.

to insert a SmartArt graphic

1 With slide 8 as the active slide, click the Home tab. In the Slides group, click the New Slide button arrow, and then click Title and Content to insert a new slide.

2 In the title placeholder, type How to Decide In the content placeholder, click the Insert SmartArt Graphic button 🔲, and then compare your screen to Figure 10.22. The SmartArt dialog box is divided into three sections. On the left is a list of the SmartArt categories. The middle section displays images of the different SmartArt graphics, organized by category. On the right, you can see a preview of the currently selected graphic, along with an explanation of when to use this type of graphic.

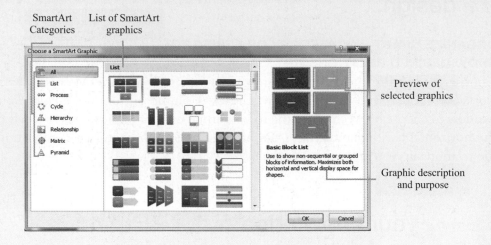

SmartArt Categories

List of SmartArt graphics

Preview of selected graphics

Graphic description and purpose

FIGURE 10.22

3 **In the middle section, scroll the list and click on different layout types, reading the explanation and purpose in the right section.** There are seven SmartArt categories, which are detailed in Table 10.2.

MICROSOFT SMARTART GRAPHIC TYPES

List	Shows information that is not sequential.
Process	Shows steps in a process or workflow.
Cycle	Shows steps that repeat continuously.
Hierarchy	Shows organizational structure or decision tree.
Relationship	Shows connectional relationships between two or more things.
Matrix	Shows how parts relate to the whole.
Pyramid	Shows proportional relationships, usually with the largest portion on the top or bottom.

TABLE 10.2

4 **On the left side of the Choose a SmartArt Graphic dialog box, click Process. In the third row, locate and then click the Chevron List layout shown in Figure 10.23.** This graphic is used to show progression through several steps in a process, as explained on the right side of the dialog box.

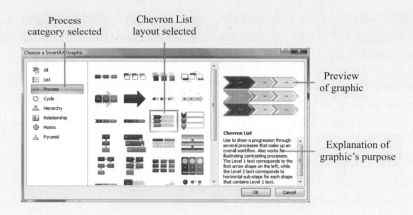

Process
category selected

Chevron List
layout selected

Preview
of graphic

Explanation of
graphic's purpose

FIGURE 10.23

5 **Click OK to insert the graphic.** Two SmartArt Tools tabs—Design and Format—
display on the Ribbon. Text can be entered directly in the graphic, or you can enter
text using the Text pane.

6 **On the SmartArt Tools Design tab, in the Create Graphic group, if necessary
click the Text pane button to display it on the screen. In the Text pane, with the
first bullet point selected, type** `Find Costs` As you type, the letters display in the
Text pane and in the first chevron graphic on the slide.

7 **In the Text pane, click the bullet point under** *Find Costs* **and type** `Current
bills` **Then click the third bullet point and type** `Amount of energy` As you
type, the font size for both subpoints adjusts as necessary to fit all of the text in the
chevron graphic and maintain the same font size. Compare your screen to Figure 10.24.

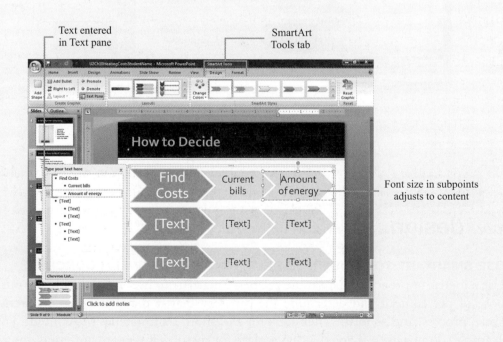

Text entered
in Text pane

SmartArt
Tools tab

Font size in subpoints
adjusts to content

FIGURE 10.24

8 On the slide, in the second row of the SmartArt, click the first chevron graphic and type `Discover Infrastructure` The font size decreases to accommodate the text and the *Find Costs* graphic font adjusts to match it.

9 Click the middle chevron and type `Type of insulation` In the next chevron on the same row, type `Type of furnace`

10 Using either method—typing in the Text pane or directly in the graphic—enter the next three steps in the process:

```
Develop a Plan

Prioritize

Investigate changes
```

11 Save your changes and compare your screen to Figure 10.25.

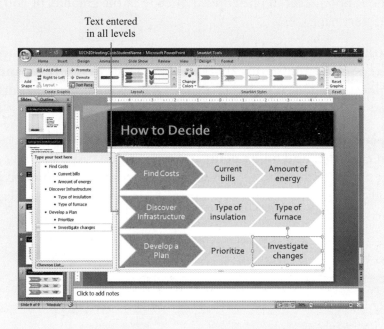

FIGURE 10.25

good **design...**

USE SMARTART TO ILLUSTRATE RELATIONSHIPS BETWEEN CONCEPTS

Use a logical approach to determine the best SmartArt to use. First, decide the purpose of the content and determine the category that it matches—list, hierarchy, cycle, process, and so forth. Then look for a diagram that matches the content. For example, do not use a shape that has a place for pictures if you are not going to use pictures.

You are not limited to the number of graphics that display in a particular layout. You can add or delete the shapes as necessary to accommodate your text.

to add shapes to a SmartArt layout

1 **In the Text pane, click to the right of** *Type of furnace* **and press** Enter. A new bullet point is added in the Text pane at the same level as the previous one. On the slide, a fourth shape is added at the end of the second row.

2 **Type** `Type of windows`

3 **On the slide, click the last shape in the third row. On the SmartArt Tools Design tab, in the Create Graphic group, click the Add Shape button arrow to display the list. Compare your screen with Figure 10.26.** Here, you can add a shape before or after the currently active shape. Depending on the type of SmartArt layout that you are editing, you may also be able to add shapes above or below the active shape.

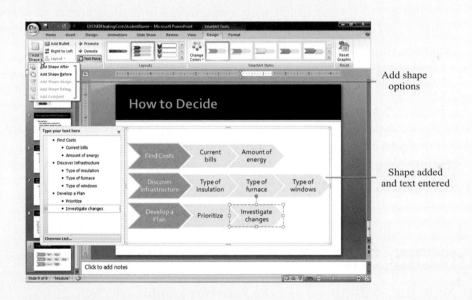

FIGURE 10.26

to extend **your knowledge**

TO REMOVE UNUSED SHAPES OR BULLET POINTS

If the SmartArt contains more shapes than you need, select the shape by clicking the edge of it. When a solid border displays around the shape, press Delete. You can also use the Delete or Backspace keys to remove unused bullet points.

4 From the Add Shape menu, click *Add Shape After,* and then type `Cost/Benefit analysis` **In the Create Graphic group, click the Text pane button to close the Text pane.**

5 **On the outside border that surrounds the SmartArt, point to the upper right sizing handle. When the** ⬉ **pointer displays, drag up and to the right to expand the graphic to the edge of the slide. Point to the lower left sizing handle and drag down and to the left to expand the graphic to the left.** As you do so, all of the shapes are resized proportionally and the font size is increased in each shape.

6 **Save** 💾 **your changes.**

good design...

KEEP IT SIMPLE

Do not try to do too much with a diagram. Limit the number of shapes, words, and images used. Create a clean image that conveys your message without clutter. Remove unused shapes or bullet points.

The theme applied to your presentation controls the colors used in the tables, charts, and SmartArt that you have added. After the theme has been applied, you can change the colors for these objects. Because the theme colors will override colors applied to objects, it is important to apply the theme first and then adjust the object colors as you choose.

to modify SmartArt

1 **With slide 9 displayed and the SmartArt graphic selected, click the SmartArt Tools Design tab. In the Layouts group, click the More button** ▼ **to display the SmartArt Layout gallery.**

2 **Move your pointer slowly over the different layouts and watch as the Live Preview feature applies the different layouts to your slide.** Live Preview gives you the chance to see other shapes and layouts applied to your text. Do not make any changes.

3 **Click on the slide to close the gallery.**

4 **In the SmartArt Styles group, click the Change Colors button to display the Colors gallery. Move your pointer over the colors and watch the preview of each color combination on your slide.**

5 **Under Colorful, click the third option:** *Colorful Range - Accent Colors 3 to 4.*

6 In the SmartArt Styles group, click the More button ⬇ to display the gallery. Move your pointer over the styles to see the live preview of each style applied to your slide.

7 Under 3-D, in the first row, locate and then click Inset. If you decide that you do not like the results, you can click the Reset Graphic button to return the graphic to its original design.

8 Save your work and compare your results with Figure 10.27.

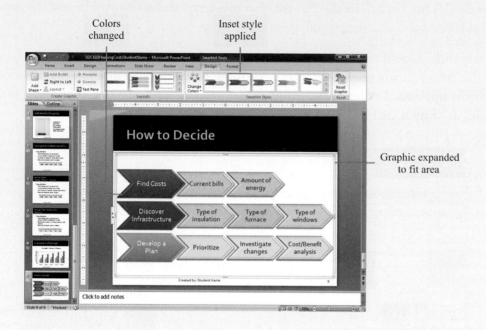

FIGURE 10.27

▶▶▶ *lesson*
SIX | Adding Animations

Transitions control how slides come onto the screen. ***Animations*** control how text and other objects come onto the screen. Animations can also attach a motion path to an object or control how items exit from the screen.

In this lesson, you will add transitions to the slides and apply animations to objects on the slides.

to add transitions and animations

1 On the status bar, click the Slide Sorter button 🔲. Click slide 2, hold down ⬆Shift, and then click slide 9 to select all but the title slide.

2 Click the Animations tab. In the Transitions to This Slide group, click the More button ⏷. Under Wipes, locate and then click *Uncover Right-Down* to apply this transition to the selected slides.

3 Click the Transition Speed arrow, and then click Medium.

4 Click slide 1. In the Transition to This Slide group, click the Dissolve button, and then change the Transition Speed to Slow.

5 On the status bar, click the Normal button to return to Normal view. To apply animations to slides, the presentation must be in Normal view.

6 Click slide 2, and then on the slide, click the text box. On the Animations tab, in the Animations group, click the Animate box arrow to display the preset animation options. Under Fade, point to *All At Once* and observe this effect on the slide, as shown in Figure 10.28.

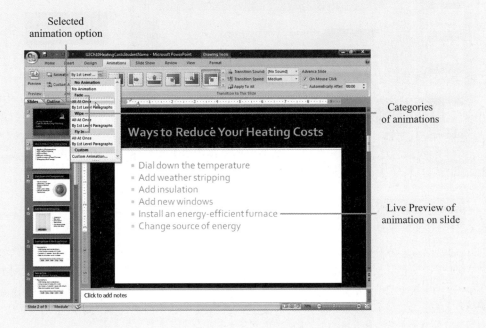

FIGURE 10.28

7 Under Wipe, point to *By 1st Level Paragraphs* to observe this effect. Bullet points can be displayed all at once on the slide, or line by line by the first-level paragraph bullet points. If the there are subpoints, they display at the same time as the first-level bullet point.

8 Under Wipe, click the *By 1st Level Paragraphs* to apply this effect to slide 2. Unlike transitions—which can be applied to a group of slides all at once— animations are applied to each slide individually, because they apply to the text box placeholder and other objects on the slide.

9 Click slide 3 and click the text box placeholder. In the Animations group, click the Animate arrow, and under Wipe, click *By 1st Level Paragraphs.* Using this option gives the presenter time to discuss each topic without the audience reading ahead. It helps you control the pace of your presentation and the focus of the audience.

10 On slide 3, click the thermostat graphic, click the Animate box arrow, and then click Fly In. The animation for objects is slightly different in that the item displays all at once. Because you set the animation for the graphic after you have set the animation for the text box, the graphic displays after all of the text has been displayed.

11 Using the procedure in step 9, on slides 4 through 7, select the text box and apply the animation *Wipe By 1st Level Paragraphs.*

12 Save 💾 your changes.

good design...

USE THE SAME ANIMATION FOR TEXT ON ALL SLIDES

It is better to use the same animation for the text on all of the slides rather than using a different animation on each slide. It is important not to overdo animations. Animations create interest until the point at which they become a diversion and your audience becomes more interested in the animations than in the content. They should enhance, not distract.

You can add more sophisticated animations using the custom animation options. Custom animations offer a wider range of motions—entrance, motion path, and exit—in addition to a greater variety of styles. Customizing animations is particularly useful with tables, charts, and SmartArt because you can control how each of these objects come onto the screen.

applying custom animations to tables

1 Click slide 5. On the Animations tab, in the Animations group, click Custom Animation. The Custom Animation task pane displays on the right side of the screen. On the slide, a small *1* displays next to each of the text items. This indicates that this block of text is animated as a group—it will come onto the screen all at once.

2 On slide 5, click the table to select it, which activates the Add Effect button on the Custom Animation task pane.

3 On the Custom Animation task pane, click the Add Effect button to display the list of actions, and then point to Entrance to display the list of Entrance effects

as shown in Figure 10.29. Entrance effects can be added to the selected object—the table—from this list, or you can choose the More Effects option. The submenu displays the effects that have been used most recently in alphabetical order. The effects listed on your submenu may be different from the ones shown in the figure.

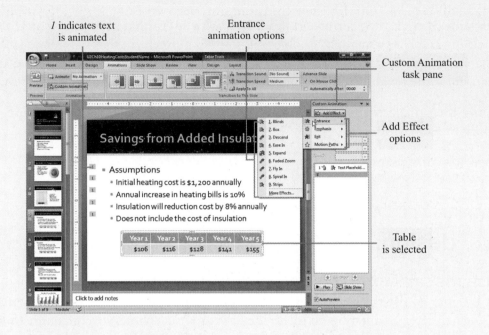

FIGURE 10.29

to extend **your knowledge**

TESTING CUSTOM ANIMATIONS

If you click one of the options listed from the Entrance list, it will be added to the selected object. If you click another one to try it, it too will be added to the object. Testing animation effects in this manner can result in multiple animations applied to one object. Multiple numbers will display next to the animated object, and a corresponding number and description will display in the Custom Animation task pane. To remove unwanted animations, in the task pane, click the arrow next to the item you want to remove, and on the displayed shortcut menu, click Remove. Do this for each animation you want to remove.

4 **On the Add Effect list, point to the other options—*Emphasis, Exit, Motion Paths*—to see the available options. Point to Entrance again, and then from the submenu, click More Effects.** The Add Entrance Effect dialog box that displays is organized into categories of effects: *Basic, Subtle, Moderate,* and *Exciting.* Notice that the *Preview Effect* check box is selected. Using the Add Entrance Effect dialog box, you can test an animation without applying it to the object. When you click an effect, it displays on the selected object but will not be applied until you click OK.

5 Click on different effects to test them and see how the effects display on the table. If necessary, point to the Add Entrance Effect dialog box title bar and drag it out of the way so that you can see the effect applied.

6 Under Basic, click Strips, and then click OK, which closes the Add Entrance Effect dialog box. On the Custom Animation task pane, click the Direction arrow, and then click Right Down to change the direction of the effect. A *2* displays next to the table and the effect is listed as *2 Table* in the task pane. The speed and direction can be controlled on most animation effects. If you click the Table animation notation in the task pane, the Add Effect button displays *Change* as the button name—the action you would need to alter an animation that is applied. Compare your screen with Figure 10.30.

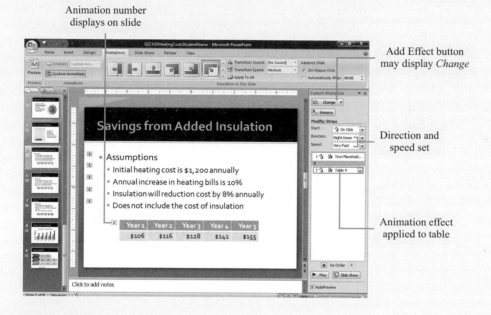

FIGURE 10.30

7 Click slide 6, and then click the table. Click the Add Effect button, point to Entrance, and then click Strips to apply it to the table. In the Custom Animation task pane, change the direction to Right Down.

8 Click slide 7, and then click the table. Using the technique you just practiced, add the Strips entrance effect and change the direction to Right Down. The three tables all have the same animation applied so that when these three slides are shown, the animations will be the same.

9 Save 🖫 your changes.

USE THE SAME ANIMATION FOR EACH TYPE OF OBJECT
When animating the same type of object, use the same animation, direction, and speed.

When you animate a chart, consider the point that you want to emphasize. You can animate the lines on a line chart or bars on a bar chart so that the lines or bars display one at a time. This gives you the ability to focus on each data element in the chart.

applying custom animations to charts

1 Click slide 8 and click the chart to select it. On the Custom Animation task pane, click the Add Effect button, point to Entrance, and then click Blinds. If necessary, click More Effects, and then under Basic, click Blinds and click OK.

2 On the Custom Animation task pane, display the Direction list, and then click Vertical. This applies the Blinds animation to the entire chart, and it displays in a vertical orientation, which matches the vertical orientation of the columns.

3 On the Custom Animation task pane, click the Content Placeholder arrow as shown in Figure 10.31. This displays a list of options for further controlling the animation to the chart.

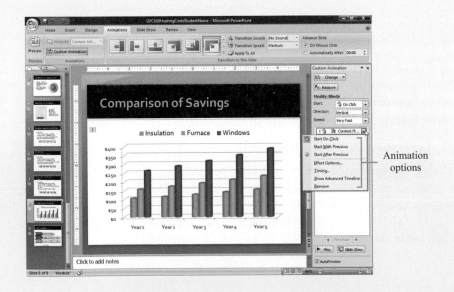

FIGURE 10.31

4 **From the displayed list, click Effect Options.** The dialog box displays the animation effect that has been applied in the title bar—Blinds. Because the animated object is a chart, one of the tabs available is Chart Animation.

5 **Click the Chart Animation tab. Click the Group chart arrow to display the options available, as shown in Figure 10.32.** You can elect to display the bars of the chart by series (*Insulation*, *Furnace*, and *Windows*) or by category (the years). If you choose *By Element in Series*, or *By Element in Category*, each of the bars will display one at a time. This requires the presenter to click the mouse button or press a key to move through each of the elements on the chart.

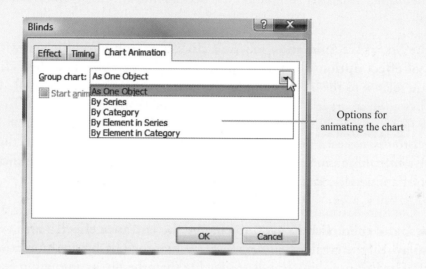

FIGURE 10.32

6 **From the displayed list, click By Series, and then click OK.** The animation displays on the chart so that you can see how it will work. This choice displays each of the three energy cost-savings options one at a time and will only require three clicks to display the series during the presentation.

7 **Save** 💾 **your changes.**

SmartArt is another graphic element that can benefit from customized animations. Rather than having the entire design display all at once, you can control the individual shapes and the timing of their entrance onto the slide. This enables you to discuss each component of the graphic and explain its relevance to the whole concept that is being presented.

applying custom animations to Smartart

1 **Click slide 9 and click the SmartArt graphic to select it. On the Custom Animation task pane, click the Add Effect button, point to Entrance, and then click Fly In. If necessary, use More Effects to locate the Fly In effect. Click the Direction arrow, and then click From Left.** This applies the Fly In animation to the entire SmartArt graphic.

2 **On the Custom Animation task pane, click the Content Placeholder arrow, and then from the displayed list, click Effect Options.** The Fly In dialog box displays, and it includes a SmartArt Animation tab because the affected graphic is a SmartArt diagram.

3 **Click the SmartArt Animation tab, and click the Group graphic arrow to display the list of effect options for this graphic. Click *One by one*, and then click OK.** Levels are related to the bullet-point levels in an outline. The darker-colored shapes in the first column are level one, and the rest of the shapes are level two. To control this in a horizontal fashion, the one-by-one animation is applied. This enables the presenter to discuss each point as it displays on the screen and to explain the steps in the decision-making process. Eleven numbers display on the screen to indicate the number of animations that have been applied—one for each shape.

4 **On the Custom Animation task pane, click the Change button. Point to Entrance, and then click Expand to change the entrance effect.** The new animation displays on the graphic and demonstrates that the one-by-one animation is still in effect. The Expand animation is less jarring than the Fly In animation and is a better choice when you are bringing many items onto the screen one at a time.

5 **Close the Custom Animation task pane. Save 💾 your presentation.**

good design...

CHOOSE ANIMATIONS THAT SUPPORT THE PURPOSE OF THE GRAPHIC

Consider the point that you are trying to make with a particular graphic, chart, or SmartArt, and apply an animation that is consistent with your purpose. For example, a line chart that shows an upward trend could be displayed with a wipe from left to right so that the line appears to rise as it is displayed. Use the Play button or Slide Show button to preview your animations to ensure that they have the intended effect.

seven | Adding Hyperlinks and Saving as a Web Page

When a presentation is shown as a slide show, you can easily link to related topics on the Internet by including a hyperlink in the presentation. Recall that a *hyperlink* is text or a graphic that you click to go to a file, a location in a file, or a Web page. This can be particularly effective when you want to direct your audience to locations where they can obtain additional information about a topic on their own.

A presentation can be shared with a wider audience by posting it to a Web site. Depending on the site, you may first need to save the presentation as a Web page file so that it can be viewed properly.

In this lesson, you add another slide, create a hyperlink, and save the presentation in a Web format.

to insert a hyperlink

1 With slide 9 selected, click the Home tab. In the Slides group, click the New Slide button arrow, and then click the Two Content layout.

2 In the title placeholder, type Next Steps

3 In the left content placeholder, type the following bullet points:

Make it a goal to reduce your energy costs

Request a home energy audit

Contact your local energy provider

Investigate energy-saving alternatives

4 Click in the third bullet point, and on the Home tab, in the Paragraph group, click the Increase List Level 🔠 button to move this to a second-level bullet point.

5 In the content placeholder on the right, click the Insert Picture from File button 🖾. In the Insert Picture dialog box, navigate to the student files for this chapter. Locate and select the *U2Ch10EnergyStarLogo* file, and then click Insert.

6 Use the corner sizing handles to increase the size of this image, as shown in Figure 10.33. Click the text on the left. On the right side of the placeholder, point to the middle sizing handle, and when the ⟷ pointer displays, drag to the right to the 1-inch mark on the horizontal ruler. Compare your screen with Figure 10.33.

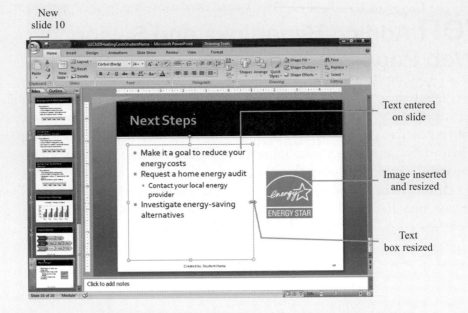

New
slide 10

Text entered
on slide

Image inserted
and resized

Text
box resized

FIGURE 10.33

7 **Click the inserted image. Click the Insert tab, and in the Links group, click the Hyperlink button.** Alternatively, you can right-click the image and choose Hyperlink from the shortcut menu.

8 **In the Insert Hyperlink dialog box, under Link to:, be sure that Existing File or Web Page is selected. In the Address box, type** `http://www.energystar.gov`

9 **Click the ScreenTip button. In the ScreenTip text box, type** `Energy Star Program` **Compare your screen with Figure 10.34.**

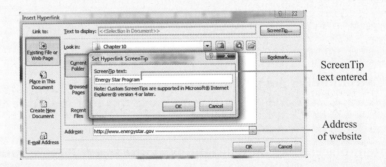

ScreenTip
text entered

Address
of website

FIGURE 10.34

10 **Click OK in both dialog boxes.** The hyperlink does not show or work until you view this as a slide show. If you need to make changes to the hyperlink, you can right-click the hyperlinked image and choose to edit, open, copy, or remove the hyperlink.

11 **On the status bar, click the Slide Show button to view the slide. Point to the Energy Star image to display the ScreenTip, as shown in Figure 10.35, and then**

click the image to test the link. The Energy Star Web site displays with information about home energy measures.

Next Steps

- Make it a goal to reduce your energy costs
- Request a home energy audit
  - Contact your local energy provider
- Investigate energy-saving alternatives

ScreenTip displays

FIGURE 10.35

12 Close ☒ **the displayed Web page, and then press** Esc **to close the slide show.** A transition and text animation still need to be added to this slide so that it matches the rest of the presentation.

good **design...**

USE HYPERLINKS TO AUGMENT THE PRESENTATION

Presentations should be simple and in outline form. Additional information can be provided by including hyperlinks to related Web pages. Test the hyperlinks to make sure they work properly.

13 **Click the Animations tab. In the Transition to This Slide group, click the More** ⊽ **button to display the gallery. Under Wipes, locate and click Uncover Right-Down.** This is the transition that was used on the other slides.

14 **Click the Text box on the left of the slide. In the Animations group, click the Animate arrow, and then under Wipe, click** *By 1st Level Paragraphs.* This is the text animation used on the other slides.

15 **Click the Energy Star image. In the Animations group, click Custom Animation. On the Custom Animation task pane, click the Add Effect button, point to Entrance, and then click Faded Zoom.** If this animation is not listed, click More Effects, and then under *Subtle*, click *Faded Zoom* and click OK. A transition and animations have been applied to the last slide in the presentation.

16 **Close the Custom Animation task pane. Save** 🖫 **your changes.**

You can save your presentation as a Web page and post it to a Web site. When you save your presentation as a Web file, you can view it with your browser to preview how it will display on the Web site. Before you publish your file, it is important to check for errors and add your name and other documentation to the file.

to prepare a presentation for web posting

1 **Click slide 1 to make it the active slide. Click the Review tab, and in the Proofing group, click the Spelling button to check the spelling.** If everything is spelled correctly, a message box displays to advise you that the spelling check is complete.

2 **Correct any spelling errors that you may encounter, and then click OK to close the message box.**

3 **Click the Insert tab. In the Text group, click the Slide Number button.** The Header and Footer dialog box opens and the Slide tab is displayed.

4 **Click the Slide number check box. Click the Footer check box, and in the Footer box, type** `Created by:` **and then type your name. Click the *Don't show on title slide* check box, and then click Apply to All.**

5 **Click slide 2 and verify that the footer displays as intended. Compare your screen with Figure 10.36. Save 💾 your file.**

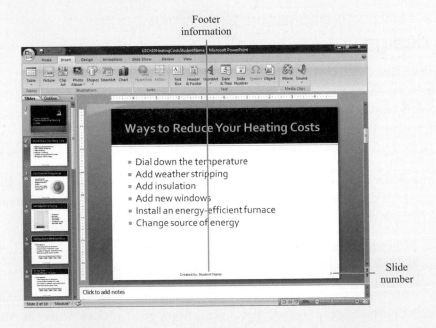

Footer
information

Slide
number

FIGURE 10.36

You can save a PowerPoint presentation as a Single File Web Page or as a Web Page. With the former, it creates a single integrated file that can be uploaded and viewed using Microsoft Internet Explorer. The Web Page save option creates a file and a folder; the folder contains supporting files such as bullets, backgrounds, and pictures, and both the file and the folder have to be uploaded to the Web site. This combination of file and folder is viewable by all types of browsers. In this task, you will save your presentation as a Single File Web Page and view it using Internet Explorer.

to save presentation as a web page

1 **Click the Office button, and then click Save As. In the Save As dialog box, if necessary, navigate to the Chapter10 folder where you are saving your files.**

2 **Click the Save as type arrow, and then click Single File Web Page.** The lower portion of the dialog box changes to include some additional options that are available for a Web page.

3 **Click the Change Title button. In the Set Page Title dialog box, in the Page title box type** Reduce Heating Costs **Compare your screen with Figure 10.37.** This is the title that will display on the title bar of the browser when the presentation is displayed.

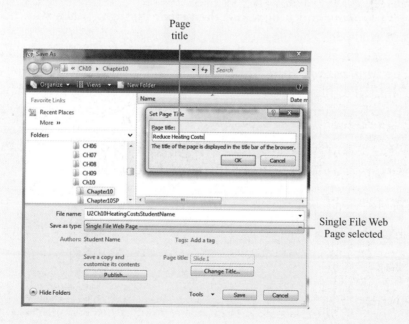

FIGURE 10.37

4 **In the Set Page Title dialog box, click OK.**

5 **In the Save As dialog box, click the Publish button.** The Publish as Web Page dialog box displays. Here, you can limit the slides you publish, choose the browsers that you want to support, decide if you want to display speaker notes, and make other selections. Compare your screen with Figure 10.38.

Options for
what to publish

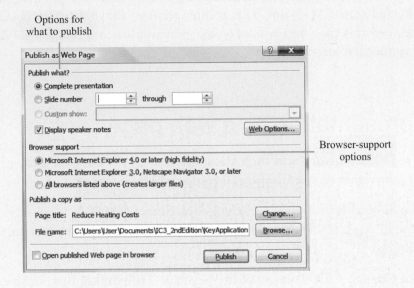

Browser-support
options

FIGURE 10.38

6 At the bottom of the Publish as Web Page dialog box, click the *Open published Web page in browser* check box, and then click Publish. When you click Publish, several things happen. The file is saved in your folder as an *MHTML* file, which is the format used for single-page Web files. Your browser opens, but the file does not display. The *Information Bar* displays at the top of the window to warn you of security issues related to files that you want to open. In this case, security has restricted this Web page from running *ActiveX controls*—small programs developed by Microsoft that add functionality to existing programs. See Figure 10.39.

Information
Bar

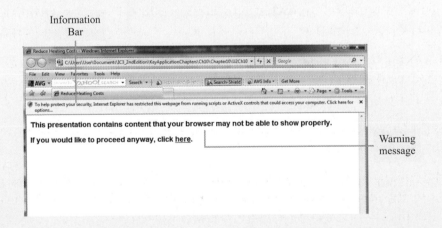

Warning
message

FIGURE 10.39

7 **Click the Information Bar, and then click *Allow Blocked Content*. In the next warning dialog box, click *Yes* to confirm that you want to run the ActiveX controls.** The first slide displays, and the left pane displays the first bullet point from each slide. Buttons along the bottom of the window enable you to navigate the slides, expand or collapse the outline, or view the presentation as a slide show. Compare your screen with Figure 10.40.

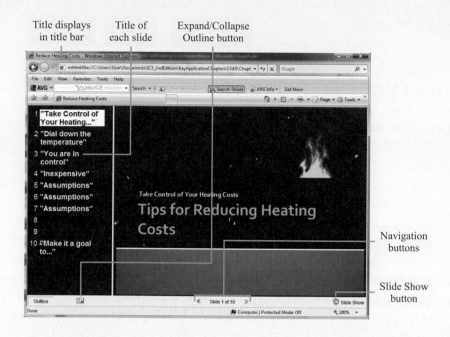

FIGURE 10.40

8 **Click the Slide Show button.** If an Information Bar dialog box displays, click Close to close the dialog box.

9 **At the top of the window, click the Information Bar. From the list, click *Allow Blocked Content*, and then click *Yes* to continue and display the presentation.**

10 **Click as necessary to pace through the presentation and observe the transitions and animations that display on the slides.** The custom animations that were applied to the chart and SmartArt graphic may not display in this environment.

11 **On slide 10, point to the Energy Star logo, and then click the image to display the Energy Star Web page.**

12 **On the Energy Star Web page, right-click, and then click the Back button to return to the presentation. Press** ⟨Esc⟩ **to stop the slide show.** When you click the Back button, the first slide in the presentation displays.

13 **Close ▨ the browser.**

CHOOSE ELEMENTS APPROPRIATE TO VIEWING ON THE INTERNET

If you save a file as a Web page, review it with your browser before you post it to a Web site. Animations and other content items may not work as expected on the Web. If you have a lot of pictures in your presentation, they may be slow to display. It may be necessary to make adjustments to the presentation before uploading it to a server. Review it with the browsers that your audience is likely to use to see if it will play as expected.

to extend **your knowledge**

SAVING DOCUMENTS IN WEB FORMAT

If you have a Web site that is shared with your intended audience, saving documents in a Web format is a good way to distribute documents when you want everyone on that site to view the information. When you use the Single File Web Page format, the file is saved with the MHTML format (MIME HTML)—an HTML format that binds the components of a file together in one file. MHTML files can only be viewed using Internet Explorer. With MHTML format, all of the supporting files are stored together with the document, using one file name.

If it is likely that your intended audience will use other browsers such as Firefox, Safari, Chrome, or others, then save it as a Web Page, which uses HTML formatting. The HTML format saves supporting files, such as images, in a separate folder that must also be uploaded to the Web site, along with the HTML file.

Create handouts to have a printed version of your presentation to share with others.

to create handouts

1 Click the Insert tab. In the Text group, click the Header & Footer button.

2 In the Header and Footer dialog box, click the Notes and Handouts tab. Click the *Footer* check box, and in the Footer box, type `U2Ch10HeatingCostsStudentName` Click Apply to All.

3 Click the Office button, point to Print, and then click Print Preview. In the Page Setup group, click the Print What arrow, and then click Handouts, (6 Slides Per Page). The header and footer information displays on the handouts.

4 In the Preview group, click the Next Page button to view the second page.

5 If you are required to print your results, in the Print group, click the Options button. Point to Color/Grayscale, and then click *Pure Black and White*, which will use less ink.

6 If required, print the handouts, or click Close Print Preview to close this window and return to Normal view. Save 🖫 your file and submit your work as instructed.

Advanced Skills or Concepts

In this section, you are introduced to skills that are not taught with step-by-step instructions.

Compressing Images

If your presentation contains many digital pictures, it will increase the overall size of your file. Compressing images helps reduce the file size. You can compress an image by permanently removing portions that have been cropped, reducing the resolution of the image, or changing the file format to a compressed format such as JPEG. To compress images that you have inserted, click one of the images to activate the Picture Tools Format tab. On this tab, in the Adjust group, click the Compress Pictures button. In the Compress Pictures dialog box, click the Options button and set the options to control or change the compression options. After you click OK, to accept your settings, in the Compress Pictures dialog box, you can choose to limit the compression to the selected image. If you do not click this check box, the compression setting will be applied to all images that can be compressed. Go to Help and type *reduce picture size* to read more information.

To see the change in file size, open the Computer window and display the details to see the size of a presentation or of images that you intend to use. After compressing the images, look at the file size again to see if compression reduced the size of the presentation.

Creating a Drawing with Shapes

In addition to the clip art, pictures, tables, SmartArt, and other graphic tools that you have used, you can also create drawings by using the Shapes that are available from the Insert tab in the Illustrations group. In particular, if you want to illustrate a specific process, it may require a combination of images, shapes, arrows, and text. The Shapes gallery provides a wide variety of tools that can be used to construct an illustration—such as a map to a location. Once created, you can use fill colors to shade the object, add text, change the line color surrounding a shape, and in some cases use arrows to connect one shape to the next. Shapes can be layered one on top of another and grouped together so that they move together as one image.

Copying a Presentation to a CD

You may need to save your presentation to a CD for portability, offsite storage, or distribution. This may be necessary to ensure that any linked files—such as videos or sound files saved on your computer—are included in your presentation. This process also packages the PowerPoint Viewer with the presentation in case the PowerPoint program is not available to display the file. To copy a presentation to a CD, open the presentation file. Display the Office menu, point to Publish, and then click Package for CD. In the Package for CD dialog box, in the Name the CD box, type the name for the CD or the folder that you want to copy your presentation to. Click the Options button, and under *Package type*, select how the presentation will play. You can also choose to include linked files and embedded TrueType fonts. After you have selected your options, click OK to return to the Package for CD dialog box. Depending on the location where you are copying the file—a folder or a CD—click the appropriate button. To learn more about this feature, display the PowerPoint Help dialog box, and then type *Package for CD* in the search box.

CHECK YOUR WORK

Here is a list of items your instructor will probably look for when grading your work. To improve your evaluation, take time to check the items yourself before you turn in your work.

Heating Presentation
- Module theme applied to all 10 slides.
- Slide 1 is a title slide and includes a movie clip inserted on the slide.
- Text is inserted from the Word outline for slides 2 through 5.
- Slides 5 through 7 include a table inserted below the text.
- Slide 8 is a cylinder bar chart.
- Slide 9 is a SmartArt graphic that includes three rows of chevron shapes.
- The SmartArt has three shapes in the first row and four shapes in the next two rows.
- The color on the SmartArt is changed to *Colorful Range – Accent Color 3 and 4*.
- The SmartArt has a Design effect of 3-D Inset.
- Slide 10 includes the Energy Star logo, which is formatted as a hyperlink to the Energy Star Web site.
- Slide 1 has the Dissolve transition applied.
- Slides 2 through 10 have the Uncover Right-Down transition applied.
- The text boxes on slides 2 through 7 and 10 are animated using Wipe By, 1st Level Paragraphs.
- The thermometer graphic on slide 3 is animated using the Fly In effect.
- The tables on slides 5 through 7 have the Strips animation applied with a Right Down direction applied.
- The chart on slide 8 is animated using Vertical Blinds by Series.
- The SmartArt on slide 9 is animated with Expand one by one.
- The image on slide 10 is animated using the Faded Zoom effect.
- The presentation is set to print as a Handout with six slides to a page.

KEY TERMS |

activeX controls

animations

hyperlink

information bar

movie clips

SmartArt

ASSESSING LEARNING OUTCOMES |

SCREEN ID

Identify each element of the screen by matching callout numbers shown in Figure 10.41 to a corresponding description.

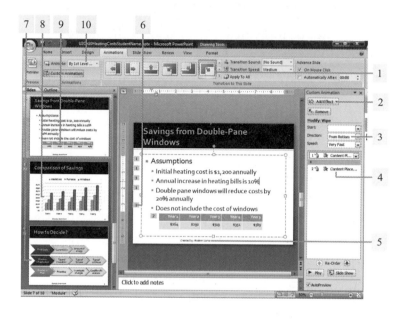

FIGURE 10.41

_____ **A.** Table

_____ **B.** Chart

_____ **C.** Applied transition

_____ **D.** Animation effect applied to text

_____ **E.** Indicates order of animation

_____ **F.** Animation applied to table

_____ **G.** SmartArt graphic

_____ **H.** Animation direction

_____ **I.** Footer information

_____ **J.** Used to add a custom animation

MULTIPLE CHOICE

Circle the letter of the correct answer for each of the following. The lesson in which the term or concept was introduced is indicated at the end of the sentence.

1. To apply custom animations to slides, it is best to use the _____ view. [L6]
   a. Normal
   b. Slides
   c. Slide Master
   d. Slide Sorter

2. To import content from a Word document using the Slides from Outline command, the Word file must be formatted as _____. [L1]
   a. a bulleted list
   b. a numbered list
   c. an outline with heading levels
   d. a table list

3. Tables can be used for _____. [L3]
   a. parallel data
   b. financial information
   c. weather data
   d. all of the above

4. Text imported from an outline _____. [L1, L2]
   a. changes to the default font used in PowerPoint
   b. retains the font from the Word file
   c. changes to the font used when a theme is applied
   d. uses a plain-text font

5. When formatting a table, all of the following are true **except**: [L3]
   a. The Table Tools tabs used in Word are available to use in PowerPoint.
   b. Changes made to the font size or text alignment are not affected when a theme is applied to a presentation.
   c. A change to the table style is not affected when a theme is applied to a presentation.

d. A presentation theme can change the placement of a table on a slide.

6. When you apply a theme to a presentation, it is important to review your presentation for _____. [L2]
   a. text boxes that may have moved
   b. objects that may have moved
   c. text that may not be visible
   d. all of the above

7. To show trends over time, the best chart type to use is the _____ chart. [L4]
   a. line
   b. pie
   c. area
   d. column

8. SmartArt diagrams can be used to show all of the following **except** _____. [L5]
   a. organizational charts
   b. bar charts
   c. process diagrams
   d. cyclical relationships

9. A SmartArt graphic whose purpose is to show a decision tree would be found in the _____ category. [L5]
   a. Pyramid
   b. Cycle
   c. Hierarchy
   d. Matrix

10. Animations can be applied to _____. [L6]
    a. a group of slides all at once
    b. graphic or text objects
    c. text boxes only
    d. cells in a table

MATCHING

Match the term or concept to its description.

_____ 1. Text or a graphic that, when clicked, connects you to a location in a file or a Web page.

_____ 2. A graphic that creates a visual representation of concepts or information.

_____ 3. By 1st Level Paragraphs.

_____ 4. A graphic diagram that shows how parts are related to the whole.

_____ 5. An animation applied to a chart.

_____ 6. An animation applied to a SmartArt graphic.

_____ 7. An area that displays to warn you of security issues related to files that have you opened.

_____ 8. A graphic diagram that shows information that is not sequential.

_____ 9. Controls how text and other objects come onto the screen during a slide show.

_____ 10. Small programs developed by Microsoft that add functionality to existing programs.

A. ActiveX control

B. Animations

C. By Series

D. Hyperlink

E. Information Bar

F. List diagram

G. Matrix diagram

H. One by one

I. SmartArt

J. Text animation effect

SKILL DRILL

The skill drill exercise is a repeat of the lessons in the chapter but with a different set of data. The instructions are less detailed, and your speed and familiarity should increase with practice. There is a figure at the end against which you can check your results. The purpose of this exercise is to build your confidence and speed in using these skills and to set them in your memory for later recall. The section numbers correspond to the lesson numbers. You are welcome to refer back to the lesson's illustrated and detailed instructions if necessary.

In this exercise, you create a presentation about petroleum that will be used to start a discussion about independence from Mideast oil.

1. Importing Text from an Outline

1. **Start** PowerPoint. On the **Quick Access Toolbar**, click the **Save** button. Navigate to the **Chapter10** folder that you created earlier. In the **File name** box, type U2Ch10OilStudentName and then click **Save**.

2. Click in the title placeholder and type Achieving Independence from Mideast Oil Click in the subtitle placeholder and type What will it take?

3. **Start** Word 2007. From your student files, locate and open the **U2Ch10Oil** file. Review the content of the file and verify that it is in an outline format with heading levels. **Close** Word.

4. In the PowerPoint window, on the **Home** tab, in the **Slides** group, click the **New Slide button arrow.** From the list, click **Slides from Outline.**

5. In the Insert Outline dialog box, navigate to the student folder for this chapter. Locate and select **U2Ch10Oil**, and then click **Insert.**

6. Click on each slide and review the content; then **Save** your file.

2. Applying a Theme and Adding Graphics

1. Display slide 1 on the Slide pane, and then click the **Design** tab. In the **Themes** group, click the **More** button. From the Themes gallery, under Built-In, locate and click the **Concourse** theme.

2. Click **slide 2** and observe that the font did not change for the imported text.

3. Hold down ⬆Shift and click **slide 6** to select all of the slides from 2 through 6.

4. Click the **Home** tab, and then in the **Slides** group, click the **Reset** button to apply the font format from the Concourse theme to the selected slides.

5. Display slide 1, and then click the **Insert** tab. In the **Illustrations** group, click **Clip Art.**

6. In the Clip Art task pane, click the *Results should be* arrow, and click **Movies** to select it and clear all other check boxes. In the *Search for* box, type oil and then click **Go.**

7. Click the image shown in Figure 10.42 or one that is similar. Move the image and resize it, as shown in Figure 10.42.

8. On the status bar, click the **Slide Show** button to view the animation on the inserted graphic. Press Esc to return to Normal view, and then close the Clip Art task pane.

9. **Save** your work.

3. Adding Tables to a Presentation

1. Click **slide 4.** On the **Home** tab, in the **Slides** group, click the **Layout** button, and then click **Title and Content.**

2. In the content placeholder, click the **Insert Table** button. In the Insert Table dialog box, Change the *Number of columns* to 2 and the *Number of rows* to 7 and then click **OK.**

3. In the top row of the table, type Regional Source Press Tab⇆ and type Energy from Petroleum (TerawattHours)

4. Press Tab⇆ and enter the rest of the data in the table as follows:

North America	2,474
South America	906
Mideast	1,222
North Africa	421
Sub-Saharan Africa	1,019
Asia	294

5. Click the **Table Tools Layout** tab. In the **Table** group, click the **Select** button, and then click **Select Table.** In the **Alignment** group, click the **Center** button, and then click the **Center Vertically** button.

6. On the bottom edge of the table, point to the middle sizing handle and drag down to the 2-inch mark on the vertical ruler to expand the table.

7. Click the **Home** tab, and in the **Font** group, click the **Increase Font Size** button until the font size is **24.**

8. Click the **Insert** tab. In the **Illustrations** group, click the **Shapes** button. In the Shapes gallery, under *Recently Used Shapes* (or under *Basic Shapes*), click the **Oval** shape. On the table, in the second column, fourth row—*1,222*—drag to place an oval around this amount. The oval covers the amount because it has a solid fill color.

9. With the oval selected, click the **Drawing Tools Format** tab. In the **Shape Styles** group, click the **Shape Fill button arrow,** and then click **No Fill.** Use the sizing handles or move the pointer to adjust the placement of the oval as necessary. Compare your results with Figure 10.42.

10. **Save** your work. Click **slide 5.** Change the slide layout to **Two Content.** This layout has a dark background. In the placeholder on the left, type: `Need to create 1,222 TwH of energy to replace Mideast oil`

11. On the lower edge of the placeholder, point to the middle sizing handle and drag up to the 1-inch mark, above the 0 on the vertical ruler. On the right of the placeholder, point to the middle sizing handle and drag to the right to the 4.5-inch mark on the horizontal ruler. This creates a narrow text box at the top of the slide under the title.

12. Using the technique you just practiced, resize the right-side placeholder into a horizontal shape in the lower half of the slide, starting at the 0-inch mark on the vertical ruler.

13. In the bottom placeholder, click the **Insert Table** button and create a 3-column and 4-row table. Enter the following data in the table:

Source	Energy Currently Generated (TwH)	Multiple of Installed Capacity Needed
Wind and Solar	96	12.8x
Hydro	289	4.2x
Nuclear	787	1.5x

14. Point to the top edge of the middle column, and when the ⬇ pointer displays, drag to the right to select the last two columns in the table. Click the **Table Tools Layout** tab, and in the **Alignment** group, click the **Align Text Right** button.

15. Select the top row of the table, and then in the **Alignment** group, click the **Center Vertically** button.

16. In the **Table** group, click the **Select** button, and then click **Select Table.** Click the **Home** tab. In the **Font** group, click the **Increase Font Size** button until the font is 24 pt. **Save** your changes and compare your results with slide 5 in Figure 10.42. Adjust the position of the table on the slide if necessary.

4. Adding Charts to a Presentation

1. Click **slide 3.** On the **Home** tab, in the **Slides** group, click the **Layout** button, and then click **Title and Content.**

2. In the content placeholder, click the **Insert Chart** button. In the Insert Chart dialog box, on the left, click **Pie.** On the right, under Pie, click the second option—*Pie in 3-D*—and then click **OK.**

3. In the displayed *Chart in Microsoft Office PowerPoint – Microsoft Excel* window, click cell **B1** and type Sources

4. Point to the corner of cell **B5** and drag down to cell **B7** to increase the range for the chart data. Beginning in cell **A2,** enter the following data:

Coal	1,990
Petroleum	64
Natural Gas	813
Nuclear	787
Hydroelectric	289
Wind and Solar	96

5. Confirm that the numbers you typed are correct, and then close the Microsoft Excel window.

6. With the chart selected, click the **Chart Tools Layout** tab. In the **Labels** group, click the **Chart Title** button, and then click **None.** The title on the slide is sufficient, and a chart title is redundant.

7. On the **Layout** tab, in the **Labels** group, click the **Legend** button, and then click **Show Legend at Bottom.** Click the **Data Labels** button, and then click **Outside End.**

8. **Save** your work.

5. Inserting Diagrams Using SmartArt

1. Click **slide 6** and change the layout to **Title and Content.** In the content placeholder, click the **Insert SmartArt Graphic** button.

2. On the left side of the Choose SmartArt Graphic dialog box, click **List,** and then in the fourth row, locate and click the **Vertical Chevron List** layout. Click **OK.**

3. On the **SmartArt Tools Design** tab, in the **Create Graphic** group, click the **Text pane** button. In the Text pane, with the first bullet point selected, type Wind / Solar Click next to the second bullet point and type Best sites in oceans or Great Lakes Then click next to the third bullet point and type Need sunny locations

4. On the slide, in the second row of the SmartArt, click the first chevron graphic and type `Hydro` Click next to the bullet point to the right and type `Most effective sites already in use` and then press ⌈Delete⌉ to remove the second bullet point from this graphic.

5. Using either the Text pane or the graphic for the last chevron, type `Nuclear` and then for the bullet points, type:

   `Many existing sites have room for a second plant`

   `Fuel-recycling and waste-disposal issues`

6. Close the Text pane. On the **SmartArt Tools Design** tab, in the **Layouts** group, locate and click the **Vertical Arrow List** to change the SmartArt layout.

7. In the **SmartArt Styles** group, display the styles gallery, and then click **Subtle Effect.**

8. Compare your results with slide 6 in Figure 10.42, and then **Save** your changes.

6. Adding Animations

1. On the status bar, click the **Slide Sorter** button. Click **slide 1,** hold down ⌈⬆Shift⌉, and then click **slide 6** to select all of the slides.

2. Click the **Animations** tab. In the **Transitions to This Slide** group, click the **More** button. Under **Wipes,** click **Box Out.** Click the **Transition Speed** arrow, and then click **Medium.** On the status bar, click the **Normal** button.

3. Click **slide 2,** and then on the slide, click the text box. On the **Animations** tab, in the **Animations** group, click the **Animate box** arrow**.** Under **Fade,** click **By 1st Level Paragraphs.**

4. Click **slide 5,** and click the text box. In the **Animations** group, display the **Animate** list, and then under **Fade,** click **All At Once.**

5. On slide 5, click the table. In the **Animations group,** click the **Custom Animation** button. In the Custom Animation task pane, click the **Add Effect** button, point to *Entrance,* and then click **Faded Zoom.**

6. Click **slide 3,** and then click the pie chart. In the Custom Animation task pane, click the **Add Effect** button, point to *Entrance.* and then click **Spiral In.** If necessary, use the More Effects button to locate this effect in the Exciting group.

7. Click the **Content Placeholder** arrow, and then click **Effect Options.** In the Spiral In dialog box, click the **Chart Animation** tab. Click the **Group chart** arrow, and then click **By Category.** Click **OK.** Change the **Speed** to **Medium,** and then click **Play** to test this effect.

8. Click **slide 6,** and click the SmartArt graphic. On the Custom Animation task pane, click the **Add Effect** button, point to *Entrance,* and then click **More Effects.** In the Add Entrance Effect dialog box, under *Moderate,* click **Descend,** and then click **OK.**

9. On the Custom Animation task pane, click the **Content Placeholder** for the effect that you just added, click the arrow to display the list, and then click **Effect Options.** In the Descend dialog box, click the **SmartArt Animation** tab. Click the **Group graphic** arrow, and then click **By level one by one.** Click **OK.**

10. Close the Custom Animation task pane. **Save** your changes.

7. Adding Hyperlinks and Saving as a Web Page

1. Click **slide 4.** Click the **Insert** tab, and in the **Text** group, click the **Text Box** button. On the slide, under the table, click to place the text box and type `Click here for more information`

2. Select the text you just typed. On the **Insert** tab, in the **Links** group, click the **Hyperlink** button.

3. In the **Insert Hyperlink** dialog box, under Link to:, be sure that *Existing File or Web Page* is selected. In the Address box type `http://eia.doe.gov`

4. Click the **ScreenTip** button, and in the Screen Tip text box, type `Oil Imports` Click **OK** in both dialog boxes.

5. On the **Insert** tab, click the **Header & Footer** button. Click the **Slide number** check box and the **Footer** check box. In the Footer box, type `Presented by:` and then type your name. Click **Apply to All. Save** your changes.

6. Click the **Office** button, and then click **Save As.** In the Save As dialog box, if necessary, navigate to the Chapter10 folder where you are saving your files.

7. Click the **Save as type** arrow, and then click **Single File Web Page.** Click the **Change Title** button. In the Set Page Title dialog box, in the Page title box, type `Oil Independence` and then click **OK.**

8. In the Save As dialog box, click **Publish.** At the bottom of the Publish as Web Page dialog box, be sure the *Open published Web page in browser* check box is selected, and then click **Publish.**

9. Click the **Information Bar,** and then click *Allow Blocked Content.* In the next warning dialog box, click **Yes** to confirm that you want to run the ActiveX controls.

10. In the browser window, click the **Slide Show** button and allow the blocked content. Pace through the presentation and look for any items that may need to be corrected. Test the hyperlink to be sure that it works as expected. Close the browser window.

11. Check the spelling in your presentation. If you are required to submit printed documentation, display the Header and Footer dialog box. On the **Notes and Handouts** tab, click the **Footer** check box, and in the Footer box, type `U2Ch10OilStudentName`

12. Display the Print Preview window. Change the Print What box to **Handouts (6 Slides Per Page).** Click the **Options** button, and change the Color/Grayscale option to *Pure Black and White.*

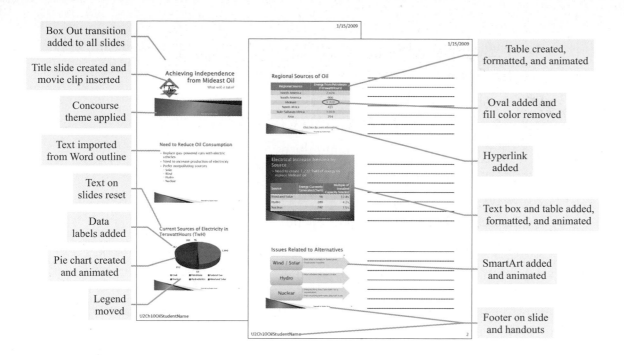

Box Out transition added to all slides

Title slide created and movie clip inserted

Concourse theme applied

Text imported from Word outline

Text on slides reset

Data labels added

Pie chart created and animated

Legend moved

Table created, formatted, and animated

Oval added and fill color removed

Hyperlink added

Text box and table added, formatted, and animated

SmartArt added and animated

Footer on slide and handouts

FIGURE 10.42

fix *it*

One way to appreciate the value of good design is to fix a file that is not designed well. In this exercise, you open a file that has several errors and design flaws and fix it according to the good design elements, using the skills that you practiced in the lessons.

Navigate to the folder with the student files, open **U2Ch10FixIt,** and save it as U2Ch10FixItStudentName

Examine this presentation and modify it, using the skills you have practiced, to create a professional presentation. Review the content and make changes to the design, layout, formats, and animations that are needed to comply with the good design principles covered in this chapter. Include the file name and slide number on the slides. Here is a list of design principles introduced in this chapter, along with some tips on how to fix the presentation. Use the principles that are appropriate for each slide.

- Change the slide layouts where graphics are needed.

- Use consistent fonts from the applied theme on all the slides. Each bullet point and the main title words begin with a capital letter.

- Add relevant clip art or pictures to enhance your slides and balance the text. Adjust placement of figures and text as needed.

- Format tabular data as a table. Place appropriate information in tables so that it is easy to compare numbers.

- Keep fonts large enough to be readable from the back of the room. Divide topics onto two slides when necessary.

- Include charts to illustrate relationships and trends in numerical data. Use the appropriate chart type for the trend or relationship. Adjust the data range to include your data and not any sample data.
- Organize chart by category or series to show desired relationship.
- Use SmartArt to illustrate relationships between concepts.
- Keep your SmartArt simple. Limit the number of items and shapes.
- Use the same animation for text on all slides.
- Use the same animation, direction, and speed for each type of object.
- Choose animations that support the purpose of the graphic.
- Use relevant hyperlinks to augment the presentation.
- Choose elements appropriate to viewing on the Internet.

A successful result will apply the theme font on all slides and good design principles for capitalizing titles and bullet points. Images will not overlap text but will be balanced with the text. Tabular data will be displayed in a table and sized so that the text is readable. The chart will display only the relevant data that was entered on the Excel worksheet. A correct chart type will be selected to display the numerical relationship. Consistent animations will be applied to the text, table, and SmartArt. The chart will include an animation to emphasize the difference in the cost of the two types of bulbs. The presentation will be error-free and include the file name in the slide footer area. Submit the file as required by your instructor. Save and close the file.

ON THE JOB

Information workers add value to data by organizing, selecting, displaying, communicating, interpreting, and using data to communicate information and support decisions. On the Job exercises simulate a situation where you are given data, and your job is to add value to it using the skills you practiced in this chapter. Success in these exercises indicates that you have a valuable skill to offer an employer.

1. LED Presentation

In this On the Job exercise, you will assist the facilities manager. He has gathered information about the cost of replacing incandescent halogen spotlights used throughout the building with LED spots. He would like to present this information at the next board meeting as part of the Green Initiative. Refer to the e-mail from the facilities manager, and then, using the skills you have practiced in this chapter, create a presentation.

> *Rob,*
> *We are in the process of reviewing all of the lighting in our building, and I have gathered some information about the cost of replacement versus the cost of operating. (Refer to U2Ch10LED.) Create a short presentation—6 slides should be enough. I would like a chart of the difference in costs because it is pretty dramatic. Make sure that it is easy to compare the actual numbers, and use some of that fancy art that you showed me last week.*

I need this in time for the board meeting on Friday. I am counting on your good sense of style and creativeness to create a professional and appealing presentation.
Thanks,
C.J.

1. Create a new presentation and save it in your Chapter10 folder as `U2Ch10LEDStudentName`

2. Follow the good design principles listed in the Fix It exercise.

3. On the title slide, use `Light-Emitting Diode Spots` as the title of the presentation and `Cost Benefit Analysis` as the subtitle.

4. Import the text from the *U2CH10LED* Word file provided. Apply the Aspect theme and reset the slides so that the font is consistent throughout.

5. On slide 2, change the layout to a Two Content layout and insert the U2Ch10Spot image on the right. Adjust the placement of the text box and the image so that the bullet points do not wrap to more than two lines.

6. Make the same changes to slide 3, and insert the U2Ch10LEDBulb image. Insert a hyperlink to the image to the `http://www.earthled.com/evolux-led-light-bulb.html` site, and use `LED Comparisons` as the ScreenTip.

7. On slide 4, change the information in the last three bullet points to an appropriate SmartArt graphic. Place the SmartArt on the bottom half of the slide and the text on the top. Remove the bullet points from the text area after you have inserted the SmartArt.

8. On slide 5, change the information in the second and third bullet points to a table to compare the two types of bulbs by lumen, cost, watts, and hours of use. Remove those points from the bulleted list. Maximize the size of the table and the font, and center the text.

9. Open the **U2Ch10LED** Word document, and use the information shown in the table at the end of the outline to create a chart on slide 6. Display the chart so that the type of bulb is in the legend.

10. Add a transition to the slides. Apply custom animations to the text boxes so that each first-level paragraph displays one at a time. Animate the images and the table to display after the text is displayed. Add a custom animation to the chart so that the chart elements display by each of the bulb types.

11. Add your name and the slide number in the footer area, and Save the file.

12. Save the file as a Single Page Web File, and use `LED Lights` as the title.

13. Create a handout with six slides to a page, and include the file name in the footer area of the handout. Print the handout and note page, or submit the file as directed by your instructor. Save the file and then close it.

2. Capacity Rating Presentation

In this On the Job exercise, you will add a table, chart, movie clip, and SmartArt graphic to a presentation about electrical capacity. Then you will add transitions and animations before saving it as a Single File Web Page. Refer to the specifications provided below.

1. Open the file **U2Ch10Capacity** and save it as `U2CH10CapacityStudentName`

2. Follow the good design principles listed in the Fix It exercise.

3. On slide 4, change the content to a SmartArt graphic that is appropriate to the data, and change the color and apply a 3-D SmartArt style.

4. On slide 5, insert a movie clip that invokes the concept of wind.

5. On slide 6, create a table of the following data. On the same slide, create a 3-D column chart of the same data.

Wind Speed	12 mph	10 mph	8 mph	6 mph
Power Output	1,000 KW	578 KW	296 KW	125 KW

6. Add transitions to the slides. Add animations to the text so that the text on each slide comes onto the screen all at once. Add a custom animation to the SmartArt, table, and chart.

7. Add your name and slide number to the slides. Include the file name in the footer of the handout page, and set it to print in grayscale.

8. Save the file.

9. Save the file as a Single File Web Page. and then close it. Print the handout or submit the files as directed by your instructor.

DISCUSSION OF ADVANCED SKILLS OR CONCEPTS

The questions in this section are based on the topics in the Advanced Skills or Concepts section of the chapter.

1. Have you sent or received images electronically that took a long time to download? What are the advantages or disadvantages of compressing images?

2. Describe an image or drawing that you might need to create where using shapes to create your illustration would be useful.

3. Other than the Excel chapter—in which callouts were used—describe other circumstances where you have used shapes to create a drawing such as a map.

4. In your experience, how does creating a drawing using shapes and lines compare with using pictures, SmartArt, or other graphical tools? Which do you prefer and why?

ON YOUR OWN

Once you are comfortable with the skills in this chapter, you can apply them to new situations of your own choosing. In this section, you choose data that you have in your possession or that you can find elsewhere. To successfully complete this assignment, you must apply good design practices and demonstrate mastery of the skills that were practiced. Refer to the list of skills and design practices in the Fix It exercise.

1. Create a Presentation About Lighting for an Organization

Work with an organization such as a church, fraternal organization, club, or apartment building. Investigate the type of lighting used in the organization's building. Obtain copies of their electrical utility bills for the past year or two. Using the information provided in the previous presentations and the information that you obtain from the organization, create a presentation about the steps necessary to reduce their electrical bill. Include a chart, table, and SmartArt. Use the good design principles that have been emphasized in this chapter. Apply a theme, transitions, and animations to the slide text and objects. Include your name on the slides and the file name on a handout copy. Save the file as U2Ch10LightsStudentName and submit the file as instructed.

2. Create a Presentation About Gasoline Prices

Using the Internet, research historical gasoline prices at the pump and create a presentation that discusses the changes in gasoline prices over the past 10 years. Look for data in your state or region. Select two specific days per year—one in the winter and another in the summer. Gather the gas prices for these dates for the last 10 years from your source. In your presentation, include a hyperlink to your source. One possible source to research is http://tonto.eia.doe.gov/dnav/pet/pet_pri_gnd_dcus_nus_w.htm

In your presentation, display the gas price information with a chart and a table. From this information, determine if there is a historical trend or a seasonal difference. Use the information to persuade your class of your point of view regarding gas prices and how it affects your decisions about the type of vehicle you drive or the type of vehicle you would purchase. Consider other issues such as commuting distance between school, work, and home. Include appropriate SmartArt, movie or clip art, animations, transitions, or other tools that you have practiced in this chapter. Include the file name on the slides.

Save the file as U2Ch10GasolineStudentName and submit it as directed.

ASSESS YOUR PROGRESS

At this point, you should have a set of skills and design concepts that are valuable to an employer and to you. You may not realize how much you have learned unless you take a few minutes to assess your progress.

1. From the student files, open **U2Ch10Assess.** Save it as U2Ch10AssessStudentName

2. Read each question in column A.

3. In column B, answer Yes or No.

4. If you identify a skill or design concept that you don't know, refer to the learning objective code next to the question and the table at the beginning of the chapter to find the skill and review it.

5. Print the worksheet if your instructor requires it. The file name is already in the header, so it will display your name as part of the file name.

6. All of these skills and concepts have been identified as important by surveying hundreds of individuals working at over 200 companies worldwide. If you cannot answer all of the questions affirmatively even after reviewing the relevant lesson, seek additional help from your instructor.

Glossary

800 band Range of frequencies from 824–894 MHz

8.3 convention An early DOS file-naming convention that used up to eight letters or numbers to the left of a period and up to three characters to the right of a period

1900 band Range of frequencies from 1850–1990 MHz

3-D pie chart A 3-dimensional disk that is divided into wedges that resemble pieces of a pie

A

AAC (.aac) Popular audio compression method

absolute cell reference In a formula, a reference to a cell location that is stored as a given row and column and does not change when the formula is filled

activated Process of recording the service provider's SID and the user's MIN into a phone

active cell The cell where data will display when you type

active-matrix display An LCD monitor type that charges each pixel as necessary

ActiveX Programming language suitable for automating functions on Web pages

ActiveX controls Small programs developed by Microsoft that add functionality to existing programs

adaptive computer device Input devices designed for special needs of people with different types of disabilities

address bar Displays your current location in the folder structure as a series of links separated by arrows

address book Feature that stores a list of names and e-mail addresses with other information

address box Area of a browser in which the Web address is entered

administrator Top level of computer access that enables a person to add or delete programs, add users, and make other significant changes

add-on Program that extends the capability of an application

advanced mobile phone system (AMPS) Early standard for 1G mobile phones

Advanced Research Projects Agency (ARPA) Government agency that created a network of computers named ARPANET that was the forerunner of the Internet

Advanced Television Systems Committee (ATSC) Standard for high definition TV

adware Programs that display advertising without the user's permission

Aero The advanced graphical user interface introduced in Vista

algorithm A set of instructions that a computer can follow to accomplish a task

alignment The horizontal placement of text, whether it is between the left and right margins in a Word document, in a cell on an Excel worksheet, on a PowerPoint slide, or in a graphic object

All Programs Option on the Start menu that displays all installed programs

alpha version The first version of a software program; it comes before beta testing

Alternate (Alt) key Key on the keyboard intended for use with other keys to provide new functions

American Psychological Association (APA) One of two commonly used styles for formatting research papers and reports

American Standard Code for Information Interchange (ASCII) A group that chose which eight bit numbers would represent letters, decimal numbers, and special function characters

amplify Make stronger

amplitude Strength of a wave

amplitude modulation (AM) Varying the strength of a signal

analog An electronic signal or system that varies in time in a way that is similar to the event it is portraying

analog to digital (A to D) converter A device that takes an analog input, such as a voice recorded by a microphone, and converts it to a digital signal

anchor A symbol that indicates the paragraph with which a graphic object is associated

and Logical operator that requires that all criteria be met

animation The process of making objects on the screen move; in PowerPoint, controls how text and other objects come onto the screen during a slide show

antenna Device that conducts charged particles to generate or receive EM wave energy

appliance A computer that is dedicated to a particular task or function

application program Programs with which you can accomplish tasks such as word processing, photo editing, or sending e-mail

application service provider (ASP) Software provided online for special purposes on a license or per-use basis

application software See *application program*

archive Inactive storage

archiving Removing from active use to a storage location

argument A value or expression used by the function, which instructs Excel how to execute the function

ARPANET Network of computers managed by the Advanced Research Projects Agency

asynchronous Communications that do not require the participants to take part at the same time

asynchronous digital subscriber line (ADSL) Type of fast connection to the Internet provided by telephone companies

atomic clock Time-keeping device that uses vibrations of atoms for high accuracy

attenuation Weakening

auction Offer for sale to the highest bidder

AutoArchive Feature for automatically moving files from active use to inactive storage

AutoComplete A feature that begins to complete a cell entry based on other entries in the same column

AutoFit Automatic process to adjust the width of a column or height of a row to fit the largest content

automatic teller machine (ATM) Computer terminal that can dispense cash and accept deposits

AutoRecover A feature that saves a copy of open files at regular intervals to create a version of the file that can be recovered in the event of a computer malfunction

B

backbone Connections between networks

backdoor Program that bypasses normal security measures to allow outside access

backlight Fluorescent light used with LCD panels

backwardly compatible The ability of a newer version of a program to open and display files that were created using an earlier version of the program

bandwidth Range of frequencies used for transmission

bar chart Uses horizontal rectangles whose length represents the value of the data

bar code reader Device that reads a series of vertical bars and spaces that represent a code that can include price and inventory information

BD-R A Blu-ray disc that can be recorded one time

BD-RE A Blu-ray disc that can be erased and recorded many times

BD-ROM A Blu-ray disc that is read-only

beta tester Person who evaluates a prerelease version of software

beta version Early version of the software released to a limited audience for testing

bibliography A list of sources used in a report, which are listed at the end of the document

binary System that has two states that can be represented using zeros and ones

biometric device A security device that can match a user's biological information—comparing fingerprints, retinal scans, or voice prints—with patterns stored in a database to confirm the identity of authorized users

bit (b) A single digit—either a zero or a one—in a binary number

bitmap (.bmp) Rectangular array of picture elements where each has a number to indicate color

blind carbon copy (Bcc) The address to which a copy of an e-mail message is sent that is not revealed to the other recipients

blog Online personal journal, short form for *weblog*

blogosphere Collection of all blogs

Blu-ray Optical disc technology that enables you to save 25 GB on a single-layer disc and 50 GB on a dual-layer disc that is the standard for recording HDTV

Bluetooth A wireless standard used for short distances. Used to connect cell phones and headsets, MP3 players and headphones, and wireless keyboards and mice

body The main part of an e-mail message containing the principle information to be conveyed

body language Communication by gestures and body position

Bookmarks List of website addresses for future reference

Boolean logic Formal rules for making decisions

boot To start the computer

borders Lines on the edges of the cells

bots Automated programs

bridge Connection between two similar networks that use the same protocols

broadband Using multiple signals of different frequency on the same medium to provide fast Internet connections that are always active

broadband coax Type of coaxial cable that can carry signals farther than normal coaxial cable

browser Program that displays Web pages

buffer Memory used to store data temporarily while downloading

bug Errors found in programs that cause the program to fail to complete its operation successfully

build Subdivision of a version used for large software projects

bullet A symbol—often a small round dot—that precedes items in a list

bulleted list A list of information that is in no particular order; each item in the list is preceded by a small symbol or bullet point

bullet point A line of text that is preceded by a small dot or other symbol

burn To write data to an optical disc

business-to-business (B2B) Exchanges between two businesses

business-to-consumer (B2C) Exchanges between businesses and consumers

byte (B) A group of eight bits used to represent characters, decimal numbers, and other special characters

C

cable modem Device that separates data from television signals

cache Temporary storage area

call center Group of people at one location who use audio communications to provide service

callouts Shapes that have a pointer and that contain text

CAPTCHA Distorted word that is recognizable by humans but not computers

carbon copy (Cc) Duplicate of the message

cash flow analysis The process of tracking money coming in and going out

cathode ray Beam of electrons

cathode ray tube (CRT) Analog imaging device that uses a beam of charged particles in a glass vacuum tube that uses an electron beam to create pictures on the end of the tube that is covered with light-emitting phosphors

CDMA2000 Advanced code-division access standard used in 3G phones

CD-R Optical disc to which data may be written

CD-ROM Optical disc from which data may be read

CD-RW Optical disc from which data may be read and to which data may be recorded and rewritten

cell The intersection of a row and column in a worksheet or a table or the area around a mobile phone tower

cell address The column letter and row number that are used to identify a cell in an Excel worksheet

cell phone Mobile phone that uses the cell system

cell phone tower Antenna used in mobile phone systems

cell reference In Excel, the identification of a specific cell by its intersecting column letter and row number

center Text that is aligned horizontally in the middle of an area

central processing unit (CPU) The "brains" of the computer; performs calculations and controls communication in the computer

certificate authority (CA) Entity that warrants the identity of a member

chain e-mail Messages intended to be duplicated and forwarded

channel Pair of frequencies used for full-duplex communications

chat Text-based exchange that takes place when both parties are present

checksum The total of the numbers in a packet

Children's Online Privacy Protection Act (COPPA) Law that protects the rights of children on the Internet

chip Another term for microchip

cipher text Encoded document

circuit breaker Safety device to disconnect electric power

circular reference An error in a formula that is caused when the cell that contains the formula results is included in the formula argument either directly or indirectly

circuit switching Wires that make up a circuit are connected at a central location

citation A reference in a text to the source of the information

classified ad Advertisement that is categorized

click through Using a hyperlink to get to another Web page

client Computer or program that requests services from a server

clip art Images used to illustrate a variety of topics that come with Microsoft Office or are obtained from other sources

clock A device that sends out pulses used to coordinate computer component activity

clock speed The rate at which the clock circuit emits pulses

Close button Closes a file or the application if only one file is open

clustered column chart Groups columns together for convenient comparison between values of the same type

coaxial cable Wire within a tube of metal, both of which are insulated

cochlea Portion of the ear that converts pressure into nerve impulses

cochlear implant Device that converts sound waves into electrical signals that are transmitted to the cochlea where they are converted to nerve impulses

codec Program or hardware that codes and decodes files to make them smaller

code-division multiple access (CDMA) Method of distributing a call over available frequencies

code group Subset of a coded message

column chart Uses vertical rectangles whose height represents the value of the data

column heading In the Computer window Content pane, identifies the columns; click on the headings to sort the file list

Command key Macintosh key similar in function to the Alternate key on other keyboards

command-line interface A way of interacting with the operating system using the keyboard

comment A note that an author or reviewer adds to a document that displays in either a balloon-shaped graphic or in the Reviewing pane

compact disc (CD) Portable, round optical storage medium

compact flash card Removable electronic memory that does not need power to retain data; typically used in digital SLR cameras

comparison operators Symbols that are used to compare two values

compatibility mode Office 2007 files that a saved with a previous version file format

compression Method of reducing file size

Computer In the Computer window, a toolbar that provides buttons to perform common tasks

computer-based training (CBT) Training that is delivered and assessed using a computer

Computer Security Resource Center (CRSC) Government site for security information

conditional formatting A selected format that is applied if a criterion is met

consumer-to-consumer (C2C) Exchanges between individuals

Content pane In the Computer window, displays the contents of the folder selected in the Navigation pane—the active folder

context sensitive Choices that display on a shortcut menu that are related to the specific area in the window or document where you clicked

contextual tabs A tab that contains tools that are related to the selected object and only displays when a related object is selected

contrast ratio The range between the darkest black on the screen and the brightest white

Control (Ctrl) key Key on the keyboard intended for use with other keys to provide new functions

control channel Frequency used to manage mobile phones

Control Panel A set of options that sets default values for the operating system

cookie Text file that contains identification numbers

Copy A command used to duplicate selected data and place it in temporary storage for use in another location in a file or in another file

copyright The legal right of the artist, author, composer, or playwright to exclusive publication and sale of artistic, literary, musical, or dramatic work

country code top-level domain (ccTLD) Two letter code that designates a country at the end of a URL

course management system Software that provides components of a class, either online or in combination with face-to-face instruction; usually provides a syllabus, calendar, lectures, chatrooms, a gradebook, and other features

crimeware Program designed to steal information for the purpose of impersonation in order to gain financially

crop To hide a portion of an image by removing unnecessary parts of the image

cumulative total Also known as a *running total*; the sum of the current value plus the previous total

currency Standard unit of value

currency format Similar to accounting format but it places the currency symbol next to the number on the left

Cut A command that removes text or images from its original location and makes it available for use in another location

cybercafé Place that serves food and drink and provides Internet access

D

data Raw, unprocessed facts and figures

database Lists of data organized in tables where each column is a type of information and each row is one person, event, or interaction

database management system (DBMS) A relational database that controls large amounts of data, and provides data security, multi-user access, and can be customized to fit the user's needs

database server Manages requests for data from a database

data source A mail merge file that contains organized data that includes names, addresses, and other information necessary to merge with a document for mailing purposes

dead zone Area without cell phone service

debugging The process of removing bugs or errors from a software program

decryption Reversing the encoding process to make a message readable

default printer The printer that a document is sent to when the Print button is clicked

defragment Rearrange data on a hard disk so that files are written on adjacent sectors

denial of service (DOS) Overloading a server with requests for service so that it denies service to legitimate users

desktop The basic screen from which Windows and applications are run. The desktop consists of program icons, a taskbar, a Start button, an optional Windows Sidebar, and a mouse pointer

desktop computer A personal computer that fits well in an individual workspace but is not mobile

desktop publishing Creating professional-quality newsletters, flyers, brochures, and booklets on a PC; also a type of software

device driver A small program that is written to provide communication instructions between a peripheral device and the computer's operating system; also called a *driver*

Device Manager Windows dialog box that provides information about devices connected to the computer

dialog box A box where you select settings and choose what actions you want the computer to take

dial-up Connection to the Internet that uses telephone voice circuits

diff Feature that highlights changes made to a document

digital Uses digits; typically refers to a binary system

digital radio Broadcast radio that includes a digital signal

digital signal processor (DSP) Microprocessor that is dedicated to converting and compressing signals

digital signature Identifying characteristics that are encrypted with a private key

Digital Subscriber Line (DSL) Digital subscriber line; uses high-pitch tones people cannot hear to transmit data

digital to analog (D to A) converter A device that takes a digital file, such as an image from a digital camera, and converts it to an analog signal

digital light processing (DLP) Projection technology that uses thousands of mirrors that are controlled by the computer

digital single lens reflex (DSLR) Semi-professional and professional still cameras that use interchangeable lenses and give the photographer complete control over the photography process

digital versatile disc (DVD) See *digital video disc*

digital video disc (DVD) Optical storage that can be recorded in layers on both sides; also called *digital versatile disc*

digital video recorder (DVR) Video recording and replay device that uses a hard drive

digital video interface (DVI) port A standard digital video interface that used to connect video sources to digital monitors or display devices

digitizing tablet Flat surface with an array of crossed wires built into the surface that can sense the vertical and horizontal position of a pointing device

direct deposit Electronic transfer between the employer's bank and the employee's bank

direct mail Advertisements sent by postal service

direct marketing Advertisement that uses direct mail

directory harvest attack (DHA) Attempt to create a list of valid e-mail addresses

disc Optical media such as CDs and DVDs

disintermediation Removing intermediate steps, people, or processes

disk Magnetic media such as hard disks and floppy disks

Disk Operating System (DOS) An early operating system with a character-based interface

distance education Teaching students who are not physically present using communication technology

distributed database Related records stored on more than one computer

distributed processing Dividing a task into component parts that can be distributed to other computers

docking station Device into which a camera or other device is attached to transfer data to a computer

document Word processing file; the main work area in the Microsoft Word window

documenting Providing information about the source, author, and creation date of a workbook

document scanner Scanner that can scan a number of individual pages of text but that cannot be used to scan books or magazines

domain name A unique combination of a domain name and top-level domain

domain name server Computer that provides a directory that relates domain names to host computers

Domain Name System (DNS) The combination of an easy-to-remember domain name and the numerical address of its host computer

dongle A device resembling a USB drive needed to connect a computer to a Bluetooth wireless device on computers without built-in Bluetooth capabilities

Do Not Call registry List of phone numbers maintained by the U.S. government of people who do not want to be solicited by phone

dot matrix printer Type of impact printer

dots per inch (dpi) Measure of printed image quality; usually the higher the number of dots per inch, the better the image quality

double-data-rate 2 (DDR2) A type of SDRAM typically used in personal computers

drag See *drag-and-drop*

drag-and-drop A technique for moving text, an image, or other object from one location to another by selecting an item and dragging it with the mouse to a new location

driver See *device driver*

dropped call Interrupted connection resulting in a lost connection between callers

dual boot The option of selecting an operating system when you turn the computer on

dual-core processor A multi-core processor with two processors

dumb terminal A communication device with a keyboard and monitor that depends on another computer for processing and storage

DVD-ROM Optical disc that is read-only; uses the digital versatile disc method of encoding data

DVD-RW A rewritable DVD

DVD-R/RW (+R/RW) One of two competing DVD formats

E

E1 Transmission capacity equivalent of 30 twisted pairs of telephone lines (European)

e-book An electronic book that can be read on a computer or a special e-book reader

edit Revise and change information

e-learning Education that uses a computer to deliver instruction

electronic learning (eLearning) Computer supported education

electromagnetic (EM) Waves of energy comprised of electric and magnetic fields

electronic commerce Doing business online

electronic data interchange (EDI) Standard for exchanging billing and invoices

electronic mailing list (e-list) List of e-mail addresses

electronic serial number (ESN) Code programmed into a cell phone for identification purposes

electrostatic plotter A plotter that can print large graphics, similar to a laser printer

e-mail Electronic mail

embedded chart A chart that is on the same worksheet as the data

embedded operating system Compact, efficient, and often single-purpose operating systems that are used in computer appliances and special-purpose applications, such as an automobile, an ATM machine, or a portable media player

em dash Name for a long dash in a sentence that marks a break in thought, similar to a comma but stronger

emoticons Symbols that indicate emotions

Encrypt Document A command that enables you to set a password for a file

endnote A reference that is placed at the end of a document or section of a document

end-user license agreement (EULA) Software license that you agree to when you purchase and install commercial software

enterprise resource planning (ERP) Set of applications that automate coordination of separate processes and functions in an organization

ergonomics Applied science of equipment design to reduce operator fatigue and discomfort

Ethernet Standard for connecting a network; usually refers to a twisted pair cable

eTrust Privacy certification service

euro European Union's currency

eWaste Discarded electronic equipment

exchange rate Adjustment factor for the difference between currency values

Extensible Markup Language (XML) Framework for writing a language as simple text along with information on how the application software should interpret that text

external social network (ESN) Social network that is available to everyone

external hard drive A hard drive that plugs into a computer, usually using a USB connection

extranet Local area network connected to another over the Internet by a secure connection

extrapolation To extend a trend beyond the known data

F

fair use Rule that allows use of copyrighted material for certain purposes without paying royalties

Favorites In the Computer window, a list of commonly used folders; in a browser, it is a list of website addresses for future reference

Federal Communications Commission (FCC) Government agency that allocates EM frequencies for public use

feed aggregator RSS reader that displays RSS files

fiber optic cable Glass strands used to carry data as flashes of light

field In a template, e-mail message, or database, a predefined area where a specific type of data is entered, such as file name, page number, or date. In Access, the smallest useable fact collected for each record; a category of data

field area An area on a document that is coded to insert a specific value

field placeholders Field names that are inserted to reserve spaces for the final data that will be inserted during the mail merge process

file compression program Program that reduces the size of files

file extension The letters following a period after a file name that identifies the type of file and often the software that was used to create it

file server A networked computer that stores and finds files or data, delivers the information to the user, and manages updates to the files

File Transfer Protocol (FTP) Rules for transferring files between computers over the Internet

fill handle In Excel, the small box at the lower right corner of a selected cell that is used to fill content across a row or down a column

filter To display only data, Web pages, or incoming messages that meet certain criteria

Find A command that is used to locate a word, phrase, or specific formatting

finite element analysis Dividing a model into small elements and calculating how they interact to simulate behavior of a real system

firewall Software that can block unwanted or unsafe data transmission

FireWire High speed connection developed by Apple and used for data transfer

first line indent A paragraph style that extends the first line of a paragraph to the right of the rest of the paragraph

first generation (1G) First cell phones

flame Insulting or provocative posting

flame war Exchange of insults or flames online

flash drive See *USB drive*

flash hard drive Hard drive that uses flash memory and has no moving parts. They use less energy, break down less frequently, and generate less heat than magnetic hard drives

flash memory Memory with no moving parts; retains its information after the power is removed. Flash memory is used for such things as USB drives and camera digital picture storage

flat panel Thin display that often uses LCD technology

flat screen CRT display with a less curved screen

flatbed scanner Device to transfer documents or pictures one sheet at a time

Folders list At the bottom of the Computer window Navigation pane, displays a list of folders that are contained within the selected folder

font A set of numbers and letters that have the same design and shape

footer An area at the bottom of a page reserved for information that should appear on every page

footnote A reference that is placed at the bottom of the page

form Access object that is used to input, edit, or view data, typically one record at a time

format The appearance of a document

formatting marks Characters displayed to represent keystrokes when you press ⏎Enter, Tab⇆, or Spacebar but which do not print

formula Symbolic representation of mathematical process

formula bar The area on a worksheet that displays the contents of the active cell

forward Sending a received message to a subsequent address

fragmentation Files stored on the hard disk as separate parts in non-adjacent tracks

frames per second Rate at which video images are displayed

fraud Hoax that is intended to make personal gain from another person

freeware Software that is copyrighted by the programmer but for which there is no charge

frequency The number of variations of the medium per second

frequency modulation (FM) Changing the frequency of an EM wave

frequency-shift keying (FSK) Method of sending binary data using two frequencies

friend-to-friend (F2F) File sharing between acquaintances

full duplex Ability to send and receive simultaneously

function A prewritten formula that is used to solve mathematical problems or manipulate text fields

Function (Fn) key Key on notebook keyboards intended for use with function keys to provide additional functions

G

gadget Small program—such as a currency converter, a calendar, or a clock—that displays in the Windows Sidebar

gallery A list of potential results

gamepad A game controller held in both hands with buttons and control sticks, which is used to play computer games

gateway Connection between different networks

general packet radio service (GPRS) Data connection used with 1G and 2G mobile phones

generic top-level domain (gTLD) General category

gigabyte Approximately a billion bytes

global positioning system (GPS) 3D location system using satellites as reference points

global system for mobile communications (GSM) Standard for mobile phone connections used in most countries outside North America

gold version The final copy of software at the end of the beta process

google Act of searching for information, typically using the Google search engine

Graphic Interchange Format (GIF) Image storage format that uses only eight bits of data for each picture element

Graphical User Interface (GUI) A program interface that includes screen elements such as dialog boxes, windows, toolbars, icons, and menus—that is manipulated with a mouse and keyboard to interact with the software

graphics tablet See *digitizing tablet*

grayscale Shades of gray that represent color, which are applied to slide images when they are printed

gridlines Lines that separate cells

group A collection of related commands on a tab that enable you to interact with the software

H

H.261 Early video compression standard

H.264/MPEG-4 Part 10 Recent video compression standard

H.320 Standard for video conferencing over public switched telephone networks, digital , T1, and satellite networks

H.323 Standard for video conferencing over LANs

H.324 Standard for video conferencing over standard telephone lines and 3G mobile telephones

hacker Clever programmer

handheld computer A small computer that fits in a pocket or purse

handout A printable output in PowerPoint that displays one to nine slides to a page for the purpose of providing an audience with a copy of a presentation

hanging indent A paragraph style that leaves the first line at the left margin, and the rest of the lines of the paragraph to the right of the first line

hard disk Magnetic media made of metal; part of a hard drive

hard drive Device to read and write hard disks; usually the main storage device in a computer

head Devices in a hard drive that read and write data in magnetic form on a stack of thin metal disks

header An area reserved at the top of a document for information that should appear on every page in a document; also the label at the top of a column or at the left of a row of data

header area The top part of the e-mail form used for identifying the recipients and subject

heading In Excel, the number at the far left of a row or letter at the top of a column used to identify a location on a worksheet

heat sink The radiator fins attached to a processor that help cool the processor when a fan is running

hertz Measure of frequency equal to one repetition per second

high-definition multimedia interface (HDMI) Connector used to transfer digital signals

high definition (HD) radio Digital radio

high definition television (HDTV) Television system that uses digital signals

hoax Lie intended to convince someone of the reality of something that is not real

home page Primary Web page with links to other pages in a group, or the page displayed first when a browser opens

hop-off gateway Device that connects the data networks to the public switched telephone network

horizontal (category) axis Bottom border of the chart with category labels

host Computer that contains a program or file

hot thread Most active Web discussion

hot-swappable Can change connected devices without shutting down the computer

hyperlink Text or an object that that you click to connect to another file, location or Web page where information is located

Hypertext Markup Language (HTML) A language that is used to create Web pages that can be viewed in a Web browser

Hypertext Transfer Protocol (HTTP) Rules used to move Web pages on the Internet

I

IBM compatible Platform that used Intel processors and DOS or Windows operating systems

identity theft Impersonating someone online for fraudulent purposes

impact printer Transfers ink to the paper by striking an ink-impregnated cloth ribbon

in-band on-channel (IBOC) Method of adding digital signal to analog signals using the basic frequency

indent To move text in from the left and/or right margin

infected State of computer security has been compromised by malware

information Data that has been processed so it is organized, meaningful, and useful

information bar Displays at the top of a window to warn you of security issues related to files that you want to open

infrared (IR) light Form of invisible light used to send signals or data

ink-jet printer Creates an image on paper by spraying ink on a page

input The action of adding instructions and data to a computer

insertion point Position where input will go; a blinking vertical line on your work area that indications where text or graphics will be inserted

insourcing Having work done in the same country

instant messaging (IM) Exchange that takes place over the Internet when both parties are present

integrated circuit (IC) Arrays of transistors and other electronic devices that perform a function

interest rate The amount charged to borrow money

interlaced Refreshing an image by refreshing half of the lines at a time

internal hard drive The main storage device in a computer

internal rate of return (IRR) A financial measurement that is used to evaluate an investment and is comparable to the percent interest you earn on a savings account

internal social network (ISN) Social network that may be joined by invitation only

International Bank Account Number (IBAN) Bank identification number

International Business Machines (IBM) Computer company that popularized personal computers in traditional businesses

International Telecommunications Union (ITU) Standards setting body for international radio and telecommunications

Internet Corporation for Assigned Names and Numbers (ICANN) Organization that coordinates domain names and IP addresses

Internet forum Web-based discussion (see *message board*)

Internet message access protocol (IMAP) The set of rules for either delivering or managing e-mail on the server

Internet Protocol (IP) address Internet protocol number for a computer on the Internet

Internet Service Provider (ISP) Companies that connect individuals or other companies to the Internet

Internet Storm Center (ISC) Emergency-response information for dealing with security breeches

intranet Private network that uses the same communication protocols as the Internet

ISO 6392 code International bank identification number

J

Java Programming language suitable for automating functions on Web pages

Joint Photographic Experts Group (JPEG) Very popular image format that allows variable compression

joystick Pointing device which is a rod connected to a track ball

jumpers Connectors that fit over pairs of pins

junk e-mail Unsolicited and unwanted e-mail (see *SPAM*)

justified Text that is aligned evenly between the left and right margins; the spaces between words are adjusted to ensure that the text aligns evenly

K

key Information used to encrypt or decrypt messages

keyboard shortcut Pressing two keys at a time to perform an action

keylogger Program that records keystrokes

keyword search Strategy for selecting Web pages that contains certain words

kilohertz (KHz) One thousand hertz

L

land An unmarked spot on a CD that represents the number 1

landscape A horizontal page orientation that is wider than it is tall

laptop computer A mobile computer that can be used anywhere and can run on batteries when a power outlet is not available; also called a notebook or portable computer

laser diode (LED) A solid crystalline device that converts electricity to a narrow beam of light that is one color

laser printer Uses a light beam to transfer images or text to paper where powdered ink is attracted and melted onto the paper

last mile Reference to the smallest branches of a branching structure

layout The arrangement of placeholders on a slide

leader Dots or other marks that provide a visual connection between widely separated text

leader character The dot, dash, or other character used in a tab leader

leader line A graphic that connects a label to a chart element

left-aligned Alignment on the left margin, with the right edge of the paragraph uneven

legacy Older model or version

legend Identifies the data series on a chart

libel A false and malicious publication printed for the purpose of defaming a living person

line chart A chart that uses lines whose height on the vertical axis represents the value of the data

line spacing The distance between lines of text in a paragraph—1.15 is the default line spacing in Microsoft Office Word 2007

linklog Blog devoted to links to other blogs or sites

Linux An operating system for personal computers based on the UNIX operating system

liquid crystal display (LCD) Type of digital display that uses electric fields to change the transparency of liquid cells to pass red, green, or blue light to create an image; typically much thinner than older-style monitors

live preview A technology that shows the a preview of formatting changes on selected text or graphics before it is applied

Local Area Network (LAN) Group of connected devices that are usually close to each other

Lock mode Command from the Shut Down menu that enables a person who wants to leave the computer for a little while without logging off to come back to his or her own personal settings without having to log on again

locking Preventing the user from using a GSM phone with another provider

log Off Command from the Shut Down menu that closes personal settings and requires you to supply your username and password to log on again before using the computer

lossless Compression method that recovers all the details in a file after coding and decoding

lossy Compression method that permanently loses details of a file during coding and decoding

lumen Measure of brightness of light sources

M

Macintosh (Mac) Model of personal computer by Apple Corporation

mail merge A Word feature that joins a main document and a data source to create customized letters, labels, or envelopes

mail server Manages delivery and submissions of electronic mail

main document In a mail merge, the document that contains the text and formatting that remains constant

mainframe computer Large computer systems, usually very reliable and secure, used to process large amounts of information

malware Software that is designed with malicious intent

manual column break An artificial break between columns to control the flow of text

manual line break An artificial end to a line without creating a new paragraph

manual page break An artificial break between pages to control the flow of text, also referred to as a hard page break

margin The space between the edge of the paper and the text

Mark as Final A command that changes a document to Read-only status

markers Small rectangles on a line chart that identify each data point

maximize The process or button that increases the size of a window to fill the screen

Maximize/Restore Down button Expands a window to fill the screen or restores it to its previous size

media player Plays audio or video files of many different formats

megabyte Approximately a million bytes

megahertz (MHz) One million hertz

megapixel Measurement of the number of pixels (in millions) in a digital camera image

memory Integrated circuits designed to store data before and after it is processed by the CPU

message board Web-based discussion

MHTML format (MIME HTML) HTML code used in single-file Web pages

microchip Integrated circuit for computers

microcomputer Another term for a personal computer

minicomputer At one time, the category of computer between a workstation and a mainframe; used primarily as file and Web servers

microprocessor In personal computers and workstations, the central processing unit (CPU) that consists of millions of transistors

microSD card Removable flash memory that does not need power to retain data; typically used in point-and-shoot cameras, smartphones, and PDAs

Microsoft Office A suite of applications that perform tasks commonly used in an office environment, such as writing documents, managing finances, and presenting information

minimize The process or button that hides a window and represents the window with a button on the taskbar

mixed cell reference Cell location where either the row or the column remains constant, but not both

mobile identification number (MIN) Code derived from the ESN and assigned telephone number

mobile telephone switching office (MTSO) Coordination center of the cell phone system in an area

moblog Blog designed for use on mobile devices

modeling Using formulas to simulate the behavior of real systems

modem Device that translates small voltage switches from a computer into two tones on a telephone line

moderator Person who has administrative rights to an e-list and can delete members or postings

Modern Language Association (MLA) One of two commonly used styles for formatting research papers and reports

monitor Display device used with computers

Mosaic Early Web browser

mouse Pointing device that moves on the desktop and controls a screen pointer

mouse pad Pad to give traction to the rubber ball in a mouse

movie clips Animated clip art or video clips

Mozilla Firefox Early Web browser

MP3 (.mp3) Popular audio compression method

multi-core processor Multiple processors on a single chip

multimedia messaging service (MMS) Extension of the short message service that manages transfer of text plus audio and video files

N

Name box The area on the Excel window that displays the cell address or name of the currently active cell

namespace File that contains the definitions and relationships of an XML file

nanoseconds Billionths of a second

National Television System Committee (NTSC) Analog TV standard used in North America and several other countries

Navigation pane The area on the left side of a folder window that enables you to view the folder structure in a vertical list. In the Computer window, displays the Favorites list and the Folders list

netiquette Rules of appropriate behavior on the Internet

Netscape Popular Web browser

network Group of connected devices

network license A software license that allows anyone on the network to use a piece of software

network server Manages flow of data between computers on the network

neuron Nerve cell

node Any device on the network

nondisclosure agreement An agreement not to share the product's new features with anyone else during beta testing

nonprinting characters See *formatting marks*

non-volatile memory Memory that does not need constant power to function

Normal view The main view in PowerPoint that is used to create a presentation

not Logical operator that reverses a true or false value

Notes pane In PowerPoint, in Normal view, the portion of the window at the bottom that is used to create notes for the speaker

notification area An area on the right side of the taskbar that keeps you informed about processes that are running in the background, such as antivirus software, network connections, and other utility programs; it also typically displays the time

null Empty or nonexistent

numbered list A list of items preceded by numbers that are arranged in a particular order—chronological, importance, or sequence

Num Lock key Key on the keyboard that toggles the function of the numeric keyboard keys from navigation to numeric functions

O

Occupational Safety & Health Administration (OSHA) An agency in the Department of Labor

Office button A button that displays commands related to files

Office Clipboard A temporary storage area in Microsoft Office applications where copied or cut text or images are stored

on demand Available on request

OpenOffice Suite of productivity applications available for free download that works with Linux, Windows, and Mac platforms

open source The source code for software that is free to distribute and use that meets the criteria of the open-source initiative

opening post (OP) First posting in a thread to start the discussion on a topic

operating system A type of software program that determines how the processor interacts with the user and with other system components

optical character recognition (OCR) Software that converts images of text on paper into editable electronic text

optical mouse Mouse that detects motion using the reflection of a beam of light

option button Element of a page that can be toggled on or off to record a choice

Option key Macintosh computer key that is similar to the Control key on other computers

opt out Choose not to participate

or Logical operator that requires that either or both criteria are met

OS X An Apple Macintosh operating system

output The process of displaying, sharing, or otherwise communicating information that has been processed by the computer

outsourcing Having work done in another country

P

packet Group of about 1,000 bytes of data that includes addressing and error-checking labels

parenthetical citation A citation in the MLA style that uses the

author's last name and the page number, surrounded by parentheses

passive-matrix display An LCD monitor type that scans and refreshes the screen a row or column at a time

password A code used to identify a user to grant access to the network

Paste A command that inserts copied or cut text or images in a new location

Paste Options A button that displays formatting options for recently pasted text

patch A software program that modifies and existing program to repair minor problems

patent Protection for an invention

payload Program that is carried by malware that performs a function

peer-to-peer Relationship between computers that are connected directly to each other without the use of a network server

pen plotter A plotter that uses individual pens and different colored inks to create large line drawings

peripheral Device attached to the system unit or case

personal computer A computer typically operated by one person who can customize the functions to match personal preferences; sometimes called a microcomputer

personal digital assistant (PDA) Appliance that tracks calendars, tasks, and contact information; often supports e-mail functions

Personal Information Manager (PIM) Software that tracks calendars, tasks, and contact information that may be expanded to include other functions such as e-mail

petabyte Approximately a quadrillion bytes

phase alternating line (PAL) Analog TV standard used in Europe and many other countries

phishing Fraudulent attempt at tricking someone into divulging sensitive or private information

photo detector Device that converts light into electrical voltage

photoblog Blog devoted to photos

pie chart Uses a circle to represent the whole of a group of data and slices to represent how each piece of data contributes to the whole

pin To attach a program to the Start menu

pit An indentation burned into a CD that represents the number 0

pixel A single picture element or subdivision of a picture

placeholders Preformatted areas that define the type of information to place in each area on the slide

plain text Decoded or original document

plain text format Document format that saves the text and paragraph marks, but none of the text or paragraph formatting

platform The combination of a particular operating system and the processor that it controls

plug-and-play Windows feature that recognizes new hardware and automatically searches for the correct software driver to install the new hardware

plug-in Program that adds functionality

plug strip Device with several power outlets

podcast Distribute multimedia files over the Internet

point (pt) Measurement for font size; one point is one seventy-second of an inch

point-and-shoot camera Small, inexpensive digital still camera with mostly automatic functions

pointing stick A pointing device that senses directional pressure

point-of-sale (POS) terminal A type of dumb terminal used for managing and recording transactions

pop-up A window that appears when activated from a Web page

port Connection device on the computer

Portable Document Format (PDF) A document format developed by Adobe that can be read on most platforms, but cannot be edited without special software; maintains document formatting, graphics, and layout

Portable Network Graphics (PNG) Graphics format designed for the Web

portal Web site that is an entry point to a variety of services and information

portrait A vertical page orientation that is taller than it is wide

post office protocol (POP) The rules for delivering e-mail

power strip An extension cord with a box of additional electrical receptacles

present value Amount of the loan before it has been repaid

primary key field Unique identifier field in a database table

primary storage The type of storage that is used while the computer is processing data and instruction; also known as memory

print driver Software that communicates between the computer and the printer

print on demand (POD) Ability to print books as required

print queue A waiting area for documents that have been sent to the printer

print server Manages printing requests from network computers

private branch exchange (PBX) Device for routing telephone calls within an organization and connecting to the telephone company

private key Non-published information used to encrypt or decrypt a message that cannot be used to reverse the process

probe Sensor used to explore places that are unsafe or not easily accessible

processing Manipulating data according to a set of instructions to create information that can be stored

programmable Computers that can change programs

programmer A person who writes computer programs

programming The process of writing software

programs See *application program*

progressive Refreshing an image by refreshing each line sequentially from the top

projector Projects monitor image for group viewing

Properties A command that displays the document properties, which includes the author, document title, subject, keywords for searching, or other information

protocol Group of rules

proxy server Security software or device that requests Internet services using its own identity to hide the address of the computer that is actually requesting the service

public key Published information used to encrypt or decrypt a message that cannot be used to reverse the process

public switched telephone network (PSTN) Older circuit switching telephone system

Q

quad-core processor A multi-core processor with four processors

query In a database, a set of criteria intended to extract the records and fields that would answer a particular question and display the table with only those records

Quick Access Toolbar A customizable toolbar to the right of the Office button that contains the Save, Undo, and Repeat/Redo buttons

Quick Launch toolbar An area to the right of the Start button that contains shortcut icons for commonly used programs

Quick Style gallery A list of available styles in a document; found on the Home tab

QuickTime (.mov) Video compression method from Apple Computer

qlog Blog devoted to answering questions

R

radio Electromagnetic waves

radio frequency ID (RFID) A device that enables remote retrieving of information using radio waves

random access memory (RAM) Integrated circuits that work with the CPU

range A contiguous group of cells that are identified by the cell at the upper left, a colon, and the cell at the lower right

readme File with notes from programmers on changes made since the manual went to press

read-only A file that can be opened and read but not edited

really simple syndication (RSS) Method of delivering content to subscribers using XML

record Database information about one person, item, place, object, or event divided into fields and displayed in a single row of a data source

Redo A command that reverses the action of the Undo command

reflector E-mail address to which a message is sent that will be distributed to the e-list

refresh rate Frequency of replacement of images

registry Company that manages a top-level domain

relational database A type of database that divides data into several tables that can be related to each other by a common field; Access is a relational database

relative cell reference Cell location that is stored as a certain number of rows and columns from the currently selected cell

relay A device that uses an electromagnet to connects circuits

release to manufacturing (RTM) A software version following beta testing that is sent to the companies that process the product for distribution

remote control Wireless control unit typically used with an appliance such as a music player, a television, or a media center on a computer

Repeat A command that repeats the previous action

repeater Device that amplifies and retransmits a signal

Replace A command that replaces found text or formatting with new text or formatting

reply New message automatically addressed to the original sender

reply to all New message automatically addressed to the original sender and those to whom it was copied

report The Access object that is used to summarize information for printing and presentation of the data

resolution The level of detail on a computer monitor, measured in dots per inch for images and pixels for monitors

resolution setting Choice of pixel size to display on a computer monitor

response time The amount of time it takes to change the color of a pixel on an LCD monitor

restore down Process or button that reduces the size of a maximized window

restore point A representation of the state of your computer's system files at a particular point in time

Restrict Permission A command that enables you to specify the users who have permission to read, change, or have full control over a document

retina Part of the eye that converts light into nerve impulses

reverse auction Request for lowest bid to provide a service or quantity of goods

Reviewing pane A pane at the bottom or side of the screen that displays comments and tracked changes

revision history Log of changes

revolutions per minute (rpm) Rate of spin of a disc

Ribbon The area at the top of a Microsoft Office 2007 window that contains groups of buttons for the most common commands used in applications

rich text format (RTF) A universal document format that can be read by nearly all word processing programs and that retains most text and paragraph formatting

right-aligned Text that is aligned on the right margin, with the left edge of the paragraph uneven

robot A mechanical device programmed to perform special functions

rootkit Program that gives outsiders access to a computer and administrator rights

rotation handle A small green circle that displays at the top of some graphic objects that is used to rotate the object in a circle

router Computer that selects the route that data should take

R-squared (R^2) value A measure of how well the calculated trendline fits the data; the closer the number is to 1, the better the fit

S

Safari Web browser by Apple

Safe Mode A method of rebooting a computer that runs only the essential parts of the operating system, and does not load many of the utilities that typically run in the background

salutation Courteous recognition or greeting

sampling rate Frequency of measurement

sans serif fonts Fonts that do not have lines or extensions on the ends of letters and are often used as headings and titles and for shorter documents

scanner Device to transfer documents and pictures into a digital format; also, a device that checks several different frequencies to detect and receive those that are in use

scanning Act of transferring a document or picture to a digital format one line at a time

screen saver A moving image that displays on a monitor after a set period of inactivity

ScreenTip A description that displays the name of a screen element, button, or area on a window

scroll bar Horizontal or vertical bars that enable you to navigate in a window, menu, or gallery by manipulating the display of content within the window

scroll box A box in scroll bars that can be used to drag a work area up and down or left and right; it also provides a visual indication of your location in the work area

search engine Program that displays links to Web pages that meet search criteria

second generation (2G) Cells phones using digital transmission

secondary storage Type of storage that is used to record information for later retrieval, and does not require constant power to retain the information that is stored

Secure Digital (SD) card Removable flash memory that does not need power to retain data; typically used in point-and-shoot cameras, smartphones, and PDAs

Secure Sockets Layer (SSL) Rules for using cryptographic methods to provide secure communications over the Internet

self publishing Using affordable software to create and distribute books

sensor Device that reacts to changes in the environment and produces an electrical signal that corresponds to the change

Séquentiel couleur á mémoire (SECAM) French and Soviet analog television standard

serif fonts Fonts that have lines or extensions on the ends of the letters and are typically used for large amounts of text

server A powerful computer that provides a service, such as running a network or hosting an Internet site

service pack Major software updates that are just short of an upgrade

shareware Software that can be used for a trial period but must be paid for if used regularly

Shift key Key on the keyboard used to produce capital letters or to be used in combination with other keys to provide new functions

shopping cart Program that aggregates orders on a commercial Web site

short message service (SMS) Wireless service for sending short messages

shortcut menu When you click the right mouse button, a list of actions that displays related to the area on which you clicked

Sigma (Σ) Greek letter associated with the Sum function

signature block Name, title and contact information at the end of a formal message

simple mail transfer protocol (SMTP) The rules for structuring and sending e-mail

simple payback period The number of years that it takes to recover the cost of an investment, which is a measure that is commonly used to compare investment alternatives

single-spaced Line spacing set to 1.0 that has no additional space between lines of text in a paragraph

site license A software license that allows anyone in an organization or group to use a piece of software

sizing handle Small squares and circles that display around the perimeter of an object that are used to resize the object and which indicate that the object is selected and can be moved, resized, or formatted

sketchlog Blog of portfolio drawings

Sleep mode Command from the Shut Down menu that shuts down nearly all of the power to the computer but keeps power to the CPU and to RAM, while greatly reducing energy consumption

slide Screen intended for projection (see *slide show*); the main work area in PowerPoint

slide master Slide layout images that contain all of the placeholder formats for each slide layout within a theme, which are used to change theme formats for all slides

Slide Master view In PowerPoint, a view that contains each slide layout, where you can change placeholder formatting characteristics for the selected theme

Slide pane In PowerPoint, in Normal view, the center pane that is used to enter slide content

slide show Series of screens used to present ideas to an audience

Slide Show view The view that is used to display slides electronically using a computer and overhead projector

Slide Sorter view In PowerPoint, thumbnail slides images displayed on a single page that is used to rearrange slides and add transitions

Slides/Outline pane In PowerPoint, in Normal view, the left pane that is used to display thumbnail images of the slides or an outline

slope The angle of a straight line compared to horizontal

small caps A text effect that displays the capital letters in a normal manner but the lowercase letters as capital letters that are approximately 3/4 height

Small Computer System Interface (SCSI) A peripheral connection method used for high-speed data transfer

smartphone A cellular telephone that has a small keypad and can run software applications, store and play music, display pictures, and send and receive email; often includes features of PDAs

SmartArt A diagram that creates a visual representation of concepts and information; use it to illustrate hierarchies, steps in a process, relationships, cycles, or lists

social network Social groups that are interconnected on the Internet

software Written instructions that direct a computer's processor on how to complete tasks; also called *programs*

source code Computer program in text form before it is translated into machine code

spacing after Space added between paragraphs when the enter key is pressed

spam Unsolicited bulk messages

speaker notes A printable output in PowerPoint that provides a copy of the slide image and related notes for the speaker during a presentation

spider Automated program that searches for Web pages

spim Form of spam directed at instant messaging services

sponsored links References to Web pages that are placed with highly ranked websites for a fee

spoofing Replacing the name of the originator of a message with a name from a contact list to disguise the origin

spreadsheet Generic term for financial data arranged in rows and columns with formulas that can recalculate automatically if values in cells change

spyware Program that records and reports user activity to an unauthorized party

star Configuration of connections that radiate from a central location

Start menu List of programs or menus of programs displayed by clicking the Start button on the taskbar

status bar Displays information about the document or other file on which you are working

storefront software Programs that enable a Web site to sell goods and services

style Combinations of formatting characteristics that are grouped together and named, and then are applied with a single click

stylus A pen-like input device that is used to tap a touch screen

subscriber Member of an e-list

subscriber identification module (SIM) Flash memory card in a mobile phone that records the subscriber's identification information and the provider's SID

subscript Characters that are placed below the regular text in a line

subwoofer Audio speaker designed for low range sounds and music

Sum A function that chooses adjacent cells that contain numbers, adds the values, and displays the total in the cell that contains the SUM function

supercomputer Extremely fast computers used for research, modeling, and large-scale data analysis

superscript Characters that are placed above the regular text in a line

supply chain Sequence of steps that produce products and deliver them to the consumer

surge suppressor Protects the computer from pulses of higher-than-normal electric voltage

S-video port Port on the video card that enables you to connect your computer to cable and view television programs

switch user mode Command from the Shut Down menu that closes personal settings and allows another user to log on

switchboard operator Person who made the connections between circuits in early telephone systems

symmetric key Information used to encrypt and decrypt the same message

synchronous Interactions between parties that are present at the same time

synchronous dynamic random access memory (SDRAM) Type of memory typically used in personal computers (see *double-data-rate 2 [DDR2]*)

synonym A word that is similar in meaning

syntax The order of arguments in a function

system administrator Person who controls the computers

system clock Circuits that keep time in the computer

system identification (SID) Code assigned to each cell phone service provider

system restore Process of reinstating a previous set of values used by the operating system

system unit The part of the personal computer that contains the central processing unit

T

T1 Transmission capacity equivalent of 24 twisted pairs of telephone lines

table The Access object that stores the data that makes up the database; each table stores a set of related data; inn Word a list of information set up in a column-and-row format; in Excel data that is organized into adjacent columns and rows and define as a table

tablet computer A laptop computer designed to enable the user to write on the screen as a mode of input

tab stop A location on the horizontal ruler to which you can move the insertion point by pressing the Tab key; used to align and indent text

tabs On the Ribbon, used to access commands related to a category of actions for each application

taskbar Displays the Start button and the names of any open files and applications. The taskbar may also display shortcut buttons for other programs

telecommute Go to work electronically rather than physically

telework Work from home

Telnet Program to allow remote login over the Internet

templates Preformatted and designed documents that can be used repeatedly

terabyte Approximately a trillion bytes

terminator Required device at the end of some types of buses such as SCSI connections

texting Sending text messages between mobile digital devices

theme A collection of design elements, fonts, colors, and graphics that create a uniform look for a

presentation, Word document, or Excel worksheet

thesaurus A research tool that provides a list of synonyms

third generation (3G) Mobile telephone system that provides high-speed data and Internet access on cell phones

thread Postings on a topic

thumb drive See *USB drive*

thumb mouse A portable mouse that uses a trackball operated by the thumb

thumbnail Icons that display a small representation of a file, or a slide

time-division multiple access (TDMA) Method of sharing the same frequency by dividing its use into time slots

time-division synchronous code-division multiple access (TD-SCDMA) Advanced version of CDMA used in 3G phones

title bar The bar at the top of a window; often displays the program icon, the name of the file, and the name of the program. The Minimize, Maximize/Restore Down, and Close buttons are grouped on the right side of the title bar

toggle A button that activates or deactivates a feature or command

toner Dry ink used with copiers or laser printers

top-level domain (TLD) Group of domain names

touch pad A small, rectangular, flat area below the space bar on many notebook computers that performs the functions of a mouse

touch screen Input device that senses touch on a monitor

track ball A pointing device with a moving ball in a cradle

Track Changes A feature that records changes and comments made to a document by others

trademark A word or symbol that indicates ownership of a product or service that is reserved for exclusive use by the owner

transformer Converts electrical voltage from high to low or low to high

transistor An electronic device that can switch on or off in response to an external signal

transitions Added to slides to control the direction, timing, speed, and manner in which slides enter and exit the screen during a slide show

Transmission Control Protocol/ Internet Protocol (TCP/IP) Rules used to control the transmission of packets on the Internet

Transport Layer Security (TLS) Rules for using cryptographic methods to provide secure communications over the Internet that followed SSL

trendline A calculated line that can be extended to predict values beyond the end of the data

trial version Software that is intended for temporary use to evaluate a product

Trojan Program that disguises itself within another program that the user agrees to install

true color System that can display all of the colors that the human eye can perceive

tumbleblog Blog that contains a mixture of media types

twisted pair Two insulated wires that are wrapped around each other

type A USB Connector on the upstream or computer side of the cable

type B USB Connector on the downstream or device end of the cable

U

Undo A command that reverses one or more previous actions

Unicode A code that uses up to 32-bit numbers to represent characters from numerous languages, including the older ASCII codes

Uniform Resource Locator (URL) Unique name used as an address on the Internet

uninterruptible power supply A device that uses batteries to keep a computer running when the power fails

Universal Serial Bus (USB) Connection method that replaces many other types of peripheral connectors

Unix Popular operating system on mainframe computers; the basis for the Linux operating system on personal computers

update Changes to a version of software to fix problems or add minor feature improvements

upgrade Replaces current version with a newer one that has significant changes

USB 1.1 First version (see *Universal serial bus*) of USB

USB 2.0 Second version (see *Universal serial bus*) of USB

USB drive Flash memory that plugs into a USB port on a computer

USB hub Provides multiple USB ports and may provide additional power

user name a name that is unique on a particular computer system

utility program Small program that does one task

V

venture capitalist Someone who loans money to startup companies in exchange for part ownership

vertical (value) axis The left side of the chart used to indicate the magnitude of the value of the data

video graphics adapter (VGA) Digital to analog adapter to use analog monitors with digital computers

video graphics array (VGA) port A personal computer display standard

video on demand (VOD) Download video at a time chosen by the viewer

video RAM (VRAM) Dedicated video memory

Views Different ways to display data on the screen

virtual Having the appearance of reality

virtual memory Space on a hard disk used to supplement physical memory

virtual team Group whose members are separated by time or distance

virus Program that makes copies of itself and distributes them as attachments to files or e-mail

vlog Blog devoted to discussions of videos

voice gateway router Device that connects the LAN and PBX to the phone company

Voice-over-the-Internet Protocol (VoIP) Audio conversation using Internet packets

voice recognition Ability to convert speech into digital files or commands

voice synthesizer Software that translates electronic words into spoken words

volatile memory Memory that needs constant power to function

W

WAV (.wav) Popular uncompressed audio file format

Web archive, single file Combined elements of a Web page saved as one file

Web cams Video camera intended for use over the Internet

webcasting Broadcasting video online

Web crawler Program that examines Web pages and gathers data about them

Web log (blog) A personal online journal

Web page A document that is written in HTML and displayed by a browser

Web server Computer that runs software that provides Web pages and runs scripts

website Collection of Web pages

what-if analysis Process of substituting values to see the effect on dependent calculations

Wide Area Network (WAN) Network of devices some of which are much farther away

wide band code-division multiple access (WCDMA) Advanced version of CDMA used in 3G phones

wiki Server program that allows users to collaborate to create the content of a website

Wikipedia Online encyclopedia that uses wiki

window Rectangular area of the screen with a title bar, Close and Minimize buttons, and a Maximize/Restore Down button

Windows Name of Microsoft's operating system that uses a GUI

Windows-based applications Programs that are written to work on computers that use a Microsoft Windows operating system

Windows Explorer The program within Windows that displays the files and folders on your computer

Windows Sidebar An area on the side of the screen that displays information you want to access quickly. Gadgets are added to the Windows Sidebar that display information such as weather or stock market data

wire transfer Electronic transfer of money

wireless Radio waves used instead of wires

wireless application protocol (WAP) Rules for connecting mobile devices to the Internet

wireless Enhanced 9-1-1 (E9-1-1) Enhanced emergency calling service that locates mobile phones

wireless fidelity (WiFi) Wireless standard used to connect computers and peripherals

WMA (.wma) Popular audio compression method

WMV (.wmv) Video compression method from Microsoft

word The unit of data with which a processor can work

WordArt A feature that turns words into a graphic that can be moved, resized, and modified to create decorative text

word processing The process of using a computer to write, store, retrieve, and edit documents

word size The amount of data that is processed in one operation

wordwrap As you type, the text on the line moves to the right, and words move down to the next line as necessary to adjust the spacing on the line to remain within the established margins

work area The area on the screen where you enter text, numbers, or graphics to create a document, a worksheet, or presentation slides

workbook A collection of worksheets in a spreadsheet program

worksheet The main work area in Excel, which is a grid of rows and columns, generically referred to as a spreadsheet

workstation A high-powered personal computer designed for specific tasks, such as graphics, medicine, and engineering; the term is also sometimes used to describe a networked personal computer

World Wide Web The resources and users on the Internet that are using the Hypertext Transfer Protocol

WorldWideWeb Name of Berners-Lee's first Web browser (see *World Wide Web*)

worm Malware program that duplicates itself on a network

X

X-Y scatter chart Similar to a line chart but it forces equal intervals on the horizontal axis

Z

Zoom bar A bar that is used to change the magnification of the document or worksheet

Photo Credits

COVER

Courtesy of www.istockphoto.com

CHAPTER 1

CO-1   istockphoto.com

CHAPTER 2

CO-2   istockphoto.com

CHAPTER 3

CO-3   istockphoto.com

CHAPTER 4

CO-4   istockphoto.com

CHAPTER 5

CO-5   Kris Butler\istockphoto.com

CHAPTER 6

CO-6   Leif Norman\istockphoto.com

CHAPTER 7

CO-7   Sue Colvil\istockphoto.com

CHAPTER 8

CO-8   Anna Pustovaya\istockphoto.com

CHAPTER 9

CO-9   Toos van den Dikkenberg\istockphoto.com

CHAPTER 10

CO-10   istockphoto.com

CHAPTER 11

CO-11   istockphoto.com

CHAPTER 12

CO-12   istockphoto.com

Index

A

Absolute references, **362–364,** 396
Access, 24–26, 262
Active cell, 287
ActiveX controls, 572
Add Entrance Effect dialog box, 562
Add-ins, installing, 203
Alignment/indents, 73–75, 98, 111, 135, 148
American Psychological Association (APA), 131
Animations
    adding, 559–561, 583
    charts, 564–565
    custom, 562
    presentation design, 561, 564, 566
    SmartArt, 565–566
    tables, 561–563
Applications
    closing, 14
    defined, 4
    elements, identification of, **6–11,** 500
    starting, **6–11,** 50
    version issues, 211
    views, 15
    Windows-based, 4
Arguments in Excel, 296, 345
AutoCorrect customization, 129–130, 157
AutoFit, 90–91
AutoRecover, 212, 261
Availability issues, 210
Average function, 349–351
Axes labels, formatting, **442–444,** 460–461

B

Backspace key, 20
Backups, 209
Backwards compatibility, 211
Balloons (reviewing pane), 238, 240
Bibliographies, 147–149, 161
Borders, 188–190, **309–310,** 332
Bulleted lists, 68–70, 111, 486
Bullet points, 479
Buttons, 27, 36, 51

C

Callouts, 423–425
Cash flow analysis, 356, **367–369,** 396–397
Cells
    absolute references, 362–364, 396
    address, 287

borders, 309–310, 332
colors, 311–312, 332
data entry, 289–291, 330
entries, confirming, 344
gridlines, 309
mixed references, 363
navigating, 286–288, 378
relative references, 349, 360–361, 396
shifting, 291–292
Center-alignment, 73
Chart design
    callouts, 425
    contribution to whole, showing, 428
    data comparisons, 418, 421
    decimal point alignment, 416
    errors, catching, 429
    extrapolation, 447
    fixing exercise, 465
    labels, 417, 433
    moving/separate sheet, 441
    time intervals, 437
    vertical axis units, 422
Charts
    animations, 564–565
    axes in, 418
    axes labels, formatting, 442–444, 460–461
    bar, 419
    callouts, 423–425
    clustered column, 421
    column, **415–421,** 458
    data entry, 415–417, 425–426, 435–437
    data selection, 418–421
    documenting, 447–450, 461–464
    elements, editing, 421–423, 429–432, 458–459
    elements, selecting, 429, 431
    embedded, 433
    legend, 418
    line, **435–441,** 460
    moving/separate sheet, 440–441
    pie, **425–433,** 435, 459–460
    presentations, 530, **548–553,** 564–565, 582
    printing, 433–435
    trendlines, **444–447,** 460–461
    type, changing, 427–428
    type, selecting, 453
    X-Y scatter, 437
Circular reference error correction, 345–347
Citations
    parenthetical, 143
    print, 143–145

Web, 145–147
Word, 143–147, 159–161
Clip art
    design, 493
    slides, inserting, 490–493
    Word, 79–82, 112
Clipboard task pane, 29
Close button, 9
Column charts, **415–421,** 458
Columns
    AutoFit, 379–380
    breaks, manual, 198–200
    hiding, 376
    inserting/deleting, 294–295, 330, 364
    multiple, 180–183, 216–217
    tables, 88–89
    text formatting, 182–183
    width, adjusting, 292–293, 330
Comments
    applications of, 232
    described, 236
    inserting, 240–241, 268
    reading, 237–239
    responding to, 241, **247–248,** 269–270
Comparison operators, 375
Compatibility mode, 184
Conditional formatting, 372–373, 397
Context sensitive, 24
Contextual tabs
    Table Tools, 546–548
    text formatting, 35–36, 52–53
Copy command, 27
Copyright law, 151
Count function, 349–351
Cropping pictures, 84
Cumulative total calculation, 370
Currency, formatting, 297–299

D

Data sources
    contents of, 254
    described, 249, 250
    document merging with, 256–257, 271–272
    editing, 252
    opening/adding, 251, 270–271
Default printer, 44
Default settings, changing, 261–262
Delete key, 20
Device drivers (drivers), 43
Dialog boxes, **12,** 51, 209
Dialog Box Launcher, 28–29

Documents
borders, adding, 188–190
copying between, 30–31
Find/Replace commands,
22–23
formats, saving to, 200–204,
218
headers/footers, **99–102,** 114,
133–134
hyperlinks (*See* Hyperlinks)
main, 249
management, 151–152
margins, setting, 175–177
navigating, **14–18,** 50
new, creating, 66–68, 110
printing, 15, 37–39, 53,
150–151, 161–164
protecting, 262
spelling/grammar, checking,
24–26, 51
symbols, adding, 21–22,
190–192, 218
text, importing, 131–132, 157
Track Changes (*See* Track
Changes)
transmission of, 106
Web page, saving as, 206–208,
220, 574
work area, 7, 8
Down button, 9

E

E-mail, 106
Encrypt Document, 262
Endnotes, 141–142, 159
Envelopes, printing, 262–263
Errors, 25, 345–347
Excel
arguments, 296, 345
AutoFit, 379–380
automatic features, 366
average function, 349–351
charts (*See* Charts)
closing, 14
comparison operators, 375
conditional formatting,
372–373, 397
copy/paste from, 179–180
count function, 349–351
currency, formatting, 297–299
error messages, 370–371
file extensions, 184
formulas (*See* Formulas)
IF function, 374–375, 397
internal rate of return (IRR)
function, 377–379, 398
labels, 438
loan conditions, documenting,
351–354
MIN/MAX functions, 347–349
page numbers, adding, 383–384

payment function, 354–357,
395
percentage format, 352
percentage increase/decrease
calculations, 362–366, 396
screen elements, 9–10
settings, changing, 262
spelling/grammar, checking,
24–26, 51
spreadsheets (*See* Spreadsheets)
Sum function, 295–297, 331,
345–347
syntax, 296
tables (*See* Tables)
templates, 390
trend identification, 389–390
what-if analysis, 354, 389
worksheets (*See* Worksheets)
Extrapolation, 447

F

Fair use guidelines, 151
Field placeholders, 250
Fields, mail merge, 251, 253–255
Files
corrupted, 211
extensions, 184, 200, 204,
210–211
management of, 14, 209
navigating, 14–18
opening/saving, **11–14,** 50
troubleshooting, 208–212
Filtering, tables, 319–321, 333
Find/Replace commands, 22–23
First line indent, 135
Fonts
described, 21
emphasizing, 308–309, 332
formatting, 34, 51–52, 71–73
letter design, 72, 178
Footers. *See* Headers/footers
Footnotes, 141–142, 159
Format Painter button, 187
Formatting marks, 15, 73–74
Format Trendline dialog box, 447
Formulas, 353–354
arithmetic operators, 354–357
cell references in, 349
circular reference error
correction, 345–347
point and click technique, 361
recalculation of, 353

G

Galleries
described, 21
text formatting, 34–36, 52–53
Graphical user interface (GUI), 4
Graphics. *See* Images
Grayscale, 511
Group, 8

H

Handouts, 508, **511–513,** 522,
574–575
Hanging indents, 148
Headers/footers
designing, 102, 501, 503
documents, **99–102,** 114,
133–134
page numbers, adding, 383–384
slides, 499–503, 521
tables, 316
worksheets, 321–322, 450–452
Headings, 293
Help programs, 40–43, 53
Horizontal (category) axis, 418
HTML, 208
Hyperlinks
adding, 204–206, 220
described, 40
in presentations, 567–569, 584
removing, 177

I

IF function, 374–375, 397
Images
benefits of, 64
compressing, 575
design, 493
file extensions, 184
inserting/modifying, **83–85,**
112–113
slides, inserting in, 487–489,
520
Information Bar, 572
Insertion point, 8
Insert Object button, 177
Insert Table button, 541–543
Interest rate calculations, 355
**Internal rate of return (IRR)
function,** 377–379, 398

J

Justification, 73, 181

L

Labels
axes, formatting, **442–444,**
460–461
chart design, 417, 433
Labels (mailing), 249, **259–261,**
272–275
Labels (worksheets)
data, entering, 289–291, 330,
344–345, 394–395
design, 290, 291
printing, 380–381, 438
Landscape orientation, 322
Language tools, 138–140, 158–159
Left-alignment, 73
Legend, 418

Letter design
accuracy, 26
balance, 39, 75, 102
block-style, 19
colors, 190
columns, 183
comments, 238, 241
complimentary close, 32
consistency, 188
data organization, 70
dates, 31
error introduction, 244
fixing exercises, 54–55,
   116–117, 165, 221–222, 276
fonts, 72, 178
footers, 102
graphics, 85
hyperlinks, 204
leaders, 198
letterhead, 30
page breaks, 151
punctuation, 255
reviewer identification, 238
reviewers, responding to, 249
salutations, 254
sort for mailing, 252
spacing, 31, 132, 255
style guides, 131
tabbed list alignment, 198
tables *vs.* lists, 91
titles, 79
track changes, 243
Line charts, 435–441, 460
Lists, numbered/bulleted, 68–70,
   111, 486

M

Magnification, changing, 16
Mailing labels, 249, **259–261,**
   272–275
Mail Merge Recipients dialog box,
   252
Mail Merge Wizard, 259–261,
   272–275
Mail merging
data sources, **249–252,** 254, 270
document/data source, 256–257,
   271–272
envelopes, printing, 262–263
fields, inserting, **253–255,**
   270–271
main document creation,
   249–250, 270
Manual column breaks, 198–200
Margins, setting, 175–177
Mark as Final, 262
Markers, 438
Maximize button, 9
Microsoft Office, 4
MIME HTML, 208
Minimize button, 9

MIN/MAX functions, 347–349
**Modern Language Association
(MLA),** 131
Money management
annual cash flow calculation, 369
average function, 349–351
cash flow analysis, 356,
   367–369, 396–397
count function, 349–351
cumulative total calculation, 370
financing costs calculation,
   367–368
loan conditions, documenting,
   351–354
MIN/MAX functions, 347–349
payback, calculating, 376, 397
payment function, 354–357, 395
percentage increase/decrease
   calculations, 362–366, 396
savings calculation, 367
Movie clips, 537–539

N

Name box, 287
Newsletters, 172
borders, adding, 188–190
columns, multiple, 180–183,
   216–217
Excel, copy/paste from, 179–180
manual column breaks, 198–200
margins, setting, 175–177
special text formatting,
   186–188, 217–218
symbols, adding, 21–22,
   190–192, 218
tab stops, 193–198
templates, 103–106, 114–116,
   183–185, 217
text, inserting, 18–19, 177–179,
   215–216
Nonprinting characters, 15
Numbered lists, 68–70, 111, 486
Numbers
displaying, 292, 356
formatting, 300–301, 331, 359,
   395–396
page, adding, 383–384
sequences, filling, 357–359,
   395–396

O

Objects, 35, 177. *See also* Images
Office button, 8
Office Clipboard, 27
Optical media, 211
Overtype, 106

P

Page breaks, 147, **151,** 382
Page numbers, adding, 383–384

Paragraphs, 188–190. *See also*
   Documents
Parenthetical citations, 143
Paste command, 27
Paste Options button, 29
Paste Special option, 180
Payback, calculating, 376, 397
Payment function, 354–357, 395
Pictures. *See* Images
Pie charts, 425–433, 435, 459–460
Pixels, 293
Plain text format (.txt), 200
Points, 293
Portable document format (.pdf),
   184, 200
Portrait orientation, 322
PowerPoint
closing, 14
file extensions, 184
Notes pane, 477
placeholders, 477
presentations (*See* Presentations)
screen elements, 10
settings, changing, 262
Slide pane, 477, 479
slides (*See* Slides)
Slides/Outline pane, 477,
   480–481
spelling/grammar, checking,
   24–26, 51
Presentation design
animations, 561, 564, 566
bullet points, 486
charts, 551, 553
consistency, 536
data, tabular, 544
diagrams, 556, 558
documentation, 501
error review, 511
fixing exercises, 523–524,
   585–586
fonts, 548
handouts, 513
headers/footers, 501, 503
hyperlinks, 569
images, 489, 493
Internet viewing, elements for,
   574
layout, 535
parallel structure, 482
speaker notes, 509
themes, 496
title slide, 478
transitions, 506
Presentations, 474
adjustment/review of, 497–498
animations, 559–566, 583
applications of, 514
bullet points, 479
charts, 530, **548–553,** 564–565,
   582
creating, 476–478, 518–519

Presentations (*continued*)
distribution of, 514, 530
drawings, creating, 575
handouts, 508, **511–513,** 522,
574–575
hyperlinks in, 567–569, 584
images, compressing, 575
movie clips, 537–539
outlines, importing, 532–534,
579–580
preparation for, 514
saving to CD, 576
slides (*See* Slides)
SmartArt diagrams, 553–559,
582–583
speaker notes, 508–511, 522
tables, 530, **539–548,** 561–563,
580–582
testing, 495
text entry, 479–481
themes, **493–496,** 520–521,
535–536, 580
tips, 514
Web posting, 570–574, 584
Printer management, 43–44
Printing
charts, 433–435
documents, 15, 37–39, 53,
150–151, 161–164
envelopes, 262–263
Help topics, 42
labels, 380–381, 438
orientation, 322, 379–380
page breaks, setting, 382
page setup, multiple worksheets,
386–388
page size reduction, 381–382
paper sizes, changing, 152
print area, setting, 385–386
print queue, 44
settings, changing, 261
troubleshooting, 44–45
worksheets, 322–325, 333–334,
379–388, 398–400
worksheets, large, 379–388,
398–400
Print Preview tab, 38, 39
Programs. *See* Applications
Properties, 262
Public computers, 209

Q

Quick Access Toolbar
buttons, 36, 201–202
described, 8, 33
Quick Launch bar, 11
Quick Style gallery, 134

R

Range, 288
Records, mail merge, 252

Redo command, 36
Relative references, 349, **360–361,**
396
Restore button, 9
Restrict Permission, 262
Ribbon, 8, 27
Rich text format (.rtf), 200
Right-alignment, 73
Rotation handles, 80
Rows
hiding, 376
inserting/deleting, 294–295,
330, 364
tables, 88–89
R-squared values, 445
Ruler, displaying, 193

S

ScreenTips, 15
Scroll bars, 7, 9, 16
Scroll box, 16
Searching, 80, 209
Section, 181
Shortcuts, 11, 18, 24
Simple payback period, 370
Six-by-six rule, 486
Sizing handles, 35, 423
Slide Master view, 501
Slides
adding, 482–484, 519–520
clip art, inserting, 490–493
duplicating, 485–486, 545
editing, 481–482, 519–520,
535–536, 545
headers/footers, 499–503, 521
images, inserting, 487–489, 520
imported text formats, 537
layout, changing, 541–543
masters, 499
navigating, 487–489
removing, 484
Slide Sorter view, 504
text entry, 479–481
title, layout of, 477
transitions, 504–506, 521–522
Slide shows, 506–507, 521–522
Slide Sorter view, 504
Slope, 445
Small caps, 186
SmartArt diagrams
animations, 565–566
graphic types, 554
inserting, 553–556, 582–583
modifying, 558–559
shapes, adding, 556–557
Spacing after tab, 67
Speaker notes, 508–511, 522
Spelling/grammar, checking,
24–26, 51
Spreadsheets, 284, 342. *See also*
Worksheets

Start menu, 11
Status bar, 9
Styles in Word, 134–138, 157–158
Sum function, 295–297, 331,
345–347
Superscripts/subscripts, 192
Symbols
adding, 21–22, 190–192, 218
currency, 298
Syntax in Excel, 296

T

Table of contents (TOC) creation,
152
Tables
alignment, 98
animations, 561–563
AutoFit, 90–91
benefits of, 64, 315
cells, merging/splitting, 97–98
defining/formatting, 315–317
draw table command, 90
filtering, 319–321, 333
formatting, 94–95, 113–114,
332–333
headers, 316
inserting, 86–88, 113
insert table button, 90
orientation, 99
presentations, 530, **539–548,**
561–563, 580–582
rows/columns, 88–89
sorting, 96, 317–319, 332–333
text, conversion to, 92–93
Tabs (ribbon), 8
Tabs dialog box, 196
Tab stops
modifying, 196–198, 218–219
setting, 192–195, 218
types, 193, 196–198
Taskbar, 6, 9, 11
Templates, 103–106, 114–116,
183–185, 217
Text
copying/pasting, **27–31,** 52
cutting/moving, **31–33,** 52
editing, 20, 50–51
formatting (*See* Text formatting)
importing, 131–132, 157
inserting, 18–19, 177–179,
215–216
selecting, 20, 26
tables, conversion to, 92–93
Undo/Redo commands, 36
Text formatting
alignment/indents, 73–75, 98,
111, 135, 148
automatic, control of, 130
benefits of, 64
columns, 182–183
contextual tabs, 35–36, 52–53

cut/paste, 26–27
fonts, 34, 51–52, 71–73
galleries/contextual tabs, 34–36,
  52–53
objects, 35
spacing, 67
special, 186–188, 217–218
Undo/Redo, 36
Themes, 493–496, 520–521,
  535–536, 580
Title bar, 8
Titles, creating, 75–79, 111–112,
  186
Toggle buttons, 67
Track Changes
  adding, 243–244, 268–269
  described, 232, 242
  hiding, 247
  responding to, 245–246
  reviewing, 242–243
Transitions, 504–506, 521–522
Trendlines, 444–447, 460–461
Trends, charting, 435–441, 460
Troubleshooting
  files, 208–212
  printing, 44–45
  taskbar, 11

U

Undo command, 36

V

Vertical (value) axis, 418
Views, 15

W

What-if analysis, 354, 389
Word
  add-ins, installing, 203
  AutoCorrect customization,
    129–130, 157
  bibliographies, 147–149, 161
  citations, 143–147, 159–161
  clip art, 79–82, 112
  comments (*See* Comments)
  documents (*See* Documents)
  error flagging in, 25
  file extensions, 184

footnotes, 141–142, 159
language tools, 138–140,
  158–159
lists, numbered/bulleted, 68–70,
  111
mail merging (*See* Mail merging)
Outline, 151–152
overtype, 106
page break, manual, 147
paper sizes, changing, 152
screen elements, 7–9
spelling/grammar, checking,
  24–26, 51
styles, 134–138, 157–158
system settings customization,
  128–129, 156, 261
tables (*See* Tables)
templates, 103–106, 114–116,
  183–185, 217
Track Changes (*See* Track
  Changes)
work area, 7, 8
WordArt
  margins, setting, 175–177
  titles, creating, 75–79, 111–112,
    186
Word Options dialog box, 239
Work area, 7, 8
Workbooks, 286, 312. *See also*
  Worksheets
Works cited, 147–149, 161
Worksheet design, 389
  cell usage, 288
  colors, 312
  column widths, 379
  currency, 299
  date formats, 303
  documentation, 307, 369
  elements of, 325–326
  empty cells, 350
  fixing exercises, 335, 401
  formula recalculations, 353
  formulas, filling, 364
  labels, 290, 291
  naming conventions, 315
  negative number display, 356
  number formats, 298, 301
  page numbers, 383
  rows/columns, hiding, 376

saving, 325
tables, 315
title emphasis, 309
Worksheets, 10
  cells (*See* Cells)
  circular reference error
    correction, 345–347
  column width, adjusting,
    292–293, 330
  copying, 313–314, 332
  dates, formatting, 302–304, 331
  deleting, 314–315, 332
  described, 286
  documenting, 307, **321–322,**
    333–334, **450–452,** 461–464
  fonts, emphasizing, 308–309,
    332
  headers/footers, 321–322,
    450–452
  headings, 293
  labels, printing, 380–381, 438
  labels/data, entering, 289–291,
    330, 344–345, 394–395
  large, printing, 379–388,
    398–400
  navigating, 286–288, 330
  numbers, displaying, 292, 356
  numbers, formatting, 300–301,
    331, 359, 395–396
  number sequences, filling,
    357–359, 395–396
  page setup, multiple, 386–388
  printing, 322–325, 333–334,
    379–388, 398–400
  rows/columns,
    inserting/deleting, 294–295,
    330, 364
  tables (*See* Tables)
  text alignment, 304–306,
    331–332
  text wrapping, 306–308
  values, shifting, 291–292

X

X-Y scatter charts, 437

Z

Zoom bar, 15